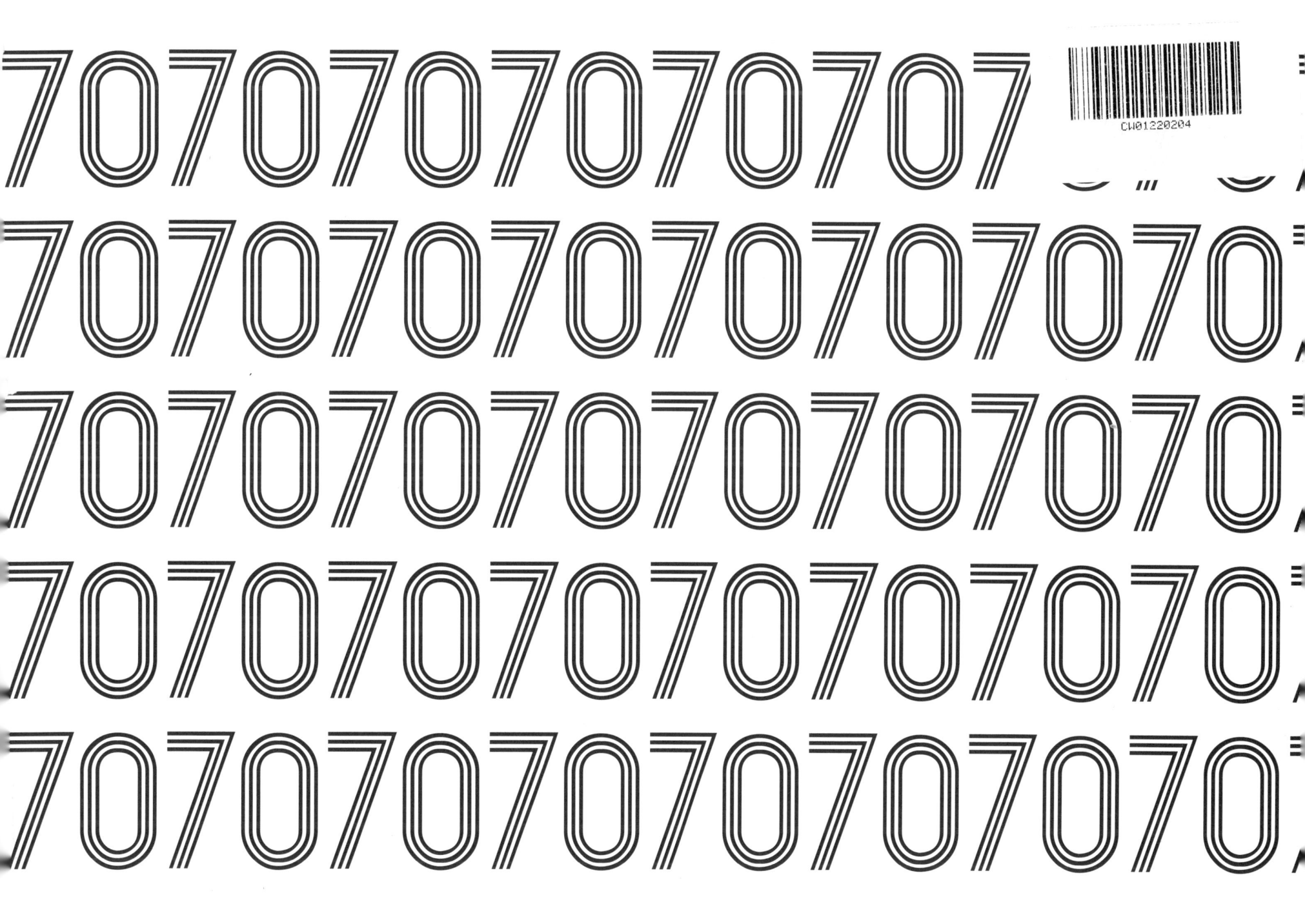

THE BIG ASTON VILLA BOOK OF THE SEVENTIES

THE BIG ASTON VILLA BOOK OF THE SEVENTIES

© Copyright 2016
Legends Publishing

E-mail david@legendspublishing.net
Website www.legendspublishing.net

978-1-906796-74-7

Notice of Rights

All rights reserved. Unless it is part of a published review, no part of this book may be reproduced or transmitted in any form or by any means, electronically or mechanically, including photocopying, recording, or by any other information storage and retrieval system, without prior written permission from the publisher. For information on getting permission for reprints and excerpts, contact Legends Publishing.

All views expressed in this book are the personal opinions of the individuals concerned and not necessarily those of the author, the publisher or the football club. All efforts have been made to ensure the content of this book is historically accurate, but if any individual named feels they have been misrepresented, your right to reply will be exercised if you so wish.

Mirrorpix and Aston Villa FC have given their permission to use the photographs within this book – every effort has been made to trace any other photographer. Thanks to David Scripps at MirrorPix for your help and assistance.

Every attempt has been made to ensure that the statistical data in the book is as accurate as possible. It has primarily been taken from meticulously kept personal records and verified where possible; including Aston Villa FC publications, Rothmans Yearbooks, PFA Published Records, newspaper archives and other sources. Every endeavour has been made to provide records that are as complete as possible and where there are gaps, then no previously published information has been discovered.

FOREWORD

The 1970s didn't begin too kindly for Aston Villa Football Club; starting the decade plying our trade in the unaccustomed third level of the English game. Aston Villa had always been one of the most famous clubs and not just throughout the British Isles; so to see them sink to those depths was simply unheard of and very sad.

I had been onboard in my role as Chairman from December 1968, taking over from the retiring Norman Smith. It was a proud moment for me as I had been a supporter of the club taking my place on the terraces for the previous twenty years.

My immediate aim on joining the Board at Villa Park was to make certain we stayed in the Second Division, no easy feat. In spite of us sitting bottom of the table, with only three wins from our 23 League fixtures, my initial thoughts were that we could claim enough points to cast aside fears of relegation to the Third Division. To achieve this it was imperative we had everyone pulling in the same direction. I gave a little speech about there being no substitute for hard work and the staff and players responded magnificently by pledging their allegiance and loyalty to the club.

I brought in Tommy Docherty as my new manager – he was a useful player in his time, he'd done well in management at his previous clubs and Tommy was a Scotsman – they breed them hard in Glasgow! He was the ideal candidate to restore the club to its former glories and the transformation in performances, and the results achieved after his arrival, ensured our short-term goal of surviving in the division was met.

Notwithstanding the fact there had been a distinct possibility of Aston Villa Football Club going bankrupt due to its commitments and debts, with unequivocal support from my Board of directors, the Aston Villa team our manager assembled for the start of the 1969/70 season would be the most expensive side the division had ever witnessed. This was a significant and bold statement from the club that we meant business.

Unfortunately, even the best laid plans fail; we started off badly and never recovered our momentum from the previous season. We, as a Board, then took the decision to alter direction mid-term after evaluating the situation and changed both management and coaching staff. It wasn't a decision we took lightly, but felt it was a necessity, and in the interests of the club.

In replacing Tommy Docherty with Vic Crowe – a Villa man through and through and who needed no introduction to our supporters – we handed our new manager an unenviable and difficult task. As happens in this game, there are no guarantees, Vic was unable to turn things around in the short time allowed and we subsequently fell from grace to the third tier of the football pyramid.

[Left] Tommy Docherty (pictured with Villa director Harry Parkes) wasn't the long-term solution according to Doug Ellis

Fresh faces were brought in on the playing side and we were sitting in a position of promotion throughout the early season and into the New Year. We had a lovely distraction in the shape of a League Cup final, and a very memorable semi-final that will long live in the memory of our supporters, where we beat the best that a Charlton, Best and Law inspired Manchester United could throw at us. We simply could not replicate our early season form post-Wembley and missed out narrowly on promotion at the first time of asking.

With a season of experience under our belts, we also had in our favour the financial muscle the club could generate due, in part, to our incredible fanbase and in the strength of our name, which attracted sponsorship. We had the foresight and ability to lure Pele and his Santos touring side to Villa Park.

What I remember most about Pele was from our chat in the Rolls Royce that I was driving him round Birmingham in, I said; "Pele, you and I both came from humble beginnings, you've excelled to the absolute top of your profession. Tell me what else would you have liked to have achieved in your lifetime?" He immediately said, "I'd like to own another bank," was his reply sitting in the car next to me.

We broke both club and Third Division transfer records twice in the space of a few weeks when we signed Ian Ross and then Chris Nicholl. Both players choosing to drop divisions to join our crusade.

The season ended with us amassing a record points tally for the Third Division and the record attendance. I know other Chairmen were sorry to see the back of Aston Villa because we took such huge numbers with us around the country, which boosted their own coffers considerably.

Without being disrespectful to the other clubs, it is a level of our game that, quite frankly, a club of Aston Villa's standing should never have had to endure, but we did and I swore it was something that would never happen again. Not in my lifetime.

I remember specifically being at Rochdale. I walked into the dressing room with all the boys there and I said; "Lads, just look around you, don't bring me back here!" I was consistent in begging all the players to give 110% to enable us to get out of that division because I didn't wish to go to the Rochdales of the division again.

Vic Crowe did splendidly well for us and we took our winning mentality and positive form into a new season of Second Division football. We finished third, but fell just short as only the top two were promoted. The rules were changed before the new, 1973/74 season, which enabled the top three to go up... If only? Had the Football League implemented their new ruling a matter of 12 months earlier we would have achieved our goal of First Division football ahead of schedule.

We slipped backwards somewhat and it was felt we would need to bring in fresh blood to take that further step up the ladder. So, in June 1974, Ron Saunders was appointed our new manager at the very time the club were looking to mark their one hundredth anniversary.

After a mediocre start we gained in confidence and won through to lift the League Cup trophy at the expense of fellow Second Division side Norwich City, a special day. I walked up from the director's car park at Wembley; I went up the steps and came to a platform, which was the level of the entrance. There were at least a thousand Villa supporters there and I was very proud in the way in which they were harmonising whilst singing, "One Dougie Ellis, there's only one Dougie Ellis."

[Left] Pele signing for the Villa apprentices after the Santos friendly at Villa Park

[Right] Doug Ellis shares his thoughts with Villa manager Vic Crowe

The motorway was a mass of claret and blue on the way back that night – a truly wonderful way to celebrate 100 years of the club, I'm sure you'll agree? It gave me immense satisfaction to be both Chairman and supporter at such a momentous occasion.

We didn't rest on our laurels; the 1970s also saw the club achieve the distinction of competing on the European stage, albeit still in its relative infancy. We consolidated our position in the First Division as our manager sought to strengthen the squad for this demanding level. Our record transfer fee was exceeded on numerous occasions in the decade as we sought to get the correct balance of experience – through seasoned professionals, as well as home grown, talented, youngsters.

We became a favourite team for the game's neutrals around the country due to our attacking and hugely entertaining brand of football. We competed, and competed well, for the top spot in the First Division, but injuries and fixture congestion took its toll and we had to settle for a commendable fourth place, a position which guaranteed another opportunity to rub shoulders with Europe's finest, and to further endorse the good name of the club.

Further silverware, in the shape of the League Cup, was added to our expanding trophy room following a marathon duel between fellow founding League members Everton. There was plenty of activity in the transfer market as the decade advanced as Saunders latest assembled side started to take shape with encouraging displays and results.

All in all, the Seventies will be remembered fondly by supporters of any age – a very eventful, very special decade, for a very special football club.

Sir Doug Ellis

We then put together an extraordinary run following our day out at Wembley, which culminated in Aston Villa Football Club assuring itself of a place back at the very pinnacle of the English game when we won in style on a balmy evening in Sheffield. I was wearing a new, very special, hand-made Italian suit that night, and as I walked into the dressing room to congratulate the lads, four players surrounded me, then threw me into the bath, still in my suit. Someone, and I never found out who, held me down under the water!

THE BIG ASTON VILLA BOOK OF THE SEVENTIES

INTRODUCTION

Aston Villa Football Club, who had exited the swinging Sixties and entered the 1970s as a relative non-entity when compared to the Liverpools, Evertons, Arsenals, Chelseas and Leeds Uniteds of the footballing world – not to mention both of the Manchester clubs. This hadn't always been the case, in fact with the exception of Everton, none of the other sides were around for the inaugural season of William McGregor's Football League in 1888.

The Villa along with Accrington, Blackburn Rovers, Bolton Wanderers, Burnley, Derby County, Everton, Notts County, Preston North End, Stoke, West Bromwich Albion and Wolverhampton Wanderers made up the dozen teams that were ultimately the pioneers to today's game of global significance.

Of those twelve sides, Blackburn Rovers and Aston Villa had the longest unbroken sequence in the top-flight, ironically both were relegated in the very same season (1935/36). This was somewhat of a shock, their record around that time had been one of consistency, with six successive top-six finishes between the late 1920s and the mid-'30s. Villa were the most decorated club in the land, six League titles, runners-up on no less than eight occasions, six FA Cup victories with two more unsuccessful appearances in the final.

As Villa's dominance started to wane, north London side Arsenal grew in stature. Regardless of what would become of Aston Villa in the future, nobody could deny they had greatness in their DNA. Under the leadership of Herbert Chapman, Arsenal landed two Division One titles, the same manager had guided Huddersfield Town to back-to-back titles in the previous decade. Both sides tasted FA Cup glory under the great man too.

After only two seasons in the Second Division, Villa were back to their rightful place, although this era could be described as mediocre at best, certainly when compared to the feats of years gone by.

It's safe to say the club lurched from one season to another merely making up the numbers. What would the old Villa guard make of it? The club clung on to its Division One status for fourteen straight seasons, with two sixth placed finishes the highest they would achieve. The only silverware to show for their exploits, the FA Cup of 1957, after a painstakingly long 37-year exile.

The victory, with old boy and Villa legend Eric Houghton in the manager's chair, made headline news – the win over Busby's Manchester United Babes set a new record for the competition (the first time a team had lifted it for a seventh time), but equally as important, it denied the red side of Manchester from taking the coveted 'Double' as they'd landed the First Division title with an eight-point margin over Tottenham Hotspur. Coincidentally, the Villa had been the last team to do the 'Double' – back in 1897. The Villa's triumphant day,

THE BIG ASTON VILLA BOOK OF THE SEVENTIES

beneath the Twin Towers, merely papered over the cracks as the club would drop for the second time in their 83 year history within 24 months of their day out at Wembley. Houghton had been sacked in November 1958, so his name was saved from the ignominy.

The footballing gods smiled down on the club as they made an instant return. Joe Mercer was at the helm, although it was largely down to the prolific goal-machine, Gerry Hitchens. Hitchens' 42 goals (1961/62) were enough to command a large fee from AC Milan for his signature. A goal-getting replacement, Tony Hateley, was also sold – again, for big money.

After just two terms back in the top-flight the side struggled to live up to the expectations and history of Aston Villa Football Club. The antiquated, 'Dickensian', board didn't help the situation – the club even sold their training ground in December 1964.

Apparently, according to chairman Chris Buckley, the £88,000 received from a development company was so good they couldn't afford to turn it down. It forced the team to train in public parks around the city, or to go cap in hand to the bigger companies such as HP Sauce and Dunlop, to use their sports grounds.

Doug Ellis attempted, but failed, to get involved at this time, after being given the impression he would be invited into the inner sanctum. Mr Ellis even agreed to put in £30,000 (a significant amount in the day) of his own money to match other investors.

These were anxious times for the club and its enormous fanbase – the envy of clubs the length and breadth of the country. After four seasons of looking over their shoulders and not reaching the required points mark the inevitable happened – for the third time the Villa found themselves falling through the trapdoor amid regular Villa Park protests and demonstrations with calls for the board to resign. This sad episode occurred at the end of the 1966/67 season.

[Left] Ron Saunders, who changed the destiny of the club, parades his Manager of the Year trophy for 1975

Don Revie and Alf Ramsey were named as potential managers, with the former being told he could name his price – Bill Shankly at Liverpool was also approached. Up and coming Brian Clough, at Hartlepools, was considered. Instead, we got Tommy Cummings from Third Division Mansfield Town who said; "I am in no way frightened by the club's great past. Tradition is no handicap. In fact, it still thrills me just to walk into Villa Park."

He continued; "You can feel that it's a great club. Mind you, I'm not going to go along continually looking over my shoulder at what has been done. Put it this way – we are a club of the present – proud of our past, and building for the future. It's my ambition to have people say in 30 years' time, 'What a marvellous club Villa were when that chap Cummings was in charge.' I'm not promising miracles. What I do promise is hard work and all-out endeavour. It's going to be difficult getting out of the Second Division, but I believe we have the players who can do it." Prophetic words indeed.

With no magic wand, sadly, life in the Second Division proved equally difficult. A 16th position was followed by 18th (Cummings was history by November 1968, to be replaced by Tommy Docherty) followed by the unthinkable – another relegation. The 'Doc' was also jettisoned 15 months down the line, his role as manager taken by Vic Crowe. Villa, known as the 'First Superclub', were now to play in the third-tier. It was nothing short of humiliating for such aristocrats of the game, and the demise sent shockwaves around the globe.

An article, under the heading 'Can Aston Villa and Preston North End Come Back?', appeared in the *Football Pictorial*. The piece went on to mention how 20 teams (who'd appeared in the top-flight had sunk to the depths of the 'Third'). Of that number, 14 had tried and failed to resurrect their fortunes. Only Wolves, Stoke, Forest, Derby, Grimsby and Cardiff had successfully achieved a return to the top flight. It went on to say that both Villa and Preston were on the point of bankruptcy. However, on reading through the Director's Report and Accounts for 1971, I found the claim to be inaccurate.

It was also suggested that the supporters of that fine club might never witness First Division football at Villa Park again in their lifetime. With hindsight this was found to be wide of the mark.

With the club's Centenary season looming (est 1874), and Villa fighting to get out of the Third Division, even the most optimistic of claret and blue persuasion couldn't have forecast what was on the horizon – a Wembley League Cup final as a third-tier outfit, where the Villa were damned unlucky not to beat a top Spurs side. Villa then finished a creditable third in their first season back in the Second Division, 1972/73, but only two teams went up.

Aston Villa's centenary year was celebrated in true style, with promotion and a League Cup trophy – the club then went on to proudly represent the nation in Europe, with further League Cup glory to follow. It was a hugely exciting period, with real momentum starting to build – progress that saw Ron Saunders fine-tuning a side to was finally able to make an assault on the biggest prize in domestic football – the First Division League title.

The Seventies… what a decade.

Colin J Abbott

[Right] League Cup final – Aston Villa v Tottenham, 27th February 1971. Referee Jim Finney tosses the coin watched by captains Brian Godfrey and Alan Mullery

1970-71

THE BIG ASTON VILLA BOOK OF THE SEVENTIES

[Back Row] Keith Bradley, Ian 'Chico' Hamilton, Charlie Aitken, Pat McMahon, George Curtis, Lew Chatterley [Middle Row] Ron Wylie (Coach), Bruce Rioch, Andy Lochhead, John Dunn, Fred Turnbull, Michael Wright, Vic Crowe (Manager) [Front Row] Jimmy Brown, Davie Gibson, Brian Godfrey, Brian Tiler, Willie Anderson.

Football League	Division Three
Manager	Vic Crowe
Asst. Manager/Coach	Roy Wylie
Physio	Fred Pedley
Captain	Brian Godfrey
Final Position	Fourth
FA Cup	First Round
League Cup	Finalists
Leading Goalscorer (all competitions)	Andy Lochhead – 13 goals

Vic Crowe had been given the task of leading the club back to where it belonged – out of the Third Division and back towards the top flight. After all, the Villa had more domestic honours at the time of their relegation to the third tier than any other member of the Football League – but changes needed to be made.

Gone were the likes of Alan Deakin and Dick Edwards, along with two players who'd been the club's record transfers within five months of each other – Mike Ferguson (£55,000 in May '68) and Barrie Hole (£65,000 in Sep '68). With first-team coach Stuart Williams' departure, Crowe recruited his former Villa team-mate, Ron Wylie, who'd recently hung up his playing boots.

Villa kicked-off their Division Three campaign with a victory at Chesterfield, and after three games unbeaten, sat joint top along with two other teams. It was not all positive news however, before the month was out influential midfield general Bruce Rioch was sidelined with cartilage trouble, an injury that would require surgery.

Losing at home to Mansfield 0-1 came as a real surprise, but it sparked a response from the team, who embarked on an unbeaten run of nine league games, which saw them well placed, only two points behind leaders Fulham. Villa had also negotiated ties against Notts County, Burnley and Northampton to progress to the last 16 of the League Cup.

Davie Gibson joined from Leicester City where he and Andy Lochhead had formed a lethal partnership, and by late December, with half of the fixtures played, Villa were sitting

continued >>>

Total Home League Attendances 603,027
Average Home League Attendance 26,218
Highest Home League Attendance 37,640
Lowest Home League Attendance 16,694

		P	W	D	L	F	A	W	D	L	F	A	Pts
1	Preston North End	46	15	8	0	42	16	7	9	7	21	23	61
2	Fulham	46	15	6	2	39	12	9	6	8	29	29	60
3	Halifax Town	46	16	2	5	46	22	6	10	7	28	33	56
4	**Aston Villa**	**46**	**13**	**7**	**3**	**27**	**13**	**6**	**8**	**9**	**27**	**33**	**53**
5	Chesterfield	46	13	8	2	45	12	4	9	10	21	26	51
6	Bristol Rovers	46	11	5	7	38	24	8	8	7	31	26	51
7	Mansfield Town	46	13	7	3	44	28	5	8	10	20	34	51
8	Rotherham United	46	12	10	1	38	19	5	6	12	26	41	50
9	Wrexham	46	12	8	3	43	25	6	5	12	29	40	49
10	Torquay United	46	12	6	5	37	26	7	5	11	17	31	49
11	Swansea City	46	11	5	7	41	25	4	11	8	18	31	46
12	Barnsley	46	12	6	5	30	19	5	5	13	19	33	45
13	Shrewsbury Town	46	11	6	6	37	28	5	7	11	21	34	45
14	Brighton & Hove	46	8	10	5	28	20	6	6	11	22	27	44
15	Plymouth Argyle	46	6	12	5	39	33	6	7	10	24	30	43
16	Rochdale	46	8	8	7	29	26	6	7	10	32	42	43
17	Port Vale	46	11	6	6	29	18	4	6	13	23	41	42
18	Tranmere Rovers	46	8	11	4	27	18	2	11	10	18	37	42
19	Bradford City	46	7	6	10	23	25	6	8	9	26	37	40
20	Walsall	46	10	1	12	30	27	4	10	9	21	30	39
21	Reading	46	10	7	6	32	33	4	4	15	16	52	39
22	Bury	46	7	9	7	30	23	5	4	14	22	37	37
23	Doncaster Rovers	46	8	5	10	28	27	5	4	14	17	39	35
24	Gillingham	46	6	9	8	22	29	4	4	15	20	38	33

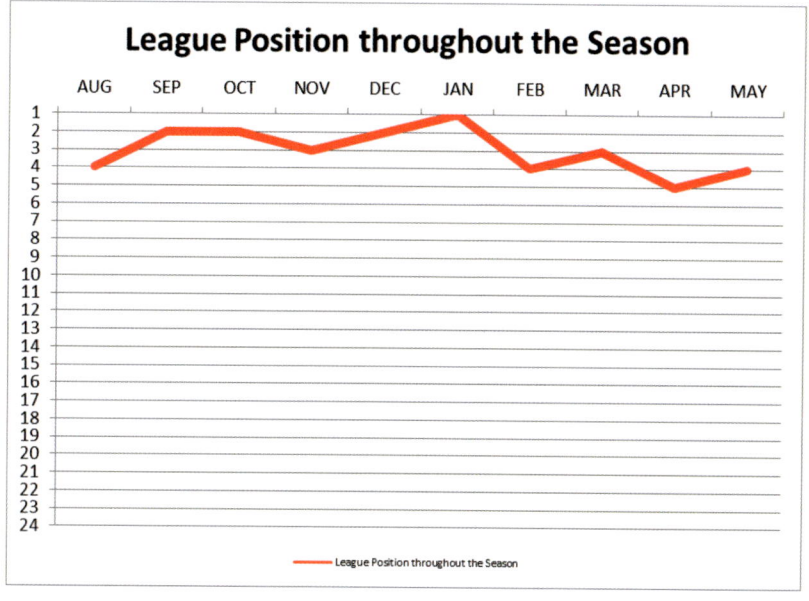

THE BIG ASTON VILLA BOOK OF THE SEVENTIES

1970-71

Sat 15th August   **Chesterfield (A)**
Won 3-2   **Att 16,689**
McMahon, Rioch B (2)

It was a tense Villa side who stepped out into the unknown world of third-tier football at Saltergate. Pat McMahon settled the nerves, putting the visitors ahead after persistent work by Hamilton. A defensive lapse brought Chesterfield level, but this spurred Villa on, and after a spell of pressure, they were back in front from a Bruce Rioch free-kick in the 28th minute. In the second-half Villa went further ahead 3-1, after a 25-yard strike, again from Rioch. Chesterfield pulled one back nine minutes from the end when the Villa's defence was pulled out of position, but the home side couldn't fashion an equaliser.

Wed 19th August   **Notts County (H) League Cup 1st round**
Won 4-0   **Att 17,843**
Anderson, McMahon, Rioch B, Hamilton

Fresh from the morale boosting opening day victory, Aston Villa showed no sympathy for their Fourth Division Midland neighbours. Already three goals to the good at half-time from Anderson, McMahon and Bruce Rioch, only the heroics of the Notts keeper Watling prevented a cricket score. One unhappy County fan shouted, "Why don't Villa declare?" The visitors had a player sent off for sending Aitken sprawling and Villa wrapped the scoring up just after the hour with a delicate glancing Hamilton header.

Sat 22nd August   **Plymouth Argyle (H)**
Drew 1-1   **Att 29,230**
McMahon

A big crowd turned out to welcome in a new era at Villa Park, but they were stunned in the sixth minute when Charlie Aitken's comfortably in second position – a promotion berth – two points ahead of third placed Torquay United.

Villa had also seen off a Manchester United side – that included Best, Charlton and Law – in a two-legged League Cup semi-final, although they fell at the first hurdle in the FA Cup 1st round to Torquay United at Plainmoor.

In the third week of January Villa finally hit top spot for the first time that season when a 1-1 draw at Rotherham was sufficient to lift them above Bristol Rovers, then a 1-0 victory, also against Rotherham, in Villa's last home game before their Wembley date, maintained the side's position at the summit.

Villa had a two-point gap over PNE and with two-thirds of the campaign played – things were shaping up well for promotion.

Aston Villa faced First Division Spurs at Wembley in the showcase League Cup final, however, two late goals, which came very much against the run of play, meant that Villa lost out on silverware and a place in Europe.

Crowe's boys struggled to come to terms with the challenges of Division Three football post-Wembley – a run of five consecutive draws and a defeat saw a five-point gap open up between Villa and the leaders.

With that in mind, Geoff Vowden was brought in during March to beef up the attack, however, the team would only taste victory three more times in the remaining nine games, a sequence that meant that Villa would be in the 'Third' for a little while longer.

attempted clearance sailed beyond keeper John Dunn. Relentless pressure saw Villa efforts cleared off the line and numerous woodwork strikes. Pat McMahon eventually saved the home side's blushes when he expertly trapped the ball before unleashing an unstoppable left-foot shot into the net. Manager Vic Crowe warned his players not to get frustrated in the second-half, they didn't – nor could they find a winner.

Sat 29th August   Swansea City (A)
Won 2-1   Att 13,535
Hamilton, McMahon

On Villa's previous two visits to the Vetch – to face Swansea Town – they had finished the season as champions of their division, could lightning strike a third time? Swansea had lost their two opening games! Villa dominated the first-half only to see the Swans take the lead through a debatable penalty. Chico Hamilton levelled at 1-1 when he fired into the bottom corner after fine wing work from Anderson. Spurred on by a huge following, McMahon went close, and with the Villa faithful still buzzing, Pat rifled home the winner. Early days but third position was promising.

Mon 31st August   Mansfield Town (H)
Lost 0-1   Att 30,862

Villa created chances but couldn't finish them, with two Lochhead headers going begging. On the half hour mark Brian Tiler, back after suspension, replaced McMahon, only for Bruce Rioch to then limp out of action – Villa were down to 10 men. In the second-half the crowds' anxiety transferred onto the pitch, Villa were being matched by a less effective outfit. Things weren't helped when Mansfield finally ventured forward and scored what turned out to be the decisive winner.

Sat 5th September   Doncaster Rovers (H)
Won 3-2   Att 23,619
Lochhead 2, McMahon

With only one point from their opening Villa Park matches, two points were a necessity. With boss Crowe's "Don't let's start feeling sorry for ourselves" message, Villa went out and bagged three goals. Andy Lochhead finally on target, after his arrival the previous February, hit two, with McMahon scoring the other. Plucky Doncaster had twice drawn level but to no avail. Substitute Jimmy Brown (for Curtis), still only 16-years of age, got a run out, coming into a team that would be without the services of Bruce Rioch, sidelined for the foreseeable future, following cartilage surgery.

Wed 9th September   Burnley (H) League Cup 2nd round
Won 2-0   Att 28,341
Hamilton, Martin

Centre-half, Fred Turnbull, back from a Halifax Town loan spell, was called in to face First Division Burnley. He was commanding at the back. Half-time was reached goalless. Hardly relishing a trip to Turf Moor for a replay Villa scored twice through Ian Hamilton and sub Lionel Martin to progress to the next round of the competition.

Sat 12th September   Barnsley (A)
Drew 1-1   Att 13,644
Simmons

Barnsley tried to put on a show against a Villa team who were 'all over the place,' not helped by missing flair players Anderson and Hamilton. Dave Simmons, an arrival during Tommy Docherty's spell, scored the all-important Villa goal to cancel out Barnsley's opener from the spot after Godfrey had handled on the line. John Dunn had initially saved the penalty, but the ref hadn't signalled for it to be taken – hence the retake – much to Dunn's disgust.

Sat 19th September   Preston North End (H)
Won 2-0   Att 26,896
Lochhead 2

Preston boss Alan Ball had gone on record as saying Villa would provide his team with a severe test. The home side welcomed

THE BIG ASTON VILLA BOOK OF THE SEVENTIES

Hamilton and Anderson back. Villa fans had complained they hadn't seen Andy Lochhead score enough – and many were still taking their places when the big 'Scot' rifled home in the second minute. For good measure, Andy scored one they could all witness eight minutes before the interval, which came after good work from Villa's returning widemen. Villa played the possession game for the entire second period, content to sit on their two-goal lead. 'Bally's' pre-match prediction had been proved correct.

Wed 23rd September   Gillingham (H)
Won 2-1   Att 29,416
Hamilton, McMahon
Backed by another big gate at Villa Park, expectancy of a victory was high – Gillingham were without an away win in four. A Brown free-kick, helped on by Godfrey, set up 'Chico' Hamilton to smash the opener with just three minutes on the clock. The noise hadn't abated, Lochhead gained possession – the 'Gills' had kicked-off remember – sent in an inch perfect cross and a McMahon looping header did the rest – straight into the top corner. Four minutes played. Villa's play thereafter was faultless, totally denying the visitors. Until, they went to sleep and allowed a free-kick to remain unchallenged and ultimately converted, beyond a surprised John Dunn and an even more dumbstruck crowd.

Sat 26th September   Wrexham (A)
Won 3-2   Att 18,536
Lochhead, Gibson, Hamilton (pen)
Wrexham were unbeaten on home soil and Villa hadn't lost away. The hosts went ahead, and without keeper Dunn on his toes, Villa could have fallen further behind. Villa levelled after clever work by debutant Davie Gibson, who set up Lochhead to drive in off the upright. A Hamilton pass deflected by the Wrexham wing-half fell into the path of Gibson who lifted the ball over the outstretched goalkeeper to make it 2-1. Only three minutes into the second half Aitken conceded a penalty, which was blazed over. Villa were then awarded one when Lochhead was elbowed in an off the ball incident, Hamilton tucked it away. Wrexham pulled a goal back to make a game of it but Villa held on to take a 3-2 win on their first competitive visit to the Racecourse.

Wed 30th September   Bristol Rovers (H)
Drew 1-1   Att 32,103
Lochhead
Villa's biggest gate so far came out to see if the club could go top of the league. Rovers had finished third last season and wouldn't be a walkover. Villa went ahead after McMahon won possession; Gibson delivered an inch perfect cross for Lochhead to head home – his sixth goal in as many matches. The home side then squandered easy chances to close the game and this came back to haunt them in the 76th minute when the lively Rovers winger Ray Graydon crashed in a deserved equaliser.

Sat 3rd October   Brighton & Hove Albion (H)
Drew 0-0   Att 26,092
The blustery conditions had a big part to play in the proceedings. Chatterley back after a lengthy spell out was kept busy as 'The Seagulls' looked the most likely to score. With the wind on their backs, the Villa's supporters expected to see a glut of goals but the home side huffed and puffed but couldn't find a way through with the few chances they created.

Tue 6th October   Northampton T (A) League Cup 3rd round
Drew 1-1   Att 15,072
Hamilton
The Division 4 side unbeaten at home were content to stifle Villa's creative midfield playmakers. It certainly worked, even though Villa went ahead through 'Chico' Hamilton - scoring from 18-yards after being played in by Lochhead – after 23 minutes. It would be the visitors last attempt on target. 'The Cobblers' drew level in the 37th minute when a speculative shot was deflected off full-back Aitken

into the path of their centre-forward who coolly slotted into the net. The Villa tightened up in the second period and were fortunate to escape when Turnbull dragged an opponent down en route to goal. The 1-1 draw ensured a Villa Park replay.

Sat 10th October   Rochdale (A)
Drew 1-1   Att 7,537
Lochhead

Spotland was a ground that Villa chairman Doug Ellis wasn't very impressed with, it was his first and hopefully last visit there with his club. Villa were trailing leaders Fulham by a point, their cause helped by Lochhead firing them into a ninth minute lead. A quickly taken free-kick by Godfrey nearly doubled the advantage but their keeper stuck out a leg and saved his team. Rochdale drew level in the first half with a well-placed header. Villa missing Bruce Rioch through injury gave his brother Neil a rare run-out. The performance and the 1-1 result were both seen as hugely disappointing.

Tue 13th October   Northampton T (H) League Cup 3rd replay
Won 3-0   Att 25,822
Lochhead 2, Anderson

The visitors nearly scored within two minutes, Dunn raced out to win the ball but they still got their shot away - on target too - only to see left-back Aitken clear off the line. Lochhead connected with a Jimmy Brown centre to give Villa a slender 1-0 half-time lead. With the second-half only ten minutes old Willie Anderson cut in from the wing and sent an unstoppable shot into the top corner. Villa added a third when a perfect pass from defender Turnbull allowed Andy Lochhead to get his second of the night.

Sat 17th October   Chesterfield (H)
Drew 0-0   Att 27,042

New signing Harry Gregory made his debut in a game where the visitors were intent on keeping numbers behind the ball. Gregory beat the goalkeeper on one occasion only to see his effort cleared off the line. Fred Turnbull nearly won it in the closing stages but was denied by a truly wonderful save. The dropped point meant Villa slipped down to fourth.

Mon 19th October   Port Vale (A)
Lost 0-2   Att 11,224

Twice in the opening minutes Villa nearly conceded directly from corners, saved by Wright and then Turnbull. Vale took the lead in the 32nd minute through their centre-forward. The Villa's only real chance of the half was a Hamilton shot from close quarters saved with ease. With five minutes remaining Port Vale scored a second to seal a deserved victory and bring to an end the league's only unbeaten away side. Villa had now played a game in hand over their promotion rivals.

Sat 24th October   Tranmere Rovers (H)
Won 1-0   Att 20,569
Hamilton

A considerable drop in the crowd from the last league match at B6, their worst so far. Keith Bradley stepped in for the injured Wright. With heavy tackles from the visitors going unpunished the fans vented their anger. Villa were awarded a penalty when Lochhead was felled but Anderson's spot-kick was pushed round the post. With Rovers players still celebrating their good fortune, the corner came over unchallenged and it was left for Hamilton to poke the ball in from close range and secure the two valuable points.

Wed 28th October   Carlisle United (H) League Cup 4th round
Won 1-0   Att 26,779
Tiler

Luckily for the hosts Carlisle didn't show the form that took them to the competition's semi-finals last season. Cup-tied Gregory was out. Villa played at a fast tempo and used the wings well with Hamilton going close a few times, a header just wide and an effort scrambled off the line. With 20 minutes to go a Villa free-kick was

[Left] Ray Graydon in action against Carlisle United in the League Cup 4th round clash at Villa Park

headed down by Lochhead, Aitken's drive was blocked on the line but Brian Tiler reacted sooner and stabbed the ball in. Aston Villa were in the last eight.

Sat 31st October   Reading (A)
Won 5-3   Att 13,479
Lochhead, Tiler, McMahon, Anderson (pen), own goal

In the Reading programme notes they expected a side of Villa's stature to come and attack – not just avoid defeat. Villa opened the scoring through centre-forward Lochhead – who'd passed a late fitness test – in the 17th minute. With further goals by Tiler and McMahon, Villa went in at the interval leading 3-0. Anderson made it four when he was fouled and took the resultant penalty himself. Two Reading goals reduced the deficit before Anderson's deflected shot made it 5-2. Still it wasn't finished. With two minutes left on the clock the hosts bagged their third of the afternoon though it counted for nothing.

Sat 7th November   Torquay United (H)
Lost 0-1   Att 28,112

Leaders Fulham had lost last week to Torquay (now 4th in the table) but the Villa faithful were expecting a win after last week's five star showing at Elm Park. Villa squandered three very good chances through, McMahon, Tiler and Lochhead while Dunn at the other end was a spectator for the first 45 minutes. A McMahon effort struck the upright, Tiler put the rebound wide and it had stalemate stamped all over it. The ground was silenced late on when a Torquay player broke through and finished with a clinical 25-yarder which Dunn was helpless to keep out. Torquay leapfrogged Villa who'd now won only four of their ten Villa Park league fixtures.

Wed 11th November   Bury (H)
Won 1-0   Att 17,029
Hamilton

Last time Villa Park had witnessed such a small gate Tommy Docherty was still clearing his desk at QPR before coming to Aston. Villa had the ball in the net early on but it was chalked off for offside. They then peppered the woodwork before finally notching a goal when Hamilton got on the end of a Tiler free-kick, heading into the net. Lochhead had already been subbed when Curtis was plagued by a reoccurring knee injury. It would keep George out for the remainder of the season.

Sat 14th November   Halifax Town (A)
Lost 1-2   Att 5,845
Turnbull

New territory for Villa and their large contingent of supporters. With a far bigger than average gate, Halifax could be excused for thinking Villa were something special, they were far from it. The hosts took a deserved lead with only five minutes gone and this was doubled just after 20 minutes played. The hosts were unfortunate not to score a third and put the game to bed. Villa's determined second-half showing was rewarded with a rare Fred Turnbull goal, a result of a corner – his first in Villa colours in 76 apps. An empty-handed Villa were now four points behind the leaders.

Tue 17th November   Bristol Rovers (A) League Cup 5th round
Drew 1-1   Att 28,780
McMahon

The pitch was in a very poor state but Villa took the conditions in their stride. They were a goal up in the first minute through McMahon and thought they'd gone two in front after 12 minutes. Referee Partridge ruled Lochhead's header out, apparently Hamilton had strayed offside. A McMahon effort was cleared off the line, this was becoming a far too regular occurrence this campaign! Roared on by a crowd three times the norm at Eastville, Rovers won a free-

THE BIG ASTON VILLA BOOK OF THE SEVENTIES

kick deep in Villa's half. The home side's big centre-half volleyed home a spectacular equaliser. Conditions were so bad the ref consulted with both sides but it was decided to carry on. The game saw no more goals and a replay would be necessary.

Sat 21st November   Torquay United (A) FA Cup 1st round
Lost 1-3   Att 9,227
Aitken

In their first ever visit to Plainmoor Villa took the lead through Aitken though it lasted all of four minutes. Ironically it was Torquay's left-back that hit the equaliser. A Villa chance went wide and Torquay made them pay when they went in front, albeit from a Bradley deflection. Ex-Villa defender Dick Edwards made it three when he rose to head in a corner and basically put the game to bed. In the second half the hosts soaked up what little pressure the Villa could muster. Lew Chatterley played his last game in the claret and blue shirt in the 3-1 reversal.

Wed 25th November   Bristol Rovers (H) League Cup 5th replay
Won 1-0   Att 37,525
McMahon

Rovers started the game asking the questions with Ray Graydon being a particular nuisance. Villa were restricted to shooting from distance and with each team cancelling out the other, half-time was reached with no score. Villa had more urgency about their play and it was late on when they finally broke the stalemate. A gloriously struck Hamilton free-kick was too hot for the keeper and as the ball spilled McMahon stole in to slide it home. Villa Park erupted, they knew they would face Man Utd in the semi.

Sat 5th December   Bradford City (H)
Won 1-0   Att 23,589
Hamilton

Gibson was back in the side to face a Bradford team who'd won four games on their travels. Villa created a hatful of chances to take

Chairman Doug Ellis enjoys a dressing room drink with (L to R) Ian Hamilton, John Dunn and Fred Turnbull – Villa had just beaten Manchester United over two legs in the League Cup semi-final

the lead before a Hamilton thunderbolt crashed in off the post. Further goals looked likely, a cleverly anticipated backpass fell invitingly to Willie Anderson who was denied by the keeper. The one goal proved sufficient to deliver both points. Manager Crowe had been awarded 'Manager of the Month' prior to kick-off.

Wed 16th December   Man Utd (A) League Cup semi 1st leg
Drew 1-1   Att 49,000
Lochhead

Utd weren't the all-conquering team they later became and went into the match having won only 27% of their home games. Roared on by 10,000 travelling fans Villa had the ball in the net after six minutes but Utd's goalie Rimmer was seemingly fouled. Man Utd had a few chances before Villa took the lead just before the break. A Hamilton shot was blocked on the goalline but the ball fell to Lochhead who made no mistake from the rebound. The fans were still celebrating when United raced up field and through Kidd scored an equaliser. Gibson and Godfrey controlled the midfield in the second period but Villa had to settle for the draw.

Sat 19th December   Plymouth Argyle (A)
Drew 1-1   Att 12,996
Lochhead

Third placed Villa had only won once in four attempts at Home Park. An uncharacteristic mistake by Dunn required Bradley to avert the danger, Turnbull later cleared off the line before an Aitken slip let Argyle in to finally go in front. The hosts should have added further goals but good luck and even better saves kept Villa in it. An undeserved equaliser from Lochhead – his 12th of the season – ensured Villa left with a point and lifted the club to 2nd in the table.

THE BIG ASTON VILLA BOOK OF THE SEVENTIES

Wed 23rd December   Man Utd (H) League Cup semi 2nd leg
Won 2-1   Att 62,500
Lochhead, McMahon

Villa Park rocked. Crowe named the same starting XI from Old Trafford while Utd made five changes. The visitors took the lead but it didn't last and Villa were on equal terms via their prolific Scottish forward, following clever work from Godfrey and Bradley. Tiler required treatment following an altercation with Denis Law but the Villaman would have the last laugh. A quick throw-in to Bradley, the ball was floated into the area, Lochhead knocked it down to Anderson who chipped it for McMahon to head in at the far post, giving Rimmer no chance. Gibson nearly extended Villa's lead but it mattered not – the ref blew up, Villa were in the final!

Sat 26th December   Shrewsbury Town (H)
Won 2-0   Att 31,177
McMahon, Rioch B

On a frozen pitch Villa looked the more dangerous but without carving out any real chances until McMahon rattled the woodwork and the Town keeper made numerous vital stops. Villa picked up in the second-half and a big cheer went up when Bruce Rioch came on for Gibson. A flag-kick led to Villa's first when McMahon headed into the top corner and the victory was assured when Villa were awarded a free-kick after Lochhead had gone down in the area. Up stepped Villa's midfield maestro to send a trademark Rioch screamer in to make it 2-0. Villa had played exactly half their fixtures, ideally positioned in a promotion berth.

Sat 2nd January   Walsall (A)
Lost 0-3   Att 19,203

Villa made the short journey to Fellows Park and were expected to take both points home with them. Villa started well but wasted their chances. Crash - the home side went ahead in the 22nd minute. Walsall's players rose in stature and Bang – two nil to the good, the scorer hadn't found the net all season yet scored twice in a 13 minute spell. A McMahon effort from a corner was cleared off the line just before half-time. Ex-Villan's Deakin and Woodward severely punished their former employers before Wallop – 3-0 to the home side. The points remained in Walsall.

Sat 9th January   Bristol Rovers (A)
Won 2-1   Att 25,486
Rioch B, own goal

Villa faced leaders Bristol with rookie keeper Geoff Crudgington, Dunn had been involved in a car smash. The visitors ran non-stop and were one up after 30 minutes when Rioch capitalised on a defensive error. The ball was hit with such venom it was in the net before the keeper blinked. Young Crudgington preserved Villa's lead more than once and was relieved that the second period was played in the opponents half. Rovers drew level with 11 minutes remaining but the visitors took a vital win at Eastville when a hopeful ball from Anderson on the left was deflected in by a full-back.

Sat 16th January   Port Vale (H)
Won 1-0   Att 28,933
Rioch B

Mid-placed Vale had lost seven on the road, could Villa make it eight? The home side took charge from the off but wayward shooting prevented a goal arriving. Hamilton was felled on the edge of the box, Godfrey poked the free-kick sideways where Rioch was waiting. He caught the ball perfectly and it rocketed in before the wall had heeded the goalie's instructions. It was his third in four matches, how the Villa had missed him. Villa dominated after the break but were nearly caught out, only frantic defending saved the day. Villa held onto their slender 1-0 lead to earn the victory.

[Right] The Villa team emerges for the Wembley showdown against Spurs (L to R) Willie Anderson, Davie Gibson, Pat McMahon and Ian Hamilton. **[Next spread]** Tottenham full-back Joe Kinnear foils Pat McMahon

Sat 23rd January   Rotherham United (A)
Drew 1-1   Att 12,817
Hamilton

John Dunn was back for the visit to Millmoor but the evergreen Aitken was out injured. The poor pitch was definitely advantageous for the home side. Villa had a scare when McMahon tried to clear a centre, he sliced it towards his goal, it hit the post, clipped Dunn, back against the upright and away from danger. Villa's luck didn't hold though and a free-kick on the stroke of half-time led to Rotherham going in a goal up. Dunn saved a penalty and moments later a Lochhead knock down enabled Hamilton to ghost in and level the score. The point was enough to put Villa on top of the pile.

Sat 30th January   Fulham (H)
Won 1-0   Att 33,344
Anderson (pen)

Despite the driving rain Aston Villa's biggest gate so far came to witness the 'first' versus 'third' encounter. A decisive through ball from Rioch put Anderson through on goal but the Villa winger was taken from behind. He got to his feet and despatched the penalty himself placing the ball high to the goalie's right. In a game of few clear-cut chances Crowe's men held on for their third victory in four games. This sequence had propelled them three points clear at the summit.

Sat 6th Feb   Bradford City (A)
Lost 0-1   Att 10,029

Villa started with urgency and were denied a stonewall penalty when Willie Anderson was hacked down. The visitors had many efforts kept out by the superb handling of Bradford's keeper and Villa should have had the match sewn up long before the break. They didn't and would they regret it! Bannister who'd scored four in City's 5-3 victory last week scored the only goal of the game when he rolled a gentle shot beyond Dunn.

Sat 13th February   Rotherham United (H)
Won 1-0   Att 27,211
Anderson

For the third consecutive game Villa would go in 0-0 at half time, the 'Millers' had come to defend and at any cost. Their tackles were high and crude and at one stage both Rioch and Anderson were prostrate and in need of medical attention. Anderson, having been robbed of a blatant penalty earlier in the game had the satisfaction of bagging the 89th minute winner when he poked the ball over the line following a Lochhead attempt rebounding off the woodwork. Villa were still two points clear, Preston were second.

Sat 20th February   Bury (A)
Lost 1-3   Att 7,516
Own goal

With Bury sitting in the bottom four both points were a mere formality at Gigg Lane, surely? With Villa again creating but not converting their chances it was inevitable they would fall behind. Only six minutes into the second half they were 0-2 down. A Rioch volley was close to going in before Villa halved the deficit when under pressure from McMahon, the Bury centre-half steered the ball into his own net. Villa with their tails up went looking for the equaliser but inadvertently let the home side counter and seal it with their third goal of the afternoon.

Sat 27th February   Tottenham Hotspur League Cup final
Lost 0-2   Att 97,024 (Wembley)

It may well have been the starting XI from last weekend but it was certainly a different side. Villa took the game to Spurs from the off and were desperately unlucky not to go in front, most notably from Hamilton (who should have been named 'Man of the Match') and Lochhead efforts. Dunn was by far the quieter of the keepers but was unable to keep out two very late Chivers strikes to give a very unbalanced 0-2 scoreline.

THE BIG ASTON VILLA BOOK OF THE SEVENTIES

Fri 5th March   **Tranmere Rovers (A)**
Drew 1-1   **Att 6,579**
Hamilton

Geoff Vowden had signed earlier in the day but didn't feature at Prenton Park. In a nice gesture the Tranmere players formed a guard of honour for the Villa players. That was the end of the respect and even though Crowe's men dominated, they had to come from a goal down. This they did when 'Chico' Hamilton reacted quickest and tapped in from close range after an Anderson shot had been deflected.

Wed 10th March   **Gillingham (A)**
Drew 0-0   **Att 10,812**

A memorable experience for Villa's first ever trip to the Priestfield Stadium – only if you were on the supporters' coach commandeered by the team when their bus broke down! Bottom placed 'Gills' were content to take a point. The bone hard pitch didn't help Villa's promotion charge, neither did their lethargic looking midfield. Only Turnbull and Godfrey could take any credit for their performances. Without a win in three, Villa had slipped to fourth.

Sat 13th March   **Halifax Town (H)**
Drew 1-1   **Att 33,533**
Turnbull

A big gate – their biggest so far – turned out to see Vowden make his first full start. Lochhead without a goal this calendar year went close to opening the scoring after being set up by the debut boy. On the half hour the Villa won a corner, Turnbull made his way upfield, when he returned to his own half he was celebrating his second goal in the claret and blue colours. Villa were leading 1-0. Halifax unbeaten in eleven knew the Villans should have been out of sight. Villa skipper Godfrey went off injured, they failed to take their chances and bang – Halifax broke forward and scored, they had stolen a draw and a share of the points.

Wed 17th March   **Walsall (H)**
Drew 0-0   **Att 37,640**

Another big crowd under the AV floodlights. Gibson was in for the injured McMahon. Vowden had a header smartly saved in the first minute. The visitors - just above the drop zone - showed no fear and challenged like their lives depended on it, three names taken more than proved the point. Anderson went close to breaking the deadlock twice after the interval, one attempt sailing just wide and one over. Deakin back at Villa Park showed he still had loads to offer.

Sat 20th March   **Torquay United (A)**
Drew 1-1   **Att 6,963**
Vowden

The 'Gulls' had already done the double over Villa having dumped them out the FA Cup. To make matters worse Lochhead was out, Harry Gregory in for the 'Scot.' Torquay took the lead very much against the run of play but Aston Villa were level within 60 seconds. Geoff Vowden scored in what was only his third start to give his side their fifth consecutive draw and keep them within two points of second placed Fulham.

Fri 26th March   **Doncaster Rovers (A)**
Lost 1-2   **Att 7,879**
Gregory

Doncaster had recently been thumped 0-4 by PNE and were destined to go down. Harry Gregory piled more misery on them when he scored his first goal for the Villa after clever link up play via Anderson and McMahon with only ten minutes showing on the clock. The visitors should have added to the tally but in a mad three-minute spell which saw the hosts win five corners it was Rovers who found the net, not once but twice. Doncaster sat on their lead after the break and Villa were incapable of penetrating the defence. Villa had now gone 630 minutes since they'd tasted victory.

Sat 3rd April   **Swansea City (H)**
Won 3-0   **Att 23,510**
Vowden 2, Gregory

The 'Swans' were unbeaten in 12 on the road. Big Andy was back but with McMahon ruled out Gregory remained in the side. Villa were one up after five minutes when Vowden majestically rose to head in a free kick. The home side doubled their lead, Lochhead causing a nuisance allowed the unmarked Gregory to volley in from distance. Villa reached the interval two goals to the good, the first time this had occurred at Villa Park since September. Aitken cleared a Thomas effort off the line before the Swansea keeper pulled off two good saves in front of the Holte. Villa weren't finished yet, with a dozen minutes left 'Chico' fed Vowden who made no mistake from the edge of the box. Villa 3 Swansea 0, their biggest winning margin of the campaign.

Fri 9th April   **Brighton & Hove Albion (A)**
Lost 0-1   **Att 22,613**

Unfortunately for the Claret and Blues, Albion were struggling and that meant Villa would probably suffer if recent results were anything to go by? The windy conditions wouldn't help nor would Hamilton's absence but at least Willie Anderson was back. A Lochhead effort struck the post while Dunn pulled off four top class saves. In a very even game the home side fashioned a goal in the 75th minute when their sub ploughed through the Villa defence and set up Napier to score.

Sat 10th April   **Shrewsbury Town (A)**
Lost 1-2   **Att 13,636**
Turnbull

Aston Villa's first competitive visit to the Gay Meadow was anything but a happy occasion. Allowing the opponents space from a throw-in Groves was allowed to drift into the box and deliver a low drive into the net. Lochhead saw a header sail over the crossbar and a shot go wide of the mark before new goalscoring sensation Fred Turnbull drilled a shot into the top corner from the edge of the area. He'd scored as many as Anderson in the league. His and Villa's joy didn't last more than a minute, probing for a winner the 'Shrews' hit Villa on the counter, scoring with only six minutes remaining.

Mon 12th April   **Barnsley (H)**
Drew 0-0   **Att 20,718**

With five games remaining Villa had it all to do, trailing second placed Preston by seven points. Godfrey and Gibson were back in the side. Plenty of the ball and three penalty claims waved aside but not for the first time an inability to do anything of note with it. The game unsurprisingly finished 0-0 with the home fans almost resigned to another season in the Third. The point was sufficient to leapfrog Bristol Rovers but in turn Chesterfield jumped over Villa.

Sat 17th April   **Rochdale (H)**
Won 1-0   **Att 18,406**
Vowden

Villa's early pressure was rewarded with a right-sided corner. Gibson precisely floated it over and Geoff Vowden stooped and headed it beyond the 'Dale' keeper to settle the home side's nerves. The win was vital. Geoff then neatly chested down a Hamilton pass but his shot struck the woodwork. Davie Gibson nearly notched his second goal in a Villa jersey but his shot was blocked on the line – by team-mate Brian Godfrey. Villa held on for the slender but all-important win but were still five points behind Preston.

Sat 24th April   **Preston North End (A)**
Drew 0-0   **Att 22,616**

Villa had not only Preston's unbeaten home record to contend with but also the atrocious conditions if they were to keep their slim promotion hopes alive. Villa used the flanks well with Hamilton and Anderson while Lochhead tormented the defence with his aerial prowess. The visitors almost took the lead two minutes after the interval when Hamilton headed wide from two yards out. Brian

THE BIG ASTON VILLA BOOK OF THE SEVENTIES

Godfrey also had a couple of chances and made the keeper pull off an outstanding save. Villa were good value and unlucky not to take both points.

Mon 26th April   **Mansfield Town (A)**
Lost 0-2   **Att 9,655**

Mansfield were only four points behind Crowe's lads. Michael Wright was back for the first time since November. Villa went all out, a Rioch header was cleared off the line and Godfrey made their keeper work yet Mansfield took the lead in the 17th minute. It wasn't long before Villa were two down, another high ball doing the damage and the defence failing to clear. Villa's cause wasn't helped when Turnbull had to leave the field of play due to him being unable to shake off an earlier concussion. Third Division football next season was a certainty now.

Sat 1st May   **Wrexham (H)**
Lost 3-4   **Att 17,302**
Vowden, Godfrey 2

The Welsh side had lost 12 on their travels, not that you'd think it. Against the run of play Wrexham went in front. Vowden levelled the game only for Villa to go behind again. Brian Godfrey made it 2-2 before half time with his first goal of the campaign. Four minutes into the second period the visitors went 3-2 in front. Godfrey then capitalised on a clever Rioch pass to incredibly hit his second of the afternoon. A mix up between Wright and Dunn (the keeper's last game) led to a Wrexham winner.

Tue 4th May   **Reading (H)**
Won 2-1   **Att 16,694**
Anderson, own goal

Villa signed off their 1970/71 - against the team who'd conceded most and scored the least - with a win in front of their lowest attendance since Dec '68. Willie Anderson set them on the way in the first minute - giving fans the hope that a walloping was on the cards.

[Above] Davie Gibson goes for goal against Wrexham

This wasn't to be and Reading drew level just before the hour mark. With only their pride to play for Villa took both points but it took an own goal to settle it. The curtain came down with Villa sitting in fourth position.

PRE-SEASON

- Dick Edwards - Tommy Cummings first signing - left in June for Torquay United for a fee of £8,000.
- Villa's most expensive player Barrie Hole was gone in July, back to his native Wales to join Swansea Town for £20,000.
- Ron Wylie and Leo Crowther joined the coaching staff.
- During the close season Vic Crowe insisted his players come in for two days training a week.
- Villa embarked on a four-match tour of Ireland/Scotland.

AUGUST

- In the first three days of the month the club faced Motherwell and Clydebank having played Coleraine and Glentoran the previous week.
- Villa played host to top-flight neighbours West Bromwich Albion in a friendly.
- The Aston Villa Traveller's Club was formed.
- At the club's AGM an operating profit of £35,000 was announced.
- The club invested in some farmland near the Belfry golf course for a training ground.
- Brian Tiler returned to the side after a three-week suspension.
- Bruce Rioch limped off in the game at home to Mansfield.

SEPTEMBER

- Bruce Rioch underwent cartilage surgery on his right knee.
- Villa lost George Curtis to a long term injury.
- Dave Simmons scored at Barnsley, his last game for Villa.
- Davie Gibson came in from Leicester City less than 48 hours after being handed a 'free.' He was reunited with his former team-mate Lochhead. They had been very effective together for the 'Foxes.'
- Lionel Martin would play twice in the month of September. His lot for the campaign.

OCTOBER

- Crowe was keen to sign Birmingham City's Dennis Thwaites but bizarrely the player couldn't decide!
- Neil Rioch came on for Brian Godfrey at Rochdale. It would be Rioch's only appearance of the season.
- Harry Gregory was signed for £7,777 from Charlton Athletic. He was quoted as saying it was the highlight of his career.
- Michael Wright limped off at Port Vale. Cartilage trouble!

NOVEMBER

- George Curtis underwent an operation to sort out his cartilage problem.
- Fred Turnbull returned to Halifax - where he'd had a spell on loan – and scored his first goal for the Villa in 76 apps.
- The FA Cup 1st round tie at Torquay would be Lew Chatterley's last game in the Villa jersey. He was the club's longest serving player at that time.
- John Dunn was looking forward to returning to Torquay with his new side - to show them why he'd left them - the defeat was somewhat unexpected.
- Crowe was nominated November's Third Division Manager of the Month.

DECEMBER

- Bruce Rioch returned to action, albeit in the Central League.
- Aston Villa were followed by 10,000 of their supporters for the League Cup semi-final 1st leg at Old Trafford.

THE BIG ASTON VILLA BOOK OF THE SEVENTIES

- Cup-tied Harry Gregory watched from the stand as Villa reach Wembley at the expense of Manchester United. Harry said the Holte End were Villa's twelfth man.
- Bruce Rioch scored on his return after coming off the bench at home to Shrewsbury.
- National Manager of the Month for December was added to Vic Crowe's growing list of achievements. It was the first time a manager from the third tier had won this particular accolade and the points accumulated made him a strong contender for the prestigious Manager of the Year title.

JANUARY

- John Dunn was out for the Bristol Rovers match after being in a car accident. Youngster, Geoff Crudgington, would take his place.
- Bruce Rioch started a game for the first time since August 31st. Eastville was the venue and he scored.
- A point at Rotherham put Aston Villa top of the pile.
- A crowd of 33,344 – the season's largest Third Division attendance – turned up for the visit of Fulham.

FEBRUARY

- Villa played three league matches, but won only once in Feb.
- Aston Villa were desperately unlucky to lose to Tottenham Hotspur in the 1971 Wembley League Cup final having outplayed them for almost the entire match.

MARCH

- Villa signed Geoff Vowden from Birmingham City. Ron Wylie, having played at St Andrews, knew exactly what quality Villa would be getting.

[Above] Manager Vic Crowe (right) and his assistant Ron Wylie

[Left] Keeper Geoff Crudgington, far right, shakes hands with captain Brian Godfrey on arriving from Wolves. The others in the Villa Park welcoming committee are (L to R) Aitken, Bradley, Lochhead and Chatterley

- Aston Villa announced that four of their youngsters would be playing in the States during the summer – Barry Lynch and Mick Hoban with Atlanta Chiefs, with Neil Rioch and Geoff Crudgington going to Toronto Metro's (later to become Blizzard).
- Lionel Martin and Lew Chatterley joined Doncaster Rovers on loan for the remainder of the season.

- An impressive 33,533 came out for the visit of Halifax, Villa's biggest of the League campaign so far.
- Villa took Birmingham City's Scottish international goalkeeper Jim Herriot on loan until the end of the season.
- Apprentices Gordon Knowles, Brian Little and Paul Child were awarded professional contracts.
- The Walsall match drew an attendance of 37,640, Villa Park's season best.
- The club didn't win a solitary match all month – drawing five and losing one.

APRIL

- Injured Brian Godfrey sat out the Shrewsbury encounter, only the second league match he'd missed all campaign. It was the Shrews' biggest gate for three seasons.
- Michael Wright returned to the side in place of Charlie Aitken, his first run out since November.
- A Defeat at Mansfield meant another year in the Third at the very least.
- "The prospect of another season in the Third Division is not something to make me jump for joy." – was Vic Crowe's verdict.

MAY

- Villa scored three at Villa Park in their penultimate fixture. Unfortunately visitors Wrexham scored four. John Dunn had played his last game.
- Reading came to Villa fighting for Third Division survival facing Geoff Crudgington in goal – they lost the fight and went down in front of Villa's lowest gate of the season.

[Right] Turnbull, Wylie (asst), Crowe (manager) and Vowden toast a job well done. The 1-1 draw at Mansfield guaranteeing promotion from Division Three

1971-72

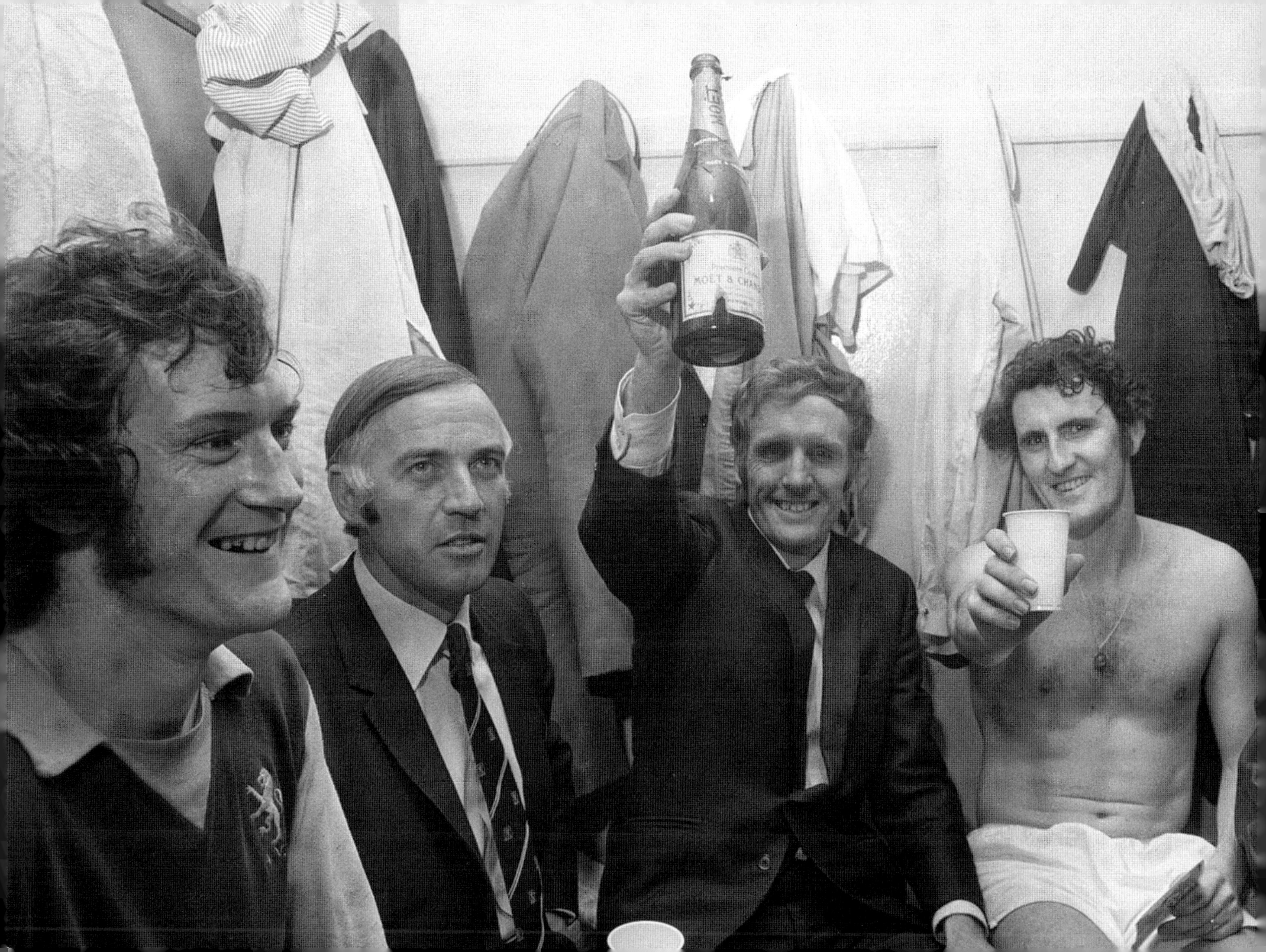
MOET

THE BIG ASTON VILLA BOOK OF THE SEVENTIES

[Back Row] Jimmy Brown, Ray Graydon, Lew Chatterley, Andy Lochhead, Malcolm Beard, Davie Gibson, Michael Wright [Middle Row] David Rudge, Lionel Martin, Charlie Aitken, Geoff Crudgington, Fred Turnbull, Tommy Hughes, George Curtis, Bruce Rioch, Willie Anderson [Front Row] Vic Crowe (Manager), Brian Tiler, Harry Gregory, Pat McMahon, Ian 'Chico' Hamilton, Neil Rioch, Keith Bradley, Geoff Vowden, Ron Wylie (Coach)

Football League	Division Three
Manager	Vic Crowe
Asst. Manager/Coach	Ron Wylie
Physio	Fred Pedley
Captain	Harry Gregory / Bruce Rioch
Final Position	Champions
FA Cup	First Round
League Cup	Fourth Round
Leading Goalscorer (all competitions)	Andy Lochhead – 25 goals

So, Aston Villa had failed in their first attempt to escape the clutches of the Third Division. At the turn of the New Year they were comfortably placed, and looked set for a quick return, but performances - more importantly results - highlighted the fact that Villa had struggled to come back down to Earth following a lengthy League Cup run that had culminated in a Wembley appearance.

A lack of goals, plus an average defence, hadn't helped the Villa's cause, but these deficiencies would be remedied. Vic Crowe upset many fans by dispensing of team captain, Brian Godfrey, in return for the silky skills of wide-man Ray Graydon – a player who would not only supply goals but score his share also. However, Crowe was vindicated – Ray went on to score 15 goals in all competitions during the 71/72 campaign.

The team set off at quite a pace – recording seven victories from their first ten league fixtures and were perfectly positioned at the summit, and in the November, the squad was added to when goalkeeper, Jimmy Cumbes, made the short journey from West Bromwich Albion.

A 6-0 demolition of Oldham (away) on his debut was followed by four consecutive wins, the new keeper's worth to the team was immediately apparent and Jim would end the season with an astonishing 18 clean sheets from 29 league games.

Villa would remain undefeated in an eleven-game sequence stretching from mid-January 'til the middle of March – a sequence that included the eagerly anticipated visit of Bournemouth for a match that attracted a new record attendance for the old Third Division (League One in today's money) of 48,110. The win saw Villa hold a two point cushion over

continued >>>

Aston Villa News & Record

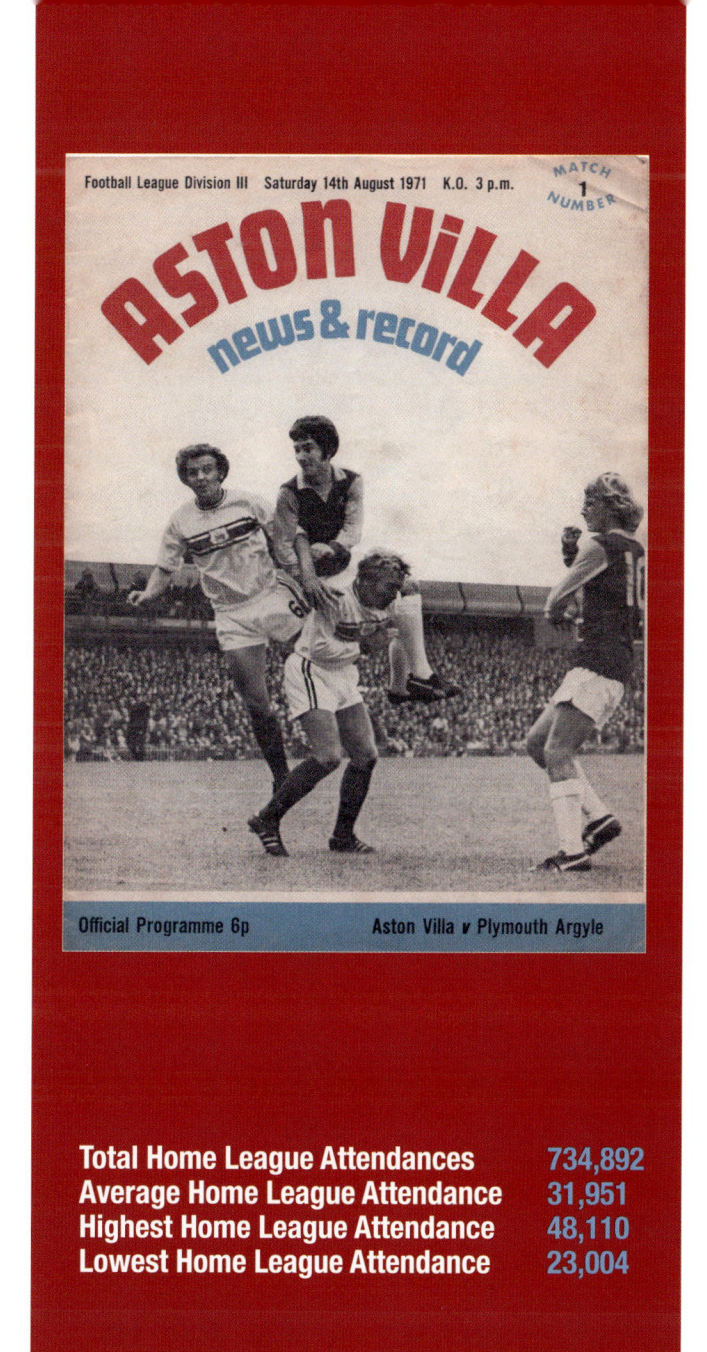

Football League Division III — Saturday 14th August 1971 K.O. 3 p.m.

Match Number 1

Official Programme 6p — Aston Villa v Plymouth Argyle

Total Home League Attendances 734,892
Average Home League Attendance 31,951
Highest Home League Attendance 48,110
Lowest Home League Attendance 23,004

		P	W	D	L	F	A	W	D	L	F	A	Pts
1	**Aston Villa**	46	20	1	2	45	10	12	5	6	40	22	70
2	Brighton & Hove	46	15	5	3	39	18	12	6	5	43	29	65
3	Bournemouth	46	16	6	1	43	13	7	10	6	30	24	62
4	Notts County	46	16	3	4	42	19	9	9	5	32	25	62
5	Rotherham United	46	12	8	3	46	25	8	7	8	23	27	55
6	Bristol Rovers	46	17	2	4	54	26	4	10	9	21	30	54
7	Bolton Wanderers	46	11	8	4	25	13	6	8	9	26	28	50
8	Plymouth Argyle	46	13	6	4	43	26	7	4	12	31	38	50
9	Walsall	46	12	8	3	38	16	3	10	10	24	41	48
10	Blackburn Rovers	46	14	4	5	39	22	5	5	13	15	35	47
11	Oldham Athletic	46	11	4	8	37	35	6	7	10	22	28	45
12	Shrewsbury Town	46	13	5	5	50	29	4	5	14	23	36	44
13	Chesterfield	46	10	5	8	25	23	8	3	12	32	34	44
14	Swansea City	46	10	6	7	27	21	7	4	12	19	38	44
15	Port Vale	46	10	10	3	27	21	3	5	15	16	38	41
16	Wrexham	46	10	5	8	33	26	6	3	14	26	37	40
17	Halifax Town	46	11	6	6	31	22	2	6	15	17	39	38
18	Rochdale	46	11	7	5	35	26	1	6	16	22	57	37
19	York City	46	8	8	7	32	22	4	4	15	25	44	36
20	Tranmere Rovers	46	9	7	7	34	30	1	9	13	16	41	36
21	Mansfield Town	46	5	12	6	19	26	3	8	12	22	37	36
22	Barnsley	46	6	10	7	23	30	3	8	12	9	34	36
23	Torquay United	46	8	6	9	31	31	2	6	15	10	38	32
24	Bradford City	46	6	8	9	27	32	5	2	16	18	45	32

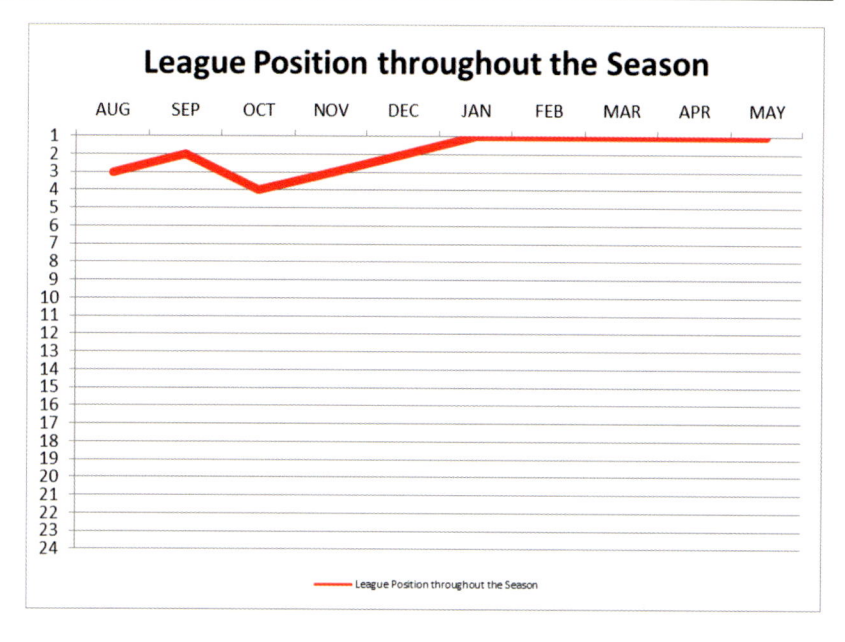

League Position throughout the Season

THE BIG ASTON VILLA BOOK OF THE SEVENTIES

1971-72

Sat 14th August   Plymouth Argyle (H)
Won 3-1   Att 26,343
Vowden, McMahon, Anderson (pen)

Despite atrocious weather, a large crowd turned out to watch Villa kick off their second season in the 'Third'. Inspired by new skipper, Gregory, Villa were in front after ten minutes through Vowden. McMahon doubled the lead when he drilled in from an acute angle, but Argyle pulled one back on the stroke of half time. After the break, the visitors pushed up for an equaliser, but despite the loss of McMahon through serious injury, Villa wrapped the game up after they were awarded a penalty for the felling of Hamilton. Anderson converted to get the season off to a 3-1 win.

Wed 18th August   Wrexham (H) League Cup 1st round
Drew 2-2   Att 24,552
Lochhead, Anderson (pen)

'Chico' Hamilton, who was sub the previous Saturday, started the game with Lionel Martin on bench duty. It was a drab first half with very few chances. Lochhead netted after getting on the end of an Anderson cross but Wrexham were level just six minutes later. With ten minutes left Anderson stroked home a penalty to book Villa's passage to the next round – or so it seemed. With seconds remaining the Welsh side made it 2-2 against the odds to earn a replay.

Sat 21st August   Walsall (A)
Drew 1-1   Att 13,092
Vowden

Bruce Rioch retuned to the side, but new signing, Ray Graydon, was out. Things didn't look good for the claret and blue visitors when Walsall took an early lead. The Saddlers then conceded

second place, but more importantly, six points (equivalent to three wins) over Brighton & Hove Albion in third place.

Additional recruits were then brought in to maintain the club's promotion drive – Ian Ross from Liverpool for a Third Division record transfer fee in late February, a figure that the Villa smashed again within weeks by landing the giant centre-half, Chris Nicholl, from Luton Town.

Following a solitary defeat in late March, Villa then recorded five wins on the bounce, and with fixtures running out, had established a seven point gap. After the disappointments of the previous year, it was now more a case of when and not if promotion would be achieved.

The final table showed the Villa had won the title at a canter, with a record points tally of 70 and having scored 85 goals – the most in the division. Four players had achieved double figures, whilst the miserly 32 conceded by the bolstered claret and blue defence was by far the meanest in the 'Third.'

a cheap free kick, which Rioch took quickly, catching his opponents unaware with the diagonal ball; Vowden read the situation and scored an easy equaliser. New keeper, Tommy Hughes, made some important stops.

Mon 23rd August   Wrexham (A) League Cup 1st round replay
Drew 1-1   Att 12,113
Anderson

Lochhead had the ball in the net after 11 minutes but the effort was offside and half time was reached goalless. Both keepers were busy in the second period and Wright - in for the injured Aitken - cleared one off the line. Incredibly the 90 minutes couldn't separate the two teams. In extra-time Villa went ahead for the third time in the tie through Willie Anderson, but just like they had only five days earlier, Wrexham managed to bag an equaliser right at the death.

Sat 28th August   Rochdale (H)
Won 2-0   Att 24,280
Lochhead, Graydon

Charlie was back in the No 3 shirt, with Crudgington in goal. Anderson turned a defender inside out before setting up Lochhead to put Villa in front after eight minutes. The home side then went two-up just before the interval when Bruce Rioch unleashed an unstoppable thunderbolt, the keeper couldn't hold it, and as it spilled, Graydon nipped in to make sure. By good fortune Rochdale conceded no more, a Gregory lob was just over, a Graydon effort slightly wide and Vowden's shot hit the bemused keeper on the shins.

Tue 31st August   Wrexham (N) League Cup 1st round 2nd rep
Won 4-3   Att 20,697
Lochhead 2, Anderson (pen), own goal

Villa were one up in the third minute of the match played at The Hawthorns thanks to Lochhead, but within 60 seconds it was all square again. Andy then had a glancing header strike the woodwork, while the recalled Aitken was on hand to clear off the line. Wrexham then took the lead, an advantage that was held for 20 minutes, until Anderson was fouled in the box – he converted the penalty himself. Wrexham then made it 2-3 with a header, before Villa pushed men forward – pressure that resulted in the Red Dragons' full-back turning into his own net, 3-3. Villa had their tails up now, and with seconds remaining, Lochhead got on the end of Graydon's perfectly flighted corner delivery to head home the winner.

Sat 4th September   Bolton Wanderers (A) Lost 0-2
Att 11,782

After initial Villa pressure Bolton took the lead when their 1966 World Cup star, Hunt, lobbed Hughes who'd advanced off his line. Tommy held it, but as he fell backwards, the ball squirming from his grip and into the net. Ten minutes after the break a Hughes clearance fell short with the defence caught square – the ball was then played forward for Byrom to side-foot home. Villa were two-down and chasing shadows. Bolton upped the tempo and struck the woodwork twice – Crowe's men were fortunate the defeat wasn't heavier.

Wed 8th September   Chesterfield (A) League Cup 2nd round
Won 3-2   Att 14,000
Lochhead, Vowden, Anderson (pen)

Villa were 1-0 up with six minutes gone when a Geoff Vowden cross was met by Lochhead. Andy then turned provider when he set Vowden up to volley home in spectacular style on 17 minutes. Turnbull then conceded a penalty by pulling a player back to make it 2-1. Chesterfield's full-back tried a speculative 25-yard free kick which Hughes let slip, Randall nipped in to poke it home. With a replay on the cards Anderson was hacked down by two defenders. As in the last round, he picked himself up and despatched the kick to give Villa the victory. Anderson had scored in all four League Cup ties.

URANT, NELSON SQ , BOLTON.
MAGEE'S ALE
REFRESHMENTS
IDEAL
SERVICE

[Left] Bruce Rioch and Fred Turnbull look on as Villa goalie Tommy Hughes denies Bolton at Burnden Park

Sat 11th September   Brighton & Hove Albion (H)
Won 2-0   Att 25,812
Graydon, Hamilton

In front of the 'Match of the Day' cameras Villa played a cautious game against a Brighton side only a point behind the leaders. It was no surprise that the break was reached in stalemate. Gregory made way for Hamilton and a more ambitious Villa took the lead on the hour through Graydon. Villa then hammered away at the Albion defence and a second goal duly arrived after smart footwork from Lochhead set Hamilton up to steer a shot into the net. It was a valuable victory that lifted Villa six places.

Sat 18th September   Halifax Town (A)
Won 1-0   Att 7,462
Graydon

In Crowe's absence, Villa nearly went one down through former player Bill Atkins following a Turnbull error, thankfully Hughes saved to spare Fred's blushes. Hamilton had the ball in the net with the second period only a minute old, but the ref ruled it out for offside. Halifax then went close, but Villa managed to hook the effort off the line. With time running out Anderson beat two defenders on the wing, his centre was met by Graydon who'd stolen in on the blind side to sweep the ball into the Halifax net to make it 1-0. Villa's first away win in 14 attempts.

Wed 22nd September   Mansfield Town (H)
Lost 0-1   Att 28,112

A win would have put Villa level at the top, while Mansfield were bottom with a single point. Curtis was back for his first start in ten months. The Stags' keeper, Book, was kept busy throughout with Rioch shooting on sight, while Lochhead, Vowden and Hamilton should have each scored hat-tricks, such was Villa's dominance. With ten minutes to play Mansfield broke forward and stole a goal on the counter. The whistle sounded to stunned disbelief. Mansfield had done exactly the same the previous season.

Sat 25th September   Wrexham (H)
Won 2-0   Att 23,004
Anderson (pen), Graydon

With the campaign in only its second month, Villa and Wrexham locked horns for the fourth time, perhaps the midweek defeat, and the fans being sick of the sight of Wrexham, contributed to the lowest crowd of the season so far? It took a foul on Lochhead and the award of a penalty to break the deadlock – Anderson scoring from the spot for the third time against John Neal's side. Ray Graydon then got on the end of a Hamilton cross to fire Villa into a two goal lead and get their promotion push back on track.

Tue 28th September   Barnsley (A)
Won 4-0   Att 8,632
Lochhead 2, Hamilton 2

But for an uncharacteristic miss by Hamilton Villa would have been in front after only three minutes, but he made amends by teeing up Lochhead with an exquisite cross to put Villa in front. After the interval, the visitors were rampant and bagged two goals in six minutes. Anderson's corner saw Hamilton head home and a Bradley centre was met by big Andy who hammered home Villa's third of the night. Hamilton then added a magnificent solo goal with two minutes remaining to ruin Barnsley's previous unbeaten record at Oakwell.

Sat 2nd October   Bristol Rovers (A)
Won 1-0   Att 20,442
Anderson

Sixth placed Rovers would offer a stern test. Graydon nearly put Villa ahead when his fierce shot struck the keeper's leg, much to the home fans' relief. Brian Godfrey also went close for the hosts,

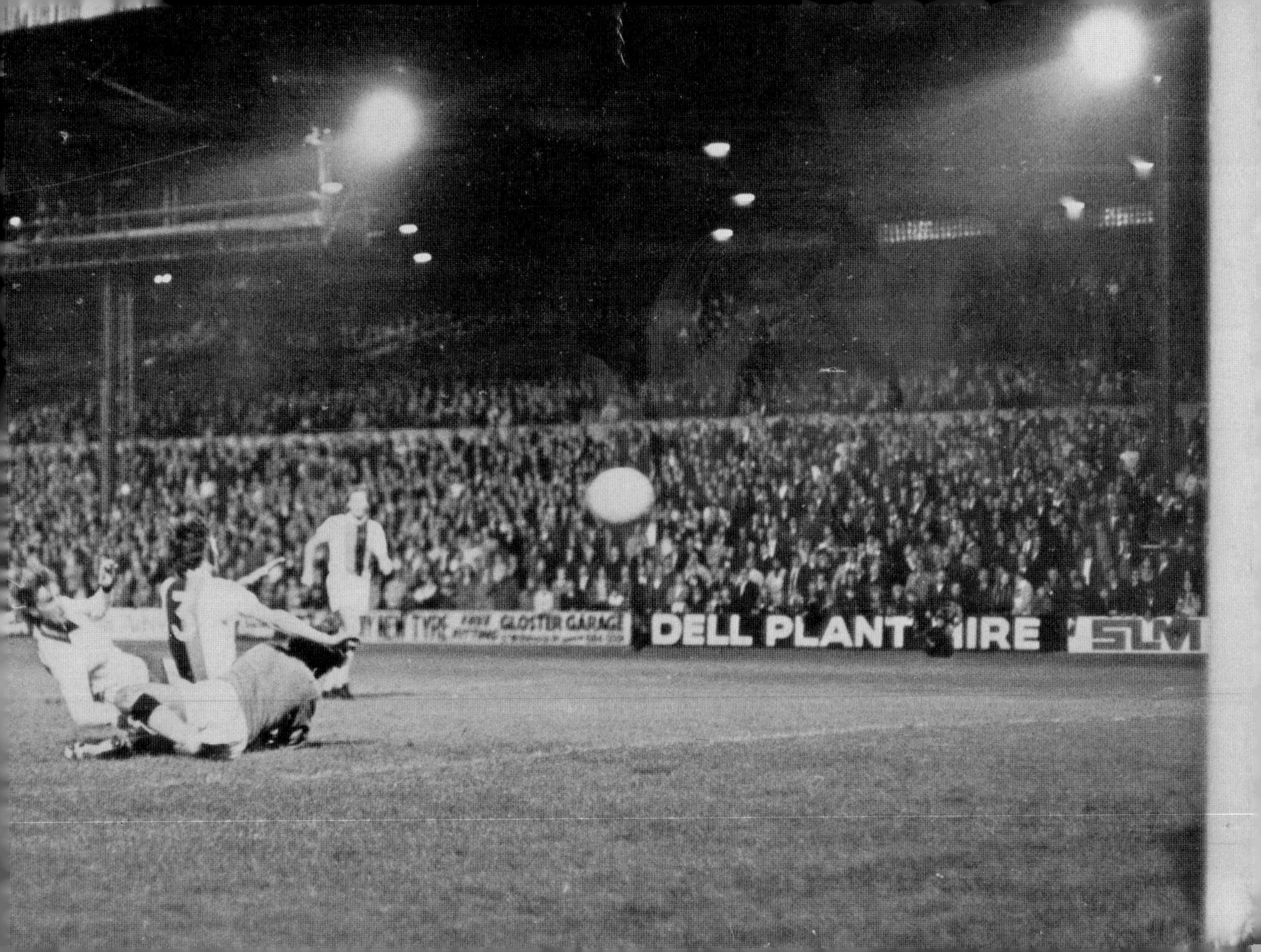
GLOSTER GARAGE
DELL PLANT HIRE

[Left] Ian Hamilton scores Villa's first in the 2-2 League Cup third round at Selhurst Park.

he beat Hughes, but Bradley cleared off the goal-line. Beard then conceded a penalty, but Hughes was equal to it, and kept Villa in the game. Anderson scored the only goal of the game, to the delight of Villa's large band of followers, when he cut in from the wing to fire a low right-footed shot into the net.

Tue 5th October   **Crystal Palace (A) League Cup 3rd round**
Drew 2-2   **Att 21,179**
Hamilton, Lochhead

Villa undeservedly fell behind against the top-flight Eagles in the 34th minute, though it was a goal of sheer quality. Palace added to their lead early in the second half after Hughes gave away a soft penalty. Villa reduced the deficit when Vowden fed Hamilton to fire in a great shot, before Lochhead got on the end of another cross by Geoff to bring Villa level at the death and give them another crack at Palace in a replay.

Sat 9th October   **Rotherham United (H)**
Lost 1-2   **Att 30,251**
Lochhead

Villa were all over their opponents like a rash, but Rotherham played with nine men behind the ball, so it was ironic that their first venture up field led to them going in front. Lochhead forced an equaliser just after the half-hour mark following dazzling wing play from 'Chico' Hamilton. The home fans expected a second-half rout, but Graydon was denied and a Lochhead header went just the wrong side of the post. Villa then lost their way, and due to farcical defensive errors, Rotherham stole a second to give them victory. The large Villa Park crowd had expected a totally different outcome.

Wed 13th October   **Crystal Palace (H) League Cup 3rd round rep**
Won 2-0   **Att 24,978**
Lochhead, Graydon

In poor conditions, caused by torrential rain, both sides cancelled each other out. A Graydon effort was turned round the post and a Vowden volley was fisted over the bar. Lochhead was pushed in the box but penalty appeals were refused. Villa finally took the lead when Graydon crossed from the right to set up Lochhead, who fired in his sixth League Cup goal. Graydon then put the result beyond doubt when he added a second with seven minutes remaining.

Sat 16th October   **Plymouth Argyle (A)**
Lost 2-3   **Att 18,570**
Rioch B, Vowden

Plymouth were one of only four teams to remain unbeaten at home and Crowe's boys discovered exactly why when Argyle scored twice in the space of four minutes late in the first period. Bruce Rioch fired in on the hour to make the scoreline 2-1, but Villa's celebrations were muted when Argyle restored their two-goal cushion shortly afterwards. A Vowden header brought Villa back into contention at 2-3 before a Hamilton effort was 'a coat of paint' away from snatching the Villa an unlikely point.

Wed 20th October   **Tranmere Rovers (H)**
Won 2-0   **Att 24,231**
Rioch B, Lochhead

Following successive defeats (the only time in the entire season) Villa had lost ground on the pacesetters. They would also be without the suspended Bruce Rioch after the game. His name was sung on the terraces and he duly responded with a trademark goal from a free kick a full 30-yards out. Goal number two arrived when Anderson found his route on the flank blocked, he simply cut inside before delivering a peach of a centre – food and drink to a certain Mr Lochhead. Villa were up to third.

THE BIG ASTON VILLA BOOK OF THE SEVENTIES

Sat 23rd October   **Bournemouth & Boscombe Athletic (A)**
Lost 0-3   **Att 20,305**

John Bond's side had won all seven league games at Dean Court, so Villa knew they were in for a rough ride on their first ever visit to the ground. Crowe dropped Aitken to make a defensive wall of Curtis, Tiler and Turnbull, but Villa were torn apart. They trailed after only five minutes, and were two down with 22 minutes on the clock. Lochhead's frustration at the lack of service led to him kicking out and being cautioned. To rub salt in, Bournemouth added a third with eight minutes left. It had been an emphatic display by the Cherries.

Tue 26th October   **Blackpool (A) League Cup 4th round**
Lost 1-4   **Att 20,193**
Anderson

Blackpool had beaten Bournemouth in the previous round, even so, Villa forced two early corners and only John Burridge's bravery between the sticks kept the visitors at bay. Blackpool then opened the scoring close to the interval when a half-clearance was crashed in with force from 25-yards. The hosts went further ahead three minutes into the second period and, by the hour mark, they were 4-0 in front. Willie Anderson hit a beauty from distance, but it was no more than a consolation and the Villa were knocked out.

Sat 30th October   **Blackburn Rovers (H)**
Won 4-1   **Att 25,558**
Rioch N 2, Hamilton, Anderson

With Bruce suspended it was strange that the headlines would be all about Rioch, albeit his younger brother, Neil, who gave Vic Crowe plenty to mull over by scoring a brace in the 4-1 win. It could have been a hat-trick had a powerful shot not been deflected late on. Hamilton and Anderson also got their names on the scoresheet. Brian Little, who was the leading scorer in the reserves, came off the bench to replace Davie Gibson who'd received a knock. Villa remained fourth.

Sat 6th November   **Port Vale (A)**
Drew 4-4   **Att 11,118**
Hamilton, Anderson (pen), own goal, Graydon

Villa were behind only three minutes in, but Hamilton brought them level in the seventh from a Graydon cross. Vale again took the lead, only for the visitors to equalise again through an Anderson spot-kick. Villa bizarrely went in front when an intended back-pass cleared the stricken goalkeeper. Graydon increased the lead when he rounded the keeper, but Port Vale fought back, firstly through Sammy Morgan – a Villa target later on – and then Vale scored a fourth five minutes later. Villa had dropped a point. Central League star, Micky Hoban, was on the bench.

Sat 13th November   **Notts County (H)**
Won 1-0   **Att 37,462**
Graydon

Villa trailed County by four points going into the game. In front of the BBC cameras Villa, without full-backs Wright and Bradley, appeared nervous. County hit the woodwork, Villa cleared off their line twice through Turnbull and Curtis. Just before the half hour mark, and against the run of play, the Villa were in front when Graydon dived to head home a Hamilton cross. Turnbull again cleared off the line, but this time with his hands – penalty to County. Hughes, who'd had a torrid afternoon, saved from Don Masson, it would be his last league game in the first-team jersey. Villa had taken a valuable two points.

Sat 20th November   **Southend United (A) FA Cup 1st round**
Lost 0-1   **Att 16,929**

Villa looked nervy from the start, especially their keeper, Tommy Hughes. Southend, on the other hand, played with a relaxed air, they had nothing to lose as they weren't expected to win. The Shrimpers went ahead in the 34th minute following an unnecessarily conceded free kick. Villa failed to control the midfield and were unable to cope with the high balls Southend kept floating into their area and Crowe's

44

side were knocked out of the competition a good six weeks before the 'big' sides would even kick an FA Cup ball in anger.

Sat 27th November   Oldham Athletic (A)
Won 6-0   Att 12,175
Lochhead 3, Anderson, Rioch B 2
Goalkeeper Jimmy Cumbes was drafted in to make his debut – having signed on the Thursday – but only with the help of a cortisone injection. The Villa raced to a two goal advantage after only 11 minutes through Lochhead and Anderson, before Rioch, back from suspension, made it three to give Villa a commanding 3-0 half-time advantage. Oldham fell further behind to yet another Rioch thunderbolt, then big Andy scored his second of the afternoon to the delight of Villa's travelling army. Lochhead wasn't finished, he bagged his hat-trick to round off a stunning 6-0 victory.

Sat 4th December   Bradford City (H)
Won 3-0   Att 27,847
Anderson (pen), Rioch B 2
Only three points behind leaders Bournemouth, Villa, led through an inspired Bruce Rioch, went all-out from the start. Bruce was upended, penalty to Villa. Up stepped Anderson to convert his seventh successive spot-kick. Rioch scored the second of the half following clever build up play by Hamilton. The hosts wrapped the points up after the interval when they went 3-0 up after a 'Chico' Hamilton cross was headed out to the 18-yard line, where Rioch read the bounce perfectly before unleashing a half-volley beyond the helpless keeper. The gap at the top was reduced to two points.

Sat 18th December   Bolton Wanderers (H)
Won 3-2   Att 27,767
Lochhead, Graydon, Aitken
Recently relegated Bolton were struggling with only two wins on the road, however, the visitors took a deserved lead before Villa pegged them back through Lochhead, who scored his 15th of the campaign. Within a minute they had gone in front, a huge Cumbes kick was met by Lochhead who headed down for Graydon to race through and beat the goalie. Bolton went one better, and were level within 40 seconds to go in at half time all square. Charlie Aitken scored the winner - his second in six seasons - getting on the end of an Anderson free kick.

Mon 27th December   Swansea City (A)
Won 2-1   Att 24,404
Aitken, Graydon
The Welsh side were fourth but level on points with Vic's side. Swansea took the lead with a goal crafted by ex-Villan Barrie Hole. Their joy was short-lived as Villa, roared on by 8,000 of their fans, levelled within seven minutes of the second half. An Anderson free kick was anticipated by the Swansea defence, and with Lochhead watched closely, Aitken stole in to score in successive games (unbelievable) to make it 1-1. In a rough and fiercely fought match, Villa snatched a dramatic winner with only three minutes remaining. Aitken floated in a free kick and Graydon applied the finishing touch. Notts County led the table, with Villa poised only a point behind.

Sat 1st January   Halifax Town (H)
Won 1-0   Att 32,749
Graydon
Villa had been held to a draw at home to Halifax last season, they weren't going to make the same mistake against a team who'd scored only six goals on the road. The home side pressed but couldn't find the necessary goal. Half time was reached with the fans venting their frustration. Villa flew out of the traps in the second period and were in front within 25 seconds of the restart. Hamilton gained possession, played in Rioch who squared for Lochhead, his header down picked out Graydon who did the rest, 1-0.

Sat 8th January   Rochdale (A)
Lost 0-1   Att 5,874

Vowden was back after being subbed the previous week, Hamilton was recalled, whilst Brown made way. Villa dominated the midfield, and with a Rioch shot shaking the woodwork, and the 'Dale' keeper in inspired form, the visitors found it difficult. With this, Rochdale grew in confidence and ventured forward. A hopeful centre struck Curtis on the hand and a penalty was awarded. Cumbes, who'd had nothing to do all afternoon, stood no chance. Villa had unexpectedly lost to a side 17th in the table.

Wed 19th January   Shrewsbury Town (H)
Won 3-0   Att 27,140
Hamilton, Graydon, Lochhead

Would Villa heads fall? With Rioch injured, Gregory made his first start since September. Anderson and Aitken had efforts ruled out before Villa legitimately went ahead through Hamilton after good work from Gregory and Anderson. With Turnbull and Curtis in defence the Shrews were going nowhere. Villa doubled the advantage when 'Chico' turned provider for the 'Grayder' to claim his 11th of the season. Jimmy Cumbes assisted for the third when his lengthy kick landed on the edge of the opponent's box, and as the ball fell, Lochhead caught it with precision to launch it into the net. He then left the field, to be replaced by Lionel Martin, but Villa were back in business.

Sat 22nd January   Barnsley (H)
Won 2-0   Att 30,531
Lochhead, Rioch B

Villa had won 4-0 at Oakwell and, with the points expected, a big crowd turned out in anticipation. The visitors were content to play with nine men behind the ball, so Villa struggled to break them down and the first goal didn't materialise until two minutes before the interval. It was worth waiting for, Vowden, Curtis and Hamilton all played a part before Graydon tore down the flank to tee up for Lochhead to tap the ball in. Bruce Rioch added the second, Villa's 50th of the League campaign, with a pile-driver fully 30-yards out, which gave the keeper no chance whatsoever. Villa were top of the pile.

[Right] Hamilton celebrates after putting Villa ahead at home to Shrewsbury Town

Fri 28th January   Tranmere Rovers (A)
Won 1-0   Att 12,054
Aitken

Vowden and Hamilton made way for Brown and Gregory, but before Villa were allowed to impose thier own game, they had to suppress Tranmere. Half-time was reached goalless, though Cumbes, back at his old stamping ground, had made some crucial saves. Villa attacked more after the break and were rewarded in the 68th minute when an Anderson free-kick from the left side found Aitken lurking in the box. The full-back met the ball squarely to head home and give the team their third successive victory. With Villa playing the day before their promotion rivals, they'd opened up a three-point cushion.

Sat 5th February   York City (H)
Won 1-0   Att 26,905
Anderson (pen)

York's first visit to Villa Park saw them under the cosh from the start. Several of Graydon's shots flew over, wide or required good saves from their keeper, whilst Gregory also went close with a long-range shot, but the 20-yarder took a deflection. A Graydon shot finally looked to have broken the deadlock, but it was handled on the line by the left-back. Anderson duly slotted the penalty home, but was forced to retake it by the referee due to encroaching in the area. He scored to secure maximum points yet again.

Sat 12th February   Bournemouth & Boscombe Athletic (H)
Won 2-1   Att 48,110
Vowden, Lochhead

This was the 'big one' and a record crowd for the division came out to witness it. The visitors took an interval lead through their goal machine Ted MacDougall in front of the 'Match of the Day' cam-

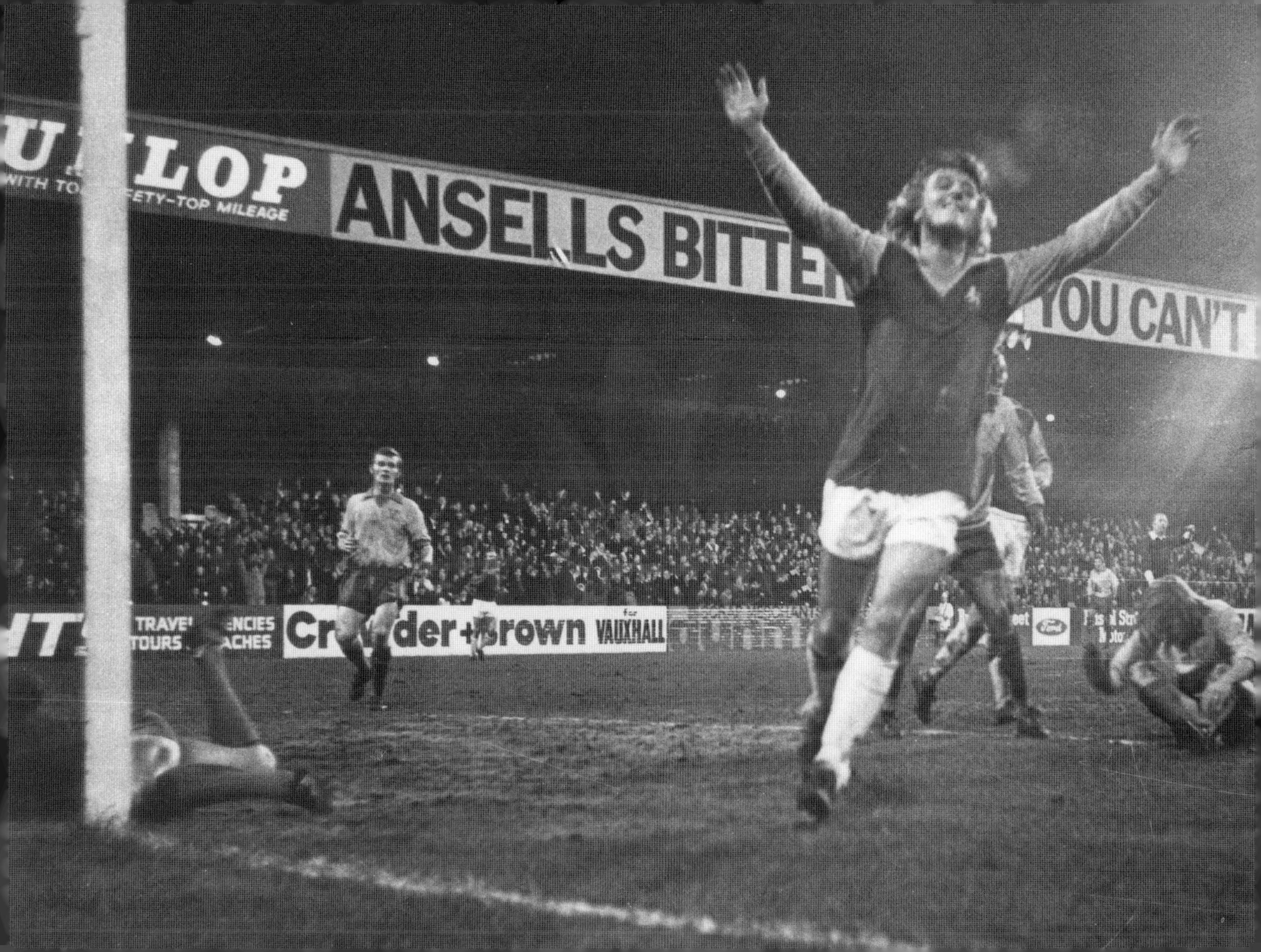

ANSELLS
YOU CAN'T
VAUXHALL
MILEAGE
TOURS

THE BIG ASTON VILLA BOOK OF THE SEVENTIES

eras, and Turnbull left the field concussed. In front of a screaming Holte End, Villa levelled when Geoff Vowden popped up to head the ball home. Game on. In a cauldron of noise Villa pushed on and found the winner through their big rugged Scot, Andy Lochhead. A Curtis free-kick was lofted to the left-side of the area, Andy's head sent the ball skywards, then as he watched it come back down, swivelled on the spot to smash it home, which caused an eruption on the terraces. The 2-1 win pushed Bond's team down a place to third.

Sat 19th February   **Blackburn Rovers (A)**
Drew 1-1   **Att 15,562**
Lochhead

Villa made the trip to mid-placed Rovers on the back of five straight victories. Blackburn had no answer to Villa and were behind on ten minutes – Ray Graydon's free-kick was met by Lochhead, his 19th of the season. Ray thought he'd increased Villa's lead but it was ruled out, Andy had fouled McNamee. The Claret and Blue's half-time advantage was cancelled out when a Rovers forward outjumped Cumbes to nod in, and the home side went close to taking both points – thankfully Turnbull was on hand to clear off the line.

Sat 26th February   **Port Vale (H)**
Won 2-0   **Att 32,806**
Lochhead, McMahon

A big crowd came out to see if Villa could maintain their position at the top. The side were buoyed by the 'blooding' of Ian Ross, who had recently signed from Liverpool. Villa were poor for the first 45 minutes but picked up the tempo after the interval – their play was more positive and led to Lochhead breaking the stalemate with a header from a McMahon right-wing cross. Ten minutes of sustained pressure saw Andy return the compliment and provide Pat McMahon with the easiest of chances to bag his second of the season and Villa's second of the afternoon. Not a pretty performance, but the points were priceless.

[Right] Andy Lochhead heads goalwards during the 2-0 win over Port Vale

Sat 4th March   **Notts County (A)**
Won 3-0   **Att 34,208**
McMahon 2, Graydon

Villa's appearance resulted in Meadow Lane's biggest gate for 15 years, and with so much at stake, it was going to be a blood and thunder enounter. Tony Hateley and George Curtis clashed in the first minute, the Villa man was covered in blood, his nose smashed. It took until the second half before the visitors asserted their authority, a McMahon goal, then one from Graydon, putting Villa two up. County were deflated and with 12 minutes left on the clock Pat McMahon bagged his second to give Villa an emphatic 3-0 victory.

Sat 11th March   **Rotherham United (A)**
Won 2-0   **Att 15,743**
Lochhead, Graydon

Villa paraded and played their £90,000 signing, centre-half Chris Nicholl, and started the game with an emphasis on containing The Millers, with the midfield dropping back to assist the defence. Their patience was rewarded with two goals in the space of eight minutes, first through Lochhead and then Ray Graydon. The side held the 2-0 advantage to the half-time whistle. Rotherham went close to pulling a goal back within four second-half minutes after Cumbes could only parry a lobbed attempt, but from there on, Villa's resolute midfield gave nothing away. An eighth win on away soil kept them a point ahead off the chasing pack with a game in hand.

Wed 15th March   **Shrewsbury Town (A)**
Drew 1-1   **Att 16,336**
Nicholl

In only his second start in the famous claret and blue, Chris Nicholl scored for his new club to the delight of the 10,000 Villa support-

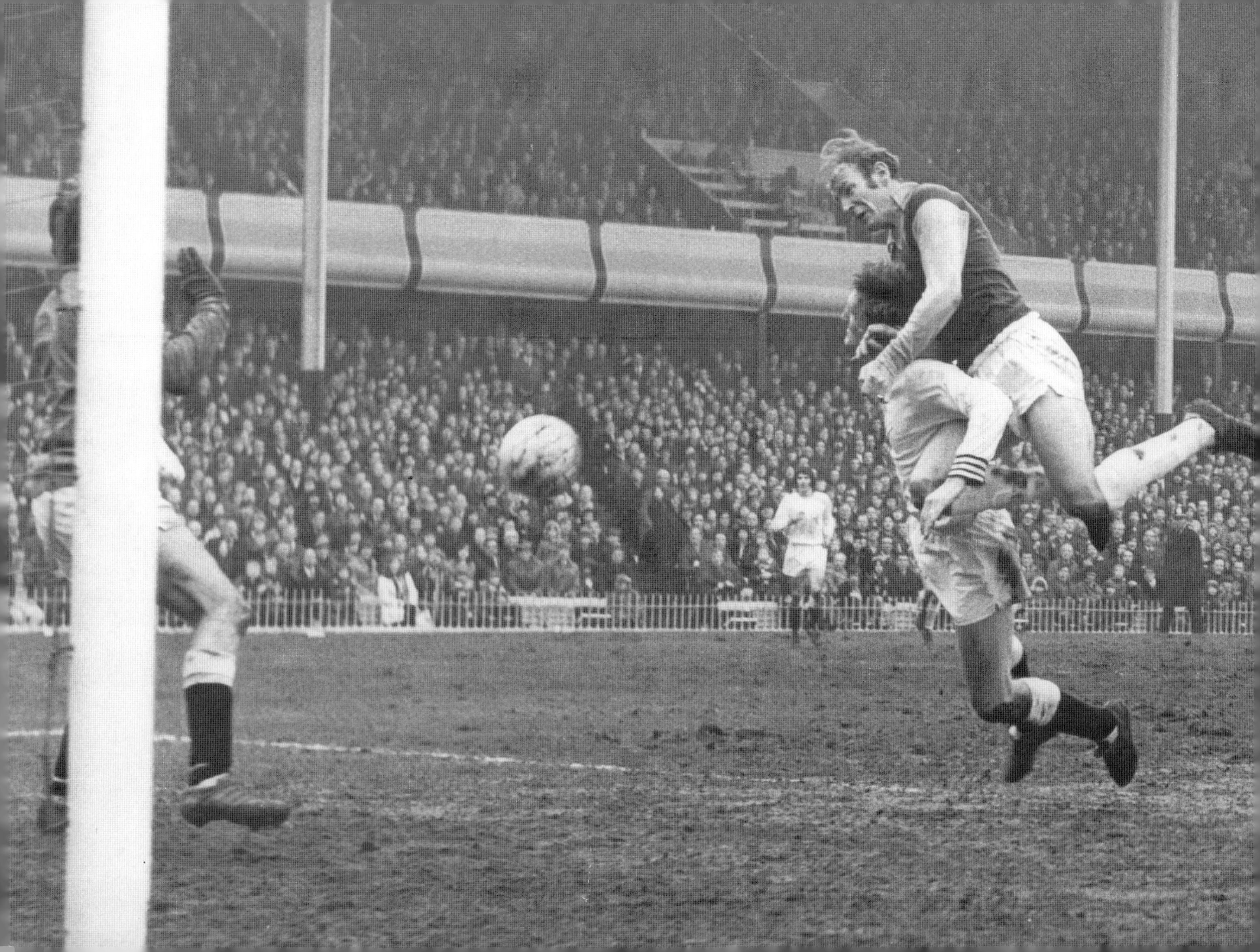

ers who'd made the comparatively short journey to Gay Meadow. Villa were trailing at the break to a robust and overly physical side, and in the second half, Willie Anderson, who'd been subjected to many crude challenges, was once again hacked down. His cleverly-floated kick was met by the imposing figure of Nicholl, who'd stolen in on the blind side, to head home with force. The point from the 1-1 draw was enough to remain at the summit.

Sat 18th March   **Walsall (H)**
Drew 0-0   **ATT 45,953**

A whopping crowd gathered at Villa Park, to become part of the second biggest in the history of third flight football. Walsall faced a Villa side unbeaten in ten – their intention obviously to prevent Villa's fluent play. This they did very well, the poor first period closed with few chances created. The second half was little better with both Villa's widemen, Anderson and Graydon, starved of service. Walsall's players left the field far happier than the hosts'.

Sat 25th March   **Brighton & Hove Albion (A)**
Lost 1-2   **Att 28,833**
Rioch B

Third placed Brighton, with an eye on a promotion berth, started with four attackers (much to Villa's surprise) and it paid off for them when they went in front after six minutes. In the second period Villa would have fallen further behind but for the intervention of Nicholl, who made two goalline clearances. Villa drew level from an attack initiated by Aitken, then Graydon played Rioch in to score his eighth of the campaign. McMahon missed a late chance to earn Villa victory, however, in the closing stages, Brighton seized on an error in the Villa box to stab home a winner.

Andy Lochhead scores his 19th of the season during Villa's 1-1 draw at Blackburn Rovers

Fri 31st March   **Wrexham (A)**
Won 2-0   **Att 17,162**
Anderson, Graydon

Graydon and Anderson tormented Wrexham from the start, with Rioch and McMahon dominating the centre of the park. Anderson scored the first goal of the game, seizing on a mis-hit clearance from Turnbull's free-kick. The second duly arrived when Wrexham's keeper and a defender got in each others way as a Michael Wright cross came over, and Graydon pounced to put the result beyond doubt. Villa took the sting out of Wrexham after the break and played the game at their own pace and ensured they bagged both points.

Sat 1st April   **Swansea City (H)**
Won 2-0   **Att 33,394**
Anderson, McMahon

Vic Crowe named an unchanged side for the sixth successive game. Villa attacked from the off and saw two efforts shake the woodwork. They eventually took the lead nine minutes after the interval through Anderson. The second, 14 minutes later, was from a Graydon corner – McMahon jumping highest to force a header past the helpless goalie.

Mon 3rd April   **Bristol Rovers (H)**
Won 2-1   **Att 41,518**
Lochhead 2

Rovers, in fifth position, were still hopeful of landing a top two finish. Villa full-back Wright was the visitor's biggest threat. Graydon, playing against his former team-mates, had a hand in the opening goal – after receiving the ball from McMahon he centred for Lochhead – who made no mistake at the far post. Lochhead's second came courtesy of a corner on the hour mark. The hosts were made to sweat when Rovers pulled one back, but they doggedly held on. No Villa side in history had achieved so many victories in one season.

Sat 8th April   **York City (A)**
Won 1-0   **Att 9,419**
Rioch B

Aston Villa travelled to York City – their first ever visit to Bootham Crescent – knowing they had six games in only 17 days, this would determine their season and possibly their future. With players of the calibre of Rioch, Graydon and Anderson etc, Villa were far superior, and after subjecting York to a constant battering, Villa got their noses in front on 28 minutes. A Willie Anderson corner was lashed home by Bruce Rioch from 25-yards out. York created a few chances but they were no more than routine saves for Jimmy Cumbes in goal.

Mon 10th April   **Oldham Athletic (H)**
Won 1-0   **Att 32,226**
Graydon

Another 6-0 was never on the cards, although Villa created enough openings, they just couldn't get them on target – the ball flying high or wide on numerous occasions. Was it going to be one of those days? Fans had been leaving in droves but, with only 30 seconds left on the watch, Graydon scored from the edge of the box with a right-footed shot. The result was paramount, the performance very much secondary in importance, but Villa's quest for promotion was still very much alive.

Wed 12th April   **Torquay United (A)**
Lost 1-2   **Att 9,928**
Vowden

Villa, seven points clear at the top, the hosts, three points adrift at the bottom – a banker? Villa hadn't won at Plainmoor and were without Lochhead, allowing Vowden to wear the No 9 jersey. Credit to Geoff, he scored on the night, unfortunately Torquay had already scored twice and there was no way back for Villa. This defeat needed to be put to the back of their minds… and quickly.

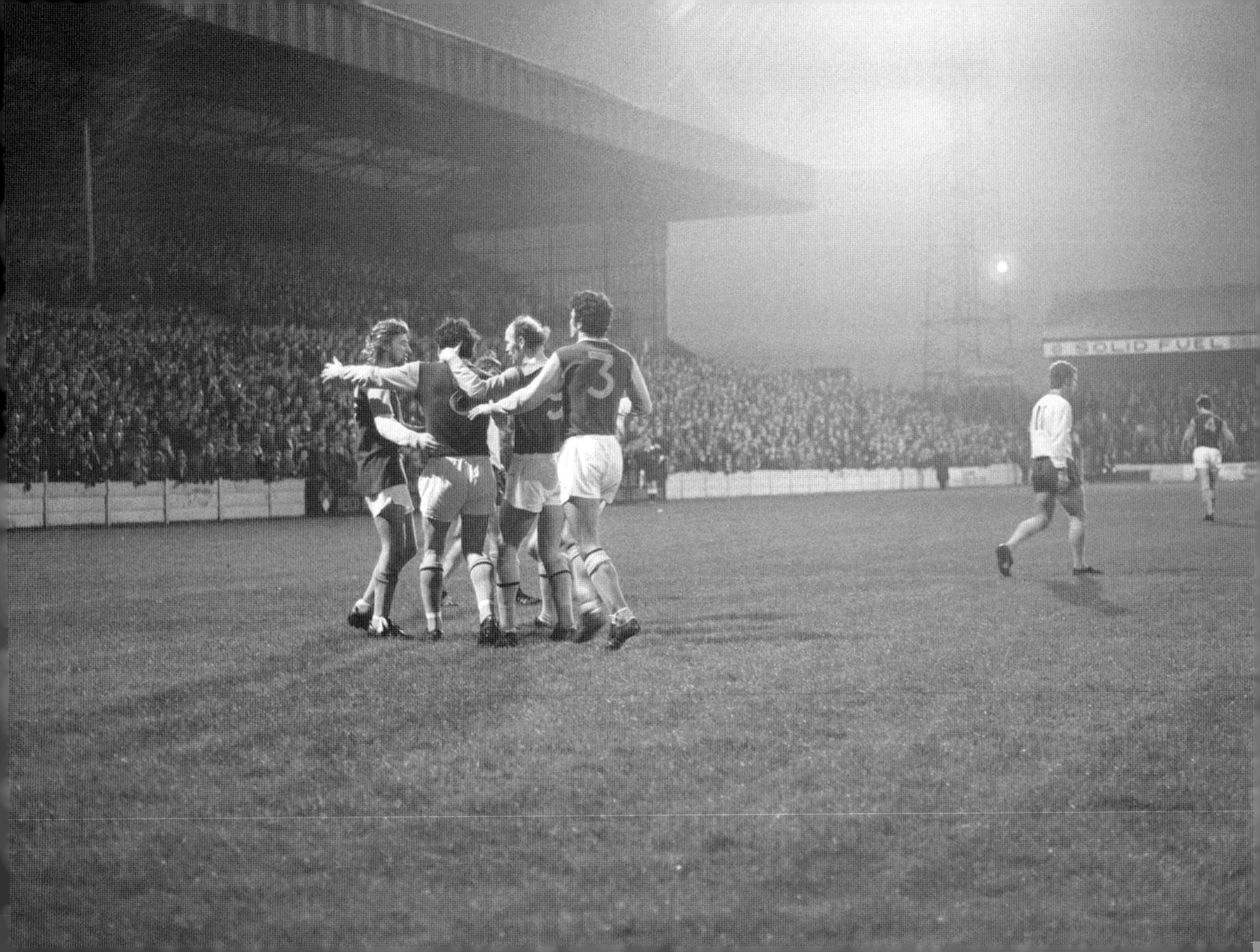
SOLID FUEL

[Left] Hamilton, Lochhead and Aitken congratulate Vowden on scoring the Villa goal that clinched promotion at Mansfield Town

Wed 19th April   Chesterfield (A)
Won 4-0   Att 12,510
Lochhead, Vowden 2, Hamilton

Crowe's team made no mistake against a side that hadn't won at home in six games. Rioch was told to play more to the left and give Anderson more of the ball. This worked like a dream, both of Villa's first-half goals resulted from Anderson crosses with Lochhead and Vowden sending the Villa in at the break two to the good. A Geoff Vowden volley made it 3-0 on the night, before Hamilton rounded off the scoring deep into injury time.

Sat 22nd April   Bradford City (A)
Won 1-0   Att 9,285
Aitken

If Bournemouth and Notts County failed to win, and Villa took both points, they would be up. Villa went ahead eight minutes in, Graydon's shot was turned over the bar, Hamilton's corner only half cleared, he crossed it again, and with Bradford's defenders attending to the threat posed by Lochhead, Aitken ghosted in and steered a header into the net. Despite a determined Bradford performance Villa held on to snatch both points. Results elsewhere had gone against Vic Crowe's team, meaning the Champagne remained on ice.

Mon 24th April   Mansfield Town (A)
Drew 1-1   Att 12,476
Vowden

Aston Villa only had 48 hours to wait before their next match – away to Mansfield. The Stags had won all three encounters in Division 3 up to now, but could Villa snatch the all-important win? Curtis was back for the first time since Hateley had refashioned his face at Meadow Lane. Villa thought they had taken the lead within five minutes only to see it chalked off, Lochhead was offside. Half-time was reached with no score. Within eight minutes of the resumption a short Graydon corner was helped on by Hamilton to Vowden who hooked the ball in from a near post position. Brown in the Mansfield goal prevented Villa from adding to their tally, and totally against the run of play, Mansfield drew level two minutes into injury time. It mattered not – with 66 points on the board Villa had secured a place in Division 2 for the following season.

Sat 29th April   Torquay United (H)
Won 5-1   Att 37,179
Vowden 2, Lochhead, own goal, Little

Curtis was out, he'd played his last game for Villa, in came youth sensation Brian Little, who'd shown immense promise against Blackburn in October. Vowden made it 1-0 before Little squared to Lochhead to double the advantage. An own goal added another before Brian Little scored the first of many in the claret and blue when he side-footed home from a corner. Torquay pulled one back, but it was no more than a token. Villa's fifth of the afternoon came from a Geoff Vowden dipping shot. Villa had guaranteed themselves promotion the previous Monday, this win confirmed they were going up as champions!

Fri 5th May   Chesterfield (H)
Won 1-0   Att 45,714
Ross

In front of yet another incredible gate, Aston Villa drew a line under their Third Division 'sentence'. It had lasted 24 months, kicking off in August 1970 and against the same opponents. Villa had started with a win and bowed out in similar fashion. Classy playmaker, Ian Ross, scored the only goal of the game, his only one of the campaign. Villa were now on 70 points, the club's best-ever tally, one that was also a record for the division.

THE BIG ASTON VILLA BOOK OF THE SEVENTIES

PRE-SEASON

- Scottish U-23 international, Tommy Hughes, signed from Chelsea.
- Villa land the exceptional Bristol Rovers winger Ray Graydon in a deal that saw Brian Godfrey go in the opposite direction.
- Goalkeeper John Dunn joined Charlton Athletic on a 'free'.
- July also saw Malcolm Beard move across the city from Birmingham on the recommendation of Ron Wylie. He would only play seven first-team matches in total.
- Villa embarked on a six-day, four-match tour of Germany.
- Local radio had announced George Curtis would remain club captain, while Harry Gregory would be short-term team captain following Godfrey's move to Bristol.

AUGUST

- Bitter rivals Birmingham City were beaten at Villa Park in a friendly in front of over 36,700.
- In the season's curtain raiser Pat McMahon dislocated his ankle against Plymouth Argyle.
- Bruce Rioch was left out of the Argyle game having missed the tour of Germany due to the birth of his son.
- Villa took three games to get past Wrexham in the League Cup 1st round. It would be keeper Geoff Crudgington's last game for the Villa first team. He'd played five times and Villa had won the lot.

SEPTEMBER

- Aston Villa were fined £3,000 (suspended for two years) by the FA for the collective number of cautions their three teams had incurred in recent seasons.

[Right] Willie Andreson scores from the spot during Villa's 1-0 win over York City

- Villa lost their first match of the season, away to Bolton, a venue they had suffered more defeats at (33) than at any other ground.
- Vic Crowe missed the trip to Halifax, he was on a scouting mission.
- Lew Chatterley, Villa's longest serving player, joined Northampton Town on a temporary transfer.

OCTOBER

- Brian Tiler came back into the side after missing four games.
- Villa skipper Bruce Rioch was handed a 28-day suspension, plus a £100 fine, at a disciplinary hearing. The outcome had club chairman Doug Ellis livid.
- Second Division Blackpool crushed Villa - minus their captain - at Bloomfield Road to end claret and blue involvement in the League Cup.

NOVEMBER

- Aston Villa's new training ground, Bodymoor Heath, was officially opened on November 9th.
- The shock FA Cup First round defeat at Southend would be Tommy Hughes, Keith Bradley and Davie Gibson's last match in Villa's senior side.
- Jimmy Cumbes made his debut at Boundary Park, Oldham. The victory would be Villa's biggest post-war win on the road.

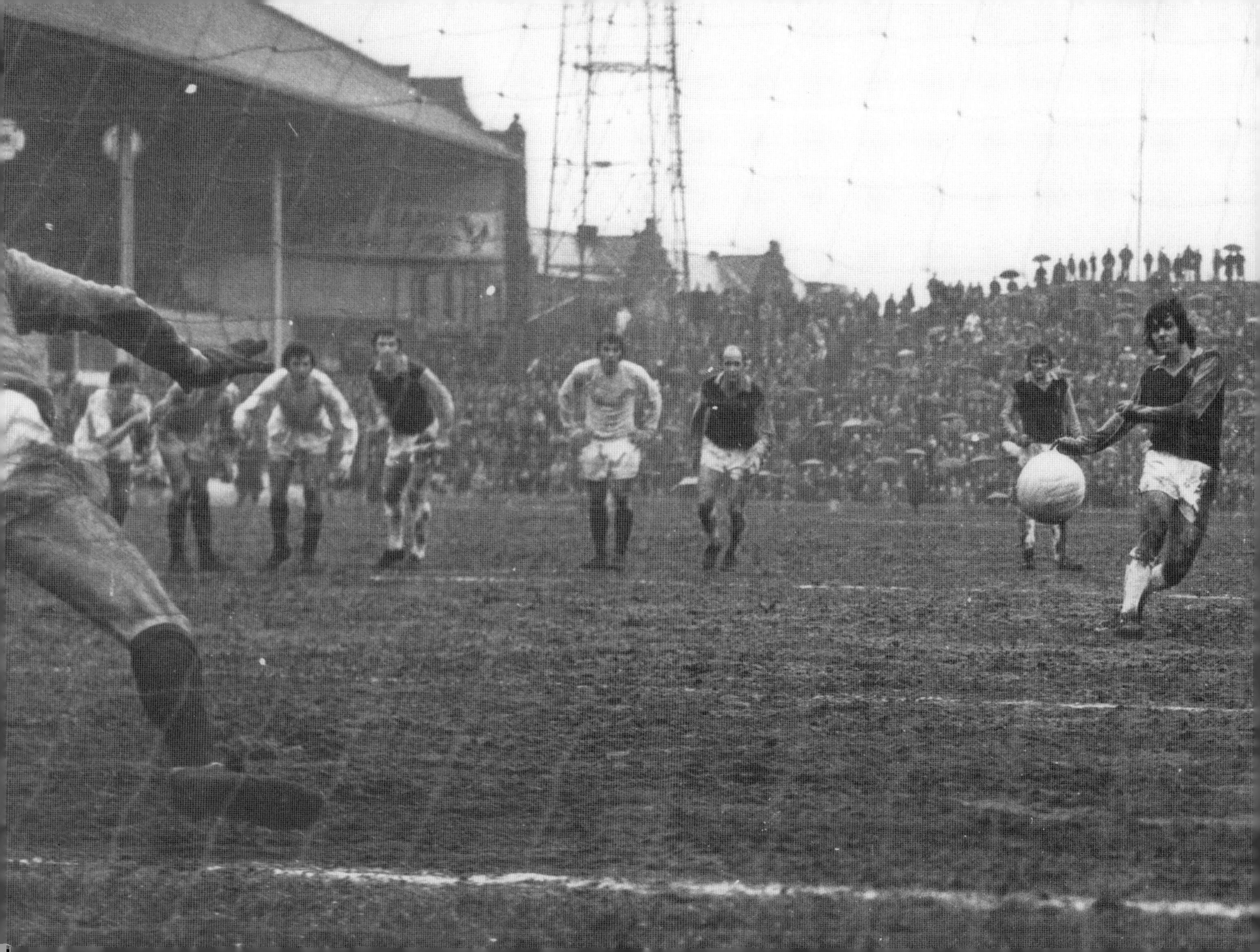

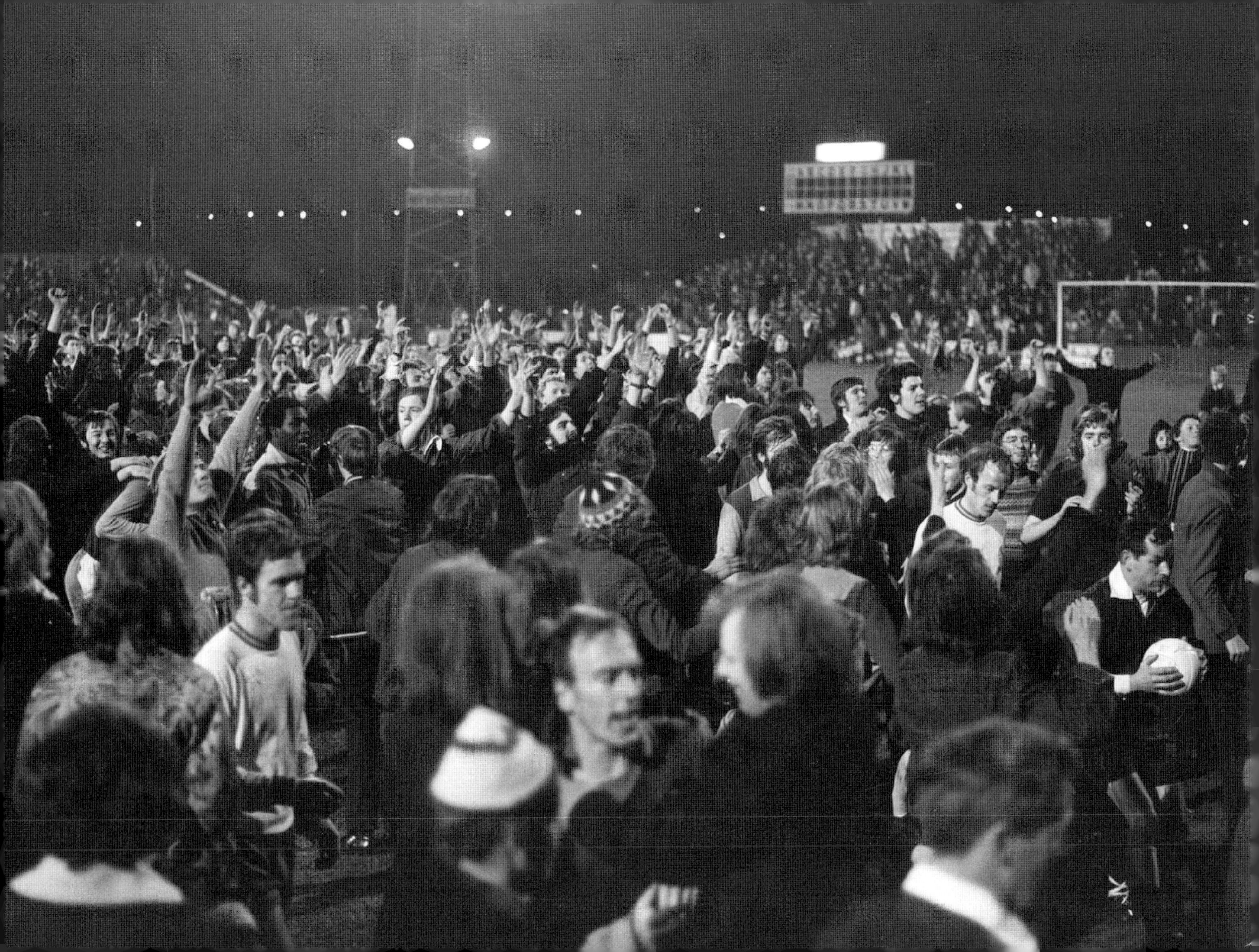

DECEMBER

- Aston Villa played only three fixtures in the month, but won them all to stay within distance of the leaders.
- Charlie Aitken's goal in the victory at home to Bolton Wanderers was his first in six seasons.
- Against all odds, full-back Aitken scored in the following game at Swansea.

JANUARY

- Villa saw the New Year in with a win at home to Halifax Town, their sixth straight victory.
- Lionel Martin came off the bench in the Shrewsbury (home) match. It was his only appearance of the season, and his last in the first-team, to bring closure to his Villa Park career.
- Keith Bradley underwent surgery to sort out ongoing injury problems.

FEBRUARY

- Harry Gregory played his last game in Villa's first team after signing from Charlton, October 1970.
- A new Third Division record gate of 48,110 was posted for the top of the table clash between leaders Villa and second placed Bournemouth. McMahon started for the first time since the opening match of the season.
- Pelé and his Santos (Brazil) team played at Villa Park during their 1972 UK tour. The hosts won 2-1 in front of over 54,000 supporters.
- Ian Ross signed from Liverpool for a record Third Division transfer fee of £70,000.

MARCH

- Ex-Villan, Tony Hateley, playing for Notts County, broke George Curtis' nose during the Meadow Lane clash. George refused to come off and played the entire game with the injury.
- £90,000 was the fee required to prise centre-half Chris Nicholl from Luton town. Yet another record transfer fee for the division.
- After recovering from a bad leg-break, Dave Rudge was back in hospital for surgery to sort his cartilage trouble.

APRIL

- Geoff Vowden wrote his name into the Villa history books with the goal at Mansfield that guaranteed promotion to Division Two.
- Curtis also starred at Field Mill having missed the last 12 games. It would be his last in the claret and blue.
- Aston Villa's youngsters, coached by Frank Upton, won the prestigious FA Youth Cup – the first time a side in the third-tier had landed the trophy.

MAY

- Aston Villa signed off the campaign with a Villa Park victory over Chesterfield – their 20th win from 23 home League fixtures. Ironically, it was against the same opponents that Villa kicked-off their Third Division spell in August 1970.
- Villa set a new 70 points tally record for Division Three.

[Left] Ray Graydon can be seen in the foreground attempting to leave the field as Villa fans celebrate the club's promotion

[Right] Aston Villa and Manchester City contest the 1972 Charity Shield at Villa Park

1972-73

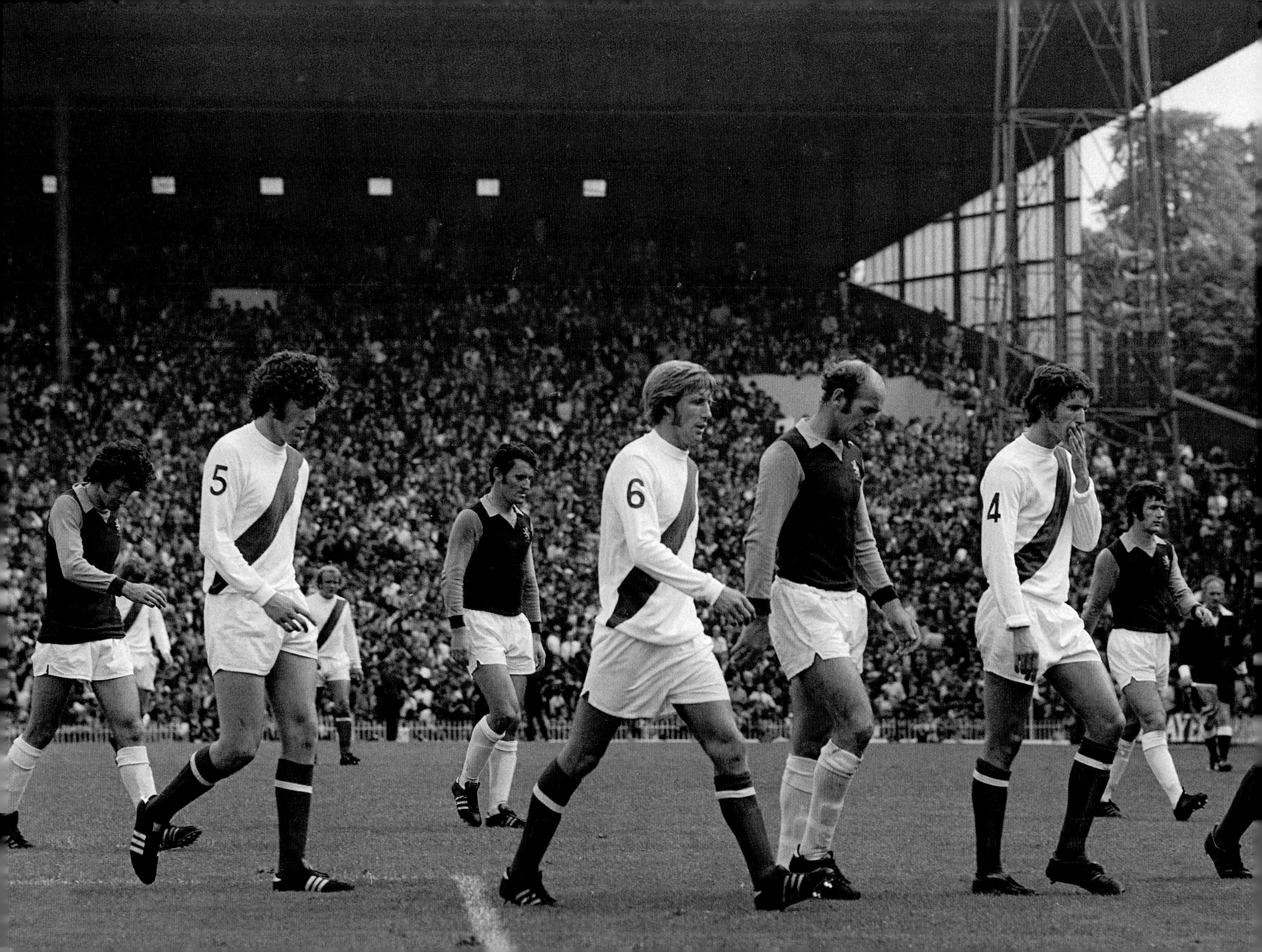
5
6
4

THE BIG ASTON VILLA BOOK OF THE SEVENTIES

[Back Row] Ian Ross, Ray Graydon, Jim Cumbes, Chris Nicholl, Tommy Hughes, Charlie Aitken, Malcolm Beard [Middle Row] David Rudge, Brian Tiler, Andy Lochhead, Fred Turnbull, Neil Rioch, Keith Bradley, Jimmy Brown, Pat McMahon, Alun Evans [Front Row] Ron Wylie (Coach), Brian Little, Harry Gregory, Geoff Vowden, Ian 'Chico' Hamilton, Bruce Rioch, Michael Wright, Willie Anderson, Vic Crowe (Manager)

Football League	Division Two
Manager	Vic Crowe
Asst. Manager/Coach	Ron Wylie
Physio	Fred Pedley
Captain	Bruce Rioch
Final Position	Third
FA Cup	Third Round
League Cup	Third Round
Leading Goalscorer (all competitions)	Ray Graydon & Alun Evans – 10 goals

Even before a ball was kicked there were rumblings of discontent at boardroom level, which eventually led to former Villa player, Harry Parkes, losing his seat to former England Test cricketer, Alan Smith. Doug Ellis was deposed as chairman by Jim Hartley, but he remained a director.

On the field, Villa signed teenage sensation Alun Evans from Liverpool, who had cost the Reds a six figure fee when they'd bought him from the Wolves – Villa paid somewhat less.

Unusually, Villa's curtain-raiser to the season was the 1972/73 Charity Shield, which came about when both the FA Cup winners (Leeds United) and First Division champions (Derby County) declined to take part. Instead, it was decided the match would be played between Manchester City (fourth in the top-flight) and Third Division Champions Villa – City won the game, which was held at Villa Park, by a single goal.

Brian Tiler and Michael Wright were deemed surplus to requirements as early as August, although no less than four of the FA Youth Cup winning side would wear the first team shirt during the months ahead – Brian Little, Jimmy Brown, John Gidman and Bobby McDonald.

Two wins at the start of the League campaign was great for morale, with the 1-4 setback at Burnley a mere blip. There followed a sequence of seven matches unbeaten (five wins), which culminated in Aston Villa FC sitting proudly at the summit, albeit on goal difference, from Sheffield Wednesday.

A League Cup run was halted at the Third Round – after disposing of Hereford United and Nottingham Forest, Villa were held

continued >>>

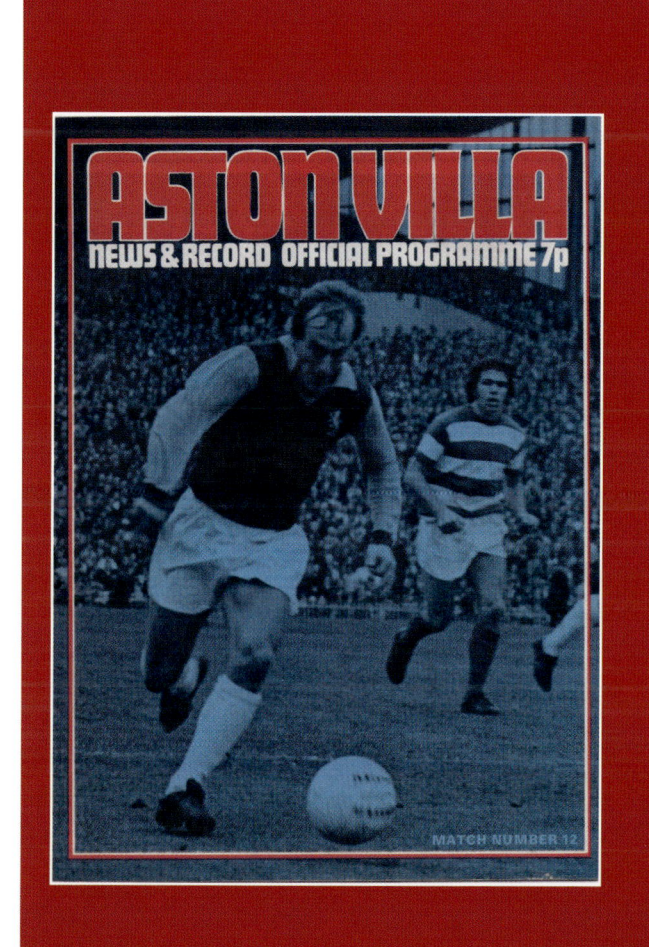

		P	W	D	L	F	A	W	D	L	F	A	Pts
1	Burnley	42	13	6	2	44	18	11	8	2	28	17	62
2	Q.P.R	42	16	4	1	54	13	8	9	4	27	24	61
3	**Aston Villa**	**42**	**12**	**5**	**4**	**27**	**17**	**6**	**9**	**6**	**24**	**30**	**50**
4	Middlesbrough	42	12	6	3	29	15	5	7	9	17	28	47
5	Bristol City	42	10	7	4	34	18	7	5	9	29	33	46
6	Sunderland	42	12	6	3	35	17	5	6	10	24	32	46
7	Blackpool	42	12	6	3	37	17	6	4	11	19	34	46
8	Oxford United	42	14	2	5	36	18	5	5	11	16	25	45
9	Fulham	42	11	6	4	32	16	5	6	10	26	33	44
10	Sheffield Wed	42	14	4	3	40	20	3	6	12	19	35	44
11	Millwall	42	12	5	4	33	18	4	5	12	22	29	42
12	Luton Town	42	6	9	6	24	23	9	2	10	20	30	41
13	Hull City	42	9	7	5	39	22	5	5	11	25	37	40
14	Nottingham Forest	42	12	5	4	32	18	2	7	12	15	34	40
15	Orient	42	11	6	4	33	15	1	6	14	16	35	36
16	Swindon Town	42	8	9	4	28	23	2	7	12	18	37	36
17	Portsmouth	42	7	6	8	21	22	5	5	11	21	37	35
18	Carlisle United	42	10	5	6	40	24	1	7	13	10	28	34
19	Preston North End	42	6	8	7	19	25	5	4	12	18	39	34
20	Cardiff City	42	11	4	6	32	21	0	7	14	11	37	33
21	Huddersfield Town	42	7	9	5	21	20	1	8	12	15	36	33
22	Brighton & Hove	42	7	8	6	32	31	1	5	15	14	52	29

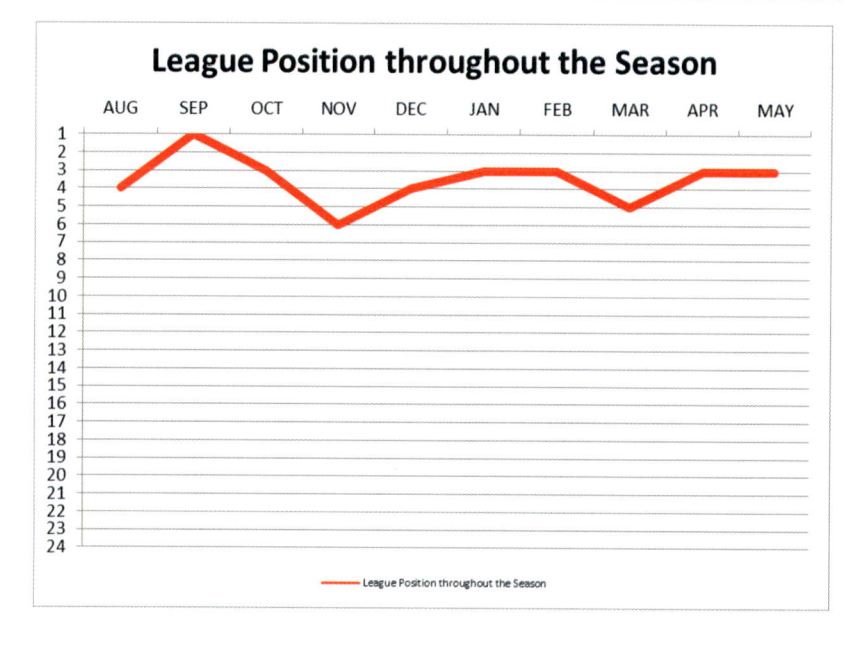

Total Home League Attendances 584,460
Average Home League Attendance 27,831
Highest Home League Attendance 38,637
Lowest Home League Attendance 15,902

League Position throughout the Season

61

THE BIG ASTON VILLA BOOK OF THE SEVENTIES

1972-73

Sat 5th August   **Manchester City FA Charity Shield (H)**
Lost 0-1   **Att 34,890**

This fixture lacked the kudos it does today, meaning Division One Champions Derby County and FA Cup holders Leeds United both declined to play the match. So it was down to high-flying City and the Third Division champs Villa, who certainly weren't overawed by a City side who'd finished fourth in the top flight. Villa took the game to them and Corrigan in goal had to be at his best to stop Lochhead from scoring. At the other end McMahon charged down a goal-bound Doyle effort. New signing Alun Evans came on for the big Scot but couldn't prevent City taking the silverware, thanks to a late goal when Franny Lee converted a penalty.

Sat 12th August   **Preston North End (A)**
Won 1-0   **Att 17,371**
Anderson

Division Three champions 1971 versus Division Three champions 1972. PNE had the ball in the net within two minutes - luckily for Crowe's boys it was offside – and dominated for the majority of the match as Villa gave the ball away repeatedly. If flair was required to win the game, Rioch provided it, forcing the goalkeeper into full length saves. His team-mates followed the example and Anderson finally broke the deadlock with six minutes remaining following good work from Graydon on the right.

Wed 16th August   **Hereford United (H) League Cup 1st round**
Won 4-1   **Att 32,113**
Rioch B, Graydon, Vowden, Evans

The fourth-tier team started the game full of aggression and took the game to Villa backed by 5,000 Bulls fans, but a Rioch goal in the

at home to Leeds United in front of 46,000 fans, although the Elland Road replay attracted a gate of less than 29,000, which included a substantial following from Birmingham.

November was a bit of a disaster for the club, with no wins registered and the team falling to sixth, after losing ground on the top two.

December was a more upbeat month, with England U-23 full-back, John Robson, signed from Derby County and the side unbeaten – two wins were followed by three draws. Villa ended the calendar year back in contention, just two points behind second-placed Queens Park Rangers.

The second half of the season mirrored the first, with little consistency shown. A narrow 2-3 defeat at First Division Everton put paid to any hopes of an FA Cup odyssey – a set back that was instantly forgotten with three impressive victories – plus an international friendly when a powerful Bayern Munich side visited Villa Park. Unfortunately Villa then suffered the same consecutive number of losses.

A 0-3 defeat at Bristol City's Aston Gate on 27th March turned out to be Villa's last reversal of the campaign as the team finished strongly, taking 11 of the 14 points on offer. Their third place finish was considered remarkable for a promoted club, despite being 11 points adrift. But, with only the top two promoted, it counted for very little, and it would be sod's law when, the following season, the Football League altered the format so the top three went up!

Fans favourite, Andy Lochhead, left for pastures new – it wasn't a fitting farewell for a prolific and popular player, his last game in the shirt was away to Carlisle in front of just 6,000 fans.

[Right] Ray Graydon scores as Villa defeat Hereford United 4-1

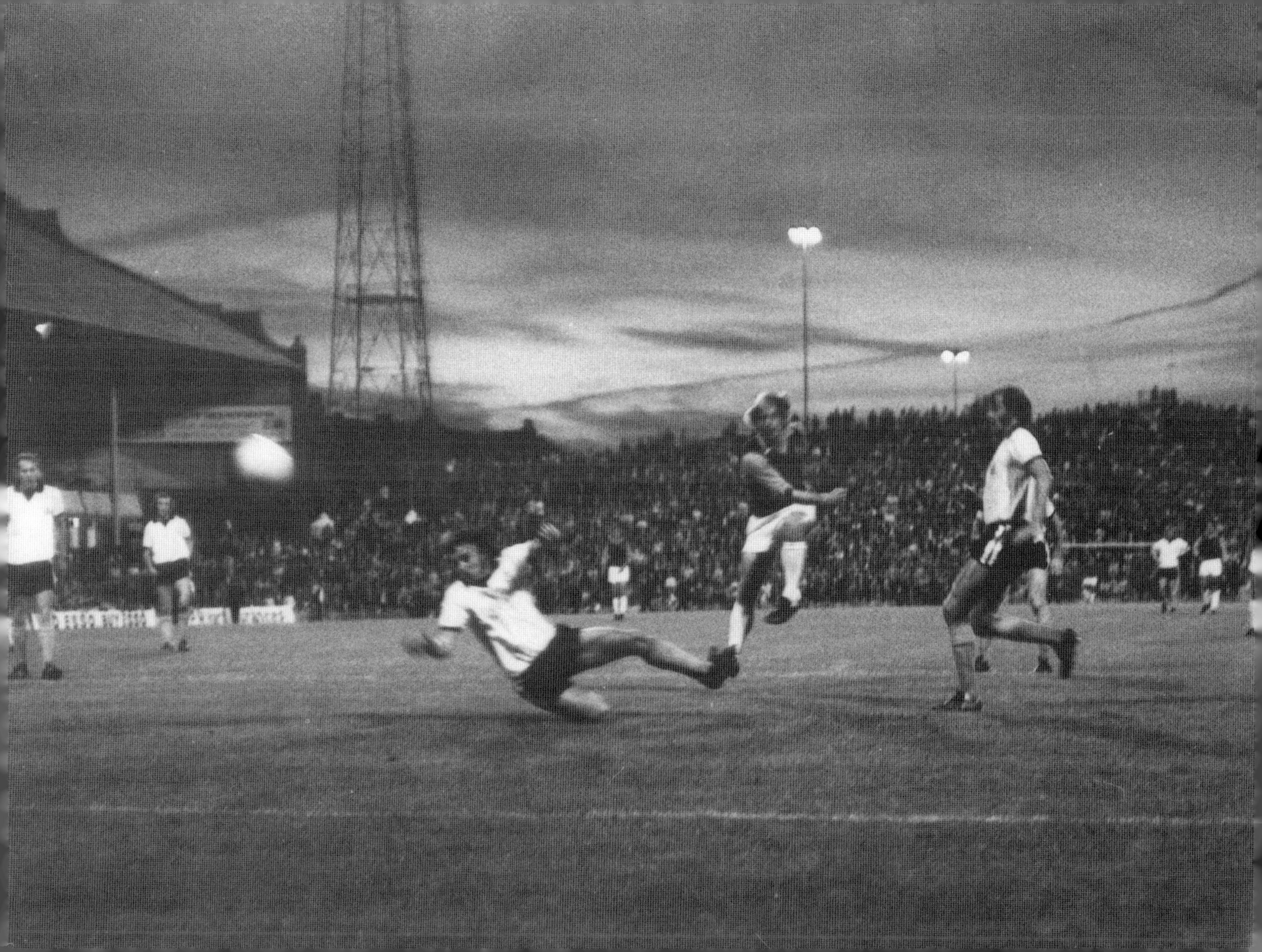

24th minute calmed things down somewhat. Graydon then made it two a minute after the break with a hard, left-footed shot from the edge of the box. Ex-Villa strike-cum-keeper, Fred Potter, kept the score down with some superb saves, before Vowden made it 3-0 following neat footwork from sub Evans. Hereford reduced the deficit with eight minutes to go, but Villa added a fourth when Evans scored his first in the claret and blue.

Sat 19th August   Huddersfield Town (H)
Won 2-0   Att 34,843
Vowden, Graydon

Villa played mostly down the flanks against recently relegated Huddersfield, who packed numbers behind the ball, and would have gone in front had Lochhead's header been a few inches closer. Geoff Vowden eventually fired Villa ahead late in the first half from a Graydon corner. The side was rocked when Rioch left the field with a broken wrist, but sealed the win with an 87th minute strike from the 'Grayder' after Evans had helped on a McMahon cross. Early days, but joint top wasn't too bad at all.

Sat 26th August   Burnley (A)
Lost 1-4   Att 14,941
Hamilton

Villa opened with a flourish, and despite going behind early in the game, were back on level terms only four minutes later through a cleverly worked goal. Aitken's free-kick found Lochhead, who nodded the ball to the feet of Ian Hamilton – 'Chico' did the rest and forced the ball home between the post and the keeper. It looked like the visitors would go on and take both points, but they were left reeling when Burnley scored two decisive goals in the space of only four minutes, then another in the 76th minute to record a 4-1 win.

Tue 29th August   Carlisle United (H)
Won 1-0   Att 29,047
Rioch B

Bruce Rioch, just 11 days after breaking his wrist, and wearing a light protective covering, was the surprise inclusion to face an unbeaten Carlisle side – Gidman debuted at full-back. Villa looked disjointed and Carlisle were unlucky not to score when they failed twice with players clean through on goal. The visitors also struck the upright when it looked easier to score. Rioch was Villa's salvation when he snatched both points with a scorching shot from distance in the 74th minute.

Sat 2nd September   Brighton & Hove Albion (H)
Drew 1-1   Att 30,750
Lochhead

Villa were well below par and half time was reached with very little to show in a drab game – then Brighton scored within 30 seconds of the restart. Willie Anderson went off in the 58th minute and Evans' appearance produced immediate results when he and Lochhead combined for the equaliser – Evans turned at speed on the left edge of the box and hooked the ball in for Lochhead to move in and send it soaring into the net. It was the big man's first of the season.

Tue 5th September   Nottingham Forest (A) League Cup 2nd round
Won 1-0   Att 17,665
Evans

Gidman retained his place in the side at the expense of Wright, and with Andy Lochhead missing, teenage sensation Alun Evans was given his first full start – he rewarded Vic Crowe's belief by putting his new team in front on 13 minutes. Rioch had started the move, which skidded off the head of a Forest player, before Evans struck, firing into the corner of the net. Villa were faster on the night and more direct – Graydon had a shot saved and an Aitken header was tipped over the bar – and although the home side created a few chances of their own – Villa held on.

Sat 9th September   **Cardiff City (A)**
Won 2-0   **Att 16,707**
Rioch B, Lochhead

Aston Villa went ahead in the 13th minute when Rioch picked the ball up 10-yards inside the Cardiff half, he then moved forward and let fly from 30-yards straight into the far corner – Lochhead doubled the advantage 12 minutes later. Vowden fed Anderson who beat the full-back, before putting over a centre that was food and drink to the likes of Lochhead. Cardiff were stunned, while Villa were described in one paper as playing 'copybook football.' Crowe's boys were sitting in a very healthy third position, just a point behind leaders Sheffield Wednesday.

Sat 16th September   **Swindon Town (H)**
Won 2-1   **Att 30,775**
Evans, Lochhead

In a match that lacked much in the way of sparkle and excitement, both Villa full-backs impressed – Aitken for continually breaking up Swindon attacks, while young Gidman demonstrating what would become his trademark overlapping runs down the wing. Don Rogers gave the visitors an interval lead, before 'Supersub' Evans levelled things up just after the hour – Rioch's corner was helped on by Vowden, then Evans connected to send the ball high into the net. Within four minutes Villa had turned the game on its head when Lochhead got on the end of a Rioch free-kick to make it 2-1. Villa pressed the opposition but couldn't add to the scoreline, nonetheless, they were top of the pile on goal average.

Sat 23rd September   **Nottingham Forest (A)**
Drew 1-1   **Att 18,082**
Own goal

But for their wasted chances, poor finishing and the saves of Jim Barron in the Forest goal, Villa should have had the game sewn up by half time. After the break Nicholl pumped a free-kick into the danger zone, it was headed down only for McMahon to mis-hit six yards out, Graydon instinctively swung at the loose ball but the shot was deflected to safety. It eventually took an own goal to put Villa in front, but the visitors couldn't see the game out and Forest earned a point with a goal with a little over ten minutes to go.

Wed 27th September   **Sunderland (H)**
Won 2-0   **Att 29,918**
Evans, Rioch B

Jim Montgomery parried Graydon's fierce free-kick only to see Evans nip in to put Villa ahead. Sunderland continued to pressure shaky Villa, and if it wasn't for Chris Nicholl the Black Cats would have been in front on 15 minutes. Despite Villa stuttering, a Bruce Rioch 20-yard special in the second period calmed the nerves and claimed both points.

Sat 30th September   **Millwall (H)**
Won 1-0   **Att 31,451**
Rioch B (pen)

Millwall were just two points off the bottom though you wouldn't have thought it – Jim Cumbes pulled off two great saves to stop a very real shock. Villa continued to struggle to piece passes together, but went ahead in the 76th minute thanks to a penalty. Bruce Rioch fired home the 12-yard spot-kick (in Anderson's absence) leaving Millwall boss Fenton peeved by the result and claiming his side had had 75% of the ball.

Wed 4th October   **Leeds United (H) League Cup 3rd rnd**
Drew 1-1   **Att 46,185**
Rioch B

A sizeable crowd came out to see how Villa would cope with Don Revie's formidable Leeds United - FA Cup winners and Division One runners-up. Villa and Leeds slogged it out like "Navvies in the Sahara" according to one report. United went in front through

THE BIG ASTON VILLA BOOK OF THE SEVENTIES

Jackie Charlton after only five minutes, and sensing Villa's threat, put men behind the ball, but it didn't stop Bruce Rioch firing home an angled 15-yard shot in the 68th minute to earn Villa a deserved replay at Elland Road. In fact Leeds were probably the happier team for having a second chance to progress.

[Right] A young John Gidman in action at Portsmouth's Fratton Park ground

Sat 7th October   **Fulham (A)**
Lost 0-2   **Att 17,576**

Fulham had certainly done their homework, they knew Cumbes big kicks launched numerous Villa attacks. They simply pushed up field where Villa would be offside. The home side went in front early on following a twice taken free-kick. The 'Cottagers' added a second through Alan Mullery with a well executed goal. Villa chased the game too late with Evans pulling two good saves out of the Fulham goalie and also striking the woodwork. The defeat cost Villa their pole position, Burnley now led the table.

Wed 11th October   **Leeds United (A) League Cup 3rd rnd replay**
Lost 0-2   **Att 28,894**

The game at Leeds was played in a strong wind, this caught out Cumbes when a long ball changed direction, he pushed it against the post only for it to hit Nicholl and creep over the line to put Leeds ahead. Seven minutes later the Yorkshire side made it 2-0 through Jones. Cumbes acrobatics kept the score down while Crowe took some flak from the travelling Villa supporters who were upset with the withdrawal of Vowden even though they'd been calling for Graydon to come off the bench.

Sat 14th October   **Queens Park Rangers (H)**
Lost 0-1   **Att 34,045**

Rangers gave Villa a stern test with Gerry Francis at the heart of everything, he and Aitken collided heavily and both needed treatment. Vowden had a shot go marginally wide but Villa then had two narrow escapes. Keith Leonard came off the bench – for the second game running - after the break and was well placed at the far post, but Graydon chose to shoot himself and forced Phil Parkes into a good save. With QPR looking dangerous it was no surprise when they scored. Their 61st minute goal just reward for their enterprising play.

Tue 17th October   **Blackpool (A)**
Drew 1-1   **Att 15,043**
Evans

A string of brilliant saves from Jim Cumbes prevented Villa slumping to a fourth consecutive defeat. Although Villa had gone ahead three minutes before the interval – Evans notching his fifth of the campaign – Blackpool were back on level terms on the hour, before Cumbes came into his own to keep out three certain goals. Villa had taken a point they hardly deserved and sat fourth in the table.

Sat 21st October   **Portsmouth (A)**
Won 1-0   **Att 13,524**
Vowden

Villa were without big centre-half Chris Nicholl, who'd gone off in the mid-week match, Fred Turnbull was in for his first start. In a sub-standard game Geoff Vowden put Villa in front after hesitancy in the Pompey defence. John Gidman, improving with every match, was unlucky not to score when he found himself unmarked just outside the box, his shot flew into the side netting. Portsmouth tried to level the game but they were somewhat erratic once in the Villa's area and, ultimately, the visitors were good value for the two points.

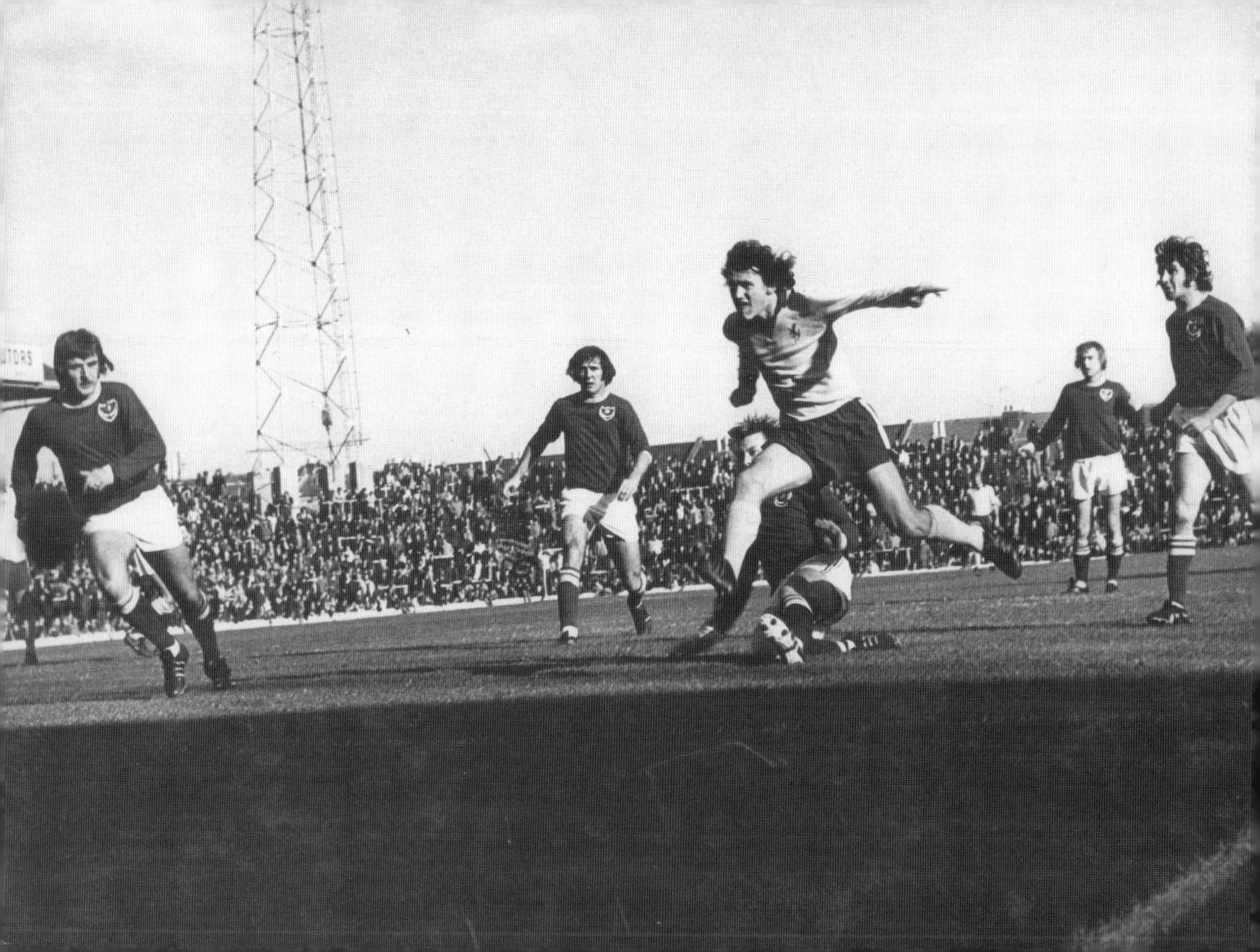

THE BIG ASTON VILLA BOOK OF THE SEVENTIES

Sat 28th October   **Middlesbrough (H)**
Drew 1-1   **Att 30,345**
Vowden

Stan Anderson's 'Boro, with just one win on the road, faced Vic Crowe's lads having won five of seven at home, and Villa not played it too casual after getting an early lead through Vowden's hooked shot, it would surely have been six victories. Instead, the home side were to rue their missed chances. A Rioch left-footer skidded narrowly wide of the mark, an Evans header glanced the wrong side of the woodwork and a Gidman shot, after being set up by Rioch, was on its way in before Jim Platt in the Middlesbrough goal dived full length. As Villa lost their grip, the visitors upped their game and drew level.

Sat 4th November   **Sunderland (A)**
Drew 2-2   **Att 18,717**
Rioch B, Little

Villa were trailing on Wearside after only 55 seconds following a rare Bruce Rioch error. He made amends mid-way through the first half to score the equaliser and the ref signalled the end of the first period with the game finely poised at 1-1. Sunderland regained the lead after the hour mark following a well placed free-kick only for Brian Little - making his second start in eight days - to bag his first goal of the season with a well placed header, which went over Montgomery following Willie Anderson's centre.

Sat 11th November   **Blackpool (H)**
Drew 0-0   **Att 31,651**

The game perfectly highlighted Villa's lack of punch in front of goal. Their 19-goal tally was 12 less than QPR, who were just above them in the table. Graydon's return from injury meant Villa played with more width and the lasting impression from the match was youngster Little's ability to read situations, coupled with his tidy ball control. Luckily for the home side, Blackpool were just as toothless during the dreary deadlock.

[Right] Rioch bags Villa's first in the 2-2 draw at Roker Park – Alun Evans and Brian Little are following up

Sat 18th November   **Luton Town (H)**
Lost 0-2   **Att 29,044**

The Hatters promised to play attacking football and they did just that by taking a 21st minute lead to give Villa an uphill battle – although, had Lochhead been on target from an accurate Ian Ross free-kick, things could have been very different. Villa staged a spirited second-half display, but a second goal for Luton wrecked chances of a Villa recovery.

Sat 25th November   **Oxford United (A)**
Lost 0-2   **Att 13,647**

Due to fighting on the terraces the game kicked-off 11 minutes late. Villa started promisingly - with Burton having to save from Lochhead - but lost the impetus when Oxford forged ahead just before the half hour. Villa's case wasn't helped when Anderson had to be replaced by McMahon because of a reoccurrence of his ligament trouble. Villa were still trying to get back into the game when they were stung by Oxford scoring a second, which put the result beyond doubt. Villa had lost back-to-back games for the second time in the campaign and dropped two places to sixth.

Sat 2nd December   **Hull City (H)**
Won 2-0   **Att 21,213**
Graydon (pen), Hamilton

After 270 minutes without scoring a goal it took Villa just two more to find the net against a Hull side without a win in five. Even though it was a controversial decision to award the penalty, Graydon

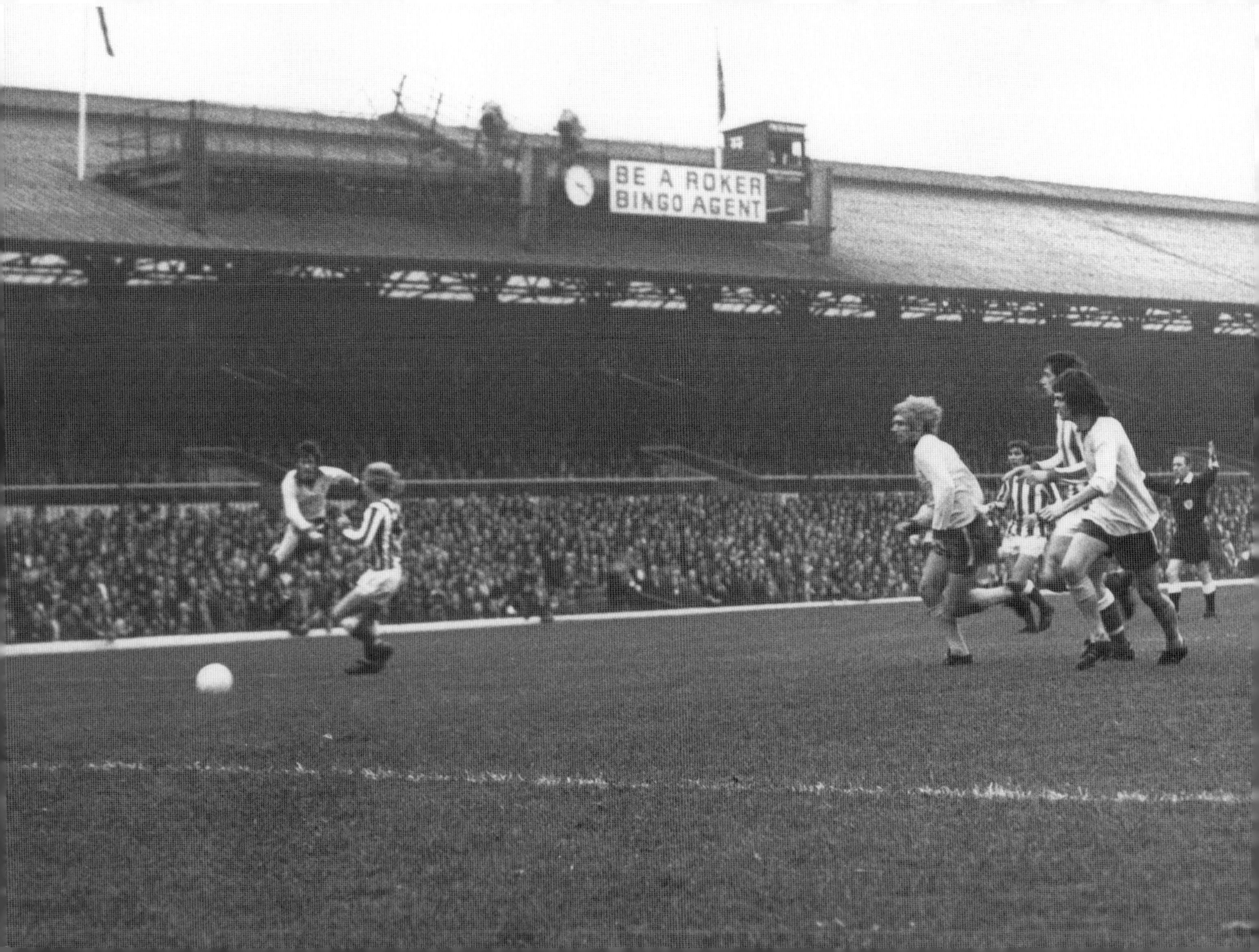
BE A ROKER
BINGO AGENT

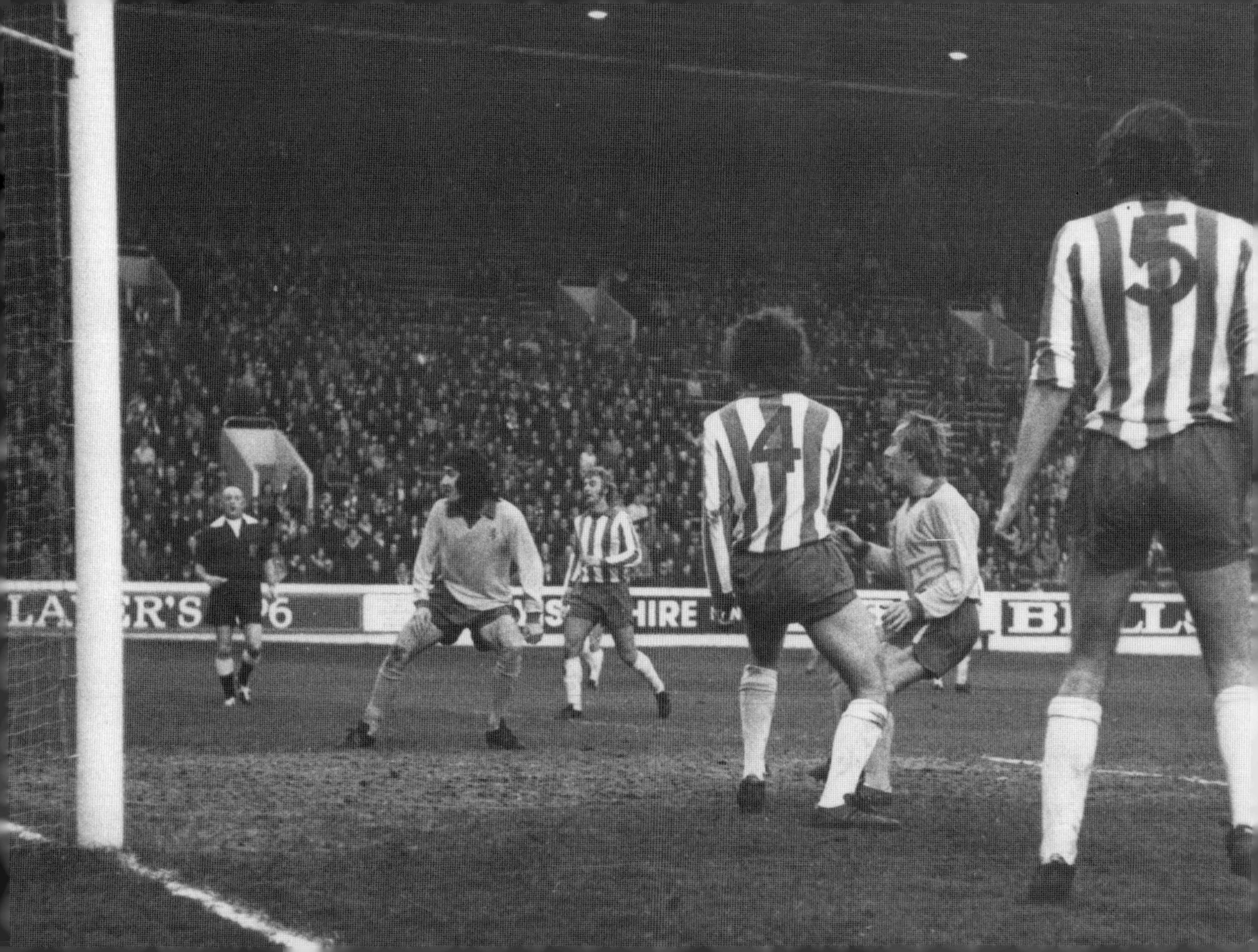
SHIRE

[Left] Graydon scores during Villa's drew 2-2 at Sheffield Wednesday as McMahon looks on

remained calm to blast it in. Villa could have added to their lead ten minutes later when a Vowden header was parried and Evans fired it back in with force, only to see it blocked. It took until the 75th minute for Villa to establish a two goal cushion - thanks again to a touch of good fortune – when Rioch's 25-yard shot was deflected off Hamilton to wrong-foot keeper Wealands.

Sat 16th December   Orient (H)
Won 1-0   Att 20,572
Evans

With Vowden missing, Malcolm Beard was recalled for his first start of the campaign (and what would be his last in the first team). Against one of the poorer away teams – one win in ten – Villa showed signs of encouraging attacking play, but were let down by sloppy finishing. One goal was enough to win this contest and it duly arrived after just two minutes – Evans latching onto the ball after it had fallen invitingly into his path after deflecting off a defender's legs.

Sat 23rd December   Sheffield Wednesday (A)
Drew 2-2   Att 20,561
Graydon 2

No team had won more matches on home soil than Wednesday, so it was always going to be a tricky visit. Ray Graydon put Villa ahead in the 36th minute with The Owl's Tommy Craig (a future Villa player) cancelling it out within two minutes. The home fans were still cheering when Graydon restored Villa's advantage, to make it three goals in a frantic four minute spell. Despite Villa blooding John Robson in defence, Wednesday were able to salvage a point when they found the net in the 64th minute. This was the first time during the campaign that a Villa player had scored two in a game – this from someone who'd only scored twice in open play.

Tue 26th December   Nottingham Forest (H)
Drew 2-2   Att 37,000
Lochhead, Evans

Villa desperately needed both points to keep in touch with Burnley and QPR, who'd both won the previous day. Roared on by Villa Park's biggest gate so far, the home side had a couple of early chances, Lochhead and Evans both being teed up by the impressive John Robson. Forest then forged a two goal lead before the break, only for Lochhead and Evans to earn Villa a share of the points in a 2-2 draw. Rioch and Evans both had good chances late on as Villa tried in vain to find a winner.

Sat 30th December   Huddersfield Town (A)
Drew 1-1   Att 9,719
Evans

Crowe's team, who produced one of their worst performances of the season, fell behind with seconds to go in the first half – this after Cumbes had been caught by surprise long-range shot that forced him into making a despairing lunge. Even though Huddersfield looked like relegation fodder, Villa were lucky to salvage something from the game through the ever-dependable Alun Evans. As the ball was hammered into the crowded area by Rioch, after being sent through by Graydon, Evans seized onto the loose ball to make it 1-1.

Sat 6th January   Burnley (H)
Lost 0-3   Att 38,637

It was ironic that, in front of what would be Villa's biggest crowd of the season, they suffered their worst defeat on home soil. Two down at the interval, things got even worse as, according to one paper, "the Villa defence opened like a door" and Burnley walked

71

THE BIG ASTON VILLA BOOK OF THE SEVENTIES

through to add a third. The Villa fans chanted that "Crowe must go!" It was of little consolation to the Villa boss that Burnley were undefeated on their travels.

Sat 13th January
Everton (A) FA Cup 3rd round Lost 2-3
Att 42,222
Vowden, Evans

Villa raised their game against a top-flight opposition unbeaten in their last four outings. Everton struck first, but Villa were soon on level terms again when an Aitken free-kick was headed on by Evans for Vowden to finish. The home side added another before a third was awarded at the stroke of half time, even though it appeared Cumbes had beaten the ball away without it crossing the line. A late Evans goal led to Villa staging a rally to force a replay, but it wasn't to be. Out at the first hurdle for the fourth season in a row.

Sat 20th January
Brighton & Hove Albion (A) Won 3-1
Att 12,212
Evans, Graydon, Brown

Villa met an Albion outfit in freefall, with ten straight defeats under their belts. An Alun Evans goal – his tenth – was the difference between the sides at the break. It must have been a massive shock to Vic Crowe when Brighton were on equal terms four minutes into the second period. Villa had countless opportunities to restore their lead before Ray Graydon picked the lock to nod home in the 75th minute. Jimmy Brown, back from the wilderness, added to the scoring to make it 3-1 on 84 minutes, giving the result a more balanced look.

Sat 27th January   **Cardiff City (H)**
Won 2-0   **Att 28,856**
Graydon (pen), Rioch B

Third from bottom Cardiff offered very little in the way of resistance, although Villa had trouble with their finishing yet again and it took

[Right] Talented Villa winger Ray Graydon turns the Burnley defenders inside out

until the stroke of half time before they finally broke the deadlock, which came from a Graydon spot-kick after Brian Little had been launched into the air by the Bluebirds' right-back. Hamilton came on for the injured Little after the break. Bruce Rioch scored a spectacular second in the 59th minute after he played a one-two with Evans before pulling the trigger on the 18-yard line. The ball went in off the inside of the keeper's left-hand post.

Sat 10th February   **Swindon Town (A)**
Won 3-1   **Att 13,855**
Evans, Graydon 2

Evans, who had passed a late fitness test, scored on 40 minutes with a fine header at the far post to put Villa in the lead in the howling wind. Villa's dominance was rewarded with a second goal five minutes into the second half; Ray Graydon applied the finishing touch following a superb run and centre from Charlie Aitken. Cumbes made one world class save before Robson cleared another effort off the line, but Swindon fought on and scored a solitary goal when their No 7 found the net. Two minutes later the home side were reduced to ten men following Bunkell's dismissal. A late Ray Graydon goal meant the skilful winger had scored four in three games.

Sat 17th February   **Preston North End (H)**
Drew 1-1   **Att 27,717**
Aitken

Villa laid siege to Preston's goal – a Rioch 35-yard pile-drive was saved, then a dangerous cross-shot from Graydon was deflected wide – but it was a question of when, not if. Aitken provided the answer when his glancing header put Villa firmly in the driving seat.

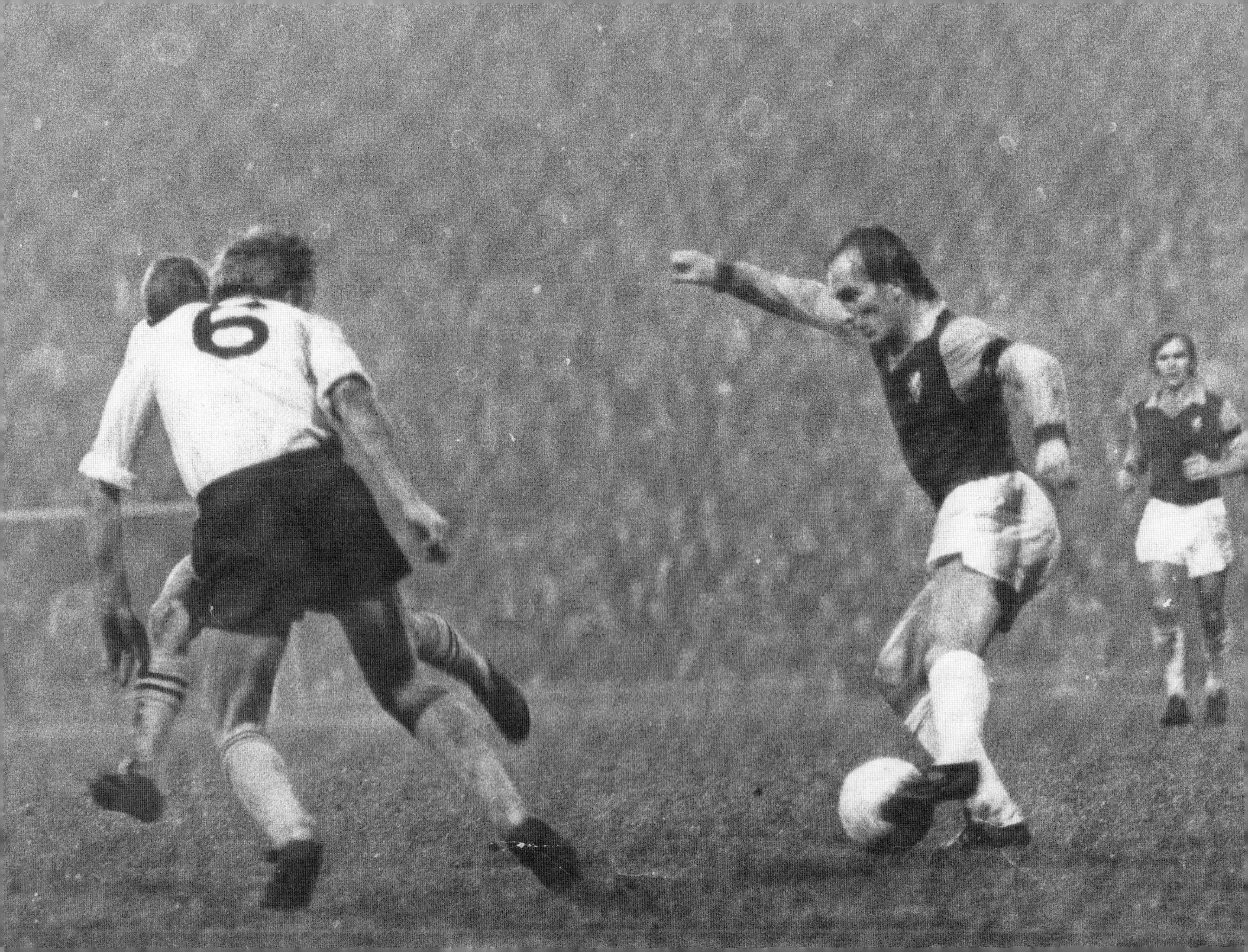

North End then came into the game and were level after 35 minutes when a shot took a slight deflection to beat Cumbes. Rioch and Graydon caused panic in the North End defence, but Villa couldn't fashion a decider.

Sat 24th February   Orient (A)
Lost 0-4
Att 9,085

Orient, second from bottom and with a solitary win in eight, took the lead after just eight minutes, and to make things worse for the visitors, Ian Ross was stretchered off soon afterwards with a badly gashed leg. Villa had to reorganise, and from there on, hardly anything in the way of a Villa attack was seen. Orient caught the opposition cold with two quick goals after the interval and, for good measure, they found the net again with quarter of an hour to go to make it a thoroughly dismal East End afternoon for Crowe's side.

Sat 3rd March
Fulham (H) Lost 2-3
Att 24,007
Little, Rioch B

Fred Turnbull was back in to replace the injured Ross. Brian Little ended a neat four-man move to put Villa ahead within two minutes, before a Robson 30-yard drive went close to increasing the lead. Within a minute of the restart Rioch delighted the Holte Enders when he sprung the Fulham offside trap, raced through and side-footed home. Fulham, only two points behind Villa at the start of play, pulled a goal back on 57 minutes, then four minutes later, the visitors were on equal terms – then, with 20 minutes remaining, The Cottagers scored their third of the afternoon to nick a 3-2 victory.

Sat 10th March   Queens Park Rangers (A)
Lost 0-1   Att 21,578

With back-to-back defeats Villa were losing touch with the top two – QPR in second were seven points better off. It was a dour game,

[Right] Neil Rioch and Chris Nicholl in action during the 2-1 win over Oxford United

although Chris Nicholl was outstanding. Villa were forced to defend but Rangers finally went in front through midfielder Mick Leach after missing several opportunities. Cumbes then brought Dave Thomas down and was lucky not to concede a spot kick, while Villa were restricted to one effort on goal when Graydon teed up McMahon, whose header was only inches over.

Sat 17th March   Portsmouth (H)
Won 2-0   Att 18,432
Vowden, McMahon

With Villa languishing in seventh, a win to stay in contention was vital. There had been jeers from the crowd before the hosts went two goals to the good – Geoff Vowden and Pat McMahon netting to set the Villa up for their first win in five. Fortunately Portsmouth offered very little and Bobby McDonald, making his first start in the Villa jersey, had a relatively quiet afternoon in defence.

Sat 24th March   Middlesbrough (A)
Drew 1-1   Att 9,776
McMahon

Bobby McDonald remained in the team in the absence of Charlie Aitken, while Graydon, hurt in training, was also a casualty. The Villa were subjected to constant first half pressure which saw Middlesbrough's Alan Foggon hit the woodwork. Villa had a few chances, the most notable of which was when Lochhead beat Platt to fire in, but it was ruled off-side. Within two minutes of the second half

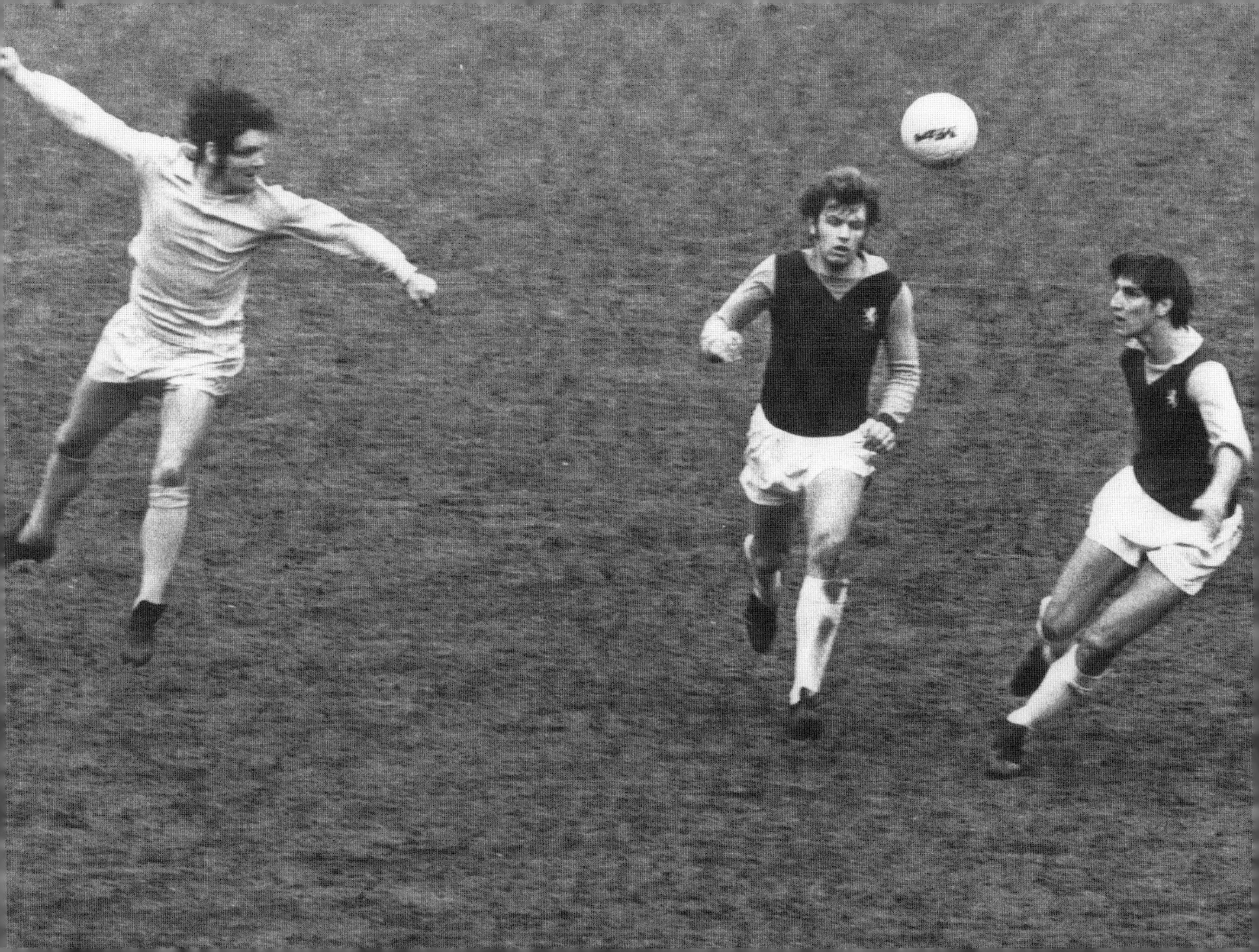

THE BIG ASTON VILLA BOOK OF THE SEVENTIES

Villa shocked the home support with a well taken goal through Pat McMahon – unfortunately Hickton equalised for Boro six minutes from time – but a point from Ayresome Park moved Villa up a position into fifth.

Tue 27th March   Bristol City (A)
Lost 0-3   Att 15,654

With right-back John Robson out of action, Neil Rioch was called up for only his second appearance of the campaign. Villa fell behind to go in one down at the break, then conceded two more second-half goals in a comprehensive defeat at Aston Gate. It was the third time is six games that Villa had leaked three or more goals.

Sat 31st March   Oxford United (H)
Won 2-1   Att 15,902
McMahon, Vowden

With promotion almost an impossibility the Villa Park attendances had fallen to 50% of the levels achieved at the start of the season. Oxford were in front on eight minutes and, with little at stake, the Villa players failed to find any real momentum. The goal was cancelled out when McMahon let fly, more in hope than expectation, from 30-yards out. It took until the hour mark to finish off an average Oxford side (four away wins) with a grabbed winner from Geoff Vowden.

Sat 7th April   Hull City (A)
Won 2-1   Att 8,072
Hamilton, Little

The signs weren't good as Villa had lost on their last three visits to Boothferry Park – but 'Chico' Hamilton headed in from a Jimmy Brown free-kick to give Villa a sixth minute lead. The Tigers then clawed themselves back into the game with an equaliser on the hour mark, also from a free-kick. Their moment was short lived however, Vowden ran down the right-wing before crossing for Brian Little and, with all the coolness of a veteran, the youngster fired a rising shot into the net from 10-yards out.

Sat 14th April   Bristol City (H)
Won 1-0   Att 19,545
Rioch N

Aston Villa totally dominated proceedings and Geoff Vowden should have had a first-half hat-trick against his name. When Villa finally broke the deadlock it was a thing of beauty. Neil Rioch's intelligent run was picked up by John Robson, the full-back's perfectly lofted ball was controlled by Rioch, before he hit it squarely beyond the helpless goalkeeper to the appreciation of the vast Holte End terrace. Three wins on the trot had hauled the claret and blues back up to third, albeit a distance behind second placed QPR.

Sat 21st April   Luton Town (A)
Drew 0-0   Att 10,981

The game had 'end of season' stamped all over it. Jimmy Brown tried hard to get Villa going, but he was the exception on the day. Both teams took a while to settle, Andy Lochhead saw a shot go narrowly wide, while a Hamilton cross-shot barely troubled Barber in goal. Only late in the game was Cumbes called on, to keep two Hatters attempts out when the tempo was raised as both sides went all out for the win.

Mon 23rd April   Millwall (A)
Drew 1-1   Att 9,932
Graydon

Millwall went ahead in the 16th minute from a penalty, but the lead lasted only ten minutes before Graydon netted to claim his tenth of the season. Unfortunately for Ray – after 75 minutes of being kicked black and blue – he finally snapped and gave a bit back to his tormentor Cripps and was sent off for his trouble. Two minutes from time Millwall thought they'd fashioned a winner, but were denied by the ever alert Jim Cumbes.

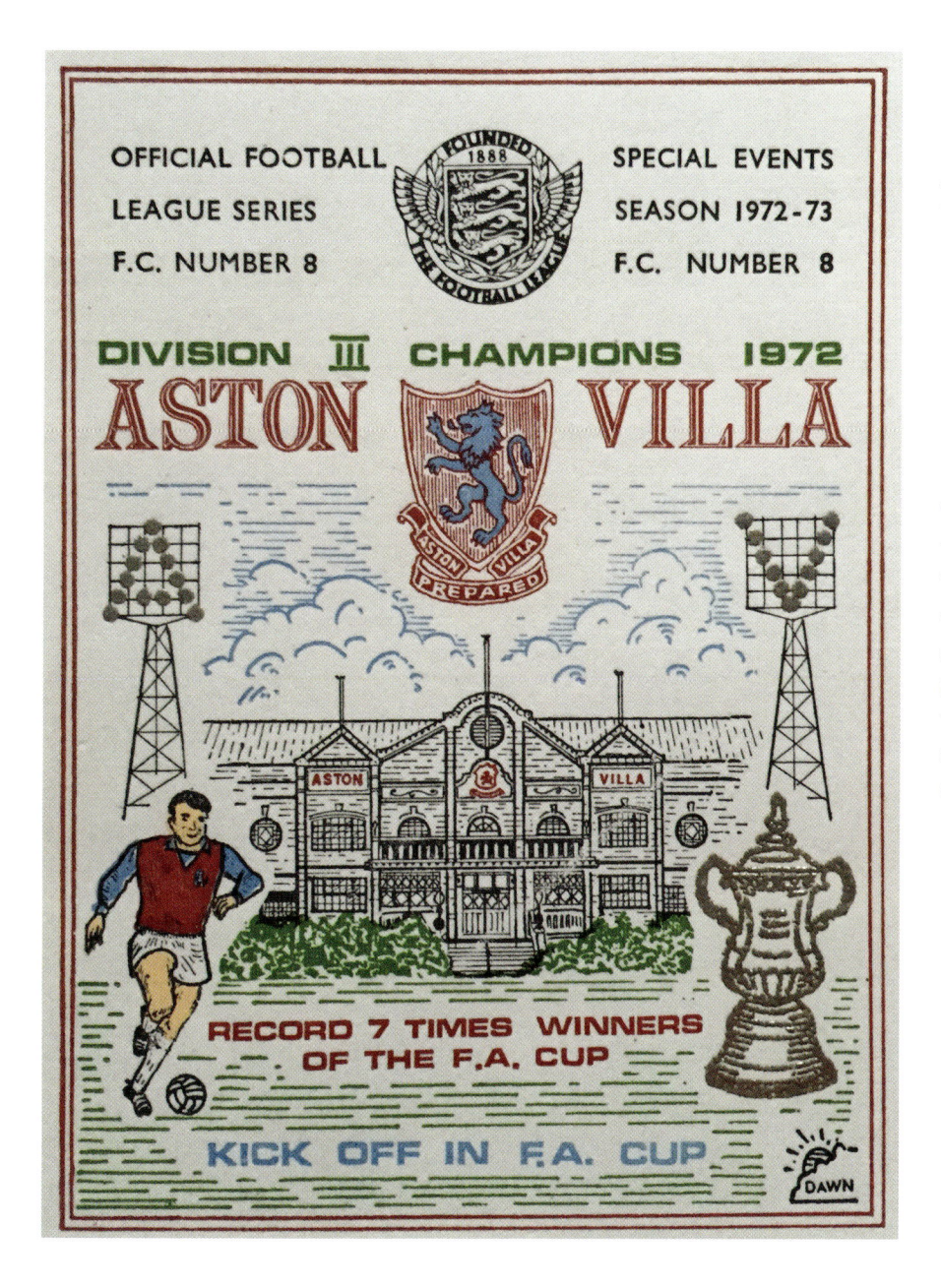

Sat 24th April   **Sheffield Wednesday (H)**
Won 2-1   Att 20,710
Lochhead, Hamilton

A win, their twelfth on home soil, against a Wednesday side with only three wins on their travels, came courtesy of Andy Lochhead and Ian Hamilton notching second-half goals, after The Owls had audaciously led 1-0 at the interval. Villa's home form wasn't great, but it their away record that would ultimately keep them down.

Mon 28th May   **Carlisle United (A)**
Drew 2-2   Att 6,178
Lochhead, Hamilton

Villa brought the curtain down on their 1972/73 campaign in front of a modest Brunton Park crowd – the smallest since Villa's visit to Rochdale in the Third Division. Carlisle, who would beat the drop by a singl, point ,took a 2-1 interval lead after Villa had opened the scoring through Lochhead on 20 minutes. 'Chico' Hamilton spared Villa blushes to maintain their unbeaten sequence (seven games) when he hit a screamer in the 76th minute. With only two teams promoted (three from the following season) Villa had missed out.

THE BIG ASTON VILLA BOOK OF THE SEVENTIES

PRE-SEASON

- Alun Evans arrived from Liverpool – the costliest teenager in the game when he moved from Molineux to Anfield for £100,000.
- The club went on a two-match tour of Holland – playing Groningen and Nijmegen – winning both games.

AUGUST

- Aston Villa and Manchester City contested the 1972 FA Charity Shield at Villa Park.
- Vic Crowe was presented with the Divisional Manager of the Season award (Division Three). Ron Saunders of Norwich City won the equivalent for Division Two.
- Bruce Rioch broke his wrist in the second game of the campaign, while Michael Wright played his last match for the Villa.
- Brian Tiler emulated Wright, playing his last match at Turf Moor the following weekend.
- John Gidman made his debut in the Carlisle game.

SEPTEMBER

- Alun Evans scored in his first full appearance in a League Cup win at recently relegated Nottingham Forest – he'd scored in the 1st round as substitute the previous month.
- There were 46 arrests when Villa played at the City Ground in a League match.

OCTOBER

- Keith Leonard made his debut at Craven Cottage.
- Scotland boss, Tommy Docherty, picked Bruce Rioch for the Denmark World Cup qualifying game, only to be told by Vic Crowe it couldn't happen. He was needed for the Blackpool game the same evening.
- Brothers Bruce and Neil Rioch started a match together for the first time since November 1969.

NOVEMBER

- Full-back John Gidman underwent surgery for cartilage trouble.
- The kick-off was delayed at Oxford for nearly 15 minutes due to crowd disturbances.
- Willie Anderson was substituted at the Manor Ground due to ligament trouble – he didn't feature for the rest of the campaign.

DECEMBER

- The 37,000 for the visit of Forest was the division's biggest so far.
- Villa signed John Robson, the classy England U-23 full-back, from Derby County for £90,000.
- Malcolm Beard's appearance versus Orient was his first in over a year. It would also be his last.
- Keith Leonard suffered a broken leg on Boxing Day in a car accident.

JANUARY

- Villa's biggest gate of the season (38,637) was for the home match with eventual champions Burnley.
- Villa lost at Goodison Park against First Division Everton in the FA Cup Third round – it was Willie Anderson's swansong.
- Villa faced the crack German outfit Bayern Munich in a prestigious home friendly – the game ended in a 1-1 draw.

FEBRUARY

- Villa sufferered their heaviest defeat of the season, 0-4 at Brisbane Road. Orient were fighting a relegation battle.
- Manager Vic Crowe was able to select an unchanged side for all three fixtures during the month.

MARCH

- Ian Ross missed all six March fixtures following a badly gashed leg.
- FA Youth Cup winner Bobby McDonald made his first appearance in the victory at home to Pompey.
- McMahon was back after being sidelined for nearly two months. Pat found the back of the net three times all season. All three goals came in a four match spell in March.

APRIL

- Three of Chico's five goals were scored in April. Both he and Lochhead netted in consecutive games, the last two of the season.
- Villa remained unbeaten during the month, registering three wins and three draws.
- Andy Lochhead brought the curtain down on his claret and blue career with a goal at Carlisle. It was the smallest crowd (6,178) of the season to watch the Villa.
- Jimmy Cumbes was the only ever-present in the side, while Nicholl missed just one match.

MAY

- The Villa squad (pictured left) leaving Villa Park bound for their tour of Tanzania in Africa.

John Gidman in full stride evades a Notts County challenge in front of a spellbound Trinity Road

1973-74

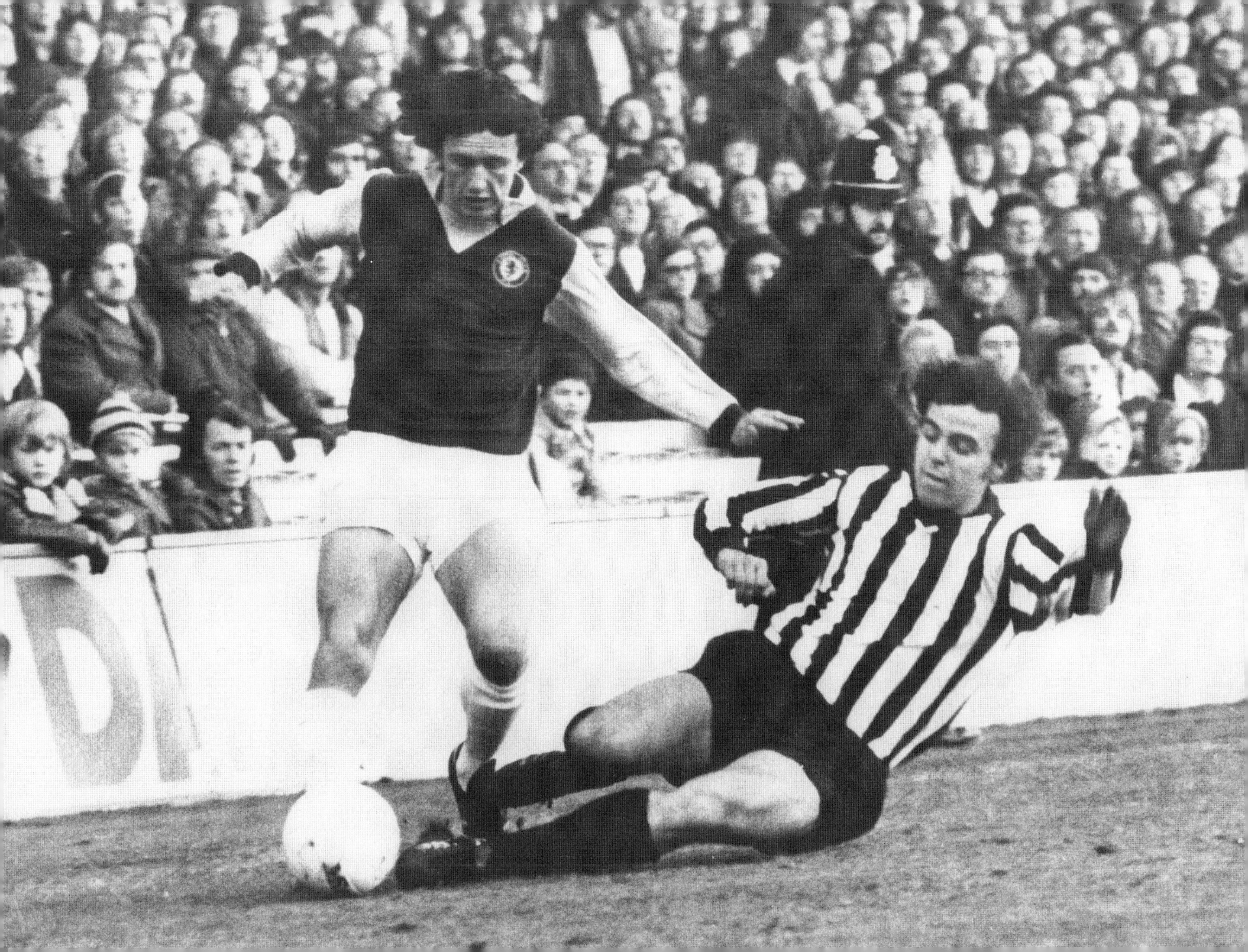

THE BIG ASTON VILLA BOOK OF THE SEVENTIES

[Back Row] Ray Graydon, Bruce Rioch, Chris Nicholl, Keith Leonard, Neil Rioch, Alun Evans, Ian Ross [Middle Row] Frank Upton (Youth Team Coach), Malcolm Beard, Brian Little, John Robson, Roy stark, John Findlay, Jim Cumbes, Tommy Hughes, Fred Turnbull, Charlie Aitken, Sammy Morgan, Leo Crowther (Second Team Coach), Fred Pedley (Physio) [Front Row] Ron Wylie (Asst. Manager), Alan Little, Tony Betts, Jimmy Brown, John Gidman, Vic Crowe (Manager), Ian Hamilton, Geoff Vowden, Trevor Hockey, Bobby McDonald, Michael Wright.

Football League	Division Two
Manager	Vic Crowe
Asst. Manager/Coach	Roy Wylie
Physio	Fred Petley
Captain	Bruce Rioch & Jimmy Brown
Final Position	Fourteenth
FA Cup	Fifth Round
League Cup	Second
Leading Goalscorer (all competitions)	Sammy Morgan – 9 goals

Notwithstanding the loss of consistent scorer Andy Lochhead to Oldham Athletic, hopes were high that Aston Villa were poised to return to the top flight. Had the 'three up' rule been in place the previous season, Villa's objective would have already been realised, and the club would be preparing for fixtures at the Baseball Ground, Elland Road and Anfield etc.

Further evidence that the club were on the rise was landing players of international calibre such as Sammy Morgan of Northern Ireland and Trevor Hockey of Wales.

Villa had played seven league fixtures before they tasted defeat and stood third in the table. Following four wins and a draw during October, and with Villa just trailing the eventual champions Middlesbrough, the wheels well and truly fell off. An horrendous sequence of results was to follow – a dozen games without a win, seven of them defeats, saw the Claret and Blue's plunge out of the reckoning and towards mid-table obscurity.

A well earned 1-1 draw at Highbury in the FA Cup 4th round, in which Sammy Morgan was sent off, ensured a replay against Arsenal in front of a crowd in excess of 47,000, who cheered the Villa on to beat the Gunners.

A four win run from mid-March propelled Villa up to tenth, but from there on in it was a bit of a mixed bag and the team finally concluded the campaign in a disappointing 14th position. They had scored nearly 30 goals less than 'Boro (77 compared to 48) whilst conceding 45. This scoring defi-

continued >>>

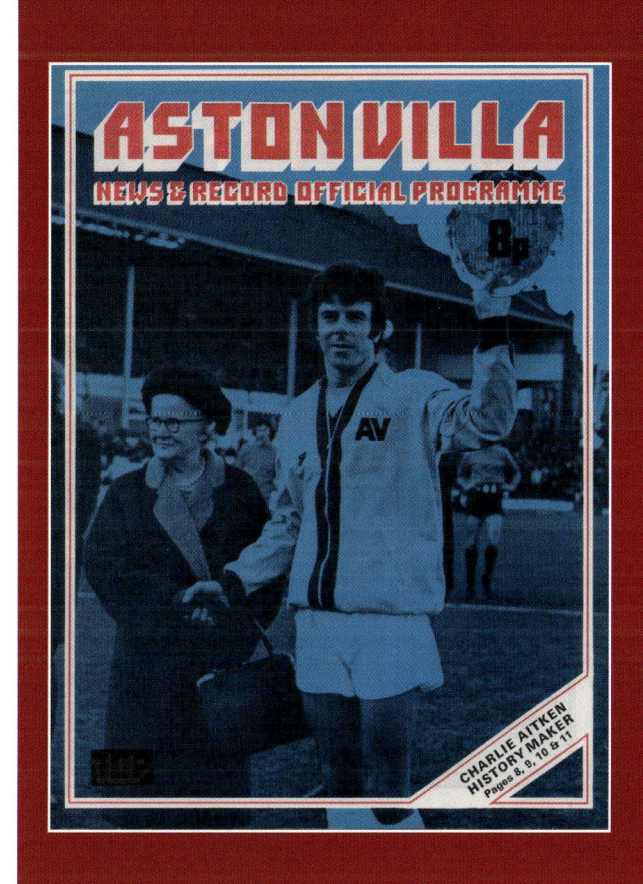

		P	W	D	L	F	A	W	D	L	F	A	Pts
1	Middlesbrough	42	16	4	1	40	8	11	7	3	37	22	65
2	Luton Town	42	12	5	4	42	25	7	7	7	22	26	50
3	Carlisle United	42	13	5	3	40	17	7	4	10	21	31	49
4	Orient	42	9	8	4	28	17	6	10	5	27	25	48
5	Blackpool	42	11	5	5	35	17	6	8	7	22	23	47
6	Sunderland	42	11	6	4	32	15	8	3	10	26	29	47
7	Nottingham Forest	42	12	6	3	40	19	3	9	9	17	24	45
8	West Bromwich	42	8	9	4	28	24	6	7	8	20	21	44
9	Hull City	42	9	9	3	25	15	4	8	9	21	32	43
10	Notts County	42	8	6	7	30	35	7	7	7	25	25	43
11	Bolton Wanderers	42	12	5	4	30	17	3	7	11	14	23	42
12	Millwall	42	10	6	5	28	16	4	8	9	23	35	42
13	Fulham	42	11	4	6	26	20	5	6	10	13	23	42
14	**Aston Villa**	**42**	**8**	**9**	**4**	**33**	**21**	**5**	**6**	**10**	**15**	**24**	**41**
15	Portsmouth	42	9	8	4	26	16	5	4	12	19	46	40
16	Bristol City	42	9	5	7	25	20	5	5	11	22	34	38
17	Cardiff City	42	8	7	6	27	20	2	9	10	22	42	36
18	Oxford United	42	8	8	5	27	21	2	8	11	8	25	36
19	Sheffield Wed	42	9	6	6	33	24	3	5	13	18	39	35
20	Crystal Palace	42	6	7	8	24	24	5	5	11	19	32	34
21	Preston North End	42	7	8	6	24	23	2	6	13	16	39	31
22	Swindon Town	42	6	7	8	22	27	1	4	16	14	45	25

Preston North End had one point deducted for fielding an ineligible player

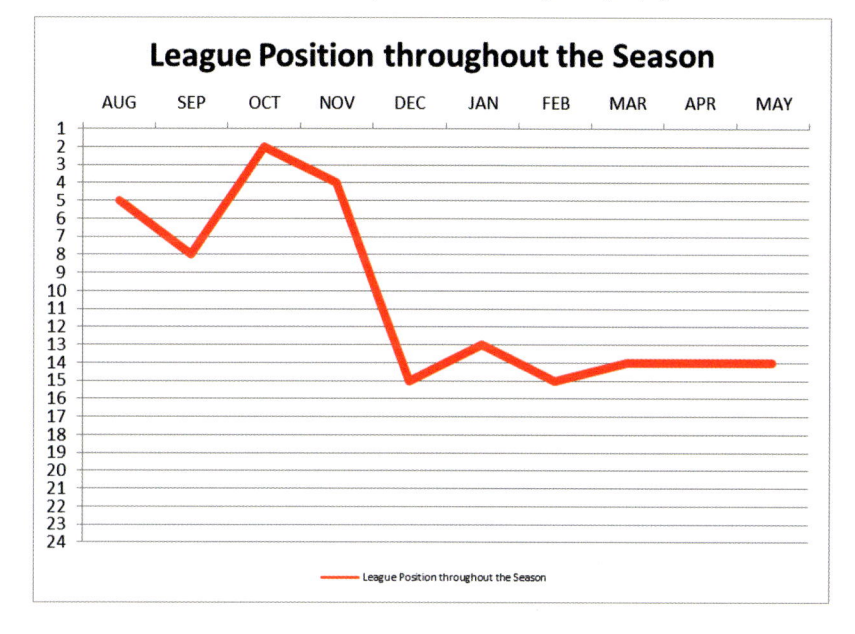

League Position throughout the Season

Total Home League Attendances 491,664
Average Home League Attendance 23,412
Highest Home League Attendance 37,323
Lowest Home League Attendance 12,007

83

THE BIG ASTON VILLA BOOK OF THE SEVENTIES

1973-74

Sat 25th August   **Preston North End (H)**
Won 2-0   **Att 28,861**
Aitken, Hockey

Villa started the new campaign without the suspended Ray Graydon and Sammy Morgan, while North End's Bobby Charlton nearly started his managerial career with an undeserved draw. Villa attacked Preston from the off but it took until the 82nd minute until Charlie Aitken broke the deadlock. Trevor Hockey made a dream start to his Villa career when he added a second two minutes later.

Sat 1st September   **Millwall (A)**
Drew 1-1   **Att 12,009**
Little

Villa took the lead in a niggly but evenly contested encounter through Brian Little after a Rioch corner was helped on by Evans. Cumbes, superb in the air all afternoon, was beaten once when Wood got on the end of a cross. The Villa keeper was instrumental in avoiding a defeat, a fact not lost on one Millwall lunatic, who launched a missile which caught the goalie just above the eye at the final whistle. "I'd settle for a bang on the head every week for an away point," was the Villa goalkeeper's response.

Sat 8th September   **Oxford United (H)**
Won 2-0   **Att 28,078**
Rioch B (pen), Vowden

Oxford's defensive mindset and midfield swamping tactics strangled Villa's hopes and kept the match goal-less at the interval. A Rioch penalty in the 59th minute finally got Villa going. Little won the spot kick after lobbing Burton in goal, but as the youngster followed through to stroke the ball home, the keeper flattened him. Geoff Vowden added a fine second goal in the 68th minute, to which the visitors had no answer. Unbeaten and top, not a bad start!

ciency would have been high on the agenda for the Crowe/Wylie partnership to rectify.

However, the duo weren't given that opportunity by the board and both were dismissed on 6th May, three days after the season had ended with a draw at Orient.

One positive, six of the successful 1972 FA Youth Cup winning side featured in the first team during the course of the campaign, with Jake Findlay and Roy Stark joining Brown, Little, Gidman and McDonald, who'd already graduated and demonstrated the Villa academy was bearing fruit.

Irishman, Bobby Campbell, who'd regularly scored in the previous season's Central League, also made the transition and scored in one of only three appearances.

Tue 11th September   Crystal Palace (A)
Drew 0-0   Att 20,838

Crowe had the luxury of naming an unchanged team for the fourth game on the spin. Palace, relegated the previous season with only seven home wins to their name, looked like they'd finally discovered some belief. They outplayed the Villa with Jim Cumbes pulling off many magnificent saves with one from Don Rogers "unlikely to be bettered all season" according to one paper report. Hockey was booked in a tense affair.

Sat 15th September   Middlesbrough (A)
Drew 0-0   Att 14,742

Villa and Boro were two of three sides on six points and, for the third match running, Cumbes was forced to make too many saves. While his team-mates struggled to get to grips with the opposition 'Boro created chance after chance. Little had a rare opportunity, but he hesitated fractionally and the moment was gone. Villa's only other real goal attempt came when Rioch and Robson combined to win a corner, from which big Chris Nicholl powered in a strong header that was cleared off the line by Craggs. It was a point earned rather than one dropped.

Wed 19th September   Fulham (H)
Drew 1-1   Att 30,162
Rioch B

For the fifth time in six outings, Villa failed to score in the first 45 minutes. Fulham were on top for the entire first half and went close twice through Alan Mullery's free-kicks. Villa, penned back for so long, finally broke and Rioch forced the Fulham keeper into two good saves from fierce long-range shots before finding the back of the net on 54 minutes. Villa were on top for a while, before the visitors hit back following a shot that took a wicked deflection to beat Cumbes in goal.

Sat 22nd September   Orient (H)
Drew 2-2   Att 26,685
Rioch B, Vowden

Villa attacked from the off. Vowden was fouled outside the area and his quickly taken kick found Rioch who caught it first time to put Villa one-up inside 70 seconds. They lost their lead in the 33rd minute when a low shot was deflected out of Cumbes line of sight by Ross. Villa's lead was restored three minutes later when Sammy Morgan created an opening for Vowden to bag an easy goal, but Orient weren't finished and levelled to the Villa fans' dismay two minutes later. The second half was played out with no further goals, meaning that Forest leapfrogged Villa into second place.

Sat 29th September   Notts County (A)
Lost 0-2   Att 15,872

Villa played the more polished football, but it was the newly promoted side who were able to put the ball in the back of the net. Brown fired over, Little took on three defenders getting fouled twice for his troubles before putting the ball narrowly wide of the post, and after Rioch sent Robson away down the wing, the full-back's cross was met forcibly by Vowden, but the keeper saved it. On 26 minutes Notts scored the first despite Villa's constant attacking and the visitors continued in the same vein, wrapping up both points with another goal with 19 minutes remaining.

Tue 2nd October   Fulham (A)
Lost 0-1   Att 11,776

Just thirteen days after playing The Cottagers, Villa were down on the banks of the Thames to meet them again. It appeared that Villa had gone south looking for a point as they played with ten men behind the ball for long periods, with only Fulham prepared to venture forward. Villa held out for the first half, but fell to a goal from the home side's substitute. With Robson picked up his third booking of the season, meaning an automatic ban was looking likely.

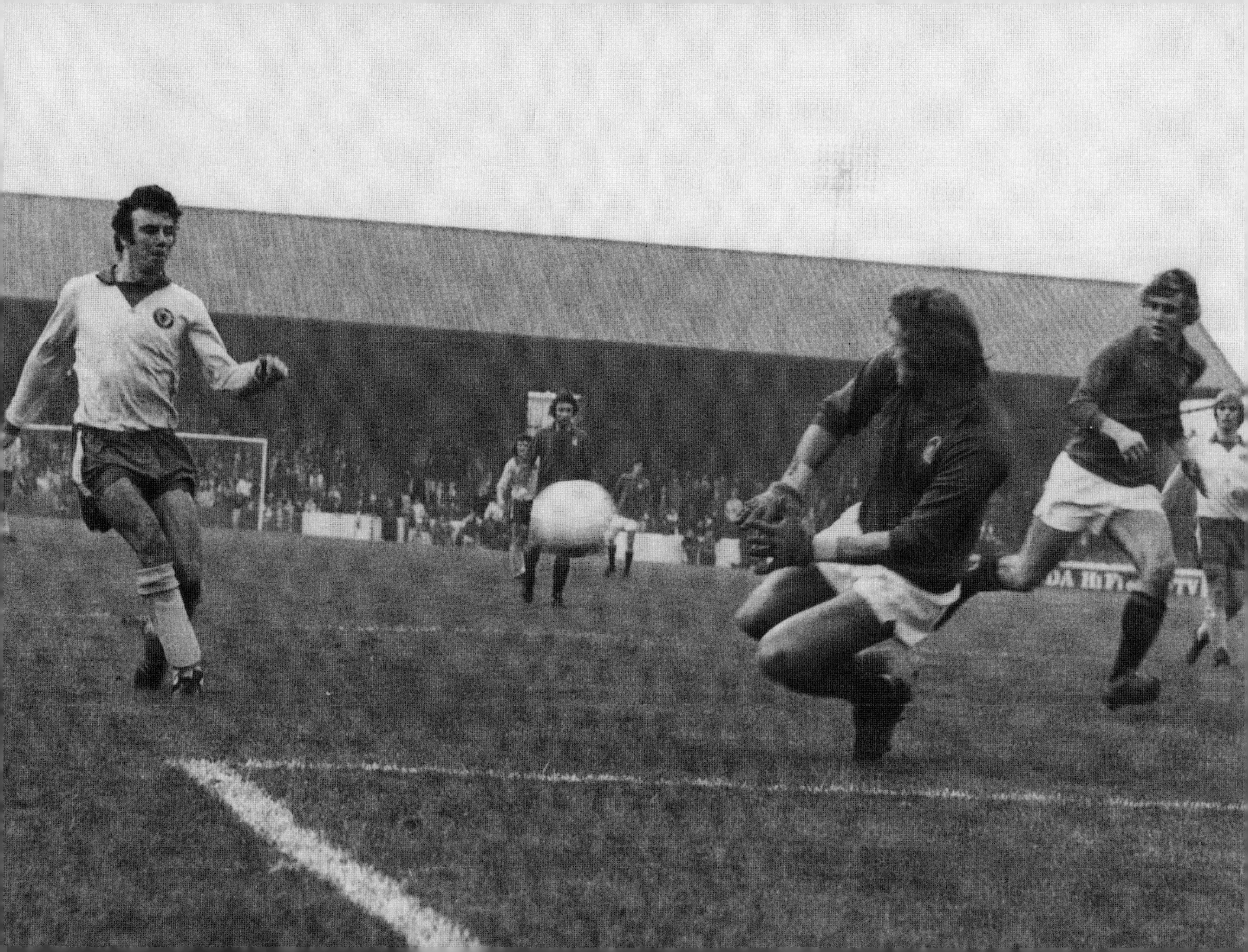

Charlie Aitken seals both points at the City Ground with a shot past Jim Barron the Forest keeper

Sat 6th October   Cardiff City (H)
Won 5-0   Att 24,483
Own goal, Graydon, Rioch B 2, Morgan

Villa made up for not winning any of their previous six games by destroying Cardiff City. The hosts were on their way after an own goal in only the fourth minute, yet they could have been trailing by that stage when McCulloch rounded Cumbes, but the City number eight failed to convert. An unmarked Ray Graydon added a second when he side-footed home from five yards to send Villa in two-nil up at the break. Rioch made it three with one of his specials and Sammy Morgan bagged his first goal since arriving from Port Vale, heading home a Robson centre. Rioch notched his second, and Villa's fifth, with a 30-yard pile driver.

Tue 9th October   York City (A) League Cup 2nd round
Lost 0-1   Att 7,981

With Villa fielding the same XI that romped to a 5-0 win only three days before, hopes were high. But Villa were swamped by a York side who made a storming opening and, after squandering a series of chances, and without their two regular strikers, they relied on a lad who'd only ever played at non-league level – the debutant scoring the only goal of the game when a right foot volley flew beyond a bemused Cumbes.

Sat 13th October   Bolton Wanderers (A)
Won 2-1   Att 19,496
Evans 2

Aston Villa responded to their cup exit with a powerful performance at Burnden Park having lost Robson and dropped Morgan. Villa bossed the midfield and were nearly in front when a Hockey free-kick was met by Gidman whose effort was deflected inches wide of the post by Evans' boot. Alun made amends when he found the target in the 37th minute with his head. Four minutes after the interval Evans struck again, and in spite of Bolton clawing a goal back in the 76th minute, Villa took both points back to B6.

Sat 20th October   Bristol City (H)
Drew 2-2   Att 26,918
Little, Graydon

Bruce Rioch was missing for the first time of the campaign through injury, Hockey pulling the strings in his absence. Villa were in front from a spectacular header on the 20 minute mark from Brian Little. It was all Villa, but in a token raid, City drew level. Ritchie then audaciously put the visitors in front with a firm header after Cumbes had fumbled the first attempt. Villa came out after half time more determined and were level within four minutes, a corner was played to Hockey, then onto Graydon, who moved the ball to his right and unleashed an outswinging shot from 30-yards out that flew into the top corner.

Tue 23rd October   Crystal Palace (H)
Won 2-1   Att 26,670
Little, Graydon

Villa were too much for a Palace side rooted at the bottom with only three points. Little got the team on their way with a fine header in the tenth minute. When the Eagles' keeper kept a McMahon certainty out it gave the strugglers hope and they then pushed up and found an equaliser. All level at the break. Hammond kept Villa at bay single-handedly, firstly Gidman, then a Graydon shot, he then partially saved an Evans effort, but the rebound fell to Graydon who slotted home to make it 2-1 on the night.

Sat 27th October   Nottingham Forest (A)
Won 2-1   Att 17,718
Graydon, Aitken

Forest struggled to contain the visitors from the start and paid the price in the seventh minute. Forest goalie, Jim Barron, did well to push Hamilton's shot out, but Graydon arrived at the far post to knock the ball in from a couple of yards. A minute later Ray just failed to connect with an Evans knock down. Forest made a game of it, pulling level before the interval, but Charlie Aitken scored the winner on 58 minutes to put them second, three points behind leaders 'Boro.

Sat 3rd November   **Sheffield Wednesday (H)**
Won 1-0   **Att 28,599**
Little

Wednesday asked all the early questions, but a magnificent goal after 20 minutes put Villa in a commanding position that they never relinquished. Gidman robbed an Owls player, ran the flank, played a one-two with Graydon, before turning a defender inside out and crossing to the far post. Fellow Youth Cup winner, Brian Little, rose above his marker to add the perfect finishing touch to a very fine move – one reminiscent of the youth team days under coach Frank Upton.

Sat 10th November   **Portsmouth (A)**
Lost 0-2   **Att 12,678**

Even without wideman Graydon who'd scored in three consecutive games before his injury, Villa rattled the suspect home defence. Sadly the possession counted for nothing and due to Milkens display between the posts the Villa couldn't break through. Villa had a penalty appeal turned down when Little was floored in the box. Portsmouth went in front following a fine Marinello run which ended with his shot being deflected beyond Cumbes by Piper. Pompey added a second with minutes remaining to firmly shut the door on an Aston Villa comeback.

Sat 17th November   **Hull City (H)**
Drew 1-1   **Att 23,773**
Little

Kicking off the game in second place and five points behind the leaders, Villa were hoping that home advantage would help in turn-

> **Brian Little out jumps his marker to get on the end of John Gidman's cross to score the only goal of the game at home to Sheffield Wednesday**

ing Hull over. However, it was a scrappy game, and Little's opener was cancelled out a minute before the break. Villa's lead had lasted all of 13 minutes. Morgan replaced Jimmy Brown just after the hour, but in front of a dissatisfied home crowd, the game petered out to finish 1-1.

Sat 24th November   **Swindon Town (A)**
Lost 0-1   **Att 8,666**

Morgan was on from the start with Evans on the bench, Vowden also began for the first time in six. There was little good football on show against 21st placed Swindon, although it could be argued the strong wind played its part. That said, Villa started positively and mustered a few half chances, Vowden and Hamilton going close, but neither could take full advantage of the numerous defensive errors occurring in the Swindon rearguard. They paid the ultimate price when Swindon stuttered up field in the 88th minute and snatched a late goal.

Sat 8th December   **Sunderland (A)**
Lost 0-2   **Att 20,784**

Sunderland had been struggling at Roker Park, with only three wins under their belts. Villa put up a good fight but were behind on 32 minutes when Dennis Tueart volleyed home after Trevor Hockey had failed to clear. This inspired the Black Cats, though Little was close to wiping out Sunderland's advantage five minutes later, Jim Montgomery charged out to block the ball. Chris Nicholl twice rescued Villa from going further behind with perfectly timed clearances, but the home side's pressure told when Vic Halom headed in to make it 2-0. There was to be no way back for the visitors.

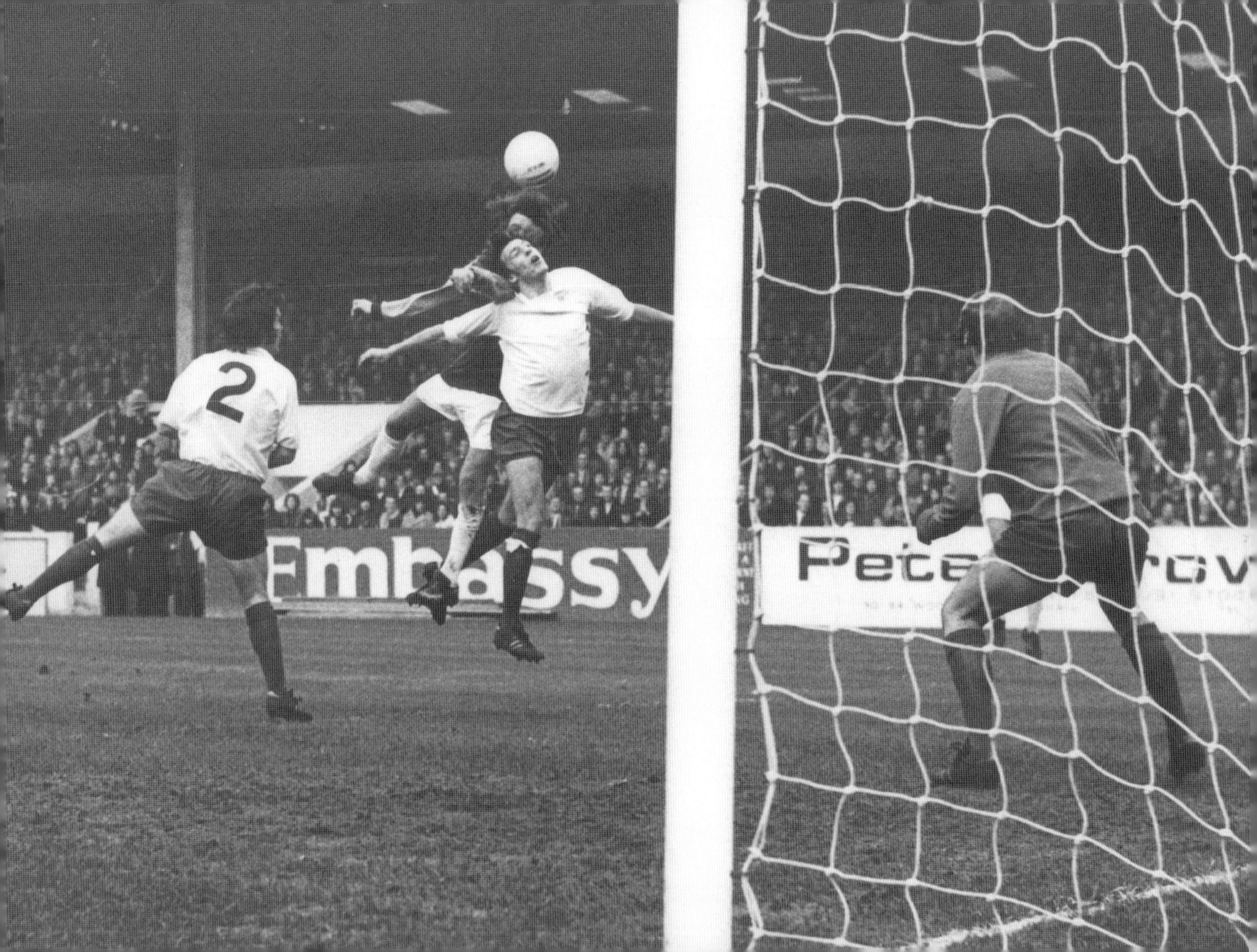
2
Embassy

THE BIG ASTON VILLA BOOK OF THE SEVENTIES

Sat 15th December   **Luton Town (A)**
Lost 0-1   **Att 10,020**

With three defeats from their last four fixtures Villa had slipped alarmingly down to tenth in the table. To make matters worse, they were up against an in-form Luton side sitting third in the table. Play was fast and open with Town the far more lively in attack, and the Hatter's scored the only goal of the game eight minutes into the second half with a cleverly crafted and well taken glancing header. Charlie Aitken equalled Villa legend Billy Walker's total of 478 League appearances.

Sat 22nd December   **Notts County (H)**
Drew 1-1   **Att 20,825**
Rioch B

Coming into the game on the back of three straight defeats, only a left-footed rocket from Bruce Rioch, back in the team after missing nine games, broke the dull and disappointing stalemate. Villa's joy was short lived, three minutes to be precise. Nicholl was adjudged to have fouled in the area and the subsequent penalty allowed County a share of the points.

Wed 26th December   **West Bromwich Albion (A)**
Lost 0-2   **Att 43,029**

A big crowd – three times the norm at the Hawthorns - greeted the first meeting of the teams in seven years at West Bromwich. Albion made the most of their limited chances, while the visitors flopped in front of goal with another glaring example of good possession, but no punch. Neil Rioch, starting only his third game this season, twice went close on the rare occasions the visitors threatened.

Sat 29th December   **Oxford United (A)**
Lost 1-2   **Att 10,390**
Graydon

Aston Villa tried hard to turn the tide, which had seen them drift away from the promotion race. With only two goals from the previous seven

Oxford goalie, Roy Burton, can't keep winger Ray Graydon from scoring his fifth of the season as Alun Evans looks on

games Villa started adventurously, and within ten minutes, they had the lead when Ian Hamilton unleashed a long-range shot from the left, the keeper spilled the ball and Graydon was in the right place at the right time again to tap in from point blank range. Oxford drew level two minutes before the half-time whistle, and against all the odds, found a winner late in the game to add to Villa's misery.

Tue 1st January   **Millwall (H)**
Drew 0-0   **Att 20,905**

Villa's failure to find the net had been responsible for their promotion collapse, but on this New Year's Day showing, some of the blame had be laid squarely at the feet (or hands) of Millwall keeper King. Outstanding saves from Rioch and Little in the first period were followed by more of the same in the second. He was only beaten once but Evans' last minute effort was chalked off for offside and didn't count.

Sat 5th January   **Chester (H) FA Cup 3rd round**
Won 3-1   **Att 16,545**
Nicholl, Morgan 2

A disappointing crowd by Villa Park standards watched on as Division Four Chester came back to level the tie after Nicholl had headed the home side in front following a corner kick. Morgan replaced Evans for the the second period and put Villa ahead in the 67th minute before Sammy lashed in his second, and Villa's third, ten minutes later to put his team in the hat for the last 32.

Sat 12th January   **Middlesbrough (H)**
Drew 1-1   **Att 26,906**
Rioch B

Villa were promising early on against Jack Charlton's pacesetters, but as the game wore on, 'Boro became far more confident and

verseas Travel
ST. EBBES OXFORD 44177
OTS
OF OXFORD
LARK
ATON
glass merchan
for
CHERWELL
TEL. 480

aggressive. The visitors took the lead when John Craggs fired through a crowded area and past the unsighted Cumbes. Geoff Vowden then tested Jim Platt with a looping header. Not long afterwards, chants of 'Ellis must go' rang around Villa Park, with most of the noise emanating from sections of the terraced Holte End. Bruce Rioch, with a just two minutes left on the clock, drilled home after a Graydon cross had been chested out.

Sat 19th January   **Preston North End (A)**
Drew 0-0   **Att 10,766**

Fives places, but a solitary point, separated the Villa (11th) and North End (16th). With both teams out of form a scrappy encounter was on the cards from the start at Deepdale, and it was no surprise the game ended in stalemate. Villa were let off the hook twice in as many minutes when Preston first missed a penalty, then Holden blazed over an empty goal. Villa had brief spells of play, but their inter-passing in the midfield wasn't attack orientated enough to inflict any pressure on Preston's suspect defence.

Sat 26th January   **Arsenal (A) FA Cup 4th round**
Drew 1-1   **Att 41,682**
Morgan

The Gunners had drawn 1-1 the previous weekend at Old Trafford, but were a mid-table top flight side at this time. Villa, without a win in 11 games, somehow contrived to take a first half-lead when Ian Hamilton sent a low cross in for Sammy Morgan who dived full length to rocket a header beyond Bob Wilson. When the home side broke, Chris Nicholl in the heart of the defence, was superb. In a moment of controversy Morgan was sent off for going in on what could best be described as a 50-50 ball with Wilson, who many on the terraces and in the press thought made a complete meal of it. Arsenal equalised against a ten-man team with a get-out-of-jail second-half goal. Aston Villa had been denied a famous victory after thoroughly deserving to go through at the first attempt.

Big Sammy Morgan leaps out of the way as Alun Evans smashes home the winner to knock First Division Arsenal out of the FA Cup

Wed 30th January   **Arsenal (H) FA Cup 4th round replay**
Won 2-0   **Att 47,821**
Morgan, Evans

Villa Park was up for it, as were the team. The claret and blue army turned out in their thousands to see justice served. Villa started with a pride and purpose in their play. Bob Wilson, the villain of the piece on Saturday, was booed and jeered throughout for 'feigning injury'. Sammy Morgan put Villa in front in the 12th minute to absolute thunderous applause – it was his fourth in the cup run – and Villa never looked back. Evans rounded off a truly great night under the famous 'AV' floodlights when he added a second on 68 minutes.

Sat 2nd February   **Luton Town (H)**
Lost 0-1   **Att 26,180**

Highflying Luton came to Villa Park, but apart from them hitting an upright in the tenth minute, their performance was not in keeping with their third placed ranking. Evans had the ball in the visitors net but the keeper had been fouled by Morgan so it didn't stand. Luton were then awarded a penalty, dubbed "a diabolical decision" by Vic Crowe, and duly scored. Villa's unbeaten home record had fallen.

Sat 16th February   **Burnley (A) FA Cup 3rd round**
Lost 0-1   **Att 29,301**

There were fears the game would be called off and two pitch inspections were required. Villa made a spirited attempt at Turf Moor to force a replay against a more than handy First Division Burnley side who would finish the season a creditable sixth in the top flight, and had taken an early eighth minute lead. The best chance fell to Ray Graydon on the stroke of half time, but the wide man fired margin-

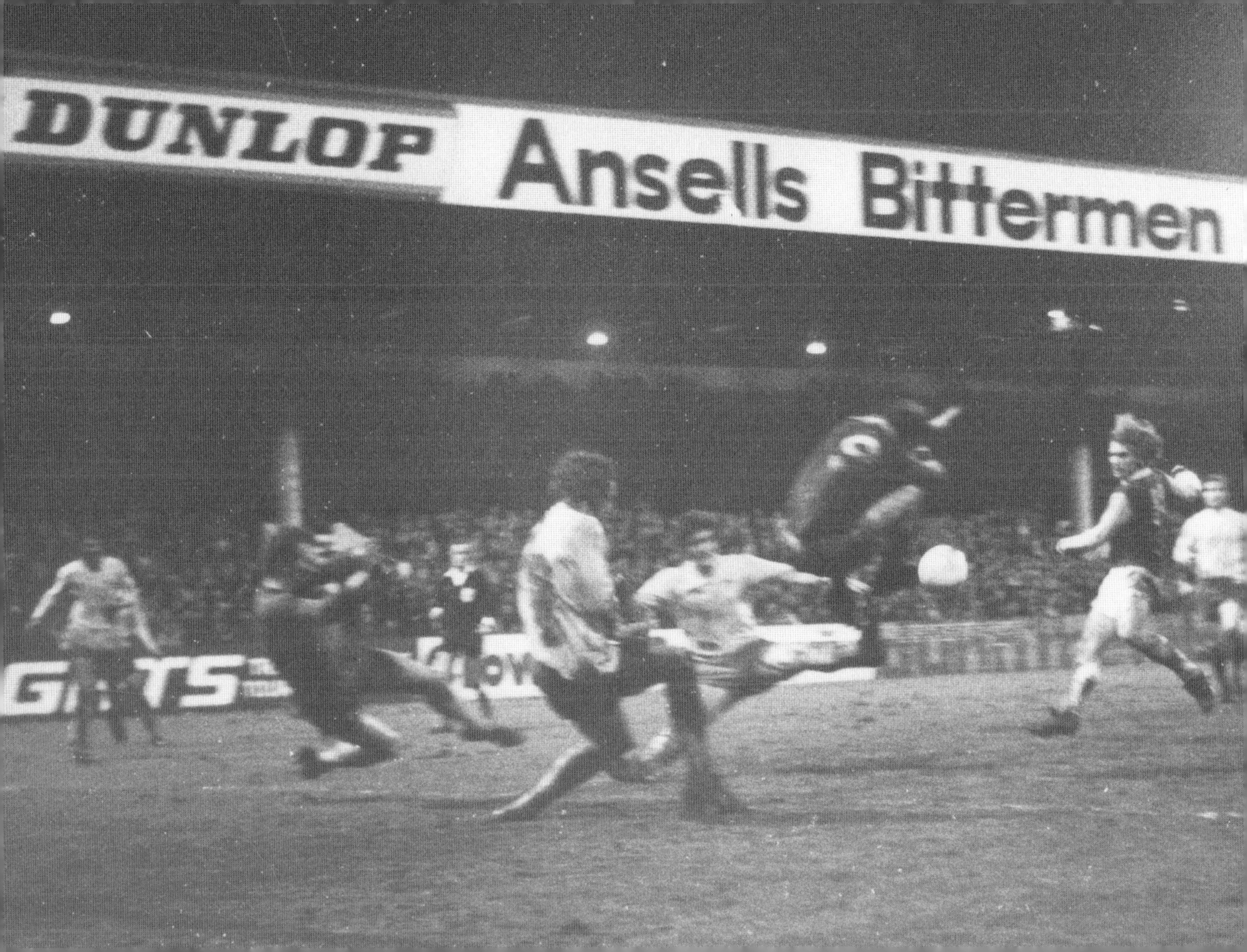
DUNLOP
Ansells Bittermen

ally over. Sammy Morgan fared no better when his header was blocked by Noble. The Villans hadn't disgraced themselves, but it was the end of the cup run for another year.

Sat 23rd February   **Cardiff City (A)**
Won 1-0   **Att 12,184**
Graydon

Villa sat in lowly 16th place, hovering just five points above a relegation berth, and desperately needed to kick-start a winning habit; something they had failed to experience in the league for 12 games. To make matters far worse Bruce Rioch – a player of genuine class – had been sold, very much against the fans wishes. But Villa sealed a deserved victory through Graydon, who had put them in front with only 68 seconds on the clock. The early goal gave the visitors confidence, and a visibly rattled Cardiff were unable to penetrate a resolute Villa defence.

Wed 27th February   **Bolton Wanderers (H)**
Drew 1-1   **18,952**
McMahon

Villa fans amongst the lowest home crowd of the season do date staged a vocal protest at the recent sale of Bruce Rioch to Derby County. With Bolton Wanderers doing all the attacking Villa were grateful to snatch an unlikely lead when Pat McMahon headed home a 'Chico' Hamilton cross. But despite Cumbes making numerous outstanding saves, Villa couldn't see the game out and The Trotters levelled after the break to take a share of the points back to Lancashire. Villa's three point haul from the last two games moved them up one position to 15th.

Sat 2nd March   **West Bromwich Albion (H)**
Lost 1-3   **Att 37,323**
Morgan

Morgan passed a late fitness test to spearhead the Villa attack, while Brian Little was relegated to bench duty. A speculative Charlie Aitken lob had The Baggies defence in trouble early on, and the game was played in a typical derby atmosphere and at an electric pace that saw four goals scored in the space of eight first-half minutes. West Brom's John Wile made it 1-0, a lead that was doubled from the penalty spot after the ball had bounced up and caught Aitken on the hand – a very harsh decision! Sammy Morgan reduced the deficit when he tapped in the rebound after a Ray Graydon shot had hit an upright, only to see Albion restore their advantage within two minutes. Despite further attempts at both ends all the scoring had been wrapped up before the half-time break.

Wed 13th March   **Carlisle United (H)**
Won 2-1   **Att 12,007**
Evans, Hamilton (pen)

Not since April 1966 had such a low attendance turned out under the shadows of Aston Hall – a clear sign that supporters resolve was being tested during a disappointing season. Villa were in front after 22 minutes when a long Fred Turnbull ball was headed on by Little for Evans to run onto and fire in from the edge of the area. Brian Tiler, back at Villa Park for the first time since his transfer, then fouled Little in the box and Hamilton was successful with the spot kick, 2-0. Alan Ashman's Carlisle pulled one back with 15 minutes to go.

Sat 16th March   **Bristol City (A)**
Won 1-0   **Att 12,759**
Morgan

Villa won their second game in a week when Sammy Morgan was gifted a goal midway through the second half, but had played for long spells deep in midfield without threatening the Robins, and had relied on brave Cumbes a number of times. The winner, which came in the 68th minute, came as a result of goalie Ray Cashley dropping the ball after Nicholl had floated in a free kick.

Sat 23rd March   Portsmouth (H)
Won 4-1   Att 15,517
McMahon 2, Morgan 2

Villa trooped off at the interval trailing after conceding a 21st minute goal, even though they had dominated the first period. Pat McMahon drew Villa level with a well taken goal on 54 minutes, then Morgan put them ahead 13 minutes later. The home side were now playing with authority and McMahon and Morgan added further goals in the last ten minutes to put the result beyond doubt.

Mon 1st April   Sheffield Wednesday (A)
Won 4-2   Att 22,504
Little 2, McMahon, Leonard

Seemingly, there was no stopping this Villa side now, and they were ahead after just five minutes. Wednesday then subjected the visitors to a battering but could only level. McMahon put Villa back in front only for the Owls to score again. Leonard, scoring his first Villa goal, restored the lead and Little wrapped things up with his second of the evening. The four straight wins was their best sequence of the season, yet it had only lifted the side to tenth in the table.

Sat 6th April   Swindon Town (H)
Drew 1-1   Att 20,709
Little

It had taken until the second half to see Villa's supremacy rewarded with a goal, Brian Little's low drive breaking the deadlock. From that point Swindon, seven points adrift at the bottom, totally outplayed a Villa side who were expected to score a hatful. Town equalised on 65 minutes with a point blank header then, in the dying seconds, had the ball in the Villa net again, luckily it was ruled out for a push on Cumbes.

Sat 13th April   Hull City (A)
Drew 1-1   Att 7,810
Own goal

Centre-half Chris Nicholl was back in the defence following his two match suspension. Villa settled down quicker than Hull and were playing the better football. Keith Leonard was put through by Hamilton but his shot narrowly cleared the bar. Hull then took the lead, much against the run of play, but Villa fought back after the interval. A John Gidman free kick was covered by The Tigers keeper but a defender attempted to clear and succeeded only in deflecting the ball into his own net to earn a share of the points for Villa in a game they should have won.

Mon 15th April   Blackpool (H)
Lost 0-1   Att 18,351

Alun Evans was back on the bench after missing the last five matches. A Blackpool team chasing promotion snuffed out Villa's unimaginative attack. The visitors scored with ten minutes to go in the first period and Villa rarely threatened thereafter. Sammy Morgan was substituted making way for Evans.

Tue 16th April   Blackpool (A)
Lost 1-2   Att 10,787
Hamilton

The hosts took a ninth minute lead when a cross was steered past Charlie Aitken and Jim Cumbes. Villa, inspired by Pat McMahon, were back on equal terms when Ian Hamilton forced the ball in, but it counted for nothing when Blackpool got a late goal that proved to be the decider. The Seasiders had taken four points off the Villa in a little over 24 hours.

Sat 20th April   Sunderland (H)
Lost 1-2   Att 17,321
McMahon

Villa tore the Rokermens' defence to shreds and took a deserved lead when McMahon finished off following smart work by youngster Bobby McDonald. But, ultimately, more indecisive finishing would let them down. McMahon, back helping out in defence, watched in

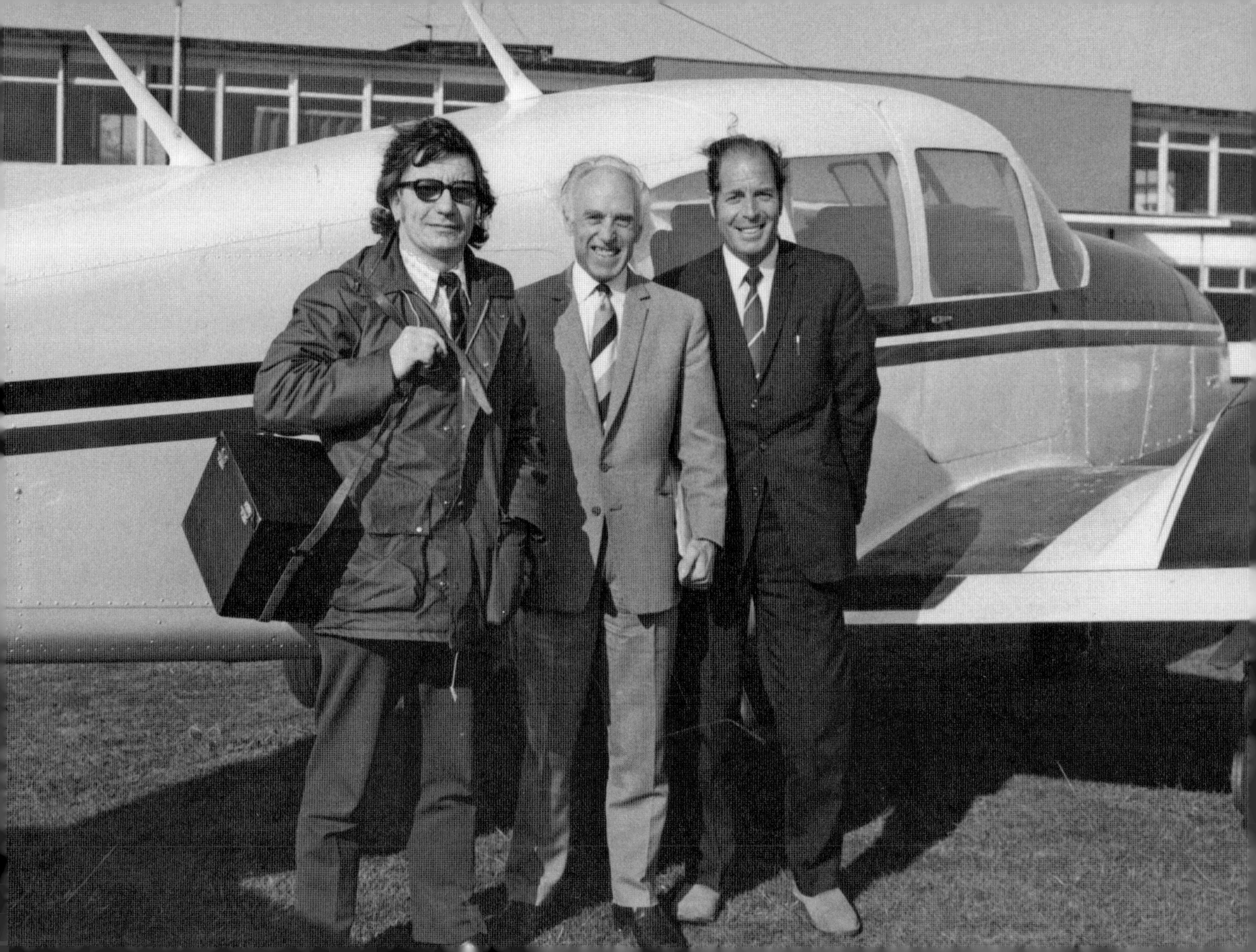

All aboard (L to R) Villa photographer, Terry Weir, accompanies Vice-Chairman Harry Kartz and chief scout Neville Briggs on the flight to Brunton Park before Villa's penultimate game of the season

horror as an attempted block veered beyond 1972 FA Youth Cup winning keeper Jake Findlay (making his first-team debut) to level the game, much against the run of play. To round off a miserable week Sunderland snatched a 77th minute winner to subject the hosts to a third consecutive defeat.

Wed 24th April   Nottingham Forest (H)
Won 3-1   Att 12,439
Hamilton, Campbell, Graydon

The tiny Villa Park crowd witnessed a rare home victory – only the third of the calendar year – and an eighth of the campaign. A lunging Hamilton header set them on the way in the fourth minute, only for Forest to cancel the goal out moments later. Irish youngster, Bobby Campbell, at only 17-years of age, came off the bench and hit an 18-yard volley to restore the Villa's advantage. Ray Graydon's blazing shot made it 3-1 before the break. With no further score in the second period Villa secured both points in what proved to be Fred Turnbull's swan-song.

Sat 27th April   Carlisle United (A)
Lost 0-2   Att 12,494

Carlisle's opening flourish earned them a 12th minute lead, although McMahon went close to levelling things up when he hit the upright on the stroke of half time. Graydon then thundered in a header on 54 minutes only to see it strike the bar. Campbell, making his first start, went off injured to be replaced by Vowden. Promotion seeking Carlisle (they'd finish third and went up) rounded the afternoon off when they made it two-nil after 66 minutes to record a fifth successive victory at Brunton Park.

Fri 3rd May   Orient (A)
Drew 1-1   Att 29,766
Graydon (pen)

In front of a packed Brisbane Road crowd, Villa turned party poopers to deny Orient the win that would secure their promotion. The home crowd were stunned when Villa were awarded a spot-kick after Brain Little had been felled, Ray Graydon stepping up to made no mistake from the spot and become Villa's top scorer for the season. Orient equalised ten minutes later and would have won the match had it not been for a superb reflex save from Cumbes two minutes from the end.

THE BIG ASTON VILLA BOOK OF THE SEVENTIES

PRE-SEASON

- Aston Villa signed footballing nomad Trevor Hockey – the Claret and Blues becoming his seventh club.
- One of the club's new apprentices is a certain John Deehan.

AUGUST

- Villa signed Port Vale centre-forward Sammy Morgan.
- Vic Crowe presented John Robson with his latest England U-23 cap.
- Villa played a friendly match in Germany, the opponents Oldenburg St Paul.
- Charlie Aitken scored Villa's first goal of the new season, bit it was only his 12th in 537 apps.
- Hockey made a dream start scoring on his debut in the 2-0 home win v PNE.

SEPTEMBER

- In only the second league match of the campaign, at Millwall's 'Den', Jim Cumbes was extremely lucky to avoid serious injury when he was hit by a chunk of terracing.
- Sammy Morgan made his debut coming on as a substitute in the Oxford United win at Villa Park.
- Welsh international Trevor Hockey was sent off in Poland during Wales' 0-3 defeat in a World Cup qualifier.

OCTOBER

- Villa ended a winless six-match sequence with a victory at home to Cardiff City. The 5-0 win was their biggest of the season.
- Keith Leonard made his comeback in the Central League after suffering a broken leg in a car crash the previous Boxing Day.
- Ray Graydon was on the mark four times in a five game spell.
- Villa registered four league wins, making October their most productive month.

NOVEMBER

- A share issue raised £65,000 to strengthen playing squad.
- Brian Little scored Villa's only two goals in the month. They picked up three points from a possible eight.
- Bruce Rioch missed the whole of the month due to injury.

DECEMBER

- Charlie Aitken equalled Billy Walker's number of league appearances for Aston Villa - 478 - at Kenilworth Road.
- The 0-0 draw at Luton was Villa's third successive match without scoring.
- At home to Notts County the following week Aitken was presented with a silver salver from Mrs Sally Walker (widow of Billy) to mark his achievement of most team appearances – he'd played in 555 competitive claret and blue matches.
- West Bromwich Albion and Villa met for the first time in the Second Division. A crowd of 43,029 turned out at the Hawthorns.

Charlie Aitken being presented with a silver salver from Mrs Sally Walker to mark his appearance record

JANUARY

- Villa negotiated the first hurdle of the FA Cup for the first time in five years beating Chester, thanks to a Morgan double.
- With power cuts commonplace, the club hired generators to ensure the Arsenal FA Cup 4th round replay went ahead. The two games were watched by a combined attendance of 89,503.

FEBRUARY

- Bruce Rioch joined Derby County citing he couldn't wait any longer for Villa to gain promotion. His last appearance in the claret and blue - against Luton Town, the side Villa bought him from.

MARCH

- Villa Park's biggest gate of the season (37,323) turned out for the visit of West Bromwich Albion.
- The 12,007 for the following game (Carlisle United) was the lowest of the campaign at B6. This started a purple patch of four straight wins, scoring 11 goals in the process.

APRIL

- Roy Stark, Captain of Aston Villa's victorious 1972 FA Youth Cup side, played back-to-back matches in the first-team. They were his first and last.
- Villa put seven past Dutch giants Feyenoord in a home friendly.
- Fred Turnbull's last game for the Villa was for the visit of Nottingham Forest, while Geoff Vowden played his last in the Carlisle game at Brunton Park.
- Another FA Youth Cup winner, keeper Jake Findlay, made his first team debut at home to Sunderland. Forward Bobby Campbell also debuted as a sub.

MAY

- Ray Graydon fired in the Villa's last goal of the campaign via the penalty spot in the 1-1 draw at Orient.
- Ian Ross is the only ever-present in the league. Cumbes played 41 games, Nicholl 40.
- Having failed to land promotion in only the second season back in Division Two, Vic Crowe and Ron Wylie were shown the door. Initial favourite for the job was deposed England boss Alf Ramsey.

Physio, Fred Pedley, Ron Saunders and Alun Evans get comfortable at Bootham Crescent for the 1974/75 curtain raiser at York City

1974-75

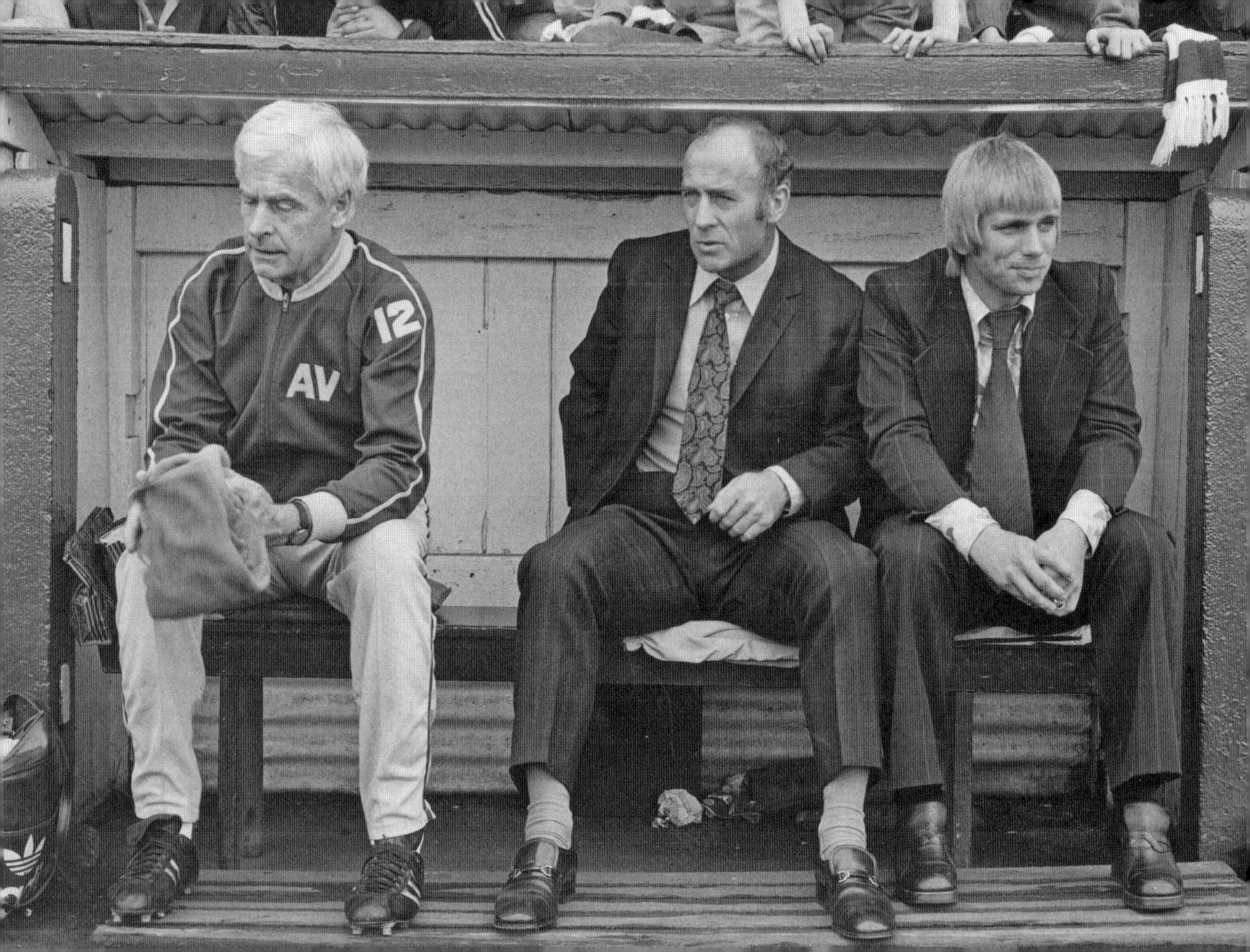
12
AV

THE BIG ASTON VILLA BOOK OF THE SEVENTIES

[Back Row] Sammy Morgan, Ray Graydon, Brian Little, Pat McMahon, Tony Betts [Middle Row] Alun Evans, Fred Turnbull, Jim Cumbes, Keith Leonard, Jake Findlay, Frank Carrodus, Alan Little [Front Row] John Robson, John Gidman, Ian Ross, Ron Saunders (Manager), Ian 'Chico' Hamilton, Chris Nicholl, Charlie Aitken.

Football League	Division Two
Manager	Ron Saunders
Asst. Manager/Coach	Roy McLaren
Physio	Fred Pedley
Captain	Ian Ross
Final Position	Second
FA Cup	Fifth Round
League Cup	Winners
Leading Goalscorer (all competitions)	Ray Graydon – 27 goals

Aston Villa unveiled their new manager, Ron Saunders, on 4th June 1974, the man who had taken Norwich City up as Second Division Champions in 1972, led them to the League Cup final in 1973 and then led Manchester City to Wembley in the same competition the following year. Saunders was a winner! His first signing took him back to Maine Road where he signed Frank Carrodus, a midfielder with a fantastic engine, a player that could run 'all day.'

Villa started the new campaign in mediocre fashion, but after three score draws, Hull were hit for six with Sammy Morgan bagging a hat-trick. Villa then encountered two away losses either side of a home win against Orient. The only other signing was the capture of Welshman Leighton Phillips from Cardiff City.

Unbeaten during October with four wins and a draw, Villa sat third, before a disastrous spell that saw three defeats on the spin, however, they had negotiated the first two hurdles in the League Cup, although both had required replays. By the end of the calendar year Villa were seventh, but with eight defeats under their belts thus far, promotion looked highly unlikely. Ray Graydon was the division's leading scorer with 18, not bad for a winger.

Away from the pressures of the league, Villa had added the scalps of Colchester and Hartlepool to Crewe and Everton and the fans had something to look forward to in the New Year in the shape of a League Cup semi-final against Fourth Division Chester. Youth Cup winners Alan Little and Tony Betts, along with Pat McMahon, had played their last games for Villa. January was a productive month – two league wins; Oldham (3-0 away) and top-flight Sheffield United (4-1 home) were put to the sword in the FA Cup, then Chester were narrowly beaten 5-4 on aggregate over two-legs, to book a date at Wembley. Villa were also hanging on the coat-tails of the top three. A fine win at Meadow Lane brought an end to

continued >>>

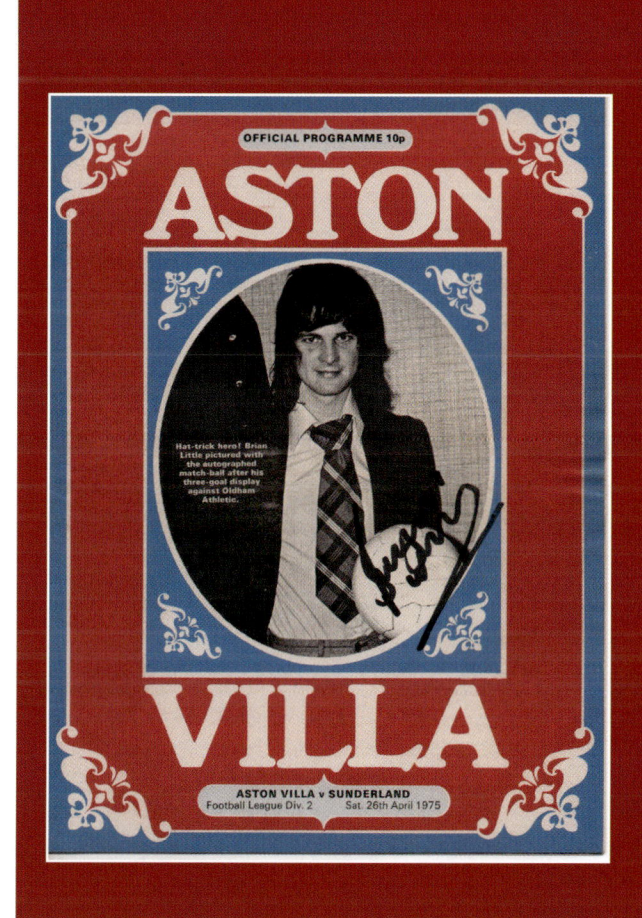

ASTON VILLA

OFFICIAL PROGRAMME 10p

Hat-trick hero! Brian Little pictured with the autographed match-ball after his three-goal display against Oldham Athletic.

ASTON VILLA v SUNDERLAND
Football League Div. 2   Sat. 26th April 1975

Total Home League Attendances	580,739
Average Home League Attendance	27,654
Highest Home League Attendance	57,266
Lowest Home League Attendance	15,840

		P	W	D	L	F	A	W	D	L	F	A	Pts
1	Manchester United	42	17	3	1	45	12	9	6	6	21	18	61
2	**Aston Villa**	**42**	**16**	**4**	**1**	**47**	**6**	**9**	**4**	**8**	**32**	**26**	**58**
3	Norwich City	42	14	3	4	34	17	6	10	5	24	20	53
4	Sunderland	42	14	6	1	41	8	5	7	9	24	27	51
5	Bristol City	42	14	5	2	31	10	7	3	11	16	23	50
6	West Bromwich	42	13	4	4	33	15	5	5	11	21	27	45
7	Blackpool	42	12	6	3	31	17	2	11	8	7	16	45
8	Hull City	42	12	8	1	25	10	3	6	12	15	43	44
9	Fulham	42	9	8	4	29	17	4	8	9	15	22	42
10	Bolton Wanderers	42	9	7	5	27	16	6	5	10	18	25	42
11	Oxford United	42	14	3	4	30	19	1	9	11	11	32	42
12	Orient	42	8	9	4	17	16	3	11	7	11	23	42
13	Southampton	42	10	6	5	29	20	5	5	11	24	34	41
14	Notts County	42	7	11	3	34	26	5	5	11	15	33	40
15	York City	42	9	7	5	28	18	5	3	13	23	37	38
16	Nottingham Forest	42	7	7	7	24	23	5	7	9	19	32	38
17	Portsmouth	42	9	7	5	28	20	3	6	12	16	34	37
18	Oldham Athletic	42	10	7	4	28	16	0	8	13	12	32	35
19	Bristol Rovers	42	10	4	7	25	23	2	7	12	17	41	35
20	Millwall	42	8	9	4	31	19	2	3	16	13	37	32
21	Cardiff City	42	7	8	6	24	21	2	6	13	12	41	32
22	Sheffield Wed	42	3	7	11	17	29	2	4	15	12	35	21

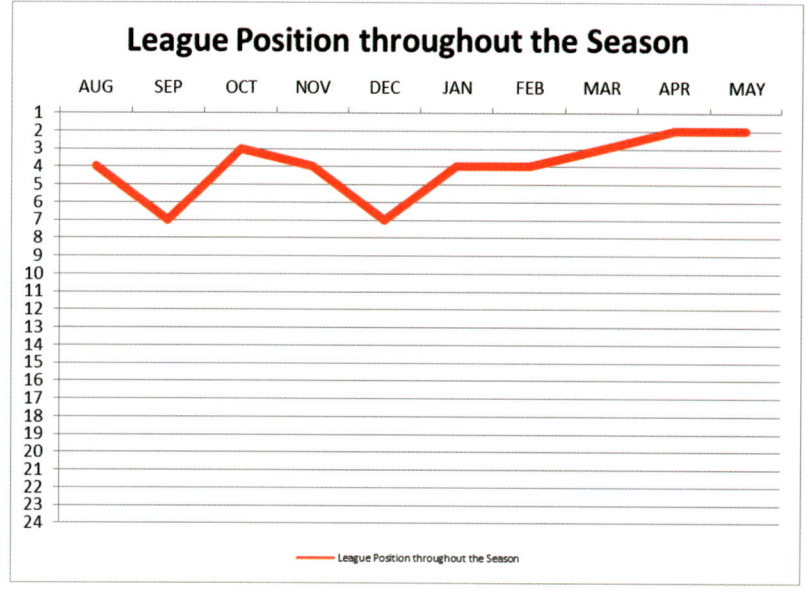

League Position throughout the Season

THE BIG ASTON VILLA BOOK OF THE SEVENTIES

1974-75

York's keeper, Graeme Crawford, is powerless to prevent Ray Graydon from heading the equaliser

Sat 17th August — **York City (A)**
Drew 1-1 — **Att 9,396**
Graydon

Newly promoted York City stung Aston Villa with an eighth minute goal – with new manager Ron Saunders watching from the dugout, his men soon applied heavy pressure with a Brian Little shot rattling the underside of the crossbar. Forward Sammy Morgan was caught offside on numerous occasions before Ray Graydon scored Villa's first of the new campaign on the half-hour mark.

Tue 20th August — **Hull City (A)**
Drew 1-1 — **Att 8,712**
Robson

Villa soaked up a lot of pressure in the first half and it was Hull who broke the deadlock in the 75th minute after their player skipped over two tackles to slot the ball home. Villa responded five minutes later when full-back John Robson, playing in midfield, was allowed space to volley in an equaliser from just inside the Hull area. It would be the only goal for the Consett born player in 176 appearances.

Sat 24th August — **Norwich City (H)**
Drew 1-1 — **Att 23,297**
Graydon

Villa, without Frank Carrodus who'd been injured at Hull in mid-week, were made to work hard to break down a nine-man City defence. A Nicholl header following a corner flew fractionally over, before Ray Graydon finally made the breakthrough in the 52nd minute. Villa's superior midfield were responsible – Little's swerving centre deceived both the defence and ex-Villa keeper, Kevin Keelan, and Graydon was there to deflect the ball across the line. The Villa's lead lasted barely half an hour with Colin Suggett's 25-yard shot snatching a point for the Canaries.

Notts County's unbeaten home record, Brian Little's brace taking his tally to a dozen, Frank Carrodus' goal being his first in claret and blue. Villa went out to Ipswich in the FA Cup 2-3 having lead at half-time – it was Alun Evans' last game, but he'd signed off with a goal.

Villa warmed up for Wembley with a fine 2-0 win over run-away leaders Manchester United (Aitken's only goal of the campaign), the points meant Villa were only one behind Sunderland and Norwich who sat in second and third. Without reaching the levels of a classic, Villa did enough to lift the League Cup thanks to a Ray Graydon penalty after a Mel Machin (not the keeper) diving save had denied Chris Nicholl. Villa would march into Europe next season as a consequence.

Following the euphoria of the cup win, Villa saw March out with three wins to add to a draw and a defeat. The 0-1 loss at Orient's Brisbane Road the only defeat of 1975 so far. Over 47,500 fans came out to see Keith Leonard hit the double that beat WBA 3-1 at Villa Park. It was tight at the top, Tommy Docherty's United had 52 points from 37 games, Sunderland had 45 from 37, Villa were sitting in the last promotion berth with 44, having played two games less. They would need to hold their nerve for the final push of seven games.

The goals came thick and fast – Millwall were hit 3-1, Cardiff beaten 2-0; Oldham were convincingly turned over 5-0, including a Brian Little hat-trick. A 3-0 victory at Blackpool meant Villa had scored 100 goals in the season and this was bettered by a 4-0 win at Hillsborough where Villa guaranteed themselves promotion. Villa's last home game of the season was played out in front of a carnival atmosphere, 57,266 (with up to 20,000 locked out) saw promotion hopefuls Sunderland beaten by two late goals. Villa rounded off their Centenary year in true style, along with a promotion and cup double they inflicted Norwich City's heaviest home defeat with the 4-1 victory.

Come Co-operative Shopping
RAILWAY STREET · MICKLEGATE & BRANCHES
Just say
RING Reynard's RENT-A-CAR YORK
FOR SELF DRIVE

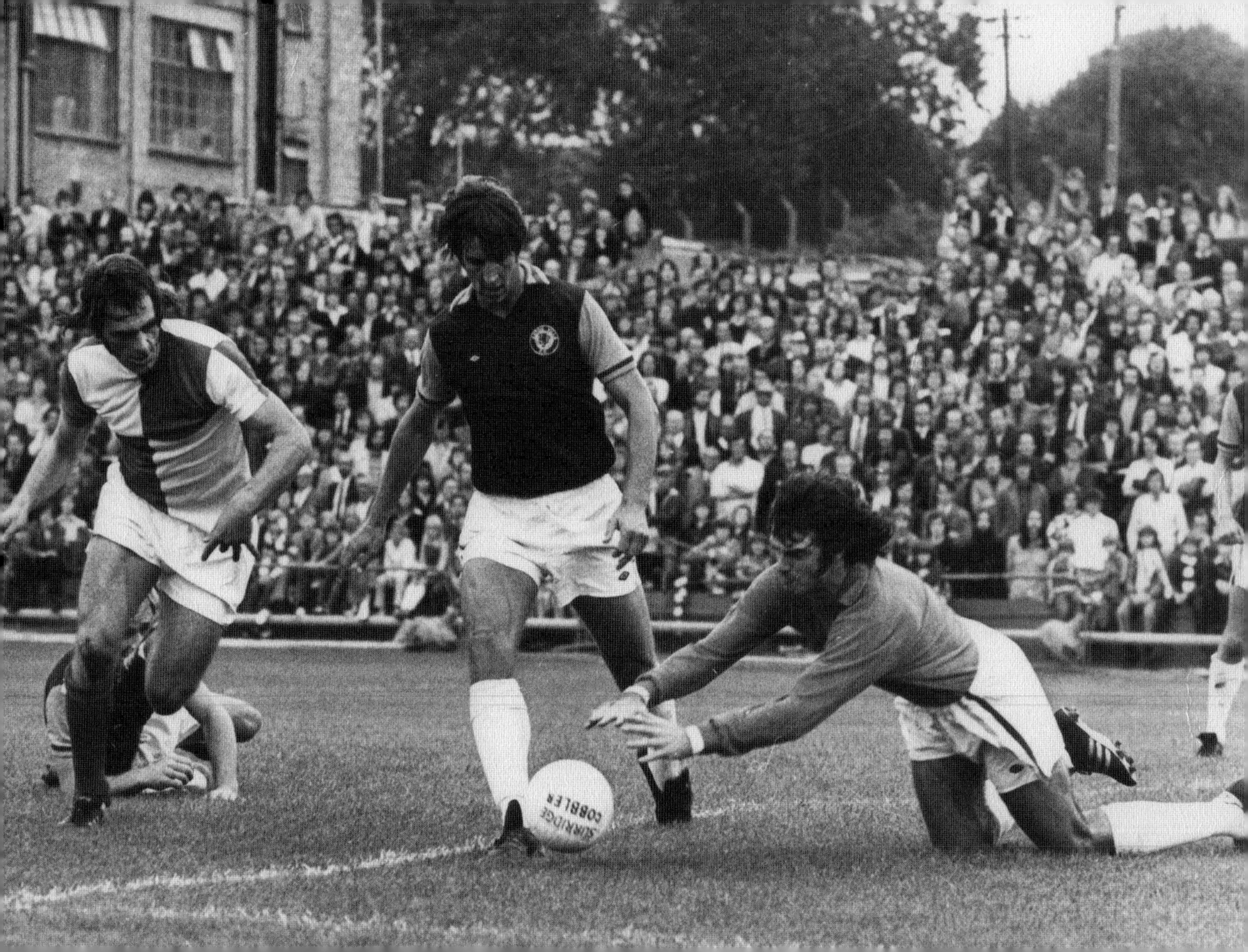
SURRIDGE
COBBLER

Chris Nicholl shields Graham Moseley as the on-loan keeper gathers the ball at Bristol Rovers

Wed 28th August　　**Hull City (H)**
Won 6-0　　**Att 18,973**
Morgan 3, Graydon, Little B, Hamilton
A Sammy Morgan goal in the 27th minute (his tenth in claret and blue) gave Villa the half-time advantage over an unbeaten Hull side. Morgan had a goal ruled out a minute after the interval before claiming the match ball with a hat-trick. It cost Villa a tidy amount, the club had agreed to pay Port Vale £10,000 once Morgan had scored 10 goals and £1,000 for every goal thereafter. Graydon (his third in four games), Little and Hamilton also found the net in the demolition of City.

Sat 31st August　　**Bolton Wanderers (A)**
Lost 0-1　　**Att 13,265**
Villa had rushed though the loan of Derby goalie Graham Moseley after keepers Cumbes and Findlay were ruled out injured. Having scoring six in midweek, Villa struggled, and took until the 75th minute to remotely trouble Barry Siddall in goal. By then Bolton had led for 50 minutes and missed a penalty – the spot kick thundered against the underside of the bar and Jimmy Brown cleared.

Sat 7th September　　**Orient (H)**
Won 3-1　　**Att 16,902**
Morgan, Graydon 2 (1 pen)
Villa were only one point, but 11 places, ahead of opponents Orient and put the Bolton defeat behind them with a polished, solid performance. Villa simply outclassed, outchased and outfought a poor Orient side. Morgan set them on the way when he hammered in a low shot, Graydon made it 2-0 with a spectacular rising drive, then Ray's second of the afternoon made it three on 71 minutes, but Orient scored a consolation three minutes later.

Wed 11th September　　**Everton (H) League Cup 2nd round**
Drew 1-1　　**Att 29,640**
Nicholl
Everton had the ball in the net within five minutes, but it had been handled prior to crossing the line. Villa went close on 18 minutes when Chris Nicholl set Little up, but the visiting keeper was well placed to save. Everton then squandered an easy chance before Nicholl put Villa in front with a powerful header from Graydon's corner kick – their performance earned a standing half-time ovation as they left the pitch. Bob Latchford, Britain's costliest player, cancelled out Villa's lead to take the tie back to Merseyside.

Sat 14th September　　**Bristol Rovers (A)**
Lost 0-2　　**Att 14,045**
In what turned out to be loanee Moseley's last game, Rovers kept Villa under constant pressure and were only let down by their inaccurate finishing. Saunders' men went off at the interval relieved to still be level. Immediately after the break Graydon worked himself some space but his shot went narrowly wide of the post. Nicholl then went closer but the headed effort was still inches over. Bristol fashioned an opening in the 55th minute when they were awarded an indirect free-kick, it was played backwards and their centre-forward made no mistake. The Pirates secured the win with a second goal with five minutes remaining.

Wed 18th September　　**Everton (A) League Cup 2nd round replay**
Won 3-0　　**Att 24,595**
Morgan, Carrodus, Graydon
Villa, inspired by midfielder John Robson, totally outclassed Everton. The only surprise was they had to wait until the second half to stamp their authority with goals. Sammy Morgan struck fon 49 mins and Frank Carrodus made it two, ten minutes later. Ray Graydon rounded off an comfortable night by fired home from the edge of the area to make it 3-0 – an emphatic result. The referee held play up when broken bottles and cans were launched into Cumbes box

by the upset Evertonians in the Gwladys Street End and policemen had to stand between them and the field of play for the remainder of the game.

Cool as you like! Graydon steers the ball to the right of Millwall's Bryan King to put Villa two-up

Sat 21st September   Millwall (H)
Won 3-0   Att 21,375
Graydon 3

Millwall had lost all three on the road before arriving in B6. With only 12 minutes gone Villa's Bobby Campbell was forced to make way for Leighton Phillips (his Villa debut) because of a badly gashed leg. Within two minutes the Welshman had robbed a Millwall player of possession, moved forward, before pushing a perfectly weighted ball into the path of Graydon who fired in off the far post. What an introduction! Graydon made it 2-0 from the penalty spot and, on 70 minutes, he then sealed his first career hat-trick by side-footed home following Ross' telling pass.

Sat 28th September   Southampton (A)
Drew 0-0   Att 18,599

Keith Leonard was given his first run out of the campaign. In a game of one-way traffic at The Dell, Villa were spared from an avalanche of goals by the acrobatics of Jimmy Cumbes between the sticks. He repeatedly denied Mick Channon – a constant thorn – and leapt high to pluck the ball of Peter Osgood's head. Villa had one chance in the match but 'Chico' Hamilton's volleyed shot thundered off the upright after Frank Carrodus had made all the running.

Wed 2nd October   Nottingham Forest (H)
Won 3-0   Att 20,357
Graydon, Hamilton, Leonard

This was a thoroughly convincing performance, which augered well for the future. Aston Villa were described in one paper as a side who 'displayed all their First Division potential.' Graydon – leading scorer in the Football League – put Villa ahead in the 22nd minute with his tenth of the season. A minute before the break Leonard flicked on Nicholl's free kick for Hamilton to put the home side firmly in the driver's seat. Keith Leonard helped himself to a goal to make it a fourth consecutive home victory. Carrodus was yet again outstanding in midfield.

Sat 5th October   Oldham Athletic (A)
Won 2-1   15,574
Own goal, Graydon

Villa attacked from the start, but couldn't take advantage before the break. Oldham went in front five minutes after the restart, but Villa were level shortly afterwards when Hicks put through his own goal – Graydon's cross had hit the centre-half's legs and rebounded in. Gidman was sent off in the 67th minute having been booked earlier when tangling with the same player. Alan Little, on his debut, also went into the ref's book. He had the last laugh though when Villa snatched a dramatic late winner when the ever-alert Graydon got on the end of a Leonard header.

Wed 9th October   Crewe Alexandra (A) League Cup 3rd round
Drew 2-2   Att 12,290
Morgan, Leonard

This was a dull match that never lived up to the atmosphere generated, even though there were five cautions and a sending off. Morgan, back after missing three games, put Villa in front. Crewe pulled level and looked the more likely of going in front, until a ball played upfield by Hamilton was collected by Morgan, he bustled his way through before teeing up Leonard to score his second in the space of eight days. Crewe then forced a replay with barely five minutes on the clock, then had a player sent off before the end.

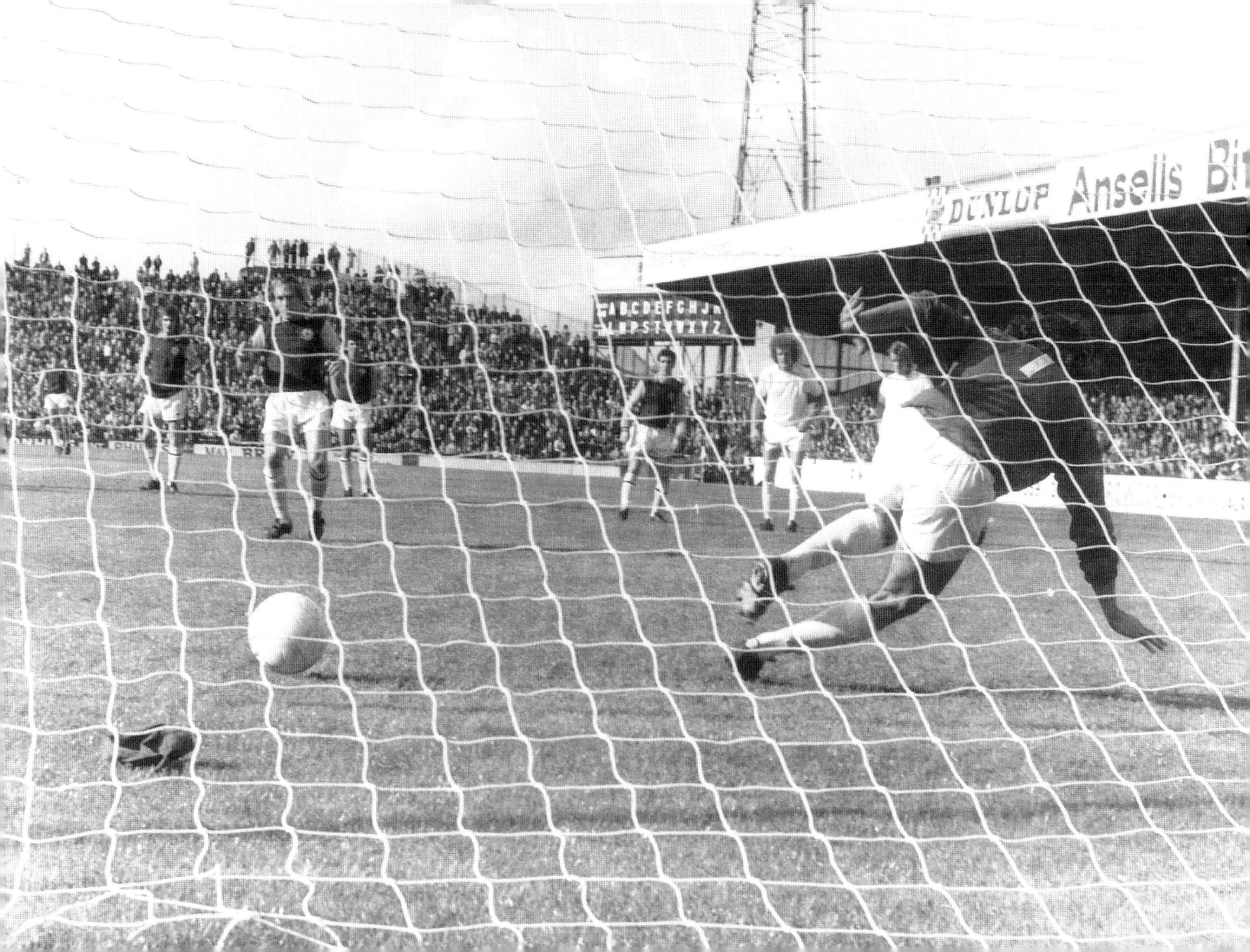
DUNLOP
Ansells Bi
ABCDEFGHJK
LMPSTWXYZ

Sat 12th October   Blackpool (H)
Won 1-0   **Att 25,763**
Graydon

Villa were being overrun by a Blackpool team sitting sixth in the table and only two places behind. Saunders' team were constantly caught in possession, or their passes were being intercepted. Cue Ray Graydon to score his 12th of the season a mere 24 seconds into the second half in what was the first moment of entertainment for the home supporters.

Wed 16th October   Crewe Alexandra (H) League Cup 3rd round rep
Won 1-0   **Att 24,007**
Hamilton

Geoff Crudgington, playing back at Villa Park for the first time since his free transfer, defied his former club with save after save, especially in the second half. Jim Cumbes on the other hand didn't have a solitary save to make. The Fourth Division outfit held Villa all the way, and it took a goal with less than two minutes remaining to decide the tie. 'Chico' Hamilton fired in a left-footed shot from just outside the area to save Villa's embarrassment and earn them a place in the last 16 of the competition.

Sat 19th October   Sunderland (A)
Drew 0-0   **Att 33,232**

Third-placed Sunderland, and fourth position Villa, were separated by goal average only. There was very little between the teams on the Roker Park pitch either. Sheer hard work and a refusal to give in gained Villa a valuable point from one of their main promotion challengers. Preoccupied with defence and midfield, Villa didn't mount many serious attacks, although Carrodus went close when he connected with a Nicholl knock down, but his attempt was just wide of the mark.

Sat 26th October   Sheffield Wednesday (H)
Won 3-1   **Att 23,977**
Phillips, Nicholl, Graydon (pen)

The Villa beat a struggling Wednesday side even though the visitors had the upper hand in midfield and attack. On another day their defensive frailties could have been punished. Phillips opened the scoring (and his account) when he curled a free kick into the top corner. Despite falling behind The Owls played the better football and Cumbes was called on twice to deny them. Tommy Craig drew the Sheffield side level on 22 minutes, before Nicholl powered in number two with a fine header. Graydon then added another to his already impressive tally to make it 3-1. All the goals coming in the first half.

Sat 2nd November   Fulham (A)
Lost 1-3   **Att 10,979**
Little B

For the visit of Villa, Fulham adopted new tactics and aimed deadballs at the far post, and within 90 seconds this ploy bore fruit when a corner played deeper was headed home by big John Lacy. From then on the visitors were on the rack with only brief respite. Cumbes was courageous and kept out three certainties before Fulham made it 2-0. The hosts had the ball in the net a third time before Brian Little scored what was no more than a consolation.

Sat 9th November   Notts County (H)
Lost 0-1   **Att 22,182**

County had the ball in the net after 35 seconds but, luckily for Villa, it was adjudged off-side. County were then attacked at will and were making it tough for Villa. Hamilton and Graydon were restricted to shooting from distance. Villa were awarded a penalty in the 37th minute following a handling incident, however, Ray Graydon, with three successful spot-kicks to his name, hit it hard and true but The Magpies keeper tipped it round the post. Needham broke the deadlock just before the half-time whistle and Villa were unable to peg the visitors back.

Tue 12th November   **Hartlepool (A) League Cup 4th round**
Drew 1-1   **Att 12,305**
Aitken

Hartlepool had knocked a decent Blackburn side out (eventual Division Three champions) in the previous round. Villa went ahead after 34 minutes through their full-back Aitken's right footed shot – following an exquisite through ball from Nicholl – and were comfortably in control. They also had two penalty appeals turned down. Hartlepool responded to their biggest and most frenzied crowd since the Busby Babes visited 17 years previously and duly levelled on the hour.

Sat 16th November   **Manchester United (A)**
Lost 1-2   **Att 55,615**
Hamilton

Skilful and full and know how, Villa controlled the first half and totally outplayed the Division's pace-setters. They took an early lead when Phillips found Aitken, who nodded down for Ian Hamilton to swivel and drill into the net. United threatened they didn't get a look in thanks mainly to Ross and Nicholl. Leighton Phillips should have doubled Villa's lead but he slammed the ball against a post with only Alex Stepney to beat. United, roared on by their biggest crowd of the season, came out fighting in the second period and were given a penalty when John Robson was harshly adjudged to have handled. They levelled from the unfair spot-kick advantage, then an un bagged an undeserved winner late on.

Sat 23rd November   **Portsmouth (H)**
Won 2-0   **Att 16,821**
Hamilton, Little B

Following three consecutive defeats, Villa needed to get back on track. Ahead on three minutes through Hamilton, and with a two goal advantage mid-way through the first half thanks to a Brian Little dipping header, Villa had virtually sewn the game up before the interval. But, to the supporters' frustration, the home side looked content to sit on their lead and it was fortunate that Portsmouth were incapable of mounting any serious challenge.

Mon 25th November   **Hartlepool (H) League Cup 4th round replay**
Won 6-1   **Att 17,686**
Hamilton 2 (1 pen), Little B 2, Graydon 2 (1 pen)

Brian Little celebrated his 21st birthday partnering his younger brother Alan up front. In the seventh minute Brian's darting run was ended by a trip, Hamilton scored from the spot. 'Chico' scored the second just before the interval, it was also created by Villa's Geordie. Villa simply ran riot in the second period, Brian got on the scoresheet twice (Hartlepool scored in between) before Graydon added a fifth. Ray also slotted home a last minute penalty to complete a 6-1 rout.

Fri 29th November   **Oxford United (H)**
Drew 0-0   **Att 18,554**

So poor was the first half that the only thing of note was a booking for an over zealous tackle on Hamilton. A Graydon corner after the interval was met and headed accurately, but with four defenders on the line, it was cleared. Frank Carrodus was fouled, the resulting free-kick was delivered by Graydon – Little dived to head it goalwards but it struck an Oxford full-back. In the dying minutes the Villa players and crowd screamed for a penalty alike when a Little shot was clearly handled on the line, but the referee claimed Brian had handled first.

Tue 3rd December   **Colchester United (A) League Cup 5th round**
Won 2-1   **Att 11,871**
Little A, Graydon

Colchester had eliminated three sides from a higher divisions to get to this stage. Alan Little, making a rare appearance, put Villa in front to give the visitors an interval lead. Ray Graydon then added to his impressive tally of 15 to double the advantage. Saunders' side were comfortably ahead against the Third Division outfit, but that all changed when the hosts pulled a goal back. The Villa penalty area was besieged from that point on and Villa were lucky to survive the frenzied finale.

Sat 7th December — Bristol City (A)
Lost 0-1 — Att 13,390
Alan Little was given the coveted No 9 shirt following his successful strike in mid-week. Villa started the more promising, but it was the home side that went in front mid-way through the first half. Villa staged a territorial fight back, but were unable to snatch an equaliser. They had only registered one win from the previous six.

Sat 14th December — York City (H)
Won 4-0 — Att 15,840
Graydon, Nicholl, Little B, Hamilton
Aston Villa's four-goal flourish against York put them firmly back into the promotion mix, trailing third placed Norwich by only two points. Ray Graydon opened the scoring when he ran unmarked into the box and connected with Little's cross. Five minutes later, centre-half Nicholl made it 2-0, his header coming from a Brown free-kick after Little had been hauled down. Villa's third was scored by Brian Little, with his back to goal he spun brilliantly and fired in from close range. The pick of the bunch was surely Ian Hamilton's – he unleashed a fierce, low drive into the bottom corner following a flowing move down the right.

Sat 21st December — West Bromwich Albion (A)
Lost 0-2 — Att 29,614
In a game of little constructive football, and littered with many errors, West Brom took the lead when a Johnston cross was spilt by Jim Cumbes. Unfortunately for Villa's custodian the ball squirmed over the line. To their credit Villa battled to turn the tide, and were unlucky when Bobby Campbell narrowly missed Graydon's right-wing centre. John Robson pushed forward, but his shot swerved the wrong side of the post. Albion scored a second on 69 minutes

Chico Hamilton chasing for the ball while others around him appear to be disorientated at The Hawthorns

to seal the win, and both points. Only a weak Little header and a Campbell cross/shot were on target for the visitors.

Thu 26th December — Bristol Rovers (H)
Won 1-0 — Att 21,556
Graydon
Villa looked to be suffering a Christmas Day hangover, but they finally created an opening through John Robson, only for Bobby Campbell to waste it. The hosts upped the ante after the break (what had Saunders said in the confines of the dressing room?) but it was a gift, presented to them by Rovers, that allowed Graydon to bag the decisive winner and keep the Claret and Blues on the fringes of the promotion zone.

Sat 28th December — Cardiff City (A)
Lost 1-3 — Att 11,060
Hamilton
Keith Leonard was the preferred striker, while Campbell had played his last Villa game the previous week. Cardiff, languishing in 18th position, were three goals up with just over half an hour gone. The swirling wind played a part in the Bluebirds' first goal with only 73 seconds on the clock when Cumbes couldn't hold a free kick. It was 2-0 twenty minutes later. 'Chico' Hamilton pulled one back for the visitors in the second half, but it was no more than a consolation. Bobby McDonald came on for Jimmy Brown.

Sat 4th January — Oldham Athletic (A) FA Cup 3rd round
Won 3-0 — Att 14,510
Little B, Nicholl, Graydon
Bobby McDonald made his first start of the campaign, while Frank Pimblett debuted. After a shaky start, Villa commanded the last 15

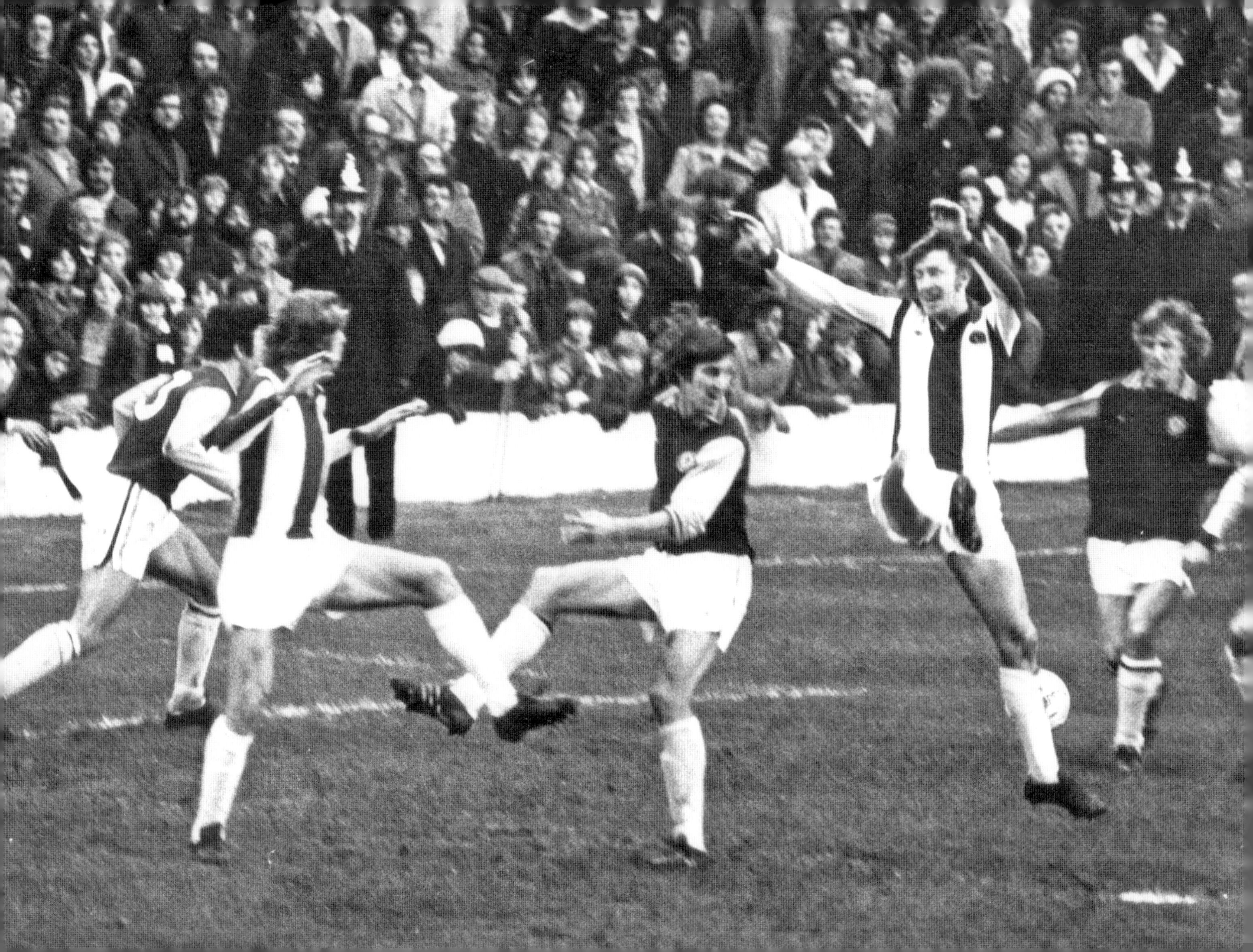

Dormie
Men's Wear
Hire Service
Morning Suits
Dinner Suits
Hipkiss
ROWE FOR

Brian Little wheels away in delight having fired Villa 3-2 in front against Chester in the semi-final 2nd leg. Villa won 5-4 on aggregate in a fiercely contested tie

minutes of the first half, during which Brian Little struck to score what was described as a 'killer' goal from close range a minute before the break. Chris Nicholl went a long way to making the tie safe when he headed in to make it 2-0. Graydon scored his 19th of the season, five ahead of second placed Mike Channon in the leading scorers' chart.

Sat 11th January   Bristol City (H)
Won 2-0   Att 22,422
Little B, Hamilton

In perfect conditions, Villa had quickly taken charge of the game without seriously worrying the City keeper, when Brian Little's cunning shot beat Cashley to put his side ahead. There was purpose and determination to Villa's play, with the youngster Pimblett particularly prominent. City were keen to wipe out their opponent's slender lead, and had almost scored when Nicholl was required to head off his own line. Hamilton finally made the game safe when he added a second for Villa after 83 minutes.

Wed 15th January   Chester (A) League Cup semi final 1st leg
Drew 2-2   Att 19,000
McDonald, Graydon

Bobby McDonald headed Villa in front just after the quarter of an hour mark, but Fourth Division Chester came back into the tie when they scored a shock equaliser on the stroke of half time. Their lead was short-lived when Graydon did what he had threatened all evening – to put the ball between the posts! Villa were coasting until defiant Chester cashed in with another goal to level the tie.

Sat 18th January   Oxford United (A)
Won 2-1   Att 10,064
Little B, Nicholl

It took a spirited performance from Villa to end Oxford's impressive run of eight consecutive home victories. The visitors dominated proceedings, and had Little's shot not been cleared off the line, they would surely have taken a half-time lead. As it was, Brian had to wait until the hour to break the stalemate. A Keith Leonard throw was nodded on by Nicholl, then Little executed an acrobatic overhead kick to put Villa ahead only four minutes after Cumbes had kept a penalty out at the other end. Leonard then had a shot saved on the line prior to Oxford drawing level. Villa's winner, a result of another Leonard throw in, came when Nicholl's header found its way into the net.

Wed 22nd January   Chester (H) League Cup semi-final 2nd leg
Won 3-2   Att 47,632
Leonard 2, Little B

A large crowd turned out knowing Villa would have to commit to going forward after being held at Sealand Road, and they were two up within twenty minutes thanks to headed Leonard goals, his second from a shrewd Carrodus cross. Chester pulled a goal back before the interval, then drew level on the hour through John James. The tie looked destined for extra time when Brian Little stole in late on – lifting the Holte End's roof off and breaking Fourth Division hearts in the process. He slammed the ball home to book Villa's date beneath the Twin Towers.

Sat 25th January   Sheffield United (H) FA Cup 4th round
Won 4-1   Att 35,881
Leonard 2, Nicholl, Graydon

First Division United arrived at Villa Park on the back of a fine 3-1 win at White Hart Lane. It was soon apparent they would have their work cut out – Villa were superb! Aggressive, attacking play bought a 1-0 interval lead, Leonard on the mark. Nicholl got onto the end of

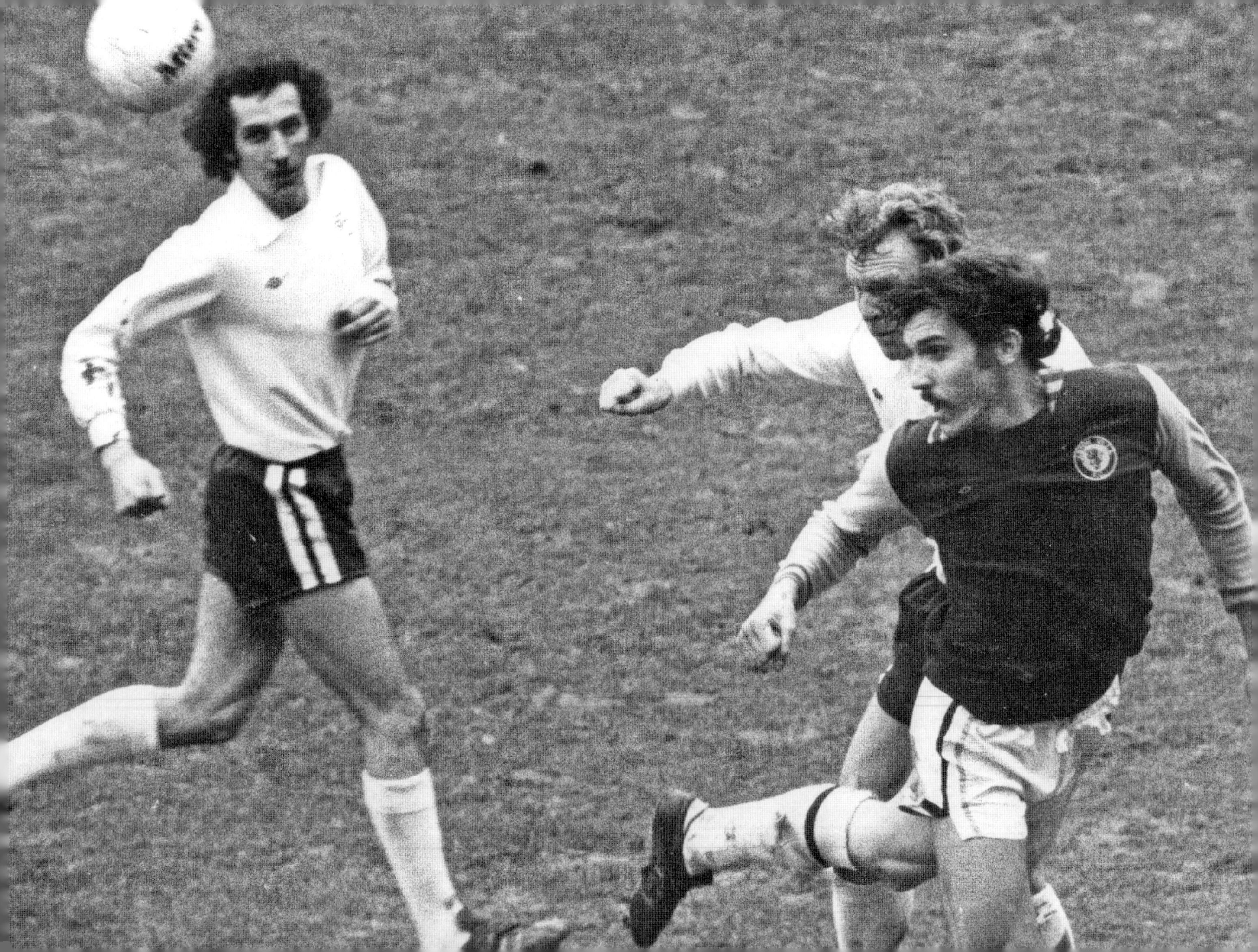

Keith Leonard remains calm despite the close attention of Fulham's Bobby Moore at Villa Park

a curling cross to make it two, and Ray Graydon showed he could torment Division One defenders when he fired Villa 3-0 in front. The Blades pulled one back before Leonard restored the margin with three minutes remaining.

Sat 1st February   Notts County (A)
Won 3-1   Att 16,651
Little B 2, Carrodus

Notts County were unbeaten at home until that stage, but Villa rolled into town and promptly turned them over. The hosts even took an early lead, though Villa looked unconcerned at conceding. They were level on the half hour when Little finished a neat Aitken/Hamilton move. Nicholl bought down Scanlon in the box to give away a penalty, but Cumbes was equal to it, to save his second in a fortnight. A minute later Villa had their noses in front when the skilful Little bagged his second of the afternoon. Frank Carrodus then got in on the act to put the game beyond doubt in the 86th minute. Villa remained fourth.

Sat 8th February   Fulham (H)
Drew 1-1   Att 28,551
Nicholl

Villa were held to a draw by lowly Fulham following three successive victories. They started like a whirlwind against a side marshalled by Bobby Moore, yet went behind mid-way through the half. A 'Chico' Hamilton penalty shortly after the interval was expected to restore parity, but Mellor in goal had other ideas. The keeper then followed this up with a superb one-handed save from a Little header. Five minutes after the spot kick miss, Villa were all square when Hamilton served up an accurate cross for Nicholl to bury in the Fulham net.

Sat 15th February   Ipswich Town (A) FA Cup 5th round
Lost 2-3   Att 31,297
McDonald, Evans

With Nicholl and Little out, Neil Rioch and Alun Evans were given rare starts. It was teenager Bobby McDonald who put Villa in front with a smart drive, after neat build up play involving Rioch, Evans and Hamilton. Villa were put into a commanding position when Evans headed in a simple goal after Leonard's effort had rolled along the crossbar. Johnson pulled one back for Town, before Bryan Hamilton, introduced with 20 minutes to go, hit Villa with a brace in the 78th and 84th minute. Villa were now fighting on two fronts not three.

Tue 18th February   Portsmouth (A)
Won 3-2   Att 13,355
Carrodus, Graydon, Little B

Villa bounced back following Saturday's FA Cup exit with a sharp shooting performance at Fratton Park. Carrodus had the visitors in front within 55 seconds, and it was no surprise when Graydon's name was added to the scoresheet mid-way through the first half. Pompey then shook Villa by finding the back of the net twice in as many minutes. The first, a twice-taken penalty. The fifth, and last, goal of the game arrived in the 38th minute when a McDonald cross was turned in by Little.

Sat 22nd February   Manchester United (H)
Won 2-0   Att 39,156
Graydon, Aitken

Villa went into the game seven points behind leaders United. Even without Hamilton, who'd failed a late fitness test, their feverish first-half display paralysed Manchester United who were unable to come back from Ray Graydon and Charlie Aitken goals. With Chris Nicholl back in the side, Villa looked better equipped to hold on to the points and Cumbes was rarely called upon. Keith Masefield debuted when he came on for Graydon.

THE BIG ASTON VILLA BOOK OF THE SEVENTIES

Sat 1st March   **Norwich City (Wembley) League Cup final**
Won 1-0   **Att 100,000**
Graydon

It was the first time the final had been contested by two sides from Division Two, and more remarkably, it was Ron Saunders' third final in a row as a manager. While never a classic, Villa created slightly more than a Norwich side who failed to service their dangerous frontman Ted MacDougall. Cumbes didn't have a save of note to make. Carrodus was industrious throughout and Little showed flashes of his brilliance, but it was centre-half Nicholl who should have broken the deadlock. His header was palmed away by Mel Machin to give the Villa a spot kick. Graydon's firmly struck penalty was pushed onto the left-hand upright by Keelan, but Ray was razor sharp and slammed home the rebound which was enough to give Villa victory.

Wed 5th March   **Bolton Wanderers (H)**
Drew 0-0   **Att 39,322**

With European competition guaranteed the following season, it was back to bread and butter football. Saunders' men had no answers to Bolton's defensive wall, yet they had so much of the play. Bad luck and bad finishing – a Graydon free-kick was punched goalwards but a Trotters defender was on hand to clear off the line – robbed Villa of the win. In the end the goalless draw was sufficient to lift Villa above Norwich and into the third promotion berth.

Sat 8th March   **Nottingham Forest (A)**
Won 3-2   **Att 20,205**
Graydon 2, Little B

Forest took the lead on 15 minutes only for Graydon to level the match on the half hour. The home side went ahead again, but Ray Graydon, notching his 26th of the season, pulled his side back into the match. Half-time was reached with the score finely balanced at 2-2. Villa were on a roll, unbeaten in their last seven and Brian Little, who along with big Keith Leonard gave Forest's defence a torrid afternoon, made sure of both points when he hooked the ball in smartly for the winner.

Villa push up in numbers during the Wembley League Cup final with ex-Villa keeper, Kevin Keelan, punching clear, under pressure

Sat 15th March   **Southampton (H)**
Won 3-0   **Att 31,859**
Leonard, Graydon, own goal

Villa had flown in a helicopter on the morning to assist in drying the Villa Park pitch. At half-time, with the score 0-0, it seemed a rather futile effort. But, shortly after the break, sterling work on the wing by Hamilton brought Leonard his first league goal in five months – the relief clearly visible. Villa's second was even better, McDonald chipped a delightful ball in for Leonard to head on for Graydon, who bagged number 27. But Villa weren't finished and continued to pushed forward and Charlie Aitken's fierce free-kick was turned in by Holmes. With Sunderland dropping a point Villa squeezed into second position.

Sat 22nd March   **Orient (A)**
Lost 0-1   **Att 9,719**

Villa started well and had the lion's share of possession; but they struggled creatively. Graydon was totally marked out of the game by Grealish, and although Carrodus worked hard in the Brisbane Road mud, there was something lacking over all. With a draw looking a cert Orient broke – Nicholl was outjumped and the ball fell to the O's number 11 who made no mistake. Cumbes stood no chance and Villa had succumbed to their first league defeat of 1975.

Sat 29th March   **West Bromwich Albion (H)**
Won 3-1   **Att 47,574**
Leonard 2, Hamilton

Villa were welcomed out by a huge crowd, as well as the Match of the Day cameras. Albion, who held a slender half-time lead

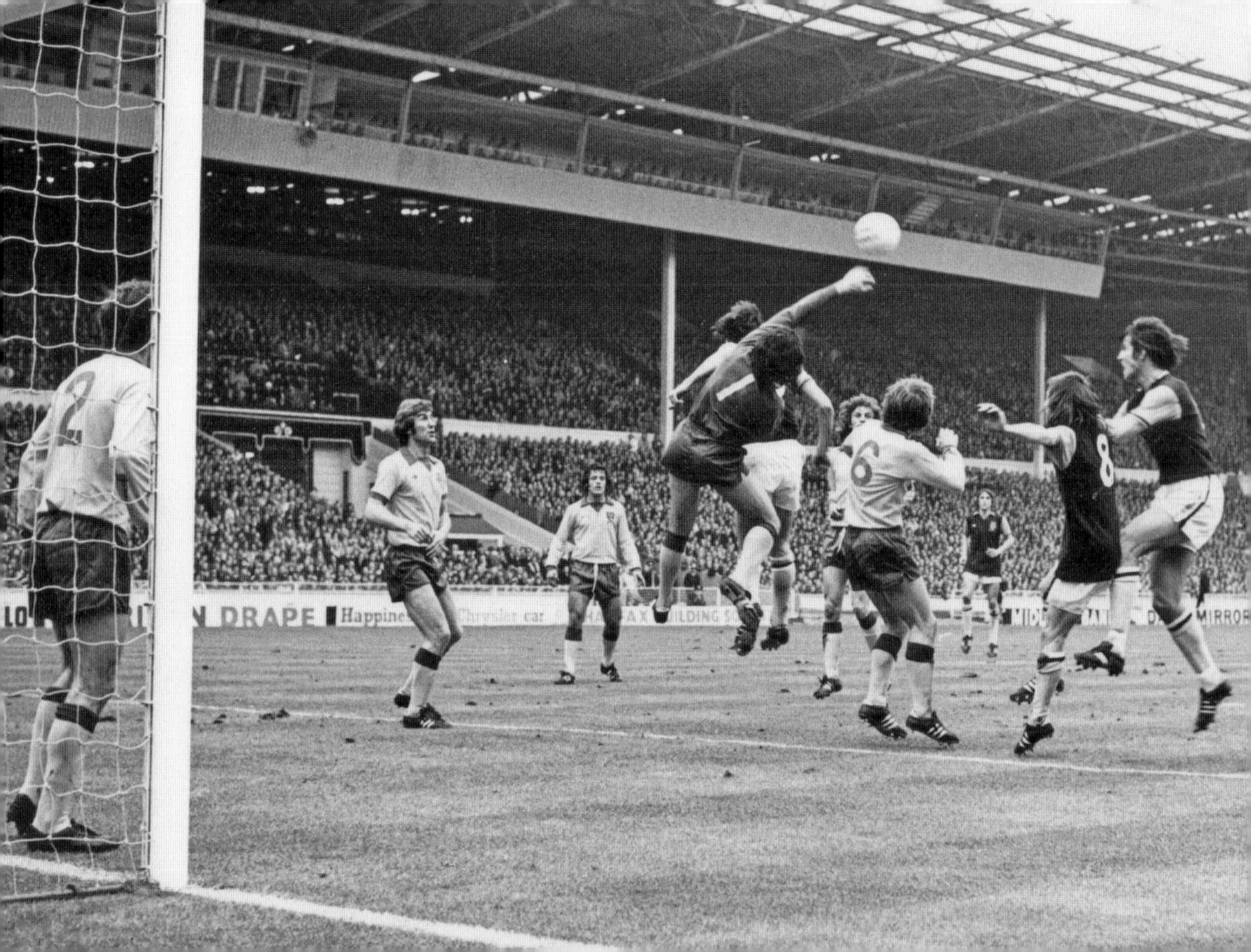
DRAPE
MIRROR

THE BIG ASTON VILLA BOOK OF THE SEVENTIES

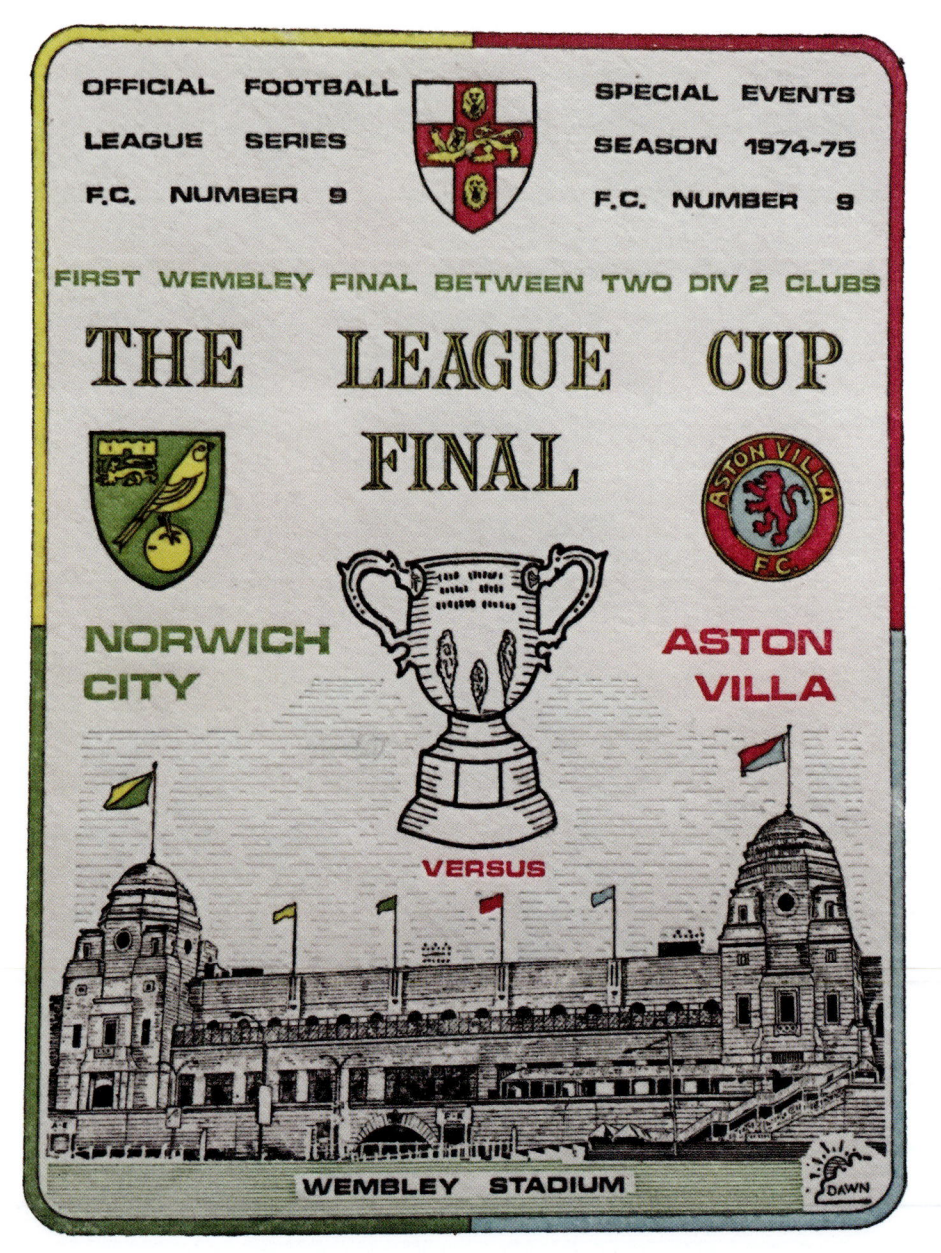

Some golden memories from Aston Villa's League Cup final win over Norwich City at Wembley Stadium – Ray Graydon's goal from the penalty spot was enough to secure the trophy

through Brown's 24th minute curling shot, came up against a transformed Villa after the break and were undone by three goals in an eight-minute spell. Graydon's shot was deflected for a corner, which he floated in perfectly – Keith Leonard beat both Osborne and Wile in the air to head home the equaliser. From then it was one-way traffic. Hamilton put Villa ahead in the 64th minute and Leonard bagged his second – again from a Graydon corner – to seal a 3-1 victory.

Tue 1st April   **Millwall (A)**
Won 3-1   **Att 13,115**
Hamilton (pen), Leonard, Little B

With any three from six still in promotion contention it was vital Villa collected both points. Millwall, fighting to stave off relegation, started at a furious pace and took the lead. Hamilton's twice taken penalty (the keeper moved) was enough to draw level, but it took until the 77th minute for Villa to get their noses in front, Leonard scoring his fourth in as many games. With a minute remaining Hamilton picked out Little who cheekily chipped the goalkeeper to finish the match in style.

Wed 9th April   **Cardiff City (H)**
Won 2-0   **Att 32,748**
Little B 2

In the end, Villa were too good for a Cardiff side destined for the drop, though for the first half, they couldn't break the visitor's resistance. Matters weren't helped by leading scorer Graydon going off with a hamstring injury early on. Just after the hour, and to the relief of another large crowd, Brian Little nodded home a Nicholl flick-on following a Hamilton corner kick. His second came 11 minutes later and was even better – a diving header into the corner of the net from a move started by Leighton Phillips and helped along by Hamilton. Brian was unfortunate not to bag a hat-trick with four minutes remaining when his shot thundered back off the crossbar with the keeper beaten before being cleared.

Sat 12th April   **Oldham Athletic (H)**
Won 5-0   **Att 36,244**
Little B 3, own goal, Hamilton

Villa started in a majestic and menacing fashion and it took just ten minutes to go ahead – Leonard's back-header into the area teed up the predatory Little who poked home from close range. Cumbes then pulled off a clever save and Aitken cut out a dangerous ball before Villa doubled their advantage through a Little cannonball of a shot. A minute later Brian missed a penalty after Phillips had been upended. An own goal made it 3-0 and then Little bagged the match ball with his third on 82 minutes – prompting the Villa faithful to chant "Little for England!" Hamilton finished off the rout when he made it 5-0 in the final minute.

Sat 19th April   **Blackpool (A)**
Won 3-0   **Att 20,762**
Phillips, own goal, Little

Blackpool, in sixth and with the meanest defence in the division, were only four points off a promotion berth, but Villa, in front of 15,000 of their own travelling fans, simply blew the Seasiders away. Phillips fired in his goal first since October before a Hatton own goal put the visitors firmly in the driving seat with 19 minutes played. A little after the hour mark a huge Cumbes goal-kick bounced just shy of the Blackpool area, and Little raced in to half-volley the ball beyond future Villa keeper, John Burridge, to score his side's 100th competitive goal of the campaign.

Wed 23rd April   **Sheffield Wednesday (A)**
Won 4-0   **Att 23,770**
Leonard, Little B 2, Ross (pen)

Two points at Hillsborough, against bottom of the table Wednesday, was all that stood between Villa and Division One! Villa held the ball and outclassed their opposition. The magnificent Carrodus played a large part in the first goal of the evening, which was scored by Leonard. He then turned provider to set Little up for the second.

Brian Little's brace helps Villa overcome Sheffield Wednesday 4-0 at Hillsborough – the victory ensured promotion back to the First Division after an eight-year absence

Keith Leonard with Sunderland keeper Jim Montgomery during Villa's 2-0 win

Steve Hunt, on for the injured Hamilton, crossed for Little to claim his eighth goal in four games, before Ian Ross scored his first goal of the campaign from the penalty spot. Villa had run out 4-0 winners and would gracing the top flight again.

Sat 26th April   Sunderland (H)
Won 2-0   Att 57, 266
Ross (pen), Little

Estimates of the number of fans locked out of Villa Park ranged from 12,000 to over 20,000, and if they'd all been allowed in, perhaps Villa's 76,588 record capacity could have been under threat. With Sunderland fighting it out for the last promotion place, it was always going to be a tight affair, and it was still 0-0 with eight minutes remaining when Little was tripped by Moncur. Ross repeated his achievement at Sheffield in the week and coolly slotted home from 12-yards. Brian scored the second, aided by McDonald's through ball, he cut-in from the left, paused, swivelled and then shot beyond Montgomery. That made it seven wins on the bounce for Saunders well disciplined outfit.

Wed 30th April   Norwich City (A)
Won 4-1   Att 35,943
Leonard, Gidman, McDonald, Carrodus

Norwich had already assured themselves of the last promotion place and would be joining Villa in Division One the following August. Hamilton, back after injury, set up Leonard to put Villa in front. John Gidman then got in on the act when he robbed a City defender of possession before burying the ball beyond Keelan's reach. Norwich pulled one back after 26 minutes, and only an incredible save from Cumbes prevented Martin Peters equalising. McDonald then bagged his only league goal of the season, while Carrodus helped himself to another (his fourth of the campaign) to wrap the season up with a satisfactory 4-1 victory.

THE BIG ASTON VILLA BOOK OF THE SEVENTIES

PRE-SEASON

- Amid all the media hype surrounding Brian Clough, Ron Saunders was unveiled as the new manager.
- Villa were prepared to smash their transfer record to bring in West Bromwich Albion and England U-23 midfielder Len Cantello.
- Villa took part in a two match tour of West Germany.

AUGUST

- Reserve coach Leo Crowther was dismissed by the club after a difference of opinion with manager Saunders.
- Ron Saunders went back to his former club Manchester City to make midfielder Frank Carrodus his first Villa signing.
- Aston Villa celebrated their 100th anniversary at home to Champions Leeds United, narrowly losing 1-2.
With injuries to both keepers (Cumbes and Findlay) Villa took Derby County's Graham Moseley on a month's loan.

SEPTEMBER

- After being held at Villa Park, the team defied all odds and won 3-0 at Goodison Park to knock top-flight Everton out of the League Cup.
- Welsh international Leighton Phillips signed from Cardiff City even though Liverpool were interested.
- Pat McMahon played his last game for Villa in the defeat at Bristol Rovers.

OCTOBER

- An FA disciplinary commission in Manchester cleared Charlie Aitken regarding his booking at the Goodison Park cup-tie. Former Villa boss Joe Mercer gave evidence in Aitken's defence.
- Port Vale offered £10,000 for Keith Leonard who had a spell on loan at Vale Park. Villa turned down the offer as Leonard was required as cover for the injured Morgan and Campbell.
- Chris Nicholl earned his first cap and scored for Northern Ireland in the European Championship tie against Sweden.
- John Gidman debuted for the England U-23 team against the Czech's.
- Leo Crowther won his fight for compensation (£1,000) following the unfair dismissal.

NOVEMBER

- Full-back Gidman was hospitalised after being hit in the eye by a stray firework (the force sent him through a glass pane) at Jim Cumbes annual bonfire night party.
- Old Trafford was the stage for Tony Betts last Villa appearance.
- Officials and players of Aston Villa and Portsmouth observed a minute's silence for those killed in the Birmingham bombings.

DECEMBER

- Alan Little played his last in the away defeat at Bristol City.
- Tony Betts joined Southport on a month's loan.
- North Warwickshire District Council threatened Villa with court action for failing to comply with planning regulations at their training ground.

JANUARY

- Chairman Doug Ellis backed the club's promotion drive with a generous interest free loan of £100,000.
- Frank Pimblett made his first-team debut in the FA Cup tie at Oldham. The following week he started his first league game.
- Villa remained unbeaten during the month, winning two league games and two FA Cup ties; drawing and winning in the League Cup.

FEBRUARY

- Alun Evans signed off in style by scoring in the FA Cup tie at Ipswich Town. Villa lost 2-3.
- Neil Rioch's last Villa appearance came at Portsmouth's Fratton Park.
- Tommy Docherty returned to Villa Park for the first time since his dismissal. Villa beat his Manchester United side 2-0 and the 'Doc' backed Villa to win the forthcoming League Cup final and gain promotion. Keith Masefield was blooded against the 'Red Devils.'
- Following his horrific firework incident John Gidman made his comeback in a Midland Intermediate League fixture at Leicester City.
- Villa president Pat Matthews was shocked to find his £25,000 shareholding of the club was sold in error to Ron Bendall while he was abroad on business.
- The £40,000 gate receipts from the Chester League Cup semi-final are a new club record.

MARCH

- Aston Villa defeated Norwich City at Wembley to lift the League Cup for the second time in their history.
- Villa made the news when they employed the services of a helicopter to dry a sodden Villa Park pitch. The game went ahead as planned and Villa put three past Southampton.
- In the match at Brisbane road, Orient fielded two No 8s. The referee said it wasn't illegal, only that the players have to carry a number on their shirt! It was Villa's only reversal in the league from the New Year till the season's end.

APRIL

- Promotion was assured in Villa's centenary year at Hillsborough.
- A crowd of 57,266 – Villa Park's largest since the Man Utd semi-final Dec 1970 – turned out to watch Villa beat promotion challengers Sunderland. An estimated 15,000 – 20,000 were locked out!
- Villa played seven games throughout the month, four away and three at home. They won the lot, conceded only the two and scored 23 times.
- The five consecutive clean sheets were the club's best sequence since 1923/24 when they managed seven straight shut-outs.

MAY

- Ray Graydon fired in the Villa's last goal of the campaign via the penalty spot in the 1-1 draw at Orient.
- Ian Ross is the only ever-present in the league. Cumbes played 41 games, Nicholl 40.
- Having failed to land promotion in only the second season back in Division Two, Vic Crowe and Ron Wylie were shown the door. Initial favourite for the job was deposed England boss Alf Ramsey.

Brian Little climbs high to head for goal during the 0-0 draw at Molineux

1975-76

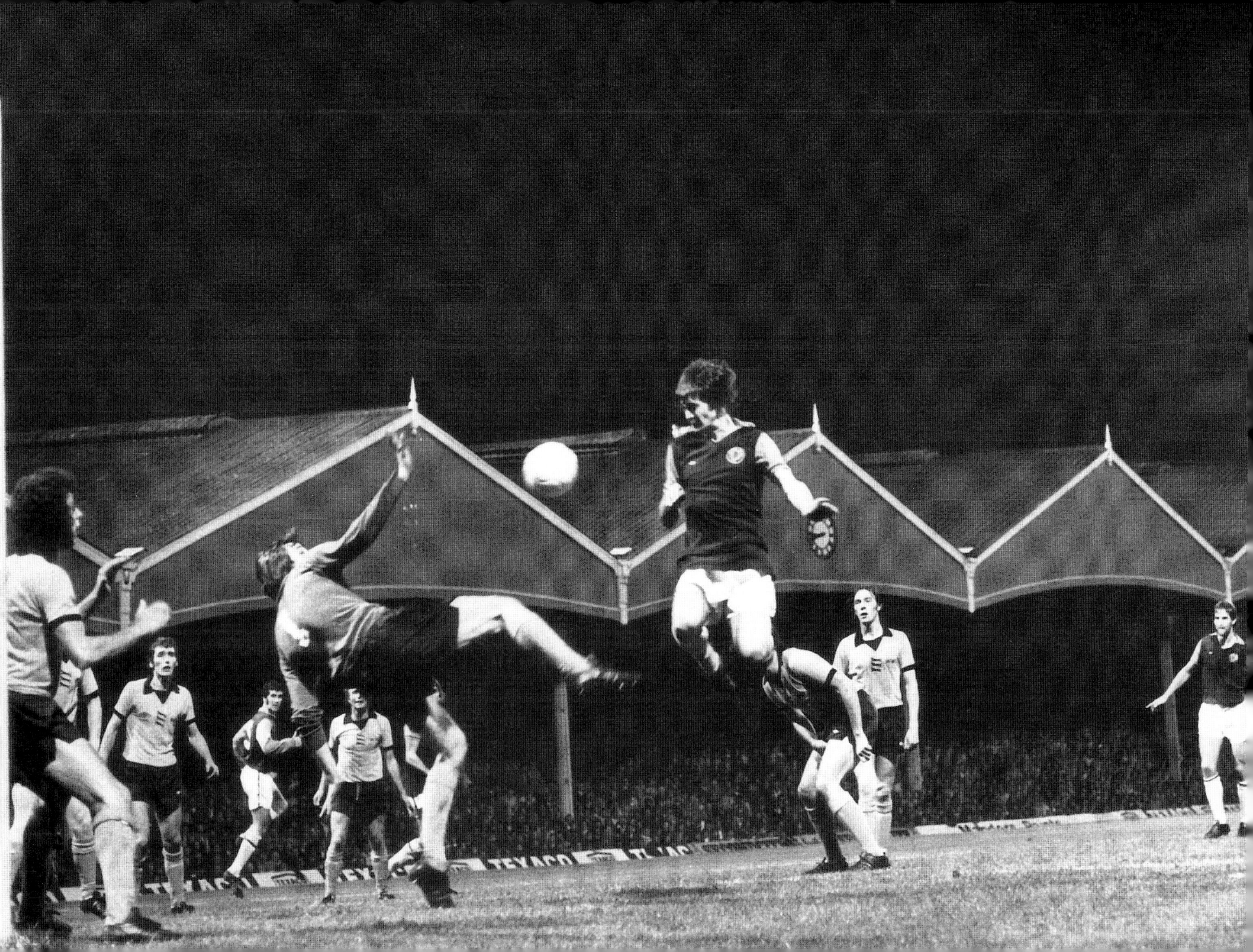
TEXACO

THE BIG ASTON VILLA BOOK OF THE SEVENTIES

[Back Row] Keith Masefield, Jimmy Brown, Keith Williams, Jake Findlay, Jim Cumbes, Steve Hunt, Ron Armstrong [Middle Row] Fred Pedley (Physiotherapist), Frank Pimblett, Pat McMahon, Sammy Morgan, Chris Nicholl, Keith Leonard, John Deehan, Leighton Phillips, Frank Carrodus, Bobby McDonald [Front Row] Alun Evans, John Overton, Charlie Aitken, John Gidman, Ian 'Chico' Hamilton, Ron Saunders (Manager), Ian Ross, John Robson, Brian Little, Ray Graydon, Roy MacLaren (Coach)

Football League	Division One
Manager	Ron Saunders
Asst. Manager/Coach	Roy McLaren
Physio	Peter Downes
Captain	Ian Ross
Final Position	Sixteenth
FA Cup	Fourth Round
League Cup	Third Round
UEFA Cup	First Round
Leading Goalscorer (all competitions)	Ray Graydon – 14 goals

Getting back into the top-flight after an eight-year absence was hard enough, but staying there would prove equally as difficult. Saunders, with the exception of two players, had basically got the club promoted with the side assembled by Vic Crowe and Ron Wylie.

Without a win in their first three games it was indeed tough at the top, but Villa closed the month of August with back-to back 1-0 home wins to lift the side into mid-table.

September saw Sir William Dugdale replace Doug Ellis as chairman. It was also at this time that forward Keith Leonard was badly hurt in a coming together with Arsenal keeper Rimmer, his short career was finished. Saunders acted fast by bringing in Andy Gray from Dundee United, he was raw, young and brave.

Villa's European odyssey was over as soon as it had begun, a 1-4 thumping in Belgium at the hands of Royal Antwerp, and a 0 -1 loss in the home leg. Cumbes, who was blamed for two of the away goals, featured no more for the Villa, Jake Findlay stepped in at Villa Park in a game where Sammy Morgan played his last.

Goalkeeper John Burridge was drafted in from Blackpool, making his debut in front of 53,782 as Villa defeated Birmingham City in the long awaited second-city derby.

Up until the New Year, Villa's form was sporadic, away they couldn't buy a win and had gleaned only four points on their travels. Home form was another story; their Villa Park record matched table-topping Liverpool's at Anfield.

"A present to the supporters" was how the arrival of Coventry City's Dennis Mortimer was described, a steal at £175,000. Over

continued >>>

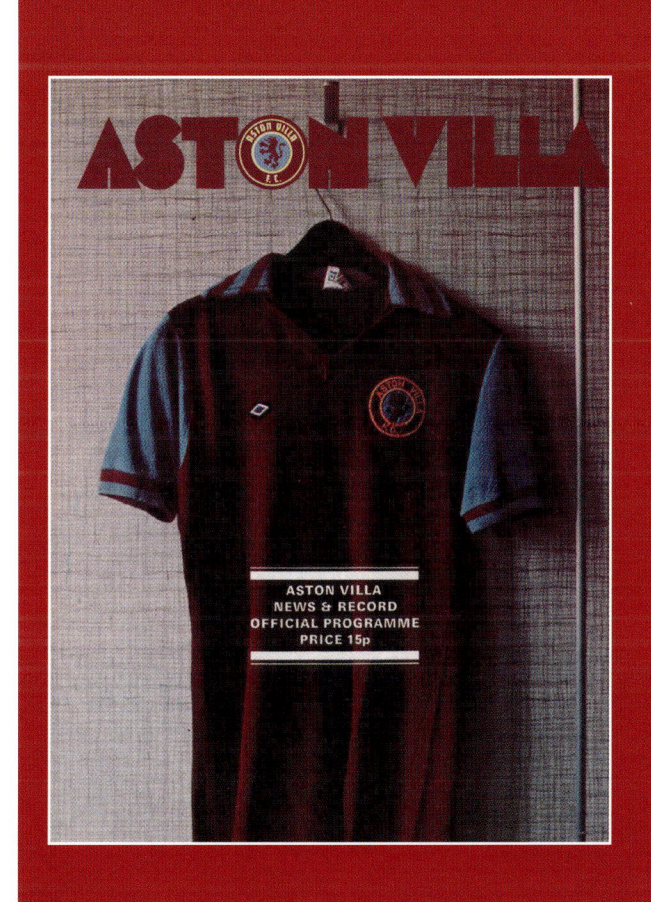

		P	W	D	L	F	A	W	D	L	F	A	Pts
1	Liverpool	42	14	5	2	41	21	9	9	3	25	10	60
2	Q.P.R	42	17	4	0	42	13	7	7	7	25	20	59
3	Manchester United	42	16	4	1	40	13	7	6	8	28	29	56
4	Derby County	42	15	3	3	45	30	6	8	7	30	28	53
5	Leeds United	42	13	3	5	37	19	8	6	7	28	27	51
6	Ipswich Town	42	11	6	4	36	23	5	8	8	18	25	46
7	Leicester City	42	9	9	3	29	24	4	10	7	19	27	45
8	Manchester City	42	14	5	2	46	18	2	6	13	18	28	43
9	Tottenham Hotspur	42	6	10	5	33	32	8	5	8	30	31	43
10	Norwich City	42	10	5	6	33	26	6	5	10	25	32	42
11	Everton	42	10	7	4	37	24	5	5	11	23	42	42
12	Stoke City	42	8	5	8	25	24	7	6	8	23	26	41
13	Middlesbrough	42	9	7	5	23	11	6	3	12	23	34	40
14	Coventry City	42	6	9	6	22	22	7	5	9	25	35	40
15	Newcastle United	42	11	4	6	51	26	4	5	12	20	36	39
16	**Aston Villa**	**42**	**11**	**8**	**2**	**32**	**17**	**0**	**9**	**12**	**19**	**42**	**39**
17	Arsenal	42	11	4	6	33	19	2	6	13	14	34	36
18	West Ham United	42	10	5	6	26	23	3	5	13	22	48	36
19	Birmingham City	42	11	5	5	36	26	2	2	17	21	49	33
20	Wolverhampton	42	7	6	8	27	25	3	4	14	24	43	30
21	Burnley	42	6	6	9	23	26	3	4	14	20	40	28
22	Sheffield United	42	4	7	10	19	32	2	3	16	14	50	22

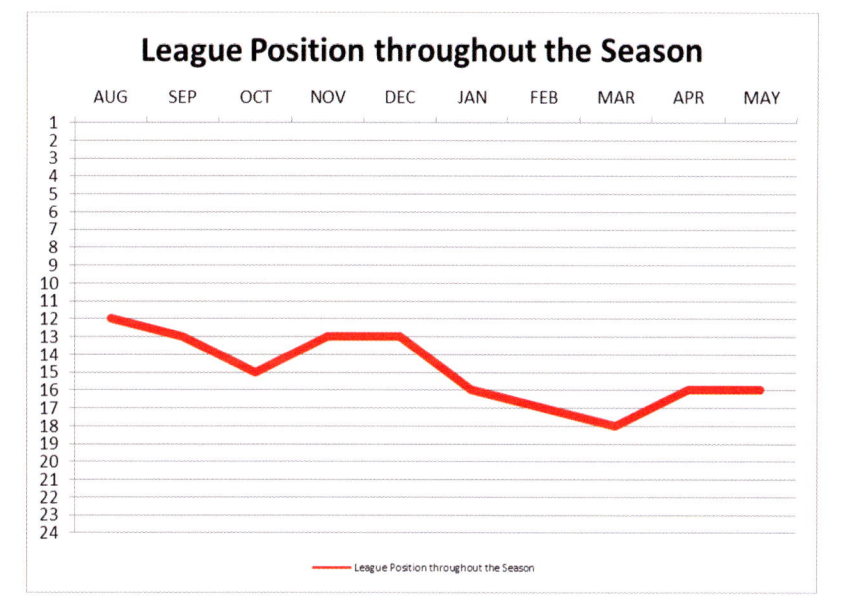

Total Home League Attendances 783,878
Average Home League Attendance 37,327
Highest Home League Attendance 53,782
Lowest Home League Attendance 30,053

League Position throughout the Season

THE BIG ASTON VILLA BOOK OF THE SEVENTIES

1975-76

Sat 16th August   **Leeds United (H)**
Lost 1-2   **Att 46,026**
Phillips

Newly promoted Villa, back after an eight year exile, gave Leeds United the run around for 20 minutes. Graydon and Little were the main antagonists, with David Harvey forced to make three crucial saves. It was from Graydon's cross that Welshman Phillips converted after only seven minutes to give Villa the lead. Leeds came back strongly and levelled through Lorimer. Nicholl saved off his own line and the visitors then had one disallowed. Leeds pressure and experience paid off in the 73rd minute when Cumbes failed to hold a header and Lorimer poked in from close range for his second and the winner.

Tue 19th August   **Queens Park Rangers (A)**
Drew 1-1   **Att 21,986**
Leonard

Villa bounced back from the opening day defeat and caused QPR all sorts of problems. Little scooped a difficult chance over the bar and Phil Parkes denied Leonard with a dramatic save. Gerry Francis then took control of the midfield and the home side dominated. It took until the hour mark for the hosts to get ahead but Keith Leonard showed the newly promoted outfit wouldn't be intimidated when he bagged a point with a 75th minute header.

A delighted Keith Leonard wheels away after bagging his first goal in the top flight to earn Villa a draw at QPR

51,000 came out to see his debut as Villa smashed West Ham 4-1. Already knocked out of the League Cup, Villa wouldn't progress beyond the FA Cup 3rd round, though after drawing 1-1 at the Dell, it was expected they would have too much for Second Division Southampton. As it happened The Saints marched all the way to Wembley where they lifted the trophy.

Villa embarked on a torrid run in the league, a loss, two draws and then three straight defeats. It was during this seqence that Charlie Aitken played the last of his staggering 660 games in claret and blue, during the home defeat to QPR. However, Villa found themselves just six points above the drop zone and anxiously looking over their shoulders.

Andy Gray hit a second-half winner to beat Manchester United 2-1, the Scot's ninth of the season, with Ray Graydon one in front on ten goals.

In March Chris Nicholl scored all four goals at Filbert Street, but they included two own goals! 'Chico' Hamilton bowed out at St Andrews then three valuable points were picked up in draws with Liverpool at home, then Coventry and West Ham away. The game at Upton Park being the last on Villa's travels, meaning for the first time in over 100 years, the club had managed to go all season without an away victory.

But Villa were guaranteed Division One survival, and managed back-to-back wins against Derby and Middlesbrough. The club's 16th place, proved a valuable foundation for the years to come, although of Villa's 39 point haul, 30 had been won at Villa Park.

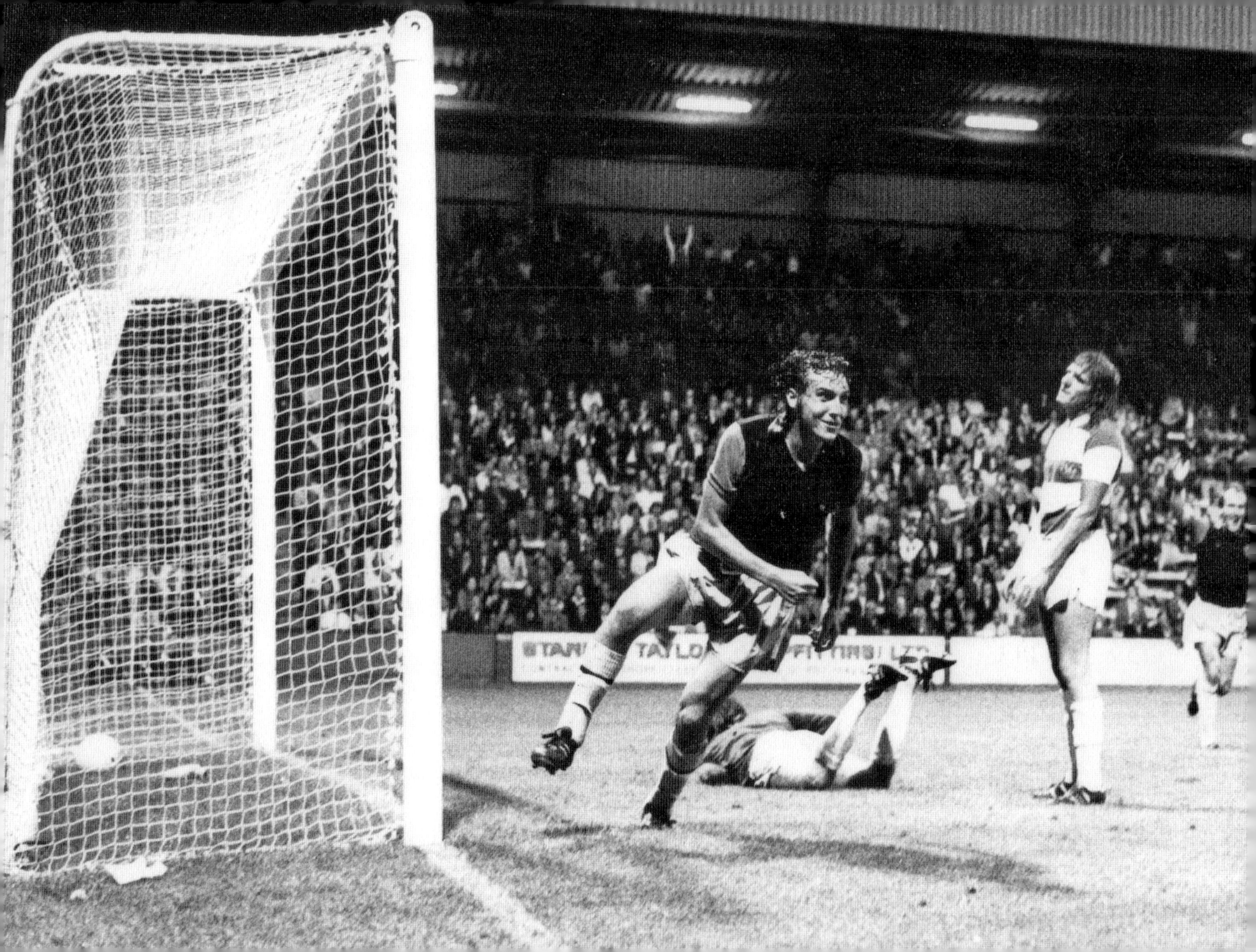

THE BIG ASTON VILLA BOOK OF THE SEVENTIES

Sat 23rd August Norwich City (A)
Lost 3-5 Att 21,195
Graydon 2 (1 pen), Aitken

Norwich went ahead through a suspect penalty, but Villa were back on equal terms within three minutes thanks to a penalty of their own – Graydon converting after Leonard was held in the box. However, due to conceding "silly goals" Villa trailed 1-4 at the break. Aitken's header reduced the arrears then Graydon scored Villa's third shortly afterwards. The visitors then went searching for an unlikely equaliser, but the result was made certain when MacDougall was allowed to run 40 yards before shooting home to bag a hat-trick in an eight goal thriller.

Wed 27th August Manchester City (H)
Won 1-0 Att 35,712
Leonard

Through hard work and endeavour, Villa at last gained a top-flight victory. Leonard would have had a first-half hat-trick had it not been for the form of Joe Corrigan in the City goal. A defence-minded City side finally conceded just after the hour when Leonard out jumped England international Dave Watson to get his head on the end of a Phillips free-kick and earn both points. On the few occasions the visitors looked remotely like attacking the ever dependable Charlie Aitken was on hand to avert the danger.

Sat 30th August Coventry City (H)
Won 1-0 Att 41,026
Graydon

The Sky Blues, having won two and drawn one, were sitting 3rd in the table and had the edge in the first half due to the dominance of a certain Dennis Mortimer. But Leonard was proving a constant thorn in the visitors' side and it was his presence in the box that led to City's keeper failing to hold 'Chico' Hamilton's centre. Ray Graydon was alert to the situation and stabbed the ball over the line from close range. Villa deserved the victory for their second-half display which pushed them up to 12th.

Sat 6th September Newcastle United (A)
Lost 0-3 Att 35,604

For the majority of the first period Villa looked the better team, yet they went in at the break two goals down. McDonald put the Magpies in front on six minutes even though Villa had asked all the questions, then went further behind three minutes before the break when Tommy Craig, later to sign for the claret and blues, found the net. Villa looked frustrated in the second-half and 'Super Mac' put the game to bed in the 86th minute to flatter the hosts. They'd won handsomely yet played badly according to some reports.

Wed 10th September Oldham Athletic (H) League Cup 2nd round
Won 2-0 Att 23,041
Leonard, Nicholl

Inspired by Leighton Phillips, holders Villa were finally too much for The Latics after struggling to overcome a heavy pitch. Only Ogden in the visitor's goal kept the game scoreless until the break, denying both Phillips and Graydon certain goals. Oldham did hit an upright before Villa broke down the left with Little, his cross was met by the in-form Leonard who forced it home. Ogden again outwitted Ray Graydon before Chris Nicholl's flying header - following a short corner played to Hamilton – guaranteed Villa's name went into the draw for the next round.

Sat 13th September Arsenal (H)
Won 2-0 Att 34,474
Phillips, Leonard

Arsenal were indebted to their keeper Jimmy Rimmer, an outstanding display meant the Gunners were still in the game at the break. Cumbes dived low to keep Alex Cropley from scoring before a rasping Phillips strike put Villa ahead. Keith Leonard made sure both points were Villa's when he headed home under pressure in the last minute. Leonard, who'd now scored four goals in only eight games, had looked badly injured earlier when he came off second best with Rimmer whilst chasing a 50/50 ball.

Wed 17th September   Royal Antwerp (A) UEFA Cup 1st round 1st leg
Lost 1-4   Att 21,000
Graydon

Villa, making their debut in European competition, started strongly and burly Sammy Morgan had the home defenders paying close attention. The Belgians gradually came into the game then romped into a four goal lead by the break, Karl Kodat bagging a hat-trick. Ray Graydon wrote his name into the Villa history books yet again when he scored the club's first ever European goal, but it was a mere consolation. Jimmy Cumbes was blamed by the manager for two of Antwerp's goals when he'd failed to hold onto the ball and it turned out to be his final match.

Sat 20th September   Liverpool (A)
Lost 0-3   Att 42,779

Villa were without top-scorer Leonard, who'd undergone cartilage surgery unaware that his career was finished. Pimblett started his first game of the season in place of Hamilton, while Jake Findlay was in goal. Villa created very few chances, and despite continuous pressure, champions Liverpool were unable to penetrate Villa's packed defence. Brian Little showed a flash of brilliance but his shot was fractionally over the crossbar. It was just a question of time however, Villa struggled in all areas, and once Liverpool found the net on 52 minutes, it was a case of how many. It was three in the end, but there could have been far more.

Tue 23rd September   Wolverhampton Wanderers (A)
Drew 0-0   Att 33,344

Findlay remained in goal even though Villa had brought in Blackpool keeper Burridge the day before and he played his part with a fine display. Phillips and Robson battled doggedly in the midfield, but the visitors lacked in attack. It took until the 50th minute for Villa to get an effort on target – a smart Chris Nicholl header. Wolves, who'd conceded five at Newcastle at the weekend, offered little and the match had nil-nil written all over it.

Sat 27th September   Birmingham City (H)
Won 2-1   Att 53,782
Hamilton, Little

In front of nearly 54,000, debutant keeper Burridge was beaten in the 12th minute when Trevor Francis stole in to poke home after Hatton's initial point-blank shot had been parried. But Villa's pace and persistence was rewarded when 'Chico' Hamilton lovelled the match when he half volleyed beyond goalie Latchford following Robson's searching cross from the right. The majority of the Blues' tackles had been totally over the top, none more so than a Kenny Burns assault on John Robson, described by Ian Ross as the worst he'd ever seen! Little pounced on a Burns mistake in the 70th minute to give Villa a deserved 2-1 victory over the arch enemy to the delight of the home fans.

Wed 1st October   Royal Antwerp (H) UEFA Cup 1st round 2nd leg
Lost 0-1   Att 31,513

Villa, with a sizeable crowd behind them, set about trying to reduce the arrears following the 1-4 reversal in Belgium. An Aitken shot was blocked before Trappeniers smothered a Little effort. Kodat fired Antwerp ahead in the 18th minute, but Villa continued to attack forcefully. Gidman's free kick was goal bound, but somehow, the agile keeper kept it out. Sammy Morgan came on after the break and created havoc with Villa having a target man to aim their crosses at, but the Belgium side knew they were home and dry and took the tie 5-1 on aggregate.

Sat 4th October   Middlesbrough (A)
Drew 0-0   Att 24,102

With just a single defeat in their last six visits to Ayresome Park, Villa

THE BIG ASTON VILLA BOOK OF THE SEVENTIES

A Carrodus header clears the bar, watched by Nicholl and Morgan, during the trip to Royal Antwerp in the UEFA Cup 1st round

travelled north in good spirits. They also had a secret weapon to unleash on unsuspecting defences in the shape of Andy Gray, a recent import from Dundee United. In fact it was outstanding work from 'Boro's defence that denied Gray a goal in the very first minute of his Villa debut. Villa soaked up tremendous pressure from an aggressive home side but nearly snatched a late winner when Little – who'd combined well with his new strike partner – was agonisingly close to getting his head on a Phillips high centre.

Wed 8th October   Manchester United (H) League Cup 3rd round
Lost 1-2   Att 41,447
Gray

Tommy Docherty's table topping United should have been overwhelmed at Villa Park, but Villa were denied by their own failings in the Manchester box. They created numerous chances but were unable to convert them, a Nicholl header was cleared off the line and Little missed when it was easier to score. Lou Macari snapped up his chance with relish in the 62nd minute, his deft back header catching Findlay off his line. Ten minutes later an unmarked Steve Coppell made it 2-0, two defensive lapses and Villa had been punished both times. Little's acrobatic overhead kick then struck the woodwork. Andy Gray, who'd won everything in the air, reduced the deficit in the closing stages with what would become a trademark header. Saunders claimed Villa should have won 8-2!

Sat 11th October   Tottenham Hotspur (H)
Drew 1-1   Att 40,048
Gray

In a tame first half Martin Chivers missed a glorious chance with the Villa defence wide open, but in the second period, battling Villa went in front with a wonderful goal from Gray. Pat Jennings almost single-handedly kept Villa at bay with countless saves. Spurs were down to 10 men just after the hour when Naylor received his marching orders, but Spurs salvaged a point from a late free kick, which came against the run of play.

Sat 18th October   Everton (A)
Lost 1-2   Att 30,376
Nicholl

Over cautious Everton were clearly troubled by a confident Villa team. Twice the inspired Brian Little forced Welsh international Dai Davies into saving his side. Just as the visitors seemed to be gaining control, Everton broke and scored when Villa's defence was caught square. A dozen minutes later the ref awarded the Toffeemen a hotly disputed penalty when Everton centre-half, Ken McNaught, was allegedly fouled by Andy Gray. Burridge saved it but the spot-kick was ordered to be retaken, either for the keeper diving too soon or Nicholl encroaching in the box. Brian Little limped off towards the end shortly before Nicholl pulled a goal back with two minutes remaining.

Sat 25th October   Burnley (H)
Drew 1-1   Att 35,204
Own goal

Ray Graydon headed over in the third minute, before Burnley went close when Gidman's intended back header fell short. Sole striker Gray (Little would be missing until mid-Feb) then saw his flicked header arrowing for the top corner – fans were already celebrating when somehow the Clarets' goalie managed to claw the ball away. The visitors went ahead when Noble cashed in after a Flynn shot had rebounded off Burridge. Villa's blushes were spared when Noble scored an own goal as Villa pushed forward.

Sat 1st November   Ipswich Town (A)
Lost 0-3   Att 24,687

Ipswich and Villa were equal on 13 points, but both sides were poor on the day, although the hosts snatched the lead a minute

THE BIG ASTON VILLA BOOK OF THE SEVENTIES

before the break. Two goals in seven minutes after the break effectively put the game to bed, but it could quite easily have been six.

Sat 8th November Sheffield United (H)
Won 5-1 Att 30,053
Gray, Hamilton 2, Deehan, Graydon (pen)
Aston Villa were full of aggression and were thirsty for goals, whilst bottom of the table United, were powerless to stop them. Andy Gray crashed in a left footed volley to give the Villans a slender interval lead, then Hamilton scored number two following good work from Pimblett. Young striker, John Deehan, who'd debuted the previous week, scored the first of many for the Villa in the 56th minute, to make it 3-0. Ted Hemsley then handled in the area, Graydon converted the penalty and Hamilton got his second of the afternoon on 84 minutes. United got a consolation in the dying seconds.

Sat 15th November Manchester United (A)
Lost 0-2 Att 51,682
Saunders side were ripped apart by United's rampant wingers Steve Coppell and Sammy McIlroy at a rain lashed Old Trafford, although Graydon tricked his way through the home defence but his shot was easily gathered by Roche. The keeper then kept out an effort from the Villa wideman with his foot. United were 1-0 to the good when Nicholl and Aitken were caught out by a low ball, then nine minutes into the second half, Villa were floored by another goal. Saves by Burridge and wasteful finishing by the home side kept the score respectable.

Sat 22nd November Everton (H)
Won 3-1 Att 33,949
Gray 2, own goal
Carrodus was back after missing the last two games and Villa were well rewarded by their fine all-round display, meaning they hadn't been beaten on home soil since the opening day. An Andy Gray brace brought his tally to four in eight league games. Sandwiched between his goals was an own goal by Everton centre-half Ken McNaught who had no chance when he deflected John Gidman's powerful drive past Lawson in goal. Saunders' team were sitting comfortably in 14th, on the same points as 11th placed Newcastle.

Sat 29th November Leicester City (H)
Drew 1-1 Att 36,388
Graydon
Villa had to come from behind against their East Midlands rivals after trailing to a 10th minute goal. Villa had chances to have led comfortably prior to this, with Gray seeing two headers stopped by Mark Wallington. John Deehan almost snatched an equaliser before Ray Graydon stole in to force a Gray goalbound header over the line following neat build up play from Nicholl and Hamilton. Desperate Leicester defending kept a surging Villa from taking both points.

Sat 6th December Stoke City (A)
Drew 1-1 Att 28,515
Graydon
The game was fought out at an astonishing pace with John Burridge kept busy as Villa were put under terrific pressure. Greenhoff gave the hosts the lead after 17 minutes, but it was short lived. Without the services of Gray, Ray Graydon showed he still had goals in him when he drew Villa level only six minutes later. It was his seventh of the campaign, although 18-year-old John Deehan was the star performer, showing touches and a maturity well above his years. In Aitken's continued absence, Gidman and Robson were forming a promising full-back partnership.

Sat 13th December Norwich City (H)
Won 3-2 Att 30,478
Graydon, Deehan 2
Graydon put Villa on the road to victory in the 17th minute by notching in his third consecutive match when he stabbed the ball

home at the near post – the goal brought Villa back on level terms after City had gone ahead after only 60 seconds through 1966 star Martin Peters. 'Dixie' Deehan's goal within six minutes of the equaliser made sure Villa went in ahead at the break. MacDougall levelled for City early in the second period, but Gray and Graydon combined well to set Deehan up with an easy opportunity that the youngster put away with relish shortly afterwards.

Sat 20th December — Leeds United (A)
Lost 0-1   Att 29,118

Leeds, in 6th place but only two points off the leaders, were expected to be a severe test for Saunders, and Villa were not helped by injuries ruling out both Gidman and Deehan. Due to the incredible Burridge, Leeds were thwarted until six minutes before the interval. Leeds approach work had been impressive, but fortunately their finishing wasn't to the same standard otherwise Villa could have been thrashed. Only Hamilton, Gray and Carrodus had seen efforts on target.

Fri 26th December — West Ham United (H)
Won 4-1   Att 51,250
Deehan 2, Gray, Hamilton

A phenomenal crowd turned out to witness Dennis Mortimer's debut following his signing from Coventry City. 'Chico' Hamilton started the move for Villa's first goal, squaring it to Deehan, who in turned played a one-two with th new boy, before swerving a shot beyond Mervyn Day. A dozen minutes later Deehan got on the end of Graydon's free-kick to make it 2-0. West Ham pulled one back, but Villa were in no mood to lie down and added further goals from Gray and Hamilton to complete a resounding win.

Sat 27th December — Derby County (A)
Lost 0-2   Att 36,230

With only a point to show from their last five away games, Villa's form on the road was very much on par with the relegation candidates. Derby on the other hand had won their last ten at the Baseball Ground. Villa did well to keep it scoreless at half time, thanks mainly to Burridge, but Derby, even without Bruce Rioch, were too much for Villa. Two second half goals, the second a penalty after Mortimer dropped Gemmill outside the box, kept Derby a point off the top.

Sat 3rd January — Southampton (A) FA Cup 3rd round
Drew 1-1   Att 24,138
Gray

Villa went in front just after the hour mark in a game of few chances – the deadlock broken when Villa were awarded a free-kick. Chris Nicholl's header thumped the woodwork and, as it came back off the crossbar, Andy Gray was on hand to poke it across the line. Promotion seeking Southampton squared the tie back in the 89th minute when a shot from distance found the back of the net with Burridge unsighted in the crowded area.

Wed 7th January — Southampton (H) FA Cup 3rd round
Lost 1-2   Att 44,623
Graydon

The Saints attacked from the start and raced into the lead, but Villa were back on level terms within seven minutes when an intended back-pass was seized upon by winger Graydon. Villa reshuffled when Ray went off, Gidman moved upfield, Robbo took the right full-back position and sub Aitken slotted in at his customary No 3 berth. The game stayed at 1-1 until the final whistle blew, and the extra time was drama all the way. Southampton restored their lead before Deehan was denied by the keeper, while Peach cleared off the line from Nicholl. Villa's efforts bore no fruit though.

Sat 10th January — Arsenal (A)
Drew 0-0   Att 24,539

Arsenal, four places below the Villa and with four home defeats under their belts, faced a Villa side still without an away victory and

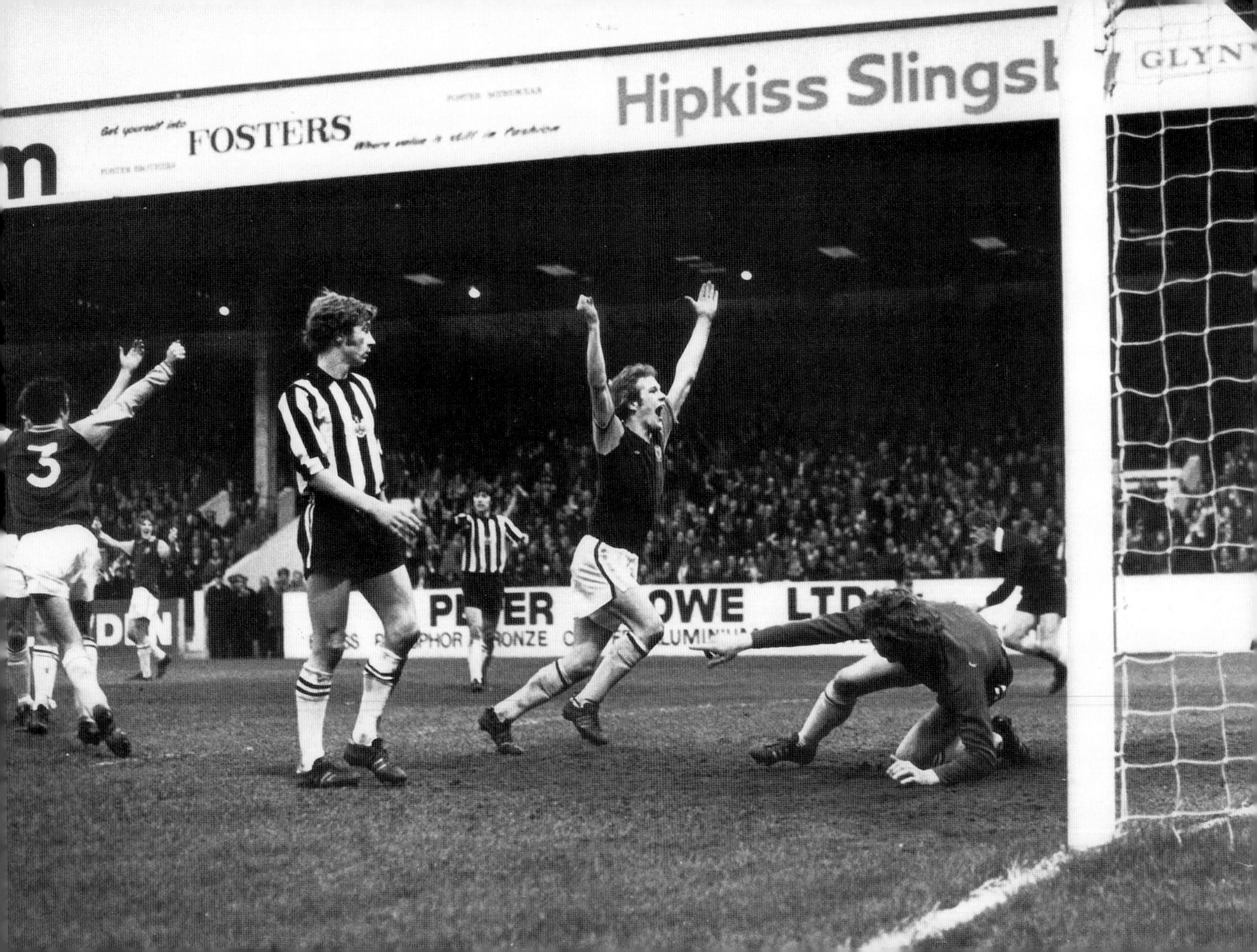

Hipkiss Slingsb
GLYN
FOSTERS
PETER
OWE
LTD

Newcastle keeper Mahoney punched the ball into his own net, under pressure from Andy Gray, to put Villa in front

missing Graydon and Deehan. Villa didn't manage a single shot on target as Gray roamed upfront on his own. All of Highbury jeered at the final whistle. Ron Saunders called the match "a joke, but not a funny one!" The only plus point - a few flashes of brilliance from Mortimer.

Sat 17th January   Newcastle United (H)
Drew 1-1   Att 36,387
Own goal
Villa were ahead only six minutes in against Newcastle when a long Carrodus cross from the right side looked easy enough for Mahoney in goal. However, Andy Gray's challenge was sufficient to distract the keeper, who fumbled his catch and watched in horror as the ball bounced over the line. Ten minutes later, while Mortimer was off the pitch being tended to, United pegged the game back following a free-kick. Gray then made a clearance in his own box by punching the ball out, luckily he got away with it. Villa did have the ball in the net after the interval only to have it disallowed for offside.

Sat 31st January   Queens Park Rangers (H)
Lost 0-2   Att 32,223
QPR, who would finish runners-up at the season's end, simply had too much in the locker for Villa who were missing key players through injury. On a frozen pitch, and with the match still goalless, Chris Nicholl went off after 30 minutes with a dislocated shoulder. Rangers domination was rewarded in the 76th minute. England captain, Gerry Francis, who'd been a revelation in spite of the close attentions of Ian Ross, sealed the win in the last minute. It brought an end to Villa's 12-game unbeaten home league run.

Sat 7th February   Manchester City (A)
Lost 1-2   Att 32,331
Gray
Decimated by injuries, John Overton debuted for the missing Nicholl, while Gordon Cowans would come off the bench to set in motion a long and fruitful claret and blue career. Villa went ahead after a superbly well taken goal by Gray, who slid it past big Joe Corrigan, Hamilton had shown great ball control down the flank. Villa almost extended their lead when Graydon's shot was blocked by the keeper's legs and then Burridge prevented a certain goal. Gidman also cleared one off the line. Gray went agonisingly close following a cute flick from Graydon late in the game, and just when Villa's travelling fans dared to think an away win was on the cards, City countered and equalised. To their horror, City then snatched a late winner to send Villa home without even a point.

Sat 14th February   Sheffield United (A)
Lost 1-2   Att 21,152
Graydon
The Blades were rooted to the foot of the table and had tasted victory only once in 28 attempts, surely Villa's away day jinx would end here? It certainly looked that way when Ray Graydon fired them into a 19th minute lead, but United fought back and Villa were undone by two lapses of concentration. The first when the defence backed off enough for Woodward to strike from distance, and then a dozen minutes into the second half, when Nicholl was outjumped. Saunders claimed United's goals were diabolical and 'Budgie' must take responsibility for both!

Sat 21st February   Manchester United (H)
Won 2-1   Att 50,094
McDonald, Gray
Brian Little returned and the game was played in an electric atmosphere. Villa were in front thanks to Bobby McDonald after 38 minutes after Graydon was hauled down, Gidman floated over the free

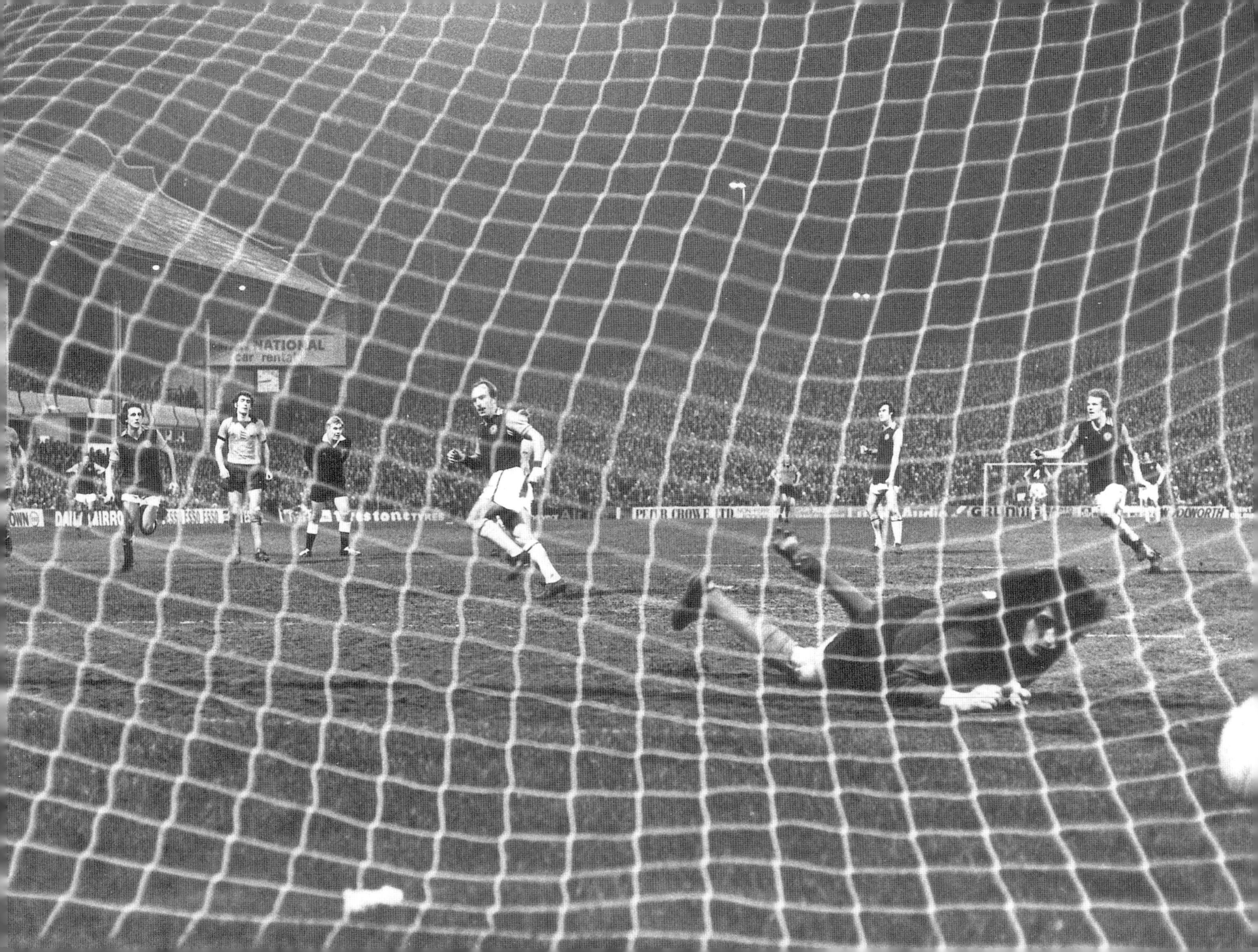
NATIONAL
car rental

Ray Graydon converts from the penalty spot to earn the Villa a draw at home to Wolves

kick and Bobby, in acres of space, was gifted a free header. United levelled before the break through a devastating Macari volley, but Villa were by far the better side in the second half and edged in front when a Gidman cross was met by Gray, who was lurking in the area with Little, and coolly slotted the ball home. Villa's first win of the New Year was greeted by a deafening roar of approval.

Tue 24th February   Wolverhampton Wanderers (H)
Drew 1-1   Att 47,693
Graydon (pen)

Three places and six points separated Villa and relegation threatened Wolves. It was tense, untidy and the referee failed to control a game full of uncompromising challenges. In one, Gidman was taken out from behind by Gould with the ball nowhere in sight. Wolves took the lead in the 53rd minute before their goalie, Parkes, denied McDonald, Little and Gray. But Wolves' keeper was later powerless to stop Ray Graydon from the penalty spot after a late slide-tackle on Gray in the box.

Sat 28th February   Burnley (A)
Drew 2-2   Att 17,174
Graydon, Gray

Villa travelled to Turf Moor with only eight goals scored in their previous 15 away games, and yet they were two up after only 20 minutes, with Graydon and Gray taking their tallies to 12 and 10 respectively and seemingly coasting to victory. Flynn pulled one back before the break when Villa failed to clear and the diminutive Welshman was at it again only three minutes after the interval when Villa's defence stood rooted. They had missed the experience of Chris Nicholl for sure, the young and willing Overton had stood in again in what was his third and final appearance.

Sat 6th March   Ipswich Town (H)
Drew 0-0   Att 32,477

Even with Dennis Mortimer back after a six match absence Villa lacked inventiveness and were unable to string much together. The only excitement came in the last two minutes of the match, Nicholl had moved up field, and from 25-yards out, he hit a full-blooded shot which Laurie Sivell blocked on the goal-line, Gray rushed in for the loose ball and caught the keeper full in the face. A stretcher was needed for the custodian and Whymark took over between the posts, but Villa couldn't capitalise. Villa had failed to find the net in 11 of their 33 games.

Sat 13th March   Tottenham Hotspur (A)
Lost 2-5   Att 24,169
Graydon, Gray

For the second consecutive away game the deadly duo of Graydon and Gray scored the goals, but unfortunately it wasn't enough to salvage even a point, with Jennings making three vital stops to prevent a 5-5 scoreline. A Nicholl own goal set Spurs on their way before Little teed Graydon up for an equaliser. Perryman restored the lead within 30 seconds and it was 3-1 at the interval with Duncan also finding the net. Gray out-jumped the Tottenham centre-half to reduce the deficit, but further goals, and Jennings in outstanding form, meant Villa were still with an away win.

THE BIG ASTON VILLA BOOK OF THE SEVENTIES

Sat 20th March   **Leicester City (A)**
Drew 2-2   **Att 24,663**
Nicholl 2

An own goal after 14 minutes by big Chris Nicholl put the hosts in the driving seat, that was until Chris scored at the correct end to save his blushes and ensure Villa were level at the break. Incredibly, on 54 minutes, Nicholl then put through his own net for a second time. Villa's performance was worthy of at least a point, and this was secured when none other than centre-half Nicholl scored his fourth of the afternoon. When the scores came through on Final Score, and we heard Nicholl had scored all four goals, we all assumed Aston Villa had chalked up the elusive away victory – sadly it wasn't the case and he'd emulated Oldham's Sam Wynne who'd done exactly the same back in 1923.

Sat 27th March   **Stoke City (H)**
Drew 0-0   **Att 32,359**

Villa stormed the first half, but were thwarted by an on-form Peter Shilton who kept out close range shots from Brian Little and Andy Gray. On the stroke of half-time Shilton rose to tip a ferocious rising drive from Villa dynamo Frank Carrodus over the bar. Villa, while industrious after the interval, weren't as menacing and looked more frustrated as the game wore on. Gidman was impressive on the flank, while Burridge had a relatively quiet afternoon.

Sat 3rd April   **Birmingham City (A)**
Lost 2-3   **Att 46,251**
Gray, Graydon (pen)

Villa were seeking to do the double over their rivals from across the city. In an entertaining duel it was the Blues who drew first blood when Hibbitt opened the scoring in the 18th minute. Andy Gray levelled a few minutes before the half-time whistle - Nicholl nodded down into space for the Scot after rising to meet a Graydon cross - much to the delight of the claret and blue masses. Burns, in a centre-forward role, made it 1-2. Villa were back on terms on 74 minutes when Graydon was felled in the box, the ref pointed immediately to the spot and was besieged by most of the home side's players. Graydon lifted his kick high to the left of keeper Latchford to level the scores, however, with time almost up, Trevor Francis scored to spark a pitch invasion.

Sat 10th April   **Liverpool (H)**
Drew 0-0   **Att 44,250**

In spite of Villa having registered only one win in 1976 thus far, and sitting just six points off a relegation position, another big crowd flocked to Villa Park to witness the game against second placed Liverpool. Saunders dropped Ross, Little and Hamilton for the match; Phillips, McDonald and Hunt starting. Villa were unsteady at the back and unable to work the ball up field. Sheer determination created a few chances, but Villa had to settle for a single point.

Tue 13th April   **Coventry City (A)**
Drew 1-1   **Att 27,569**
Nicholl

This was the first occasion Villa had visited Highfield Road for a top-flight match. City went ahead via a penalty kick after Phillips had sent Hutchison sprawling. Villa played negatively throughout, but were on an equal footing when Northern Ireland international Chris Nicholl powered home a header late in the second period. Only moments after Villa were denied a stonewall penalty, and a possible victory, when City goalie Blyth rugby tackled Bobby McDonald in the box. Saunders stormed, "It was a bad decision."

Sat 17th April   **West Ham United (A)**
Drew 2-2   **Att 21,642**
Deehan, Hunt

Villa were ahead inside four minutes through a John Deehan headed goal, then doubled their advantage when Steve Hunt was on target with an angled header only six minutes later. West Ham pulled one back on the stroke of half time. West Ham took control after the interval but with just 95 seconds remaining it looked like Villa had finally secured that elusive away victory, only for a Trevor Brooking shot to find its way through and deny the original claret and blue team. Despite this frustrating turn of events, Villa were guaranteed First Division football the following season.

Mon 19th April   **Derby County (H)**
Won 1-0   **Att 39,241**
McDonald

With the pressure off, Villa played a more relaxed game, they were better organised and more ambitious. With few chances recorded Graham Moseley, who'd been on loan the previous season, failed to hold a Deehan flick and gifted McDonald the ball to score the all-important goal, Villa's first at home in four games. In fact, the last time Bobby found the net Villa had beaten Manchester United way back in February. The result snuffed out Derby's remaining title aspirations.

Sat 24th April   **Middlesbrough (H)**
Won 2-1   **Att 33,241**
Deehan, Carrodus

Villa brought the curtain down on a season of disappointment with a win against a dogged, but uninspiring, Middlesbrough. Villa took only 90 seconds to go ahead when Gray pressured Platt in goal. He could only punch the ball out as far as the lurking Deehan, who headed it straight back and into the net. 'Boro levelled before the break. Villa stormed out of their second-half blocks, McDonald found room on the left and played in Deehan whose flick bounced off Platt – Gray had a shot parried before Carrodus stepped up to rifle into the bottom corner of the net. It was his first of the season, "That was sheer magic for me, crowed Frank."

[Above] Liverpool's defence is put under pressure from the Villa trio of Nicholl, Mortimer and Carrodus [Below] Deehan heads Villa in front at home to Middlesbrough

THE BIG ASTON VILLA BOOK OF THE SEVENTIES

PRE-SEASON

AUGUST

- Aston Villa kicked-off their season after an eight year top-flight exile at home to European Cup finalists Leeds United.
- After a solitary point from their first three league games, Villa won back-to-back matches. This wouldn't occur again until the last two games of the campaign.

SEPTEMBER

- Doug Ellis resigned as chairman on the 1st September to be replaced by Sir William Dugdale.
- Harry Kartz stepped down as vice-chairman, local businessman Ron Bendall replaced him.
- Keith Leonard sustained a knee injury against Jimmy Rimmer in the Arsenal home win. It was the end of a promising career.
- Aston Villa's first European foray ended in a 1-4 defeat at Belgium side Royal Antwerp. Graydon scored the consolation goal.
- Goalkeeper John Burridge arrived from Blackpool for £100,000.
- With Keith Leonard's career finished Saunders acted quickly to recruit the raw Dundee United striker Andy Gray. The £110,000 fee was a new club record.

OCTOBER

- Andy Gray made his debut at Ayresome Park.
- Brian Little was admitted to hospital for a cartilage operation following a bad tackle at Goodison Park. In doing so he was withdrawn from the England U-23 squad that travelled to Czechoslovakia.
- Andy Gray bagged a hat-trick in Scotland U-23s 4-1 European Championship win against Denmark.
- Villa failed to register a win during the month, three draws and a defeat in the league, defeats in the UEFA and League Cup.

NOVEMBER

- Villa recorded their biggest win of the season when they put five past Sheffield United in a 5-1 win.
- Ken McNaught scored his first goal at Villa Park, but he was still playing for Everton at the time! His own goal ensured a 3-1 home win.

DECEMBER

- Sammy Morgan was sold to Brighton & Hove Albion.
- Dennis Mortimer joined from Coventry City for £175,000. "It was the club's present to the fans," said Saunders.

JANUARY

- Charlie Aitken played for the last time in a Villa shirt.
- Villa's only league goal during January came courtesy of a Mike Mahoney own goal.

FEBRUARY

- Gordon Sidney Cowans signalled his arrival when he came on as a substitute at Maine Road, replacing Pimblett.
- John Overton was also blooded in the Manchester City game. John's only other two appearances in the first-team would be during this month.

Physio Fred Pedley and club medical officer Dr David Targett lead Chris Nicholl away for treatment after the big defender dislocated his shoulder at home to QPR

MARCH

- Chris Nicholl scored all four goals at Filbert Street. Bizarrely two were own goals and the match ended 2-2.
- Leighton Phillips was selected for the Wales v England Centenary match at Wrexham.

APRIL

- The derby defeat at St Andrews brought the curtain down on Ian 'Chico' Hamilton's Villa career.
- Captain Ian Ross spoke out publicly after being dropped for the Liverpool home game. He said he felt like he'd been kicked in the stomach and was pig sick.
- By only drawing at Upton Park 2-2, Villa failed to register an away win for the only time in their illustrious 101 year history.
- Villa ended the campaign with a 2-1 home win over Boro, it also signalled the end for both Ross and McDonald. Impressively the Villans had suffered only two defeats at Villa Park all season.
- No Aston Villa side previously had drawn 17 games in a season.

MAY

- Villa terminated the contracts of promising youngsters Alan Peters and Micky Buttress – a result of repeated breaches of club discipline.

THE BIG ASTON VILLA BOOK OF THE SEVENTIES

An acrobatic Brian Little over-head kick puts Villa in front at home to League Cup holders Man City

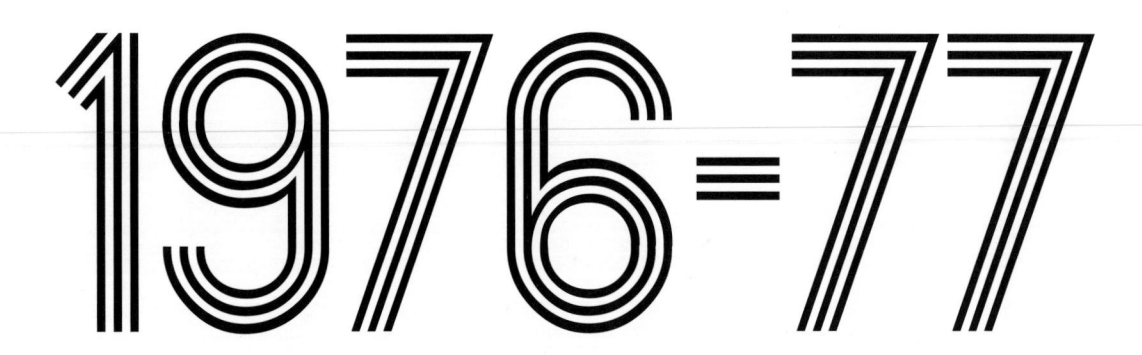

1976-77

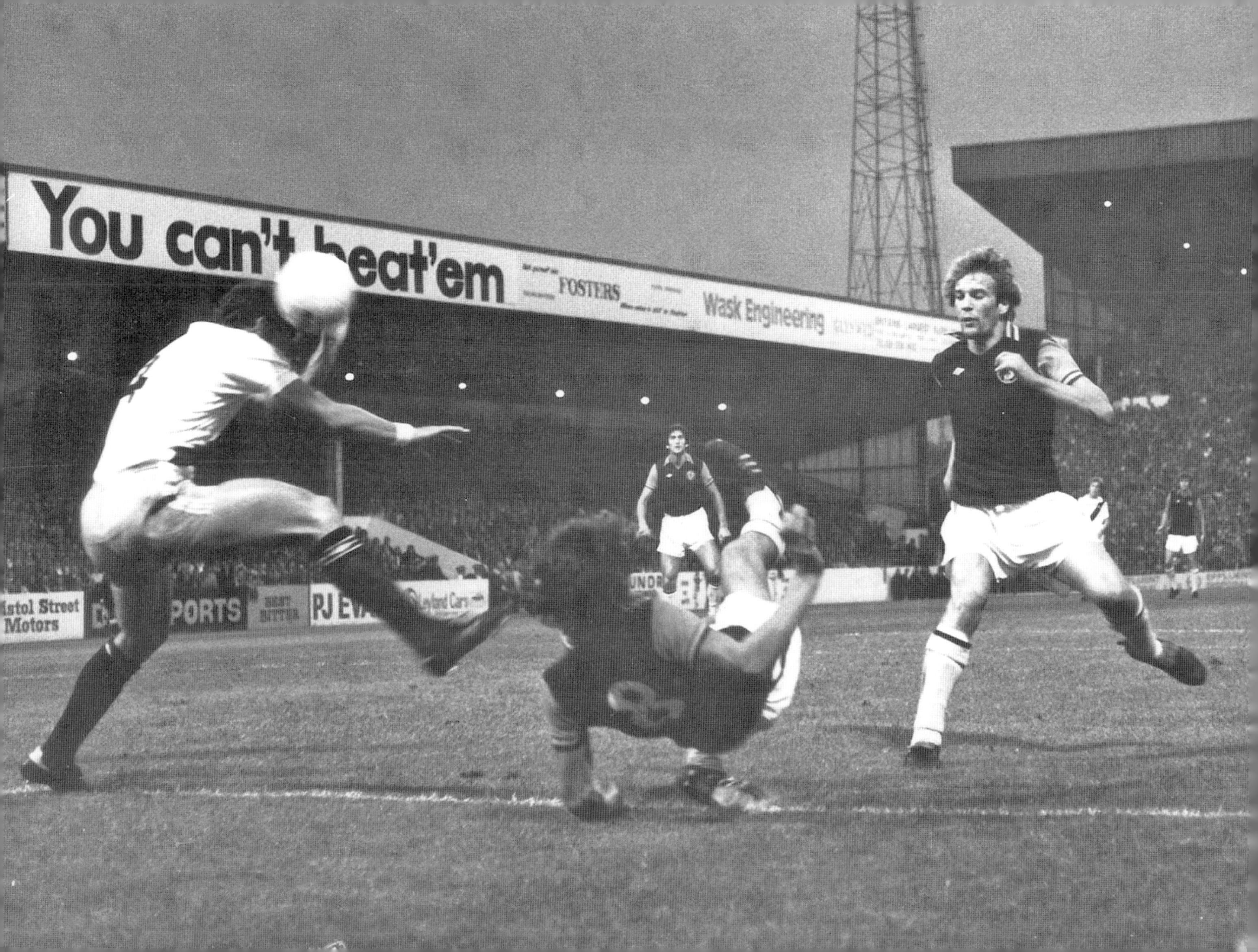

You can't beat'em
FOSTERS
Wask Engineering
Motors

THE BIG ASTON VILLA BOOK OF THE SEVENTIES

[Back Row] Charlie Young, John Deehan, David Evans, David Hughes, Keith Masefield, Keith Williams, Steve Hunt, Ian Hendrey, Gordon Cowans [Third Row] Frank Upton (Youth Coach), Peter Downs (Physiotherapist), Brian Little, Michael Buttress, Keith Leonard, Michael Parsons, John Burridge, Jake Findlay, Andy Gray, Frank Carrodus, Bobby McDonald, Dave Richardson (Youth Development Officer), Tony Barton (Manager's Assistant) [Second Row] Roy MacLaren (Coach), Ray Graydon, Gordon Smith, Leighton Phillips, John Gidman, Ron Saunders (Manager), John Robson, Dennis Mortimer, Ian Ross, Chris Nicholl, Bill Shorthouse (Reserve Team coach) [Front Row] Noel Fagan, Adrian O'Dowd, Gavin Price, Ivor Linton, Martin Stephenson, Tony Coles, John Capaldi, Gary Williams, Terry Wilson

Football League	Division One
Manager	Ron Saunders
Asst. Manager/Coach	Roy McLaren
Physio	Peter Downes
Captain	Chris Nicholl / Leighton Phillips
Final Position	Fourth
FA Cup	Sixth Round
League Cup	Winners
Leading Goalscorer (all competitions)	Andy Gray – 29 goals

Ron Saunders had set his stall out before a ball had been kicked in anger, not just for the coming season, but for the years ahead. His coaching staff had been told that every player, from the 12-year olds to the club apprentices, would be coached only in basic skills.

He didn't want them being brainwashed with methods, systems or formations. "It's important for the future of the game in this country that we make sure youngsters concentrate solely on improving their skills. There is time enough to coach method into them when they move to professional football," he added.

Full-back Gordon Smith was signed to play on the left side of Saunders' defence, though he admitted years later he was actually a right-back but he knew he'd never dispossess John Gidman, so he reinvented himself. Either that or play to 4,000 at St Johnstone.

Villa hit the ground running with a comprehensive 4-0 win against West Ham, whilst League Cup holders, Manchester City, were dumped out of the competition 3-0 at the first hurdle, a game in which Brian Little's stunning acrobatic overhead-kick was being touted as 'Goal of the Season.' Ipswich and Arsenal were on the receiving end too, both conceding five in B6, Andy Gray grabbing a hat-trick in Town's demolition. Alex Cropley signed from Arsenal and scored a wonder-goal in Villa's 1-0 win at Roker Park.

continued >>>

		P	W	D	L	F	A	W	D	L	F	A	Pts
1	Liverpool	42	18	3	0	47	11	5	8	8	15	22	57
2	Manchester City	42	15	5	1	38	13	6	9	6	22	21	56
3	Ipswich Town	42	15	4	2	41	11	7	4	10	25	28	52
4	**Aston Villa**	**42**	**17**	**3**	**1**	**55**	**17**	**5**	**4**	**12**	**21**	**33**	**51**
5	Newcastle United	42	14	6	1	40	15	4	7	10	24	34	49
6	Manchester United	42	12	6	3	41	22	6	5	10	30	40	47
7	West Bromwich	42	10	6	5	38	22	6	7	8	24	34	45
8	Arsenal	42	11	6	4	37	20	5	5	11	27	39	43
9	Everton	42	9	7	5	35	24	5	7	9	27	40	42
10	Leeds United	42	8	8	5	28	26	7	4	10	20	25	42
11	Leicester City	42	8	9	4	30	28	4	9	8	17	32	42
12	Middlesbrough	42	11	6	4	25	14	3	7	11	15	31	41
13	Birmingham City	42	10	6	5	38	25	3	6	12	25	36	38
14	Q.P.R	42	10	7	4	31	21	3	5	13	16	31	38
15	Derby County	42	9	9	3	36	18	0	10	11	14	37	37
16	Norwich City	42	12	4	5	30	23	2	5	14	17	41	37
17	West Ham United	42	9	6	6	28	23	2	8	11	18	42	36
18	Bristol City	42	8	7	6	25	19	3	6	12	13	29	35
19	Coventry City	42	7	9	5	34	26	3	6	12	14	33	35
20	Sunderland	42	9	5	7	29	16	2	7	12	17	38	34
21	Stoke City	42	9	8	4	21	16	1	6	14	7	35	34
22	Tottenham Hotspur	42	9	7	5	26	20	3	2	16	22	52	33

League Position throughout the Season

Total Home League Attendances 795,957
Average Home League Attendance 37,902
Highest Home League Attendance 50,084
Lowest Home League Attendance 28,056

THE BIG ASTON VILLA BOOK OF THE SEVENTIES

1976-77

Sat 21st August   West Ham United (H)
Won 4-0   Att 39,012
Gray 2, Graydon 2 (1 pen)

The goal-less first-half was a competitive affair, but within four minutes of the second period Villa were in front through an opportunist Gray goal. The home side surged forward and Ray Graydon got his name on the scoresheet twice within six minutes, the second from the penalty spot. Andy Gray rounded off a superb afternoon for the Villa when he fired home the loose ball after Mervyn Day could only parry Dennis Mortimer's low, long strike.

Wed 25th August   Manchester City (A)
Lost 0-2   Att 41,007

Aston Villa's wretched away form continued with a defeat at the hands of a very impressive City side who dictated the game from the off. Villa were dead and buried by half time, with both City goals coming from headers. Graydon had two half-chances, but both efforts were wide of the mark. Gray offered little up front, but in fairness, he had no support.

Sat 28th August   Everton (A)
Won 2-0   Att 32,055
Little, own goal

After an opening spell in which Villa were pinned back by the men from Goodison Park, the visitors took the lead through a first class volleyed goal by Brian Little, who later admitted, "I just hit it and hoped". The 20th minute strike set Villa on their way to a first victory on away soil for over a year. Had Ray Graydon not squandered two opportunities Villa could have been 3-0 up, however, he made amends when his shot-cum-cross was turned into his own net by Everton's

A fine 3-1 victory at Elland Road in mid-December was achieved without Chris Nicholl (nursing a broken nose), a win that was eclipsed four days later when the mighty Liverpool were silenced 5-1 at Villa Park, all goals coming in an action packed first half.

Always in and around the top five, the Villa progressed in both cup competitions, eventually running out of steam in the FA Cup at the quarter-final stage to eventual winners Man Utd.

They fared better in the League Cup and, following the City win, they put Norwich, Wrexham, Millwall and QPR to the sword, before needing two replays and extra time to land their second League Cup title in three years – Everton being the vanquished foe.

Brian Little's 10-goal spree on the cup trail ensuring he remains one of the club's leading scorers in the competition. Villa entered the season's final furlong season with as many as five games in hand over higher placed clubs due to cup commitments, but fatigue finally caught up with Ron's boys.

Nine games in the month of April were just too punishing, May was no easier, with seven fixtures to fulfil. Over all, Villa had done better than their supporters could have dared to expect, the club's best placing since the War (fourth), having scored 76 goals along the way, made them the highest scoring side in the division, not to mention reaching the FA Cup quarter-finals and lifting the League Cup.

Andy Gray had bagged an amazing 29 goals, with Little close behind on 26.

Mick Lyons. The home side struck the woodwork a number of times, but Villa kept their composure and bagged the points.

Wed 1st September   Manchester City (H) League Cup 2nd round
Won 3-0   Att 34,585
Little 2, Graydon

Villa were nothing short of rampant against the Cup holders, going ahead when a Graydon corner from the right was helped on by Nicholl and met acrobatically by Little who fired the ball into the top corner with a stunning overhead kick. Only 72 seconds after the interval Little made it 2-0. He received the ball on the edge of the box with his back to goal, then back-heeled it, turned the defender and drilled it beyond goalkeeper Joe Corrigan. Graydon added a third when he was presented with a tap in following a pass from the rumbustious Gray.

Sat 4th September   Ipswich Town (H)
Won 5-2   Att 39,916
Little, Gray 3, Graydon

Villa had struggled to score the previous season, ending with a tally of just 51, how things had changed! Villa took the lead through Brian Little, only for Ipswich to peg them back ten minutes later. One-all at the break there was nothing to suggest the impending goal-fest which was sparked with Gray's flying header, adding another after robbing Hunter to put Villa 3-1 up. Town pulled one back, but 40 seconds later, Villa's two-goal cushion had been restored, when that man Gray again completed a hat-trick. A spectacular Graydon volley completed the rout over Bobby Robson's side as Aston Villa went top of the division.

Sat 11th September   Queens Park Rangers (A)
Lost 1-2   Att 23,602
Gray

Normal away service was resumed, despite Gray putting Villa in the driving seat with a typically brave goal when he got between two defenders to reach a cross from Frank Carrodus on 30 minutes. From there on in Rangers dominated the midfield meaning there was precious little service for Villa's explosive forward. Shots rained down like confetti on John Burridge and it was full credit to the keeper that the 1-2 defeat wasn't far heavier.

Sat 18th September   Birmingham City (H)
Lost 1-2   Att 50,084
Gray

Villa were able to field the same starting XI for the sixth successive league fixture, with the fans desperate to see their high scoring home form continue against the foe. A win looked on the cards when Gray struck after 13 minutes, Brian Little was the playmaker, beating three men before pushing the ball into the middle, where Gray steamed in like an express train to force the ball home. An uncharacteristic slip by Chris Nicholl allowed Burns to level for the Blues, who then threw caution to the wind to boldly play with four attackers. They went in front just before the interval, and although Villa upped the ante in the second period, the visitors held on.

Tue 21st September   Norwich City (H) League Cup 3rd round
Won 2-1   Att 31,295
Gray 2

With Villa looking tense following the Blues' defeat, and Norwich playing a smothering game, it was never going to be an open match. Gray missed a sitter early on, but his enthusiasm never waned. Graydon did well on the wing and drilled the ball into the centre for Gray to leap above the defence and loop his header over ex-Villa keeper Keelan. Norwich levelled the tie seven minutes into the second half with a smartly taken volley. Villa regained the lead when Carrodus blocked a clearance, fed Little who released Gray to rifle home with his deadly right foot. Villa were through to the last 16. A certain Gordon Cowans made his full debut in the match.

THE BIG ASTON VILLA BOOK OF THE SEVENTIES

Sat 25th September   **Leicester City (H)**
Won 2-0   **Att 36,652**
Graydon (pen), Gray

New boy, Alex Cropley, slipped perfectly into a Villa midfield who took control of the game from the off. He added fuel to Mortimer's flair and Carrodus' graft. Villa went ahead from a penalty kick via the trusted peg of Ray Graydon. Andy Gray, already a regular name on the scoresheet, struck again when he side-footed beyond Wallington. Villa's win was impressive enough to have boss Ron Saunders whistling in admiration at the end of the match.

Sat 2nd October   **Stoke City (A)**
Lost 0-1   **Att 29,602**

Villa attacked from the start, totally dominated the game, but ended up with nothing. John Gidman had the ball in the net only to be flagged offside, before Stoke scored against the run of play six minutes before the break. Villa were thrown a lifeline on 51 minutes when a Gray header was stopped 'goalkeeper fashion' by a defender on the line, and although Graydon struck it firm and true, England goalkeeper Peter Shilton guessed correctly, diving to his right and pushing the ball out for a corner.

Sat 16th October   **Sunderland (A)**
Won 1-0   **Att 31,578**
Cropley

In only his third match for the club Cropley showed Villa's travelling support what a gem of a player he was, his goal, which turned out to be the winner, was as audacious as it was brilliant. It came in the 75th minute, just when it looked like the game Villa should have won at a canter was about to slip away from them. Cropley twisted and wriggled free of attention, found himself on the edge of the 18-yard box, saw Barry Siddell off his line and, with poise and confidence, calmly lifted it over the stranded keeper. He was congratulated by stunned but impressed teammates.

Andy Gray jumps for joy after scoring Villa's third in the 5-1 rout of Arsenal – Jimmy Rimmer is the Gunners' keeper

Wed 20th October   **Arsenal (H)**
Won 5-1   **Att 33,860**
Mortimer, Graydon (pen), Gray 2, Little

Arsenal were a point behind leaders Liverpool with a solitary defeat on their travels. Controlled and composed, The Gunners drew first blood when Alan Ball netted on 18 minutes, but Dennis Mortimer scored his first in Villa colours pulled it back to 1-1, before Graydon's penalty put Villa in front at the break. Cue Andy Gray. His first came following sterling work by Gidman and Little, with the second thanks to a courageous challenge to beat Howard and Rimmer, then proded the ball home. Brain Little rounded off the 5-1 humiliation when he scored with four minutes to go. Villa jumped up to fourth.

Sat 23rd October   **Bristol City (H)**
Won 3-1   **Att 37,094**
Nicholl, Gidman, Graydon

Villa typically struggled against a team sat in a relegation spot and trailed 0-1 at half time. The game plan of short passing, played into the hands of City's defence, but a rejuvenated Villa emerged for the second period. Carrodus had two shots charged down before Nicholl got the ball in the net, heading home a Cropley free kick. John Gidman's first goal of the season put Villa in the driving seat, and when Graydon made it 3-1, the result was beyond doubt. Villa were now second in the table behind surprise leaders Middlesbrough.

Wed 27th October   **Wrexham (H) League Cup 4th round**
Won 5-1   **Att 41,428**
Little 2, Carrodus, Nicholl, Gray

Having disposed of top flight sides in the shape of Leicester City and Tottenham Hotspur already in the competition, Wrexham warranted respect, more so when they took an eighth minute lead. But

153

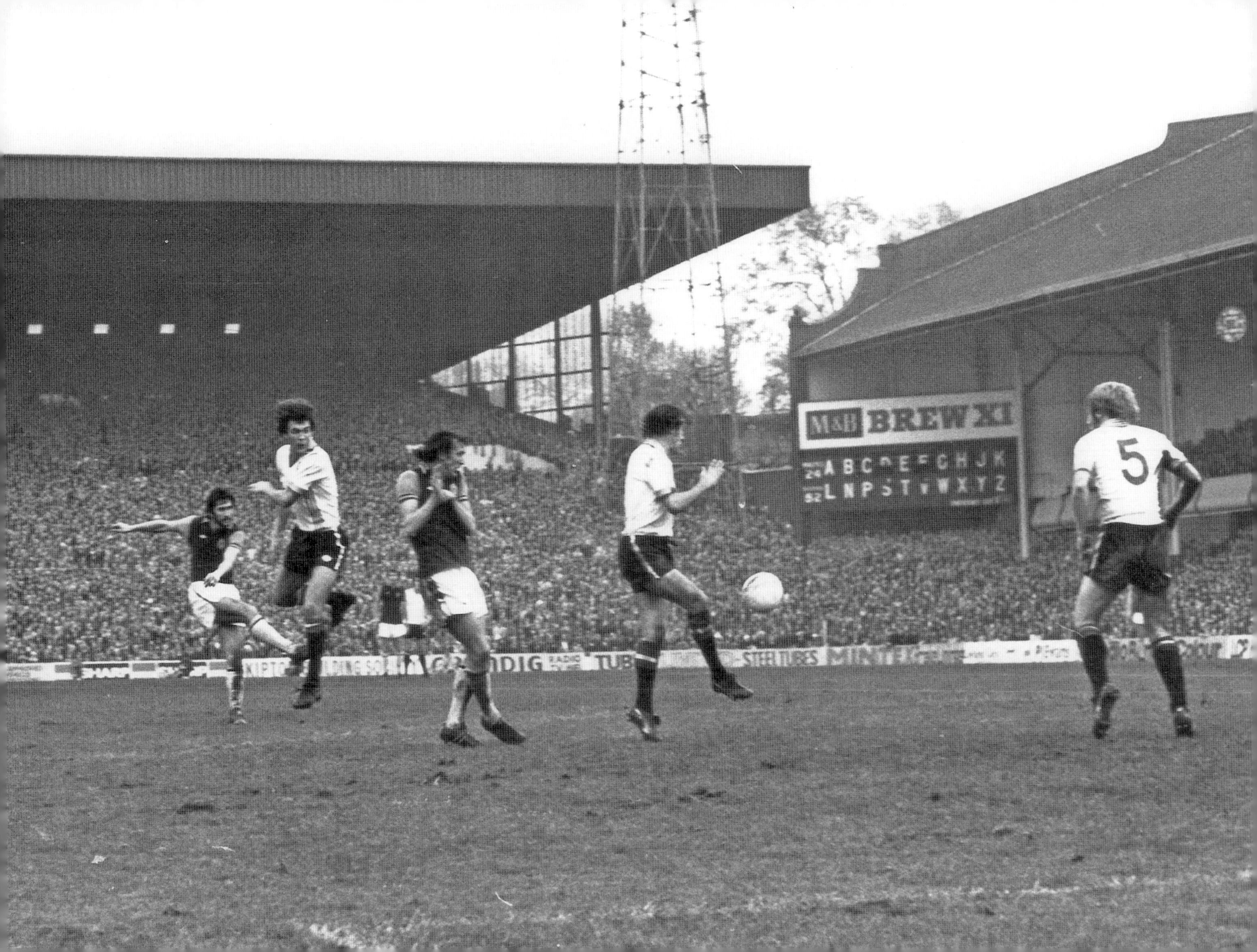
M&B BREW XI
STEEL TUBES
SHARP

Dennis Mortimer fires home from 20-yards against Manchester United in Villa's 3-2 victory

Villa recovered to take a grip of the game, with Alex Cropley very much the kingpin in a superb three-man midfield. Little opened the Villa account and Frank Carrodus doubled the advantage within 70 seconds. The siege began in earnest after the interval when Little made it 3-1. Captain Chris Nicholl made it four before Gray scored the best of the bunch bagging his 13th of the campaign.

Sat 30th October   **Liverpool (A)**
Lost 0-3   **Att 51,751**

Villa were the better side in the first half with the midfield of Cropley, Carrodus and Mortimer comfortably on top. Andy Gray wasted a golden chance to put the visitors into a deserved lead and the game remained without a goal until 16 minutes to go. This was when Liverpool managed to penetrate Villa's resolute defence and again six minutes later. Keegan then added a third on 85 minutes to give a totally distorted scoreline.

Sat 6th November   **Manchester United (H)**
Won 3-2   **Att 44,789**
Mortimer, Gray 2

The character of the game was quickly established, the fans were in for a treat. Gray created a chance within two minutes, Stepney was equal to him. United led through Stuart Pearson only for Mortimer to equalise when a Gidman piledriver rebounded off the defensive wall following applied Villa pressure. It came as no surprise when Gray did get on the scoresheet with the goal arriving only 14 seconds after the half-time interval. The game was level again when Gordon Hill made it 2-2. Gray's winner came on 54 minutes though Villa should have made the result more emphatic, Graydon and Gray going narrowly wide, not to mention a Graydon penalty saved by Stepney.

Wed 10th November   **West Bromwich Albion (A)**
Drew 1-1   **Att 41,867**
Mortimer

With Albion thumped 7-0 by Bobby Robson's Ipswich the previous weekend, Villa were expected to do a similar demolition job, by their fans at least. Dennis Mortimer hit a 30-yard curler beyond the debutant keeper - his second goal in four days - to set Villa on the way before Andy Gray was frustrated by the goalkeeper's legs. Villa then dropped their guard, which gave Albion the opportunity to take a point they hardly deserved. Graydon limped off near the end, the result of a late tackle. Saunders was fuming about the referee's performance and Albion's aggressive and dangerous challenges.

Sat 20th November   **Coventry City (H)**
Drew 2-2   **Att 40,047**
Gidman, Gray

Villa's richly deserved breakthrough in a thoroughly entertaining derby came on the stroke of half time. Gidman, who'd had a tremendous game, took a short pass from Carrodus on the right, he then cut inside before unleashing a fierce, curling shot that gave Jim Blyth no chance. City, with one away win under their belts, shocked the home side with two goals in the space of eight second-half minutes. But Gray kept up his phenomenal scoring record to make the result 2-2. Coventry finished with ten men when John Beck was given his marching orders in the 77th minute.

Sat 27th November   **Norwich City (A)**
Drew 1-1   **Att 22,110**
Little

Norwich, struggling at the wrong end of the table, took a 32nd minute lead against the Villa. A Peter Osgood pass, hit Gidman and looked to be going out for a corner, but Villa's defence hesitated. Graham Paddon kept the ball in play before squaring it for Phil Boyer who made it one nil to City. Luckily for Villa, at the other end, Brian Little was more alert and dragged Villa level within four minutes. Gray was described as "perpetual motion in Villa's threatening breakaways" by City boss John Bond, but the try and he might, he was unable to pull a winner from the hat.

Wed 1st December   **Millwall (H) League Cup 5th round**
Won 2-0   **Att 37,947**

Villa booked their sixth appearance in the semi-finals of the competition when they overcame Second Division opposition in the shape of Millwall. Villa were set on their way in the eighth minute when Chris Nicholl got his head to Cropley's corner from the right. Millwall had come to contain Villa rather than conquer, and hardly threatened. In fact, for long periods, Villa were reduced to their visitors' level, though it should have been an elementary exercise for Saunders' men. The second goal came when Brian Little took a pass from Carrodus on the halfway line, accelerated past full-back Evans, before firing a right footed shot beyond the Millwall keeper. In truth the 2-0 scoreline flattered Villa.

Sat 11th December   **Leeds United (A)**
Won 3-1   **Att 31,232**
Gray 2, Cropley

Ray Graydon was still out injured for the trip to Elland Road, as was Chris Nicholl, who'd broken his nose in training the day before. Charlie Young, who was responsible for Nicholl's nose-break, took the big man's place in defence. Andy Gray scored a brave header to give Villa a slight interval lead, and although Leeds hit back, Gray headed to restore the Claret and Blue's advantage. Cropley fired in the third, but the real star of the show, was Villa's Welsh international Leighton Phillips, who looked head and shoulders above the rest.

Wed 15th December   **Liverpool (H)**
Won 5-1   **Att 42,851**
Gray 2, Deehan 2, Little

Villa, who hadn't scored against Liverpool in three attempts since their return to the top flight, more than made up for it in a pulsating 45 minute spell. Ahead after 10 minutes through Gray, following a Cropley-Deehan-Robson move, Villa forged further ahead when Deehan rammed home two minutes later. Dixie made it 3-0, then Little hit number four following a shrewd Gidman pass. Liverpool pulled one back only for Gray to restore a four-goal cushion when he headed home a cross from Villa's man of the match, Dennis Mortimer. Saves from Clemence in the second-half kept the result from being a rugby score.

Sat 18th December   **Newcastle United (H)**
Won 2-1   **Att 33,982**
Deehan 2

Third placed Villa took on United in fifth, and although the visitors took the lead through Alan Gowling, they didn't look capable of holding on and Deehan got his head to a Charlie Young headed cross to ensure the second-half started all square. Alex Cropley failed to reappear after the break, Micky Buttress taking the Scotsman's place. Villa had to wait until five minutes from the end for the winner, which came courtesy of 'Dixie' Deehan, after he got on the end of a precise Brian Little pass.

Mon 27th December   **Middlesbrough (A)**
Lost 2-3   **Att 31,451**
Gray, Hughes

Villa, unbeaten in seven, came up against Jack Charlton's in-form 'Boro who took advantage of shaky defending to punish Villa with David Mills bagging a first half hat-trick. Andy Gray's 21st goal of the campaign kept the visitors in with a shout, and despite being without Graydon, Cropley, Nicholl and Gidman, Villa made a game of it after the break, and following debutant David Hughes spectacular goal, they pushed hard for a deserved equaliser, but it just wouldn't come.

Sat 1st January   **Manchester United (A)**
Lost 0-2   **Att 55,446**

There was no sign of Villa's new found away confidence during the first-half, even with Nicholl and Cropley back in the side and Villa were trailing by two goals by the interval. Strangely, United's fluency was lost after the break, with Villa's midfield of Cropley, Carrodus, Mortimer and particularly Little, buzzing. Villa were now in the ascendancy, Gray shot narrowly over while Stepney saved from Cropley. But The Villans knew it wasn't to be when Alex Cropley's goalbound shot struck the upright late on.

Sat 8th January   **Leicester City (A) FA Cup 3rd round**
Won 1-0   **Att 27,112**
Gray

It was Villa's first trip to Filbert Street for an FA Cup tie and 'Giddy' was back to partner Robson in defence. Saunders' side were fortunate not to be torn to pieces in the first 45 minutes, such was Leicester's fine approach play, but luckily The Foxes failed to retain that poise and rhythm and Villa started to dominate with Cropley and Mortimer pulling the strings in midfield. Villa stole the tie with a late, opportunist header from Andy Gray, who read John Gidman's long cross perfectly.

Sat 22nd January   **West Ham United (A)**
Won 1-0   **Att 27,577**
Gray

West Ham's three diminutive strikers were no match for Villa's powerful defence, no wonder they had failed to score in nine of their previous matches. Villa were effective and broke with lightning speed. It was from one such move the winning goal came, a Hammers attack was snubbed out by Robson, Frank Carrodus found John Deehan, who fed the unmarked Gray. Needless to say the Scot scored with ease. Villa were fourth.

Sat 29th January   **West Ham United (H) FA Cup 4th round**
Won 3-0   **Att 46,954**
Deehan 2, Mortimer

West Ham tried to make the game as difficult as possible for the Villa, playing with five men behind the ball at all times. These tactics didn't make for exciting football, but Villa's continued domination finally paid dividends. With every Gray movement watched closely, Deehan was able to peel away and get to Brian Little's cross for the opener. Eight minutes later Billy Bonds was robbed of possession and Deehan let fly from 20-yards out to double the advantage. Villa's impressive performance was capped by a third goal when Mortimer lobbed West Ham custodian Mervyn Day perfectly.

Tue 1st February   **QPR (A) League Cup semi-final 1st leg**
Drew 0-0   **Att 28,739**

Villa were made to fight a tremendous rearguard battle to stubbornly deny QPR any clear cut chances. The one shining light in a dour affair was the young, sinewy Gordon Cowans – Cropley's replacement didn't put a foot wrong during his non-stop display, neither was he intimidated by the occasion or by far more experienced players on the park. The determined Gray, nursing a groin injury played, and even at half-pace made a vital contribution. Brian Little went closest, snapping at a chance early in the second half.

Sat 5th February   **Everton (H)**
Won 2-0   **Att 41,305**
Gray, Little

Aston Villa provided further evidence of their title potential with another thrilling display. Andy Gray again highlighted his courageous character when he limped back onto the pitch following treatment for a hip injury. After making his way into the box he outjumped a bemused Mick Lyons to get his head to a Phillips cross to put the Villa in front. Gray only stopped being a threat to the Toffees when he had to leave the field of play injured, Cowans taking his place. Brian Little moved infield from his wide role and hit his 11th of the campaign.

Sat 12th February   Ipswich Town (A)
Lost 0-1   Att 29,766

Ipswich were unbeaten at Portman Road, but without Gray, Villa were very much on the back foot. Nicholl had to manhandle striker Paul Mariner on more than one occasion and Burridge was called on to make vital stops. When Nicholl wrestled Mariner to the floor in the box the ref didn't hesitate, luckily Kevin Beattie's spot kick was yards off target. Villa conceded on the stroke of half time when Clive Woods, in acres of space, headed home unchallenged. Villa couldn't recover from the setback and left Suffolk empty handed.

Wed 16th February   QPR (H) League Cup semi-final 2nd leg
Drew 2-2   Att 48,429
Deehan 2

There was little to separate the two teams who appeared as able and skilful as one another. Little and Carrodus both saw efforts blocked before a superb move between Phillips, Little and Carrodus, ended with Deehan smashing Villa into a 63rd minute lead. Rangers were level on 79 minutes when a Dave Clement free-kick was headed home from close range by Gerry Francis. Villa drew first blood in extra time when 'Dixie' scored again but it wasn't enough to secure his side a record fifth appearance in the final. A finely executed John Burridge penalty save helped Villa's cause considerably, only for Rangers to draw level with six minutes remaining.

Tue 22nd February   QPR (Highbury) League Cup semi-final replay
Won 3-0   Att 40,438
Little 3

Villa dictated the pace of the game from the first whistle, although Andy Gray, back from injury, was upstaged by his long-haired strike partner Little, and both of Brian's first-half goals were at the expense of Rangers defending errors. Villa were firmly in the driving seat, their superior fitness and determination key to the victory. Brian Little made it a personal triumph when he bagged the hat-trick with a minute remaining to book Villa's place in another Wembley final.

[Right] Brian Little's drive finds its way through a crowded box and into the net to put Villa 2-0 up in the Highbury semi replay

[Following page] John Gidman and Andy Gray celebrate on reaching the 1977 League Cup final

Sat 26th February   Port Vale (H) FA Cup 5th round
Won 3-0   Att 46,872
Nicholl, Little, Deehan

Villa, fighting on three fronts, were expectedly far too much for their Third Division opponents. Gutsy Vale hurried Villa into making elementary mistakes, with only Mortimer realising that Villa didn't have a divine right to progress, but Gray and Cropley were both carrying injuries and were below par. Nevertheless, Villa took a lead through their Irish centre-half Chris Nicholl after 19 minutes. Further goals from Little and Deehan secured Villa's passage to the last eight, although the result flattered them. It certainly wasn't the massacre the Holte End had envisaged.

Wed 2nd March   Derby County (H)
Won 4-0   Att 37,396
Mortimer, Gidman, Little, Cowans

Due to the cup distractions, Villa were now in sixth place, but had four games in hand over the sides around them, so points were essential to keep within touching distance. Derby, following three successive defeats, added to their own woes when they found themselves three down before the interval. Goals from Mortimer, Gidman and Little setting Villa on their way back up the table. Buttress made his second appearance in Cropley's No 10 shirt, but it was Cowans at number 9 who stole the headlines. 'Sid's' goal, Villa's fourth of the afternoon, capped a marvellous display by the youngster and the team as a whole.

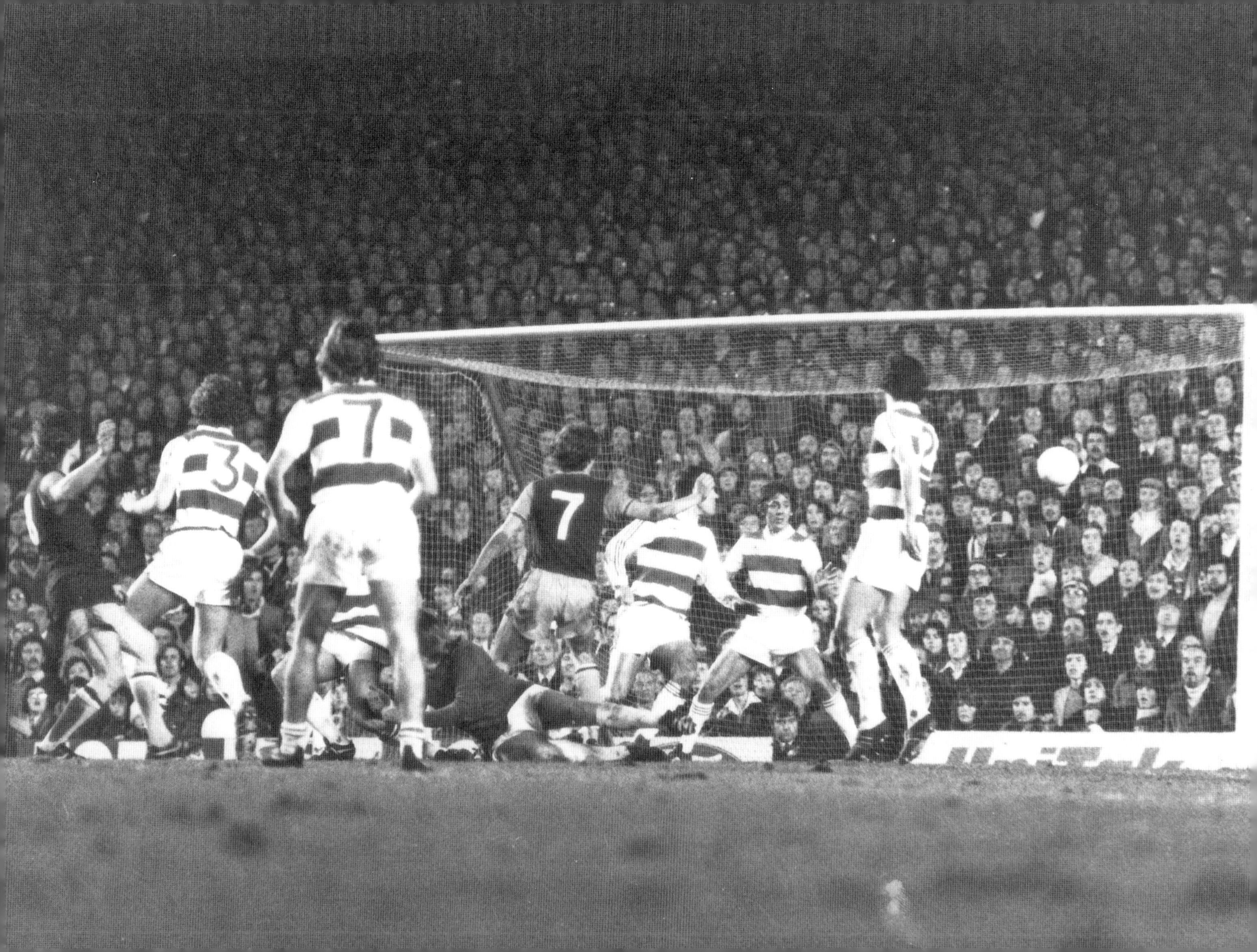

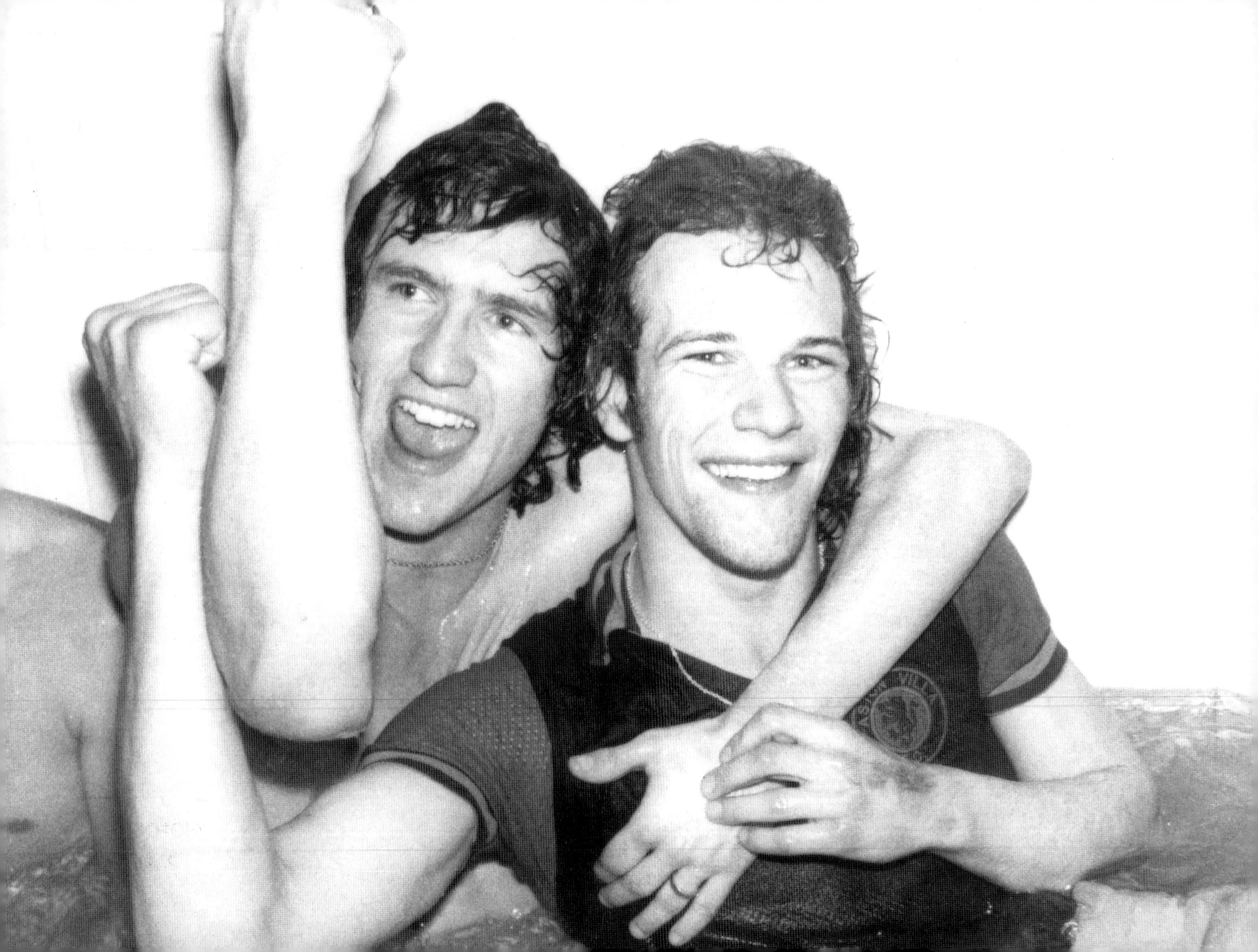

Sat 5th March   **Leicester City (A)**
Drew 1-1   **Att 22,038**
Deehan

Andy Gray missed the trip to Filbert Street, but in John 'Dixie' Deehan they had more than adequate cover, in just his 11th start he'd already found the net four times. His goal duly arrived on 23 minutes, Mortimer's ball into the box had been cleared as far as Cowans, he returned it quickly to Little, who turned and fed Deehan who made no mistake. Leicester surged forward looking to level, but just when it appeared the Villa had weathered the storm, City were given a fortunate penalty when 'Sid' fouled Alderson on the edge of the area. Findlay, in for Burridge, had no chance and the game ended 1-1.

Sat 12th March   **Everton (Wembley) League Cup final**
Drew 0-0   **Att 100,000**

After Villa's devastating display in the semis, it was expected they would run riot, sadly they didn't. The game was actually described in one newspaper as 'a significant occasion reduced to absolute ennui.' Gidman was unadventurous, Carrodus was quiet, and only Cropley seemed 'up' to supply the ammunition, however, both Little and Gray were having off days too. Everton mastered the early part of the game, only once in the first half did Villa find a gap in the Toffeemen's defence but Gray squandered what was, for him, an easy chance. The second period wasn't much better, though stopper David Lawson did block a Gray shot and then smothered the rebound from Deehan. A replay was necessary for the first time since Wembley began hosting League Cup finals in 1967.

Wed 16th March   **Everton (Hillsborough) League Cup final rep**
Drew 1-1   **Att 55,000**
Own goal

Cropley was injured, Cowans was in, otherwise it was the same XI as Saturday's bore-draw. Villa's front line threatened from the off, Deehan dispossessed Roger Kenyon to go one-on-one with Lawson, but his shot was tame and straight at the keeper. 'Dixie' was again denied, before Villa deservedly took the lead on 79 minutes. Mortimer crossed to Deehan who turned the ball goalwards, Kenyon seemed certain to clear the attempt but stumbled and virtually walked the ball into his own net. Surely the trophy was going back to Villa Park? But, with only 90 seconds remaining, Villa's defence failed to clear inside their box, Duncan McKenzie's chip found bustling centre-forward Bob Latchford who forced the ball home. Another replay was needed.

Sat 19th March   **Manchester United (A) FA Cup 6th round**
Lost 1-2   **Att 57,089**
Little

With the game barely two minutes old, Mortimer played a clever ball from midfield, Little controlled it and came up against Martin Buchan – the heart of United's defence, a brief standoff ensued before Brian Little pulled the trigger from fully 35-yards out that gave Stepney had no chance. United took time to recover from this set back, but gradually asserted their authority. Villa legs looked tired, this, their third game in eight days. John Robson's brilliant performance wasn't enough to keep United out as shots rained in from all angles. Burridge was beaten twice in the first half as Villa trailed off 1-2 down. The second period produced no more goals, numerous 'Budgie' saves kept the score respectable but there would be no more Wembley appearances for Villa that season.

Wed 23rd March   **Sunderland (H) Won 4-1**
Att 34,458
Gidman, Gray, Deehan 2

Villa were down to eighth in the table, but had five games in hand over most teams. Gidman fired Villa ahead from a stunning free-kick after Mortimer had been felled outside the box and Sunderland offered little before going two down when Gray hit his 25th of the season following a clever run from Mortimer. Ten minutes after the interval a Phillips free-kick was headed on by Gray to Deehan, who hooked the ball in to make it 3-0. The Black Cats pulled one back, but a rampant Villa side

161

carved out yet another goal when 'Dixie' struck in the 88th minute. The hosts could easily have notched seven on the night.

Sat 2nd April **Bristol City (A)**
Drew 0-0 **Att 27,266**
Newly promoted City, sitting on the same points as bottom placed West Ham, seemed more intent in not conceding than actually scoring. Villa were happy to let the hosts have the majority of the possession, knowing through Gray, Deehan and Little, they could hit hard and fast on the counter. A Charlie Young header from a corner was on its way in before Sweeney stopped it on the line, and after the match, photographers behind the goal claimed it was stopped by a hand. The ref missed the incident meaning it was only the fifth time Villa had failed to find the net in 28 League games.

Tues 5th April **Middlesbrough (H)**
Won 1-0 **Att 32,646**
Deehan
The Villa had to give a determined display to overcome a rugged 'Boro side. Before the game, boss Saunders had called for more effort, and Villa gave it – they took the lead when Deehan hit his 13th of the campaign, nodding in when Willie Maddren had deflected Mortimer's corner into his path. Andy Gray, with only one goal in his last six games, and clearly lacking confidence, missed three chances he would have buried earlier in the season. With games still in hand Villa looked a good outside bet for the title.

Sat 9th April **Derby County (A)**
Lost 1-2 **Att 28,061**
Little
The Rams' (one point above a relegation spot) plight was almost as desperate as the skipper Roy McFarland's tackling. He put Frank Carrodus out of the game mid-way through the first half. Little's 18th goal of the season had given the claret and blue side a deserved 10th minute lead, before Leighton James equalised for Derby on the hour.

A victorious Villa team do a lap of honour at Old Trafford after landing the League Cup at the expense of Everton – Villa winning 3-2 at the third attempt

The Derby captain had accounted for Gray too, but with sub Cowans already on, Villa were down to ten. Villa fought on bravely, but it was the home side that finished the scoring when Derek Hales rounded Burridge following a poor clearance from Villa's keeper.

Wed 13th April **Everton (Old Trafford) LC final 2nd rep**
Won 3-2 **Att 54,749**
Nicholl, Little 2
Carrodus (knee ligaments) and Gray (ankle ligaments) were both out, whilst Nicholl, a victim of the pot-holed Baseball Ground pitch (not McFarland), was forced to play with a heavily bandaged left ankle. Everton took the lead following a free kick on 37 minutes, and it took Villa until the final 11 minutes to pull the tie level. Nicholl, with the ball near the half way line, ran unchallenged goal-wards, then in the blink of an eye, he struck the ball with his bandaged foot which flew into the top corner. Little's goal within a minute then turned the game on its head, only for Everton to snatch an equaliser at the death. Deep into extra-time Little homed in on Gordon Smith's right-wing cross as the Everton defence were caught cold, to place the ball out of reach of the despairing keeper. Villa held out to take the trophy after 330 minutes of football.

Sat 16th April **Coventry City (A)**
Won 3-2 **Att 31,288**
Cowans, Deehan, Little
With games in hand, Villa were still in the race for the title, but City established a 2-1 lead at the break with 'Jock' Ian Wallace scoring either side of Cowans 40th minute strike. Saunders' side were simply brilliant in the second half, helped in part when the Sky Blues' Dugdale was given his marching orders for a second book-

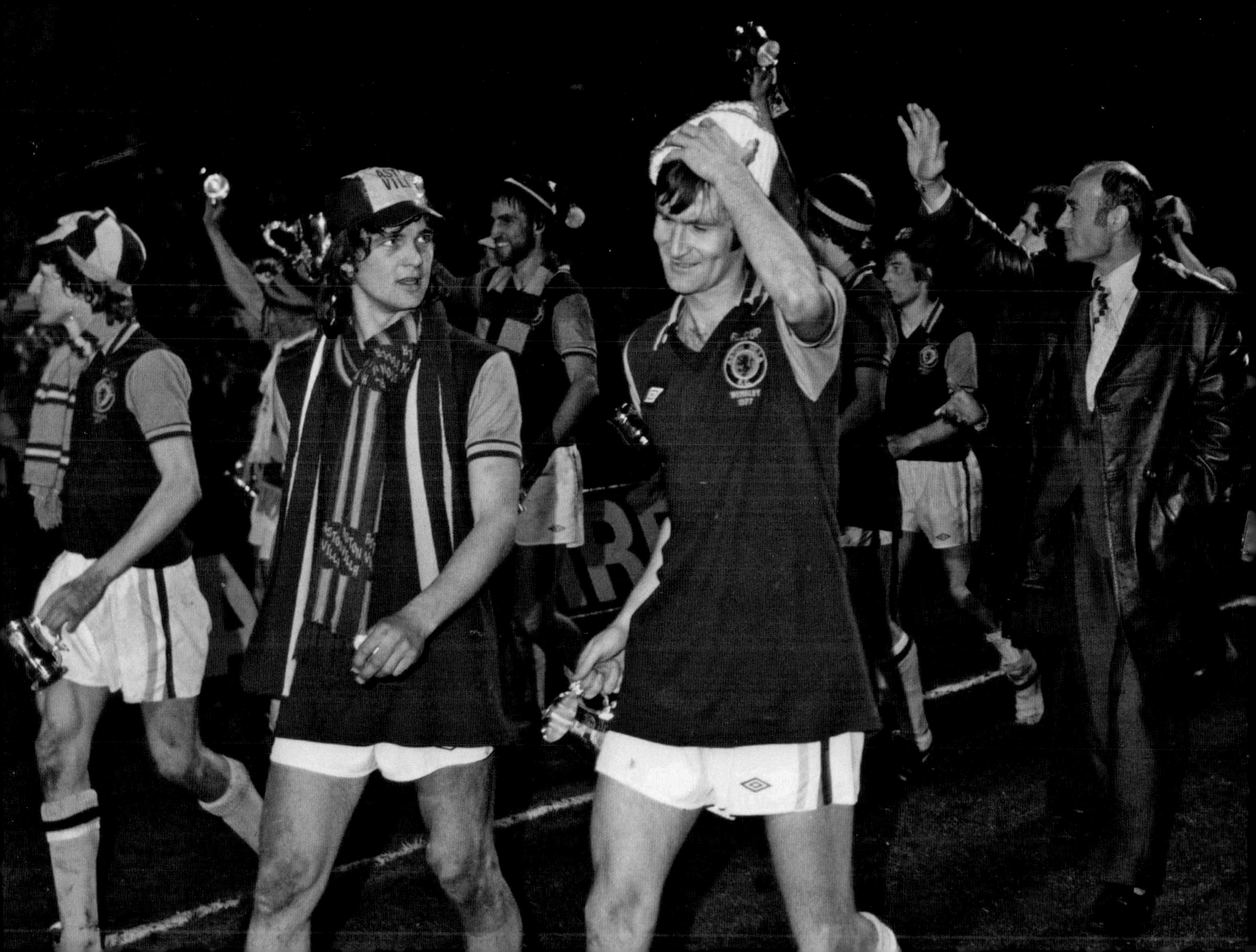

able offence. Les Sealey (later to join Villa) did well to deny Graydon within seconds of the game restarting, but it was just a question of time before Villa scored. John Deehan equalised on 80 minutes, then, for the second time in four days, Brian Little popped up to score a late, late winner.

Wed 20th April — Tottenham Hotspur (H)
Won 2-1 — Att 42,047
Little, Deehan

Still without Gray, Carrodus and Gidman (the latter two wouldn't feature again that season), Villa moved up to fifth as they over-powered Spurs. Brian Little got them on their way when he nipped in to beat Pat Jennings after sterling work on the left wing by Mortimer. Graydon and Smith then combined well to set up 'Dixie' Deehan, whose header made it 2-0. Tottenham's early second-half goal made for a totally unbalanced scoreline as Villa should been out of sight.

Sat 23rd April — Norwich City (H)
Won 1-0 — Att 35,899
Little

In spite of Norwich City's rough house tactics, which reduced Mortimer and Cropley to spectators, Aston Villa's devastating home form continued. Not only were they the highest scorers on home turf, they'd played less games than any team above them. Brian Little's cheeky header from Cropley's perfect cross was all that separated the teams at the end of an untidy and undistinguished first half. Later, Deehan was elbowed in the face for his troubles and David Hughes had to come on for Mortimer with 18 minutes to go.

Mon 25th April — Arsenal (A)
Lost 0-3 — Att 24,011

Villa's punishing season (48 matches so far, with Highbury making four games in ten days) gradually caught up with them. Decimated by injuries despite the return of warrior Andy Gray, Villa were two down long before the break. The inexperienced Hughes was

Action from Leeds as Jake Findlay punches clear with Gidman, Gray and Young in close attendance

replaced by the even less experienced Keith Masefield before Arsenal added a third on 59 minutes. It could have been worse had Malcolm 'Supermac' Macdonald not blazed a late penalty wide.

Sat 30th April — Tottenham Hotspur (A)
Lost 1-3 — Att 30,690
Deehan

Described in the papers after the event as, 'an odd match.' Villa played fluent, flowing football in the first period and took a ninth minute lead through Deehan, only for Hoddle to draw the Londoners level within two minutes. Villa's play in the second half was nothing more than scrappy, Gray shooting wide of the mark with their only real clear-cut chance. Spurs took the lead with six minutes remaining and still had time to find the net again. This would be the only time the Villa had conceded three goals in back-to-back games all season.

Wed 4th May — Manchester City (H)
Drew 1-1 — Att 36,190
Little

Following the two defeats, Villa were out of the title reckoning but Man City were still very much involved and sat in second place. City looked to have won the game with Dennis Tueart's 53rd minute header, but Brian Little pounced when Robson's 25-yard screamer came back off the woodwork and beat the stranded Corrigan in goal. Little was hauled down on 73 minutes by Willie Donachie for a stonewall penalty, but to the supporters' frustration, the referee waved play on. Villa remained fifth, still with games in hand.

Sat 7th May — Leeds United (H)
Won 2-1 — Att 38,205
Deehan, Cropley

Villa completed the 'double' over Leeds with Alex Cropley, ironically, scoring in both fixtures (he'd only scored two all season - Roker

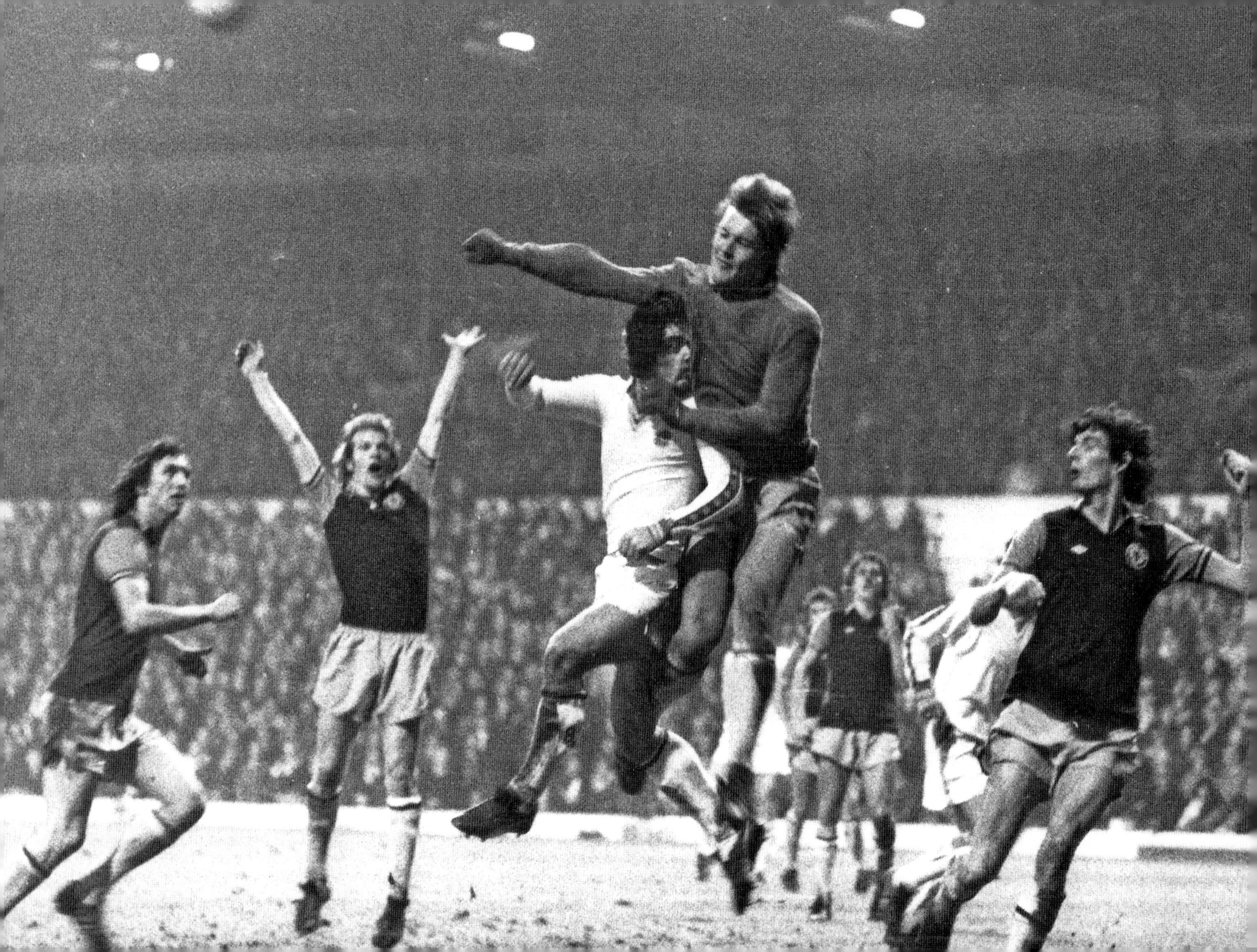

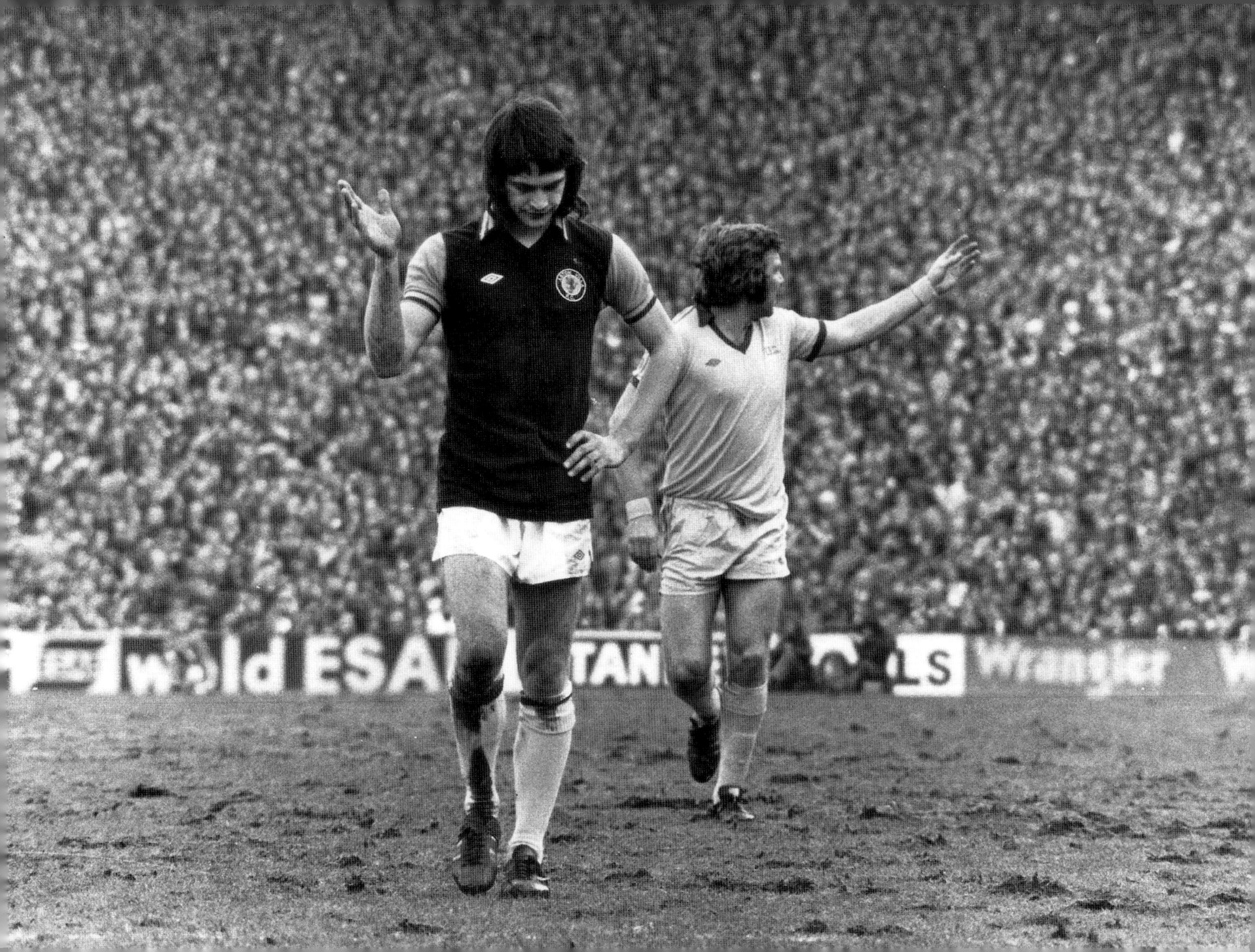
Wrangler

A dismissive Brian Little in action at home to Everton

Park and Elland Road). Villa, playing their best football for several matches, went behind to a stunning goal by McNiven. They had to wait until the hour mark to draw level, John Deehan notching his 15th of the campaign. Cropley's goal, the result of a rebound which struck Gordon McQueen's hand. Both Villa goals had been manufactured by the supremely talented Brian Little.

**Tue 10th May   Birmingham City (A)
Lost 1-2   Att 43,721
Deehan**

An ugly encounter descended to new depths when Phillips brought Trevor Francis down from behind - yellow card. Leighton then booted the ball away and when the referee ordered him to fetch it, the official was then given the V-sign - red card! But ten-man Villa took the lead when a perfectly weighted cross from Mortimer was headed home magnificently by Deehan. Birmingham were back on level terms when Francis' persistence enabled Hibbitt to gather the loose ball and despatch it beyond Burridge. With five minutes remaining Gray and Francis clashed in the Villa box, the City man fell… penalty to the home side. It was converted, they had done the 'double' over their more famous rivals.

**Sat 14th May   Newcastle United (A)
Lost 2-3   Att 29,873
Little 2**

United, on the back of three straight defeats, were left reeling when Brian Little intercepted a weak back-pass to put Villa ahead with only 50 seconds on the clock. The lead lasted all of four minutes when a Paul Cannell header made it 1-1. Mike Mahoney kept out certain goals from both Gray and Deehan before United swept into a commanding 3-1 interval lead. The quicksilver Little pounced again on 74 minutes to reduce the deficit, but never-say-die Villa couldn't find the elusive equaliser.

**Mon 16th May   Stoke City (H)
Won 1-0   Att 28,936
Gray (pen)**

In front of Villa Park's lowest crowd so far that season, the home side played scrappy and unimaginative football. With only one win in six they were awarded a penalty in the opening spell of the game. Andy Gray, without a goal in his last nine outings, put the ball on the 12-yard spot and executed it perfectly for his 26th of the season. Alan Dodd, who gave away the penalty, almost made amends but his header sailed just wide of Burridge's upright. Villa remained fifth.

**Fri 20th May   QPR (H)
Drew 1-1   Att 28,056
Cowans**

Twice in the first five minutes Chris Nicholl was on hand to clear the danger in the six-yard box. From then on Villa grew in strength, and had Ian Gillard not cleared off his line, and a Gray effort came bouncing back of the angle of the woodwork, Villa would have gone in at the break a couple of goals to the good. As it was, QPR snatched a lead through Ron Abbott before the wispy Gordon Cowans stroked home to notch his third of the campaign. The point was enough to leapfrog Newcastle for fourth spot.

**Mon 23rd May   West Bromwich Albion (H)
Won 4-0   Att 42,532
Nicholl, Gray 3**

Another large Villa Park crowd turned out to show their appreciation for what had been an extremely long, but very successful, season. Big Chris Nicholl put the Villans on the way to victory with a header after four minutes, Andy Gray made it 2-0 just before the half-time whistle as Albion were clearly being outclassed by Villa's rapier-like attack, long before Gray hit his 28th and 29th goals of the season. Brian Little, scorer of 26 goals himself, setting up Andy's last two. Villa's fourth placed finish was their highest since the War.

THE BIG ASTON VILLA BOOK OF THE SEVENTIES

PRE-SEASON

AUGUST

- Pat Matthews resigned as president, with Trevor Gill taking office.
- Villa signed Scottish U23 defender Gordon Smith from St Johnstone for £80,000, he made his debut in the Villa Park friendly against Royal Antwerp.
- Villa kicked the new season off with their most emphatic opening day scoreline since the war. West Ham were on the receiving end of a 4-0 drubbing!
- Bobby McDonald ended a six year spell at Villa when he joined Coventry City.
- Ron Saunders was named Manager of the Month.

SEPTEMBER

- Andy Gray's hat-trick in the 5-2 demolition of Ipswich Town was the first in the top flight for the club since Tony Hateley's feat in the 5-5 draw at White Hart Lane, 1966.
- Gray then scored twice in Scotland's 6-0 thrashing of Finland at Hampden Park four days later.
- The £53,000 gate receipts for the Blues clash was the biggest ever for a league match in the West Midlands.
- Alex Cropley was spotted in the dugout for the Norwich City League Cup tie. The Scottish international signed the following morning from Arsenal for £125,000.

OCTOBER

- Andy Gray, Leighton Phillips [left] and Chris Nicholl were all selected for their respective countries.
- The Villa Park friendly with Glasgow Rangers was abandoned after 53 minutes when Villa's second goal sparked a riot from the travelling Scottish fans.

NOVEMBER

- With the WBA match rearranged, plus international fixtures, Villa had a ten day break from competitive matches.
- During Villa's Coventry City clash at Villa Park the club's 1972 Youth Cup winning defence were out in force, Jake Findlay and John Gidman for Villa, along with left-back Bobby McDonald in a Sky Blues' jersey.
- Villa remained unbeaten throughout the month.

DECEMBER

- Villa signed a young 16-year old Colin Gibson – Villa had another Colin Gibson playing for them just after the war.
- Keith Leonard, only 26-years of age, announced his retirement from the game due to a serious knee injury. Leonard battled for 18-months to regain fitness following a cartilage op – to no avail.

- Aston Villa sent shockwaves throughout the footballing world when they put league leaders Liverpool to the sword 5-1. The Reds' biggest defeat since 1966 against Ajax.
- Villa had now scored five goals in four matches for the first time since the 1961/62 season.

JANUARY

- The club announced plans for a new £1million stand at the Witton End of the ground. It would seat 4,000 in an upper section with terrace standing room for 6,000 in the lower.
- After their FA Cup 3rd round victory at Filbert Street, Villa were now seen as serious contenders on three fronts by the critics.
- Villa's League Cup semi-final game at QPR was their fifth consecutive away game. It was also the first time Villa had kept a clean sheet against Rangers in a competitive match.

FEBRUARY

- Following a 2-2 draw against QPR in the semi-final 2nd leg a replay was required. The toss of the coin was called correctly, but Villa were allegedly cheated out of a tie at Highfield Road. Highbury was the venue.
- Villa booked a date at Wembley for a record fifth League Cup final appearance thanks to a Brian Little semi-final replay hat-trick.

MARCH

- The home game with Derby County was Villa's first in the league since February 5th.
- John Gidman receiveed a call-up for England's World Cup squad.

APRIL

- Villa landed the League Cup for the second time in three seasons when they defeated Everton at the third time of asking.
- David Hughes played his last Villa game, away at Arsenal.
- Ray Graydon bowed out at Tottenham.
- The Villa News & Record was voted the No 1 programme.

MAY

- Villa's defeat at the hands of Birmingham City meant they had done the double over Villa – the only team to do so in the entire division.
- Charlie Young's appearance at Newcastle was his last in claret and blue. He would go to Gillingham along with Michael Buttress.
- Burridge and Nicholl signed off their Villa careers on a high – a 4-0 win at home to neighbours West Bromwich Albion.

[Right] John Deehan nips in to score away to Fenerbahce after the keeper failed to hold a Gordon Cowans shot

1977-78

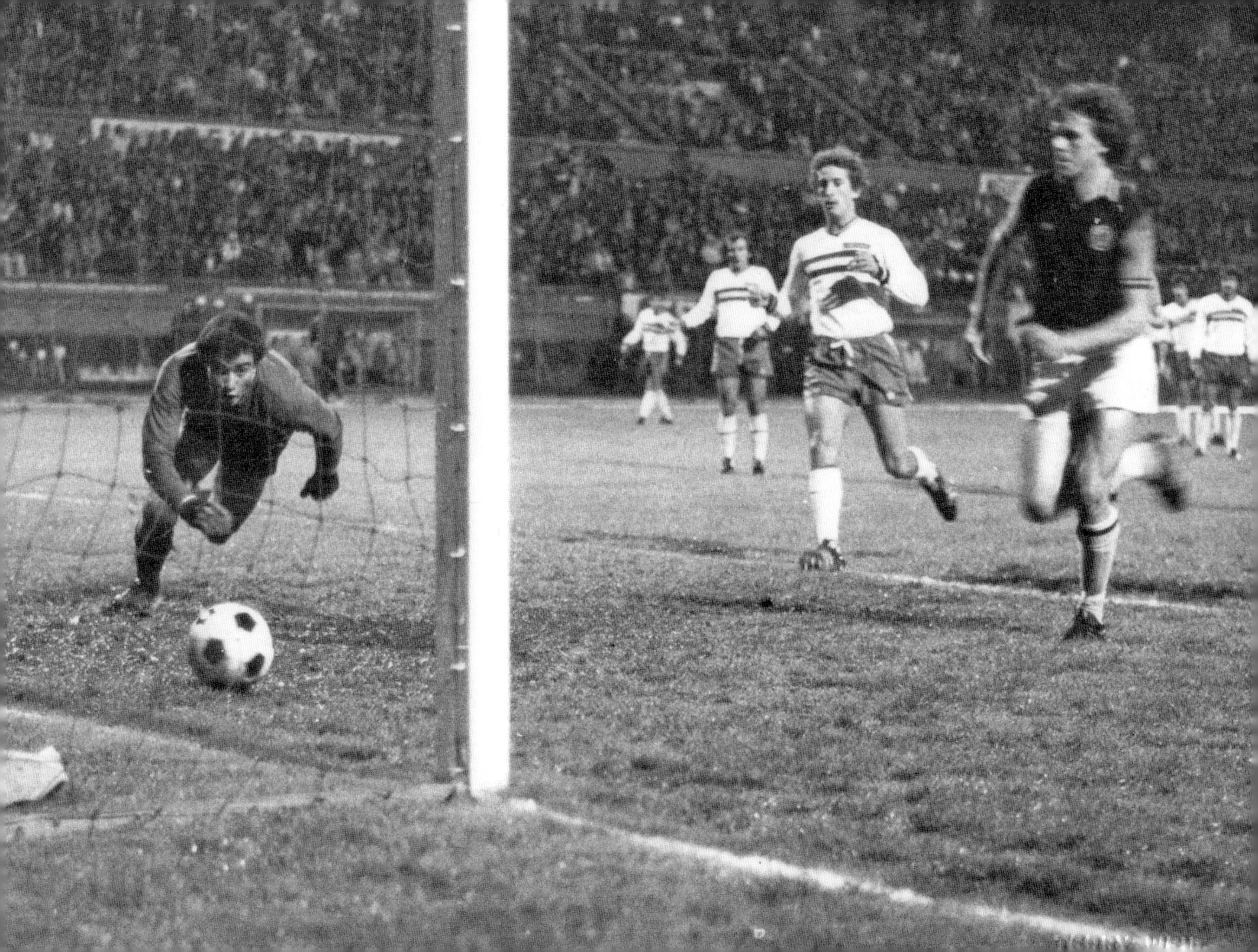

THE BIG ASTON VILLA BOOK OF THE SEVENTIES

[Back Row] **Martin Stephenson, Charlie Young, Jake Findlay, John Burridge, Michael Parsons, Nigel Spink, Allan Evans, Ivor Linton** [Third Row] **Tony Barton (Manager's Assistant), Bill Shorthouse (Reserve Team Coach), David Evans, Michael Buttress, John Gregory, Andy Gray, Gordon Smith, David Hughes, Gordon Cowans, Adrian O'Dowd, Keith Leonard (Youth Coach), Dave Richardson (Youth Development Officer)** [Second Row] **Roy MacLaren (Coach), John Deehan, Alex Cropley, Leighton Phillips, John Gidman, Ron Saunders (Manager), John Robson, Brian Little, Dennis Mortimer, Frank Carrodus, Peter Downs (Physiotherapist)** [Front Row] **Lee Jenkins, Colin Gibson, Alan Ollis, Ian Ward, Glen Beech, Ian Hendry, Gary Williams, John Capaldi, Brendan Ormsby**

Football League	Division One
Manager	Ron Saunders
Asst. Manager/Coach	Roy McLaren
Physio	Peter Downes
Captain	Leighton Phillips
Final Position	Eighth
FA Cup	Third Round
League Cup	Fourth
UEFA Cup	Fourth
Leading Goalscorer (all competitions)	Andy Gray – 20 goals

For the first time ever, the Villa, Albion, Birmingham, Wolves and Coventry were all in the top-flight. With so many 'derby' games, emulating the success of the previous season would be no easy task. Losing players of the calibre of Graydon, Nicholl, and Burridge wouldn't help the situation either. Would new signings centre-half Ken McNaught, and goalkeeper Jimmy Rimmer step in seamlessly? A relatively unknown player by the name of John Gregory also came in from Northampton Town.

Villa kicked off the new campaign with a fine win at Loftus Road, but from there on, league form was erratic. After nine games Villa had won only twice and were sitting in 14th.

European football was showing another side to Villa's game – they were assured, strong and played with a flair that was lacking on the domestic scene. Turkish side Fenerbahce (6-0 agg), and Poles, Gornik Zabrze (3-1 agg), were easily despatched.

Villa started November with a fine win at Anfield, their first in 25-years. Of the last five fixtures Villa had won four and drawn one. Typically they would then lose at home to 'Boro. Their last game that month would see their involvement in the League Cup ended for another year, Forest succeeding where Exeter and QPR had failed.

Alex Cropley was taken out with a crude tackle by Albion's Ally Brown at Villa Park, which broke his leg badly – the silky, smooth midfielder would come back in time, but was a shadow of his former self and sadly only played a handful more games. Tommy Craig was quickly signed to fill the void, the £275,000 fee breaking the club's transfer record.

continued >>>

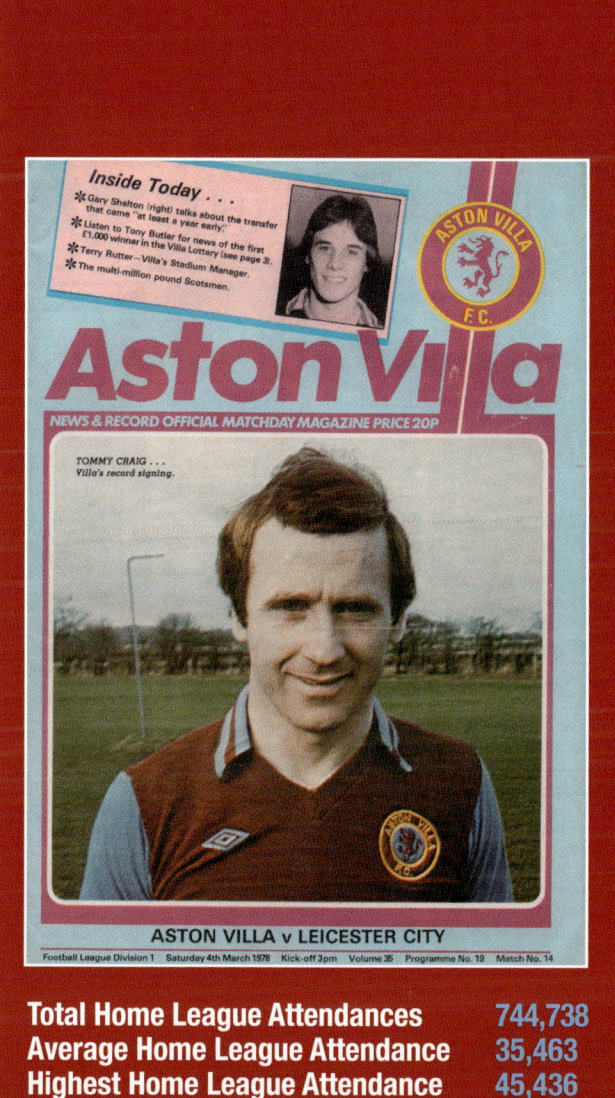

		P	W	D	L	F	A	W	D	L	F	A	Pts
1	Nottingham Forest	42	15	6	0	37	8	10	8	3	32	16	64
2	Liverpool	42	15	4	2	37	11	9	5	7	28	23	57
3	Everton	42	14	4	3	47	22	8	7	6	29	23	55
4	Manchester City	42	14	4	3	46	21	6	8	7	28	30	52
5	Arsenal	42	14	5	2	38	12	7	5	9	22	25	52
6	West Bromwich	42	13	5	3	35	18	5	9	7	27	35	50
7	Coventry City	42	13	5	3	48	23	5	7	9	27	39	48
8	**Aston Villa**	**42**	**11**	**4**	**6**	**33**	**18**	**7**	**6**	**8**	**24**	**24**	**46**
9	Leeds United	42	12	4	5	39	21	6	6	9	24	32	46
10	Manchester United	42	9	6	6	32	23	7	4	10	35	40	42
11	Birmingham City	42	8	5	8	32	30	8	4	9	23	30	41
12	Derby County	42	10	7	4	37	24	4	6	11	17	35	41
13	Norwich City	42	10	8	3	28	20	1	10	10	24	26	40
14	Middlesbrough	42	8	8	5	25	19	4	7	10	17	35	39
15	Wolverhampton	42	7	8	6	30	27	5	4	12	21	37	36
16	Chelsea	42	7	11	3	28	20	4	3	14	18	49	36
17	Bristol City	42	9	6	6	37	26	2	7	12	12	27	35
18	Ipswich Town	42	10	5	6	32	24	1	8	12	15	37	35
19	Q.P.R	42	8	8	5	27	26	1	7	13	20	38	33
20	West Ham United	42	8	6	7	31	28	4	2	15	21	41	32
21	Newcastle United	42	4	6	11	26	37	2	4	15	16	41	22
22	Leicester City	42	4	7	10	16	32	1	5	15	10	38	22

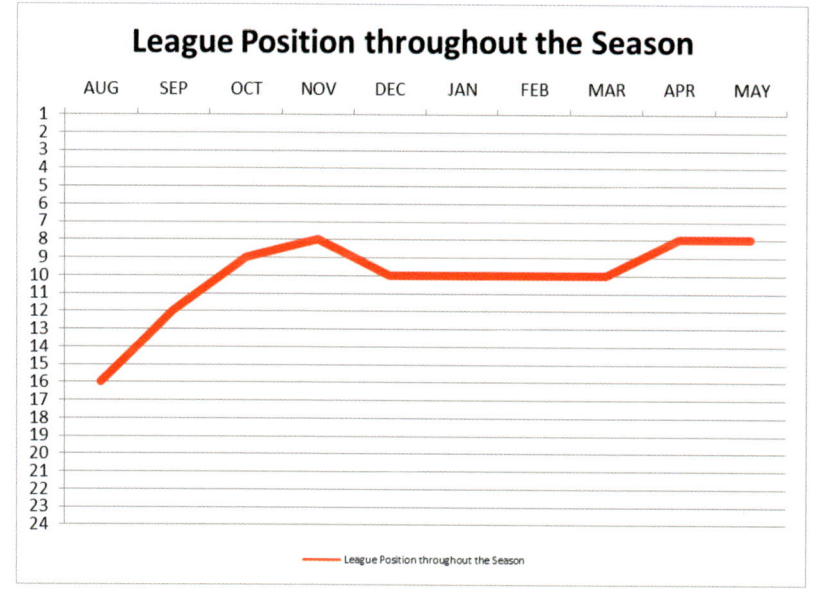

League Position throughout the Season

Total Home League Attendances 744,738
Average Home League Attendance 35,463
Highest Home League Attendance 45,436
Lowest Home League Attendance 25,493

THE BIG ASTON VILLA BOOK OF THE SEVENTIES

1977-78

Saturday 20th August   **Queens Park Rangers (A)**
Won 2-1   **Att 25,431**
Own goal, Carrodus

Ron Saunders included all three new signings – Jimmy Rimmer, John Gregory and Ken McNaught – in the starting XI, while Andy Gray was ruled out because of a pre-match injury. Villa contained QPR for most of the match and then set them up for the kill, hitting two goals within six minutes of the break. A Deehan cross-shot was bundled in by David Webb as he attempted to clear the danger, then Frank Carrodus hit the second after latching onto a Cropley pass from the right. He rode a fierce tackle, picked himself off the ground, then cooly slotted the ball home with his left peg. Rangers pulled one back with four minutes remaining, but the damage had been done.

Wed 24th August   **Manchester City (H)**
Lost 1-4   **Att 40,121**
Deehan

With the gleaming new North Stand setting a majestic backdrop, John Deehan fired Villa into a fifth minute lead. Gray was back in the side, with Cowans making way. Booth levelled within two minutes and City took a 2-1 lead into the interval when Dennis Tueart – signed for City in Ron Saunders' last act as boss – found the net. It was still the same scoreline with only three minutes remaining, however, that man Tueart struck twice to register a 1-4 loss for the Villa.

[Right] Frank Carrodus cooly drives home despite the attentions of QPR's Ian Gillard. Villa won the season's opener at Loftus Road 2-1

Only two more wins were registered in the league during 1977, Villa were 13 points adrift of leaders, and eventual winners, Forest in a mid-table tenth place.

By this time Athletic Bilbao had been eliminated from the UEFA Cup – the 2-0 win at Villa Park was followed by a very creditable 1-1 draw in Spain in front of a very volatile crowd. A quarter-final encounter with Barcelona in the New Year was eagerly anticipated.

A Johan Cruyff/Neeskens inspired Barca came to B6, and in front of a near 50,000 gate, they took a two goal lead. Cruyff left the field late-on to a standing ovation, only to see Villa battle back to snatch an unlikely 2-2 draw. In the second-leg, in front of 80,000 at the Nou Camp, Villa had the audacity to lead through a Brian Little goal. Had John Gidman not been sent off could Villa have survived instead of crashing out 1-2?

Playing in only his third league game centre-forward Allan Evans scored in a 1-1 draw away to Newcastle United. Only nine days later Villa - on the back of beating Chelsea 2-0, hammered the final nail into the Magpies' Division One coffin, hitting them with the same score-line, to send them down. Only 28 Newcastle fans showed up at Villa Park.

Villa then went on a goal-scoring spree, WBA 3-0, Leeds 3-1, saving the best 'til last, Ipswich were trounced 6-1. But Villa ended the season on a low note going down 1-3 at Molineux. They finished eighth, their defence was breached only 42 times - the fourth tightest in the division.

On a sad note John Robson was forced to take early retirement due to Multiple Sclerosis.

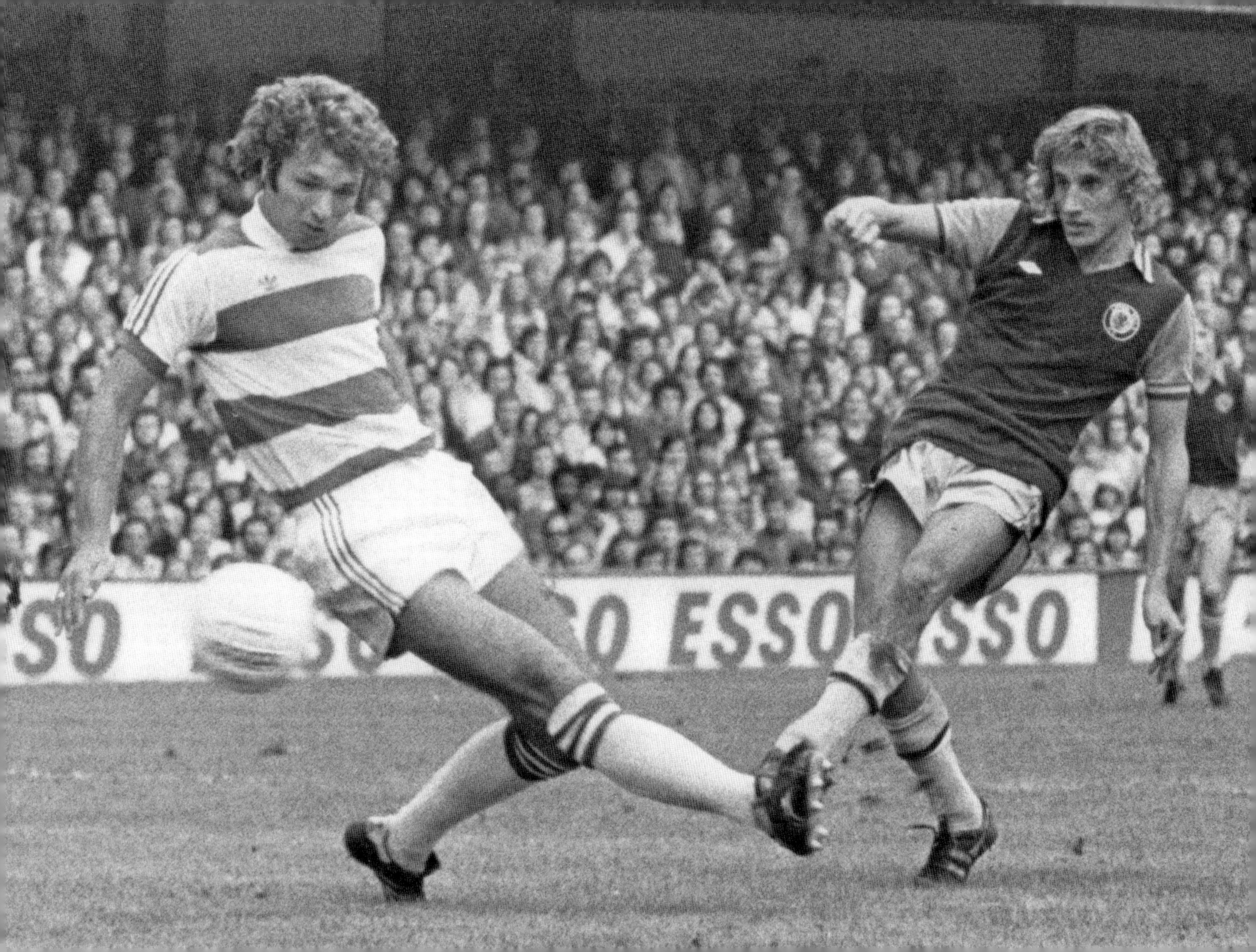
SO
SO ESSO
SSO

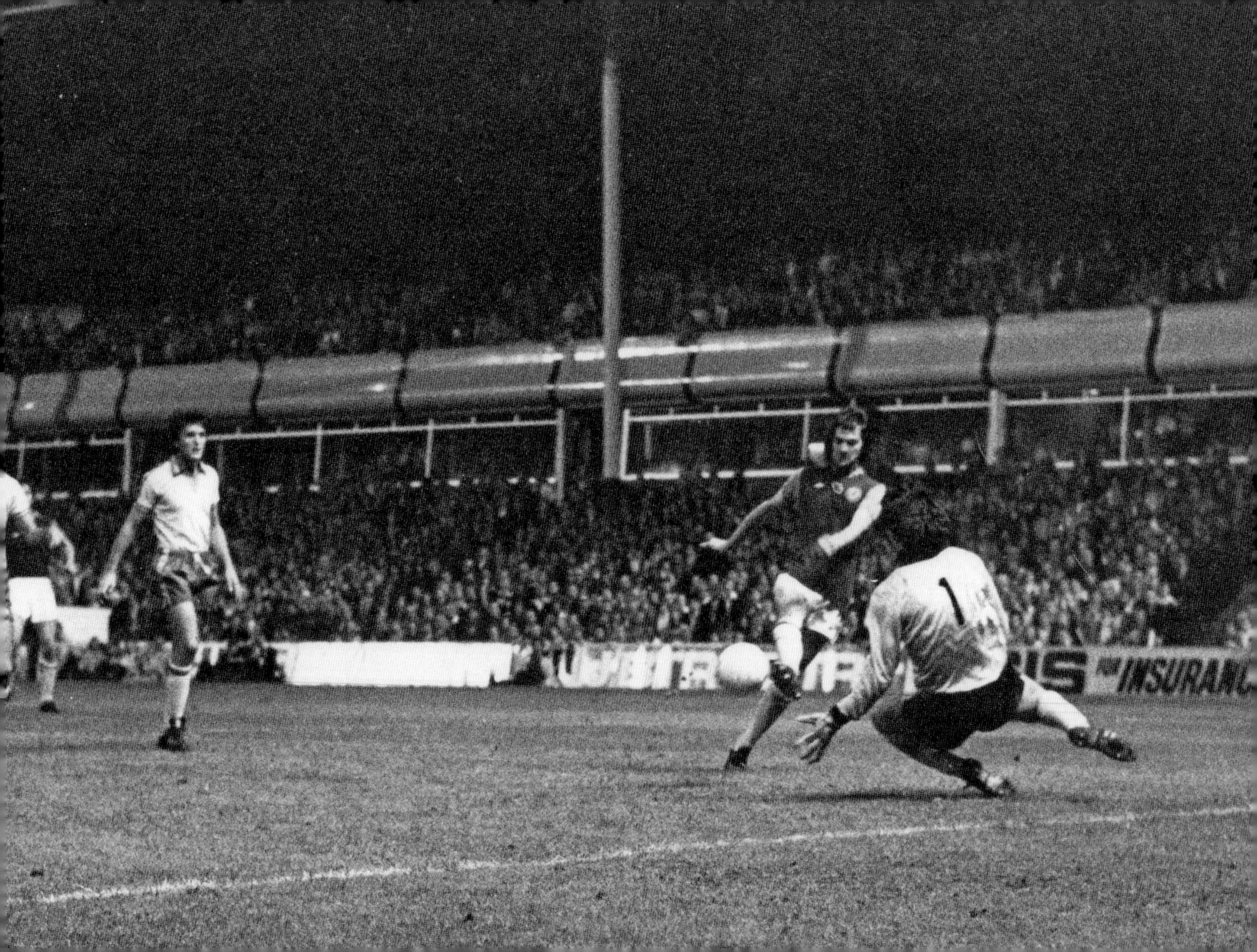
INSURANC

Brian Little goal completes the 4-0 scoreline in the UEFA Cup first round first leg tie against Turkish outfit Fenerbahce

Sat 27th August   **Everton (H)**
Lost 1-2   **Att 37,806**
Gray

Andy Gray was back on the score-sheet, his 22nd minute volley perfectly caught from Little's right wing cross. From there Villa lacked consistency in midfield, even though Carrodus toiled and Mortimer contributed as usual. Everton made Villa pay and were level on the hour before taking the lead 15 minutes later. Villa had lost more home games in the four days than they had the whole of the previous season.

Wed 31st August   **Exeter City (A) League Cup 2nd round**
Won 3-1   **Att 13,768**
Gray 3

Villa were able to overcome the first hurdle in their defence of the League Cup, even if they did play in an unfamiliar blue and gold kit due to a mix up, it was thought Exeter played in red not white. Villa's Cropley saw a 30-yard pile-driver canon off the keeper's chest before Gray spectacularly headed Villa into a slender interval lead. Gray's second of the night put Villa in control, only for Exeter to win and convert a penalty on the hour. Villa refused to panic and the Scottish forward settled the fans' nerves when he completed his hat-trick.

Sat 3rd September   **Bristol City (A)**
Drew 1-1   **Att 22,359**
Little

Brian Little scored a sublime goal in the 20th minute, latching on to Carrodus' through ball and acrobatically flicking it over the advancing goalie, underlining Villa's first-half supremacy. But, just as they did against Everton, they lost their way somewhat in midfield and let Bristol City back into a game they should have won at a canter.

Sat 10th September   **Arsenal (H)**
Won 1-0   **Att 36,929**
Cropley

Best described as unimpressive, the flow and fluency of Villa's midfield simply wasn't there. Ken McNaught, a future stalwart, was clearly struggling, trying to adapt to a system alien to the accustomed style at Everton. Apart from a Deehan header wide of the mark there was little to show from Villa's attack. But with the 90 minutes up, Cropley raced to get to Gidman's centre from the right, he succeeded and drove the ball beyond Pat Jennings into the net and Villa Park erupted.

Wed 14th September   **Fenerbahce (H) UEFA Cup 1st round 1st leg**
Won 4-0   **Att 30,351**
Gray, Deehan 2, Little

Aston Villa returned to top form and their adventurous, attacking style of play set them up comfortably for the return in Istanbul. The Turks had no answer to Gray's aerial power, yet it wasn't his head that set Villa on the way but a powerful left-footed strike. Deehan, in acres of space, made it 2-0 before the half-time whistle. Both Deehan and Mortimer hit the woodwork before the former struck again to put Villa firmly in control. Little made it four when he drew the keeper out and cheekily placed it beyond him.

Sat 17th September   **Nottingham Forest (A)**
Lost 0-2   **Att 31,016**

Forest, only a point behind the leaders, would take the Division by storm and sew the title up with games to spare. Bearing that in mind it wasn't such a disgrace that Villa were easily beaten. Shilton's only participation in the match was to pluck a 'Sid' Cowans 30-yarder out of the air. A Tony Woodcock goal after six minutes was only added to when John Robertson rolled the ball in to make it 2-0 in the last minute. According to the papers, only Carrodus could walk off the pitch with his head held high and 'Forest should have had six!'

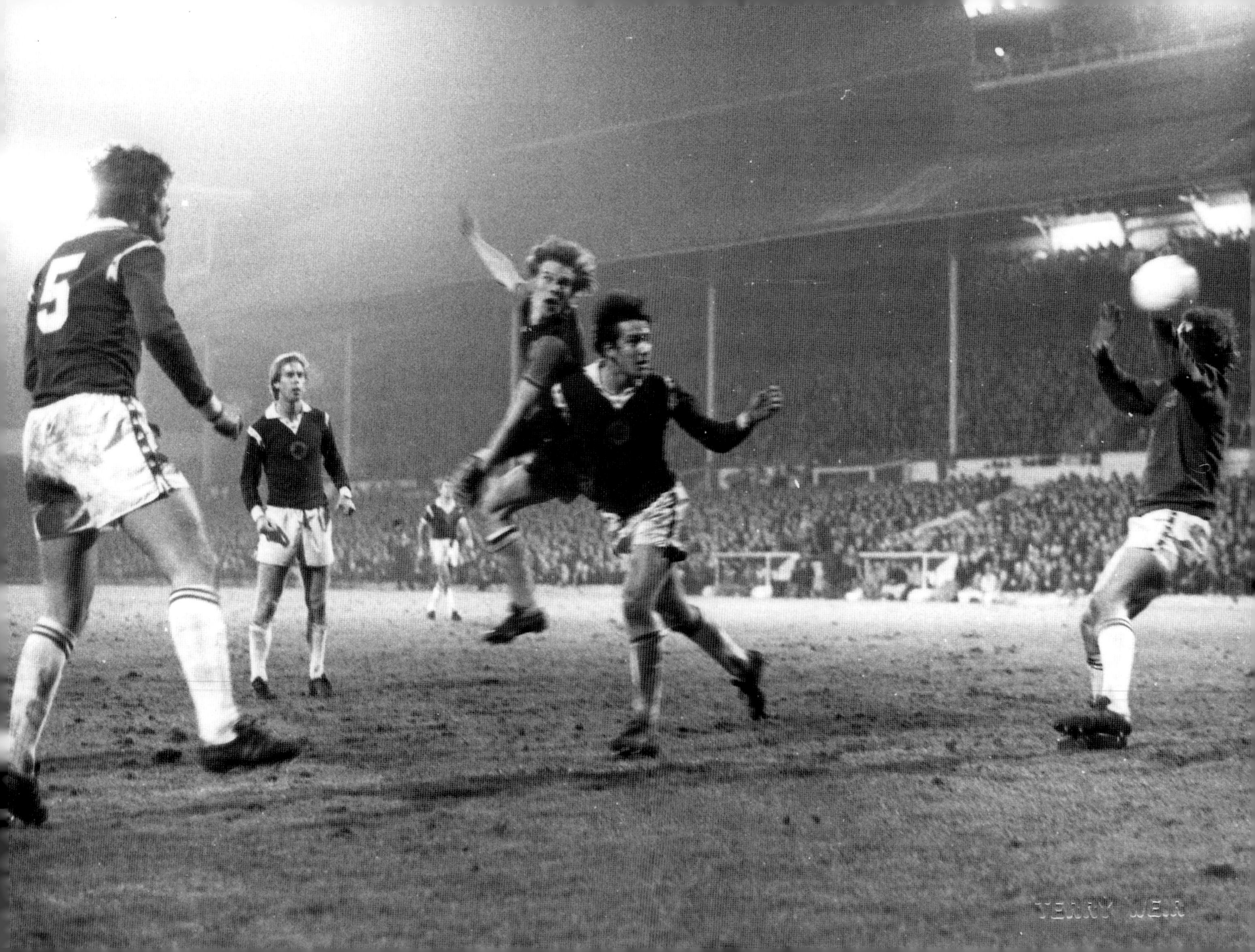
JERRY WEIR

[Left] Andy Gray's goal at Filbert Street in the 2-0 win was his seventh of the campaign thus far

Fri 23rd September   **Wolverhampton Wanderers (H)**
Won 2-0   **Att 39,403**
Own goal, Deehan

Wolves, unbeaten on the road, were 15 minutes away from taking a well deserved point at Villa Park when the game changed dramatically. Their centre-half, Colin Brazier, tried to return a short goal-kick back to Phil Parkes but managed to lob it past him. Villa had been close to taking a lead with less than three minutes played, Frank Carrodus racing round three defenders only to see Parkes block on the line. Villa full-back Gidman, with the help of a one-two, took the ball the length of the pitch, also to be denied by the Wolves keeper. A volley by Deehan in the dying minutes secured both points.

Wed 28th September   **Fenerbahce (A) UEFA Cup 1st round 2nd leg**
Won 2-0   **Att 18,000**
Deehan, Little

Andy Gray missed the trip through injury, but John Deehan's goal in the 7th minute was enough to stun Fenerbahce and silence their volatile fans. Villa then went on to play with style, safe in the knowledge they were through to the next round. When keeper Fuat punched Little's shot into his own net the fans roundly booed and jeered the home side. Deehan and Cowans went off injured, both the result of nasty tackles, to be replaced by Ivor Linton and John Gregory.

Sat 1st October   **Birmingham City (H)**
Lost 0-1   **Att 45,436**

Villa's legion of supporters urged their side to get it right on the field, but without success, this was an over anxious and seldom convincing performance. Villa lost Brian Little after 15 minutes, replaced by a subdued Andy Gray, but that was no excuse. Blues took a 38th minute lead, while Villa saw two shots cleared off the line. It was the fourth consecutive Blues derby that Villa had lost.

Wed 5th October   **Leeds United (A)**
Drew 1-1   **Att 27,797**
Gray

Villa faced a Leeds side unbeaten at Elland Road and ignored the form book. Andy Gray's 32nd minute opener was all the Villa had to show for a first-half of total domination, with Cropley, Mortimer and Carrodus bossing the midfield, but the second half and an entirely different game. Gordon McQueen's equaliser before the hour signalled Leeds all-out attack on the Villa goal. Luckily Villa's defending was heroic.

Sat 8th October   **Leicester City (A)**
Won 2-0   **Att 20,276**
Cowans, Gray

Villa turned in a thoroughly convincing display to show that they were back to their best. A 'Dixie' Deehan header that clattered the woodwork was all there was to show for 45 minutes endeavour, but as the second-half wore on, Villa gained in stature and were rewarded with two magnificently taken goals. Gordon Cowans claimed his first of the campaign with a perfectly executed diving-header to force in Giddy's right-wing cross. The second strike was equally impressive, Dennis Mortimer drove forward before releasing Gray to prod calmly past Mark Wallington in the Leicester goal.

Sat 15th October   **Norwich City (H)**
Won 3-0   **Att 32,978**
Gray, Cowans, Little

A Norwich win would see the Canaries a point off the top, yet Villa overpowered and totally outplayed John Bond's side. Gray opened the scoring, firing wide of Kevin Keelan in goal. Substitute Cowans (on for Deehan) scored in successive weekends to put Villa two-up. The best was yet to come, a long clearance by Jimmy Rimmer was headed on by Little to Gray, Brian took the return ball before advancing and unleashing an unstoppable shot, Keelan hadn't even moved. The problems that had caused Villa's slow start to the season appeared well and truly behind them.

THE BIG ASTON VILLA BOOK OF THE SEVENTIES

Wed 19th October   **Gornik Zabrze (H) UEFA Cup 2nd round 1st leg**
Won 2-0   **Att 34,138**
McNaught 2

Ken McNaught, criticised and unfairly compared with former Villa favourite Chris Nicholl, not only silenced the minority of boo boys, by full-time, he had all sides of the ground chanting his name. His first goal for Villa arrived in the 11th minute when he rose above the Polish defence to head home. His second arrived on 54 minutes when he took off and powered a flying header beyond a flailing defender and the keeper. This was a polished Villa performance, on another day Gray, Deehan and Little would have scored too.

Sat 22nd October   **West Ham United (A)**
Drew 2-2   **Att 26,599**
McNaught, Gray

Villa came up against a West Ham side yet to win on home soil and Ken McNaught didn't help the Hammers' plight when he headed a powerful effort in from 10-yards to cancel out West Ham's earlier lead. The hosts went back in front, but only after the Villa were turned down a certain penalty when Deehan was upended in the box. Gidman's surging right-wing runs were rewarded when one was met by Deehan, his weak header was fumbled by Mervyn Day and Gray moved in for the kill, 2-2.

Wed 26th October   **QPR (H) League Cup 3rd round**
Won 1-0   **Att 34,481**
Gray (pen)

Villa didn't look quite the side that had lifted the trophy only six months previously. Deehan had a chance fizz wide and Cropley had a 25-yard drive strike the post. They then were awarded a hotly disputed penalty when the referee judged that Don Givens had pushed McNaught in an off-the-ball incident. Gray took the kick and scored to register his 10th of the campaign. The QPR players continued to remonstrate. QPR had more second-half possession but their finishing let them down.

Sat 29th October   **Manchester United (H)**
Won 2-1   **Att 39,144**
Gray, Cropley

Villa kicked-off the match just a point in front of United, looking for their fourth consecutive home win against the Red Devils. Yet another brave header from Gray – who nearly wrapped himself around the upright – and a second when Alex Cropley fired through a crowded goalmouth, put Villa on the road to victory. United pulled a goal back when defender Jimmy Nicholl's cross-shot found its way in on 83 minutes. The win kept Villa within three points of second placed Liverpool.

Wed 2nd November   **Gornik Zabrze (A) UEFA Cup 2nd rnd 2nd leg**
Drew 1-1   **Att 15,000**
Gray

After a very poor first-half Villa were made to work hard for passage to the last 16, thanks in no small part to the heroics of Phillips, McNaught, Smith and Gidman in defence. Little and Deehan were rather anonymous up front, Cowans came on to replace the latter. Frank Carrodus, known for his stamina, didn't stop running all night and it was his guile and craft that led to Gray scoring a magnificent goal on 52 minutes to cancel out Gornik's 40th minute lead. Saunders was clearly pleased, "I am absolutely delighted with the result. We did not play in the first half and let them tie things up."

Sat 5th November   **Liverpool (A)**
Won 2-1   **Att 50,436**
Gray 2

With Villa having suffered nine straight defeats at Anfield, the Kop were stunned into silence when an Andy Gray double inspired the claret and blues to a valuable win, which constituted Liverpool's first home loss in 20 months. Gray's first goal arrived after Ray Clemence had touched Carrodus' header against the post, Andy steamed in to force the ball over. Liverpool were level when a Phil Neal centre was turned in by the unfortunate Carrodus, but Gray, spearhead-ing a phenomenal all-round team performance, regained Villa the lead when he fired in a perfect shot following Kenny McNaught's 40-yard free kick. The Press were now calling Aston Villa serious title challengers.

Sat 12th November   Middlesbrough (H)
Lost 0-1   Att 31,837

To many, Villa's defeat to 'Boro, following a nine match unbeaten run, was a surprise. But Villa supporters remembered that after poking five past Liverpool the previous campaign they went and lost at Ayresome Park next time out. Villa underestimated their opposition and were fortunate the winning margin wasn't greater as the visitor's defence kept a tight grip on Little and Gray, with their striker Billy Ashcroft looking the more dangerous.

Sat 19th November   Chelsea (A)
Drew 0-0   Att 31,764

For the most part Chelsea tackled with such determination there was little the Villa could do about it. A late burst underlined what Saunders' side were capable of, and when Cropley put the ball in the net there was confusion as to why the flag went up, was Cropley offside or was Gray adjudged to have fouled Peter Bonetti the Chelsea keeper? Villa's confidence grew as the game wore on and they should have punished the London side with at least a couple of goals.

Wed 23rd November   Athletic Bilbao (H) UEFA Cup 3rd round 1st leg
Won 2-0   Att 32,973
Own goal, Deehan

Under the famous Villa Park floodlights, and kitted out in an uncustomary white strip, the Villa battled impressively in atrocious conditions to take a two goal cushion to Spain. The hosts were helped by the Bilbao keeper for the breakthrough, Cropley's right-wing corner punched into his own net by Jose Angle Iribar. Poor Jose' evening got worse when Deehan headed into an empty net on 78 minutes after Gidman's free kick was misjudged, the goalie came out to meet the ball but completely missed it. Deehan was making a name for himself on the European stage, his last Villa goals had also been in the same competition.

Tue 29th November   Nottingham Forest (A) League Cup 4th round
Lost 2-4   Att 29,333
Little, Carrodus

Villa were teased, tormented and over run as Forest swept into a three goal lead within 25 minutes. A certain Peter Withe bagging the third. Rimmer pulled off a few saves to keep the scoreline somewhat respectable, but he was unable to prevent Tony Woodcock from adding number four. Brian Little volleyed the best goal of the game before a speculative Carrodus effort found its way past Chris Woods. Villa's first defeat in the competition for 13 games saw their hold on the trophy loosened.

Sat 3rd December   Ipswich Town (A)
Lost 0-2   Att 20,908

Villa met an Ipswich team with only one win in six games, nevertheless, Bobby Robson's team were only two points behind them. Elementary defensive mistakes cost Villa the game, and with the exception of the hardworking John Gregory and Gray, the side bore little resemblance to the one which beat Athletic Bilbao so comprehensively. Trevor Whymark hit the first for the hosts and Eric Gates' goal from the edge of the box in the 37th minute as good as sealed the points.

Wed 7th December   Athletic Bilbao (A) UEFA Cup 3rd rnd 2nd leg
Drew 1-1   Att 39,000
Mortimer

Aston Villa turned in one of their best ever performances to go through to the quarter-finals. Dennis Mortimer popped up to head Villa in front with two minutes of the first half remaining following a magnificent midfield display inspired by Gregory and Mortimer, that

Athletic struggled to handle. The home side spared their blushes with an equaliser with four minutes left on the clock, but the fiercely loyal Basque crowd applauded Villa's players off the field.

Sat 10th December   West Bromwich Albion (H)
Won 3-0   Att 43,196
Cowans, Gray, Gidman

Villa's triumph was attributed to skilful football and self control, notwithstanding Albion's intimidation and general thuggery, which should have been stamped out by a weak referee. Cowans, substitute for McNaught (the victim of an overzealous challenge), put Villa ahead before all hell let loose. Ally Brown went clean through Alex Cropley, and even with 40,000+ in the ground, the cracking sound of 'Crops' leg break was unmistakeable. The Holte End crowd screamed 'animal' in Brown's direction and players from both sides got involved with the pushing and shoving. Reduced to ten men, incensed Villa hit the Baggies with two further goals through Gidman and Gray.

Sat 17th December   Middlesbrough (A)
Lost 0-1   Att 14,999

'Boro, known for being a hard side to break down, proved too much for the Villa. In fact the last time the Villa had recorded a win at Ayresome Park was back in their Second Division title campaign of 1959/60 under Joe Mercer. The match had 0-0 stamped all over it, Rimmer making only two saves, while Platt in goal at the other end had a free afternoon. That was until Gidman was shown a red card for bringing down the diminutive Stan Cummins, the tackle had been fairly innocuous, but the referee responded to the baying crowd. Gray was booked during the mass protest by Villa players. Eight minutes later ten-man Villa went behind to a Hedley goal.

Mon 26th December   Coventry City (H)
Drew 1-1   Att 43,671
Deehan

A great game was never on the cards with the Villa Park pitch resembling a beach following the club's decision to give the playing surface a £6,000 patch-up. City took the lead in the 73rd minute, with a headed goal from Tommy Hutchison. Villa's response was immediate, Deehan had the ball in the Coventry net within seconds, after heading in at the far post from Mortimer's cross. It was surprising that no players were injured due to the atrocious conditions underfoot.

Tue 27th December   Derby County (A)
Won 3-0   Att 30,395
Little, Gray, Deehan

There was an inevitability about the Villa's success, equally encouraging was that all three of their potent strike-force were on target. Brian Little led the way after eight minutes and Gray put Villa further in front shortly before the interval. The versatile John Gregory played in Cropley's position after promising earlier performances at full-back and centre-half. Deehan made certain of both points going in head-first in a very congested penalty area, his bravery rewarded with his eighth goal of the campaign. This was the first time the Villa had won away by a three goal margin since returning to the top flight.

Sat 31st December   Manchester City (A)
Lost 0-2   Att 46,074

Fifth in the table City were five places higher and three points better off than the Villa. It was apparent very early on that a repeat of the Baseball Ground performance wasn't on the cards. And, when City took the lead shortly into the second half, it was obvious that Villa weren't even going to get a share of the points. Peter Barnes' goal was down to slack defending in the Villa ranks, who had no response to the setback. Brian Kidd added a second meaning it was game, set and match to Manchester City.

Mon 2nd January   Queens Park Rangers (H)
Drew 1-1   Att 34,750
Little

Frank Carrodus' name was missing from the teamsheet for the first time that season, Cowans starting in his place. Goalkeeper Jimmy Rimmer kept Villa in the game saving well from Don Givens and twice from Leighton James. Brian Little broke the deadlock on 22 minutes when he fired right-footed to send his powerful drive through a crowded goalmouth and beyond Phil Parkes. Just after the hour, John Gidman was caught from behind by Gerry Francis, the referee played the advantage only for QPR to take possession and hit Villa on the break. With Gidman still down, Givens moved into the free space and saw his shot deflected into the Villa net - much to the Villa fan's fury.

Sat 7th January   Everton (A) FA Cup 3rd round
Lost 1-4   Att 46,320
Gray

Aston Villa were unceremoniously dumped out by an Everton side hell bent on revenge for the previous season's marathon League Cup final defeat. Everton's first arrived on 20 minutes, whilst the controversial second came when Gregory challenged Duncan McKenzie fairly only for the referee to point at the spot. Leighton Phillips was booked for comments made. The spot kick was converted and Everton made it 3-0 soon after. Gray rifled in from close range in the 42nd minute to give Villa some hope, but sadly the second half belonged to Everton and they found the net again. To complete Villa's misery Phillips was given his marching orders for further comments made to the man in the middle.

Sat 14th January   Everton (A)
Lost 0-1   Att 40,630

Villa's chances of taking anything from the game were greatly reduced when Andy Gray limped off a few minutes in, they were already without the injured Carrodus and the suspended Phillips, hence Micky Buttress starting, with sub Ivor Linton being called into the fray. Andy King scored mid-way through the first half. Brian Little had a shot blocked after the break and George Wood had to react when Terry Darracott back-heeled to prevent Deehan who was powering in, but it was not enough to avoid defeat.

Sat 28th January   Bristol City (H)
Won 1-0   Att 29,676
Deehan

With the last Villa Park victory a distant seven weeks ago, Villa played host to City in front of their first sub 30,000 gate of the season, in spite of record signing Tommy Craig making his debut having joined from Newcastle United. On the day, Bristol's finishing, coupled with saves by Rimmer, ensured City didn't land their first away win of the season. John Deehan spared Villa blushes when he plundered a 50th minute lead to give his side both points, which moved them above Derby County in the table and up to tenth position.

Sat 4th February   Arsenal (A)
Won 1-0   Att 30,127
Own goal

It was a surprise the game was allowed to go ahead, the pitch was simply a mud bath. Villa adapted slighter better to the atrocious conditions, with Tommy Craig adding poise to the Villa midfield. When Arsenal did find their feet they were beaten by the heroics of McNaught, Phillips, Gregory and Smith. The first goal would always win this game and that's exactly how it panned out. A Mortimer corner was punched clear by Jennings, only to strike Malcolm McDonald and rebound into the net. One-nil to the Villa, their first 'double' of the campaign.

Sat 25th February   Birmingham City (A)
Lost 0-1   Att 33,679

Villa didn't deserve to lose this, they created enough chances to win six games let alone one. Villa's domination stemmed from Craig, Carrodus, Cowans and Mortimer, they were excellent. Villa struck the woodwork twice in a first half that they bossed. It was much the same after the interval, the woodwork shook repeatedly, Carrodus, Smith and Little should all have scored, yet it was Trevor Francis who harshly scored the only goal of the game.

Wed 1st March   Barcelona (H) UEFA Cup quarter-final
Drew 2-2   Att 49,619
McNaught, Deehan

Bullied by Barcelona's over aggressive players, Villa came back from the dead. They trailed 0-1 at the interval thanks to a Johan Cruyff masterpiece, the Dutchman picked the ball up in the centre circle, ran unchallenged before hitting a 20-yard swerver beyond Rimmer. When Barca added a second with 12 minutes remaining Cruyff took it that victory was assured and left the field to a standing ovation from the appreciative audience. Not So! Within three minutes Ken McNaught rose majestically to head home a perfectly floated Gordon Smith centre, and with only two minutes left to play, Mortimer chipped the ball forward, Allan Evans challenged the goalie in the air, the ball fell and there was Deehan to rifle it home with his trusty right-peg for twos-a-piece.

Sat 4th March   Leicester City (H)
Drew 0-0   Att 29,971

After impressing in the mid-week match Allan Evans was handed his league debut against a Leicester side sitting second from bottom. In the 57th minute Evans soared above the City defence, his header came back off the bar. 'Sid' Cowans suffered the same fate when a terrific volley smashed against the upright. Then, with time running out, Evans bent the ball past Wallington, but it too struck the woodwork. The Foxes' only chance was a McNaught clearance that flew inches wide of Rimmer's post.

[Right] Johan Cryuff evades Ken McNaught, while Gordon Smith measures up the Barcelona legend at the Nou Camp

Sat 11th March   Norwich City (A)
Lost 1-2   Att 18,575
Gregory

It was sod's law that Roger Hansbury - who'd had a nightmare the previous weekend – would be in inspired form in goal for City, his impressive display foiled Brian Little from scoring certain goals on two occasions. Villa, with a three man frontline, went behind on the half-hour mark. John Gregory came on for Evans and it was the sub who gave Norwich their second when he bundled over Martin Peters for full-back Ryan to convert the penalty. Gregory made amends of a sort when he fired Villa back into contention on 87 minutes, but Villa were unable to find a leveller.

Wed 15th March   Barcelona (A) UEFA Cup quarter-final
Lost 1-2   Att 80,000
Little

Aston Villa fought a heroic battle in the Nou Camp, but bowed out honourably. Their cause wasn't helped when Gidman, playing in midfield, was red-carded on 24 minutes for retaliating to being body checked by centre-half Jesus De la Cruz. Rimmer magnificently saved from Zuviria, Cruyff and Rexach before Brian Little seized on a mis-clearance from Gordon Smith's free kick to put Villa ahead in the tie on 57 minutes. Barca piled forward and were back on terms when Zuviria headed home from a corner. Ten minutes later Asensi put the Spanish giants ahead. Ken McNaught caused concern for the hosts when he caught the defence in array only to see his effort hit the crossbar.

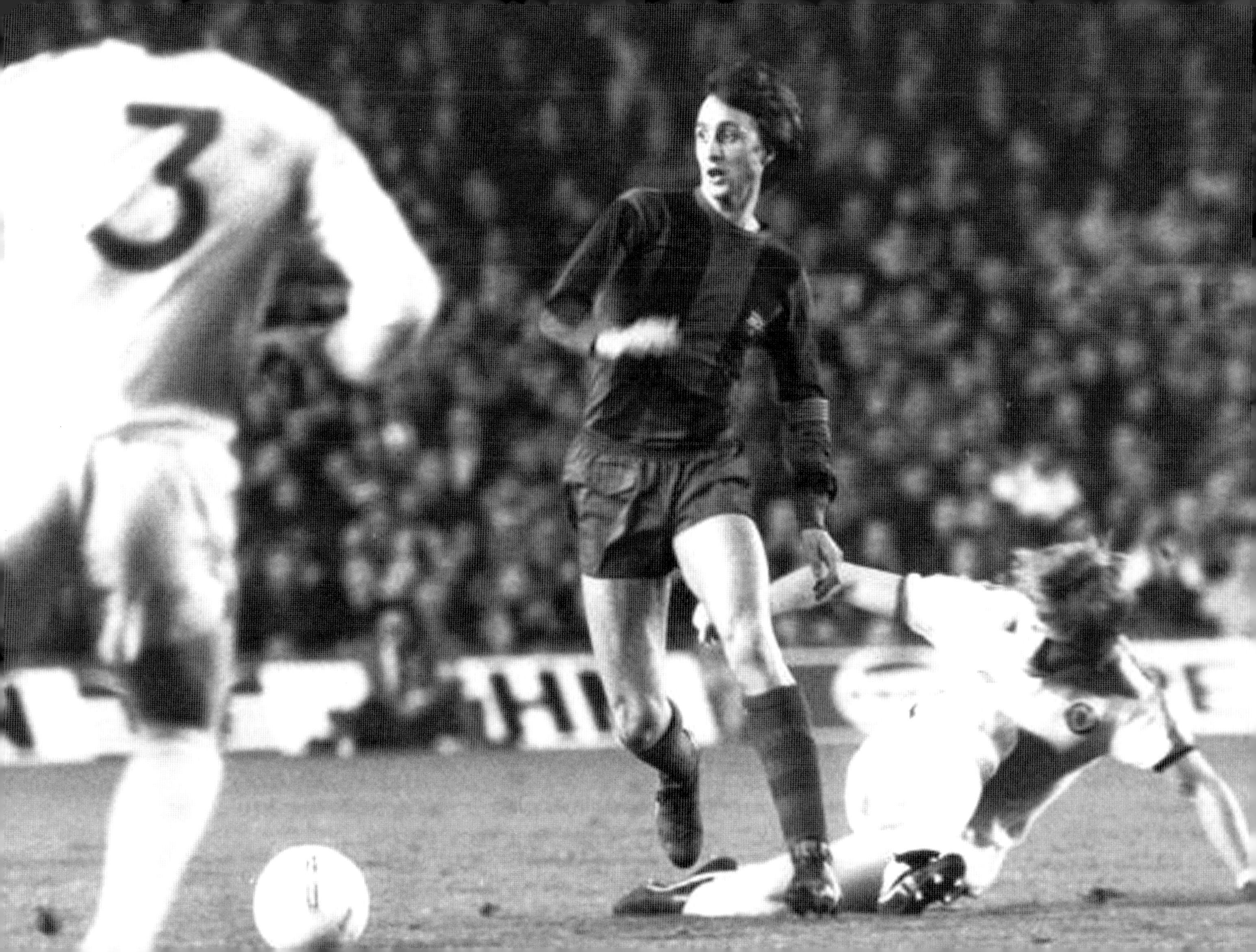

THE BIG ASTON VILLA BOOK OF THE SEVENTIES

Sat 18th March   **West Ham United (H)**
Won 4-1   **Att 28,275**
Gregory 2, Deehan, Mortimer

Villa masked their UEFA Cup elimination well by hitting West Ham for four. They were made to work hard against the relegation threatened side, Gregory's header put Villa in the driving seat, but a solo goal from Trevor Brooking brought the game back all square. Villa were ahead once again when John Deehan found the net and two more headers, from Mortimer (75 mins) and Gregory (79 mins), put the result beyond doubt. Villa were up to tenth.

Tue 21st March   **Coventry City (A)**
Won 3-2   **Att 30,920**
Little, McNaught, Gray

Coventry were sitting in the lofty sixth position for Villa's visit to Highfield Road, unbeaten in their last five games and having won the last three on home soil. This counted for nothing as Saunders' boys romped into a three goal lead, though it could have been very different had Garry Thompson put the Sky Blues in front in only the first minute – Villa had Rimmer to thank for a lightning-quick reflex save. Brian Little opened the scoring when he jabbed home from six-yards out, McNaught rose well to nod in Mortimer's right-wing corner and then Andy Gray, back from his injury-induced absence, sent the fans wild with a trademark, brave diving header. City pulled two late goals back but the points were Villa's.

Sat 25th March   **Derby County (H)**
Drew 0-0   **Att 32,793**

Derby down to ten men for the last 20 minutes easily coped with Villa's one dimensional attack. The best chance for Villa - in a game that created few – fell to Brian Little in stoppage time. Challenged by Steve Powell, Little connected just as the ball bounced up, but prodded it wide in front of an equally frustrated Holte End crowd.

Wed 29th March   **Manchester United (A)**
Drew 1-1   **Att 41,625**
Deehan

Villa suffered at the hands of an inept refereeing display. Jimmy Rimmer was penalised when he was adjudged to have fouled Stuart Pearson, but justice was done when the keeper saved the spot kick. Later, when Gray was impeded by Stepney, then bundled over by Buchan, nothing was given. The Old Trafford curse for visiting teams was alive and kicking even back then it seems. Mortimer sent Deehan clean through to put Villa in front, but the lead was short lived, 60 seconds to be exact. In the final 15 minutes Dennis Mortimer was tackled Twickenham-style, but Lou Macari got away with a lenient yellow.

Sat 1st April   **Liverpool (H)**
Lost 0-3   **Att 40,190**

Liverpool, in seventh position, were into a sequence that would bring them nine wins in an 11 game unbeaten run. Needless to say Villa couldn't live with them on the day. With a display of dazzling football Liverpool ripped the Villa apart and were 3-0 up within 21 minutes, Kenny Dalglish with two, and Alan Kennedy doing the damage. Despite the hardworking Gordon Cowans – Villa's best player by a mile – they failed to make an impression.

Wed 5th April   **Nottingham Forest (H)**
Lost 0-1   **Att 44,215**

Brian Clough's newly promoted Forest were sitting proudly at the First Division summit, however, Villa played them off the park for the entire game only to be floored with an 86th minute goal by Tony Woodcock. Deehan and Little performed well and Gray was back to his best. Indifferent decisions by the referee cost Villa dearly, Kenny Burns handled a Cowans shot on the line and within minutes Larry Lloyd barged Gray over in the area, both incidents were ignored by the man in black.

Sat 8th April   **Newcastle United (A)**
Drew 1-1   **Att 19,330**
Evans A

Villa missed Andy Gray, even so, they should have won by a margin of four or five. As it was chances went begging yet again, disappointing finishing meant Allan Evans' goal after 67 minutes was all they had to show for an afternoon of domination. It was a point lost rather than gained.

Sat 15th April   **Chelsea (H)**
Won 2-0   **Att 27,375**
Cowans, own goal

Chelsea, threatened with relegation, packed numbers behind the ball. When Villa did get beyond the wall of yellow shirts, Peter Bonetti was there to deny Mortimer, Carrodus, Cowans and Gray. 'Sid' eventually found the way through ten minutes after the interval when he crashed home following a neat Gray sideways flick. It stayed that way until three minutes before the end when a Mortimer in-swinging corner was met by Gray and the challenging Steve Wicks, the Chelsea man diverting the ball past his own keeper.

Mon 17th April   **Newcastle United (H)**
Won 2-0   **Att 25,493**
Cowans, Gray

With it still mathematically possible for Newcastle to avoid the drop it was somewhat surprising that only 28 of their Toon Army turned up in support. The Newcastle board paid the admittance of those few who bothered, according to a Northern Echo reporter. Cowans hammered the first nail in the Magpies coffin with a wonderful strike after Mortimer had slipped him a short free-kick. Andy Gray made sure when his 19th of the campaign sealed the visitor's fate. Villa would be spared the long journey to St James Park the following season.

Sat 22nd April   **West Bromwich Albion (A)**
Won 3-0   **Att 35,112**
Deehan, Cowans, Mortimer

Villa's victory was down to their decisiveness, they were sharper and more committed than an Albion side four points higher in the table. Deehan got the ball rolling with a header at the far post to give Villa the lead. Cowans, scoring for the third successive game, made it two before Dennis Mortimer wrapped up the afternoon's scoring when he helped inflict the second 3-0 defeat on the Baggies by a rampant Villa side.

Wed 26th April   **Leeds United (H)**
Won 3-1   **Att 30,524**
Deehan, Little, Mortimer

Villa, seeking a fourth consecutive win, were one place behind a Leeds side defeated three times in their last five games. The inspiration for Villa's 3-1 win was John Deehan, who scored the first with a brilliant header and then played creator for the other two. His first-half goal was cancelled out six minutes into the second period when Ray Hankin headed the equaliser, which was as good as it got for the visitors. A Deehan centre from the right on 73 minutes was met by Little and then a cross from the left was eagerly accepted by Dennis Mortimer.

Sat 29th April   **Ipswich Town (H)**
Won 6-1   **Att 39,955**
Deehan 2, Gray, Little, Carrodus, Cowans

Ipswich Town, no doubt with one eye on the forthcoming FA Cup final, were mercilessly humiliated by Villa. Deehan started the rout, the second scored by Gray, owed much to a dazzling run by Little. Villa were three-up on 24 minutes when Little claimed the best goal of the afternoon when he slipped inside George Burley before delivering a calculated drive into the top corner. Deehan made it

4-0 before the half-time whistle, but only after Gray had struck the woodwork twice. Carrodus scored only his second of the campaign, his first on the opening day of the season. But, Villa weren't finished, Cowans hit his fourth in five games to make it 6-0 before Rimmer was beaten by Whymark.

Tue 2nd May   **Wolverhampton Wanderers (A)**
Lost 1-3   **Att 30,644**
Carrodus

Wolves, who could still go down if they lost their remaining two fixtures, took a lead on the quarter-hour before Frank Carrodus levelled things on 28 minutes. Whilst not prolific, this was the third time in four seasons where Frank had scored in the last game of the campaign. Mel Eves restored Wolves advantage when he beat the outstretched reach of Rimmer, then a Rafferty near-post header ensured Villa headed home with nothing and a belated charge for European football had failed.

[Above] Marathon man, Frank Carrodus, scored in both the first and last games of Villa's 1977/78 campaign

PRE-SEASON

- John Deehan scored for England U21s v Norway in Bergen
- Aston Villa prised centre-forward Allan Evans from Dunfermline Athletic for £30,000.
- Utility/midfielder John Gregory was signed from Northampton Town.
- Villa landed Ken McNaught from Everton for £200,000. The Scot impressed Saunders with his displays against Villa in the previous season's League Cup marathon.

AUGUST

- Jimmy Rimmer arrived from Arsenal for a bargain £70,000.
- Villa's shock 1-4 defeat on home soil against Manchester City was the club's heaviest loss since September 1968 when Spurs knocked Villa out of the League Cup by the same scoreline.
- Villa were forced to turn out in a blue and gold ensemble away at Exeter. They'd turned up with their white away kit believing Exeter wore red.

SEPTEMBER

- John Gidman was recalled to the side having missed the first four games.
- England U21s trounced Norway 6-0, Deehan bags two goals.
- John Robson played his last game in claret and blue against Nottingham Forest in the City Ground encounter. Sadly he would shortly be diagnosed with Multiple Sclerosis.
- Villa cruised into the UEFA Cup 2nd round by thrashing Turkish side Fenerbahce 6-0 on aggregate.

[Above] A Brian Little chip from the edge of the box makes it 2-0 away at Fenerbahce

OCTOBER

- John Deehan hit another double for England U21s as Finland were beaten 8-1.
- Andy Gray's goal at Elland Road in the 1-1 draw with Leeds started a sequence of six league games where the marksman was on target.
- A Ken McNaught brace against Gornik Zabrze ensured Villa travelled to Poland with a two-goal cushion.
- Goalkeeper Jake Findlay played against the Poles at Villa Park. It was his sole appearance of the campaign.
- The match at Filbert Street was held up for eight minutes as trouble flared on the terracing. Debris, including a beer crate, bottles and sticks, were launched onto the pitch.

THE BIG ASTON VILLA BOOK OF THE SEVENTIES

NOVEMBER

- Andy Gray's double in the 2-1 win at Anfield meant he'd now scored in eight of his last nine games – the 14 goal total was one less than the same point in the previous season.
- Defeat at home to Boro' ended an unbeaten run of six matches
- In defeating Spanish outfit Athletic Bilbao 2-0 at home in the UEFA Cup, it meant Saunders' boys had kept clean sheets in every round at Villa Park.
- John Gidman and Dennis Mortimer played for England B against a Czechoslovakian B side in Prague. The match finished 0-0.

DECEMBER

- After defeating Athletic Bilbao over two legs, Villa's name went into the hat for the UEFA quarter-final draw along with PSV Eindhoven, Eintracht Frankfurt, Grasshoppers, Bastia, Barcelona, Magdeburg and Carl Zeiss Jena.
- A bad challenge by West Bromwich Albion's Ally Brown left midfield maestro Alex Cropley with a broken leg. The third of his career.

JANUARY

- Gary Shelton signed from neighbours Walsall.
- Ivor Linton came on for Gray at Everton in the Cup. It was one of only two appearances for the youngster during the season.
- Everton exacted revenge for the previous season's League Cup final defeat when they hit Villa for four in the FA Cup tie at Goodison.
- Villa smashed their transfer record when Tommy Craig landed for £270,000 from Newcastle United. Craig debuted in the home win against Bristol City.

FEBRUARY

- Villa gained their first win in seven attempts at Highbury (the last being 1962/63) courtesy of a Malcolm McDonald own goal to complete a double over The Gunners.
- Defeat at St Andrews meant another 'double' by the arch rivals from across the city.

MARCH

- Young full-back, David Evans, was blooded in front of nearly 50,000 fans in the Villa Park clash against Barcelona. The game ended 2-2, but it was Evans' only appearance of the season.
- Andy Gray missed the Barcelona clash at the Nou Camp through injury, however, in Gray's auobiography it is claimed Saunders said, "Gray has cheated himself, the fans and the club."
- John Gidman was sent off in Spain as the side were narrowly defeated 3-4 on aggregate by Barcelona.
- John Deehan starred for England U21 as they beat their Italian counterparts 2-1 in the Euro Champs qualifier.

APRIL

- After starting the month with two defeats, Villa then went on to win five matches on the spin – scoring 16 in the process and shipping just two.
- Villa's youngsters reached the final of the FA Youth Cup for the first time since 1972.
- The two Johns – Gidman and Deehan – featured in Ron Greenwoood's England set-up, though neither came off the substitute's bench for the England versus Brazil fixture at Wembley.

[Left] Captain Leighton Phillips during the win at QPR

- Villa's 6-1 victory at home to Ipswich Town concludeed a five match winning streak. Their best since gaining promotion in the 1974/75 season.

MAY

- Villa signed off the season with defeat at Wolverhampton Wanderers – Frank Carrodus scoring Villa's last goal of the campaign in the 1-3 loss. Carrodus had also found the back of the net in Villa's opening fixture at Loftus Road.
- Over the course of the season the Villa had done the double over two teams, Arsenal and West Bromwich Albion, although five sides had inflicted the same on them; Manchester City, Everton, Nottingham Forest, Birmingham City and Middlesbrough.

[Right] Brian Little strokes home goal number three at White Hart Lane – Villa would add another as they spoilt the Argentineans' welcome with a resounding 4-1 victory

1978-79

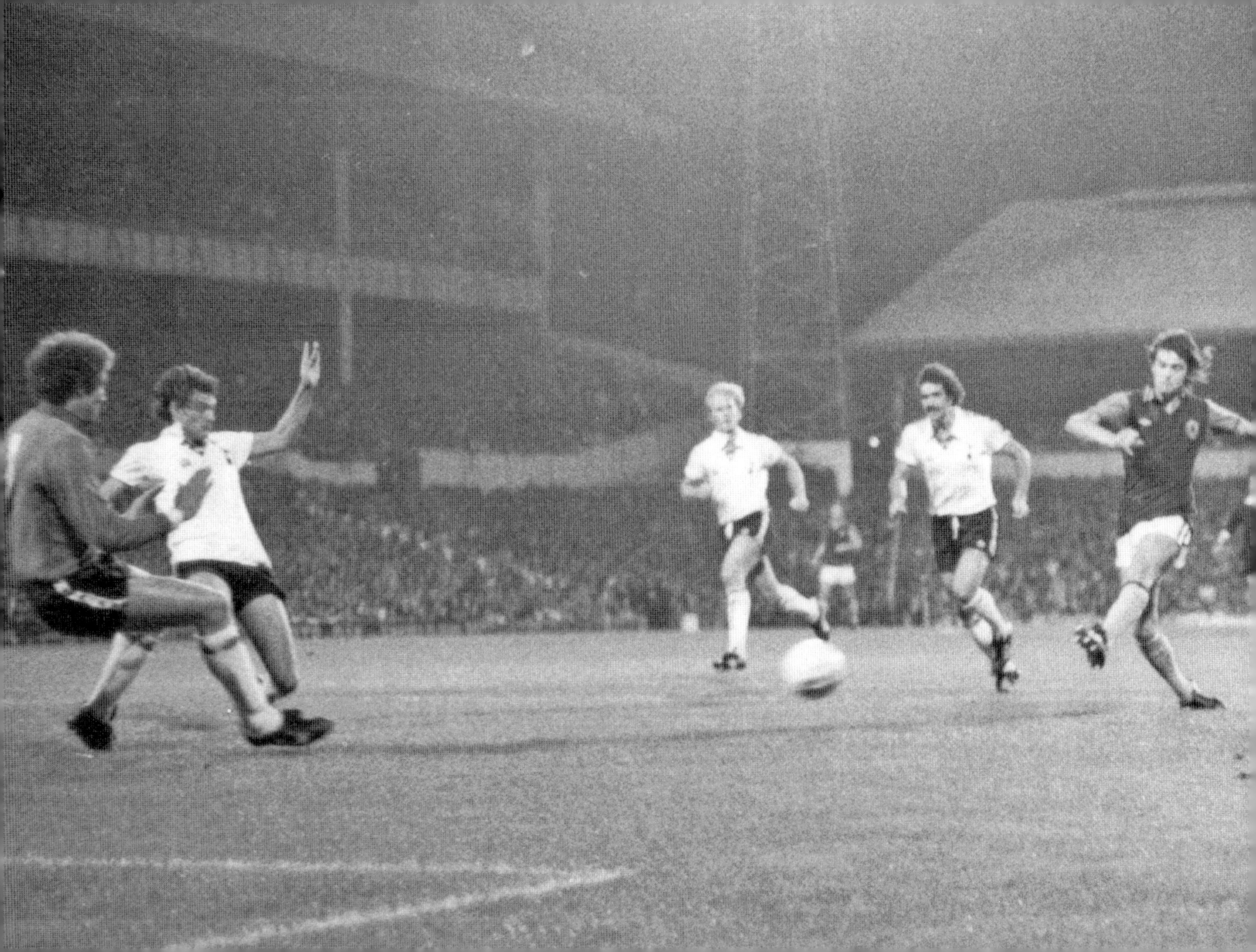

THE BIG ASTON VILLA BOOK OF THE SEVENTIES

[Back Row] Alex Cropley, Allan Evans, Jake Findlay, Jimmy Rimmer, Ken McNaught, John Deehan [MiddleRow] Roy MacLaren (Coach), Gordon Cowans, Brian Little, Andy Gray, John Gregory, Dennis Mortimer [Front Row] Frank Carrodus, Gordon Smith, John Gidman, Ron Saunders (Manager), Gary Shelton, Leighton Phillips, Tommy Craig

Football League	Division One
Manager	Ron Saunders
Asst. Manager/Coach	Roy McLaren
Physio	Peter Downes
Captain	Dennis Mortimer
Final Position	Eighth
FA Cup	Third Round
League Cup	Fourth
UEFA Cup	Fourth
Leading Goalscorer (all competitions)	John Deehan – 9 goals

With no players coming in or leaving, transfer activity at Villa was non-existent during the closed season – although West Brom put in a tentative bid for Deehan. But as the season unfolded the club would blood numerous lads from their academy; Brendan Ormsby, Colin Gibson, Gary Williams, Lee Jenkins and a certain Gary Shaw were introduced with varying degrees of success.

After a narrow win at home to the Wolves on the opening day, Villa exploded into life at White Hart Lane in front of the World's media, who had gathered to witness the arrival of Argentine World Cup heroes Ricardo Villa and Osvaldo Ardiles to English football. But it was the Aston variant, not Ricky, who made the headlines with Saunders' men running out 4-1 victors. Unfortunately the side could only muster one win from the next eight league games before a satisfactory 1-0 win at rivals Birmingham.

November was a mixed month – two good wins, that included the 4-0 rout at Wolves, meant vital points catapulted Villa up to seventh, but they were dumped unceremoniously out of the League Cup by Second Division Luton Town after it had taken three games to get past Crystal Palace from the same division.

Villa then went through December, January and February unbeaten in the league, though the five draws following a sole victory against Chelsea meant Villa were closer to bottom placed Birmingham City than leaders Liverpool. At least Villa could concentrate on the bread and butter football having lost to Forest at the first hurdle of the FA Cup.

March started well with a 'Sid' Cowans goal ensuring a double over the Blues, the seventh time this had been achieved, whilst

continued >>>

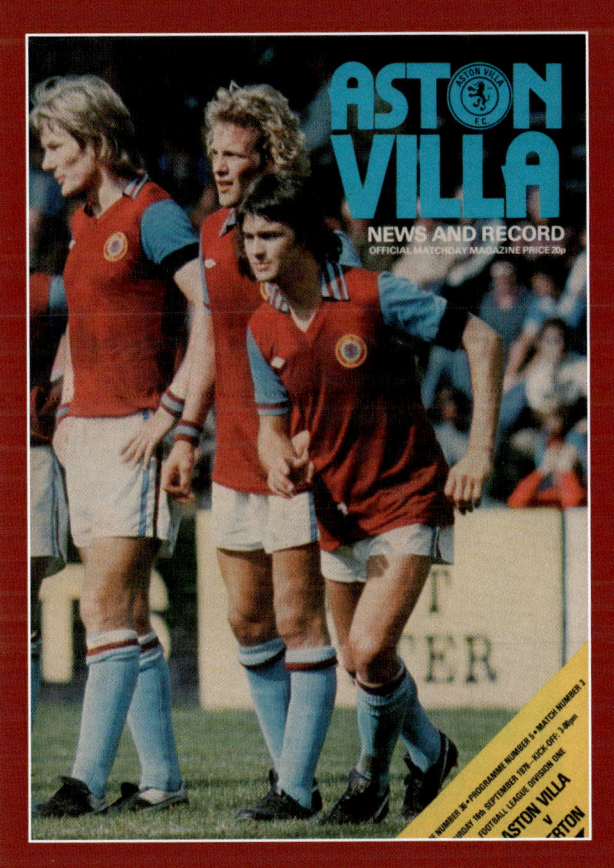

		P	W	D	L	F	A	W	D	L	F	A	Pts
1	Liverpool	42	19	2	0	51	4	11	6	4	34	12	68
2	Nottingham Forest	42	11	10	0	34	10	10	8	3	27	16	60
3	West Bromwich	42	13	5	3	38	15	11	6	4	34	20	59
4	Everton	42	12	7	2	32	17	5	10	6	20	23	51
5	Leeds United	42	11	4	6	41	25	7	10	4	29	27	50
6	Ipswich Town	42	11	4	6	34	21	9	5	7	29	28	49
7	Arsenal	42	11	8	2	37	18	6	6	9	24	30	48
8	**Aston Villa**	42	8	9	4	37	26	7	7	7	22	23	46
9	Manchester United	42	9	7	5	29	25	6	8	7	31	38	45
10	Coventry City	42	11	7	3	41	29	3	9	9	17	39	44
11	Tottenham Hotspur	42	7	8	6	19	25	6	7	8	29	36	41
12	Middlesbrough	42	10	5	6	33	21	5	5	11	24	29	40
13	Bristol City	42	11	6	4	34	19	4	4	13	13	32	40
14	Southampton	42	9	10	2	35	20	3	6	12	12	33	40
15	Manchester City	42	9	5	7	34	24	4	8	9	24	28	39
16	Norwich City	42	7	10	4	29	19	0	13	8	22	38	37
17	Bolton Wanderers	42	10	5	6	36	28	2	6	13	18	47	35
18	Wolverhampton	42	10	4	7	26	26	3	4	14	18	42	34
19	Derby County	42	8	5	8	25	25	2	6	13	19	46	31
20	Q.P.R	42	4	9	8	24	33	2	4	15	21	40	25
21	Birmingham City	42	5	9	7	24	25	1	1	19	13	39	22
22	Chelsea	42	3	5	13	23	42	2	5	14	21	50	20

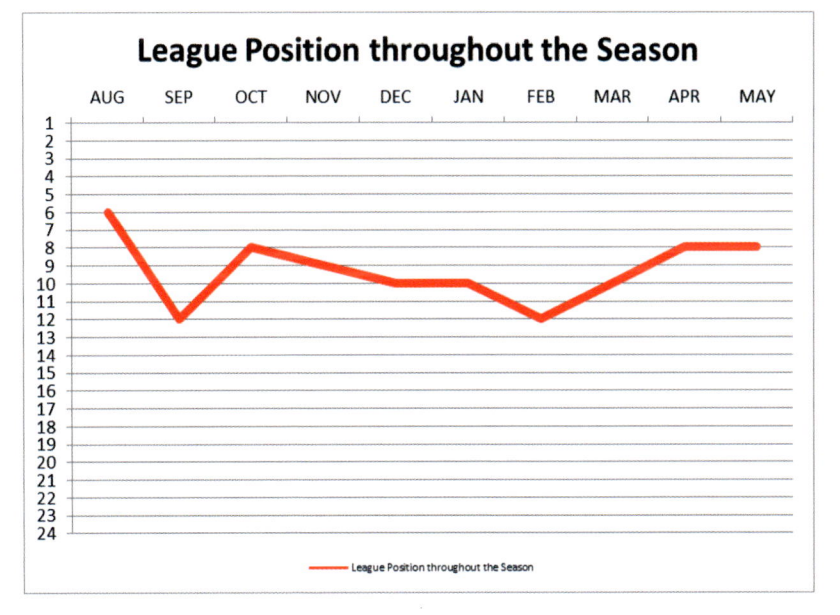

Total Home League Attendances   689,589
Average Home League Attendance   32,837
Highest Home League Attendance   44,029
Lowest Home League Attendance   21,884

League Position throughout the Season

THE BIG ASTON VILLA BOOK OF THE SEVENTIES

1978-79

Sat 19th August   **Wolverhampton Wanderers (H)**
Won 1-0   **Att 43,922**
Gray

Villa and Wolves became locked in a frustrating midfield stalemate, though encouragement could be taken from the commanding defensive display of McNaught and the ever improving Evans. Gary Shelton, making his debut, contributed to Villa's more confident second-half showing and the game was settled by an opportunist Andy Gray goal. The Villa striker, whose 20 goals last term weren't deemed sufficient to gain a place in Scotland's World Cup squad, cast a glance towards the director's box where Scotland boss Ally MacLeod happened to be sitting.

Wed 23rd August   **Tottenham Hotspur (A)**
Won 4-1   **Att 47,892**
Evans A, Gregory, Little, Shelton

All eyes were on White Hart Lane for the debuts of Spurs' new Argentinian World Cup signings, Ardiles and Villa. Greeted by a ticker-tape welcome it was Aston Villa, not Ricardo Villa, that set the pulses racing and Allan Evans opened the scoring with a scorching left-footed drive. Cowans' midfield performance overshadowed the South Americans' and his work led to John Gregory making it 2-0. A Hoddle penalty, that following a foul on Ardiles, gave the Tottenham players short-lived hope before Brian Little added a third on 82 minutes, then Shelton got on the end of a Gidman cross to add insult to injury.

[Right] Gary Shelton rounds off the scoring at White Hart Lane, bagging his first top-flight goal in the process

Andy Gray scored one as Villa led Bolton 3-0 at half time. Boss Saunders kindly let Gray slip away at the interval to open his new nightclub, The Holy City Zoo.

Following the annual Ayresome Park defeat (0-2) Villa put three past QPR, 3-1, then stuttered along without a win in six, although the side did show some resilience – after trailing 1-2 at the interval away to Derby they managed to salvage a point in a 3-3 draw. Whilst in no danger of being sucked into a relegation dogfight the side were in a lowly 14th position.

In typical fashion Villa then beat leaders Liverpool 3-1, followed it up with a gutsy 2-1 win at Carrow Road, before running amok at home to Arsenal. Losing 0-1 at the interval, Villa came out transformed, a Gary Shelton hat-trick and a Dixie Deehan double sent the Gunners crashing to a 5-1 defeat, the first time they'd conceded five since losing at Villa Park in October 1976.

Graham Wilkins' own goal set Villa on their way at home to bottom-placed Chelsea, Kenny Swain then putting the result beyond doubt by adding a second, which put another nail in his old side's coffin. By that stage Villa had hauled themselves up to eighth in the table with games in hand over many of the teams. But that was as high as they would climb. Successive draws were followed by a 0-3 reversal at Anfield to ensure Liverpool won the crown.

West Brom, who would finish third, claimed a 1-0 victory at Villa Park, but at least the claret and blues ended the campaign on a high note away at Maine Road – despite being a goal down, Ron's boys hit three second half goals to win 3-2. Of the three scorers that day, Cropley and Deehan had scored their last for the Villa.

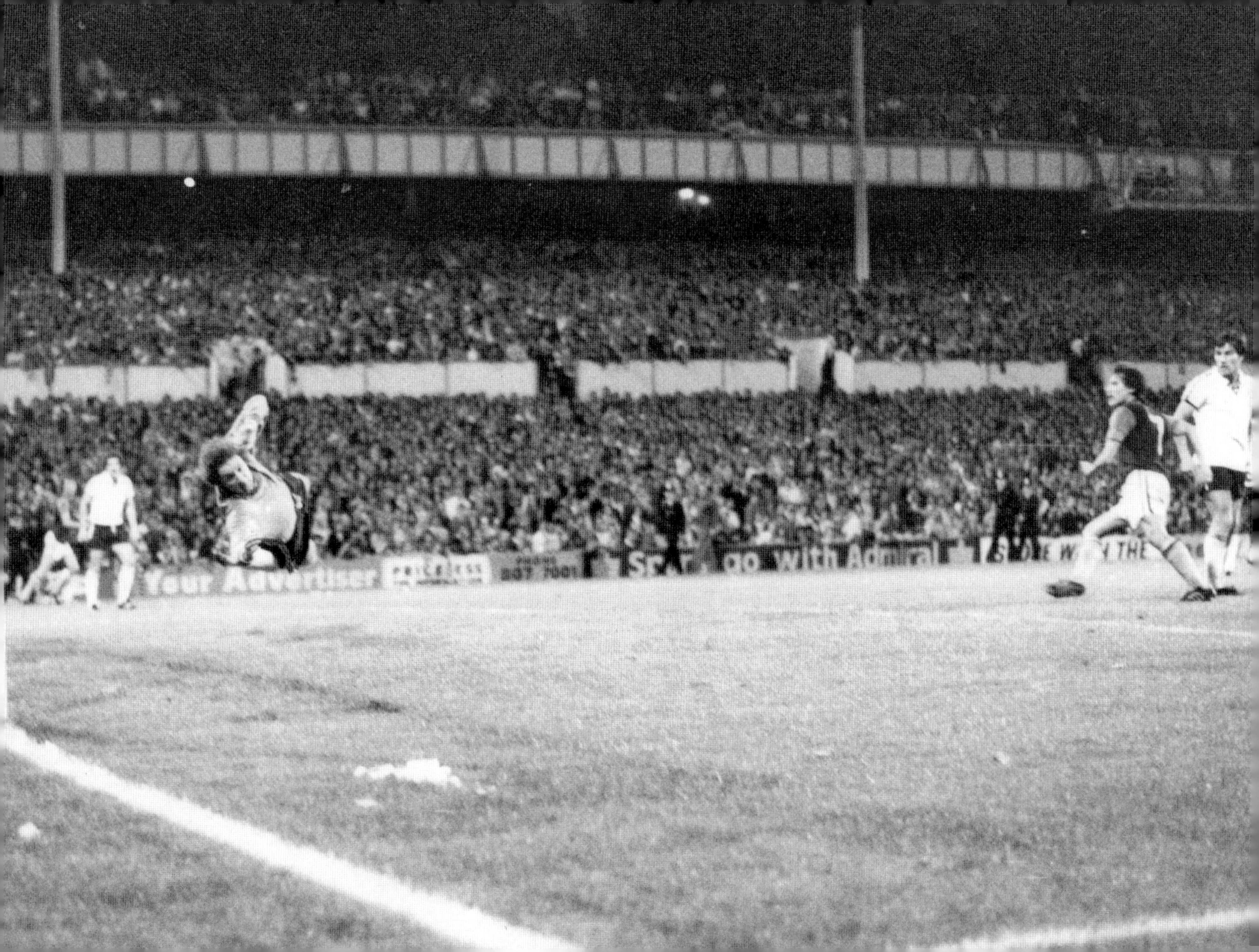
Your Advertiser
go with Admiral

Sat 26th August — Bristol City (A)
Lost 0-1 — Att 23,881

Villa were knocked off the top of the table by an unbeaten Bristol City side who could have won more emphatically. Fortunately for the Villa Jimmy Rimmer was on top of his game and pulled off superb saves from Tom Ritchie and Joe Royle. Villa were missing Andy Gray, although his deputy Gregory didn't have one effort all afternoon. On a positive note Gary Shelton showed enterprise and a certain young apprentice, Gary Shaw, came on as substitute, but Villa would need to be more consistent.

Wed 30th August — Sheffield Wednesday (H) League Cup 2nd
Won 1-0 — Att 31,152
Shelton

Following an outstanding move between Gidman and Cowans, Gary Shelton scored the all-important winner on 26 minutes with a powerful drive. Third Division Wednesday were content to counter Villa's skill with brawn (or you could say Sheffield steel). Villa were denied a certain penalty when everyone, bar the referee, saw Hugh Dowd flatten Gray. Cowans was scythed down early in the second period and Gray was also targeted repeatedly. Ian Porterfield was only the second Owl carded when he chopped down scorer Shelton. Villa couldn't find further goals to punish Jackie Charlton's side, thankfully the one proved enough on the night to progress.

Sat 2nd September — Southampton (H)
Drew 1-1 — Att 34,067
Gray

Villa took a 23rd minute lead when a Gidman free-kick was met by McNaught, his header thundered off the post for Gray to ram home the rebound. Dennis Mortimer created chance after chance and 'Sid' Cowans' numerous corners were a cause for Saints concern – but Villa failed to turn their domination into goal advantage. This came back to bite them when Chris Nicholl, on his return to Villa Park for the first time since his transfer to Southampton, headed home on 44 minutes from an Alan Ball cross.

Sat 9th September — Ipswich Town (A)
Won 2-0 — Att 22,189
Gregory, Gray (pen)

The Ipswich forwards found it impossible to break through Villa's defensive wall of Evans and McNaught, and with Tommy Craig back assisting Mortimer and Cowans, the Villa midfield were also far too strong for the hosts. Villa went in front when Gregory stole in to stroke home Little's pass, whilst Paul Cooper made three fine saves to deny the visitors before the points were made safe in the 90th minute. An Andy Gray curler was heading for the top corner but Mick Mills handled it – Gray took the resulting penalty kick and cheekily rolled it in. Lee Jenkins debuted for Gidman in this very impressive performance which lifted Villa up a place to fifth.

Sat 16th September — Everton (H)
Drew 1-1 — Att 38,636
Craig

Villa were without Gidman (who was stretched off at Ipswich), Smith and Carrodus for the visit of unbeaten Everton – David Evans debuted at right-back. Everton broke the deadlock when a Dave Thomas free-kick on the edge of the box was met by Mickey Walsh. Villa's record signing, Tommy Craig, cancelled out the visitors' lead when he drove in a powerful shot following a short Mortimer free-kick knocked squarely to Cowans, Sid's ball was inch perfect for Tommy to fire home his first for the club. Villa had the chance to win the game at the death but Everton's George Wood somehow managed to get down to Brian Little's low shot. Gary Williams came on as a sub for Shelton.

[Right] Gary Shelton fires in a powerful right-footed drive to put Villa through to the League Cup 3rd round at the expense of Sheffield Wednesday – a club he would later join

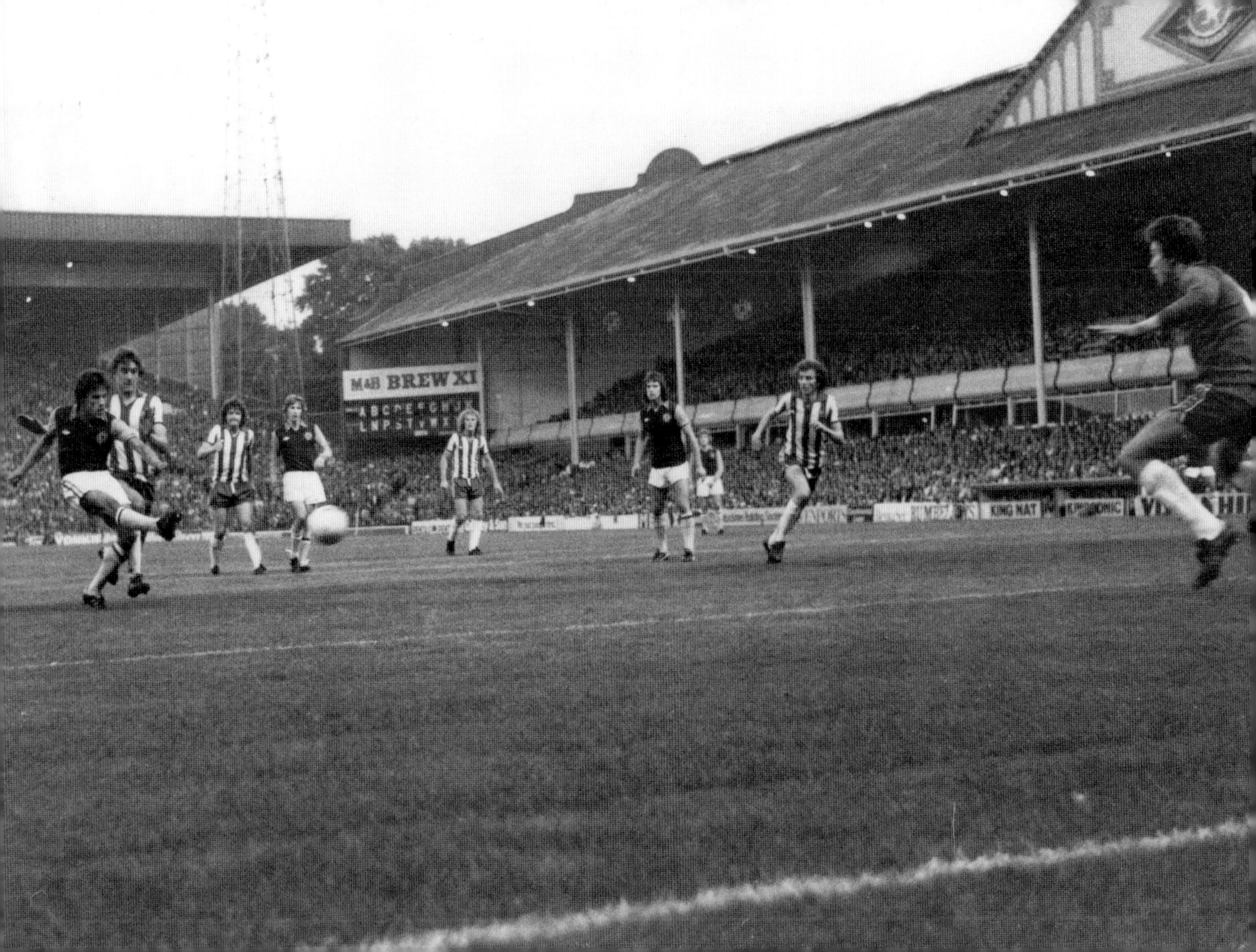
M&B BREW XI
KING NAT

Sat 23rd September   Queens Park Rangers (A)
Lost 0-1   Att 16,410

Lowly QPR rode their luck to earn both points in a game in which Villa had dominated the first period without Phil Parkes having to make a save. Deehan thumped two headers wide, Shelton timed a run to perfection only to see his effort go over the bar, then Mortimer and Little were both wide of the mark. Two minutes into the second-half a wild ball was hoisted into the Villa box, it was mis-hit by a Rangers forward but fell to Rachid Harkouk in acres of space who couldn't miss.

Sat 30th September   Nottingham Forest (H)
Lost 1-2   Att 36,735
Craig (pen)

Gary Williams made his full debut in a game that Villa were territorially superior to a Forest side looking to equal Leeds United's sequence of 34 matches unbeaten and went ahead when Craig converted a spot-kick. The penalty was the result of Larry Lloyd blocking McNaught in the area. Villa's lead lasted all of four second-half minutes when Tony Woodcock headed in at the far post. Pressure on the Villa increased when Cowans left the field of play with a broken foot and the inevitable winner for Clough's men arrived in the closing stages. But it was only thanks to a soft penalty and Ken McNaught was booked for dissent whilst voicing his opinion regarding the incident.

Wed 4th October   Crystal Palace (H) League Cup 3rd round
Drew 1-1   Att 30,690
Little

Villa were initially stunned by Second Division Palace's tactics of swarming forward en masse in search of an early lead, but Villa claimed a half-time advantage when Mortimer's corner kick was headed on by centre-half McNaught for Brian Little to nod home. Villa swept forward and were unfortunate not to double their lead when Deehan was denied by ex-Villan John Burridge. Shelton was crudely tackled in the box – penalty – but Tommy Craig saw his spot-kick saved when 'Budgie' guessed correctly and dived to his left. Palace equalised when they were awarded a fortuitous penalty of their own after a Vince Hillaire shot had bounced off McNaught's hand.

Sat 7th October   Arsenal (A)
Drew 1-1   Att 34,537
Gregory

After a 25 minute barrage, which saw Arsenal take a single goal lead, Villa weathered the storm, with Allan Evans a tower of strength in defence. Mortimer led the revival, and in spite of Brian Little squandering a chance on 80 minutes, the Villa earned a point when John Gregory snatched a goal with six minutes remaining. His first shot had been blocked by Pat Jennings but he followed up to despatch the rebound. The draw lifted Villa two places to tenth.

Tue 10th October   Crystal Palace (A) League Cup 3rd round rply
Drew 0-0   Att 33,155

Palace were eager and inventive, luckily Rimmer was at his acrobatic best to deny Jerry Murphy and Dave Swindlehurst. Like the Villa Park tie – where Ron Saunders had labelled the Palace players 'kickers' – the game was fiercely contested. Villa had the ball in the net twice through Gregory but neither stood (one for off-side and the other Deehan was adjudged to have fouled in the build up). A frustrated Allan Evans received his marching orders for a second bookable offence on 78 minutes, which meant Villa had to contend with 30 minutes of extra-time a man down.

[Right] The ever dependable Allan Evans thwarts an attack from QPR's Stan Bowles at Loftus Road

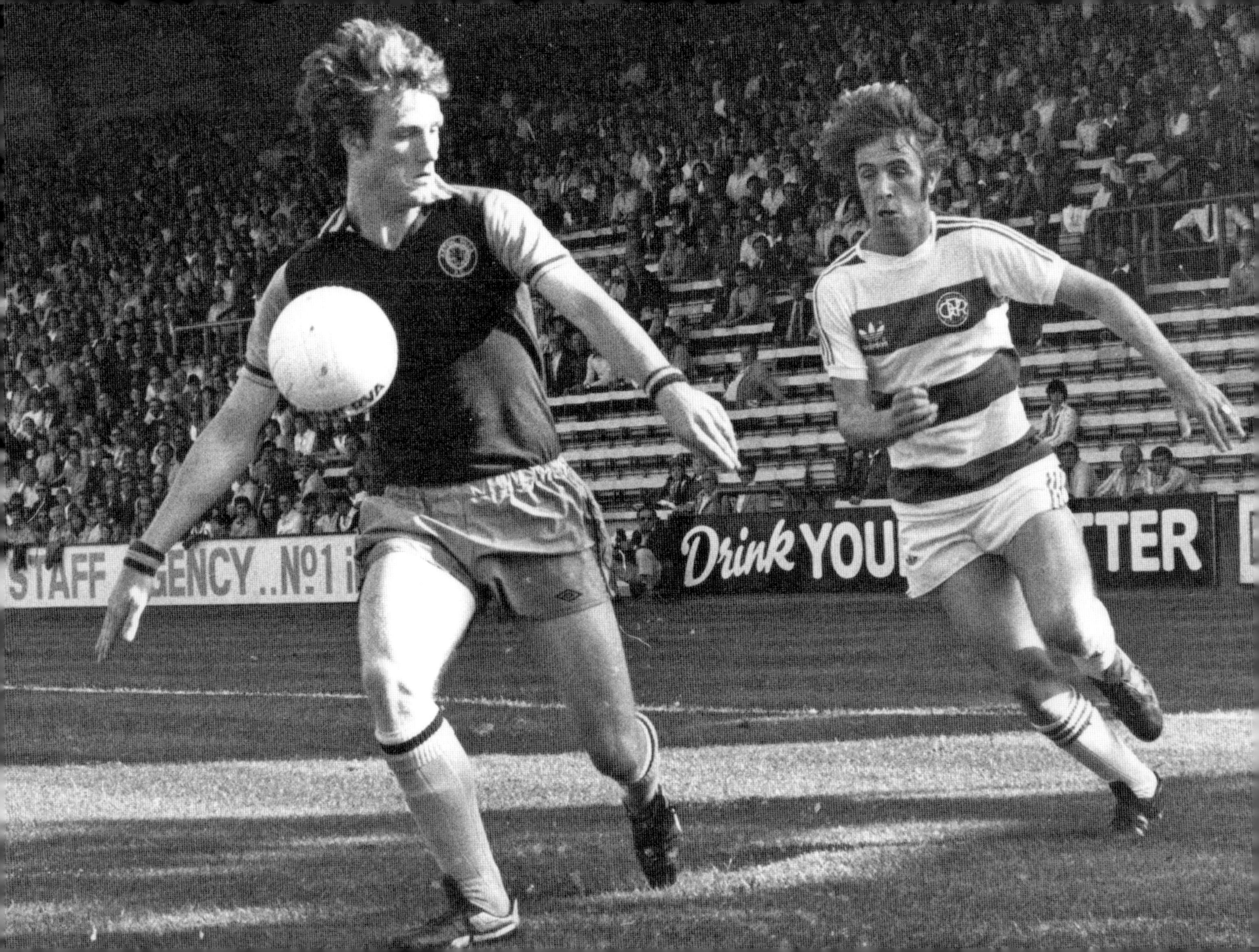
STAFF GENCY ..No1 i
Drink YOU
TTER

THE BIG ASTON VILLA BOOK OF THE SEVENTIES

Sat 14th October   **Manchester United (H)**
Drew 2-2   **Att 36,204**
Gregory 2

Aston Villa and Manchester United served up a full-blooded thriller. The first-half belonged exclusively to the Villa where debutant, Willie Young, revelled on the left flank. Villa Park lit up on 32 minutes when John Gregory latched on to Gray's header to volley the ball home from the edge of the box. Just before the break, Gray set Young away down the wing, the youngster beat Arthur Albiston before putting in an exquisite chip to the near post, Gregory made no mistake and neatly headed over Paddy Roche to make it 2-0. Two second-half goals shocked the Villa, and had Rimmer not pulled off a contender for 'Save of the Season' they could well have ended the match with nothing.

Mon 16th October   **Crystal Palace (Highfield Road)**
   League Cup 3rd round 2nd replay
Won 3-0   **Att 25,455**
Gray 2, Gregory

This tie was settled by half time as, by then, Villa had secured a two-goal cushion with Andy Gray in devastating form. Inspired by Little, Villa were in determined mood. Gray bravely got onto the end of a McNaught flick-on from Craig's corner kick on 19 minutes, then a dozen minutes later, Brian Little's mazy 40-yard run led to John Gregory getting on the scoresheet. Gray bagged his second to make it 3-0 when his sublime volley beat former teammate John Burridge in the Eagles' goal.

Sat 21st October   **Birmingham City (A)**
Won 1-0   **Att 36,145**
Gray

Villa had lost this fixture on the previous five occasions; a statistic that wasn't lost on their claret and blue army. But with Blues rooted to the foot of the table, Villa made sure their bitter rivals extended a sequence of games without victory to 11. Villa took an early lead

[Right] Dennis Mortimer goes to ground against Southampton while ex-Villa captain Chris Nicholl keeps him close

when Mortimer, Gray and Little combined – Gray eventually out-stripping the City defence before lifting the ball over a prone Jim Montgomery from an acute angle. The game was bad tempered and littered with wild kicks and dangerous tackles, which mirrored the volatile atmosphere on the terraces perfectly. Rimmer had a quiet afternoon, which was more than could be said for the referee, who had to stay on his toes to keep control. Two players from each side received bookings as the Villa moved up two places.

Fri 27th October   **Middlesbrough (H)**
Lost 0-2   **Att 32,614**

With a solitary victory on home soil, Villa slumped to their second defeat at B6. Villa began promisingly, with Gregory in particular threatening, but against a side who played with bodies in number behind the ball, Villa started to struggle. 'Boro took the lead on the half hour and doubled their advantage late on… "This is probably the worst performance I've seen at home since I arrived at Villa Park," Saunders blasted after the match.

Sat 4th November   **Manchester City (H)**
Drew 1-1   **Att 32,724**
Deehan

There were very rare glimpses that Villa might be able to shake themselves out of their poor run of form and it was hoped by the club's faithful fans that the reintroduction of Little, Gray and Deehan as a potent three-pronged strike-force might achieve the desired result. A Deehan goal with 'Giddy' supplying the ammunition, sparked the game into life on 62 minutes only for City to draw level through a hotly disputed penalty. Rimmer had an outstanding match, and even after picking up an injury, he made several stunning saves.

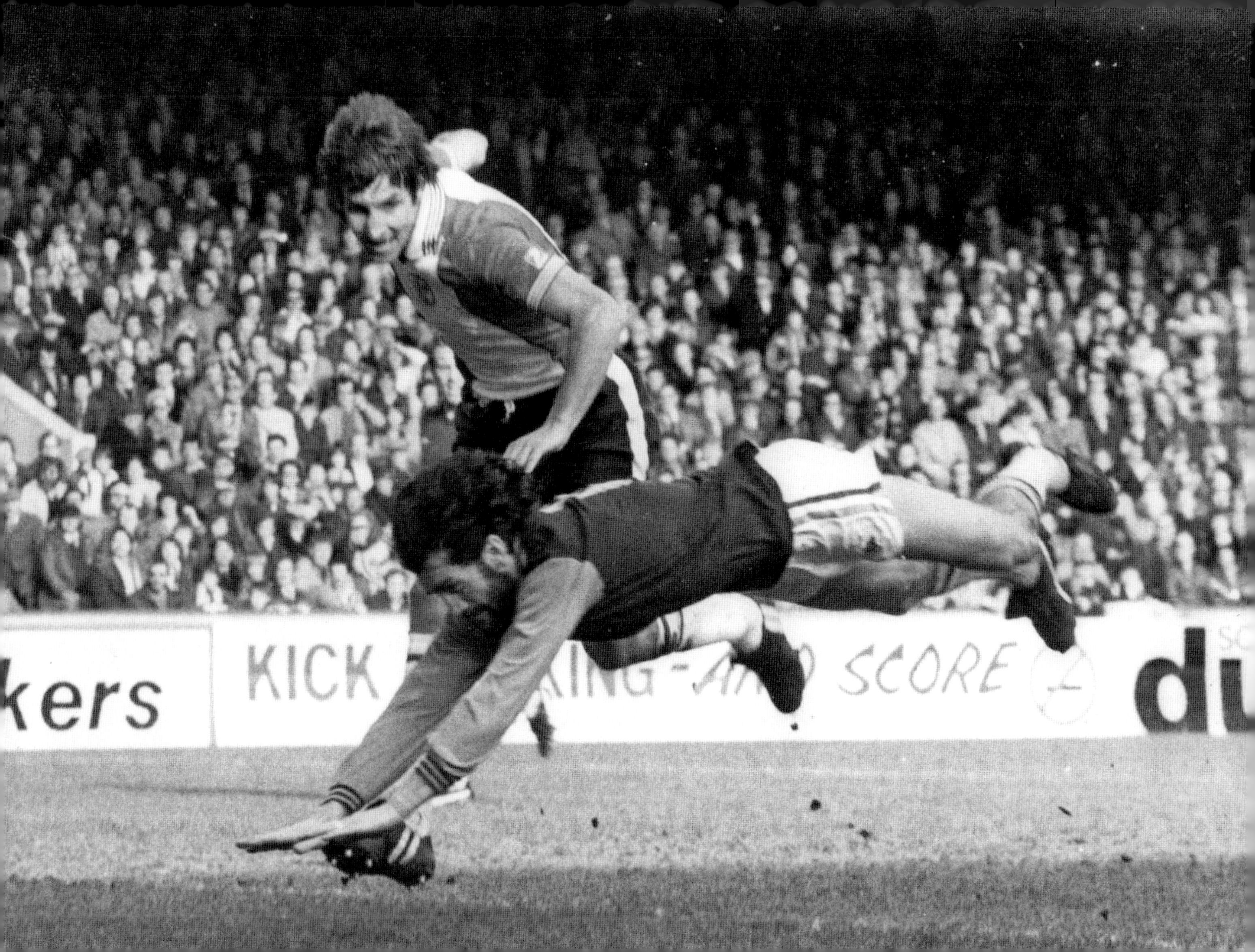
kers
KICK
SCORE

THE BIG ASTON VILLA BOOK OF THE SEVENTIES

Wed 8th November   Luton Town (H) League Cup 4th round
Lost 0-2   Att 32,727

Before Villa had settled into their game, Luton's Mal Donaghy went in over the top on Gray with nine minutes on the clock. Gray had damaged ligaments in his ankle and was off to hospital – he wouldn't play again this side of March. Villa reshuffled, with Cowans the replacement and half time was reached at nil-nil. But it was Luton who took the lead when Bob Hatton found the net for the Second Division side, in fact Villa rarely offered an attacking threat and were stunned when Brian Stein made it 0-2 in the dying seconds. Villa were out yet again at the fourth round stage.

Sat 11th November   Wolverhampton Wanderers (A)
Won 4-0   Att 23,289
Shelton, McNaught, Deehan, Mortimer

Second from bottom Wolves conceded four for the third successive match, but it took the Villa until the 39th minute to open their account when Gary Shelton headed home. Four minutes later they extended the advantage when McNaught steered his shot around the keeper. Wolves then hit a post, and Rimmer made a few bread and butter saves, before Deehan wrapped things up in the 81st minute, then Mortimer added a fourth with minutes remaining. It was Villa's biggest away victory in the League since they'd gained promotion on that glorious night at Hillsborough in April 1975.

Sat 18th November   Bristol City (H)
Won 2-0   Att 27,621
Deehan, Cowans

For the first hour it looked unlikely that Villa, would register their first home win since the opening day victory against Wolves. Not only had City held their own, they went uncomfortably close a few times. But, when England U21 striker 'Dixie' Deehan scored, it transformed the game. Within ten minutes Gordon Cowans had made it 2-0 thanks to an unstoppable shot from 25-yards out. City's Joe Royle was given his marching orders following a clash with Allan Evans.

[Right] Andy Gray scores from the penalty spot as Villa record their first ever win at Portman Road – Villa beat Ipswich 2-0

Tue 21st November   Southampton (A)
Lost 0-2   Att 20,616

Ivor Linton retained his place following a fine display the previous weekend, however, his forward partnership with Deehan didn't come off at The Dell. It was also a night when the reliable Evans and McNaught had a bit of a nightmare. Villa were killed off with two goals within a minute, which came midway through the first half. It summed up the Villan's night when Deehan rounded the keeper late on only to see his shot go a whisker wide of the upright.

Sat 25th November   West Bromwich Albion (A)
Drew 1-1   Att 35,166
Evans A

Third placed Albion must have expected both points from what turned out to be an exciting and full-blooded affair. The first half was pretty even, separated by a West Brom goal that came from the penalty spot after Tommy Craig had upended Brendon Batson – 'Bomber' Brown made no mistake. Villa came out after the break in mean mood and were rewarded in the 64th minute when Allan Evans flew through flying boots and bodies to get his head on a Cowans in-swinging corner. The industrious Mortimer had been Villa's most creative player.

Sat 9th December   Chelsea (A)
Won 1-0   Att 19,636
Evans A

Top-flight strugglers Chelsea looked a beaten side long before Villa took the lead in controversial style. John Gidman flighted a free-kick that was headed on by Gary Shaw for Evans to apply the finishing touch from, what Chelsea believed, to be an off-side position. Both Shaw and Gregory should have added to the score. The biggest cheer in this one-sided encounter was the introduction of Alex Cropley eight minutes from time, marking his first game in over a year.

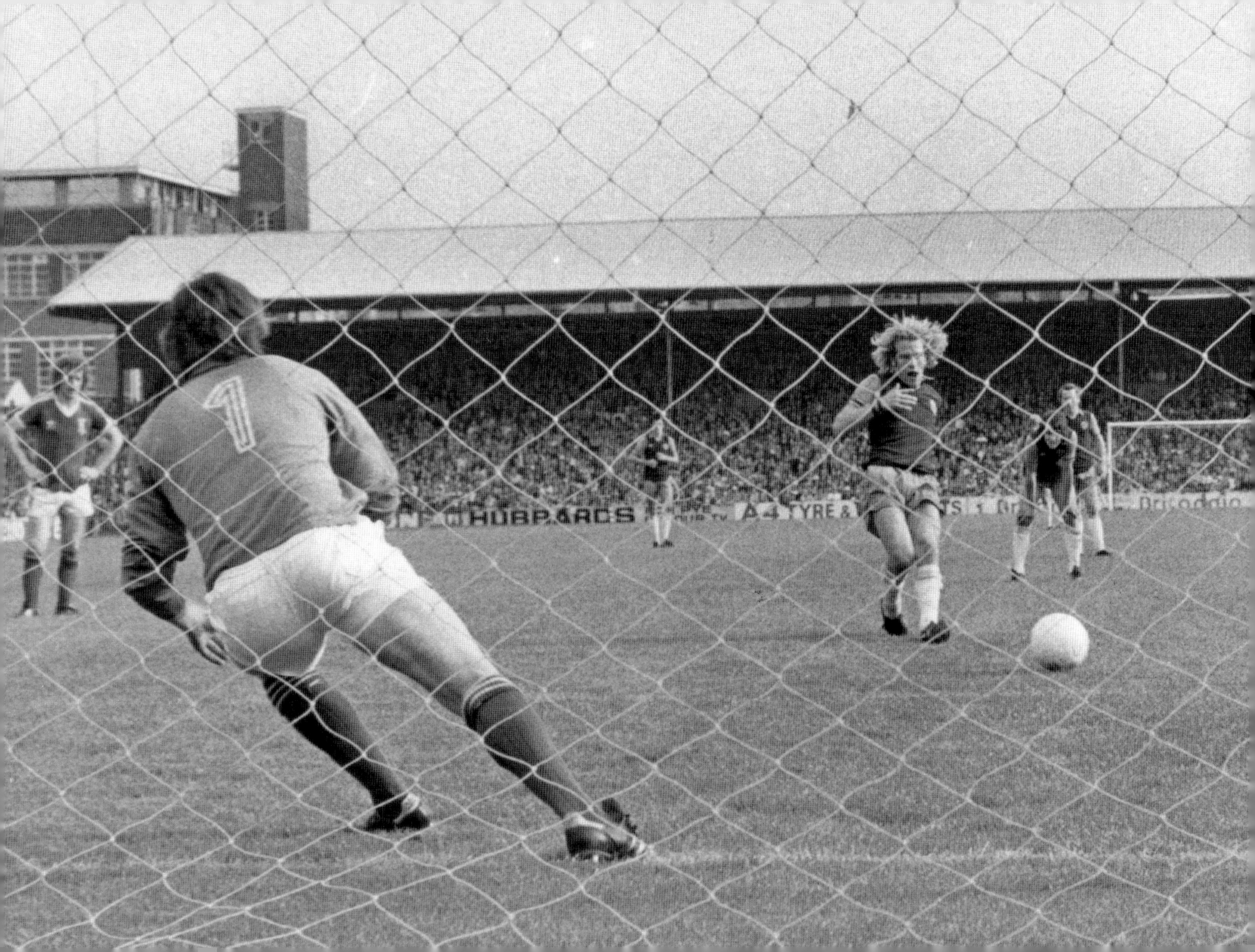
TYRE &

THE BIG ASTON VILLA BOOK OF THE SEVENTIES

Sat 16th December   **Norwich City (H)**
Drew 1-1   **Att 26,228**
Own goal

New boy, Kenny Swain, started the first of many games in what would be a long and distinguished Villa career. Norwich took an unfair lead very much against the run of play. Gidman was impeded, the linesman raised his flag, only to drop it when he couldn't catch the referee's eye. The Villa players expected the whistle to blow as the ball came over, but Norwich turned the ball into the net. The goal stood. Villa stormed forward with Swain, Gregory, Cowans and Deehan all denied by an acrobatic Kevin Keelan, however, the Canaries custodian was finally beaten when a shot from Mortimer deflected off Mick McGuire to give the Villa a well deserved point.

Sat 23rd December   **Derby County (A)**
Drew 0-0   **Att 20,109**

Villa, sitting in tenth, were four places above the Rams. Villa's Kenny Swain thought he'd scored his first for his new club when he got on the end of a Deehan cross – the ball was swept over the line and it rolled under the side-netting then onto the track. The referee consulted with a linesman and, bizarrely, awarded Derby a free-kick. The Rams did more of the attacking but came up against an outstanding Allan Evans. Villa were left reflecting a gritty performance and a share of the spoils.

Tue 26th December   **Leeds United (H)**
Drew 2-2   **Att 40,973**
Gregory 2

Villa's three-pronged attack of Swain, Gregory and Deehan were given excellent service by a midfield consisting of Craig, Cropley and Mortimer. Villa were two-up and looked out of sight before the half hour with Gregory getting them both. His first, following an intelligent run from Swain, his second arriving six minutes later when 'Giddy' flighted in a long centre that the keeper punched clear. It fell to Deehan, who knocked it back for Gregory to drill home. The second half was as dramatic as it was disappointing for the Villa faithful. Eddie Gray reduced Villa's two-goal cushion after Tony Currie was given too much space, then, with ten minutes remaining, Brian Flynn and Frankie Gray combined for brother Eddie to knock the ball past Rimmer to make it 2-2.

Wed 10th January   **Nottingham Forest (A) FA Cup 3rd round**
Lost 0-2   **Att 29,550**

For the second successive season it was Brian Clough's side that stood in the way of Saunders Villa team and a cup run and Ron's boys couldn't have asked for a tougher tie. Not only were Forest reigning champions, they were also unbeaten thus far on the banks of the Trent and looking good to retain the title. Villa, playing on a greasy pitch with an uneven bounce, were able to reach half-time without conceding, but Rimmer had been called upon to stop Woodcock, while at the other end, Peter Shilton had been fortunate to deny Deehan. Villa also had claims for a penalty turned down when Cowans was blocked. But it was Forest who broke the deadlock when David Needham swept home from eight yards, before another Villa appeal was waved away when Viv Anderson handled. Their misery continued when a Woodcock shot took a wicked deflection to make it 2-0 to Forest and John Deehan was sent off with two minutes remaining.

Wed 31st January   **Everton (A)**
Drew 1-1   **Att 29,079**
Shelton

Considering the Goodison Park pitch had been cleared of snow, it was in great shape. Villa were now without the suspended Deehan to add to the long term injured of Gray, Carrodus and Little. Allan Evans saw a 25-yarder turned for a corner in a goalless first half. Villa stunned Everton, who could go top with a win, by taking a lead when Gary Shelton was left unmarked to head home. Swain nearly added a second before the Toffees pulled out a fortunate equaliser deep into injury time to keep their unbeaten home record intact.

Sat 24th February   Manchester United (A)
Drew 1-1   Att 44,437
Swain

Joe Ward, signed from Clyde in December, made his long-awaited debut, due to several weeks' postponements due to the bad weather, and an ever growing injury list. The Villa dominated for long periods. Mortimer and Swain continually caused United problems. The pair combined well in the 58th minute, Swain ran onto Mortimer's through ball, cleverly feinting past Brian Greenhoff, before sliding the ball wide of Gary Bailey who'd advanced from his goal. One-nil to the Villa. Gregory then bought down Sammy McIlroy, and Jimmy Greenhoff made no mistake from the spot. Until then, United had looked set to lose their fourth successive match at Old Trafford.

Sat 3rd March   Birmingham City (H)
Won 1-0   Att 42,419
Cowans

After a two-month absence from playing at home due to adverse weather conditions, Villa welcomed back Brian Little and Andy Gray (having missed nine and ten games respectively). Their lack of match fitness was apparent. The game was highly competitive but there was little to choose between the sides. But with ten minutes remaining Villa broke the deadlock to ensure Blues stayed rooted to the foot of the table. A left-wing cross from Swain was half cleared and Cowans swept it into the net. 'Sid' was the toast of Birmingham, his second goal of the season giving Villa not only the bragging rights, but a 'double' over the 'old enemy' for the first time in 14 years.

Wed 7th March   Bolton Wanderers (H)
Won 3-0   Att 28,053
Gray, Swain, own goal

A huge cheer rang out around Villa Park when it was announced the tenacious Alex Cropley was playing, his first start in 15 months. Villa were too much for the previous season's Division Two champions, even without injured skipper Mortimer. Villa opened the scoring on 17 minutes through Andy Gray, Kenny Swain added a second on the half hour, before Bolton's centre-half Paul Jones rose above Gray to nod Cowans corner kick into his own net. With Villa 3-0 up at half time Saunders showed his softer side when he replaced Gray with Deehan, allowing Andy to dash off and officially open his new night club the Holy City Zoo.

Sat 10th March   Middlesbrough (A)
Lost 0-2   Att 16,558

Villa had lost only once in their last 13 games but were without McNaught, Gregory and Mortimer for the Ayresome Park encounter. Boro had lost their last two on home soil, however, the home side dominated the goalless first 45 minutes. Allan Evans had performed magnificently in defence, but the midfield had struggled to supply Gray and Little up front. Villa stormed out of the blocks for the second half and forced five corners in as many minutes, but all were sadly to no avail. Middlesbrough then hit Villa with two goals in the space of 90 seconds to seal the victory.

Tue 20th March   Queens Park Rangers (H)
Won 3-1   Att 24,310
Evans A, Gidman (pen), Mortimer

Villa didn't need to find top gear against a Rangers side destined for the drop. Villa were always in charge and went in front on 34 minutes when a Gary Williams free-kick was chipped on by Gregory – Allan Evans, who'd made a determined run, connected to rifle in his fourth of the campaign. Villa had to wait until the 72nd minute to add to the scoreline; substitute Ivor Linton, on for Little, was hauled down in the box and Gidman cooly converted the spot kick. Captain Mortimer, back after missing the last two, struck a sweet left-footed volley with a minute to go to make it 3-0. Rangers' Clive Allen then hit a consolation in injury time.

THE BIG ASTON VILLA BOOK OF THE SEVENTIES

Sat 24th March   **Tottenham Hotspur (H) Lost 2-3**
Att 35,486
Gidman (pen), Gray

Spurs were looking the more dangerous throughout the first half, but it was Villa who opened the scoring when, for the second successive match, Gidman fired home from the penalty spot. Gray then added a second on the stroke of half time with a superb left-footed volley. The points looked secure at that stage, but the game was turned on its head in a crazy six-minute spell. Hoddle fired in-off the post with 12 minutes remaining, before Jones grabbed an equaliser in the 82nd minute, with Hoddle inflicting the killer blow when he noticed Rimmer off his line and chipped home a winner.

Wed 28th March   **Coventry City (H)**
Drew 1-1   **Att 25,670**
Evans A

City were two points ahead of Villa, but they'd played five games more. The driving rain and blustery conditions contributed to a scrappy game in which Villa took the lead four minutes after the break – Allan Evans heading home from a Cowans corner. Dennis Mortimer worked tirelessly against his old club, but Villa's front two of Gray and Little failed to make any impact against a composed and compact Coventry who levelled in the 72nd minute when a clever pass by ex-Villan Bobby McDonald was met by their promising 19-year old striker Garry Thompson (who would later play for Villa).

Wed 4th April   **Nottingham Forest (A)**
Lost 0-4   **Att 27,056**

Clough's men, still unbeaten at home, were looking to retain their title, so it was a surprise that Villa were only one down at the interval – an own goal by Evans. In what was described as Villa's 'worst performance' under Ron Saunders tenure, Villa capitulated in the second period. Forest were two up four minutes into the second half, bagged number three six minutes later then future Villa manager, Martin O'Neill, added a fourth on 71 minutes.

[Right] Brian Little shields the ball during the encounter at Highfield Road. Both Villa and Coventry City had to settle for a point in the 1-1 draw

Sat 7th April   **Coventry City (A)**
Drew 1-1   **Att 23,668**
Deehan

With Gray out injured 'Dixie' Deehan made his first start of the year. Coventry took the lead on 21 minutes with their first real attack of the afternoon. Equally damaging for the claret and blue was the dismissal of Evans for headbutting fellow Scot Tommy Hutchinson. Rimmer was at his best to deny Bobby McDonald extending their lead with a headed goal. Inspirational skipper Mortimer never gave up searching for an equaliser and Alex Cropley, clearly not match fit, battled manfully. But it was against the run of play that Villa levelled, Deehan getting on the end of a McNaught clearance. With honours even the Sky Blues remained three points ahead of the Villa.

Wed 11th April   **Derby County (H)**
Drew 3-3   **Att 21,884**
Cowans 2, Gidman (pen)

Evans and Gregory were out, Brendan Ormsby and Colin Gibson were in. Villa were rocked when captain Mortimer had to be subbed on seven minutes after a bursting a blood vessel in his calf, but Gordon Cowans gave Villa's lowest crowd of the season something to cheer when he hooked the ball home in the 26th minute after Little had turned his marker to square the ball. Derby were level three minutes later and made it 1-2 on the stroke of half time. A Gidman spot kick, following a hand ball, made it 2-2 before Cowans fired home in spectacular fashion to regain Villa's lead. Debutant defender Gibson was desperately unlucky when he deflected a late corner into his own net and beyond an animated Rimmer.

208

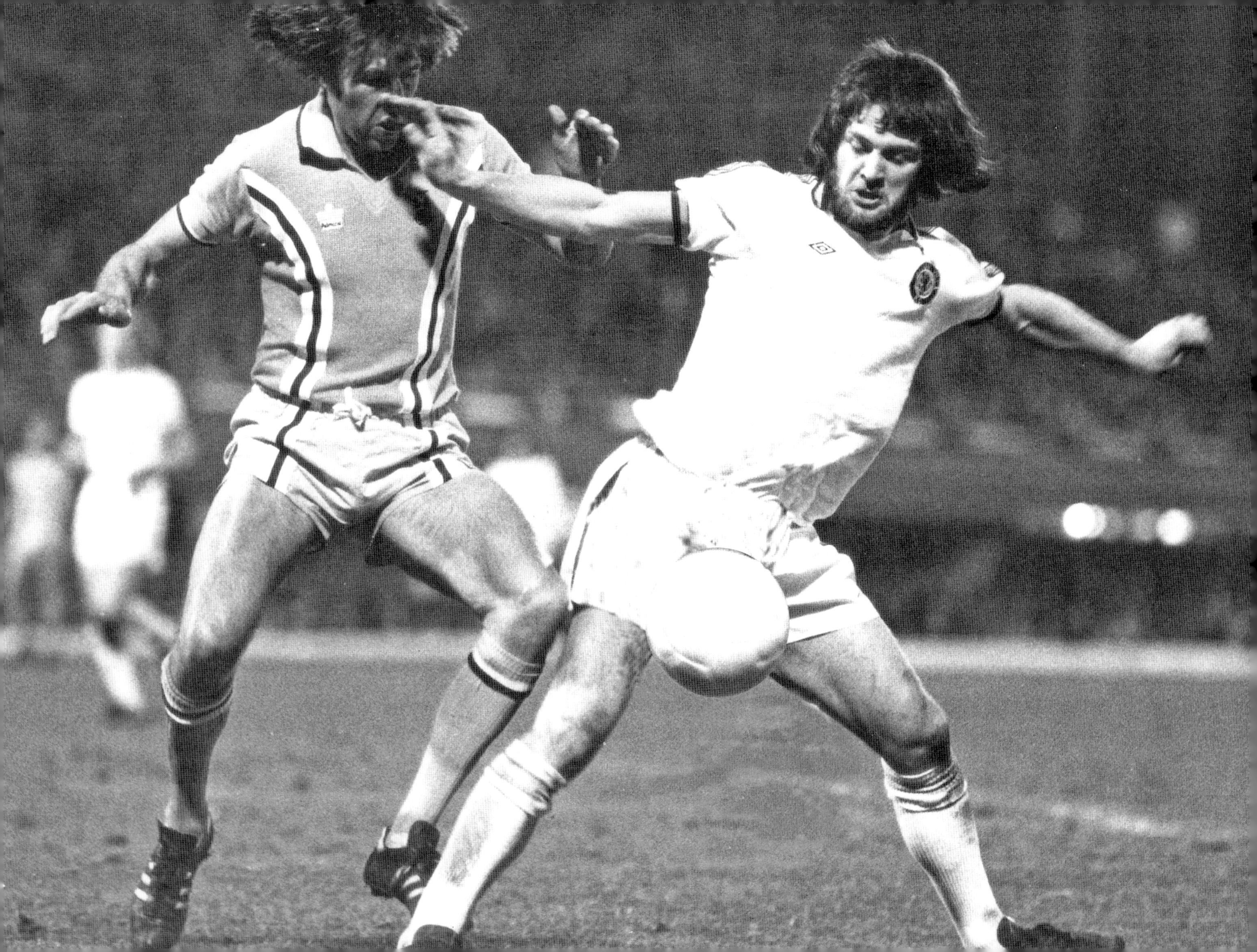

THE BIG ASTON VILLA BOOK OF THE SEVENTIES

Sat 14th April   **Leeds United (A)**
Lost 0-1   **Att 24,281**

Villa were finally beaten by a set piece in this highly entertaining match. The visitors had started well with Cowans pulling the strings in midfield. Deehan and Little had half chances on the counter-attack, while at the other end, the defence was marshalled well – Evans was back from suspension alongside McNaught who was equally dominating. A momentary lapse on 27 minutes let Paul Hart head home from a right-sided corner to put Leeds ahead. Villa tried to salvage something from the game and threw Allan Evans up front late on. The centre-half connected with a few crosses and went close, but Villa couldn't muster a goal to take a share of the points. They were now without a win in six.

Mon 16th April   **Liverpool (H)**
Won 3-1   **Att 44,029**
Evans A, own goal, Deehan

Liverpool came into the game with five wins under their belts and a six point cushion at the top. With Gray and Little out, Ron Saunders played Evans as a forward and it paid dividends when the big defender gave Villa a surprise lead on 33 minutes, knocking the ball in after Ray Clemence had spilled a half-hit shot from Cowans. Nine minutes later Villa had doubled their lead: Swain centred for Evans, his looping header deflected off Phil Thompson. However, Liverpool hit back with a vengeance and reduced the arrears only for Villa to wrap it up on 84 minutes in a move that was started by Gidman and finished by Deehan, with the assistance of Swain and Evans.

Sat 21st April   **Norwich City (A)**
Won 2-1   **Att 13,421**
Shelton, Cropley

With Evans out, Saunders reshuffled with Gregory playing deeper at centre-half and Gary Shelton taking the midfield berth. It was Shelton who opened the scoring when he prodded home from ten yards on 13 minutes, but Norwich were back in it on the half hour when Justin Fashanu scored. Villa were rocked further when McNaught limped out of the action, Deehan taking his place, which allowed sub Linton to create havoc further up field. Cropley, now with much needed match fitness under his belt, fired the winner, his first since his horrendous leg break. This was a valuable victory and only the club's second win at Carrow Road in their last 13 attempts.

Wed 25th April   **Arsenal (H)**
Won 5-1   **Att 26,168**
Shelton 3 (1 pen), Deehan 2

Villa conceded a sloppy goal only 80 seconds in against the FA Cup finalists, but came back with a vengeance, despite still trailing at the interval. Shelton evened the game just four minutes into the second half with a great opportunist goal. Then, two minutes later, he was at it again by steering home a header from Mortimer's corner kick. A Deehan header made it 3-1 before 'Dixie' got his second, which is regarded as one of the best goals ever seen at B6 – an unstoppable bullet of a drive from 25-yards out. Cowans was then hauled down in the box, which allowed Shelton to secure his hat-trick and the match ball from the resulting spot kick. A handsome victory indeed.

Sat 28th April   **Chelsea (H)**
Won 2-1   **Att 29,219**
Own goal, Swain

For the second time in four days Villa trooped off losing at the break, this time against a Chelsea side who were already guaranteed Second Division football following season. The Londoners had gone ahead on six minutes when an uncharacteristic Gregory mistake let Tommy Langley in. It then took until the 68th minute for Villa to hit the comeback trail, Graham Wilkins, under pressure from Shelton, putting into his own net. The goal inspired the Villa. Cropley went close when he struck the bar, before the match-winner arrived – Cowans played the ball to Kenny Swain on the edge of the area who beat his marker with a neat body swerve before cracking a fierce shot into the roof of the net. That made it four wins on the bounce.

Wed 2nd May   **Ipswich Town (H)**
Drew 2-2   **Att 26,636**
Swain, Deehan

A win would see the Villa leapfrog Bobby Robson's Ipswich up to seventh with the possibility of UEFA qualification on the horizon. This was very much on the cards after Kenny Swain had fired Villa into an eighth minute lead, with Deehan doubling the advantage five minutes later. Arnold Muhren then pulled one back moments after Shelton had gone close to making it 3-0. Town, with 14 points from a possible 16 before the match, warranted respect and it was no shock when Muhren's second of the evening levelled things up, the Dutchman latching onto an Evans half-clearance to volley beyond Jimmy Rimmer.

Sat 5th May   **Bolton Wanderers (A)**
Drew 0-0   **Att 17,394**

Burnden Park hadn't been a happy hunting ground for the Villa following just three wins and 14 losses since the war. Not surprisingly they seemed cautious, playing a waiting game. Defensively Villa were strong (McNaught was back) and Bolton were restricted to a handful of chances, but as the game wore on Villa became more creative. Mortimer had a legitimate goal chalked off on the half-hour when he chipped the keeper only for Deehan to be deemed as standing offside. Both full-backs, Gidman and Gibson, overlapped energetically, threatening to provide the attack with a breakthrough but when Kenny 'Mac' saw his header cleared off the line the writing was on the wall and a point was all they'd earn for their troubles.

Tue 8th May   **Liverpool (A)**
Lost 0-3   **Att 50,576**

Falling behind within a minute, Villa fans feared the worst, and although Villa had a promising spell midway through the first half, they went further behind when conceding to Kenny Dalglish on 37 minutes. Terry McDermott added number three, before Cowans went off concussed, his face coming off second best to Ray Kennedy's elbow and an x-ray after the matched confirmed a fractured cheekbone. Three-nil was becoming a familiar scoreline, Villa had lost by the same score to the Reds in the last four seasons.

Fri 11th May   **West Bromwich Albion (H)**
Lost 0-1   **Att 35,991**

Albion took a 15th minute lead, and luckily for Villa, Laurie Cunningham, Brown and Regis all squandered easy chances to put the result beyond doubt. Villa had more of the possession and were unfortunate when Allan Evans had to go off after suffering a badly gashed forehead on 35 minutes. Villa played their best football early in the second half, and had it not been for Tony Godden in the Albion goal, Villa would have surely taken a point from the game.

Tue 15th May   **Manchester City (A)**
Won 3-2   **Att 30,028**
Cropley, Mortimer, Deehan

Villa were made to fight hard all the way after City's Polish international, Kazimierz Deyna, scored in the fourth minute with what was described as a 'sloppy' goal. Villa had several chances to get back into the match before the break, but couldn't tuck any of them away. 'Dixie' Deehan missed a sitter, before Cropley had the Villa level five minutes into the second half with a rare header. But City were back in front moments later. Dennis Mortimer added Villa's second after a fine move involving Cropley and Swain to make it 2-2, and within four minutes of the leveller, took the lead when Colin Gibson's cross was met by Deehan who played a one-two with Kenny Swain before applying the finishing touch, his ninth of the campaign.

THE BIG ASTON VILLA BOOK OF THE SEVENTIES

PRE-SEASON

AUGUST

- Villa Park had undergone a £250,000 facelift including a new playing surface and the Holte End had segregation fencing installed.
- Harry Kartz was unanimously elected chairman of Aston Villa, succeeding Sir William Dugdale.
- For the third successive season Villa started with a victory.
- Villa achieved their biggest ever win at White Hart Lane on the evening Spurs showed off their new Argentinean World Cup stars, Osvaldo Ardiles and Ricardo Villa.
- Young Villa apprentice, Gary Shaw, made a substitute's appearance at Ashton Gate.

SEPTEMBER

- Keith Leonard, who retired early through injury, had a testimonial at Villa Park against an Aston Villa 1974/75 XI.
- It was announced that John Robson's career was finished due to the debilitating Multiple Sclerosis.
- Gordon Cowans broke a bone in his foot during the 1-2 defeat at home to Nottingham Forest.
- Gordon Smith underwent cartilage surgery.
- Andy Gray scored in Scotland's 2-3 European Championship defeat in Vienna.

OCTOBER

- Due to injuries, Villa had already used 18 players, with youngsters Gary Shelton, David Evans, Gary Shaw, Lee Jenkins and Gary Williams all making first-team debuts.
- Willie Young had a fine debut in the Villa Park clash with Manchester United, which ended 2-2. Young would only play for the first-team twice more.
- Frank Carrodus played his last game for the Villa in the League Cup 2nd replay versus Crystal Palace.
- Alex Cropley, on the comeback trail following his broken leg horror, featured in John Robson's Testimonial against an International XI at Villa Park.

NOVEMBER

- Andy Gray was selected for Scotland's European Championship clash with Norway.
- A bitter sweet month for Leighton Phillips, he captained Wales for the first time (his 38th cap) as they hammered Malta 7-0 in a European qualifier – four days later he played his last game for Villa in the home draw with Manchester City.
- Gary Shaw, Lee Jenkins and Brendan Ormsby were selected for the England Youth squad to play in Monaco. In the space of 13 days, Gary collected four Youth international caps and made his full Villa debut.
- John Gidman and Dennis Mortimer won 'B' caps in Czechoslovakia.

DECEMBER

- The 1-0 win at Stamford Bridge was Gordon Smith's last appearance in the claret and blue. Cropley made a return in the same match albeit as a late sub. His first action for a year.
- Kenny Swain and Joe Ward arrived from Chelsea and Clyde respectively.
- Swain made his debut in the 1-1 draw with Norwich City.
- Villa remained unbeaten during the month, a win was followed by three straight draws.

JANUARY

- Gary Shaw, a star of the future, signed his first full professional contract. Lee Jenkins also signed the same day.
- Due to the adverse weather conditions, the Villa played only one league game during the month, away to Everton on the last day. after games at Liverpool and home to Ipswich fell victim to the freeze.
- Villa were knocked out of the FA Cup at the first hurdle for the second consecutive season.

FEBRUARY

- Work got under way for the club's Sports Hall on the Serpentine Ground.
- Joe Ward debuted in the Manchester United match – his Old Trafford run out was the only appearance of the season.
- Gordon Cowans won his first England U21 cap in a 1-0 victory versus Wales at Swansea.

MARCH

- Due to the appalling weather the Birmingham City fixture was the first game at Villa Park in the new calendar year.
- Boss Saunders showed his soft side when he excused Andy Gray at half time to allow the striker to go and open his new night club. Villa were leading 3-0 at the break against Bolton Wanderers.
- John Gidman converted his first penalty for Villa in the QPR match at Villa Park. He repeated the feat just four days later against Tottenham Hotspur.

APRIL

- Tommy Craig left for Swansea after only 32 appearances (2 goals).
- Brendan Ormsby made his first full start, stadning in for Allan Evans in the 3-3 draw with Derby County. Ormsby's only other game time was from the bench against Palace in the League Cup.
- Starting with a fine 3-1 win at home to eventual champions Liverpool, Villa went on to win four games on the bounce.
- Villa hit five against Arsenal after trailing 0-1 at the interval.
- Villa played eight games in the month due to the inactivity of an icy January and February.

MAY

- John Gregory played his last game for Villa in the 3-2 win at Maine Road after appearing in every outfield position for the club and wearing every shirt, numbered 2-11, in the season with the exception of No 5, which he wore in the 1977/78 campaign.
- John Deehan was called up to the England U21 squad.
- Villa's youngsters beat Leicester City 5-1 on aggregate (4-0 & 1-1) to land the Southern Junior Floodlit Cup.
- With so many injuries, Villa had used 26 players during the season.

[Right] Ray Stewart's penalty, in the 88th minute in the FA Cup 6th round, puts paid to what many believed was Aston Villa's year to lift the famous trophy. Mortimer, Cowans and Gibson can only look on helplessly

1979-80

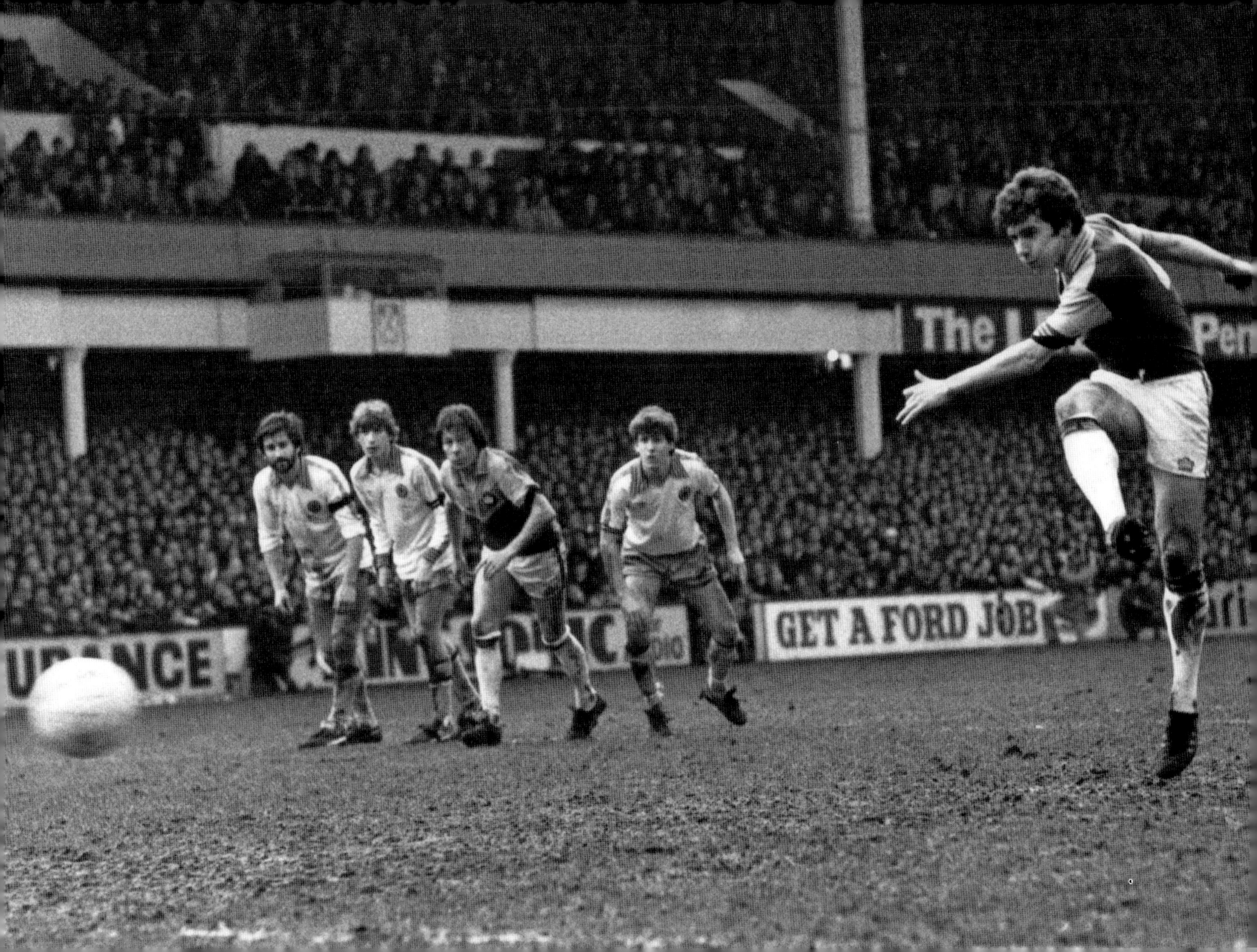
GET A FORD JOB
URANCE

THE BIG ASTON VILLA BOOK OF THE SEVENTIES

[Back Row] Ken McNaught, Jimmy Rimmer, Brendan Ormsby, Nigel Spink, Allan Evans, Gary Shelton **[MiddleRow]** George Armstrong (Coach), Gordon Cowans, Pat Heard, Des Bremner, Gary Williams, Brian Little, Colin Gibson, Mike Pejic **[Front Row]** Tony Morley, Alex Cropley, Kenny Swain, David Geddis, Ron Saunders (Manager), Dennis Mortimer, Frank Carrodus, Gary Shaw

Football League	Division One
Manager	Ron Saunders
Asst. Manager/Coach	Roy McLaren / George Armstrong
Physio	Peter Downes / Jim Williams
Captain	Dennis Mortimer
Final Position	Seventh
FA Cup	Sixth Round
League Cup	Third Round
Leading Goalscorer (all competitions)	Gary Shaw – 12 goals

The closed season rumours weren't particular encouraging, with the club's flamboyant, international pair of Gidman and Gray, both reportedly unhappy and wanting to leave Villa. Better news for supporters was the collapse of Brian Little's transfer to arch rivals Birmingham City, albeit due to fitness doubts.

Meanwhile a young Tony Morley had arrived from Burnley, right footed but operating on the left, he was quick with good feet and a striker, Terry Donovan, landed from Grimsby Town.

A draw on opening day at Bolton was followed by a solid 2-1 victory at home to Brighton – the only blot on the copy book was Alex Cropley breaking his ankle.

However, losing to very mediocre Bristol City and Palace during a winless six match sequence lessened fans expectancy levels considerably and despite Villa failing to find the net in five of them, they allowed the sale of John Deehan to West Brom, and Andy Gray headed to Molineux for a fee in excess of a million pounds. Mike Pejic, Des Bremner and David Geddis were drafted in.

It took a penalty shoot-out to dispose of Third Division Colchester United in the League Cup 2nd round, United actually having won the second-leg 2-0 at Villa Park, then John Gidman was next out the door, off to Everton.

A strange sequence of results then materialised with Villa winning then drawing four times on the bounce – Dennis Mortimer scored in all four wins, Allan Evans in three of them. Regardless, Villa had moved up ten places to ninth.

Villa then lost to high-flying Liverpool, enjoyed a great win at White

continued >>>

ASTON VILLA NEWS & RECORD
OFFICIAL MATCHDAY MAGAZINE — PRICE 30p

Football League Division One • Volume No. 37 • Programme No. 18
SATURDAY 1st MARCH 1980 • KICK-OFF: 3.00pm

ASTON VILLA v DERBY COUNTY

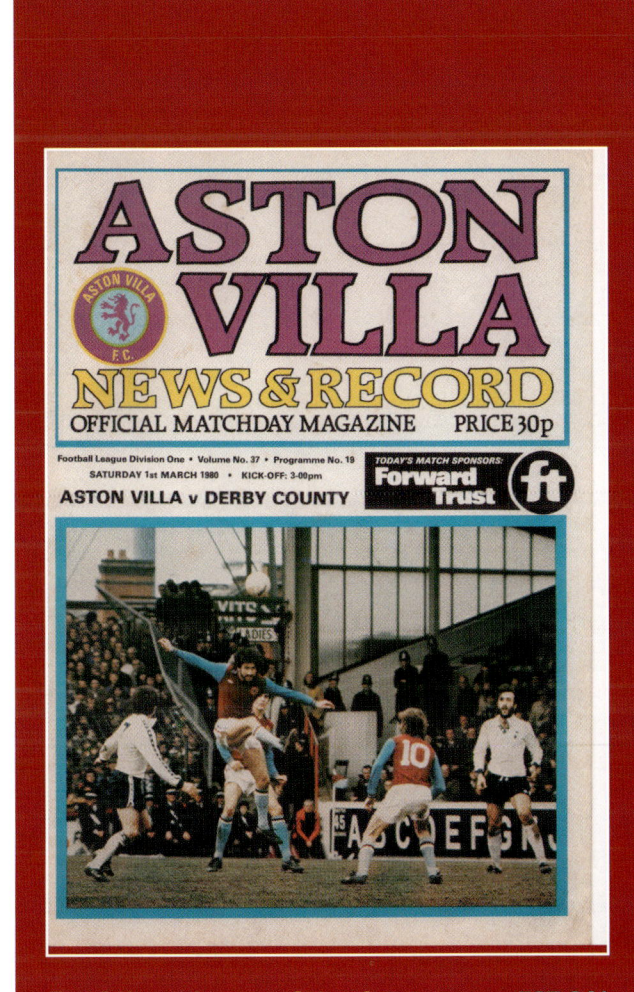

Today's match sponsors: Forward Trust

Total Home League Attendances	587,941
Average Home League Attendance	27,997
Highest Home League Attendance	41,160
Lowest Home League Attendance	15,319

		P	W	D	L	F	A	W	D	L	F	A	Pts
1	Liverpool	42	15	6	0	46	8	10	4	7	35	22	60
2	Manchester United	42	17	3	1	43	8	7	7	7	22	27	58
3	Ipswich Town	42	14	4	3	43	13	8	5	8	25	26	53
4	Arsenal	42	8	10	3	24	12	10	6	5	28	24	52
5	Nottingham Forest	42	16	4	1	44	11	4	4	13	19	32	48
6	Wolverhampton	42	9	6	6	29	20	10	3	8	29	27	47
7	**Aston Villa**	**42**	**11**	**5**	**5**	**29**	**22**	**5**	**9**	**7**	**22**	**28**	**46**
8	Southampton	42	14	2	5	53	24	4	7	10	12	29	45
9	Middlesbrough	42	11	7	3	31	14	5	5	11	19	30	44
10	West Bromwich	42	9	8	4	37	23	2	11	8	17	27	41
11	Leeds United	42	10	7	4	30	17	3	7	11	16	33	40
12	Norwich City	42	10	8	3	38	30	3	6	12	20	36	40
13	Crystal Palace	42	9	9	3	26	13	3	7	11	15	37	40
14	Tottenham Hotspur	42	11	5	5	30	22	4	5	12	22	40	40
15	Coventry City	42	12	2	7	34	24	4	5	12	22	42	39
16	Brighton & Hove	42	8	8	5	25	20	3	7	11	22	37	37
17	Manchester City	42	8	8	5	28	25	4	5	12	15	41	37
18	Stoke City	42	9	4	8	27	26	4	6	11	17	32	36
19	Everton	42	7	7	7	28	25	2	10	9	15	26	35
20	Bristol City	42	6	6	9	22	30	3	7	11	15	36	31
21	Derby County	42	9	4	8	36	29	2	4	15	11	38	30
22	Bolton Wanderers	42	5	11	5	19	21	0	4	17	19	52	25

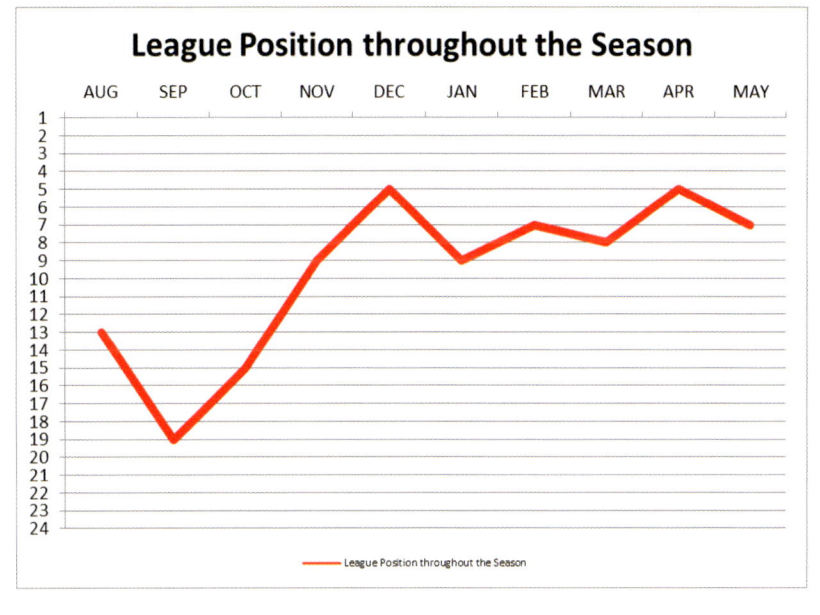

League Position throughout the Season

THE BIG ASTON VILLA BOOK OF THE SEVENTIES

1979-80

Sat 18th August   **Bolton Wanderers (A)**
Drew 1-1   **Att 19,795**
Cowans

Villa started the game with an attack-minded 4-2-4 formation and could have opened the scoring twice early on with both Deehan and Little denied by the Bolton keeper. New signing, Tony Morley, added sparkle on the wing and his accurate, whipped in crosses showed Villa fans he was adept at turning defenders and shooting with power – one such effort rattling the crossbar. Gordon Cowans, in his fifth season, opened Villa's account on 74 minutes, but the joy was short lived when Wanderers cancelled out 'Sid's' goal two minutes later.

Wed 22nd August   **Brighton & Hove Albion (H)**
Won 2-1   **Att 28,803**
Evans A (pen), Morley

Newly promoted Brighton were outclassed for much of the game, yet they could so easily have snatched both points with Jimmy Rimmer having to pull off three spectacular saves to deny them. Brian Little provided the energy up front. Albion struggled to contain him and when he was felled in the box Allan Evans stepped up to convert the penalty. The visitors were on even terms when a cross from the right evaded Rimmer and nestled in the net. Tony Morley, on his home debut, endeared himself to the Villa faithful when he bagged the winner on 66 minutes with a left foot shot. Cropley then had to leave the field of play earlier than he'd hoped with a badly injured ankle – he wouldn't wear the Villa shirt again.

Sat 25th August   **Bristol City (H)**
Lost 0-2   **Att 25,526**

Even without want-away stars Gidman and Gray, Villa were clearly intent on attacking. Cowans was impressive but he lacked support

Hart Lane, then Coventry City were smashed 3-0, with Donovan scoring his first for Villa.

Jimmy Rimmer missed his first game since his Villa arrival, with a young keeper by the name of Nigel Spink replacing him in the 1-2 defeat at Forest. Spink's name would obviously crop up again a few years down the line. Gary Shaw, scorer at the City Ground, then bagged his first hat-trick for the senior side when Villa beat Bristol City 3-1.

A win at Bristol Rovers in the FA Cup 3rd round was followed by victory against Everton, revenge for the Toffeemen having put Villa out of the League Cup three months earlier. By the end of February the side were sitting seventh and had progressed to the FA Cup quarter-finals for only the second time since 1962. Perhaps claret and blue ribbons would adorn the famous old trophy in May?

Of the eight league fixtures played in March, four were defeats – Villa had clearly lost momentum, yet they had only dropped one place. April saw a marked improvement as Villa gained their first win (3-2) against Brian Clough's Nottingham Forest since they had taken the football scene by storm by winning the title in 1978. The only loss in the month came at Old Trafford, though Villa signed off from Villa Park with a narrow victory over Spurs. The curtain came down at Anfield, Villa scored, but Liverpool grabbed four.

As for the famous colours attached to the FA Cup, it happened alright, but it was West Ham United that lifted that trophy. Villa were doing OK at Upton Park in the 6th round before the referee adjudged Ken McNaught handled in the dying seconds. Despite the protests, the Hammers full-back put away the penalty. Thirty-five years on and I still struggle to bring myself to say his name!

once the injured Little had departed. John Deehan went close on a few occasions, thwarted by the keeper on others. But Villa looked flimsy at the back and City took advantage in the 17th minute. They added to the lead when Tom Ritchie was fouled by substitute Ivor Linton, the City striker making no mistake from the spot firing to Rimmer's right.

Tue 28th August   Colchester Utd (A) League Cup 2nd rnd 1st leg
Won 2-0   Att 6,221
Shaw 2

The two rebels, Gray and Gidman, were recalled by boss Saunders due to injuries, but Colchester seemed unfazed by their illustrious visitors and were nearly ahead with only three minutes on the clock, Rimmer was alert to save from winger Bobby Hodge. Gary Shaw, in for the crocked Little, headed Villa in front on the 35th minute following a low Colin Gibson centre that was turned into his path by Morley. A confident Villa strode forward and Shaw, almost immediately, had the ball in the net again, but his effort was ruled offside. United had a chance to level in the 55th minute but midfielder, Eddie Rowles, fluffed with a weakly hit shot. Gary Shaw extended Villa's advantage when he was fed by a Morley header in the 73rd minute.

Sat 1st September   Everton (A)
Drew 1-1   Att 29,271
Morley

Everton started with such energy it was a mystery how Villa were still in the game, however, against the run of play, Tony Morley got to the far post to nod Villa ahead on 16 minutes against his boyhood team. After that is was a case of hanging on for Saunders' boys as Everton started the second half as they'd played for the majority of the first. Villa's smash-and-grab raid was undone when Everton finally found a deserved goal through John Bailey.

Wed 5th September   Colchester Utd (H) League Cup 2nd rnd 2nd leg
Lost 0-2 won 9-8 on pens Att 19,473

Villa were clearly shaken by the grit and determination shown by the third-tier side, more so when United went ahead in the 20th minute. Villa worked hard to get back into the tie, Swain had an effort disallowed but Colchester defended resolutely. With 20 minutes remaining the Villa Park faithful were further stunned when their side went further behind from a Bobby Gough volley. The game would be decided by penalties and, with the count at 8-8, the Colchester keeper missed his spot-kick which allowed Tony Morley to seal it.

Sat 8th September   Manchester United (H)
Lost 0-3   Att 34,859

On the day that Andy Gray signed for neighbours Wolverhampton Wanderers, Villa were comprehensively beaten. Deficient in most positions only the drive of Mortimer, and the deft touches of Cowans, stood out. Villa trailed to a Steve Coppell goal on 17 minutes, and although Deehan had a half chance, his header sailed high and wide. Villa had a brief spell of possession early in the second half when a Gary Shaw effort was held on the line, but United recovered to overwhelm their hosts. Goals in the 70th and 85th minute added to Villa's misery, but the defeat could have been far worse.

Sat 15th September   Crystal Palace (A)
Lost 0-2   Att 28,428

This would be John Deehan's last game for Villa before a shock move to West Brom, while new boy Mike Pejic made his debut in defence after joining from Everton. 'Unsure at the back' and unable to score goals Villa went behind four minutes before the break, with Murphy getting his second goal of the afternoon on 65 minutes. Rescued time after time by Rimmer and Gidman, Villa avoided a landslide defeat, although a third defeat in four games saw them languishing in 19th position.

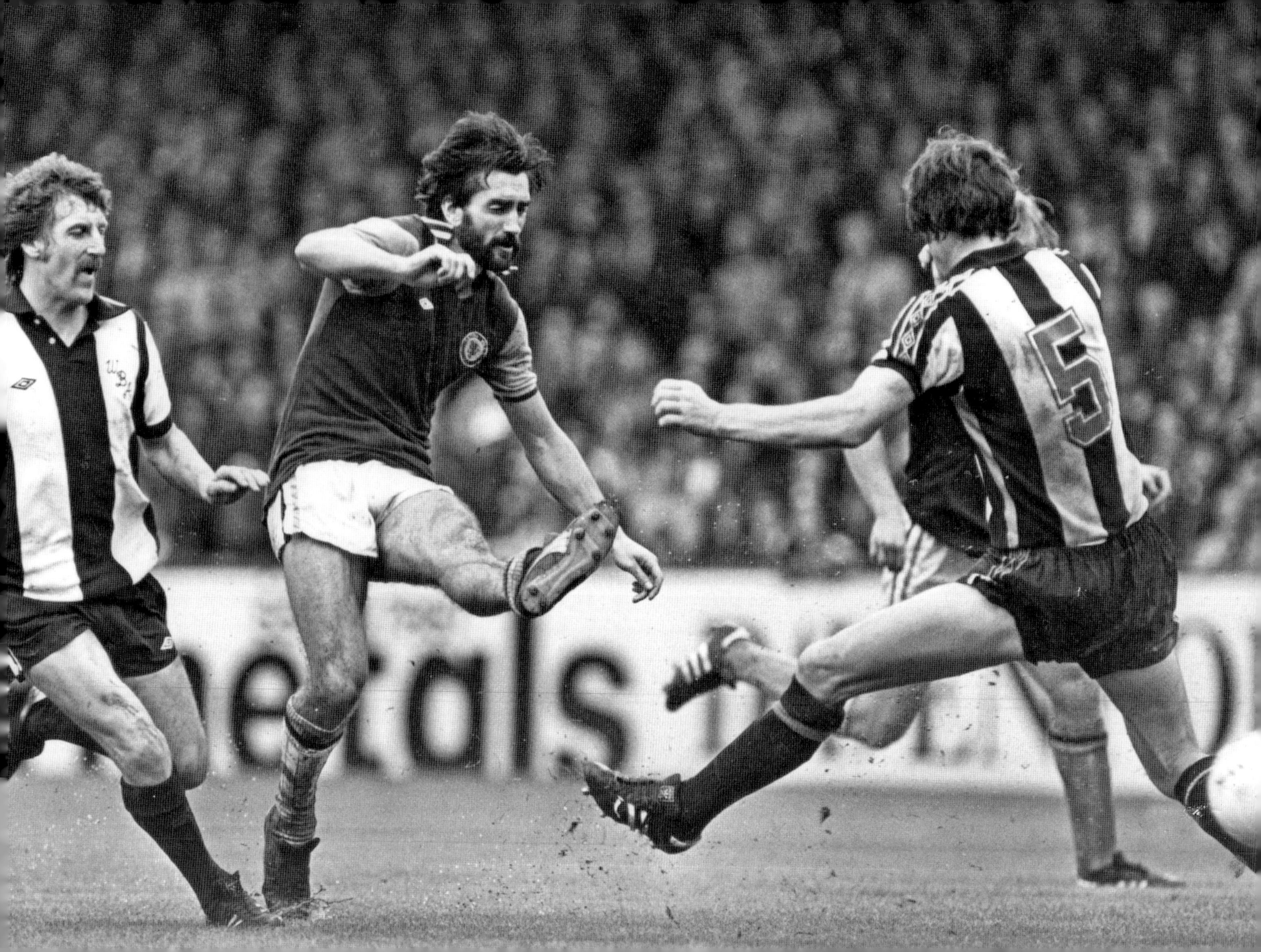

[Left] Dennis Mortimer nutmegs Albion's John Wile during the Villa Park encounter – a game that finished goal-less

Sat 22nd September   Arsenal (H)
Drew 0-0   Att 27,277

Despite an unconvincing performance the Villa at least picked up a point, though it has to be said, this was entirely due to Arsenal's appalling finishing and Rimmer's heroics. New signings, Des Bremner from Hibernian, and David Geddis from Ipswich Town, both debuted – the former an aggressive style player, the latter an unselfish worker. Villa, who clearly need time to bed in their new players, came into the game more after the interval, but were sadly short on ideas.

Tue 25th September   Everton (H) League Cup 3rd round
Drew 0-0   Att 22, 635

The scoreline was misleading - this was a thriller. Everton showed attacking intent and in David Geddis, Villa had a player who personified their fighting spirit. A Brian Little curler went just wide of the mark, while at the other end, Rimmer denied Brian Kidd's deft flick. It was end-to-end… Geddis was prevented his first goal when Mick Lyons desperately cleared, then shortly afterwards, he was pushed aside in the area but the referee chose to let it go unpunished. Further chances for both sides went wide or were saved by the brilliance of the goalkeepers Jimmy Rimmer and George Wood.

Sat 29th September   Middlesbrough (A)
Drew 0-0   Att 16,017

It was hard to believe that Villa hadn't scored in their previous five matches (incl. cup) as Cowans and Pejic tested the 'Boro keeper early on with confident, fierce efforts. Villa continued to look dangerous as they were driven on by midfielder Mortimer, irrepressible as ever. Transfer-listed full-back John Gidman failed to reappear after the break, his place taken by centre-half Gary Williams. There were encouraging glimpses as Little and Geddis combined well together upfront and Villa would likely have taken both points had Ken McNaught not been harshly dismissed on 76 minutes.

Sat 6th October   Southampton (H)
Won 3-0   Att 24,377
Bremner, Mortimer, Evans A (pen)

With four wins and a draw from their last five games, Southampton were going to be a tough nut to crack. But Villa's new boys were starting to bed in nicely, none more so than Des Bremner who opened his scoring account on 34 minutes. From there on Villa played with more fluency and confidence and went further in front when a Mortimer free-kick was driven high and wide of the Saints' keeper. The visitors rarely pressed and it was well past the hour before Rimmer was called into making a save. An Evans converted penalty rounded off a 3-0 scoreline, Swain had been scythed down by Holmes for the spot-kick.

Tue 9th October   Everton (A) League Cup 3rd round replay
Lost 1-4   Att 22,098
Swain

Villa could have taken an early lead when Kenny Swain fired into the side-netting and then proceeded to give away two sloppy goals in the opening 10 minutes – Rimmer dropping a harmless cross for the second. Brian Little struggled in front of goal and failed to put two good chances away, while Mortimer saw an effort flash just wide of the upright. A third for Everton arrived when Bob Latchford scored with ease following hesitancy from Rimmer and The Toffees made it 0-4 on 75 minutes before Swain fired a consolation two minutes from the end.

Sat 13th October   West Bromwich Albion (H)
Drew 0-0   Att 36,007

In spite of the lack of goals, the game was entertaining from the first whistle to the last. Mortimer and Cowans were outstanding in midfield creating chance upon chance for the forwards. A Gary Shaw

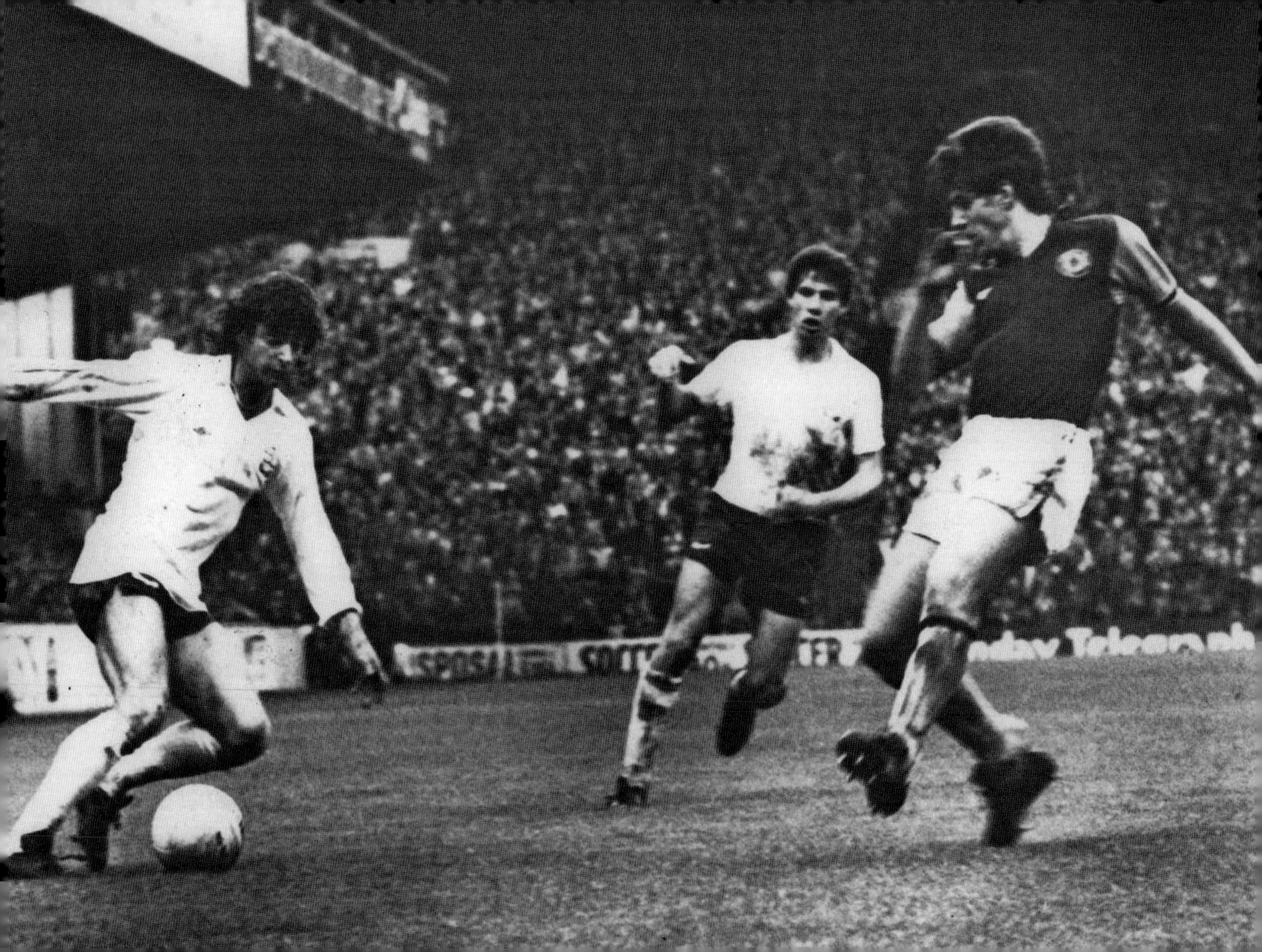

[Left] Colin Gibson, in for the injured Mike Pejic, puts pressure on Bolton's wideman in Villa's 3-1 win

shot bounced back off the crossbar as Villa racked up eight first-half attempts. Ormsby, Pejic and Swain were solid at the back when Albion attacked, although they also hit the woodwork. Unfortunately Villa were missing the goal threat provided by the departed Gray and Deehan.

**Sat 20th October   Derby County (A)
Won 3-1   Att 20,162
Little, Shaw, Mortimer**

The writing was on the wall for Derby when Brian Little (scoring his first league goal since Aug '78) fired Villa in front on six minutes. The hosts pulled a goal back through Paul Emson before the break, but it was a just question of time, when would Villa's superiority bring the deserved rewards? On 55 minutes a powerful left-footed Shaw drive restored Villa's advantage, then captain Dennis Mortimer thrashed in a low shot from the edge of the box following a superb run by Cowans out on the left wing. The win lifted Villa up two places to 15th.

**Sat 27th October   Wolverhampton Wanderers (A)
Drew 1-1   Att 36,267
Shaw**

Despite the attentions of Allan Evans and Brendan Ormsby, Andy Gray fired Wolves ahead in the 15th minute, dashing in at the far post to clip the ball in. In a game that was fiercely competitive Wolves poured forward but couldn't add to their slender lead. This came back to haunt the home side when Swain and Mortimer combined to set Gary Shaw up, the youngster showing maturity beyond his years as he unleashed a left-footed shot which goalie Paul Bradshaw failed to hold, one-all. Both sides were reduced to ten men on the hour when Ormsby and John Richards clashed following a tackle from the Villa man.

**Sat 3rd November   Bolton Wanderers (H)
Won 3-1   Att 24,744
Shaw, Evans A, Mortimer**

Apart from the return of big Ken McNaught, Villa fielded the same XI that salvaged a point at Molineux. Gary Shaw set the ball rolling in the 15th minute when he scored for the third successive game. Allan Evans' headed goal made it 2-0 four minutes before the half-time whistle. Villa let their guard down briefly and conceded but there was only going to be one winner in this one-sided affair. Skipper Mortimer added Villa's third in the dying seconds in a match where Bolton could have been really put to the sword.

**Sat 10th November   Ipswich Town (A)
Drew 0-0   Att 17,795**

Bobby Robson's Ipswich were struggling at the wrong end of the table following seven defeats in their last nine matches. Villa meanwhile were unbeaten in seven. It was the home side who put together the more positive attacks with the Villa midfield uncharacteristically overrun. Villa carved out a few openings, Shaw should have done better in sight of goal but he hesitated and Terry Butcher made the tackle. At the other end Rimmer was forced to make a headed clearance and a John Wark effort crashed against the post.

**Sat 17th November   Stoke City (H)
Won 2-1   Att 27,086
Mortimer, Evans A (pen)**

Villa's unbeaten run looked to have ended when Stoke took a tenth minute lead following a corner, but Saunders' men were nothing if not resilient and back on level terms when Mortimer took advantage of brilliant build up play from Little and Cowans to zip in a 25-yarder low into the bottom right-hand corner of the net. Just before the interval Des Bremner denied the visitors a certain goal when he cleared an Adrian Heath header off the line. Mortimer grazed a crossbar with a long range shot then forced an acrobatic save from Roger Jones. With the game looking likely to end all even Villa were awarded a

223

penalty after Swain was held back, and under immense pressure, the ice-cool Allan Evans calmly planted it wide of the keeper.

Sat 24th November   **Leeds United (H)**
Drew 0-0   **Att 29,736**

Villa suffered a series of first-half lapses, none more so than an Evans penalty miss, although Leeds' agile keeper did well to turn the ball over the bar. Shaw also kept Lukic busy, the goalie making two fine saves and a further one from Brian Little. In the second half chances were restricted for the Villa frontrunners as the service from midfield became almost non-existent. Leeds took a grip of the game and forced Rimmer into numerous saves. To round off a miserable run in front of goal for David Geddis (his 12th app without scoring), the striker somehow missed a wonderful chance at the far post in the 90th minute.

Sat 1st December   **Norwich City (A)**
Drew 1-1   **Att 15,257**
Evans A

Villa totally dominated the first half, but all they had to show for their effort was an Allan Evans headed goal. Norwich had the ball in the Villa net within 60 seconds but it was ruled out for offside. This caused unrest on the terraces. In the 70th minute John Fashanu was sent off for stamping on Evans, this led to missiles, bottles and coins raining down on Jimmy Rimmer's goal. The Villa custodian was felled by coins and received lengthy treatment. In the 88th minute Norwich were awarded a penalty for a Mike Pejic tackle on Keith Robson, Mortimer, clearly angry about the decision, made a remark and received his marching orders. City scored to remain unbeaten at home.

Sat 8th December   **Liverpool (H)**
Lost 1-3   **Att 41,160**
Little

Villa's 11-match unbeaten run, which stretched back to early September, came to a shuddering halt against second-placed Liverpool.

[Right] Villa sub, Terry Bullivant, up against Kenny Dalglish during the 1-3 defeat to Liverpool at Villa Park

In a thrill-a-minute match the Villa comfortably held the Reds, and even when the visitors took a 55th minute lead, courtesy of a Ray Kennedy goal, it was only for 50 seconds. That's all it took for Brian Little to equalise. Alan Hansen stole to in regain Liverpool's lead on the hour and Terry McDermott added number three 15 minutes later. Shaw and Little toiled and Geddis saw a shot go just the wrong side of the post. Recent signing, Terry Bullivant, came on late in the game for Colin Gibson, although it would be Mike Pejic's last game due to injury.

Sat 15th December   **Tottenham Hotspur (A)**
Won 2-1   **Att 30,555**
Geddis, Cowans (pen)

Villa denied Spurs the room to play their eye-catching football from the start and David Geddis finally broke his duck by putting the Villa ahead. With Allan Evans missing the game, it was down to 'Sid' Cowans to convert the penalty awarded in the second half to give the Claret and Blues a two-goal cushion. Ossie Ardiles pulled one back, but with Rimmer, Ormsby and Little outstanding throughout, Villa held their nerve and the lead. The victory hauled them up three places to eighth.

Wed 19th December   **Coventry City (H)**
Won 3-0   **Att 24,446**
Donovan, Little 2

The Sky Blues came into the game on the back of two defeats and Villa helped them maintain their poor form by taking an eighth minute lead through Terry Donovan, (in for the injured Geddis) heading home a Cowans corner. Villa, playing arguably their best football of the season, ran riot – Les Sealey saving from Little and Cowans, before a prone Bobby McDonald blocked another Brian Little goalbound shot. Brian made it 2-0 with an exquisitely individualist goal, holding off three defenders in the process, he then capped a wonderful afternoon by picking the ball up in the centre-circle, running half the length of the pitch, before dispatching his second and Villa's third.

Wed 26th December   Nottingham Forest (A)
Lost 1-2   Att 32,072
Shaw

Villa in fifth, but level on points with third-placed Arsenal, frequently threatened the European Champions with their lightning-quick counter attacking. Villa went close to breaking the deadlock on the stroke of half time, however, the ball bounced unkindly as Little attempted to tee-up Gary Shaw. Forest then took the lead when a theatrical dive by Trevor Francis was rewarded by a spot-kick, John Robertson converted. Little forced a world class save from Shilton before a Stan Bowles header in the 56th minute made it 2-0. Still Villa wouldn't lie down and they pulled a goal back through Shaw, who swivelled to steer Brian Little's centre beyond Forest's keeper. A certain Nigel Spink made his debut.

Sat 29th December   Bristol City (A)
Won 3-1   Att 18,799
Shaw 3

It was the same outfield ten that lost narrowly in Nottingham, while Rimmer was back between the posts. U21 international Gary Shaw took his tally for the season to nine in league and cup with a memorable second-half hat-trick. His first, a simple tap in following a Cowans corner, but the second, only three minutes later, was far more dramatic – a stunning drive from fully 35-yards out. Shaw had to wait until four minutes from time to be guaranteed the match ball, taking possession in midfield, he ran through the City's bewildered defence before slotting home after his initial strike came back off the upright. Villa's display might not have been 'vintage' but no one could deny it was effective.

225

THE BIG ASTON VILLA BOOK OF THE SEVENTIES

Fri 4th January   **Bristol Rovers (A) FA Cup 3rd round**
Won 2-1   **Att 16,060**
Shaw, Cowans

This was Villa's first pairing with Rovers in an FA Cup tie since the 1960/61 season and the plucky hosts played courageously – it took the Villa until near half-time to go in front. Gary Shaw celebrated his first FA Cup tie with a peach of a goal, a tremendous strike from well outside the box that give goalkeeper Thomas no chance, but Rovers deservedly equalised when Stewart Barrowclough stole through and rounded Jimmy Rimmer to poke the ball home. Villa sealed the victory shortly afterwards following the sterling work of Little and Shaw who carved out an opening for Cowans to scramble the ball over the line.

Sat 12th January   **Everton (H)**
Won 2-1   **Att 31,108**
Gibson, Donovan

Teenage full-back Colin Gibson, having an extended run in the first team, put the Villa in front much to the dismay of the Everton keeper. Gibson's optimistic shot from 25-yards was speculative to say the least, it bobbled and then rolled from the diving keeper's hand. Martin Hodge was at fault for goal number two, under pressure from Donovan and Shaw, he could do no more than direct a Mortimer cross to the former who gleefully seized the opportunity to roll it in from four yards. Everton pulled one back through Peter Eastoe, and despite them being outstanding all afternoon, they couldn't prevent Villa from taking maximum points.

Sat 26th January   **Cambridge United (A) FA Cup 4th round**
Drew 1-1   **Att 12,000**
Donovan

Villa were unchanged for their first visit to the Abbey Stadium and indeed facing Cambridge United, who had never reached the fourth round. The Villans expectedly took the lead when Terry Donovan found the net on 16 minutes, but the match failed to emerge as a stroll as Villa's domination ended when United drew level in the 34th minute. The claret and blue midfield were then hurried into a succession of poor passes as Cambridge chose the route of aerial attack. Ken McNaught was rock solid as others around him trembled. Villa created only a few chances, while Rimmer had to produce some outstanding saves.

Wed 30th January   **Cambridge United (H) FA Cup 4th round rep**
Won 4-1   **Att 36,835**
Donovan 2, Evans A, Little

Villa took to the field with the same XI from the Abbey Stadium encounter – Terry Donovan gave the home side the lead with only 80 seconds on the clock only for Cambridge to be on equal terms within 15 minutes. A determined Villa then upped the ante; a Donovan header made it 2-1 before Allan Evans weighed in with his first cup goal in English football, heading home a Swain free kick. Within a minute Brian Little put the result beyond doubt and Villa were through to the last 16.

Sat 2nd February   **Crystal Palace (H)**
Won 2-0   **Att 29,469**
Cowans, Mortimer

Ron kept faith with the team that disposed of Cambridge, and despite incessant rain on an already heavy pitch, Villa's strength and stamina shone through. Gordon Cowans fired Villa in front with a 30-yard skidding shot a minute after Donovan had been denied by ex-Villan John Burridge in the Palace goal. It was disappointing that the home side were unable to capitalise on their territorial superiority (though a Little shot cannoned back off the woodwork) until injury time when captain Mortimer made the game safe with his fifth of the campaign. Villa remained sixth, with games in hand over many sides.

Sat 9th February   **Arsenal (A)**
Lost 1-3   **Att 33,816**
Mortimer

Arsenal, a point and two places above the Villa, took command of the game from the off and led by a single goal at half time. In truth, it should have been far more. A further strike, a Graham Rix 25-yard cross-shot, had the Gunners coasting. Gary Shaw, who'd hardly had a touch all afternoon due to the midfield having to play deep to help the defence, was then subbed before Villa conceded a third on 64 minutes. Mortimer pulled a goal back for the visitors two minutes later, however, it wasn't the start of a comeback, merely a consolation.

Sat 16th February   **Blackburn Rovers (A) FA Cup 5th round**
Drew 1-1   **Att 29,468**
Geddis

Due to his energy and enthusiasm when coming on at Highbury, Geddis was given his first start since scoring at Spurs in December. And it was the blond-haired striker who impressively gave Villa a 40th minute lead after he ran onto a Donovan header from McNaught's free kick. Mortimer and Bremner fought valiantly for the cause in midfield, but were as stunned as their team-mates when the Third Division side grabbed an unlikely leveller right at the death. Allan Evans' attempted near post headed clearance from a Rovers corner skidded off his head and into the roof of the net.

Wed 20th February   **Blackburn Rovers (H) FA Cup 5th round rep**
Won 1-0   **Att 42,161**
Evans A

Villa Park hosted its biggest gate of the season as the fans turned out in droves to see if Villa could emulate the class of '57 – Dixon, McParland, Sims et al – but early signs weren't good. Although a Brian Little shot fizzed wide on 25 seconds, Blackburn then took charge as Villa's defence showed signs of the jitters, with Rimmer forced into numerous saves and Gibson clearing one off the line. Geddis had a clear chance at the other end, but headed wide. 'Sid' Cowans was outstanding alongside his skipper Mortimer, thankfully the winning goal arrived in the 81st minute when Villa's big Scottish centre-half rose to nod in Little's inch perfect centre, not McNaught but Allan Evans. It could only happen in the cup!

Sat 23rd February   **West Bromwich Albion (A)**
Won 2-1   **Att 33,618**
McNaught, Little

Even though Villa looked dangerous from the off, breaking at speed and Cowans going oh-so-close, it was Albion who held a half-time single goal cushion. It could have been more. Villa then toiled after the break to convert their territorial advantage into chances, and within three minutes they were level when Kenny Swain floated a free-kick into the area for the unchallenged McNaught to power home. There was then more than a touch of fortune about Villa's winner… Morley slipped the ball to Bremner, Tony Godden and Gary Pendrey were caught in two minds, and as Little and Godden went for the ball, it bounced off the Villaman and into the net.

Wed 27th February   **Manchester City (H)**
Drew 2-2   **Att 29,139**
Shaw, own goal

Villa were seventh going into the game having played four less than most teams, meanwhile, only the bottom two sides had lost more on the road than City. Though neither side could find any rhythm, Villa true to form, went ahead through scoring sensation Gary Shaw. Taking a pass from Tony Morley the youngster calmly curled the ball beyond keeper Joe Corrigan. Thereafter Villa failed to convert numerous chances that would surely have put the game to bed. City took full advantage of the situation and were equal through a penalty following a corner being handled in the area. Paul Power put the visitors in front with ten minutes left, and with time running out, a Mortimer corner-kick was headed into his own net by Willie Donachie to level things up.

Sat 1st March   **Derby County (H)**
Won 1-0   **Att 28,956**
Evans A

There was precious little to choose between two sides at the opposite ends of the table (Derby would go on to be relegated). Derby's urgency and determination matched the Villa's, but as if often the

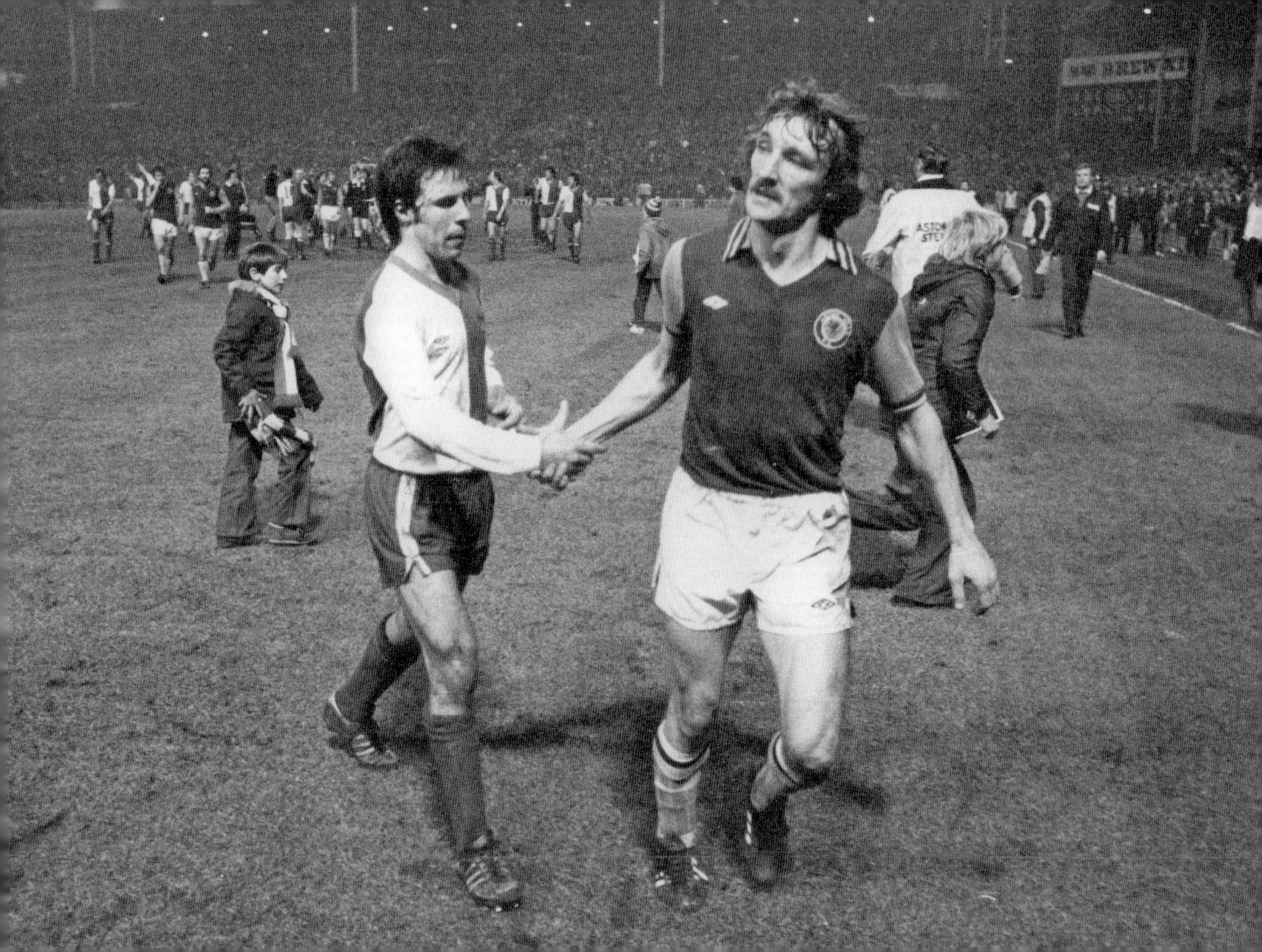

[Left] Des Bremner leaves the field knowing he'd been in a game. Blackburn Rovers had held Villa 1-1 four days earlier, however, an Allan Evans goal ensured Villa won the replay

case, they didn't get the breaks. Villa were untidy in midfield and short of penetration upfront with Little, Shaw and Morley all struggling. It eventually fell to centre-back Allan Evans to show his colleagues where the net was. His effort in the 43rd minute – a powerful header from a Cowans curling free-kick - the only goal to show in what was best described as unforgettable.

Mon 3rd March   Brighton & Hove Albion (A)
Drew 1-1   Att 23,077
Evans A

Allan Evans was the hero and Villain of the piece in a game in which Brighton took a 27th minute lead from a corner kick, Ray Clarke getting the finishing touch after Mark Lawrenson had helped it on. Evans then headed an equaliser in the 33rd minute, his ninth goal of the season, from a Cowans free-kick, which was followed shortly afterwards by a booking (his seventh). Then, straight after the interval, Evans needlessly handled and was sent off, which meant he would miss the forthcoming FA Cup tie. Rimmer prevented Brighton taking both points with a fine save from a clean through Clarke

Sat 8th March   West Ham United (A) FA Cup 6th round
Lost 0-1   Att 36,393

With West Ham going well in Division Two, Ron Saunders decided on a defensive strategy. It wasn't pretty on the eye, but swamping the midfield seemed a successful ploy. Villa contained the enthusiastic east London side by and large with Rimmer saving from David Cross, Brooking and Alan Devonshire when necessary. A replay looked on the cards, however, that all changed with only two minutes remaining when the referee claimed McNaught had handled deliberately in the box and gave a spot-kick. It was a cruel blow when Ray Stewart stroked the ball home and dump Villa out.

Mon 10th March   Wolverhampton Wanderers (H)
Lost 1-3   Att 30,432
Shaw

A mere two points separated Saunders and John Barnwell's sides, although Villa's fourth game in a nine day spell had obviously taken its toll on the players. Wolves didn't have as much possession as their hosts, but that didn't stop them leading 3-1 at half-time. "We found ourselves at the bottom of a very big hill," claimed Saunders after the game. Wolves were two-up before a magnificent headed goal from Shaw on 32 minutes gave Villa hope. But three minutes later that had evaporated as the visitors had restored their two goal cushion.

Sat 15th March   Southampton (A)
Lost 0-2   Att 20,735

Villa's season continued to collapse with a third straight defeat in eight days. Already without the injured Little, Villa trailed to an Ivan Golac goal before having to reshuffle when Shaw went off with groin trouble –Linton and Evans formed the new line of attack. Skipper, Dennis Mortimer, played the second half with his thigh heavily strapped. Villa's strike force were unable to make much impression, although Des Bremner went close to equalising on 76 minutes, and Wells in the Saints' goal saved superbly. In the closing stages Phil Boyer set Mike Channon up to put the game to bed.

Wed 19th March   Middlesbrough (H)
Lost 0-2   Att 15,319

A Villa Park crowd, less than fifty percent of the season's average, turned out for the visit of a 'Boro side only a point adrift of Villa. With McNaught, Mortimer, Shaw and Little (still) all casualties, Bullivant and Donovan were given rare starts. Unbeaten in their last four, John Neal's team played with a confidence the hosts lacked and led at the interval via a Billy Ashcroft goal. Villa missed a glorious chance to level when a Gibson cross was completely missed by Geddis in the air. Swain moved upfront and the Villa looked more positive, but it was Middlesbrough who made this their third win on the bounce at Villa Park.

THE BIG ASTON VILLA BOOK OF THE SEVENTIES

Sat 22nd March   **Ipswich Town (H)**
Drew 1-1   **Att 22,836**
Morley

On the back of four successive losses things looked even bleaker for Saunders' side when they fell behind to a John Wark goal on 15 minutes. Third-placed Town, unbeaten in 15 (12 wins), were then content to sit back. Driven on by a lion-hearted performance from Gordon Cowans, the Villa responded by taking the game to Bobby Robson's men. In an intense spell of pressure, Swain, Bremner and Evans all went close, but it took until the 73rd minute for the goal to finally arrive. A Cowans strike came back off the Ipswich defence and Morley caught it with a beautifully executed right-footed volley to send the ball screaming into the roof of the net.

Wed 26th March   **Norwich City (H)**
Won 2-0   **Att 17,956**
Cowans (pen), Hopkins

Pat Heard was given his Villa debut, and buoyed by the appetite shown against Norwich's near neighbours, the Villa started well. Heard's early ball distribution was exceptional with Swain (twice) and Evans benefitting most, and had they not erred at vital moments, Villa could have built up a commanding lead. When Fashanu hit the woodwork just after the hour it sparked the hosts into a higher gear. Swain was sent crashing to the ground in the 71st minute, the reliable 'Sid' Cowans coolly converted the spot-kick. Former Youth Cup captain Robert Hopkins came on for Ivor Linton in injury time and capped his debut with a goal from his only touch.

Sat 29th March   **Stoke City (A)**
Lost 0-2   **Att 16,558**

Villa suffered the back-lash of Alan Durban's verbal assault on his side following Stoke's humiliating 0-3 surrender at Wolves in their previous match. Stoke ploughed on energetically after Tony Morley had seen a shot come back off the bar in only the seventh minute with keeper Peter Fox well beaten. A penalty was then awarded after Linton had

[Right] Des Bremner challenges John Wark – Colin Gibson and Ken McNaught look on during the draw at Villa Park

bought down the dangerous Garth Crooks, Ray Evans stroking home. Allan Evans, playing as centre-forward, fluffed a simple chance when he failed to connect with a Cowans right-wing cross, and Villa paid the price for the miss when Stoke added a second.

Sat 5th April   **Nottingham Forest (H)**
Won 3-2   **Att 29,156**
Bremner, Evans A, own goal

Forest started brightly and asked the early questions when Villa hit them on the counter-attack by taking a 12th minute lead. A precise through pass by Cowans fed Bremner who delicately flicked the ball over the advancing Shilton. Garry Birtles scored from close range to make it 1-1, only for Villa to restore their lead when Allan Evans moved forward in attack and climbed between two defenders to head home. Immediately after the interval Larry Llloyd - under pressure from Terry Donovan – headed into his own net to make it 3-1 to the Villa and move the side up three places to fifth.

Mon 7th April   **Manchester City (A)**
Drew 1-1   **Att 32,943**
Geddis

Notwithstanding the fact City had gone 16 matches without a win, Villa were made to sweat at Maine Road for a point. The visitors created numerous first-half chances, only for David Geddis, who had an eventful match, to miss them. He eventually came good in the 44th minute when he put Villa ahead. Power levelled for the home side on 52 minutes before Geddis missed another two gilt-edged chances… it was then City who drove on looking for a winner. A Geddis last-gasp tackle robbed Dennis Tueart of a certain goal, before the two clashed shortly after, and in the flare-up, Geddis was booked for the second time and was sent off.

Ron Saunders (far right) observes proceedings with physio Fred Pedley and first-team coach Roy MacLaren

MANAGERS

Villa's Eamonn Deacy in action during the draw at Elland Road

APRIL

- Robert Hopkins came on two minutes into injury time against Nottingham Forest – 20 seconds later, with his first and only touch of the game, he steered home the winner.
- Sid Cowans earned another England U21 cap in the 1-2 defeat to the German Democratic Republic (GDR).
- A 2-0 aggregate victory over Millwall secured Villa's Youth a place in the FA Youth Cup final.
- A Trevor Ames hat-trick gave Villa's Youth Cup side a useful 3-1 advantage in the first-leg of the final at Maine Road.
- Man City pulled off a shock 1-0 win at Villa Park but it wasn't enough to prevent Aston Villa being crowned FA Youth Cup winners 1980, 3-2 on aggregate.

MAY

- Ron Saunders was granted a testimonial – Birmingham City provided the opposition for the Villa Park fixture, billed as 'The Second City Cup final' Unfortunately, Villa went down 2-3.
Villa lost the second-leg of the Southern Junior Floodlit Cup 2-3 at home to QPR but still won the trophy 5-4 on aggregate.
- Villa's 1-4 defeat to Liverpool was the fifth consecutive season they had lost at Anfield by a three-goal margin.

THE BIG ASTON VILLA BOOK OF THE SEVENTIES

- The 41,160 league attendance for the visit of Liverpool was Villa's biggest of the season.
- The Liverpool loss halted an unbeaten sequence of 11 games.
- Rookie keeper Nigel Spink played at Nottingham Forest. He would have to wait until May 1982 to get another run out.

JANUARY

- Gordon Cowans was awarded 'The Young Player of the Month' by Robinson's Barley Water.
- Colin Gibson scored his first goal in claret and blue – Villa beating Everton 2-1. Terry Donovan also scored his first Villa goal in the game.

FEBRUARY

- An impressive Villa Park crowd of 42,161 saw Villa vanquish Blackburn Rovers to make the last eight of the FA Cup.
- Villa won at the Hawthorns to remain unbeaten at WBA since gaining promotion back to Division One.
- Tony Morley returned to the side following a five month absence.

MARCH

- A 4-3 aggregate victory over WBA earned the Villa youngsters a place in the FA Youth Cup semi-finals.
- Villa defeated QPR 3-1 at home in the first-leg of the Southern Junior Floodlit Cup.
- Villa fell at the FA Cup 6th round hurdle to Second Division West Ham after a dubious late penalty was awarded.
- The 15,319 for the visit of Middlesbrough was Villa's lowest gate for six years (Forest April 1974).

Alex Cropley being helped off the pitch by Roy McLaren during the Brighton & Hove Albion 2-1 win at Villa Park – the ankle injury ended his Villa career – and the diminutive Scot would never play for the first-team again

PRE-SEASON

- John Deehan gained another England U21 cap in the 3-1 win against Bulgaria U21s in Pernik.
- Right-footed left-winger Tony Morley arrived from Burnley for £200,000.
- Terry Donovan, a centre-forward from Grimsby Town, was signed for £80,000.
- Brian Little's £600,000 departure to rivals Birmingham City was called off following an adverse medical report.

AUGUST

- Alex Cropley broke his ankle against Brighton, unfortunately, the injury would finish his Villa career.
- Tony Morley scored the winner on his Villa Park debut during the 2-1 victory over Brighton & Hove Albion.
- Lee Jenkins' time at Villa was also over after just three substitute appearances.

SEPTEMBER

- Ex-England full-back Mike Pejic arrived from Everton for £225,000.
- Third Division Colchester United won 2-0 at Villa Park in the League Cup to take the tie (2-2 agg) to extra-time and penalties. Villa went through 9-8 on spot-kicks.
- Gordon Cowans was named in the England U21 squad to face Denmark, but didn't play. Deehan scored the only goal of the game.
- John 'Dixie' Deehan departed for West Bromwich Albion – it cost the Baggies £500,000 for his signature.
- Midfielder Des Bremner was signed from Hibernian.
- An FA Cup winner with Ipswich Town, Dave Geddis came in as Villa's record transfer buy at £300,000.
- Recent signing, Terry Donovan, was selected to play for the Republic of Ireland against Czechoslovakia.

OCTOBER

- Youth goalkeeper, Mark Kendall, was invited to train with the England Youth squad.
- Kendall played against Denmark Youth in Esbjerg.
- In his last game before converting to right-back, Kenny Swain scored Villa's consolation in the 1-4 League Cup defeat at Everton.
- The team remained unbeaten in the league, winning two and drawing two during the month.

NOVEMBER

- Gordon Cowans played for England U21s, beating Bulgaria U21s 5-0 at Filbert Street.
- Both Mortimer and Evans score in consecutive Villa Park victories.
- Villa signed midfielder Terry Bullivant from Fulham.
- Villa's youngsters destroyed Port Vale 8-0 in the Midland Intermediate League.
- Villa went unbeaten for the second month on the spin.

DECEMBER

- Frank Carrodus moved to Wrexham after giving Villa five years outstanding service.
- Eric Houghton retired from his role as a director – Doug Ellis also tendered his resignation from the Board.
- Mike Pejic played in the Liverpool 1-3 home defeat, his last in Villa's colours due to serious injury.

THE BIG ASTON VILLA BOOK OF THE SEVENTIES

Sat 19th April   **Leeds United (A)**
Drew 0-0   **Att 15,840**

Ron Saunders' side were easily the better but couldn't turn superiority into goals. Cowans and Bremner dominated the midfield, with Brian Little looking lively after missing the previous seven games, and was twice denied a goal. Firstly, he was narrowly beaten to a Swain through-ball by John Lukic and then the keeper was forced to palm away Brian's dipping, goal-bound shot. Defensively Villa, who had Eamon Deacy debuting, were strong and untroubled with a point enough for them to remain in fifth position.

Wed 23rd April   **Manchester United (A)**
Lost 1-2   **Att 45,201**
Bremner

The game was described in one paper as "a messy match of mediocre entertainment value", with Villa's lack of goal power glaringly obvious. United took a fourth minute lead, although the ball had gone out of play before Coppell crossed for Joe Jordan to head home. Jordan, who later clashed with Allan Evans leaving the Villa man with a suspected broken nose, then headed a second, but again, controversy surrounding the goal. This time United were awarded a free-kick, although Villa's players protested it should have been a throw in. Villa improved slightly as the game wore on but Bremner's goal was nothing more than a consolation.

Sat 26th April   **Tottenham Hotspur (H)**
Won 1-0   **Att 29,549**
Cowans

Villa went into the game searching for their first win in four – Midland pride was also at stake as Black Country rivals Wolverhampton Wanderers were ahead of Saunders side on goal difference only. With Evans out for the rest of the season it meant a debut for Villa's Jamaican born centre-half Noel Blake with Geddis back having missed the last two fixtures. In a game of few chances it was no surprise the interval was reached with no score. Gordon Cowans scored his sixth of the campaign (league and cup) to ensure both points stayed in 'Brum.' 'Sid' would see the season out an ever-present, as he would be for the following three seasons, which was a remarkable achievement. At the other end, Rimmer had kept 15 clean sheets in all competitions.

Tue 29th April   **Coventry City (A)**
Won 2-1   **Att 17,932**
Gibson, Cowans (pen)

Noel Blake retained his place in a young Villa team whose average age was only 20. In a smash-and-grab raid Villa scored against the run of play, Shaw intercepted, the ball found its way via Pat Heard and Cowans to Gibson who hit a low shot into the Coventry net. City, who'd done all the attacking, forced further saves out of Rimmer from Ian Wallace and Tommy English, before the visitors countered and scored again. Ivor Linton chased down a long pass from Geddis and was fouled in the box. Cue Sid Cowans to stroke the ball home. Wallace pulled one back for the Sky Blues on 73 minutes.

Sat 3rd May   **Liverpool (A)**
Lost 1-4   **Att 51,541**
Own goal

Who says lightning doesn't strike twice? For the second successive year the Villa found themselves on the receiving end of a heavy Anfield defeat to guarantee the Reds the title crown. The die was cast as early as the third minute when David Johnson opened the scoring. Miraculously Villa went in at the interval on level terms, a Swain free-kick was blocked, Heard crossed it and Israeli defender Avi Cohen was on hand to sweep the ball into his own net. But Liverpool were in front again just six minutes into the second half and further goals ensured the hosts claimed their 12th title. However, Villa, who had been ravaged by injuries most of the campaign, limped over the finish line in a respectable seventh position.

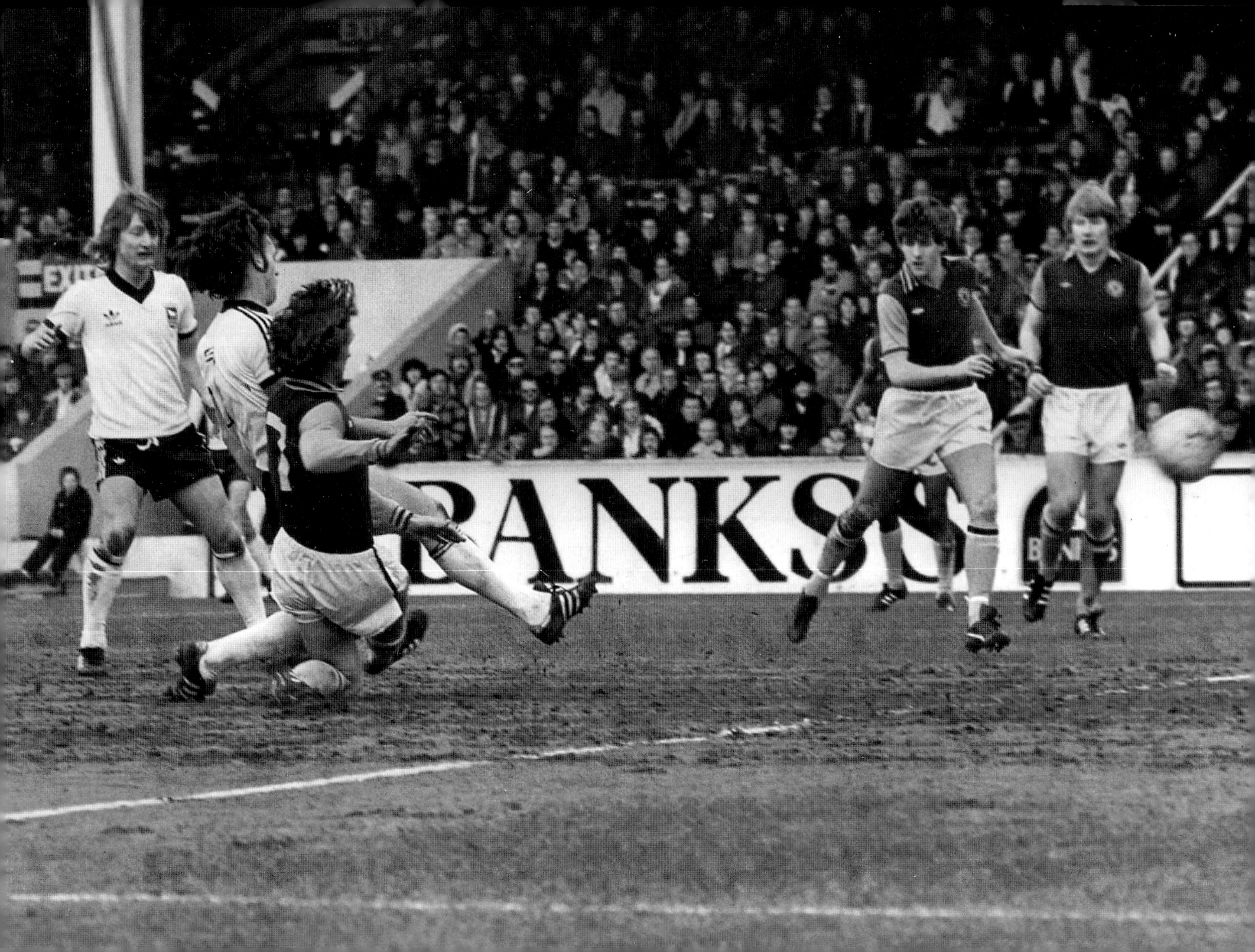
EXIT

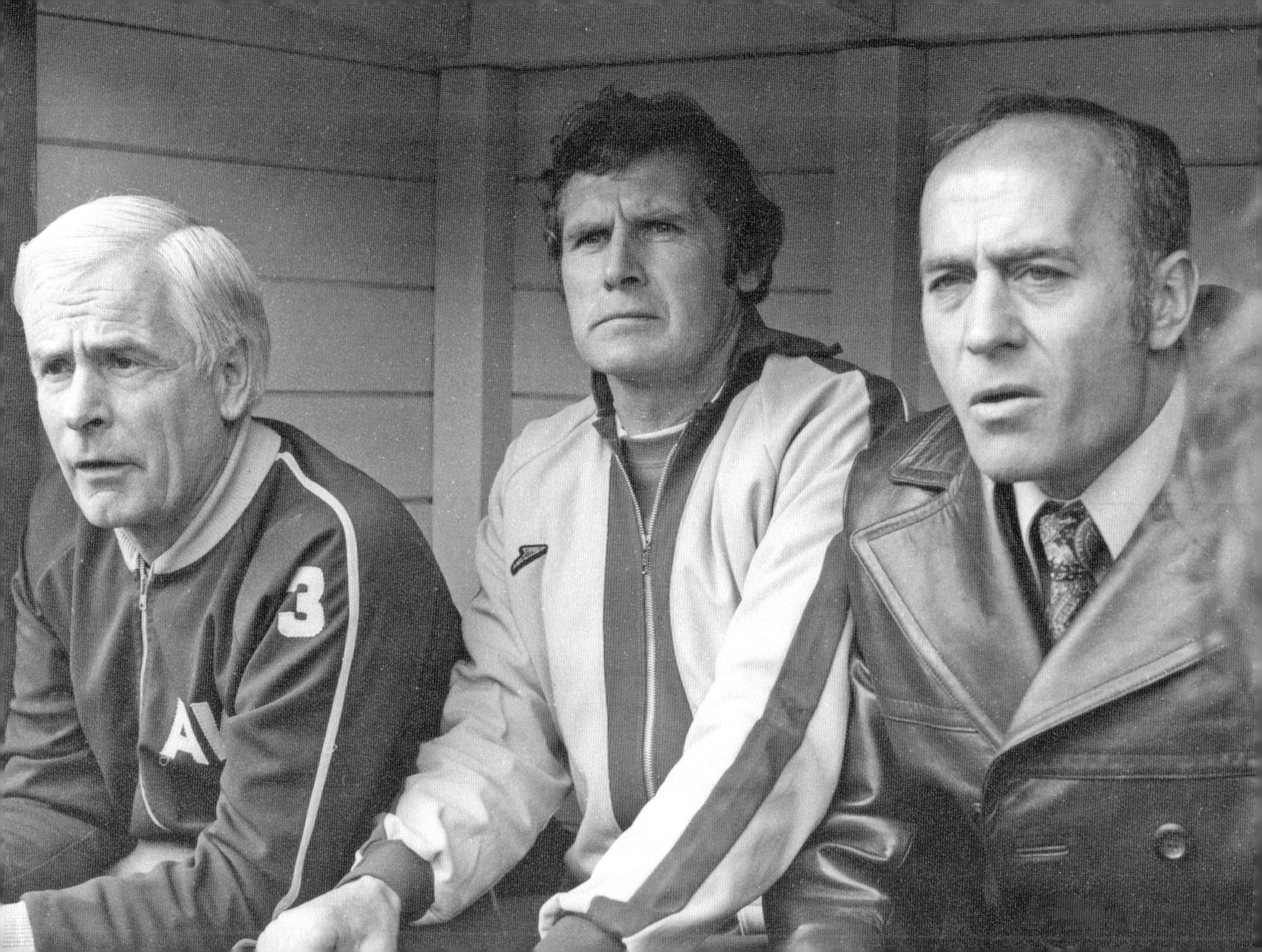

Vic Crowe

Born: 31st January 1932
Died: 21st January 2009
Birthplace: Abercynon
Appointed in 1970
Dismissed in 1974

BACKGROUND

Welshman Crowe did it all where Aston Villa Football Club was concerned, player, coach and the ultimate role – manager. He wasn't the first ex-Villan to go from boots to suit, Alex Massie and Eric Houghton had trodden the same path before him as did Ron Atkinson, Brian Little and John Gregory thereafter.

Born in Abercynon, Wales in January 1932 but bought up in the Handsworth district of Birmingham, his family having moved there when Victor Herbert was only two years of age. It was at nearby West Bromwich Albion that the teenage Crowe was given his first break in football when he joined the club on an amateur basis after playing for Erdington Albion (the 'Baggies' nursery side) on leaving school.

He had an amateur trial at the Villa the following year (1951) only for National Service to take him away. Initially to Blandford, Dorset for his basic training and then onto Scotland where he was attached to the Royal Electrical and Mechanical Engineers (REME), though Vic's son Stuart says, "God help them – he'd struggle putting a shelf up!" On the plus side Vic received more rations than most because he was in the football team. During this time he turned out for Stirling Albion, they were promoted as Scottish League Division B runners-up during 1950-51 but came straight back down the following season. They won only five of their 30 games, conceded 99 goals and had a goal difference of -60. This must have rankled with Vic who was determined to say the least.

THE PLAYER

Aston Villa finally landed their man, this time on professional terms, in June 1952 during George Martin's tenure. Vic Crowe never got to feature in Villa's first-team under the manager who signed him, Martin was sacked a few weeks prior to the start of the 1953/54 season and replaced by former Villa legend Eric Houghton.

Wing-half or more specifically right-half was Crowe's favoured position, he was 'blooded' in a 4-2 win away to Manchester City in October '54 with Irishman Blanchflower out. When Danny came back into the side Vic was the player who made way, this all changed in December of that year when Blanchflower left for pastures new, White Hart Lane the destination.

From that point on Crowe was an almost ever-present making 28 appearances in league and cup. His value to the club was plainly visible, the man was committed, wore his heart on his sleeve and shirking tackles wasn't in his vocabulary. The following season he missed only a handful of matches and weighed in with his first goal in claret and blue during the 3-0 rout of Newcastle United at Villa Park.

Crowe was injured at the beginning of the 1956/57 campaign and Bill Baxter wore the No 4 shirt for the first nine games. When Baxter was sidelined through injury Stan Crowther was given the right-half berth and his performances were such that he stayed in the side and walked away with an FA Cup winners medal for his efforts come the 4th May. Vic Crowe only managed a solitary game in what must have been a bitter/sweet experience for him. He featured sporadically in the early months of the new season but from the New Year he was back to full fitness and set to stay in the side.

Not even 'Spikes' (Vic's nickname) determination and work ethic could stop Aston Villa being relegated (1958/59) for only the second time in their illustrious history. It was hoped their prolonged cup run might have inspired some league form as they made it all the way to the FA Cup semi-final stage, (to fall narrowly to eventual winners Nottingham Forest), but sadly this wasn't the case.

Villa quickly found their Second Division feet and under captain Crowe (he missed only one match) they were back in the top flight as champions after just the one season in the wilderness. They also made it to the last four in the FA Cup but lost to Division One runners-up Wolverhampton Wanderers who also lifted the Football Association's blue ribbon event. Villa finally landed silverware the next year (1961) in the shape of the League Cup (its inaugural competition) when they defeated Rotherham United 3-2 on aggregate. In a marathon season of 58 competitive fixtures Vic Crowe featured in all but three of them.

He exceeded this in the 1961/62 campaign when he was the only ever-present first-teamer (league) in a season that saw the emergence of the latest Mercer's Minors as Villa finished a respectable seventh, albeit a dozen points shy of Alf Ramsey's surprise champions Ipswich Town, who'd won the Second Division title 12 months earlier.

Crowe's first League Cup goal for the Villa saw them take a commanding 3-1 win in the semi-final first-leg at Roker Park. Due to one of the worst winters on record the second-leg wasn't played until the following April ('63) when Villa were going through a nightmare period (eleven straight defeats). The 0-0 draw at home took them to a second final in three years only for them to lose to Birmingham City 1-3 on aggregate.

Crowe's last game in the claret and blue was in the December '63 in the 2-2 draw at home to Wolves. He'd scored his last in the colours in the away fixture just two days earlier in the 3-3 draw at Molineux. This was only a month after his testimonial, played at Villa Park, a London XI beat a Birmingham XI 6-1. All of his 16 caps for Wales came during his time at the Villa.

In the summer of 1964 he joined third-flight Peterborough United. Only admitted to the Football League at the expense of Gateshead at the start of 1960/61 the 'Posh' won the Fourth Division title and followed that up with two top-six finishes in the 'Third.' Vic stayed at London Road until 1967.

From there Vic Crowe went stateside joining Atlanta Chiefs of the National Professional Soccer League (NPSL), linking up with former Villans Phil Woosnam and Peter McParland. This league lasted only one

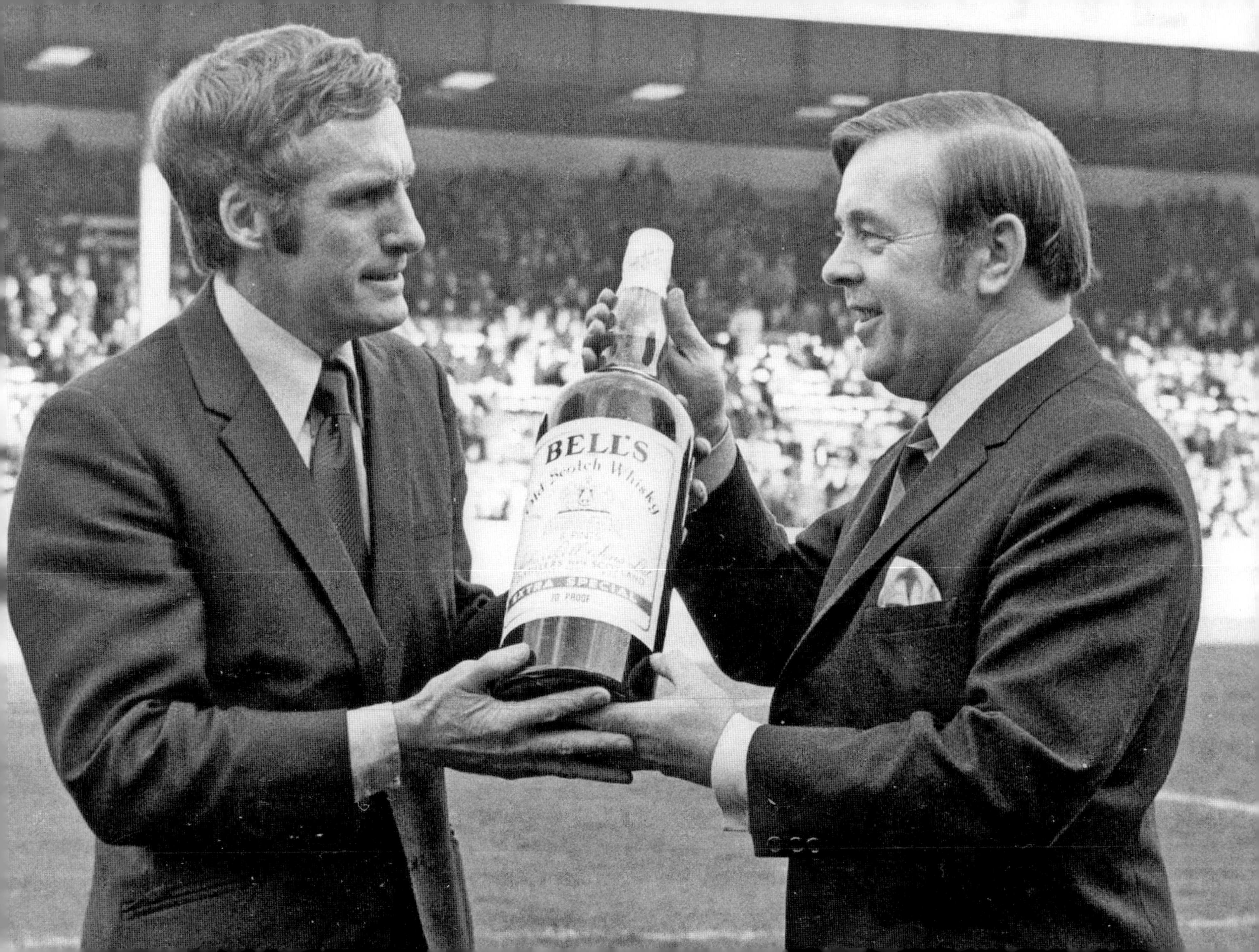
BELL'S
Scotch Whisky

[Left] Vic Crowe picks up the prestigious Bell's Manager of the Month award during Villa's promotion season

year (1967) before it merged with the United Soccer Association (USA) to form the North American Soccer League (NASL).

During the summer of '69 the Villa, under the leadership of the charismatic Tommy Docherty, arrived in the USA to take part in a five week tour. The club were based in the Atlanta area and inherited the moniker 'Atlanta Villa.' Vic was by now coaching the Chiefs. Villa winger Willie Anderson says the 'Doc' and Vic must have had conversations out there as Crowe landed up at Villa shortly after the club returned from their tour and took up a role coaching the Villa's reserve side.

THE MANAGER

By mid-January, with only four wins to show from 26 league games and anchored to the foot of Division Two, Tommy was sacked by Villa, the manager's job offered to Vic, who readily accepted it. There were murmurs that Vic had done the dirty on 'Doc' so Vic addressed the players, "People think I've done this and that but I'm willing to win you over!"

Initially coaches Stuart Williams and Frank Upton were taken on as Vic's backroom staff but after Villa's fall from grace into Division Three, Williams left to manage Payhaan of Iran. His place was taken by former Villa team-mate Ron Wylie who'd left the Villa to join Blues in the June 1965. Villa's rivals were managed by Joe Mallett (ex Forest coach) at the time. Ron respected Joe and went to St Andrews to learn off the master so to speak as he knew his future lay in coaching also.

Immediately on Vic Crowe taking up the manager's role, Barrie Hole ended his month long strike, having fallen out with Docherty and was reinstated in the team. Crowe signed Andy Lochhead, a bustling goal machine from Leicester City.

Unfortunately with games running out and time conspiring against the Villa, they dropped into the Third Division. It was a shock to their supporters, the city itself and the footballing world in general. Villa, at the time of their sad demise, were the most decorated club in English football.

Under the Crowe/Wylie double act new faces were bought in, Villa looked odds on to make a return at the first attempt. In a promotion berth prior to a Wembley League Cup show down with Tottenham Hotspur (a game Villa dominated but cruelly lost in the final 10 minutes), the wheels fell off and they had to settle for fourth position.

Before the start of the 1971/72 campaign Crowe caused an outcry by selling the popular (and captain) Brian Godfrey. It was the only way he could land winger and scorer Ray Graydon from Bristol Rovers. In time Vic was proved correct in that transfer. John Dunn's replacement between the posts Tommy Hughes didn't work out as well as expected, Crowe simply moved for WBA's Jimmy Cumbes.

On track for a return at the second time of asking Ian Ross and Chris Nicholl were both talked into dropping down the league to come to B6, showing yet again how persuasive Vic Crowe could be. Both were the division's costliest players at their time of signing proving the board were prepared to back their manager.

Villa took the Division Three title with a record 70 points tally; they had notched up the most wins (32) ever in a season by a Villa team, scored the most goals (85) and had conceded the least number (32) also. The management had done their homework in every quarter!

Vic Crowe had two 'Manager of the Month' awards for his efforts but many believe he should have had the 'Manager of the Year' crown too, beaten by Don Revie, his third title in four years.

241

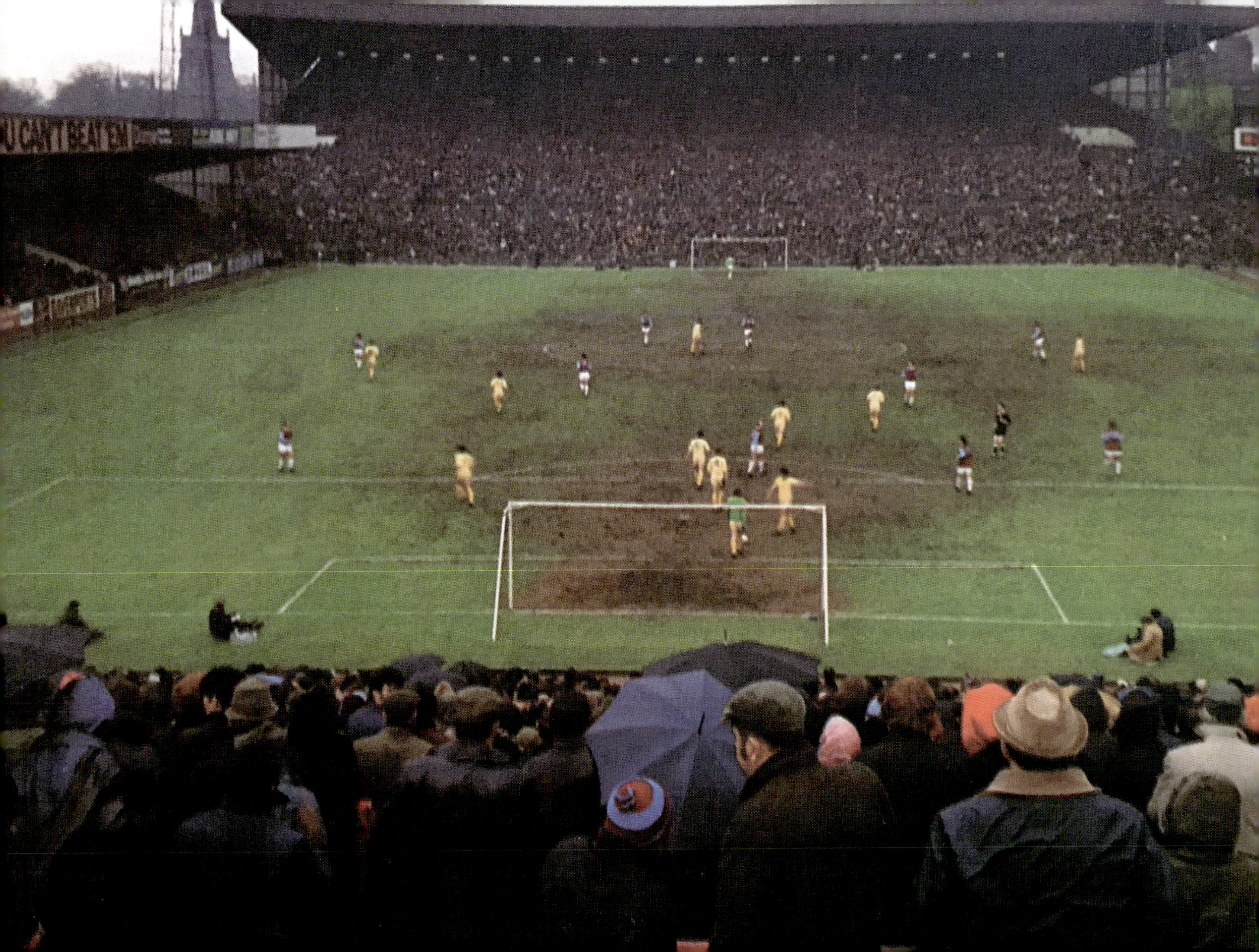

[Far Left] A rare colour photo taken looking towards the Holte End during Vic's time in charge of the club [Left] Crowe gets his man as Sammy Morgan signs on the dotted line from Port Vale

Back in the Second Division Villa were around the top of the table from the word go. Only beaten once in their first ten league games the side finally finished in a highly respectable third position. This was at a time when only the top two went up! Villa couldn't maintain the momentum the following season and with a disappointing 14th place finish Vic Crowe and Ron Wylie were pushed out of the door.

In June 1974 Ron Saunders was appointed and the rest is history...

But it's worth remembering that Saunders side which clinched promotion back to the top-flight as well as a successful League Cup campaign in the club's centenary year of 1974/75 was the side Vic built with the exception of only two signings – Frank Carrodus and Leighton Phillips.

Neil Rioch remembers Vic's appointment as a step in the right direction, "He was hard, he was fair, he was also a very shrewd boss. His man management skills were top drawer."

Ian 'Chico' Hamilton was also full of praise, "I had a great rapport with Vic Crowe, he knew what players were about and along with Ron Wylie they both knew how to treat players the right way. You had good banter with them and the atmosphere was always good."

Ray Graydon was a big fan of Vic's managing style and recalls that Vic would 'always take the time to come and have a word.' Once after a particularly heavy defeat he saw the other side to his boss who was understandably livid, "Some of you will stay in this club and some of you will leave. We are going to go forward with this team, some of you won't have a part in it!"

Ron Saunders

Born: 6th November 1932
Birthplace: Birkenhead
Appointed in 1974
Left in 1982

BACKGROUND

To a generation of Villa supporters Ron Saunders will forever be seen as the best manager in the club's history. This bold statement isn't without merit, on Saunders' arrival the club were at best a middle-of-the-road Second Division side. By the time he walked out of the club in February 1982 they were on the road to greatness with a European Cup victory against the mighty German team Bayern Munich just over the horizon.

THE PLAYER

As a player Saunders was a goal-scoring journeyman. He started at Everton close to his Birkenhead birthplace but first-team action was severely restricted. Southern League outfit Tonbridge threw Ron a lifeline and he seized it with both hands. Following a two-season spell with 'The Angels' he was given another opportunity at Football League level when Gillingham of the Third Division South came calling. His 20 goals for the 'Gills' alerted First Division Portsmouth.

Saunders spent a rollercoaster six years on the south coast at Fratton Park with 'Pompey' dropping down two divisions in the space of three years. His 145 goals in 236 appearances helped retain Second Division status when they went up as champions of the 'Third' before he moved onto Watford. At Vicarage Road his impressive scoring streak continued as the club finished in the top half of Division Three. He was there for the one season. A two-year spell followed at 'The Valley' where he netted 24 times for Charlton Athletic at a rate of a goal every 2.7 games.

Yeovil Town gave Ron Saunders his first taste of management though he also combined playing for the non-League side. Finishing a respectable 12th and 7th in 1967/68 and '68/69 respectively. He took over briefly at Oxford United where he set a 15 point target from the remain-

close run thing but they stayed in the First Division albeit by just two points and their fans also had a day out at Wembley though they were defeated 0-1 in the League Cup final at the hands of Tottenham.

With little more than a third of the 1973/74 season played (16 matches) and only two wins chalked up Norwich were sitting third from bottom. City had just suffered yet another defeat (home to Everton, 17th Nov), their eighth so far. A row ensued between the manager and the boardroom and before the end of the evening Saunders had tendered his resignation. Before the week was out Manchester City offered Ron another chance at management. The Manchester side had been rudderless since October when their boss Johnny Hart (a former City player), who'd succeeded Malcolm Allison in the hot seat, had had to call it a day, retiring through illness. Saunders readily accepted the role.

City's league form was far too inconsistent. Since Saunders came in they had only managed back-to-back wins the once, though they were able to negotiate all before them in the League Cup to earn their place at the Twin Towers. It was the second successive year Ron led a team out on the hallowed turf in the competition, it was also his second loss. His Man City side equalised through Colin Bell to cancel out Kenny Hibbitt's opener for Wolves, only to fall to a late Richards winner. Following their day out at Wembley, City would manage only one win in the next 11 league fixtures (scored 6, conceded 18), Saunders was sacked before the conclusion of the campaign as the 'Citizens' limped over the finish line in what looked a respectable 14th position. This didn't tell the whole story; they were only four points above doomed Southampton.

Come the end of the season down in Birmingham, Aston Villa relieved Vic Crowe and Ron Wylie of their duties. The general consensus was Brian Clough's imminent appointment in Aston. This wasn't to be; the board took little notice, they certainly wouldn't bow to outside pressure. In the June their new manager was unveiled before the cameras – Ron Saunders. Who? To many he'd escaped under the radar, before he was finished everyone throughout the land would know his

The journey begins here – Ron Saunders newly appointed manager at Aston Villa

ing 12 games to maintain their status in the division. They achieved this, sending Bury down with bottom-placed Fulham.

Norwich City then prised him away to Carrow Road. The 'Canaries' finished 11th and then 10th under Saunders but in his third term there the Norfolk based side took the Second Division title in 1972 to earn a place in the top flight for the first time in the club's history. It was a

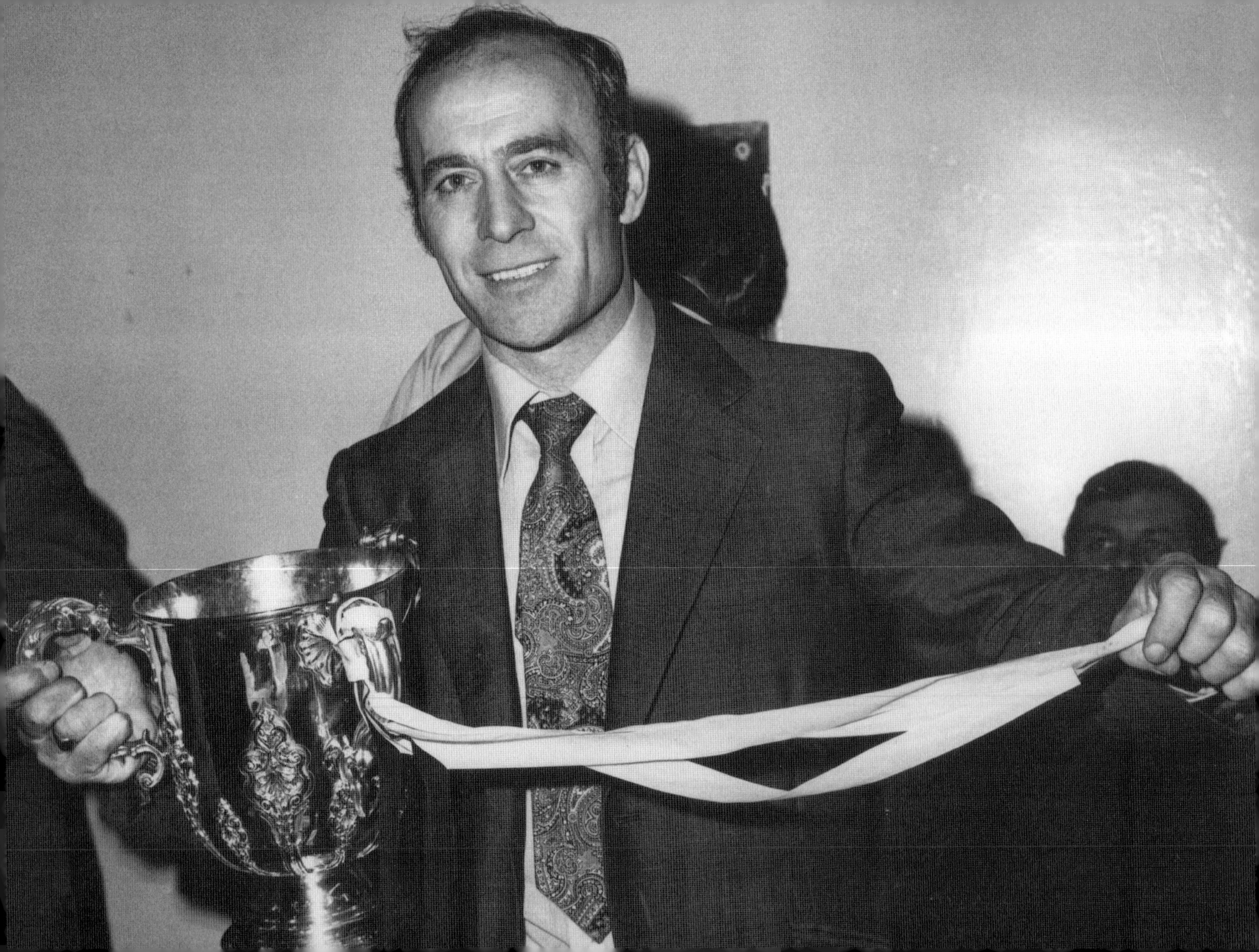

Saunders gets his hands on the League Cup at the third time of asking. He led Norwich to the final in 1973 and Manchester City the following year

name! Saunders had gone on record to say that he'd only be tempted back into the game if an offer arrived from a top club. Villa were in Division Two having finished 14th, but Ron was aware of the club's standing in the game, no team had more domestic honours than the famous claret and blue clad outfit.

Described by many as a sergeant-major type disciplinarian Mr Saunders took stock of the position. He had a healthy foundation on which to build, such was the strength in depth of his inherited squad he only dipped into the transfer market twice in his first full season at the club bringing in Frank Carrodus and Leighton Phillips. At the first attempt he managed to get Aston Villa back into familiar surroundings, their exodus from 1967 the longest the club had ever been out of the top flight. To add to their runners-up spot behind Manchester United the side lifted the League Cup when they defeated one of Saunders old sides in Norwich City, to make it a memorable centenary for one of the League's founder members. For Ron himself it was third time lucky.

Aston Villa maintained their place in Division One, they didn't pull up trees but neither did they look serious contenders to go straight back down. An injury to striker Keith Leonard earlier in the season would prove to highlight Saunders shrewd business acumen. In would come an unknown in the shape of Andy Gray who would go on to be recognised as the latest in the line of No 9 greats at B6. Dennis Mortimer was signed in December of that same season. A young stick-thin midfield player by the name of Gordon Cowans was given match time having come through the apprentice ranks. He would later be immortalised at Villa Park and rightly so. Alex Cropley arrived from Arsenal, a silky smooth player whose career was sadly finished by horrendous injuries.

Ron had quietly set about transforming Aston Villa. In the 1976/77 season they raised eyebrows the length and breadth of the country, they put five past Ipswich and Arsenal, they demolished Liverpool 5-1, they scored four goals at home on another four occasions, they finished the season in fourth place, scored the most goals in the division (76) and had it not been for a marathon run of 10 games (not to mention a myriad of injuries) to land their second League Cup in three years they would surely have landed the title.

Saunders it was claimed didn't trust the older or senior players, apparently it was player power that had got him removed from Maine Road. Whether there were any grains of truth in this we shall never know? Captain Chris Nicholl was one of the more senior players and coming up to 31-years of age at Villa Park when he was suddenly transferred to Southampton in the close season of 1977. He was replaced by the much younger (22-years old) Ken McNaught who'd shone in his League Cup final performances for Everton, against the Villa. Saunders fourth final in five years!

Other notable players to be signed in the late 1970s included Jimmy Rimmer, Allan Evans, Kenny Swain, Tony Morley and Des Bremner, while youngsters such as Gary Shaw, Gary Williams, Colin Gibson and Nigel Spink were all 'blooded' having made waves in the Central League. In the autumn of 1979 two of the bigger names at the Villa were on their way out following very public falling outs with boss Saunders, Andy Gray went to neighbours Wolves while John Gidman wound up at Goodison Park.

Notwithstanding these developments Ron's next team was taking shape; it only required the last piece of the proverbial jigsaw. It would also happen in the next decade and in the next volume!

ASTON VILLA FIRST TEAM
PLAYERS

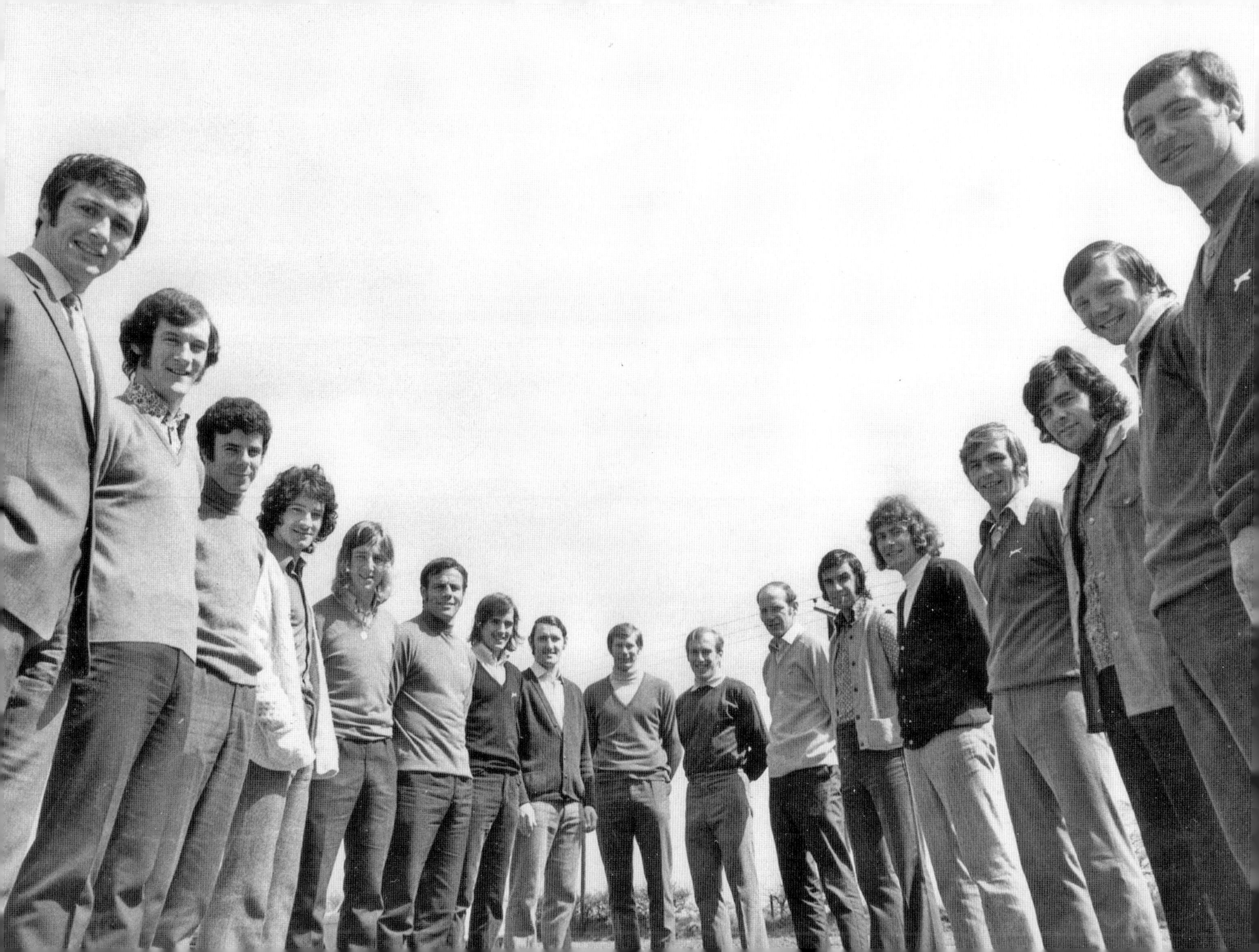

CHARLIE AITKEN

Charlie Aitken started his career with Lothians United. It was there he won the amateur cup, a competition open to the whole of Scotland. In the quarter-finals he recalls they beat Dundee Butterburn and then Drumchapel Rovers in the semis, on a pitch that consisted of crushed coke from the local brazier, the only grass - a bit on each corner.

From there he progressed to Edinburgh Thistle 'A' team, and later was invited to train a couple of times a week with Scottish First Division outfit Hibernian at their Easter Road ground. At 17 he still had a year to go in the sixth form at George Watson's college in Edinburgh, a private school that played rugby.

In his time at school Aitken was unbelievably quick, extremely fit and a very accomplished athlete, he won many races and set records. Trophies still bear his name to this day. "I used to play rugby in the morning and at 13 or 14-years of age I played for a local youth team in the afternoon. The school was upset when I left to join Aston Villa. I saw it as a challenge, it hadn't been my intention to play professional football, I played it for fun."

Along with another full-back Wilson Briggs also from Scotland, Aitken signed professional terms in August 1959. In the early days at his new club he was shocked at how unfit the players were. When Joe Mercer signed him for the Villa, Charlie held the advantage due to the grounding he'd received at school.

He moved into his Yardley digs and relied on the No 11 local bus to get to training at Villa Park. Other Villa youngsters such as George Graham and Mike Tindall would often be on the same bus. On a Saturday, matchday, the journey would be shared with supporters making their way to the game.

Struggling to adapt to his new life and being bored silly, he enrolled in night school to study.

He 'cut his teeth' in the 'Fourth' team playing in the Warwickshire Football Combination and Villa's mid-week side. In spite of overseeing a successful return to top-flight football for the senior side, manager Mercer and right-hand man Dick Taylor invested a great deal of time working with their new defender on the training ground.

"Joe and his assistant manager spent a lot of time with me, not so much speed work, it was more that I didn't have the same natural ability many of the players possessed. Joe worked hard on that side of my game. He taught me how to play within my limits as a defender on the pitch, how and when to tackle and how not to get injured."

"Once I tried something smart during a weekend game with my weaker foot. Joe went mad. Even though we won the game he shouted, "Charlie get your bloody right foot chopped up for fire wood." "By the Monday he came and apologised."

Before the close of the 1959/60 campaign Charlie was turning out in the Midland Intermediate League with the 'Third' string.

[Right] Charlie Aitken captains the Villa for the match against Notts County in December 1973

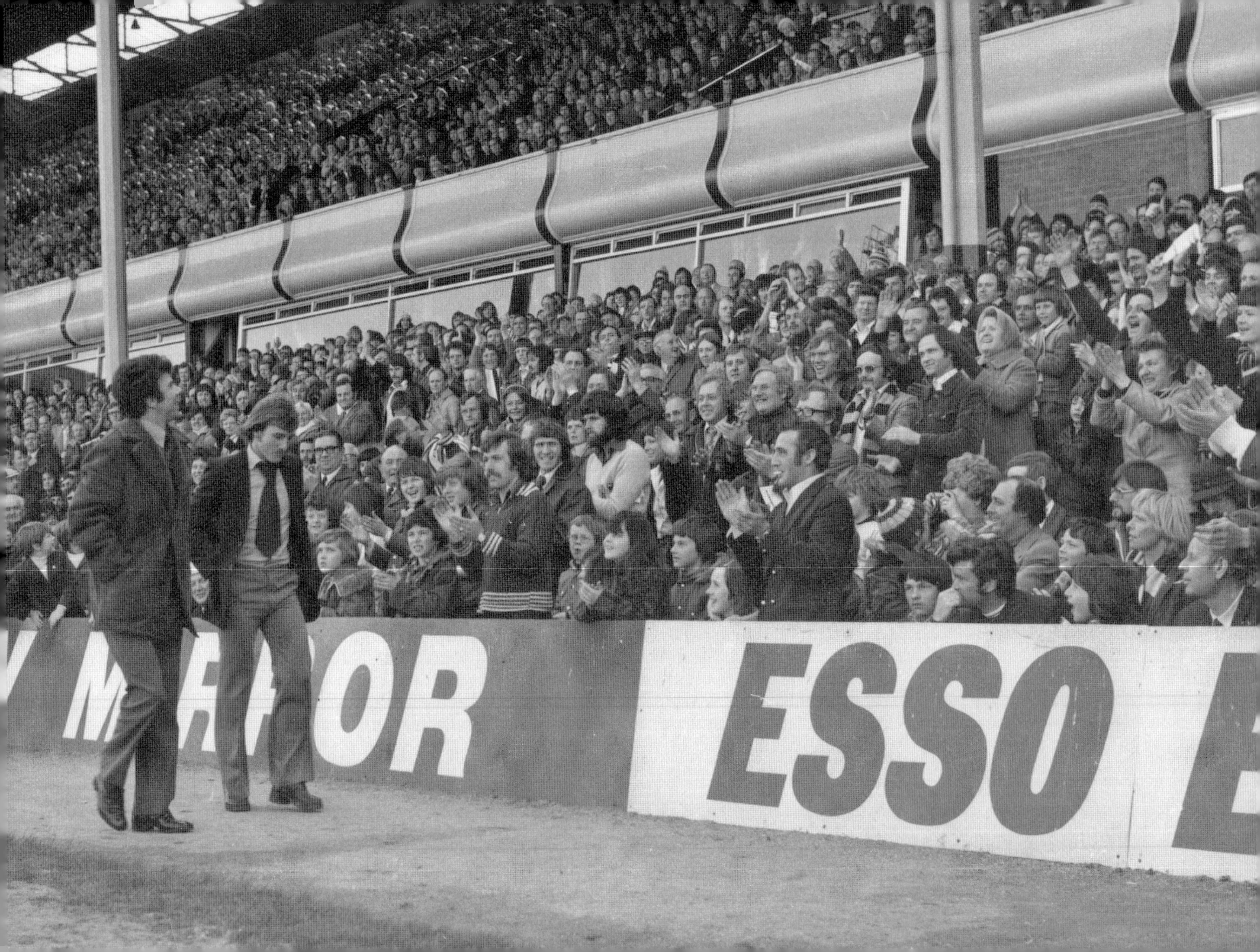
ESSO

[Left] Record appearance holder, Charlie Aitken, gets a standing ovation from an appreciative Villa Park crowd

In March of the following season Gordon Lee returned to Division One football following a two-and-a-half-year absence allowing Charlie to move up to the Central League. After assured displays Mercer threw him in at the deep end and gave him his first-team debut 'blooding' him in the final fixture of the campaign, at home to Sheffield Wednesday. Also making his only appearance of the season was legend and club captain Johnny Dixon, a veteran of 430 games.

Lee was first choice left-back at the commencement of the '61/62 but not for long. Aitken got the nod in September and was there till the end racking up 35 games.

During the next eight seasons he amassed over 300 appearances in what was 'his' No 3 shirt, ever present in many of those campaigns and dropping a mere handful of matches.

Sadly in the 1969/70 season the Villa stunned the footballing world when they dropped into the Third Division. They were the most decorated club in the English game.

"Obviously I didn't want to go down to the Third Division but we had so much experience and so many players who'd played in the top flight when we went down. Vic Crowe came in and did a very good job along with Ron Wylie. It was just a question of time before we got ourselves out of Division Three, I felt we had too good a team. I think the first year we finished fourth and got to the League Cup final. We were a pretty good team then, we could beat First Division sides but we had to battle the physical side first by getting involved."

The Villa were able to persuade players from the higher divisions, they knew Villa were there only temporarily. Ian Ross came from Liverpool. Ray Graydon was drafted in.

"I'd marked Graydon in some games and Vic Crowe asked what I thought of him. "Ray's a very good player," I told him.
"He's one of the best I've ever played against. You knew he'd get you 10-15 goals a season and from the wing. Cast from the same mould as Harry Burrows - who was also absolutely brilliant."

At this point all Aitken had to show for his time south of the border was two League Cup runners-up gongs ('63 and '71). This changed when he was one of many vital components in getting the famous old club out of the third-tier in April 1972. The club's 70 points total a new division record, not to mention most goals scored and least conceded.

Under new manager Ron Saunders further promotion in 1974/75 was achieved coupled with a Wembley League Cup final. Villa were once again going to be dining from the top table. Only Aitken remained from the previous time the club graced the 'First.'

Charlie, back in the big league where his talents deserved to be displayed, started as first choice as per normal but the manager then began playing John Robson at left-back.

Sadly at home to QPR, Saturday 31st January 1976, he made his last appearance in the claret and blue shirt he'd worn with pride for over 15 years.

He'd played under six different managers and amassed an unbeatable 661 games. The best of it was, he was still running rings around everyone else when time was called on his claret and blue career.

"Even when I left Villa to go to New York Cosmos I was still the fittest at Villa Park," stated Charlie.

BRUCE RIOCH

Bruce Rioch knew from a very early age in what direction he wanted his career path to take. Born in Aldershot to a Scottish father, he grew up in Cambridge where he watched City and United alternate weekends. Wilf Mannion the original 'Golden Boy' England legend and prolific scorer for Middlesbrough was now plying his trade at the Abbey Stadium in the Eastern Counties League. "He was a dream to watch as a youngster," recalled the budding footballer.

The park became Bruce's classroom and his father and brothers were his tutors, teaching him the art of the game, the techniques, trapping, passing volleying, shooting, heading, the lot.

He got a trial - whilst still a schoolboy - at Chelsea when Tommy Docherty was boss. Bruce bagged a hat-trick, "though nothing came of it."

He persisted with the graft in the park and the workload paid off, he got his wish to be a pro. He made his mark at Kenilworth Road establishing himself in Luton's first-team but his record of a goal in every three games soon had bigger clubs watching him. "I was playing for Luton Town. I'd been in the side a number of years playing at inside-forward and scored my share of goals. I was invited as a youngster to tour with the FA. We went to New Zealand and the Far East, playing games in New Zealand, Taihiti, Hong Kong, Singapore and Bangkok."

We came back off the tour and returned to life at Luton. At the end of one training session manager Alec Stock called me over, "We've received an offer from Aston Villa and it's been accepted."

"Their manager Tommy Docherty wanted to meet me and my younger brother Neil, also a player at Luton, I think he must have remembered that Stamford Bridge trail match. Terms were agreed and we were taken up to Birmingham where we stayed overnight with Villa director Harry Kartz. Arriving at Villa Park the next morning both Neil and I were amazed by the sheer scale of the place, it was amazing, I'd never seen the ground before. We signed our contracts that very morning, we were now Aston Villa players."

The Rioch's were now a part of the most expensive side in the Second Division, the club having spent in excess of £200,000, a considerable sum at that time!

"As the season began they played me further forward than my usual midfield role, I was now up front with Ian Hamilton. It didn't suit my game but when you're asked to play, that's what you do. Results weren't good, we couldn't score goals and Tommy Docherty paid the price for the poor start to the season when he lost his job in the January."

"Second team coach Vic Crowe took over immediately but he couldn't halt the slide. Being so far behind on points we didn't survive and got relegated. When I joined the club I thought we were going up, not down. Luton came up to Division Two as Villa went in the opposite direction. It was a huge shock, everybody involved was disappointed, the supporters, the city of Birmingham. We hadn't anticipated this at all."

Bruce Rioch's tenacity was evident early on in his claret and blue career. Just eight games into the new season he damaged a cartilage at Watford though he played on and was an ever-present during the campaign. Only one other player, right-back Michael Wright played all 42 in a side that was never really balanced.

Lightning struck again, only four games into Villa's maiden Third Division season and Rioch was badly injured, this time he couldn't play on, "We played Mansfield at home. I went to pull the ball down and a Mansfield player caught the side of my foot. This knocked my knee joint to the side, the cartilage tore completely. The cartilage was removed in an operation at the West Bromwich & District and because I'd damaged the other one the previous year it was decided to have that taken out a month or so later after I'd had some rehabilitation. It kept me out of the game for three months. Other absentees were George Curtis and Michael Wright who'd also had cartilage surgery along with Dave Rudge, he'd badly broken his leg. We did our rehab together and helped each other."

"I came back on Boxing Day as a sub against Shrewsbury and scored. Vic and Ron Wylie had told me straight that I wouldn't start the game but there was a strong possibility I'd get on for part of it. I had a few Central League games under my belt beforehand and I'd also been on the bench midweek for the League Cup semi-final 2nd leg at home to Manchester United, though I didn't get on."

With beating United 3-2 over two-legs Villa had made it to a Wembley showdown final against Tottenham Hotspur. The evergreen Davie Gibson had been outstanding in both ties but was forced out of the side with Rioch returning to some form of fitness.

"It certainly wasn't an easy decision they had to make for either myself or Davie. He'd been playing brilliantly while I'd been out and against United he was outstanding. Leaving Davie out was always going to be difficult because he was a playmaker who bought a lot to the team. He was a big influence on the pitch, he played with vast experience and had style and class. Vic Crowe and Ron must have reckoned on me having played enough matches since my return to pick me ahead of Davie."

Under the twin-towers the Villa played well above their station, belying their third-tier status, they were taking the game to Spurs. Hamilton hit the woodwork while Andy Lochhead will forever contemplate what might have been had he struck his shot with more venom denying Perryman to clear off the line.

THE BIG ASTON VILLA BOOK OF THE SEVENTIES

"While I was delighted to have played at Wembley, I genuinely felt for Davie. We had our chances on the day but Martin Chivers was on form and hit the two late goals that sunk us. We were disappointed but we knew we were a good side, tough and hard to beat, with a great mentality. No matter who we played sides were going to find it extremely difficult to beat us."

"Getting back to Third Division games after playing at Wembley was like going from caviar to baked beans. We had to adapt and adapt quickly for the next game. Unfortunately we came down to earth with a bump and lost matches we thought we should have won at a canter. Perhaps some of the players lost their focus a bit after having their heads turned in the big cup-ties with the big atmospheres?"

"My form tailed off, after a peak I was in a trough. I'd been out for 12 weeks and came back with determination and drive. From thinking my career was over I experienced a big high (Wembley) but then the adrenaline rush tapered off and the training became mundane. Geoff Vowden was brought in. He was well known to Ron Wylie in their time together at Birmingham City. Geoff was a super guy, a great player and he could score goals."

"Look we think you have lost some of your focus. Your form has dipped so for the good of the team we are leaving you out," I was informed by the management.

Villa finished the season on a low; following the Cup final the side registered only two victories from 15 games. Promotion at the first opportunity had failed. The club finished fourth, nine points behind second-placed Fulham.

"Andy Lochhead was our most influential player. An old fashioned, rugged centre-forward who could lead the line. His main strength was his aerial power but he also very good on the floor allowing us to play off him. In Willie Anderson we had a great winger. Jim Cumbes and Ray Graydon came in. Ian Ross and Chris Nicholl followed them in the New Year - we had a real team."

"It was evident that the second half of the season was the key. The first half was obviously important but from the New Year and onwards we kept 15 clean sheets in the remaining 25 games. That in itself was priceless to the final run-in because it gave us the necessary points." Villa at the second attempt were out of the third-tier.

"Picking up the trophy on 5th May at home to Chesterfield in front of 45,000 was a wonderful feeling. It meant a lot to so many, not just the board and players but the coaching staff, the medical and backup staff and the magnificent Villa supporters."

"I had five fantastic years despite the injuries and the setbacks. I've got a lot of fond memories and I enjoyed it immensely. Ambition was the only reason I left the Villa. Had Villa got promotion to Division One I would have stayed. I was happy but we finished third when only two teams go up.

Birmingham City and Arsenal made enquiries, Vic thought the 'Gunners' style of play wouldn't suit my game. Derby County then wanted me and I was told Villa had accepted their offer."
His time at B6 came to a close, he'd made 176 (5 sub) appearances in the Villa colours and found the back of the net on 37 occasions, most of his goals came from distance and hit with such force keepers didn't stand much chance.

Bruce was the first English born player to captain the Scotland national side, won a First Division title in his time at the Baseball Ground and later proved his worth as a manager at several clubs. Remembered for bringing Dennis Bergkamp into the English game during his tenure as Arsenal boss.

[Right] Rioch brothers, Bruce and Neil, arrived from Luton Town

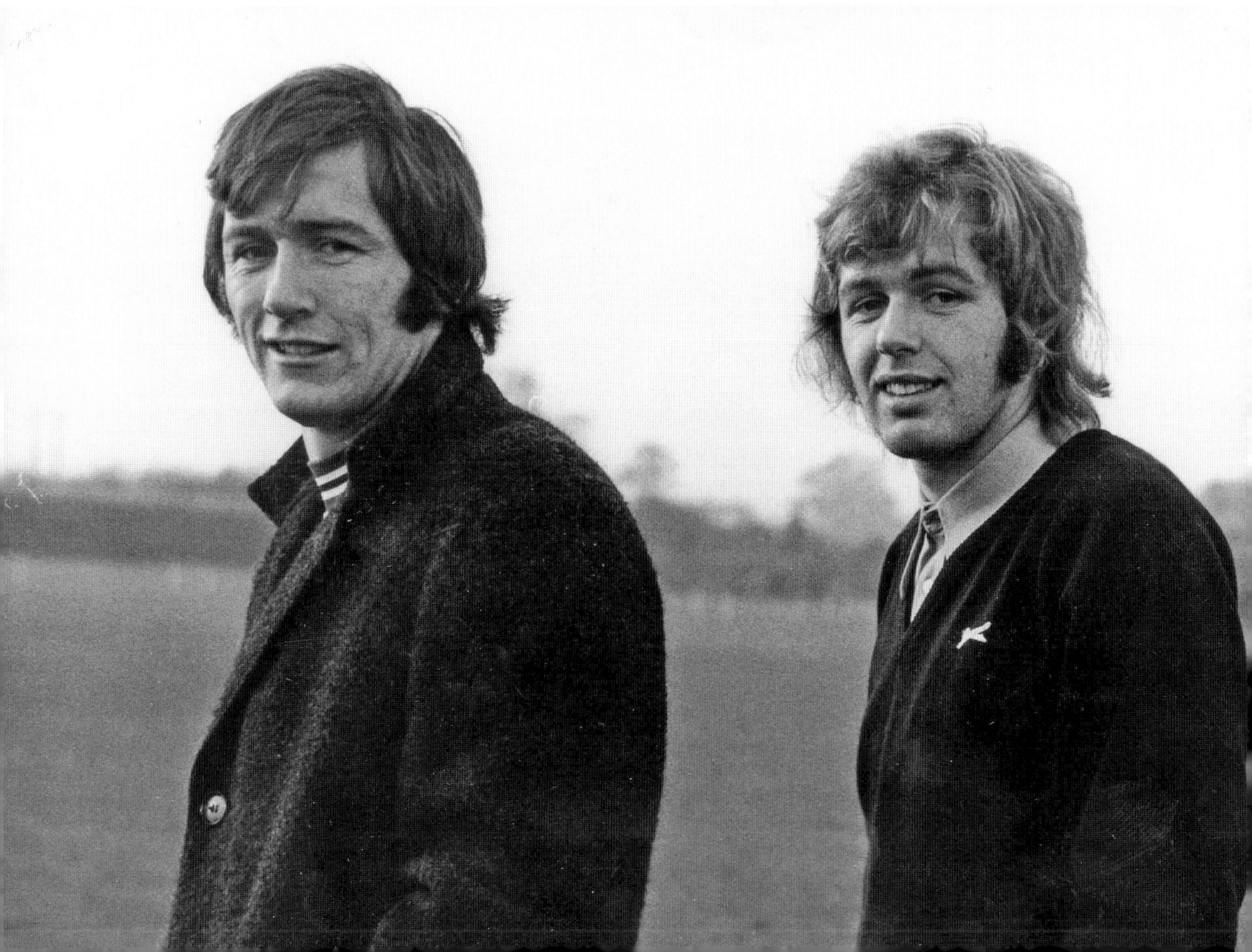

WILLIE ANDERSON

THE BIG ASTON VILLA BOOK OF THE SEVENTIES

Born in Liverpool in January 1947, Willie started out playing for Liverpool and Merseyside Boys. He greatly impressed an interested Manchester United so much they signed him on as a junior in 1962, "I joined United as a 15-year old. Me and George Best came through at the same time, we were good mates and in 1964 we won the FA Youth Cup when we defeated Swindon Town 5-2. In truth we were expected to win it as the club had won the first five tournaments when it started back in the 1950s"

Anderson was given his first-team debut at 16 and got a taste for playing in front of the vast Old Trafford support that followed the 'Red Devils' even back then. Having performed in front of large attendances, turning out in the Central League was a case of coming back down to earth with a bang, "Once you'd played in front of big crowds, playing in the reserves got kind of old, so in the end I asked manager Matt Busby and his assistant Jimmy Murphy if I could move on."

Not long after an opening appeared when Willie was called into the office and informed that Aston Villa were keen on signing the winger.

With a far better prospect of first-team football at Villa Park he met Villa boss Dick Taylor at the Old Trafford ground and signed on the dotted line. He was still a teenager.

"I was just looking for an opportunity to play on a regular basis. Villa had a great name and they were in the First Division. I got into the first-team immediately making my debut for the Villa away to Chelsea (Jan '67) and I kept my place in the team for the remainder of the season."

In the 17 starts he made Willie bagged five goals showing what he could achieve and this was playing in a wide role. Unfortunately the club had been in freefall long before his arrival and with losing 11 but more significantly, winning only two of those fixtures, Villa were doomed to the Second Division.

"Manchester United won the title while Villa went down but I didn't see this as a step backwards. Whilst it was great being at Manchester United, playing in the Central League wasn't enough for me."

The following campaign he was one of two ever-presents, along with Lew Chatterley, 28 players were called upon due to injuries or loss of form. The side struggled throughout and with 20 defeats to their name (only the two relegated teams lost more) were fortunate to remain in the division.

"Tommy Cummings came in and I don't think he made that many changes to be honest. By the time I'd signed, the club especially at boardroom level was in decline. This was more evident having come from Manchester United. The training facilities were terribly outdated and I personally didn't think Tommy Cummings - who'd replaced Dick Taylor - was a great manager. Certainly not in my eyes, and bearing in mind I'd served under Matt Busby."

"Villa could have been on par with Manchester United. Villa Park was a great ground, they attracted huge crowds even when they were struggling, they just needed better guidance from the boardroom and from the management."

"I don't remember what happened to Cummings but Villa struggled under him from day one. Everyone expected us to bounce straight back up but it didn't happen. I remember losing to Birmingham City of all teams, 50,000 supporters came out for it but we got turned over and we were on the same points as whoever was bottom of the table, it was shocking, it never should have happening. Not to a team of Aston Villa's calibre surely?"

"Tommy Docherty came in to replace Cummings sometime in the November? He was larger than life, a very charismatic man. His man management skills were legendary even then and he could motivate anyone to believe they were the best player in the world.

We trained hard under 'The Doc' and things took off straightaway. We couldn't stop winning! A good run in the FA Cup helped us too, we tied down at Southampton's place and beat them up at Villa."

"Before big matches Tommy had us staying over at Ashby de la Zouch near Leicester. I remember getting on the bus that day for the journey to Villa Park for the Southampton cup-tie. You'd think you were going to Wembley for the final itself, huge crowds everywhere you looked, it was crazy amazing."

Sadly Tommy's golden touch deserted him. Even though he was permitted to assemble the most expensive side in the division with the board's backing and support, Villa stumbled to the point they were still without a win under their belts after nine league games.

Despite the vote of confidence from the club hierarchy Tommy was moved aside, Vic Crowe who'd returned to the club to coach the reserves was installed as new boss, but Villa still fell from grace. Third Division football was on the cards.

THE BIG ASTON VILLA BOOK OF THE SEVENTIES

"When Villa went down I put in a transfer request, the last thing I wanted to do was play in the Third Division. Vic Crowe said to leave it with him and he would see what would happen. Nothing happened, in truth I don't think they wanted me to leave."

"We had to figure it out very quickly in the Third Division because it was a whole new ball game. Luckily we had an abundance of steel throughout the side which is what you need (it seemed everyone wanted Villa's scalp), we also had our share of flair players too, lads who could get their foot on the ball and dictate the pace of the game to suit our needs. We had to find a way to win because the lower down the league, the harder it is to play. There's not as much football played, so to speak, there was plenty of aggression though to make up for it."

"We never wore shinguards which was crazy in those days, we knew we were better than the opposition and they fully understood that. They soon realised the best way to compete against us – if we weren't on our feet we couldn't go past them. We had to come to grips with all of that. In the first season we put together a decent cup run so it showed we were going about it the right way. When teams came to play us on our patch it was like them going to Wembley."

"Villa regularly had 30,000+ gates at home and we would go and play at their grounds and be backed by thousands of our fans but if it wasn't us playing they'd be lucky to have 5,000 turn up. Week in and week out we went to places and grounds most of us had never been to and it wasn't like they were in great condition, some of the pitches had no grass whatsoever, they were just mud baths. It was really a physically tough division to play in and it was hard to overcome some of these other teams." Villa's good cup run was rewarded with a mouth watering two-legged semi-final against Willie Anderson's ex-side.

"We didn't face any big teams until the end. The lads wanted Bristol City in the semis but from a personal point of view, drawing Manchester United was great for me. I felt good going back there and the team playing really well. It was a great result for us because no one gave us a chance in hell of beating United."

"Getting them back to Villa Park was a night I'll never forget. It was a full house, the Holte End was packed and behind us all the way. Brian Kidd scored early on in the game for them but we fought back and Andy Lochhead scored with a great header just before the break.

In the second-half I remember crossing the ball from out on the left and Pat McMahon headed it home to make it 2-1. We held on, we'd won the semi and now we were going to the final. I could hardly believe it. It didn't sink in for weeks that we were going to be playing at Wembley, a dream come true."

On the eve of the cup final Aston Villa were level on points with leaders Preston North End. Providing they held their nerve they would be out of the 'Third' at the first attempt.

Anderson remembers being down in London ready for the showdown, "We got together at the hotel and had a team talk on the morning of the game. Vic said, "Hey, this day is going to go by really fast so take everything in as best you can because before you know it it's going to be over." And boy was he right!"

"When I watched previous finals on the television, I looked at the team buses fighting their way through the crowds and I'd think, "God how great would it be doing that? And you know what? We did. But Vic was right on the money, it was all over before we knew it, in the blink of an eye, gone."

"Going into the Wembley changing rooms and then walking out on the pitch before the game was the greatest. We get there about an hour or so before and you walk out to see what studs you need in your boots and to get a feel for the atmosphere. Everything leading up to the game was great but it went too quickly. I remember it was one hell of a game, we gave it our best shot and on another day, could have scored. We were on top or matched them until the last ten minutes and then Martin Chivers popped up and scored a couple. It was anybody's game until then."

"We were devastated not to be going up at the end of that first season. After playing in the final at Wembley it was hard for some players to adjust going back to the little grounds. Turning out on a cold night at places like Tranmere was a real turn off. Motivating yourself for them games got harder us. If we hadn't been distracted by getting to Wembley and believe we would have won promotion at the first time of asking."

Lessons were learned ready for the forthcoming onslaught for the Villa's second term in the 'Third.' Defensive issues were addressed in the signings of Cumbes and later on Ross and Nicholl. The attack also received a timely boost in the shape of winger Graydon. The result – far more goals in the scored column, fewer in the conceded equals promotion. Villa took the title at a canter.

"We went having no scorer in double figures in that first year to then having four players who scored double figures. The teams we had to play had already played us the year before so it wasn't as big a deal. We got down to business from the word go and figured out that we had to grind out results. This is what we did. All the games that season came together. We won a lot of them 1-0 or 2-0 (19 in fact). There weren't many teams that could stop us because we had so many options. The entire team was set up to attack."

Willie started the following season at the club but got injured mid-September. After returning to the side in October he had a run of games but was out again mid-November.

"I got injured and then fit, 'Chico' Hamilton was also injured at that same time." "I'd like you two to play in the reserves," Vic Crowe said. "We had Leeds United coming up and the manager wanted us to prove we were both fit. I was OK with that but 'Chico' said he wouldn't play. We got up to Leeds and Vic picked the team and I was left out. 'Chico' was substitute. I got really pissed off with that."

"I talked to Ron Wylie about it at Bodymoor and asked him what was happening? Within a week Vic Crowe called me into his office and told me they had received an offer from Cardiff City. At least I knew someone wanted me."

Needless to say Anderson left to join the 'Bluebirds.'

"It's the worst decision I ever made in soccer, I should never have left the Villa. I loved playing for them, I should've stayed at the Villa and done a Charlie Aitken. It's the biggest regret I have – ever!"
Had Willie been allowed to stay at Villa Park he would surely have added greatly to the 267 (inc 3 sub) appearances he made, not to mention his tally of 44 goals.

RAY GRAYDON

Having failed at the first time of asking to escape the clutches of Division Three, Vic Crowe went out and made a big headline signing in winger Ray Graydon from Bristol Rovers, unfortunately Villa had to let crowd favourite and captain Brian Godfrey go in the other direction.

As a child growing up in Bristol, Ray Graydon used to watch the Rovers occasionally and there was a certain player he would study that bit more than the others. Harold Jarman was that player in question who was at home making darting runs down the right-wing.

Ray went through a bit of a difficult time, he'd signed as an apprentice at Bristol Rovers at the age of 16 but a year in he felt hadn't done too well. As a result of this his enthusiasm waned somewhat. The coach was quite aggressive towards him and the enjoyment he found playing on a Saturday in the youth team had deserted him.

"I found it increasingly difficult and it all came together to the point I couldn't produce on the pitch. I decided it would be better for me if I left but Rovers wanted to keep an eye on me because they weren't one-hundred percent that I wouldn't make it as a player. During my apprenticeship I'd been doing day release with an electrical contractor so I had something to fall back on."

"In my time away from Eastville I turned out regularly for Hanbrook, a local side and it was while I was with them I played for the England amateur youth and U-18s. This proved to me that I was obviously improving. Someone at Rovers thought so too, they had been in touch and this led to me playing in youth and floodlit matches for them."

"In time I signed on as a part-timer for £5 a week. I played in the first-team making my debut at 17-years old. Over the next three years I played consistently, made over 130 appearances and just before my 21st birthday I was informed a club was showing interest in me. It sounded even more fantastic when I was told that the club was Aston Villa, they were a big team."

"Both my parents were very proud and supportive and watched me at Bristol Rovers. My dad had helped me my entire career and I couldn't wait to tell him my good news. His words were ringing in my ears," "Get up that motorway as quick as you can son. Bristol Rovers were a well supported club but Aston Villa was on another level completely. The facilities were out of this world, new training kit and as many footballs as I've ever seen. I felt like a kid in a sweetshop."

"I felt at home in my new surroundings straightaway. It was something I desperately wanted to do and the players helped me immensely. Bruce Rioch and George Curtis in particular, they went out of their way to make Sue and I feel at home. It was a terrific gesture and we greatly appreciated it."

"Even though I hadn't long since joined the Villa I accompanied Ron Wylie on some coaching missions which helped me settle in quicker." After the first six games Ray was Villa's leading scorer having found the net on three occasions and this from playing in a wide role on the right wing. In November for the visit of fellow promotion candidates Notts County, Graydon scored a wonderful goal to secure both points in front of the Match of the Day cameras, "It was one of the few headed goals I've scored in my career but it was a good one and an important one." How he found the space to head into such a miniscule gap between the upright and the keeper, only he knows.

The winger followed this up with a goal just as audacious for the visit of Bolton Wanderers, "I remember my goal against Bolton vividly, I also recall seeing it in a football magazine with the headline 'The goal with two touches.' It was a volley, a result of a long, long goalkick by new keeper Jimmy Cumbes. Lochhead flicked it on and I smashed it in."

Andy Lochhead and Ray Graydon were perfect for each other, the bullet headed centre-forward was hardly ever beaten in the air and he would knock the ball into space for Graydon to have a crack at goal. Likewise many of Andy's headed goals were a result of an inch-perfect cross from somewhere on the right flank, delivered by yours truly, "I could lob the ball in and knew that Andy would be on the end of it, a bit like Andy Gray later on. He was the first centre-forward I really thought, "Wow, this guy can get on the end of crosses.""

The BBC were back again in February for the Bournemouth encounter, a game Ray recalls, "I remember the games against Bournemouth being big games and really tough. MacDougall was playing for them as well as Boyer. They stood out in my memory, they were very good players and during our games against them we gave them the respect they deserved. This was before they'd hardly made their mark on the game and it was no surprise they went on to bigger clubs."

By the season's end Villa would rightly be crowned champions with a record points tally for the division. In League and cup the team scored exactly 100 goals, Ray weighed in with 15 of those and probably made four or five for every one he scored.

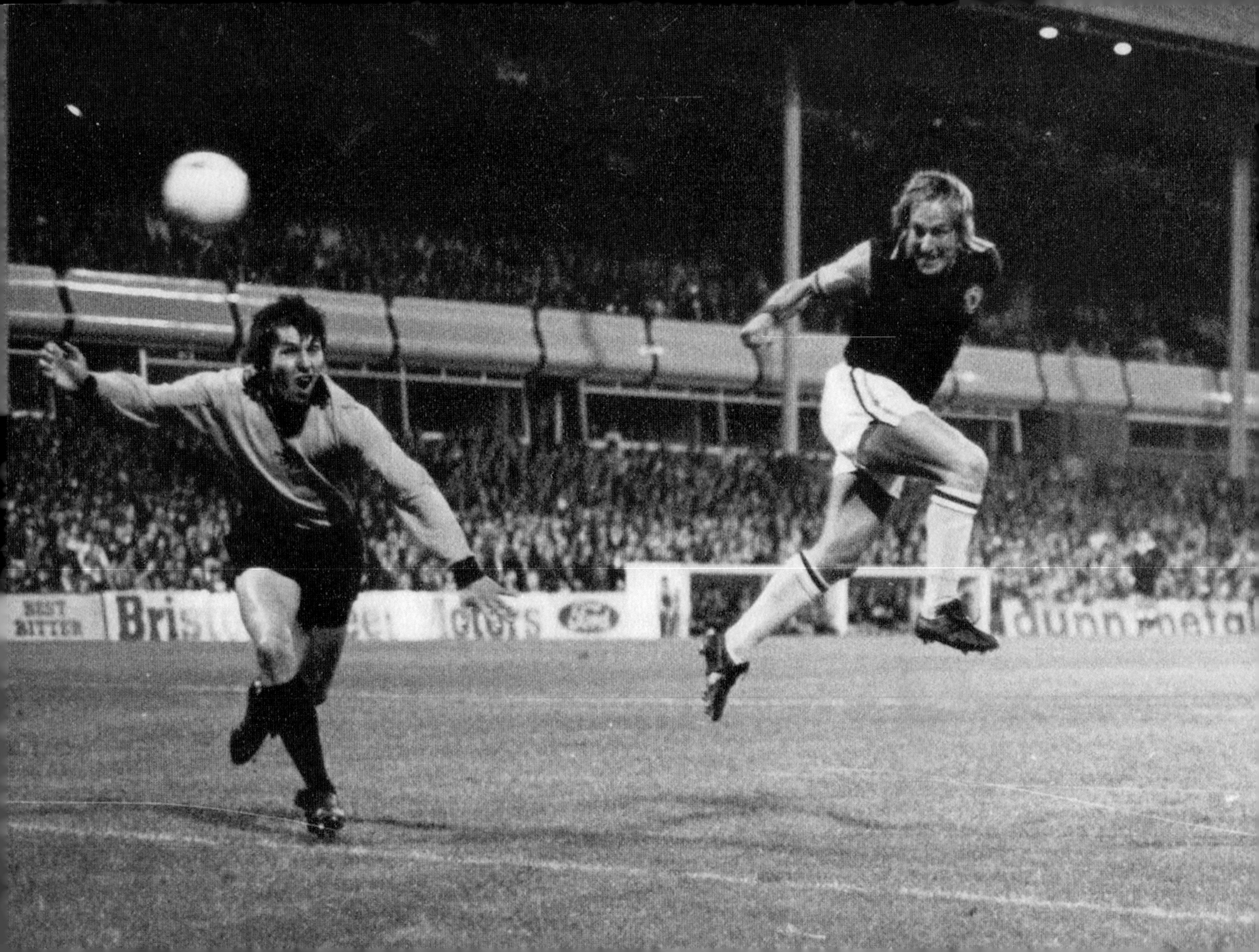

BEST
BITTER

[Left] During his time at Villa Park Ray proved quite a prolific scorer – in Villa's promotion and League Cup winning campaign 1974/75 he scored 27 goals alone

In the club's centenary season of 1974/75 Ray was just as vital a cog in the machinery. This was his moment, 27 goals in all competitions and from out wide, included in this amount the Wembley winner in the League Cup final. Under the 'Twin Towers' he saw his late spot-kick pushed onto the post but with the coolness of a winter's day, he controlled the ball before unleashing it beyond a fully stretched Kevin Keelan.

Next season the Bristolian would write his name in the Villa annuls when he scored the club's first ever European goal, albeit in a 1-4 reversal at the hands of Royal Antwerp in the UEFA Cup in Belgium. Lastly Ray would add a second League Cup winners gong when he returned from injury to face Everton in the 1977 second replay victory at Old Trafford.

Graydon would only appear four more times in the famous colours. His record of 81 goals from 232 appearances from an old outside-right position reveals his true worth to the club. Graydon still had plenty to offer Aston Villa Football Club but he was moved out. "Ron Saunders decided to get rid of several of the older players and bring in younger ones."

Unbeknown to Aston Villa fans Ray Graydon could have ended up at Filbert Street but this story never made the papers. At the end of his career at Villa the team had been on a post-season tour of Spain. Ron Saunders pulled the winger aside as they returned to Villa Park after the trip and informed him that Leicester City had made an offer for him. "I'm prepared to let you go" the manager added. Ray took it that the boss meant "I want you to go." The player was keen to talk so he travelled over to Leicester City where Frank McLintock had just taken over as manager there (his first job in management). Graydon recalled a conversation he'd had with McLintock a few months earlier when the Villa had played down at Highbury. "Frank asked me in the player's room after the game what I was doing at the end of the season?" "I don't know, I don't know where I stand," he replied.

Ray had an interesting and long chat but said he would need some time to think it over. As he was leaving McLintock told him he was also hoping to sign Kenny Burns from Birmingham. "Whether you sign Kenny or not we get on great, I don't have a problem with him, we've met a few times and he's always been okay with me," said Ray. Players talk and Ray heard some of the whispers, "It was all hearsay but apparently Kenny wasn't always the best of trainers, could go a little bit off the rails sometimes, liked a drink and the nightclubs."

Burns wound up at Forest under Cloughie did absolutely brilliantly and was Player of the Year at the end of that season." Ray and his wife Sue thought long and hard about Leicester but decided against it. With Ron Wylie now at Coventry City and the mutual admiration between them both (going back to Villa's Third Division days when Ron was assistant manager to Vic Crowe) coupled with the fact that signing for the Sky Blues meant the Graydon's didn't have to uproot their young family from their Four Oaks home, Highfield Road was the winger's next port of call.

"Through my respect of Ron Wylie and knowing he wanted me at Coventry, I joined them when I realised my Villa career was finished. Because I appreciated him (Wylie) so much it was an easy decision and I was pleased to be rejoining him."

Interestingly Bobby McDonald another ex-Villa player and Graydon would travel over to Coventry together. In later years when Ray was assistant at the Manor Ground McDonald was signed by Oxford United, Jim Smith taking onboard Ray's recommendation of the skilful Scottish versatility player.

BRIAN LITTLE

THE BIG ASTON VILLA BOOK OF THE SEVENTIES

With a solitary England cap to his name, and that was as a late substitute against Wales in 1975, Brian Little can feel rightly vexed. His talent and ability were there for all to see on pitches the length and breadth of the country. The image most remembered by supporters is of him with his socks rolled down, his shirt untucked and his cascading hair. With Little in full flow it appeared as if the ball was somehow glued to his feet as he glided across the grass. Brian was worthy of far, far more at international level and it was his country's loss.

Born Newcastle-upon-Tyne, just a mile from St James Park, 25th November 1953, he arrived at Aston Villa during the summer of 1969 as a raw teenager, "I remember leaving the train station in Durham with the £1 10/- my dad had given me."

He joined at a time when the charismatic Tommy Docherty was manager though he'd have more involvement initially with Graham Leggatt the youth team coach. In his first year at B6 Brian travelled to Amsterdam and took part in the annual Blauw-Wit tournament, something the Villa had done religiously over the years with their youngsters.

"I went to Manchester City, I'd been asked to go to Leeds United, Newcastle United and a few other clubs and was offered apprentice forms but I chose Villa. I remember saying to my dad that I liked the Villa, I'd like to go there and they were in the Second Division"

"The fact that I didn't get in my county schools football team made me think if I went to somewhere like Man City or Leeds who were Division One teams, I might not be good enough for them and I may be back home in a couple of years. Whether it was freak judgement or just a bit of good luck it was the right choice in the end."

Even though young Little couldn't get in his Durham county side he was having trials for England albeit at basketball. He'd already represented the whole of the north of England at that particular sport.

Brian was taken along with the first team on a few occasions and looked on as another kid, Jimmy Brown, was actually making it into the starting XI. Jimmy was 'blooded' as a 15-year old at Bolton and remains to this day the youngest ever first-team player for Aston Villa.

"I was part of the club, part of the youth team and for all I travelled I never played in the first-team until the year after but I'll never forget the club struggling. It was an absolute nightmare of a season and Villa went down. It was a real tough time and it wasn't enjoyable to watch. It really surprised me that a club like ours could get relegated and that was in my first season as an apprentice. It was certainly a hard thing to get used to." Brian Little, along with John Gidman and other names for the future, started making the headlines with Villa's FA Youth Cup winning side of 1972.

"The FA Youth Cup gave the younger lads the opportunity to play at Villa Park. It was great to get a game there as we played most of our league matches at Fort Dunlop, Boldmere St Michael or other little grounds around the outskirts of Birmingham, though the likes of 'Giddy,' myself and a few of the older ones had played at the big grounds like Elland Road, St James Park and Old Trafford with playing regularly in the Central League."

Brian remembers this period with fondness, "They were fantastic games with big crowds and we had a great spirit as a group. Rod Stewart was big at the time and me and John Gidman used to sing 'Maggie May' before the games, it was our sort of warm up, our get ourselves in the mood song."

On the back of winning the FA Youth Cup, Brian Little and John Gidman were selected to play for England in the European Championships at the end of the 1972 season. "We went off to Spain and won the tournament though in fairness I was mostly a substitute."

Most of the players were from the top-flight sides, the likes of Chelsea, Ipswich Town and West Ham United. It wasn't very often that kids from the third-tier would ever get the nod, but the fact that Villa won the FA Youth Cup and against a strong Liverpool outfit, it shot many claret and blue youngsters to prominence.

"The Youth Cup really catapulted John Gidman and myself especially. I'm sure Bobby McDonald and Jake Findlay became Scottish internationals? Jimmy Brown was already a Scottish Youth international. But out of the team there probably ended up five or six of us as international players which was quite something as Villa were a Third Division club."

Others from that Youth Cup side went on to feature in the Villa first team including Brian's 'kid brother' Alan, Jake Findlay and Tony Betts.

"There were a lot of us came through the youth team and Frank Upton obviously had a lot to do with that. He was a pretty tough character and very strong on discipline yet he would take me to one side and talk to me. Frank was a close figure to me and he understood the difficulties I had from time to time."

When Little came to the Villa he was more of a right-winger or midfield player. The coach could see the 'Geordies' worth to the team playing him further up field. "Frank put me up front to play off Tony Betts in the youth team, he said," "With the pace you have and the vision you have as a midfield player, I want you to push on more as a striker."

"He never saw me as an out and out goalscorer though, he just thought I may be able to do more damage to the opposition in the final third of the pitch. I never looked back from there on in to be honest, I owe a lot to him for giving me the opportunity."

THE BIG ASTON VILLA BOOK OF THE SEVENTIES

During the FA Youth Cup run, Little had been handed a chance by Vic Crowe to show what he could do in the first team. In a 4-1 win at home to Blackburn Rovers in the October he came on as a replacement for Davie Gibson and showed touches of brilliance.

"Of my first-team debut what stands out the most was that I was still only a kid. I remember being part of it, coming on as substitute for a spell towards the end of the game. It was brilliant, something I'd been looking forward to."

The team were destined for promotion and Vic couldn't afford to deviate from week to week as Villa went on the rampage. Of the next 29 games since the Rovers match, the Villa won 21, lost only three and ensured their place in next season's Second Division with a draw away to Mansfield.

Crowe had no hesitation in handing the precociously talented Little a first-team start at home to Torquay United. Villa thrashed the opposition, the win secured the club the Third Division title and Little hit his first senior goal in the 5-1 romp.

"On my full debut and at Villa Park (Torquay) and to score was great. I remember playing up front with Andy Lochhead, he was fantastic. He was a man's man and one of those you didn't mess with."

Lochhead took the youngster under his wing, "Wherever I am, whatever I'm doing, I want to see you only ten yards away. That's as far as you can go away from me and everything else will take care of its self. When the pieces are there, you just pick them up!"

"I'd stay close to him, watch when he jumped and pick the ball up when people got knocked off it. I fed off him there on in, that was my education to first-team football."

In Villa's first season back in Division 2, Brian was given an extended

The penultimate game of 1974/75 – Brian Little leads out Steve Hunt, Bobby McDonald, Charlie Aitken and Leighton Phillips

run in the side when Pat McMahon was sidelined, he racked up 20 appearances and found the net on three occasions. The following year (1973/74) he would start the campaign in the No 11 shirt but when regular centre-forward Sammy Morgan was injured the 5' 8" Little was then played as the regular target man, taking the knocks and all in his stride. He ended the season with eight goals, only one less than Morgan.

Aston Villa's centenary year was memorable for both club and player. Promotion back to the First Division after an eight year absence was achieved along with the League Cup trophy. Brian scored 20 league goals in only 33 full starts; he found the net in six successive games (10 goals) towards the back end of the campaign and scored in both cup competitions. He celebrated his 21st Birthday in style with a brace of goals in a resounding 6-1 win at home to Hartlepool in a League Cup tie. The game made even more special for the Little family when Brian's younger sibling Alan also played in the match, the first time they'd appeared together "My dad and brother Ken came down on the train with the Hartlepool supporters and I was pleased I was able to provide them with something to feel pleased about."

An even prouder moment came a month after the season's end when Brian Little received a call up to the England team to face Wales at Wembley in May 1975. Replacing Mick Channon he came on in the No 15 shirt and within seconds he'd played a one-two with Davie Thomas, evaded one tackle, ran 20 yards, sidestepped a defender before unleashing a fierce left-footed shot from the edge of the area that fizzed just the wrong side of the left hand post. David Coleman's commentary sums the move up perfectly, "Little, Thomas, Little wanted to take it on and did so rightly. Good play by Little, real skill and belief

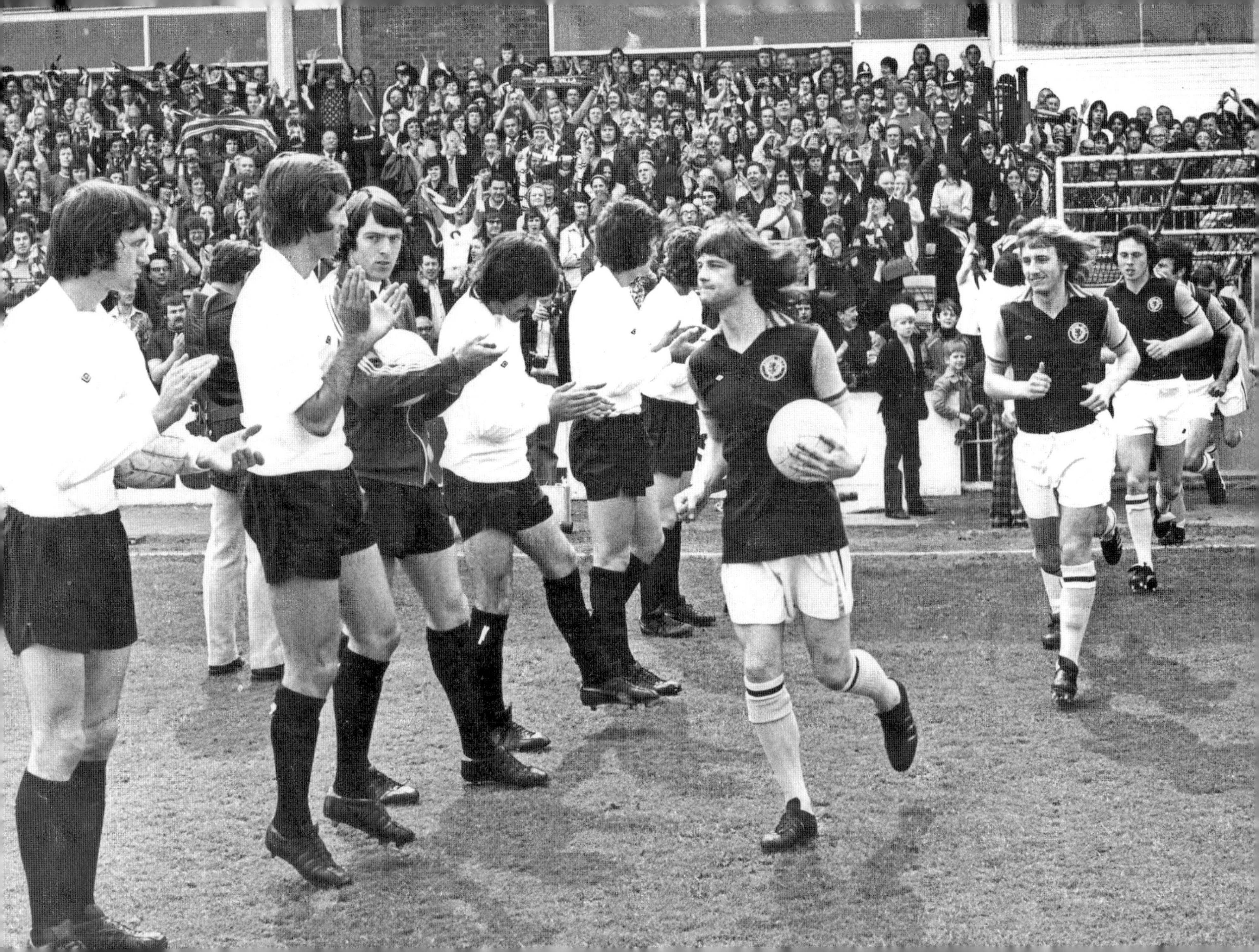

shown then. Little took it on himself from there, the jink was good enough to find space for the shot and the shot was well struck."

Still with the score 2-1 in Wales favour, Little took a pass from Whitworth, ran towards the bye-line being closely marked by the centre-half and in spite of the defender's attention, delivered a peach of a cross for David Johnson to nod in the equalizer. Despite the rave reviews Little would never be capped again for England, the latest tale in the claret and blue curse.

Injury in October virtually wiped away his top-flight campaign restricting him to less than half the club's league games. He was nothing if not resilient, and 1976/77 would be even more outstanding for the likeable 'Geordie' than the promotion season.

The club's sole ever-present he was only upstaged in the league goals tally by an Andy Gray at his peak (25 to Brian's 14), Little's 10 League Cup goals were instrumental in lifting the trophy yet again, including a hat-trick in the semi-final replay v QPR and a pair of opportunist strikes in the final's second-replay against Everton at Old Trafford. The team finished a highly respectable fourth in the table, but many believe without injuries and a glut of cup ties (14) the title was theirs for the taking.

Villa's couldn't emulate their phenomenal form in the league the following term but they progressed to the quarter-finals of the UEFA Cup where they went out narrowly 3-4 to Barcelona. Little scored Villa's goal in the 1-2 Nou Camp defeat.

Unbeknown at the time Brian only had two more seasons left in him as a Villa player. His days at B6 entertaining the fans with his silky skills were numbered. It was looking more and more likely that a switch to Birmingham City in a £650,000 transfer was on the cards. This deal fell through on medical grounds, a back problem being responsible and then at the age of only 27 his career was finished - due to a knee injury! He was given this devastating news by a Harley Street specialist on

[Left] Brian Little and Bobby Campbell spearhead an attack at home to York City during the 4-0 win in December 1974

the same day Mike Pejic was dealt the same hand, except the full-backs career was over without him knowing what the specific problem was. Both players had travelled down to the capital together. A fantastic servant to Aston Villa Football Club, he racked up 302 appearances (inc 7 sub) bagging 82 goals in the process.

On hanging up his boots Brian Little worked for the club's Development Association for a year and then Villa's youth team coach. He held this later post for three years but walked out during Graham Turner's tenure as manager.

He took up similar coaching roles at Wolves and Middlesbrough and it was during his time back in his native north east that he was given his chance in management by Darlington. Little joined them too late to stave off relegation from the Football League but led them to the GM Vauxhall Conference title at the first attempt. He then won back-to-back Divisional Manager of the Year awards as 'Darlo' were crowned Division Four champions.

Leicester City gave him his chance and were rewarded with promotion to the Premiership at the third time of asking. The 'Foxes' were losing play-off finalists in his first two seasons.

When word reached Little that Ron Atkinson had been sacked by Aston Villa the Press weren't far behind. Brian sought permission to speak to the Villa only for the Leicester City chairman to release a statement denying him the right, without having consulted with him first. A letter of resignation was written and handed to the board citing a relationship breakdown with the chairman. To save face a compromise was reached and Leicester City informed the media that Brian was free to join the club of his choice.

He was back home at Villa Park to manage 'his club' ironically on November 25th the day of his 41st birthday.

The directive from Villa's Doug Ellis was to preserve the club's status in the top flight. They were fourth from bottom with only three league wins from 15 fixtures. Ex-Villa men Allan Evans and John Gregory came in as his backroom staff. New signings were bought in as Little stamped his mark on the team, Whittingham, Parker, Richardson, Barrett, Atkinson and Saunders would be culled from the team as the season wore on with Taylor, Johnson, Charles and Wright arriving.

Villa did survive though it was a close run thing. More signings followed close-season with Southgate, Milosevic and Draper all landing for big fees. Under Brian Little in his first full season the fans were treated to breathtaking football, it started with a scintillating win at home to Manchester United – it finished with a top four finish, silverware in the shape of a fifth League Cup win and an FA Cup semi-final appearance.

The following season never scaled the same heights though a fifth place and a brief European adventure was respectable.

Stan Collymore arrived in a blaze of publicity for a club record £7,000,000 but the side lost their first four league fixtures. Brian stood down as manager in February 1998 his last game, the Wimbledon match at Selhurst Park, exactly the same fixture before Big Ron was axed!

A man with as much to offer to the game as Brian Little, he wasn't out of work for long. He managed Stoke City, Hull, Tranmere, Wrexham, restructured Gainsborough Trinity and is currently employed as Director of football for the Jersey FA.

CHRIS NICHOLL

Big, brave, fully committed and a hugely talented centre-half. Nicholl, born in the Cheshire town of Wilmslow, 12th October 1946, the son of an Irish Villa fan never followed the masses, supporting the red or blue of Manchester, "I grew up in Manchester and everyone around me was a Manchester United or Manchester City fan. I never got to go to any games but with my dad being a Villa fan I followed them more than the Manchester clubs, always looking out for their results."

Nicholl was spotted playing for Macclesfield Schools and snapped up on apprentice terms by Burnley in June 1963, one of the biggest sides of the time. After winning the First Division title in 1959/60 for only the second time, they then went on to finish runners-up the next two seasons and then 3rd in 1962/63. He signed a professional contract in 1965 but never made the first-team during his time at Turf Moor.

Even so, it was only his strong character that enabled him to follow this career path, "It was certainly no thanks to an old headmaster at the Grammar School I attended. They played rugby and he banned me from playing any sport at the school because instead of playing rugby for the school on a Saturday morning I jumped on a train to Burnley and playing for their youth team. It was a really petty thing at the time." Halifax Town then took him following a brief spell with Witton Albion and was in their side that gained promotion from the Fourth Division.

His performances at 'The Shay' were such that Luton Town broke their previous record transfer fee to land Nicholl for £30,000. With Chris as the cornerstone of the 'Hatters' defence, they went up as Division Three runners-up. The 43 goals conceded by Luton that season was only bettered by Orient who took the title.

Eighteen months later an impressed Vic Crowe spoke to the commanding centre-half regarding signing for Aston Villa – he took no convincing. It cost Villa a club and division record to land their man, a whopping £90,000 fee, though Nicholl was going to sign regardless of what was in it for him, "It didn't matter how much I was being offered, my dad's team was always Villa so as soon as I knew I had a chance to sign for them that was it!"

"To move down to the Third Division when it took me a while to get to the Second wasn't a difficult choice when I knew who the club were. Villa were in the 'Third' but only on paper! Doug Ellis and Vic Crowe came down and I remember seeing them in the manager's office. It struck me straight away that Mr Ellis was the driving force, he wanted Villa to do something and he had the future in mind. Obviously being in the Third Division wasn't good enough and he and Vic Crowe convinced me to go back down a division."

"Villa were on their way and they wouldn't tolerate anything else. The next thing that happened, I met Ron Wylie at the training ground and together with Vic he provided what was needed for the team - the tactics, the strategy, the drive, the togetherness and the standards needed on the field. Ron was also a big factor in coming to Villa. Leo Crowther the reserve coach was also a very influential figure." From Nicholl's debut away to Rotherham in March 1972 the Villa lost only two of their remaining 15 games. The signing pre-season of Ray Graydon and the later additions of Jim Cumbes and Ian Ross also key to Villa's promotion at the second attempt. Despite missing out on a successive promotion the following year when they finished third with only the top two going up, they kept their heads and under a new manager in the shape of Ron Saunders promotion to the top-flight was achieved in Villa's centenary year of 1974/75 along with the League Cup trophy. It was Chris Nicholl's header destined for the top left corner at Wembley stadium that was saved on the line by Norwich's Mel Machin that led to Ray Graydon's winning penalty.

Back in Division One Chris made the headlines in March 1976 when he scored all four goals in a 2-2 draw league encounter at Filbert Street. As captain he led what many supporters regarded as the best Villa side since the war to a highly commendable fourth position in the First Division. Without the heavy casualty list and the glut of cup games (14 in total) they could well have landed the title. As it was they had to content themselves with a second League Cup win in three seasons – Chris scoring a left-footed howitzer from - depending which match report you read – anywhere between 25 – 45 yards, in the second replay 3-2 win at Old Trafford.

It was during the three 1977 League Cup final games that boss Ron Saunders was made aware of Everton's centre-half Ken McNaught due to his fine displays against the Villa frontline. Little did Nicholl know on that momentous evening in Manchester that he would only play 10 more games for the club he supported as a boy. Against his wishes Chris was sold to Southampton in the close season (June) to make way for McNaught's imminent arrival the following month.

During his Villa Park spell Chris Nicholl gained 12 of his 50 Northern Ireland caps (he made his international debut against the Dutch playing as a centre-forward alongside George Best on Danny Blanchflower's instructions), made an impressive 252 appearances in the claret and blue and weighed in with 20 goals.

JOHN GIDMAN

John Gidman was one of the finest right-backs to ever pull on the famous claret and blue jersey of Aston Villa Football Club. As an attacking full-back he had no equal in the game. He had no idea as a child how high his star would rise and that he'd get to proudly display the three lions on his chest.

John was born in Liverpool, 10th January 1954 and grew up idolising the likes of Ian St John, Roger Hunt and Tommy Smith (he even named his dog 'Scouse'). He showed huge promise himself at the game captaining Springwood Primary School (he was a gifted player and very athletic according to team-mate Jimmy Case who at only 8-years old offered glimpses of the tough tackling he'd later be renowned for) and as a youngster he wound up on Liverpool's books, "I was in the youth team at Liverpool and went in one day to play in the 'A' team. Ronnie Moran said he had a problem, the right-back was struggling and he asked me to play full-back but to keep going forward. I never played right-wing in the old fashioned term again. That was the day that changed my life." John just didn't know it at the time!

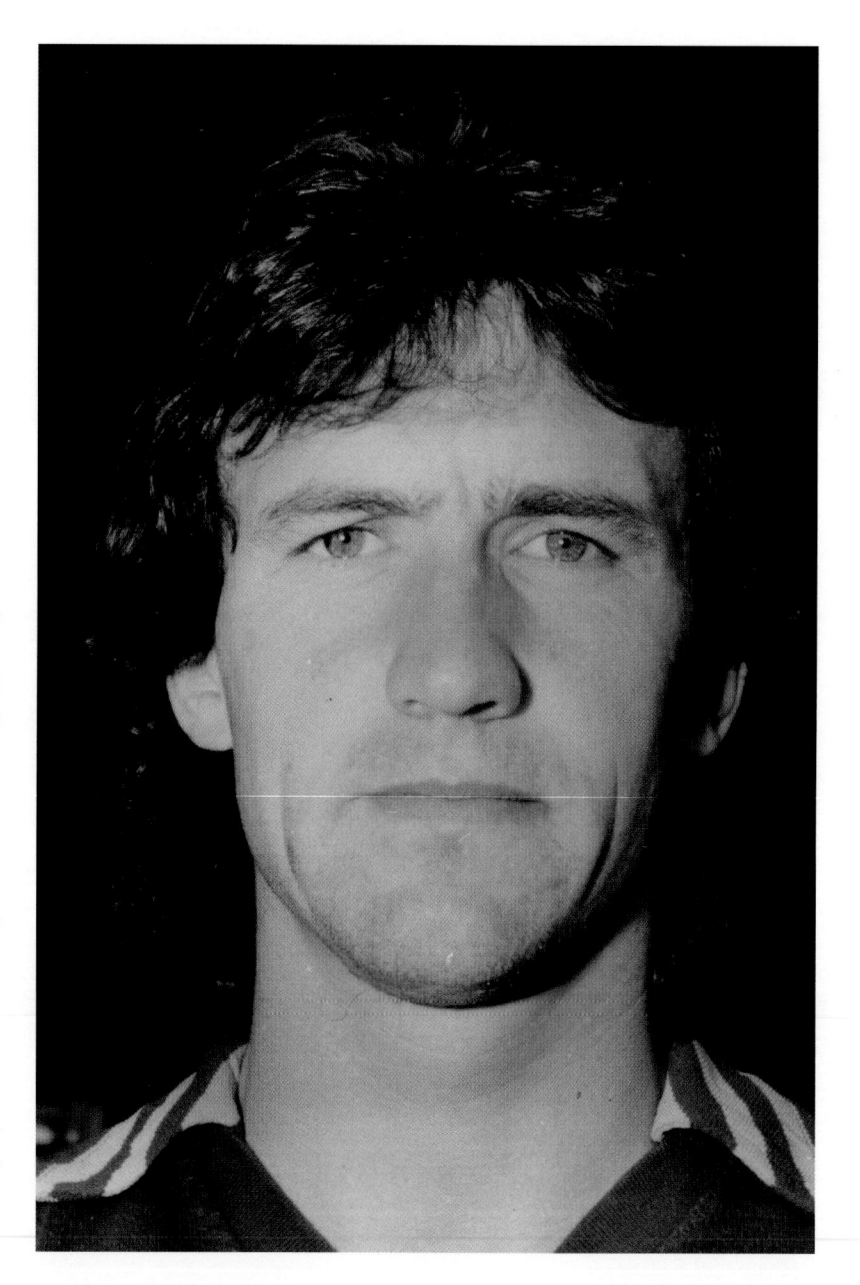

Life was going great for him at the Melwood training ground until a new head of Youth Development arrived in the shape of Tony Waiters. For some reason Waiters didn't fancy the young attacking full-back though John carried on playing well and to the best of his considerable ability.

"I was called into Shankly's office, he was the best known manager in England. I thought he was going to hand me my first-team debut; straight to the point he told me I didn't have the ability to become a professional footballer, I was shite and I was being released. It knocked everything out of me." In fairness Shankly was only saying what his youth team coach Tony Waiters had told him. Shortly after this in the May 1970 a letter arrived through the door of the Gidman household. It was from Bill Shankly.

Dear Mr & Mrs Gidman... It is with regret I must inform you the coaching staff here at Liverpool FC and myself have come to the conclusion that your son will not reach the high standards that are demanded of senior players at Anfield. We will do everything we can to place your boy with a club more suited to his ability. This isn't the letter in its entirety but you get the gist. John Gidman still has that letter dated 14th May to this day.

There's a saying, when one door closes... In John's case this other door opened wider than he could ever imagine, "I came to Villa on a month's trial, played in four friendlies and in that time I couldn't do anything wrong. It's not a long time to prove yourself but there must have been something there that Frank Upton and Vic Crowe liked and it went from there. Fortunately for me it worked out and I was offered professional terms." Another life changing event.

Gidman started the 1971/72 campaign turning out for the reserve side in the Central League, he played well and the side lost only two of their first 12 fixtures. He also featured in the Midland Youth League. The youngsters reached the semi-final stage of the Southern Junior Floodlit Cup but went one better when they went all the way in the prestigious FA Youth Cup. They beat the much fancied Liverpool team over two-legs in the final. They gained a slim one-nil advantage in the Villa Park match watched by 16,463, the only goal courtesy of a Gidman penalty.

Shankly was at the Anfield game eight days later and watched in disbelief as Frank Upton's side won 4-2 on the night (5-2 on agg). The Liverpool supremo refused to shake hands with the Villa camp. Twice in the game 'Giddy' took bangs to the head and was knocked out. He continued to play and it caught up with him at the celebrations that followed. He was rushed from the Adelphi Hotel directly to hospital where he was detained for a couple of days. That season Gidman cemented the right-back position his own, turning out two-dozen times for the second-string.

"To play in the Youth Cup final against Liverpool, going back to the Kop and beating them 4-2, incredible. Ronnie Moran came up to me after the game and shook my hand and said," "We made a mistake."

Progression was swift for the Liverpudlian, he made his first-team debut only four games into the 1972/73 season due to a serious injury to regular No 2 Michael Wright. Gidman himself would soon be sidelined, with only 16 games under his belt he underwent surgery for cartilage damage.

"When I walked out of the dressing room for the first time against Carlisle and I went down the tunnel and out in front of 30,000 it was something else. I wanted more, as soon as I came off the pitch after the game I wanted it to be Saturday. I wanted to play again."

Having got through a career threatening injury he was further hampered when he strained his Achilles tendon postponing his comeback. He returned to first-team action at Burnden Park (Oct '73) in a 2-1 win and remained in the side until the end of the season. The club's centenary year of 1974/75 was a mixed bag for the player, silverware was won but to the exclusion of Gidman. He started as first choice but by November having played 17 games he was out again, possibly for good?

Life changed abruptly on 5th November 1974. Gidman joined other Villa players at Jim Cumbes house for the goalie's annual firework display. A stray rocket caught 'Giddy' smack in the eye putting him clean through a patio window. The saving grace was that the Villa club doctor David Targett was in attendance. He was rushed to hospital and it was initially expected the badly haemorrhaging eye would need to come out. John thought his career was over but due to the fantastic efforts of Dr Cruz his sight returned though not fully.

In time his left eye compensated and balanced enabling him to get the speed and the timing of the ball. It took John eight months to return when he came on against Sunderland in April 1975, "He (Ron Saunders) put me on for the last twenty minutes. When I got out of the dug-out and took my tracksuit off I got the best feeling ever. Everything worked, the touch, the passing, the lot." Gidman was back! The following Wednesday he scored the first of his nine goals for the Villa in the last match of the season, the 4-1 win at Carrow Road.

With Villa having won promotion, not to mention a League Cup triumph, they were back in the top-flight where John more than held his own, a personal high for him as he played in 44 league and cup games. The following season of 1976/77, the Villa took the footballing scene by storm. Gidman and Gordon Smith formed an almost watertight partnership as Villa romped to League Cup victory and a phenomenal, though unexpected fourth position. Villa scored more goals than any other side in the division and only a few teams conceded fewer.

This led to Nationwide attention and media speculation for a possible call-up. He'd been in the squad a few times under Don Revie but always on the edge, "During a practice game Revie came over and informed me that I would be making my debut in England's game that

[Above] John Gidman winning the Terrace Trophy, as voted by the club's supporters, in 1973/74

evening against Luxemburg." He was wanted to mark a player out of the game. John called his old man, "Hey, you know that dream you've got, it's come true tonight, I'm playing." His father was straight down on the train.

"Going up that tunnel with the likes of Kevin Keegan, Peter Shilton and Emlyn Hughes and I was thinking to myself, I cleaned your boots three years ago and I'm playing in the England side with you. When they played the National Anthem I thought of 'Shanks,' I'd gone from the England Youth team, the Under-23s, the 'B' team and now this. I'd done the lot. What could people say?"

Like many Villans before and as many after, John Gidman would never reach the caps his talent deserved, he would be restricted to a single cap for his country. How?

He may not have had the most orthodox pre-match ritual but it certainly worked for him. "Before the match I'd go into the physio's room and down a couple of brandy and cokes. It was my routine. My first focus would be have I got a winger, and then secondly, sod defending, I'll just go forward," he added!"

Villa had two more seasons out of their swashbuckling defender before it all went pearshaped. "You ask every pro, what's said in the dressing room should stay in the dressing room but with me something happened in that dressing room and it changed my life where I had to get out of the club."

John was aware that a team-mate who shall remain nameless was the manager's eyes and ears, though he'd refer to this player as 'The Natterjack.' "If we go out or we discuss something about the manager it was relating back to the manager everything that was said in the dressing room. He was letting the manager know what was going on between players but if he had to get on in life by doing what he did – it's a disgrace. I never forgave him for that!"

Giddy's team-mate, ex-housemate and good friend Andy Gray was also on his way out of the club after falling out with the manager, having been accused of cheating the club and the fans. Andy put in a transfer request at the beginning of the season telling Mr Saunders he wouldn't play for him again, this was turned down. He then slapped another in.

The two players got a call at the training ground, the Aston Villa board wanted a meeting with them at Villa Park. They were asked if they would stay if the manager was sacked, 'Giddy' said yes. Andy said no, he wouldn't be used as the reason for them to sack the manager. John Gidman never wanted to leave the club, he'd been there nine years and he loved it. In his own words he was, "forced out!"

October 1979 and John was off to Goodison Park, Pat Heard making the reverse journey as a make weight in the transfer deal. This move didn't work out as expected, Everton's defensive game plan clearly didn't suit 'Giddy's' attacking style of play. Cue 'Big Ron' Atkinson to end the right-back's Merseyside nightmare, John knew from Ron's time with West Brom that he was a flare manager who encouraged his teams to play on the front foot, he didn't hesitate.

The flamboyant boss made Gidman his first signing after arriving at Manchester United. In his time at Old Trafford the defender helped the 'Red Devils' win the FA Cup in 1985 when they defeated Everton 1-0; he then had a brief spell at Manchester City. Not many players can say they were on the books of all four of the big north west clubs. Stoke City was another port-of-call before he later joined up with former Villa team-mate Brian Little at Darlington.

John Gidman lives in Calahonda, Spain nowadays along with his wife Mayte and their dogs, one of which John rescued from a life on the streets.

THE BIG ASTON VILLA BOOK OF THE SEVENTIES

GORDON COWANS

Born in October 1958 at West Cornforth, Co Durham, Gordon Sidney Cowans was destined for greatness. At an early age the family moved to Mansfield where dad Walter worked in the mining industry. Young Gordon took a shine to local team Mansfield Town. He played schoolboy football and before long people started becoming aware of this skinny little lad who 'could play.'

His reading of the game and passing ability belied his tender age. Among those early admirers was Neville Briggs, Aston Villa's chief scout. The club's scouting network realised they had stumbled upon an uncut diamond. They had to obtain his signature at any cost. The Villa, only a third-tier side at the time invited Cowans entire school team down as club guests to take in a Villa Park match. When this didn't have the desired effect they offered Walter Cowans the opportunity to leave mining behind and look after the club apprentices at their hostel on the Chester Road. This worked, Gordon signed apprentice forms, putting pen to paper in June 1974 the same month Ron Saunders arrived as new boss to the recently departed Vic Crowe.

Walter and wife Norma ran the hostel for a few years before Walter was given the job of kit man to the first-team.

He looked up to certain players and took pieces from their game to add to his own armoury, "As a youngster I enjoyed watching Manchester United's famous trilogy, George Best, Denis Law and Bobby Charlton. George and Denis were by far my favourites. No one could come close, they were the best in the business. 'Bestie' was a genius, he ghosted past players, the best two footed player I've ever seen. Denis was a natural at scoring, he had vision and read the game so well he was always in the right place. Bobby Charlton was the perfect midfield player and his shooting ability was well known. Gordon could score goals from anywhere."

'Sid' started on the Villa ladder in the club's centenary year 1974/75, playing in the Midland Intermediate League and the various youth competitions, alongside future first-team players Steve Hunt and John 'Dixie' Deehan.

He climbed further the following season. In August he came on as a sub against Coventry City at Highfield Road in a reserve match. "I played over 20 times in the Central League, in what was a useful reserve side. I rubbed shoulders with first-teamers coming back from injury, the likes of Ian Hamilton, Sammy Morgan, Brian Little and Pat McMahon."

Cowans then picked up the first of countless awards when he was part of Villa's Southern Junior Floodlit Cup winning team who thumped Ipswich Town 5-2 over two legs.

In February 1976 Sid realised the next step in his early claret and blue career when finally got to taste first-team football. It mattered not that he had to come off the bench, taking Frank Pimblett's place in the action at Maine Road. Villa lost that day to Manchester City having led for a long time but the result wasn't as significant as the occasion in his eyes. In spite of him getting no more call ups for the senior side and having to make do with reserve team football, Ron Saunders saw enough potential to offer him a professional contract. "It's every young lads dream to be a footballer and I'm no different. I can say I am now." The new campaign saw him make several sub appearances before his first full start came in an away fixture at Portman Road. From there on he'd play in the majority of the remaining games. His first senior goal arrived in the 4-0 demolition of Derby County. Undoubtedly the highlight of his season was being part of the victorious Cup side - playing in both League Cup Final replays against Everton and winning his second piece of silverware. His stature in the game was raised to a national level when in 1979 Cowans was voted PFA Young Player of the Year.

Sid's place in Villa folklore was cemented when he was one of the ever presents in Aston Villa's 1980/81 League Championship winning side, the clubs first title for 71 years. In fact he was an ever present for four consecutive seasons - 1979/80 to 1982/83. He reached the summit of club football in May 1982 when he took his usual berth in the midfield for the European Cup Final against the highly fancied German masters Bayern Munich in Rotterdam.

Villa somehow defied all odds and bought the trophy back to 'Brum.' Sid was also instrumental in the following campaign with Villa beating the Spanish giants Barcelona 3-1 on aggregate in the UEFA Super Cup, heady days for Aston Villa.

By now he was on the radar of several leading European clubs, most notably Napoli, and supporters were delighted when it was confirmed their favourite son was staying put. Football can be a cruel game and just weeks later, August 18th, and playing in the pre-season Zaragoza tournament (Spain) Sid suffered a double fracture of his right leg against Mexican outfit FC America and had to sit out the entire 1983/84 campaign. Putting the hours in at Bodymoor Heath and later pounding out relentless miles in nearby Sutton Park he regained his strength and

THE BIG ASTON VILLA BOOK OF THE SEVENTIES

stamina and was back to his best for the following season. Ultimately his fine performances would take him to Italian side Bari along with Villa striker Paul Rideout.

Fast forward to July 1988, Graham Taylor had just achieved promotion back to the First Division with his Villa side and wanted some much needed experience for life in the top flight. Villa had first refusal on Cowans should Bari choose to sell, he perfectly fit the bill and missing only a handful of games back in English football, helped Villa consolidate their position in Division One.

The start of season 1989/90 was unrewarding to say the least, only one win from seven games. Then a sequence of five wins on the bounce and the Cowans/Platt partnership showing real potential and the Villa were soon top of the pile. Unfortunately they ran out of steam towards the end but finishing the season as runners-up to Liverpool far exceeded fans expectations. Taylor left at this stage to manage the National team and knowing what class Cowans could bring to the England midfield he didn't hesitate in Sid adding to his cap's tally.

Big Ron Atkinson let him go in November 1991, Dalglish took Sid to Blackburn Rovers where he was a key part of their promotion winning side, defeating Leicester City in the play off final at Wembley in 1992. He was back at Villa Park in May of the same year for his testimonial against Stoke and duly signed back on for the claret and blue the following month – his third stint. Games were limited for Gordon and he played his last game for Aston Villa in December 1993.

His England career was restricted to only 10 full caps, which is a bloody insult, when you consider that Glenn Hoddle who – in my opinion - couldn't come close to Sid's ability at pin-point crossing accuracy and striking of a dead-ball, went on to reach five times that amount. Had Gordon chose to play in London or the northwest he would have reached treble figures! He represented his country at youth, under-21 and 'B' level. Bobby Robson, a figure hugely respected in the game gave him his full international call up and described Cowans as "potentially the most complete footballer and midfield man in English football." England's loss was definitely Aston Villa's gain!

Gordon Cowans, a wonderfully gifted footballer, an absolute Villa legend and third on the all time list of appearances for the Claret & Blue is 'back home' now coaching the Villa's youngsters, where there just happens to be another little terrier plying his trade for the Villa cause who carries the same Cowans surname. If young Henry turns out to be half as good as his old man, the lad is destined for a fantastic future!

John Dunn
Goalkeeper
Born; Barking, 21st June 1944

Started as a youth at Chelsea and signed as a pro under Tommy Docherty. After five years of frustration at Stamford Bridge he left for Torquay. Within 18-months Villa boss Tommy Cummings came in for Dunn who was so impressed with the Villa Park set-up and the club's phenomenal fanbase, he took no persuading to sign on the dotted line in January 1968. The fee £8,000. John debuted the same month in a 4-1 home win against Charlton. He displaced Colin Withers as keeper in making the position largely his own in September 1968 despite the arrival of Dochery as manager (Dec '68) and seeing Evan Williams and John Phillips given brief spells in goal. Dunn starred in the 1971 League Cup final and would have been an ever-present that season had he not missed two matches due to a car crash. Joined Charlton in 1971.

118 appearances (0 sub)

Michael Wright
Full-back
Born; Ellesmere Port, Cheshire, 25th September 1946

Signed as an apprentice in July 1962 and gained a pro contract slightly over a year later. Michael played for both England Youth and U18s, winning the Junior World Cup in 1964 defeating Spain 4-0, alongside the likes of Harry Redknapp, John Hollins, Don Rogers and Peter Osgood. Confounded the critics when he came back from a bad leg-break in a game at Ayresome Park (1-1 draw, Sep '67) going on to make a further 100+ appearances. Wright was outstanding in the second-half of the Third Division promotion campaign of 1971/72 but his career was later finished due to knee injuries (three cartilages removed). His last game was August 1972, in a 2-0 win at home to Huddersfield Town.

318 appearances (inc 4 sub) 1 goal

Charlie Aitken see page 250

Brian Godfrey
Midfielder
Born; Flint, North Wales, 1st May 1940

Signed by manager Tommy Cummings from Preston North End in September 1967 along with Brian Greenhalgh, with Villa having to pay £35,000 for the double transfer. Godfrey gained three Welsh caps and also represented the Under-23 side. Well respected at Villa Park, won the supporters 'Terrace Trophy' in 1968. Captained the team in the 1971 League Cup final defeat to Tottenham. The versatile Brian wore eight outfield shirts in his Villa spell but was sadly sold to Bristol Rovers in the deal that brought Ray Graydon from Eastville. Later managed Bath, Gloucester and Cinderford. Died in Cyprus, February 2010.

160 appearances (inc 4 sub) 25 goals.

George Curtis
Centre-half
Born; Dover, 5th May 1939

The hard-as-nails defender was signed by Tommy Docherty, only a month before the Villa manager was sacked. Curtis added backbone to Villa's fragile defence but was powerless to prevent the drop in April 1970. Hampered by cartilage trouble he missed most of the club's maiden season in the third flight but featured far more during the promotion campaign where he formed a formidable line of defence with Fred Turnbull. Had to have his nose rebuilt at the season's end following a coming together with Tony Hateley in a clash at Meadow Lane (March '72), George refused to leave the field and played on in Villa's 3-0 victory. He was advised to retire, which he did in May 1972. Joined Coventry City for whom he'd played and his roles included joint manager and later director at Highfield Road.

58 appearances (0 sub) 3 goals.

Lew Chatterley
Defender/midfielder
Born; Birmingham, 15th February 1945

Joined the Villa groundstaff in 1959 at the age of 15, under manager Joe Mercer after being given a trial. Lew was rewarded with a professional contract at 17. He gained England Youth honours as a teen and cites Phil Woosnam, a senior Villa star, for teaching him the craft of football. Chatterley is best remembered for being the first Villa substitute in history to score a goal, replacing Mike Tindall; the game being the Blackpool league fixture, 14th January 1967, Villa won 3-2. Related to the then Villa manager Vic Crowe, Lew was sold to Northampton Town in 1971 after 13 years at Villa Park, following a loan spell at Doncaster Rovers the same year.

166 appearances (inc 6 sub) 27 goals

Pat McMahon
Midfield/forward
Born; Croy, Scotland, 19th December 1945

Came down on a free from Celtic prior to the 1969/70 campaign commencing. Made his debut in the opening game of the season, replacing Dick Edwards in the home defeat against Norwich. This game set the tone for the new season as Villa slipped to the Third Division the following May. Pat was joint top scorer in the League Cup campaign of 1970/71 where they were unlucky to lose to top-flight Tottenham Hotspur in the Wembley final. McMahon then suffered a dislocated ankle and missed two-thirds of the 1971/72 season when Villa came up as Division Three champions. He featured in only two games during 1974/75 under new manager Ron Saunders before moving to the USA to join Portland Timbers.

150 appearances (inc 9 sub) 30 goals

Bruce Rioch see page 254

Neil Rioch
Defender
Born; Paddington, London, 13th April 1951

Featured in the same England Youth side as future team-mate Ian 'Chico' Hamilton. Michael Docherty (son of Tommy) also played in the same England set-up and before long Docherty senior was watching Neil's performances with interest. Shortly thereafter Neil knew he was off to Villa Park, long before his brother Bruce Rioch was part of the equation. Due to his versatility he played in many roles during his seven seasons at Villa Park, including weighing in with vital goals during the club's successful promotion from Division 3 in 1971/72. Made a big impact stateside where he played for the Portland Timbers side - among others - in the NASL. Later was instrumental in running the 'Aston Villa Former Players' Association.'

26 appearances (inc 7 sub) 3 goals.

Andy Lochhead
Centre-forward
Born; Lenzie, nr Milngavie, 9th March 1941

Described as a bullet-domed central striker. Lochhead ended up at Villa Park via Burnley and Leicester City. Signed in February 1970 for £30,000, he was unable to find the goals to keep Villa from going down. In 1971 he played a big part in Villa reaching Wembley for a League Cup final date with Tottenham and the following season he terrorized Third Division defenders, finding the net 19 times in the league. He was also the club's top-scorer in the cup competitions that same season. He wore the iconic No 9 shirt with a certain ruggedness and style at B6 and is still revered to this day by the claret and blue army! At a recent Villa Park book launch hundreds of fans serenaded him with a rendition of, "Andy Lochhead in the air!"

154 appearances (inc 4 sub) 44 goals

Ian 'Chico' Hamilton
Midfielder
Born; Streatham, London, 31st October 1950

Despite being Chelsea's youngest ever player and goalscorer, it didn't stop Tommy Docherty selling Hamilton to Southend. The same manager took him to Villa Park for £40,000 in the summer of 1969 though the 'Doc' was gone by January '70. 'Chico' thrived under new boss Crowe missing only two games in Villa's maiden Third Division season and hitting a dozen league and cup goals. Played magnificently at Wembley when Villa were unfortunate to lose to top-flight Spurs in the 1971 League Cup final. Hamilton went one better in 1975 when Villa won the competition beating Norwich City 1-0. Was a vital component in both Villa's successful promotion charges of 1972 & 1975 scoring vital goals along the way. After a season in the First Division with Villa, Hamilton left for Sheffield United though he stated that during his time at Villa, "even the bad times were good!"

252 appearances (inc 18 sub) 48 goals

Willie Anderson see page 258

Brian Tiler
Wing-half
Born; Whiston, nr Rotherham, 15th March 1943

Tiler was the first signing by flamboyant Villa boss Tommy Docherty, following his manager down from Rotherham's Millmoor in 1968 at a cost of £50,000. A solid and consistent performer, Brian was given the captaincy at Villa. He also played at Wembley in the League Cup final showdown with Tottenham Hotspur. He made only the one appearance in the 1972/73 campaign before leaving the Villa to go Stateside and join the Atlanta Chiefs of the NASL.

127 appearances (inc 2 sub) 4 goals

Jimmy Brown
Midfielder
Born; Wallyford, Midlothian, 3rd October 1953

Came down to Villa Park for a trial from Scotland as a 15-year old having already promised his signature to Arsenal. A few days later and in the secrecy of the Villa boardroom, discussions between manager Tommy Docherty, chairman Doug Ellis and an inebriated Mr Brown (father) led to 'Jimbo' signing schoolboy forms for Aston Villa. Making his debut at Bolton Wanderers Burnden Park in September 1969, Jimmy made history in being the youngest player ever to wear the Villa first-team shirt, aged only 15-years! The die was cast – the strong and competitive midfielder was captain by 19-years old, another record. Featured for Villa during six seasons (including the promotion campaigns of 1971/72 and 1974/5) leaving the club in 1975 due to his not getting on with Ron Saunders. Won the 'Terrace Trophy' as voted by the fans in 1972.

88 appearances (inc 4 sub) 1 goal

Fred Turnbull
Defender
Born; Wallsend, 28th August 1946

Despite his fragile appearance Fred could mix it with the best of centre-forwards, resolute and hard-tackling. Villa initially took him on a fortnight's trial from Blyth FC during Dick Taylor's tenure as manager (Taylor had played in the same Grimsby Town team as Blyth boss Norman Penrose). Within a month he'd earned a contract, turning down interest shown by Norwich City. Formed a solid partnership with George Curtis, Fred as centre-half would play on the left, George on the right. Fred claimed he wasn't the most gifted (he certainly wasn't a 'fancy' footballer but he had an uncanny ability to stop those who were in their tracks). But, he always gave 110% and the fans loved him for it. Had a brief loan spell at Halifax but was recalled by Docherty a month later. Played in the 1971 League Cup final, it was his job to mark Martin Chivers. Was granted a testimonial in 1976 against the 'Baggies.'

183 appearances (inc 1 sub) 3 goals

THE BIG ASTON VILLA BOOK OF THE SEVENTIES

Dave Simmons
Striker
Born; Ryde, Isle of Wight, 24th October 1948

Striker signed from Arsenal, February '69, he spent a spell on loan at Bournemouth during 1968. Scored on his full Villa debut and found the net five times in 10 games. Made only a handful of appearances over the next two seasons though Simmons signed off his claret and blue career with the winner at Barnsley's Oakwell Ground in September 1970. Had a brief loan spell at Fellows Park before moving to Colchester United on a permanent deal.

19 appearances (inc 6 sub) 7 goals

Lionel Martin
Forward
Born; Ludlow, Shropshire, 15th May 1947

Joined the Villa as an apprentice in July 1962 and signed professional forms in July 1964 – the same month Joe Mercer left as Aston Villa manager. Was given his start seven games into the new season, it was his only one during 1964/65. The ever-patient Lionel's next match was over two-and-a-half years later in the last game of the 1966/67 campaign in the 2-6 defeat at Southampton, Villa were already guaranteed Second Division football prior to the game. It wasn't really until the arrival of the 'Doc' that Martin got a run of games, he was the only Villa player during the 1968/69 season to score in all three competitions. Had a brief loan spell at Doncaster Rovers before ending up at Southern League side Worcester City where he helped them secure the title in 1979.

59 appearances (inc 15 sub) 9 goals

Davie Gibson
Inside-forward
Born; Winchburgh, Scotland, 23rd September 1938

Came to Villa by way of an Andy Lochhead recommendation, Davie having supplied the ammunition for the rugged centre-forward in their time together at Leicester City. Gibson featured in both 'The Foxes' League Cup finals sides of 1964 and 1965 and along with Lochhead in their 1969 FA Cup final defeat. An exceptional playmaker who could 'put the ball on the proverbial sixpence.' Starred in Villa's LC semi-final matches against Manchester United and was desperately unlucky to miss out on the final. On describing his time at Villa Park, "I had a lovely two or three seasons with Aston Villa." Left for Exeter unaware the Villa received a fee.

24 appearances (inc 3 sub) 1 goal

Harry Gregory
Forward
Born; Hackney, London, 24th October 1943

Won England Youth honours early in his career along with such notables as Martin Peters and Villa's Alan Baker. Villa signed Harry

286

for £7,777 from Charlton Athletic, October 1970. Elevated to club captain following an impressive display in a pre-season tour of Germany, July/August 1971. In his second season at Villa Park the side lost only two games when Gregory featured. In August 1972 he moved to Edgar Street with Dave Rudge to play for Hereford United.

29 appearances (inc 6 sub) 2 goals

Keith Bradley
Full-back
Born; Ellesmere Port, Cheshire, 31st January 1946

Was on Everton's books as a junior prior to signing as an apprentice at B6 in July 1962. Keith turned professional 12 months later. Made his claret and blue debut in the derby win at St Andrews, February 1965. Turned out for Villa over eight seasons and reached in excess of 100 appearances. Not bad considering the strength of competition for the right-back berth with Gordon Lee and later Michael Wright, to partner the evergreen Charlie Aitken. Bradley won a League Cup runners-up tankard in the 1971 defeat at the hands of Spurs and featured prominently in the first half of the promotion campaign of 1971/72.

144 appearances (inc 9 sub) 2 goals

Geoff Crudgington
Goalkeeper
Born; Wolverhampton, 14th February 1952

Signed professionally for Villa in September 1969 having been snapped up from his hometown club Wolves. Geoff won England schoolboy honours but couldn't cement a place in the Villa goal. His chance only came when regular keeper John Dunn was hurt in a car crash. Crudgington played well in his first two games having received a 'Good luck' telegram from Dunn prior to his debut. Villa won both with the rookie keeper conceding just the one goal though Dunn was back in immediately on his return. Another recall in the final game of the season led to another Villa win. Tommy Hughes was signed at the start of the 1971/72 season, Geoff stepped in for two more Villa victories but the club then went and signed Jim Cumbes from WBA leaving the frustrated goalie to spend spells on loan before going to play for Toronto Blizzard in Canada.

5 appearances (0 sub)

Geoff Vowden
Forward
Born; Barnsley, 27th April 1941

Signed from rivals Birmingham City on the recommendation of coach Ron Wylie for the fee of £12,500 in March 1971. Made his debut the same month and hit 5 goals in only 12 starts during 1970/71. Due to his 'Blues' history Geoff wasn't appreciated as much by the fans as he should have been. He was well respected in the dressing room and his team-mates were fully aware of his worth to the team on the pitch. Used to room with Chris Nicholl on away trips. During the successful promotion campaign of 1971/72 Vowden netted on ten occasions, including bagging the vital goal in the 1-1 draw at Mansfield Town that guaranteed Division 2 football the following season.

115 appearances (inc 5 sub) 25 goals

Tommy Hughes
Goalkeeper
Born; Dalmuir, Scotland, 11th July 1947

Another keeper with Chelsea links, Villa having bought him from the London club in June 1971 for £12,500, in readiness for Vic Crowe's (successful) promotion push of 1971/72. Hughes gained Scotland U23 caps in his time at 'The Bridge' before breaking a leg. Tommy recovered from that setback but struggled at Villa Park and after only half a season made way for the incoming Jim Cumbes. He had a loan spell at Brighton before making a permanent move to Hereford United in 1973.

23 appearances (0 sub)

Ray Graydon see page 262

Malcolm Beard
Wing-half
Born; Cannock, Staffordshire, 3rd May 1942

Vic Crowe signed Malcolm Beard on a free towards the end of his career on the recommendation of right-hand man Ron Wylie, who'd been a teammate at St Andrews. Birmingham had cheekily placed a fee of £35,000 on Beard's head only 12 months earlier when Villa had made an initial approach. His experience (over 400 appearances for 'Blues') was hoped to add strength to Villa's defensive cover. This didn't really materialise during his time in claret and blue - restricted to single figure appearances. Had later spells at Villa Park, firstly as chief scout and then as reserve team coach.

7 appearances (inc 1 sub)

Brian Little see page 266

Jim Cumbes
Goalkeeper
Born; Didsbury, nr Manchester, 4th May 1944

Signed in the November 1971 when it transpired Tommy Hughes wasn't going to remain as Villa's regular keeper. Cumbes, signed from Albion was big in stature and a big personality in the dressing room. Made his debut in a 6-0 win at Oldham (Nov '71) and in the 29 matches he played in Villa's 1972 promotion campaign the side lost just three times with Cumbes keeping 18 clean sheets. Also won 'double' League Cup and promotion to Div 1 in the club's centenary year of 1974/75. Also won honours in his time as a first-class cricketer, serving with Lancs, Worcs and Warwickshire.

183 appearances (0 sub)

Ian Ross
Defender
Born; Glasgow, 26th January 1947

Vic Crowe had pursued Ian Ross for a long time before he finally landed his man. Selling Aston Villa to the Liverpool player, a thrilled Crowe called it, "a declaration of faith." Ross was one of four major signings made during the successful promotion push of 1971/72. 'Roscoe' was a fine professional, later became captain under Ron Saunders and led Villa to Wembley victory in the 1975 League Cup final as well as promotion to the 'First' as runners-up to Man Utd in Division Two that same season. Bruce Rioch described Ross as "an extremely clever player and one of the best readers of the game I've ever seen!" Had a spell at 'The Posh' before going into management.

205 appearances (0 sub) 3 goals

Chris Nicholl see page 272

John Gidman see page 274

Alun Evans
Forward
Born; Stourport, 30th September 1949

Son of Alun Evans the former WBA player. Despite having trials with Villa as a 14-year old Alun made his name at Molineux before Liverpool took him to Anfield in 1968 for a huge £100,000, fee, making him the costliest teenager in the history of the game. With Keegan's arrival on Merseyside Evans anticipated game time would be limited and when Shankly accepted Vic Crowe's offer the writing was on the wall – his future lay elsewhere. Formed a great understanding with winger Ray Graydon, they both ended the 1972/73 campaign as joint leading scorers. Injuries (cartilages removed) ravaged Evans second term under Crowe before Ron Saunders was appointed manager in June 1974. Under the new boss he realised he wasn't going to get a game - even though the Villa never lost a league game when Alun scored - so he moved to neighbours Walsall. He played at schoolboy, youth and U23 level for England and was linked with the squad for the 1970 Mexico World Cup. Won a League Cup winners tankard in 1975 though he was an unused sub.

74 appearances (inc 12 sub) 16 goals

Keith Leonard
Centre-forward
Born; Birmingham, 10th November 1950

Came into the game late when he arrived on trial at Villa from non-League Highgate United at 21-years of age. He was deemed too small to make the grade at 15. Greatly impressed the backroom staff when he scored in only his second run out for the reserves. Made his debut away to Fulham in October 1972. The uncompromising forward formed a deadly partnership with Brian Little following the departure of big Sammy Morgan and his 12 league and cup goals during the 1974/75 campaign helped the Villa lift the League Cup at Wembley and also gain promotion to the top-flight after an eight year absence in what was the club's centenary year. Was cruelly forced to retire after colliding with future Villa keeper Jimmy Rimmer in a First Division encounter against Arsenal, September '75.

47 appearances (inc 2 sub) 17 goals

John Robson
Full-back/midfielder
Born; Consett, County Durham, 15th July 1950

Vic Crowe beat off interest from top-flight sides Wolves and Birmingham to land England U23 full-back Robson from Derby County. Already a holder of Second and First Division title medals from his time at the Baseball Ground (signed by the legendary Brian Clough who'd been impressed with Robson's throw-ins!) before arriving at B6 in October 1972. John was a no-nonsense, sure-footed player who slotted into Villa's defence with ease, making his debut December '72 at Hillsborough. Partnered Aitken before the emergence of John Gidman. At the start of the 1974/75 season Saunders played Robson in midfield (he'd started life as a right-half) though he would alternate positions. Won a promotion and two League Cups with Villa before hanging up his boots prematurely due to battling the debilitating multiple sclerosis. John sadly passed away in May 2004.

176 appearances (inc 4 sub) 1 goals

Bobby McDonald
Full-back/midfielder
Born; Aberdeen, 13th April 1955

Joined the club on apprentice forms in June 1971. Was part of the successful Aston Villa FA Youth Cup winning side of 1972, signing pro with the club in September the same year. In May 1973 Villa won the Southern Junior Floodlit Cup where McDonald played alongside other future first-teamers a month after making his full Villa debut in a 2-0 win at home to Portsmouth. Bobby had limited run outs as full-back when the evergreen Charlie Aitken was injured before he was handed a midfield role. Due to his versatility he was played all over the shop and on Aitken's retirement it was fully expected by the backroom staff that McDonald would be his natural successor. This wasn't the case and against his wishes Bobby was sent to Coventry, literally, signing for the 'Sky Blues' in August 1976.

46 appearances (inc 6 sub) 5 goals

Trevor Hockey
Midfielder
Born; Keighley, West Yorkshire, 1st May 1943

Hockey, a footballing nomad, had already played for six league sides before landing at Villa Park from Norwich City in June 1973 at a cost of £38,000. He scored on his debut in the 2-0 home win curtain raiser versus PNE; it was his only goal in a

Villa career that spanned one season. During his brief stay at B6 Trevor gained the last of his Welsh caps when he was sent off against Poland in Katowice in 1974.

24 appearances (0 sub) 1 goal

Sammy Morgan
Forward
Born; Belfast, 3rd December 1946

Already capped by Northern Ireland before arriving at Villa Park in 1973 for a nominal fee. Sammy had started as an amateur with Gorleston (in Norfolk) who were managed by ex-Villan Roger Carter. Roger recommended Morgan to an old team mate from his Villa Park days, Gordon Lee, who was managing Port Vale. Whilst playing for Vale in a Third Division 4-4 draw with the Villa, Morgan terrorised Vic Crowe's defenders - in particular Neil Rioch - to such an extent, the Villa boss had to have him for his side. A strong old-fashioned No 9 who fought like a lion for the cause once he crossed that white line. He was loved by a generation of Villa faithful. Off the field he was shy and retiring!

51 appearances (inc 7 sub) 15 goals

Roy Stark
Defender
Born; Stapleford, Nottingham, 28th November 1953

Equally at home in a full-back or centre-half role. His qualities, of which he had many, including his ability in the air, earned him the captaincy of Villa's Youth team - the victorious one of 1972 who thumped Liverpool 5-2 on aggregate in the final of the FA Youth Cup. Roy was keen as mustard and would 'run through brick walls' if Frank Upton asked him to, according to centre-half partner Alan Little. Stark made his first-team debut alongside Fred Turnbull in Villa's 4-2 victory at Hillsborough, April 1974. Featured in the following game but that was it, next stop, non-League footie.

2 appearances (0 sub)

Jake Findlay
Goalkeeper
Born; Blairgowrie, Perthshire, 13th July 1954

Offered an apprenticeship at Villa in 1970 and turned professional in June 1972, only a month after Findlay had played an important role in Villa's youngster's landing the prestigious FA Youth Cup. Big, brave and fully committed, he was seen as the replacement for Jim Cumbes. Sadly the manager had other ideas and John Burridge arrived from Blackpool in September 1975. Findlay's game time was severely restricted but he always covered himself with credit when playing in the first-team. Made his debut at home to Sunderland during the '72/73 campaign. Had a run of seven games during 1976/77, Villa lost only once and included in that sequence was the 5-1 demolition of Liverpool. Left B6 for Luton Town in November 1978.

18 appearances (inc 1 sub)

Bobby Campbell
Forward
Born; Belfast, 13th September 1956

Joined Villa's youth ranks within weeks of the club lifting the 1972 FA Youth Cup. A big, bustling old-style centre-forward who could look after himself. Scored in only his second start as a substitute when he fired home Villa's second in a 3-1 home victory against Forest during the 1973/74 season. Used sparingly during the first half of Villa's promotion/League Cup 'double' campaign of 1974/75 before being sent out on loan to Halifax and then permanently to Huddersfield Town. Went on to have an outstanding career with Northern Ireland at youth and senior level.

12 appearances (inc 3 sub) 1 goal

Frank Carrodus
Midfielder
Born; Manchester, 31st May 1949

Substitute in the 1974 League Cup final under Ron Saunders with Manchester City. Saunders hadn't been at B6 long in his new role as Villa boss (June '74) before he returned to Maine Road to make the athletic Carrodus his first signing on 15th August. The fee was £95,000. He had only to wait two days to make his debut as Villa kicked-off their new Second Division campaign away to York City. Well known for his stamina and strength, Carrodus started 47 games in his maiden season in claret and blue as he played a vital role in Villa's promotion and League Cup 'double' campaign. Was also a winner in the same competition in 1977 versus Everton. Frank racked up an impressive 187 appearances during the first four seasons of his Villa Park career averaging over 46 games per season. Joined Wrexham in 1979.

197 appearances (0 sub) 10 goals

Tony Betts
Inside-forward
Born; Sandiacre, Nottinghamshire, 31st October 1953

Came to B6 as a junior in May 1969. Tony was then part of the 1972 FA Youth Cup winning side where they played regularly in front of 20,000+ crowds at Villa Park. He signed a professional contract a month before the final but had to wait two years to make his first-team debut, coming on for 'Chico' Hamilton at York City in the first game of the 1974/75 season. It was hard on Tony that he never really got a chance, the team basically picked itself and would go on to gain promotion and the League Cup 'double.' Betts by his own admission didn't play in the first-team as much as he wanted and left in 1975 to go to America where he made a big name for himself on the NASL circuit. Won both amateur and youth international caps with England.

5 appearances (inc 4 sub)

Graham Moseley
Goalkeeper
Born; Manchester, 16th November 1953

Drafted in on-loan from Dave Mackay's Derby County towards the end of August 1974, Jim Cumbes being ruled out for nearly a month through injury. Graham played in a total of three first-team matches including a 3-1 home win against Orient. Capped for England at youth level, Moseley is best remembered for his heroics in the 1983 FA Cup final for Brighton where they went very close to defeating Manchester United.

3 appearances (0 sub)

Leighton Phillips
Defender/midfielder
Born; Briton Ferry, nr Swansea, 25th September 1949

Joined the Villa a month into the 1974/75 campaign arriving from Ninian Park in a deal worth £100,000 to Cardiff City. Leighton was the ideal team player, tenacious, clever without being flashy and he had great vision. In his first season he helped Villa achieve promotion back to Division One. Cup-tied with Cardiff he had to sit out Villa's League Cup odyssey which resulted in the not so epic Wembley final with Norwich. He more than made up for this in 1976/77 when he played in all ten League Cup games coming away with a winners tankard. Represented his beloved Wales at schoolboy, U21, U23, and senior level. In his time at Villa Park Leighton gained 26 of his 58 caps. Was almost an ever present until featuring for the last time in claret and blue in November 1978.

175 appearances (inc 7 sub) 4 goals

Alan Little
Forward/defender
Born; Horden, County Durham, 5th February 1955

Alan knew he would join older brother Brian at Villa, this he did the following year at 15-years of age as an apprentice. Started at centre-forward before Youth team coach Frank Upton converted him to the back four. Alan starred in the Villa's successful 1972 FA Youth Cup win against the much fancied Liverpool. On signing pro forms he then adapted to a midfield role though he played alongside Chris Nicholl on his first team-debut in a 2-1 win at Oldham, October 1974. The versatile Little played up front with Brian in a League Cup tie at Colchester United (en route to the 1975 final), scoring the first in a 2-1 win at Layer Road. Left Villa Park in December 1974 to join Southend United. Went into management and steered his York City side past Ferguson's Manchester United over two legs in the League Cup, masterminding a 3-0 win at Old Trafford.

5 appearances (inc 1 sub) 1 goal

Frank Pimblett
Midfielder
Born; Liverpool, 12th March 1957

The former England schoolboy and youth trialist signed professional forms at Villa Park in October 1974, 15 months after arriving as an apprentice. Starred in both victorious Villa sides that lifted the 1973 and 1975 Southern Junior Floodlit Cup, scoring in the 3-1 first-leg of the '75 competition. Made his first-team debut at Oldham in an FA Cup tie (4th Jan '75). A week later he appeared at Villa Park for a league match with Bristol City, four days later he was showing in a League Cup semi-final! Sadly Frank's fame was short lived, he made only one more appearance in that campaign and just seven the following year, in Villa's first season back in the top flight. After various loan spells he moved to Australia where he still resides.

11 appearances (0 sub)

Keith Masefield
Full-back
Born; Birmingham, 26th February 1957

Alongside Pimblett, Masefield made a name for himself in the Southern Junior Floodlit Cup teams where he was an accomplished and steady right-back. He arrived at Villa Park a month after the famous FA Youth Cup win of 1972 and was rewarded with a professional contract two years later. Made his debut at Villa Park (Feb '75) in front of 39,156 for the visit of Manchester United, replacing goalscorer Ray Graydon. Came on as sub for a sole appearance the following season and went one better in 1976/77 when he actually got to start a match. His contract was cancelled by mutual consent and Keith left to play his club football in Holland.

4 appearances (inc 3 sub)

Steve Hunt
Midfielder
Born; Perry Barr, Birmingham, 4th August 1956

Joined Villa in July 1972 and turned pro in January '74. Made his first-team debut replacing Ian Hamilton at Hillsborough (April '75) in the historic 4-0 win that guaranteed Villa promotion back to the top-flight after an eight year absence. His full debut was in front of a 57,000 Villa Park crowd in the following game (home to Sunderland). Used sparingly over the next two seasons before heading Stateside to play with New York Cosmos of the NASL. After spells at the 'Sky Blues' and the 'Baggies' Steve returned to B6 having won two England caps but couldn't halt the club's slide into Division 2 under Turner and McNeill. Played regularly in the first half of the 1987/88 promotion campaign but was forced to retire prematurely due to recurring knee problems. Later had varying roles in management and coaching.

81 appearances (inc 5 sub) 9 goals

John Burridge (see page 307)
Goalkeeper
Born; Workington, 3rd December 1951

Signed by newly promoted Villa in September 1975 for a £100,000 outlay from Blackpool to replace Jimmy Cumbes. Made his debut in front of a 53,000+ crowd for the long awaited 'derby' visit of

Birmingham City, Villa won 2-1. John kept a remarkable 19 clean sheets during the successful 1976/7 season when Villa won the League Cup, finished fourth in the table and progressed to the quarter-finals of the FA Cup. Had a brief loan spell with Southend United before moving permanently to Crystal Palace in 1978. 'Budgie' went on to make over 1000 appearances with 29 different sides in a career that spanned three decades.

80 appearances (0 sub)

Andy Gray
Striker
Born; Gorbals, Drumchapel, 30th November 1955

Joined the club from Dundee United for a club record fee of £110,000. Scored on his home debut in a League Cup defeat against Manchester United. The fans loved his cavalier attitude, he was the latest in a long line to grace the iconic No 9 shirt. His return of a goal in three games in a season when he was still finding his feet gave a clue to what his future held. The following season Andy took all that stood before him, he terrorised defences the length and breadth of the country. He plundered 25 league goals in 36 games as well as four in ten cup matches. He walked away with both 'Young Player' and 'Player of the Year' awards in the 1976/77 season, the first time this had been achieved. Behind the scenes all wasn't well in the corridors of B6 and in September 1979 Andrew Mullen Gray joined Wolverhampton Wanderers for a seven figure sum. Won honours at Wolves and Everton before playing for his boyhood team Rangers. Made a return to Villa Park in 1985.

210 appearances (inc 4 sub) 78 goals

John Deehan
Striker
Born; Solihull, 6th August 1957

Spotted playing in local Elmdon Park, Deehan was due to attend a trial at Arsenal. With both John and his father, John senior, being Aston Villa fans his dad phoned the Villa who told him, "bring him across and we'll have a look at him." Deehan scored a first-half hat-trick in his Bodymoor Heath trial and as a result the club signed him as an apprentice on the spot, the date July 1973. Was introduced to Central League football at the tail end of the 1973/74 campaign and the following year was netting regularly at that level. Starred in the victorious 1975 Southern Junior Floodlit Cup competition and was offered a professional contract that same year. Broke into the first-team during Villa's return to the top flight in 1975/76 and impressed with a return of seven goals in 14 league games. A prolific scorer thereafter. Sold against his wishes when he transferred to West Brom in September 1979. Gained youth and Under 21 caps for England.

139 appearances (inc 4 sub) 50 goals

Dennis Mortimer
Midfielder
Born; Liverpool, 5th April 1952

Started his career playing in the same Kirby Boys team as future team-mate Kenny Swain. He signed on apprentice terms at Highfield Road in 1967 and was rewarded with a pro contract two years later. He amassed over 200 appearances for Coventry City before Ron Saunders signed him in December 1975 as 'a present for the supporters.' A very underrated player, Dennis had the lot, vision, skill and determination. Picked up a League Cup winners gong in 1977 before leading the club to their first title in 71 years. Mortimer was one of seven ever-presents in that magical 1980/81 season. Eclipsed the title win by landing the European Cup at the first time of asking in 1982. Was capped at youth and Under 23 level with England yet amazingly he only gained an England 'B' cap at senior level. Only a handful of players (nine) have appeared more in the Villa jersey.

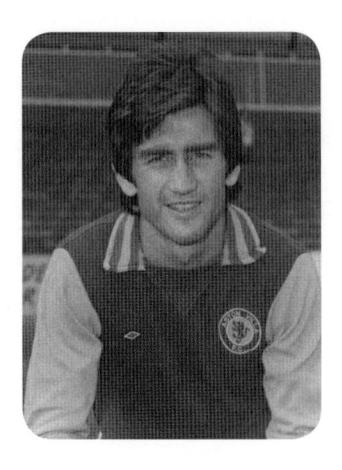

406 appearances (inc 1 sub) 36 goals

John Overton
Defender
Born; Rotherham, 2nd May 1956

Joined as an apprentice in June 1972 and signed professionally January 1974. John made his long awaited debut at Manchester City's Maine Road ground in February 1976. Two further games, one as substitute were his sum total in the Villa first-team. He had a loan spell shortly after at Halifax Town before moving to Gillingham in a permanent deal.

3 appearances (inc 1 sub)

Gordon Cowans see page 278

Gordon Smith
Full-back
Born; Glasgow, 3rd July 1954

A Scottish U23 defender who came down from St Johnstone in August 1976. Knowing he wouldn't displace right-back John Gidman, Smith bent the truth slightly and told Saunders he was a left-back. A position he'd never played in his life. Made his debut in a pre-season Villa Park friendly against Royal Antwerp. Despite his alien role he formed a water-tight back-line with 'Giddy.' Following an outstanding performance from 'Smudge' in the high-profile Tottenham game (Aug '78) which saw the arrival of Argentineans, Ricardo Villa and Osvaldo Ardiles, Gordon was signed by Spurs boss Keith Burkinshaw. Won the 1977 League Cup in his time at B6.

96 appearances (inc 4 sub)

Alex Cropley
Midfielder
Born; Aldershot, 16th January 1951

Won a Scottish League Cup with Hibernian before moving south to join Arsenal. In his short time at Highbury the tenacious Cropley gained U23 and full international honours for Scotland. Came back from a leg-break to sign for Saunders in September 1976 for a £125,000 fee. Made his Villa debut the following weekend in a 2-0 home victory over Leicester City. In only his third game in claret and blue Alex scored one of the best goals ever witnessed in Villa colours when he chipped Barry Siddall in the Sunderland goal to record a 1-0 win at Roker Park (only the team's second win on the road since promotion in April 1975). Cropley made the No 10 shirt his own before a vicious tackle at the hands of Albion's Ally Brown broke his leg for a third time in December 1977. He returned in time and played out the remaining 15 games of the 1978/79 campaign only to smash his ankle in his first game the following season. There was no way back this time, Alex had short spells at various clubs before going back to his native Edinburgh where he drives a taxi to this day.

83 appearances (inc 2 sub) 7 goals

Charlie Young
Centre-half
Born; Nicosia, Cyprus, 14th February 1958

Signed pro forms at the Villa November 1975, having spent a year and a half as an apprentice. Standing over 6 ft tall, Young made his debut at Elland Road in December 1976, deputising for the injured Chris Nicholl. Charlie broke Chris' nose in a training ground accident the day before! Enjoyed an extended run in the side, including the never-to-be-forgotten 5-1 victory over Liverpool, claimed by many to be Aston Villa's finest ever team performance. Left the Villa to join Gillingham where he broke his leg shortly after, enabling a youngster by the name of Steve Bruce to break into the team.

11 appearances (inc 1 sub)

Michael Buttress
Full-back
Born; Whittesley, nr Peterborough, 23rd March 1958

Joined the club as a junior and was handed a professional contract in February 1976. Came on to replace Alex Cropley in the stunning 5-1 win over Liverpool, December 1976 and came on in the following game for the same player, this time in the victory over Newcastle United. Played in his one and only full game up at Goodison Park in January '78, Villa went down 0-1. Joined Gillingham at the same time as Villa centre-half Charlie Young.

3 appearances (inc 2 sub)

David Hughes
Midfielder
Born; Birmingham, 19th March 1958

Picked up from Birmingham Parks football and taken on as an apprentice the same month as Saunders arrived at Villa Park, June 1974. He turned professional in February 1976. David made his Villa debut at Middlesbrough's Ayresome Park in December 1976. Trailing 1-3 at half-time to a David Mills hat-trick, Hughes reduced the arrears when he fired home, but to no avail as Villa lost 2-3. Left Villa Park in April 1977 to join Lincoln City where he played in excess of 60 times for the 'Imps.'

4 appearances (inc 1 sub) 1 goal

Ivor Linton
Midfielder
Born; West Bromwich, 20th November 1959

Following an initial trial and the mandatory apprenticeship Ivor was handed a pro contract in September 1977. The following term he was one of the stars of Villa's FA Youth Cup run which ended in final defeat. Had a couple of first-team run outs at the tail end of the 1976/7 season and did likewise in the following two campaigns. During 1978/9 Linton featured in 16 league and cup matches before making the journey to Peterborough's London Road. Later made a bit of a name for himself in Finland where he played for a couple of sides.

30 appearances (inc 13 sub)

Jimmy Rimmer
Goalkeeper
Born; Southport, 10th February 1948

Made his mark at Old Trafford where he was an amateur before signing apprentice and professional contracts. Was on the bench when the Manchester side lifted the European Cup in 1968 so received a coveted medal. He spent three and a half years at Arsenal before Ron Saunders brought him to Villa Park in August 1977. He immediately displaced John Burridge between the posts. Missed only two league games in a five season spell. Was ever-present when Villa landed the title in 1981 and was instrumental when they lifted the European Cup in 1982, none more so than his vital penalty save away to Dynamo Berlin. Remembered for having to leave the Rotterdam pitch early in the final to be replaced by Nigel Spink. Won Under 23 honours and a solitary full England cap.

287 appearances

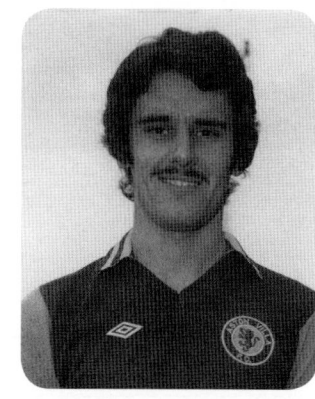

John Gregory
Midfielder/utility
Born; Scunthorpe, 11th May 1954

Arrived from Northampton Town in June 1977. A battler and grafter, John was possibly too versatile for his own good. Never held one position down, in fact he appeared in all ten outfield shirts during his two seasons as a player. Weighed in with some vital goals before transferring to Brighton. Following coaching and caretaker manager roles he made a return to Villa Park in November 1994 where he and Allan Evans were backroom staff under manager Brian Little. Villa won the 1996 League Cup during their tenure. Little stepped down in February 1998 to be replaced the day after by Gregory who'd been managing Wycombe Wanderers. Led the Villa to back-to-back 6th place finishes in his first seasons in charge.

76 appearances (inc 7 sub) 11 goals

Ken McNaught
Centre-half
Born; Kirkcaldy, Fife, 17th January 1955

The son of Scottish international Willie McNaught. Taken on as an apprentice at Goodison Park in July 1971 and made a pro within ten months. Totally dominating in the air Ken took no prisoners. His outstanding performances for Everton in the 1977 League Cup final matches – against you know who – led to Ron Saunders clinching his signature in a £200,000 move. Had his work cut out to win the Villa Park faithful around after taking Chris Nicholl's place in the side. Once McNaught was accustomed to, what for him was an alien role initially in Villa's defence alongside Leighton Phillips, he commanded respect. He and Allan Evans were possibly one of the best centre-half pairings throughout Europe. Ever-present in the 1981 title campaign and a stalwart in Villa's impressive European odyssey the following season. Captained the side to victory (and scoring) against the mighty Barcelona in the 1983 European Super Cup. Gained amateur and youth honours with Scotland. Still seen around B6 as he runs the 'Lions & Legends,' a team made up of former Aston Villa stars who play matches for charity.

260 appearances (0 sub) 13 goals

Tommy Craig
Midfielder
Born; Penilee, Glasgow, 21st November 1950

Joined the Villa mid-season 1977/78 from Newcastle United a year after gaining a full Scottish cap. His cost of £275,000 a new club record transfer, dwarfing the £200,000 paid to Everton for McNaught. Predominantly left-sided, skilful and a clean striker of the the dead ball, he arrived shortly after Cropley's horrendous leg-break. Tommy debuted for the Villa in January 1978 but was restricted to just four run-outs in that season. His first goal in the famous colours came against Everton in a Villa Park league match the following term. His free-kick from distance similar in style to a certain Bruce Rioch from a few years earlier. Sadly, this Scot couldn't emulate Bruce in his time in Aston. He moved to Swansea in July 1979 having sadly never fulfilled his potential.

32 appearances (0 sub) 2 goals

Evans Allan
Forward/Centre-half
Born; West Calder, West Lothian, 12th October 1956

A promising striker signed from Dunfermline Athletic in June 1977, a steal at only £30,000. During a run of Central League appearances Allan rattled in 9 goals inc six in one match (Sheff Utd, Feb '78). This had Saunders sitting up and taking notice. Evans made his full league debut weeks later in a drab 0-0 draw with bottom side Leicester City, having come off the bench against Barcelona four days earlier in the UEFA Cup quarter-finals. In spite of his prowess in front of goal, the Villa boss pulled off a masterstroke pairing him with fellow Scot Ken McNaught at centre-half. These two would form the cornerstone of the future title and European Cup winning side's defence. Diagnosed with Crohn's Disease in his last year at the Villa, Graham Taylor wouldn't renew his contract. Allan gained his 'A' and UEFA Licences and coached for a time in Canada. After various other appointments he ended up back at Villa Park, along with John Gregory to assist new manager Brian Little. Only Charlie

THE BIG ASTON VILLA BOOK OF THE SEVENTIES

Aitken 660, Billy Walker 531, and Gordon Cowans 527 have bettered Allan's 475 first-class appearances in claret and blue!

475 appearances (inc 9 sub) 62 goals

David Evans
Defender
Born; West Browwich, 20th May 1958

Landed at B6 the same month as new manager Ron Saunders, June 1974. He was on apprentice forms less than two years with Villa handing him a professional contract in February '76. Incredibly Saunders chose to 'blood' Evans in the highly charged atmosphere of the UEFA Cup quarter-finals, at home to Spanish giants Barcelona, complete with superstars Cruyff and Neeskens. Acquitted himself well on the night even though he would only wear the shirt on two more occasions. Reinvented himself as a midfielder and played in excess of 300 games with Halifax Town not to mention over 200 with Bradford City.

3 appearances (0 sub)

Gary Shelton
Midfielder
Born; Nottingham, 21st March 1958

Joined Walsall as an apprentice and signed professional forms four years later in 1976. Came to Villa's notice and signed in January 1978 for a fee of £60,000, but had to wait until the first game of the 1978/79 campaign (home to Wolves) to make his debut. Scored in the following game, a surprise 4-1 win at White Hart Lane when Villa upstaged the well documented arrival of Argentine World Cup stars Osvaldo Ardiles and Ricardo Villa. Shelton only featured four times in the 1979/80 season, none the following year when Villa won the title using only 14 players and after a solitary appearance during 1981/82 he left for Sheffield Wednesday. Gained an England U21 cap in his time at Hillsborough.

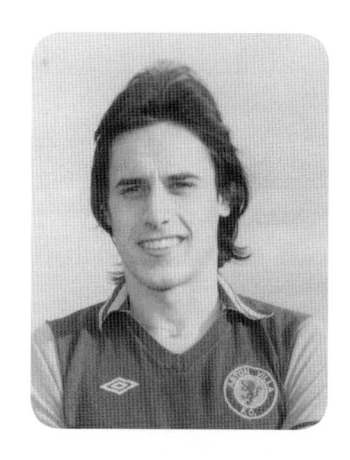

27 appearances (inc 1 sub) 8 goals

Gary Shaw
Striker
Born; Castle Bromwich, Birmingham, 21st January 1961

Prolific scorer at school and District level. Villa signed him on in July 1977 as an apprentice and as a professional 18 months later. After hitting the back of the net regularly for the reserves (22 all told during '78/79) he turned out a few times for the first-team but showed glimpses of his true potential when he was given an extended run the following year and rewarded Saunders faith by bagging goals in all three domestic competitions. His partnership with Peter Withe was key to Aston Villa's successful title bid of 1981 and the following year the pair took Europe by storm and landed the biggest trophy in club football. Gary was voted PFA 'Young Player of the Year' in 1981 and 'Outstanding Young European Player of the Year' in 1982. Sadly for Shaw, the Villa and football in general, the blonde haired striker was injured in September '83 in a league game at Nottingham Forest. He required operations on his damaged knee on no less than six occasions. He played on at Villa Park, but a former shadow of what he'd been, soldiered on albeit briefly at numerous other clubs before making a new career for himself working with OPTA (football match stats) and radio commentary. It was England's loss the lad was only capped at Youth and Under 21 level.

213 appearances (inc 9 sub) 79 goals

Lee Jenkins
Midfielder
Born; West Bromwich, 17th March 1963

Came to Villa Park in June 1977 as an apprentice, signed as pro in January '79. The attacking midfielder won England Youth honours alongside team-mates Gary Shaw and Brendan Ormsby and was part of the FA Youth Cup team that reached the 1978 final but lost by the only goal to Crystal Palace. His claret and blue first-team career was albeit brief, consisting of three substitute appearances. His first in the 1978/79 campaign in September, his second coming only three games later. Lee's last appearance was the following season when he came on against Brighton & Hove Albion for the very unfortunate Alex Cropley. Crops had fought back from a bad leg break only to 'do' his ankle, it was his last game too.

3 appearances (inc 3 sub)

Gary Williams
Defender
Born; Wolverhampton, 17th June 1960

Came to Villa Park as an apprentice. Signed pro forms within two years at the time he captained Villa's Youth Cup final team (as a centre-half) who lost narrowly to Crystal Palace. Gary could also play in midfield but made his name at full-back. Spent numerous seasons vying for the left-back shirt with Colin Gibson before partnering him with Gary switching to the right. Williams won a First Division title medal in 1981 to go with future European Cup and Super Cup gongs. Had a brief loan spell at Walsall before leaving for Leeds United in 1987. Injury ruled out his chance of Under 21 honours with England.

302 appearances (inc 5 sub) 2 goals

Willie Young
Forward
Born; Glasgow, 24th February 1956

Landed at Villa Park in July 1978 having come down from Clyde. Made a very promising start in claret and blue when he featured in a 2-2 draw at home to Manchester United in October 1978. Unnerved by a large crowd, Willie played in the next two games including a Birmingham 'derby' at St Andrews. In spite of passing his baptism of fire with flying colours he wouldn't wear the first-team jersey again. Found the net regularly in Villa's Central League side before moving onto Torquay United in 1981.

3 appearances (0 sub)

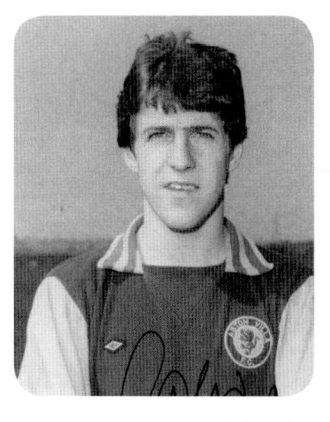

Colin Gibson
Left-back/midfielder
Born; Bridport, 6th April 1960

Was a Youth Training Scheme product but signed pro within two years (Oct 1978). Weeks later Colin had a brief run-out in a Villa shirt at Bristol City when he replaced Allan Evans. Had an extended run, playing in the remaining 11 fixtures of the season following injury to left-back Williams. Started both the following campaigns as first choice in the No 3 jersey ('79/80 & '80/81) earning a League champions medal for his efforts. Starred in the Charity Shield at Wembley, early rounds on the 1982 European Cup trail and also played in the Super Cup clashes with Barcelona. Moved to a midfield role as Williams claimed the left-back berth. Joined Manchester United in a big figure deal - £275,000 - in November 1985. Capped at three different levels for England, Youth U21 and 'B.'

238 appearances (inc 5 sub) 17 goals

Kenny Swain
Inside-forward/full-back
Born; Birkenhead, 28th January 1952

Played in the same Kirby Boys side as a certain Dennis Mortimer. Initially signed as a forward to play alongside John Deehan due to Brian Little being injured. Kenny cost the Villa £100,000 when he made the switch from Chelsea. When John Gidman left for Everton, Ron Saunders moved Swain to the right-back position he is more fondly remembered for by Villa supporters. Was one of seven ever-presents during Villa's title winning campaign of 1980/81 and starred in the 1982 European Cup final in Rotterdam where he headed one Bayern effort off the line! After being told regular first-team action couldn't be guaranteed under manager Tony Barton, Kenny was quickly snapped up by Brian Clough for his Nottingham Forest side.

179 appearances (0 sub) 5 goals

Joe Ward
Forward
Born; Glasgow, 25th November 1954

Arrived from Scottish side Clyde for £80,000 in December 1978. Joe played a part in landing the Second Division championship for 'The Bully Wee' in the '77/78 campaign as well as gaining Scotland caps at amateur and youth level. Scoring at an impressive rate of almost one-in-three games (39 in 128). Found game time severely restricted at Villa Park and returned north of the border in the deal that saw Hibernian's Des Bremner move to B6.

3 appearances (inc 1 sub)

Brendan Ormsby
Defender
Born; Edgbaston, Birmingham, 1st October 1960

Came to the club as an apprentice and was rewarded with a professional contract in October 1978. He came on as a substitute the same month in a League Cup tie away to Crystal Palace, helping to keep a clean-sheet. In the following month he was selected alongside Villa team-mates Gary Shaw and Lee Jenkins for the England Youth squad to play in Monaco. Brendan had to wait until April 1979 to make his full debut in a 3-3 draw with Derby County at Villa Park. Had his finest season during the 1983/84 campaign where he made over 40 appearances and weighed in with goals in the League and UEFA Cup. Last but not least, Brendan has the distinction of having a beer named after him – Ormsby's Bitter brewed by The Wold Top Brewery - as president of a Scarborough based Leeds United Supporter's Club. Brendan left Villa for the Elland Road side in 1986.

140 appearances (inc 4 sub) 7 goals

Tony Morley
Winger
Born; Ormskirk, 26th August 1954

Started out at Preston North End. In his time at Deepdale he helped England Youth win the mini-World Cup - defeating East Germany in Italy – and gained Under 23 honours. Turned down the chance to go to Arsenal, instead landing up at Turf Moor. Had three successful seasons at Burnley before signing for the Villa in the summer of 1979. Played sporadically in his first season but was everpresent in Villa's title success of 1981, playing as an old fashioned left winger though he was naturally right-footed, where he not only supplied the ammunition for the deadly partnership of Shaw and Withe but weighed in with vital league and cup goals (12 in all). Was Villa's leading scorer in the triumphant European Cup campaign of 1982 and supplied the cross for Withe to score the only goal in the final versus Bayern Munich. A crowd favourite at B6 who like others, was pushed out of Villa Park far too soon.

180 appearances (inc 10 sub) 34 goals

Mike Pejic
Full-back
Born; Chesterton, Staffordshire, 25th January 1950

Pejic was a big money signing from Everton, £225,000. Part of Ron Saunders' rebuilding process following the sale of Andy Gray to Wolves. Came to Villa Park with full England honours (and U23 caps) under his belt, a player with true pedigree. A gritty performer who tackled hard but fair. Mike was extremely unfortunate, after only a dozen league and cup games in a Villa career that spanned only four months, he had to hang up his boots due to injury. Had later spells as coach or manager at various lower level clubs.

12 appearances (0 sub)

Des Bremner
Midfielder
Born; Aberchider, Kirkaldy, 7th September 1962

The likable Scot came down from Hibernian in a deal that sent Joe Ward the other way. From making his debut in a home draw

THE BIG ASTON VILLA BOOK OF THE SEVENTIES

with Arsenal (September 1979), Des was an ever-present for the rest of the season. His work rate, tackling and passing very evident from the terraces and well received and respected by his team-mates. Capped only once at senior level with Scotland (a travesty) and a handful of appearances with the U23s. Bremner would be one of the final pieces of the Villa jigsaw that dominated football in the early 1980s, winning League championship, European Cup and Super Cup gongs in the process. Left the Villa for bitter rivals Birmingham in October 1984.

227 appearances (inc 5 sub) 10 goals

Dave Geddis
Forward
Born; Carlisle, 12th March 1958

Won an FA Cup winners medal with Ipswich Town in their surprise victory over Arsenal, May 1978. Ron Saunders signed Geddis in September 1979 for a club record fee of £300,000 following the departures of strikers Gray and Deehan. Found goals hard to come by scoring only three in 24 appearances in his first campaign at Villa Park. Due to Peter Withe's arrival in May 1980, David found himself down the pecking order somewhat but when required he came up with the goods during the 1980/81 title winning season scoring four vital goals in only eight starts. Gained England caps at Youth and B-level.

57 appearances (inc 5 sub) 16 goals

Terry Bullivant
Midfielder
Born; Lambeth, London, 23rd September 1956

Landed from Fulham, November 1979, in a deal worth £220,000 for 'The Cottagers.' Was used sparingly during the 1979/80 campaign (a total of only seven league and cup apps), didn't feature at all during the title win the following year and was only given limited games in his last season at Villa Park. Unsuccessful at landing a regular place in the side Terry moved back to London, signing for Brentford, July '83.

15 appearances (inc 4 sub)

Eamonn Deacy
Full-back
Born; Galway, Ireland, 1st October 1958

Signed from Galway Rovers in March 1979 after writing to Villa asking for a trial. Made his debut coming on for the injured David Geddis in a 2-1 win at White Hart Lane in December 1979. Featured in 10 of Villa's matches during their title winning 1980/81 campaign. Scored his only goal in claret and blue during a 3-2 win at home to Norwich City, March '83. A humble guy, loved by his team-mates, who sadly passed away in Galway 2012. Galway FC's ground Terryland Park has since been renamed Eamonn Deacy Park in recognition of the area's famous son.

41 appearances (inc 11 sub) 1 goal

Terry Donovan
Centre-forward
Born; Liverpool, 27th February 1958

Villa signed the prolific Grimsby Town striker in September 1979 at a cost of £75,000. Donovan had to wait until December of that year to make his first-team start for Villa though it was a dream debut, scoring the opener in the 3-0 home demolition of Coventry City. Emulated his father Don Donovan when he was called up for the Republic of Ireland, winning two caps in his time at Villa Park. Scored vital goals in the early stages of the European Cup as well as a phenomenal amount for the reserves in the Central League (70 in only 120 games) but left for pastures new before the final itself; a loan spell in the States with Portland Timbers among his many ports of call.

24 appearances (0 sub) 11 goals

Nigel Spink
Goalkeeper
Born; Chelmsford, 8th August 1958

Was signed from Chelmsford City (a top Southern League side) for the sum of £4,000 in January 1977 after impressing Tony Barton. Behind both Burridge and Findlay, Spink was pushed further down the pecking order with the arrival of Jimmy Rimmer. Made his long-awaited debut away to European Cup winners Nottingham Forest on Boxing Day 1979. Ironically Nigel would wait another three years before getting a second game in Villa colours, impressing Barton once again and seeing his name in the headlines all over the world. Replacing Rimmer after only nine minutes, Nigel was unfazed and held everything Bayern Munich could throw at him in the 1982 European Cup final. A superb shot-stopper, no keeper has played more in claret and blue (green technically speaking) though he came on as an outfield player for the injured Ian Taylor at QPR in his last game. Disgraceful he won only a solitary England cap!

460 appearances (inc 5 sub)

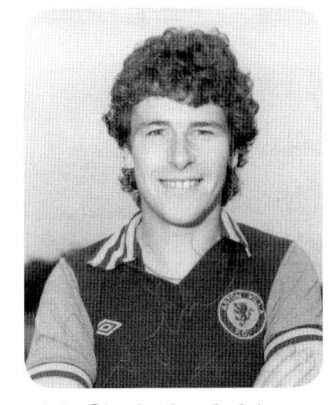

Pat Heard
Defender
Born; Hull, East Riding of Yorkshire, 17th March 1960

Pat joined Villa from Everton in October 1979 as part of the deal that saw want-away full-back John Gidman go to Goodison. After turning in good performances in the Central League (1979/80), weighing in with a solitary goal, Pat was thrown in against Norwich City in the 2-0 home win in early April. He played well enough to remain in the side for the remaining eight fixtures of the season. Was unable to get a game during the halcyon title winning campaign but was back in the action for the 1981/82 season, scoring too. The pinnacle of his career undoubtedly was as a substitute (albeit unused) for the 1982 European Cup final in Rotterdam. A steady player who could always be relied on when called into the action. Left for Hillsborough, January 1983.

27 appearances (inc 6 sub) 2 goals

Robert Hopkins
Midfielder
Born; Hall Green, Birmingham, 25th October 1961

Came to Villa Park as an apprentice and signed professional terms two years later in July 1979. Played over 20 times for the reserve side in his first season, scoring on the odd occasion. An FA Youth Cup winner with Aston Villa in 1980 and scored on his first-team debut at home to Norwich in March 1980 with his only kick of the game. Hopkins had a terrible disciplinary record and took great delight in broadcasting the fact he played for Villa with a Birmingham City badge pinned to his shirt! He joined Blues in 1983.

3 appearances (inc 2 sub) 1 goal

Noel Blake
Defender
Born; Jamaica, 12th January 1962

Signed professionally in August 1979 after two years with local side Sutton Coldfield. Appeared over 30 times in the Central League during '79/80, scoring twice. Given his first-team start at home to Spurs (April '80) in that same season and also played in the remaining two games. Blake would make only one more appearance in claret and blue (December 1981) before joining near neighbours Birmingham City in September 1982 in a deal worth £55,000.

4 appearances (0 sub)

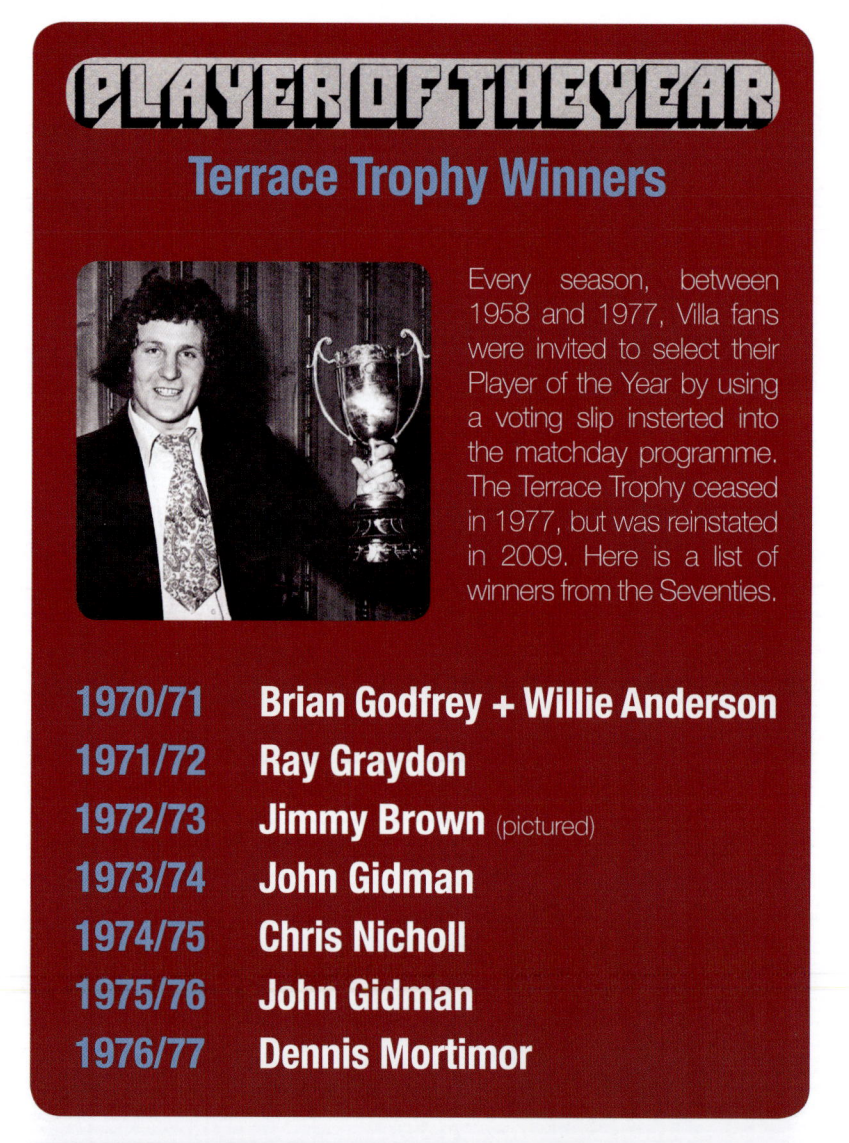

PLAYER OF THE YEAR
Terrace Trophy Winners

Every season, between 1958 and 1977, Villa fans were invited to select their Player of the Year by using a voting slip insterted into the matchday programme. The Terrace Trophy ceased in 1977, but was reinstated in 2009. Here is a list of winners from the Seventies.

1970/71	Brian Godfrey + Willie Anderson
1971/72	Ray Graydon
1972/73	Jimmy Brown (pictured)
1973/74	John Gidman
1974/75	Chris Nicholl
1975/76	John Gidman
1976/77	Dennis Mortimor

[Right] Goalkeeper ,John Burridge (centre), is welcomed to Villa by (L-R) Ian Ross, Andy Gray, John Gidman and John Robson

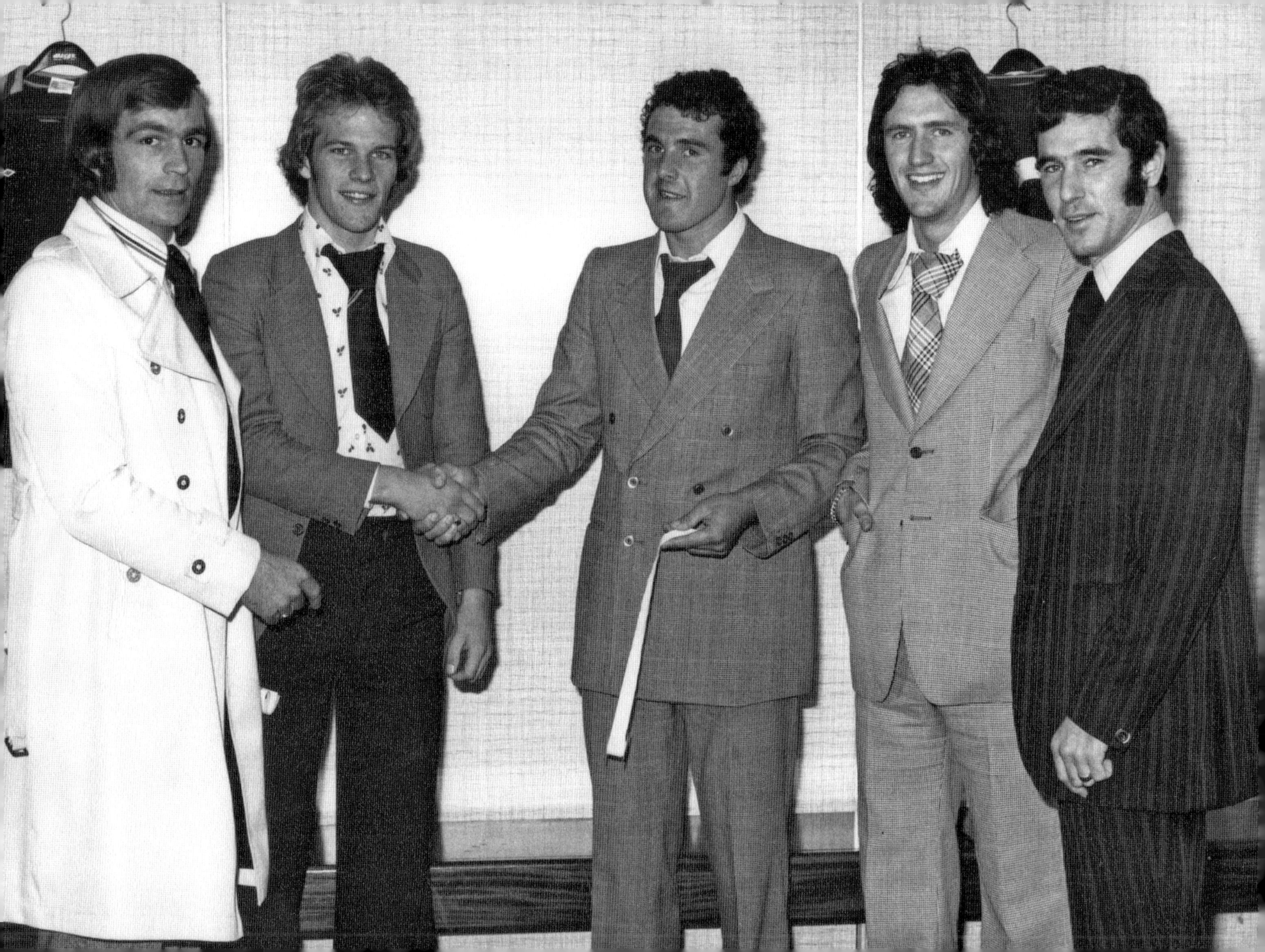

THE BIG ASTON VILLA BOOK OF THE SEVENTIES

[Right] Glasgow Rangers were the 'friendly' visitors to Villa Park in October 1976 – the game was unfortunately abandoned in the second half due to crowd disturbances with Villa 2-0 up

OTHER FIXTURES

FRIENDLIES, TESTIMONIALS AND NON-COMPETITIVE MATCHES

HITACHI T.V. and AUDIO
Ansells Bittermen
CROWDER BROWN FOR VAUXHALL
SCRAP MERCHANTS

1970-71 PRE-SEASON FRIENDLIES AND OTHER NON-COMPETITIVE MATCHES

Pre-Season Tour (Ireland & Scotland)

Shaun Dunlop Testimonial — **Mon 27th July**
Coleraine 0 — Aston Villa 4
Hamilton 2 Rioch B 2

Dunn, Wright, Aitken, Godfrey, Curtis, Chatterley, McMahon, Rioch B, Martin, Hamilton, Anderson, Subs Brown, Tiler

Friendly — **Wed 29th July**
Glentoran 0 — Aston Villa 0

Dunn, Wright, Aitken, Godfrey, Curtis, Chatterley, McMahon, Rioch B, Martin, Hamilton, Anderson, Subs Phillips, Brown, Tiler

Friendly — **Sat 1st August**
Motherwell 2 — Aston Villa 1
Chatterley

Dunn, Wright, Aitken, Godfrey, Curtis, Chatterley, McMahon, Rioch B, Lochhead (Martin), Hamilton, Anderson,

Friendly — **Mon 3rd August**
Clydebank 3 — Aston Villa 1
McMahon

Phillips, Wright, Aitken, Tiler, Curtis, Chatterley, McMahon, Rioch B, Lochhead, Godfrey, Anderson, Sub Brown

Friendly — **Sat 8th August**
Aston Villa 1 — West Bromwich Albion 1
Godfrey
Att 20,800

Dunn, Wright, Aitken (Turnbull), Godfrey, Chatterley, Tiler, McMahon, Brown, Rioch B, Hamilton, Martin

1971-72 PRE-SEASON FRIENDLIES AND OTHER NON-COMPETITIVE MATCHES

Pre-Season Tour (Germany)

Friendly   **Thurs 29th July**
Alemannia Aachen 1   **Aston Villa 0**
Att 4,000

Hughes, Bradley (Wright), Aitken, McMahon, Turnbull, Tiler, Graydon, Vowden (Hamilton), Lochhead, Gregory, Anderson.

Friendly   **Sat 31st July**
Kickers Wurzburg 2   **Aston Villa 4**
Curtis, Lochhead, Graydon, McMahon

Hughes, Wright (Bradley), Aitken, Gregory, Curtis, Tiler, Graydon (Rudge), Vowden, Lochhead (McMahon), Gibson (Hamilton), Anderson.

Friendly   **Mon 2nd August**
Bayreuth 2   **Aston Villa 3**
McMahon, Lochhead, Hamilton

Crudington, Bradley (Wright), Aitken, McMahon, Turnbull, Tiler, Graydon (Rudge), Vowden, Lochhead, Gregory, Anderson (Hamilton).

Friendly   **Tues 3rd August**
Goppingen 2   **Aston Villa 2**
Anderson (pen), Hamilton

Crudington, Wright, Aitken, Bradley (McMahon), Curtis, Turnbull, Rudge (Gregory), Tiler (Vowden), Lochhead, Hamilton, Anderson.

THE BIG ASTON VILLA BOOK OF THE SEVENTIES

Friendly   **Sat 7th August**
Aston Villa 2   **Birmingham City 1**
Anderson 2
Att 36,771

Hughes, Bradley, Aitken, Gregory, Turnbull, Tiler, Graydon (Rioch B), McMahon, Lochhead (Martin), Vowden (Hamilton), Anderson.

Friendly   **Wed 1st December**
Aston Villa 1   **Gornik Zabrze (Poland) 1**
Hamilton
Att 14,662

Cumbes, Gidman, Rioch N, Rioch B, Turnbull, Hoban (Lynch), Graydon (Rudge), Brown (Hamilton), Lochhead (Martin), McMahon, Anderson.

Friendly   **Mon 21st February**
Aston Villa 2   **Santos (Brazil) 1**
McMahon, Graydon
Att 54,437

Cumbes, Wright, Aitken (Lynch), Rioch B, Curtis (Tiler), Turnbull, Graydon, McMahon (Hoban), Lochhead, Hamilton, Martin.

End of Season Tour

Squad from, Cumbes, Findlay, Wright, Aitken, Ross, Turnbull, Curtis, Rioch B, Graydon, Lochhead, Anderson, Hamilton, Vowden, McMahon,

Friendly   **Tue 9th May**
Maccabi Natanya (Tel Aviv) 1   **Aston Villa 2**
Aitken, Lochhead

No team line-up available.

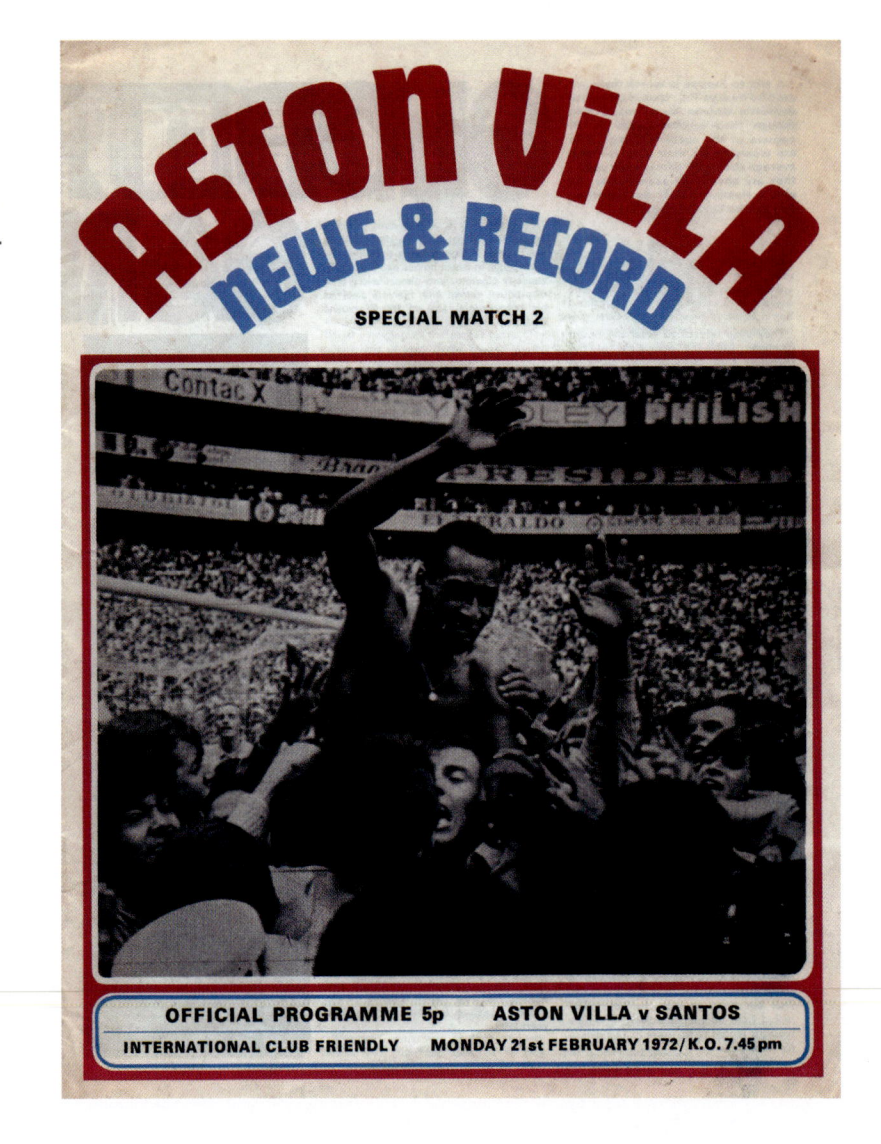

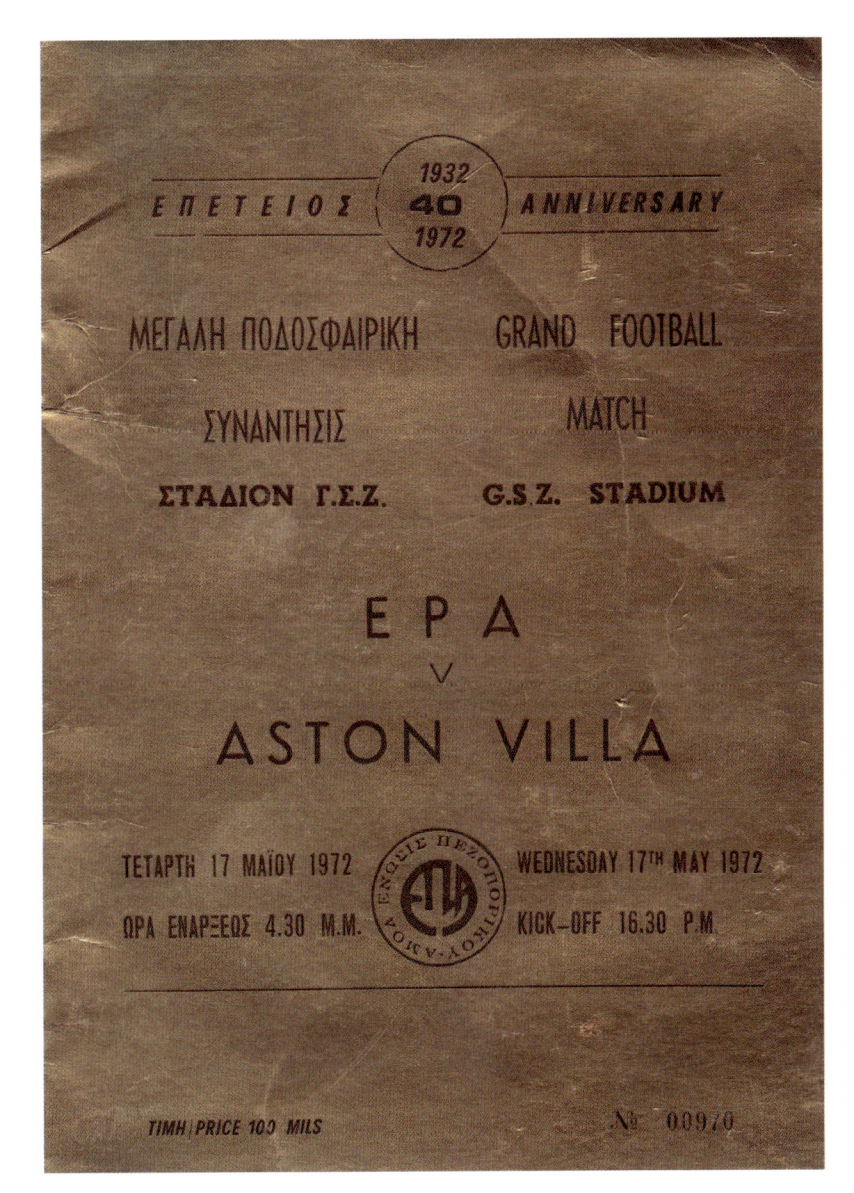

Friendly: Wed 10th May
Beer Sheba 2 Aston Villa 1
Graydon
No team line-up available.

Friendly Wed 17th May
EPA Larnaca (Cyprus) 0 Aston Villa 6
Graydon 2, Aitken, Lochhead, Rioch B, McMahon
No team line-up available.

1972-73 PRE-SEASON FRIENDLIES AND OTHER NON-COMPETITIVE MATCHES

Pre-Season Tour (Holland)

Friendly   **Wed 26th July 1972**
Groningen 1   **Aston Villa 2**
Nicholl, Graydon

Cumbes, Wright, Aitken, Rioch B, Nicholl, Turnbull (Beard), Graydon, Evans, Ross (McMahon), Vowden, Anderson (Hamilton).

Friendly   **Sat 29th July**
Nijmegen 0   **Aston Villa 3**
Lochhead, Anderson (pen), Nicholl

Hughes, Tiler, Aitken, Rioch B, Nicholl, Ross, Graydon, Evans, Lochhead, Vowden, Anderson.

Friendly   **Wed 2nd August**
Fr Aston Villa 0   **Tottenham Hotspur 0**
Att 23,538

Cumbes, Ross (Wright), Aitken, Rioch B, Nicholl, Turnbull, Graydon, Vowden (Hamilton), Lochhead (Little B), Evans (McMahon), Anderson.

Friendly   **Mon 7th August**
Shrewsbury Town 2   **Aston Villa 2**
Evans 2
Att 3,500

Hughes, Gidman, Wright, Tiler, Turnbull, Vowden, Brown, McMahon, Evans, Hamilton, Anderson Subs all played, Rudge, Stark, Rioch N, George, Little B.

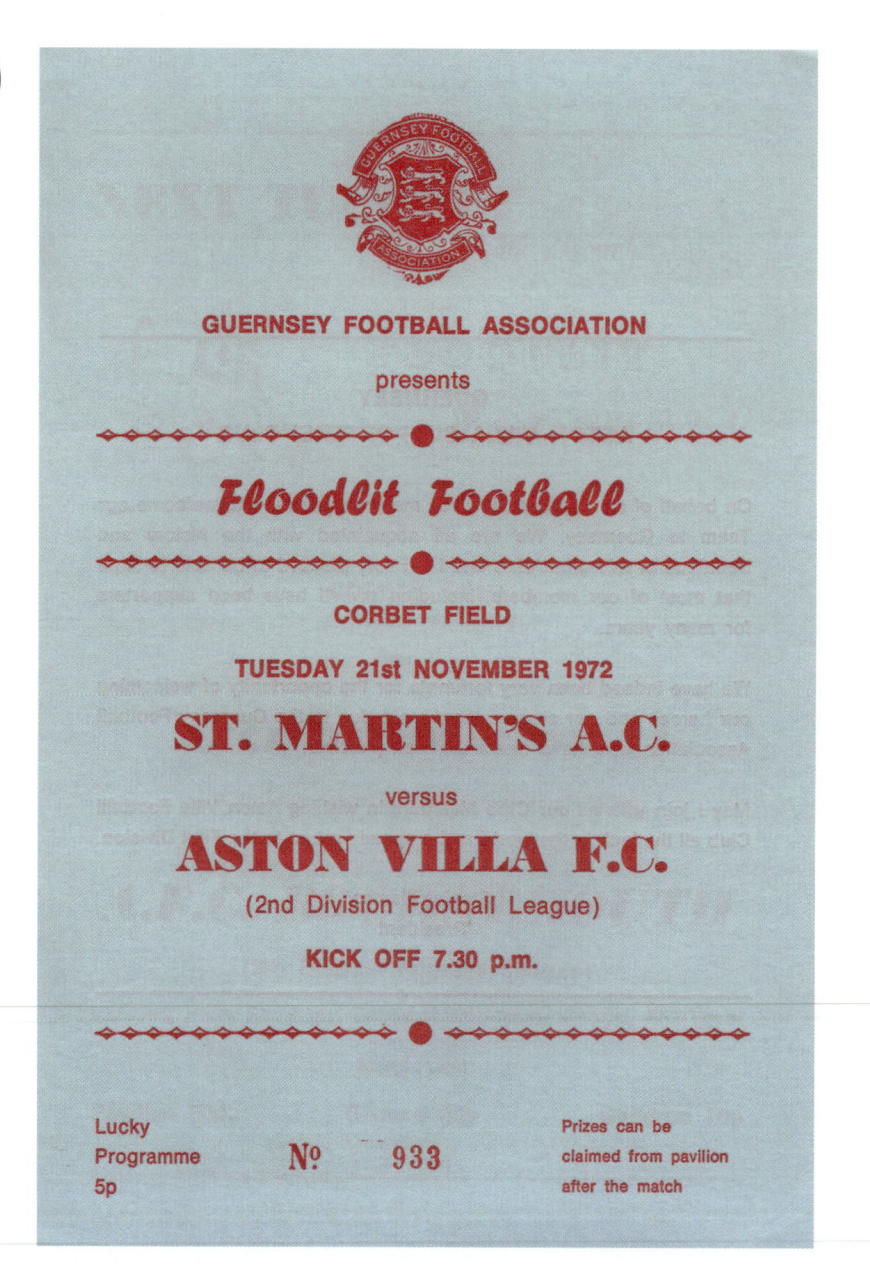

GUERNSEY FOOTBALL ASSOCIATION

presents

Floodlit Football

CORBET FIELD

TUESDAY 21st NOVEMBER 1972

ST. MARTIN'S A.C.

versus

ASTON VILLA F.C.

(2nd Division Football League)

KICK OFF 7.30 p.m.

Lucky Programme 5p   Nº 933   Prizes can be claimed from pavilion after the match

EUROPAPOKALSIEGER 1967

F.C. BAYERN MÜNCHEN E.V.

DEUTSCHER MEISTER 1932 1969 1972
DEUTSCHER POKALSIEGER
1957 1966 1967 1969
1971

Aston Villa v Bayern Munich
FRIENDLY MATCH   TUESDAY 23rd JANUARY 1973   KICK-OFF 7.45 pm

TEAMCHECK...

ASTON VILLA	TEAM CHANGES	BAYERN MUNICH	TEAM CHANGES
Claret & Blue Shirts, White Shorts		White Shirts, White Shorts	
1 JIMMY CUMBES		1 SEPP MAIER	
2 JOHN ROBSON		2 JONNY HANSEN	
3 ~~CHARLIE AITKEN~~	MACDONALD	3 PAUL BREITNER	
4 BRUCE RIOCH		4 GEORG SCHWARZENBECK	
5 CHRIS NICHOLL		5 FRANZ BECKENBAUER	
6 IAN ROSS		6 FRANZ ROTH	
7 RAY GRAYDON		7 FRANZ KRAUTHAUSEN	
8 JIMMY BROWN		8 ~~RAINER ZOBEL~~	SCHNEIDER
9 ALUN EVANS		9 GERHARD MULLER	
10 GEOFF VOWDEN		10 ULE HOENESS	
11 BRIAN LITTLE		11 WILLI HOFFMANN	

(Substitutes to be announced)

OFFICIALS...

Referee: KEN BURNS, Wordsley, Worcs.
Linesmen: A. J. HAMIL, Wolverhampton, *Red Flag*
F. LEWIS, Birmingham, *Orange Flag*

BAYERNS EUROPAMEISTERS

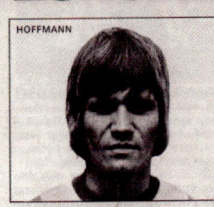

HANSEN — HOFFMANN — ZOBEL
ROTH — KRAUTHAUSEN — LATTEK

THE BIG ASTON VILLA BOOK OF THE SEVENTIES

Bryan Sharples Testimonial
Exeter City 2
Rioch B, Little
Att 4,921

Tue 24th October
Aston Villa 2

As listed on programme: Findlay, Gidman, Aitken, Turnbull, Rioch N, Rioch B, Vowden, McMahon, Hamilton, Little B, Lochhead, Evans, Anderson.

Friendly
St Martins (Guernsey) 0
Lochhead 2, McMahon, Ross 2
Att 1,400

Tue 21st November
Aston Villa 5

Findlay, Ross, Nicholl, Turnbull (Rioch N), Aitken (Brown), Rioch B, McMahon, Vowden, Graydon, Lochhead (Leonard), Evans (Little).

Friendly
Aston Villa 1
Robson
Att 22,699

Tue 23rd January 1973
Bayern Munich 1

Cumbes, Robson, McDonald, Rioch B (Hamilton), Nicholl, Ross, Graydon, Brown, Evans, Vowden (Anderson), Little B (McMahon).

Friendly
Sutton Select XI 2
Stark

Mon 5th March
Aston Villa 1

Findlay, Fellows (Overton), McDonald, Stark, Little A (Place), George, Hoban, Betts, Baker (Smith), Campbell, Child

Len Weston Challenge Cup
Hereford United 2
McMahon, Kirk
(match decided on penalties, Hereford United 3 Aston Villa 4)

Mon 19th March
Aston Villa 2

Rioch N, Graydon, Betts, McMahon, Hughes, Robson, Aitken, McMahon, Rioch N, Beard, Graydon, Lochhead, Kirk (Betts), Hamilton, Little B, Sub Stark.

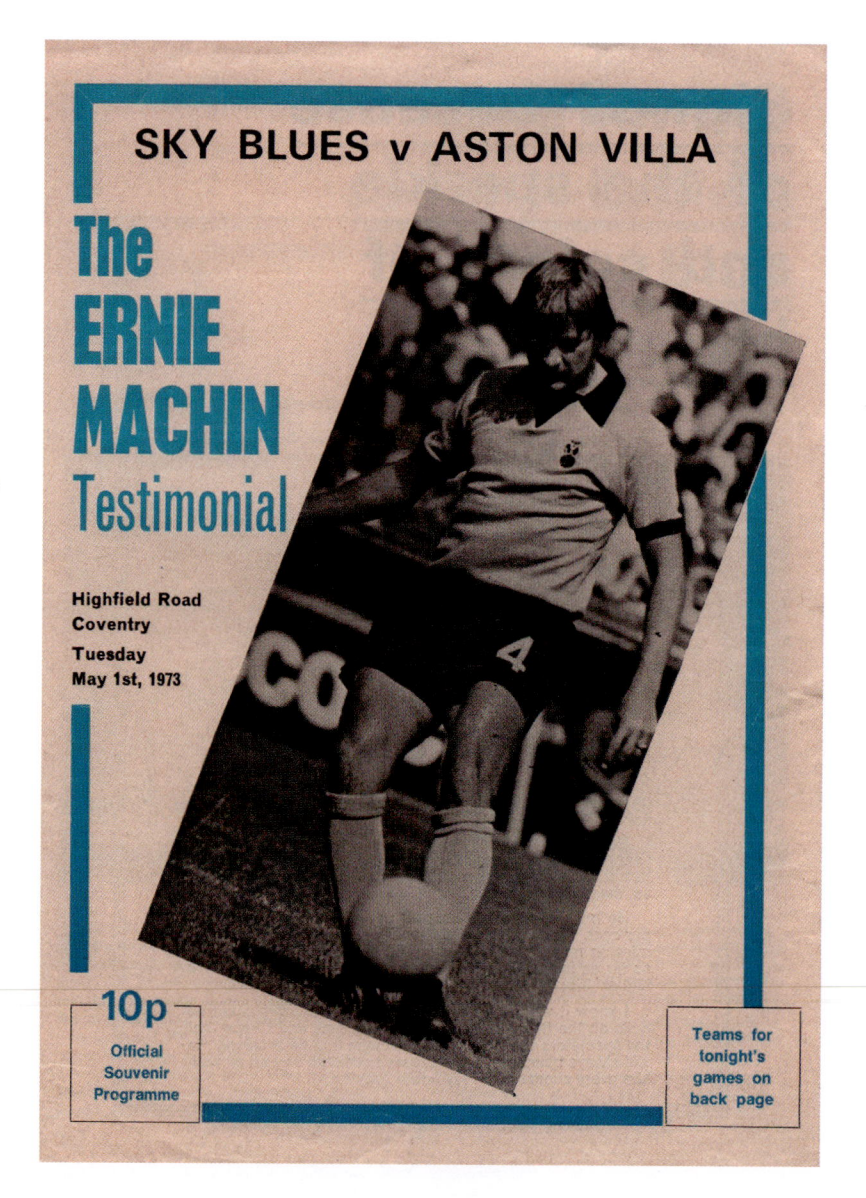

316

[Right] The Villa squad leaving Villa Park bound for their tour of Tanzania in May 1973 [L-R] Pat McMahon, John Robson, Alun Evans, Chris Nicholl, Tommy Hughes, Ian Hamilton, Fred Turnbull, Charlie Aitken, Brian Little, Ian Ross, Neil Rioch, Jimmy Brown, Geoff Vowden, Ray Graydon and manager Vic Crowe

Ernie Machin Testimonial   **Tue 1st May**
Coventry City 1   **Aston Villa 1**
Vowden

Cumbes, Turnbull, Robson, Brown, Nicholl, Ross, Graydon, Little, Evans, Vowden, Hamilton, Sub Rioch N.

Friendly: **Fri 4th May**
Wimbledon 0   **Aston Villa 2**
Graydon, Ross

As listed on programme: Cumbes, Robson, Aitken, McDonald, Rioch N, Rioch B, Nicholl, Ross, Turnbull, Graydon, Brown, McMahon, Evans, Vowden, Lochhead, Hamilton, Little

End of Season Tour (Tanzania)

Friendly   **Sun 13th May**
Young Africans 0   **Aston Villa 0**
Att 50,000

Cumbes, Robson, Aitken, Brown, Ross, Graydon, Little B (Hamilton), Evans, Lochhead, McMahon, Vowden.

Friendly   **Wed 16th May**
Zanzibar XI 0   **Aston Villa 3**
Evans, Hamilton, Little
Att, 10,000

Hughes, Robson, Aitken, Brown, Rioch N, Ross, Hamilton, Little, Evans, Vowden, McMahon, Sub Turnbull.

Friendly   **Sat 19th May**
Simba SC 1   **Aston Villa 1**
Graydon
Att 35,000

Cumbes, Aitken, Turnbull, Nicholl, Ross, Graydon, Little, Evans, Lochhead, Vowden, Hamilton, Subs McMahon, Rioch N.

Friendly   **Sun 20th May**
Young Africans SC 1   **Aston Villa 1**
Lochhead

Hughes, Rioch N, Aitken, Ross, Turnbull, Graydon, Evans (McMahon), Lochhead, Vowden, Hamilton, Sub Little.

1973-74 PRE-SEASON FRIENDLIES AND OTHER NON-COMPETITIVE MATCHES

Pre-Season Tour (Germany)

Friendly   **Wed 15th August**
Oldenburg St Paul 2   **Aston Villa 3**
Nicholl, Little B, Vowden

Cumbes, Robson, Aitken, Rioch B, Nicholl, Ross, Brown, Hockey, Evans, Vowden, Little B, Subs Gidman, Graydon, Morgan, Hamilton, McMahon.

Friendly   **Sat 18th August**
Aston Villa 0   **Leicester City 1**
Att 15,153

Cumbes, Robson (Gidman), Aitken (Hamilton), Rioch B, Nicholl, Ross, Brown, Hockey, Evans, Vowden (Graydon), Little B.

Friendly   **Sat 9th March 1974**
Aston Villa 3   **Southampton 0**
Leonard, Evans, own goal
Att 3,881

Findlay, Gidman, McDonald, McMahon, Nicholl, Turnbull, Little B, Ross, Leonard, Hamilton, Evans, Subs Hockey, Morgan.

Friendly   **Tue 30th April**
Aston Villa 7   **Feyenoord (Holland) 1**
Little B 2, Leonard 2, Evans, Betts 2
Att 7,596

Findlay, Robson, McDonald, McMahon, Nicholl, Ross, Graydon, Brown, Leonard, Hamilton, Little B, Subs Stark, Evans, Vowden, Betts.

Aston Villa v Feyenoord

INTERNATIONAL CLUB FRIENDLY MATCH TUES 30th APRIL 1974 KICK-OFF: 7.30 pm

TEAMCHECK

ASTON VILLA Claret and Blue Shirts, White Shorts	TEAM CHANGES	FEYENOORD Green Shirts, Green Shorts	TEAM CHANGES
1 JIMMY CUMBES		1 EDDY TREYTEL	
2 JOHN GIDMAN		2 WIM RIJSBERGEN	
3 CHARLIE AITKEN		3 HENRI VOS	
4 PAT McMAHON		4 JOOP VAN DAELE	
5 CHRIS NICHOLL		5 MLADEN RAMLJAK	
6 FRED TURNBULL		6 PETER RESSEL	
7 RAY GRAYDON		7 WIM VAN HANEGEM	
8 IAN ROSS		8 WIM JANSEN	
9 ALUN EVANS		9 THEO DE JONG	
10 IAN HAMILTON		10 LEX SCHOENMAKER	
11 BRIAN LITTLE		11 JORGEN KRISTENSEN	
12		Subs: Schneider, Sprangers, Israel, Wehru, Boskamp	

SCORECHECK

Arsenal v Q.P.R.
Cardiff v Crystal Palace
Oldham v Charlton
Walsall v Port Vale
Halifax v York
Exeter v Rotherham
Scunthorpe v Bury

STOP PRESS!
To celebrate ASTON VILLA'S CENTENARY we have arranged to play **LEEDS UNITED** (LEAGUE CHAMPIONS) at Villa Park on Wed., 7th August Kick-off: 7.30pm

OFFICIALS

Referee:
Mr K. BURNS, Stourbridge
Linesmen:
Mr G. W. HOLT (Red Flag)
Mr J. A. REES (Orange Flag)

Ken Burns, a legal executive, took charge of last season's F.A. Cup Final and has refereed many International matches since his appointments by F.I.F.A. in 1969 and U.E.F.A. a year later. Refereed League Cup Semi-Finals (1969 and 1970), F.A. Cup Semi-Finals (1967 and 1971) and the F.A. Charity Shield (1970).

The Tony Brown Testimonial Fund

THE HAWTHORNS, MONDAY 6th MAY 1974

Festivities commence 7-15pm

OLD ALBION v OLD VILLA

BLUES/WOLVES XI v ALBION/VILLA XI

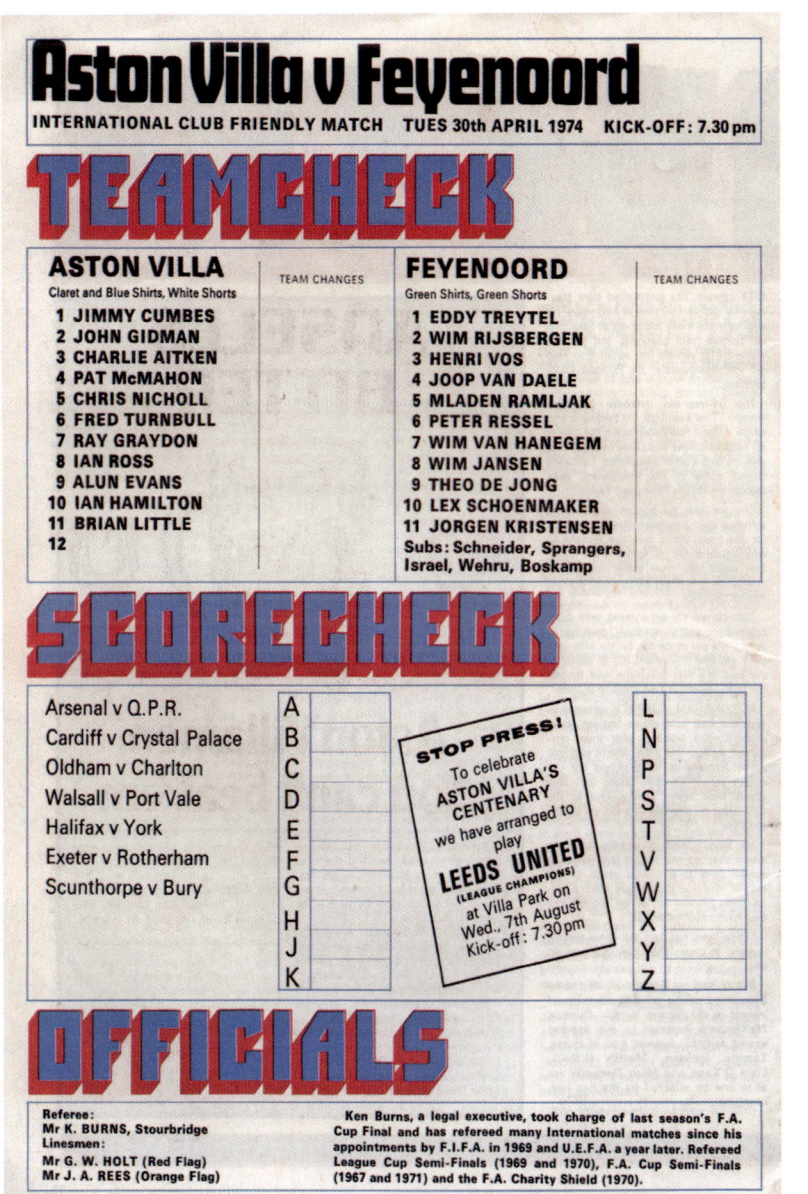

Souvenir Programme 10p

Tony Brown Testimonial Mon 6th May
Blues/Wolves XI 1 **WBA/Aston Villa XI 2**
Brown (WBA), Hamilton

Latchford, Gidman, Wilson, Cantello, Wile, Ross, Graydon, Brown, Astle, Hamilton, Hartford, Johnston.

1974-75 PRE-SEASON FRIENDLIES AND OTHER NON-COMPETITIVE MATCHES

Pre-Season Tour (Germany)

Friendly	**Sat 27th July**
Fr Osnabruck 1	**Aston Villa 1**
Leonard	

Findlay, Gidman, Aitken, Ross, Nicholl, Little A (Robson), Graydon, Morgan, Leonard (Betts), Hamilton (Evans), Brown.

Friendly	**Mon 29th July**
Borussia Dortmund 0	**Aston Villa 1**
Robson	

Findlay, Gidman, Aitken, Ross, Nicholl, Robson, Graydon, Morgan (Evans), Betts (Leonard), Hamilton, Brown.

Centenary Match	**Wed 7th August**
Aston Villa 1	**Leeds United 2**
Morgan	

Att 29,481

Findlay, Gidman, Aitken, Ross, Nicholl, Robson, Graydon, Evans, Morgan, Hamilton, Carrodus.

Friendly	**Sat 10th August**
Bury 0	**Aston Villa 1**
Graydon	

Cumbes, Gidman, Aitken, Ross, Nicholl, Robson, Graydon, Evans, Morgan, Hamilton, Carrodus. Sub Leonard, Little B.

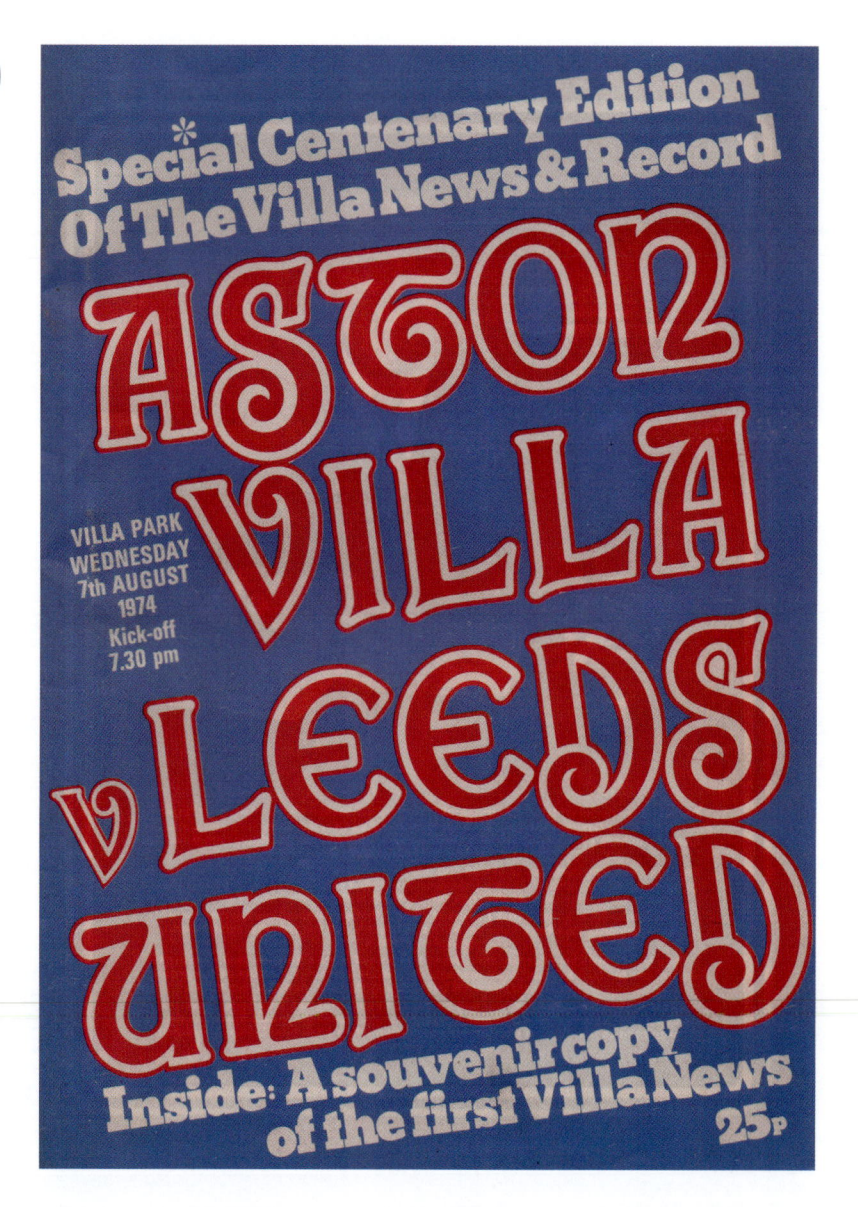

Michael Wright Testimonial   **Mon 5th May 1975**
Aston Villa 3   **Stoke City 1**
Graydon, Leonard 2
Att 16,067

Cumbes, Gidman, Aitken, Ross, Nicholl, McDonald (Phillips), Graydon (Pimblett), Little, Leonard, Hamilton, Carrodus.

Ray Wilson Testimonial   **Thur 8th May**
West Bromwich Albion 2   **Aston Villa 2**
Little, Leonard
Att 9,133

Cumbes, Gidman, Aitken, Ross, Nicholl, Phillips, McDonald, Little, Leonard, Hamilton, Carrodus. Subs Vowden, Campbell.

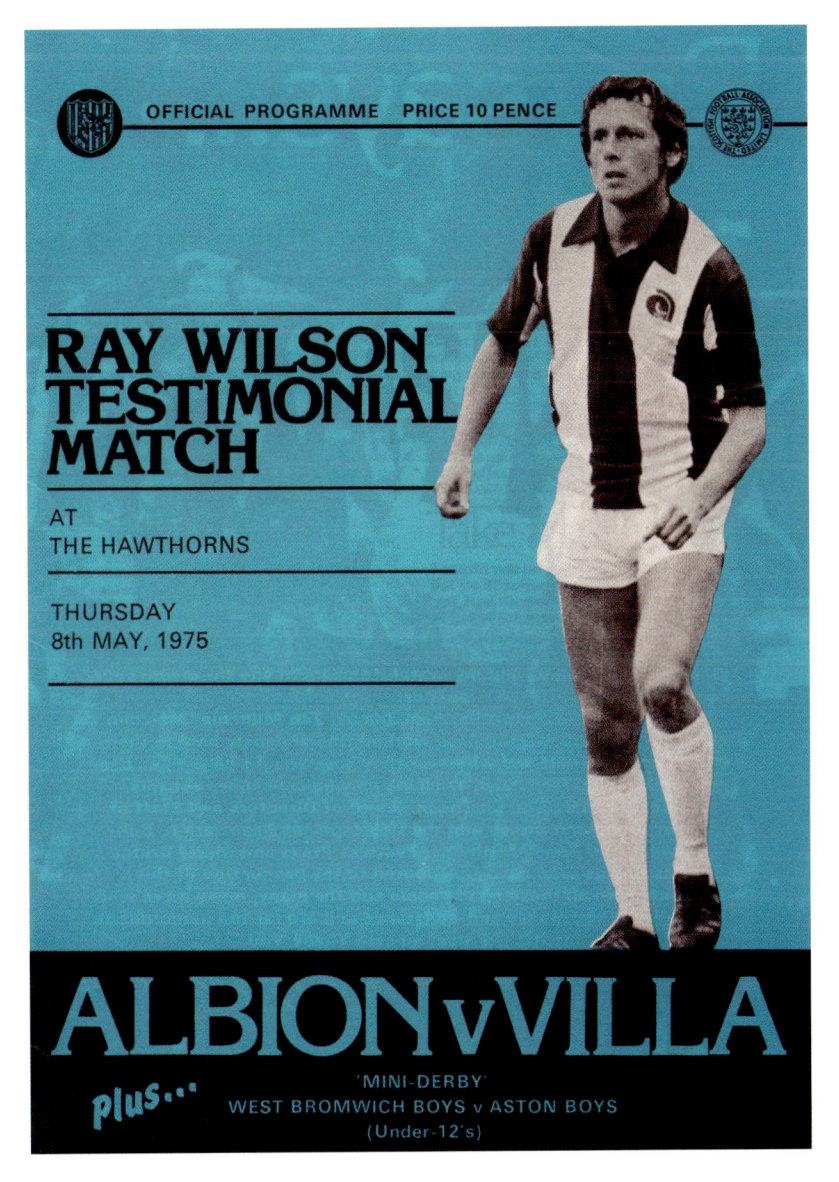

End of Season Tour (Caribbean)   **15th-29th May**

Squad from, Cumbes, Findlay Gidman, Aitken, Ross, Phillips, Nicholl, McDonald, Masefield, Hunt, Graydon, Little, Leonard, Carrodus.

Barbados International XI 0 Aston Villa 2
Leonard, Graydon

No team line-up available

321

1975-76 PRE-SEASON FRIENDLIES AND OTHER NON-COMPETITIVE MATCHES

Friendly   **Sat 2nd August**
Port Vale 2   **Aston Villa 3**
Leonard, Graydon, Hamilton
Cumbes, Robson, Aitken, Ross, Nicholl, Phillips, Graydon, Little, Leonard, Hamilton, Carrodus, Subs McDonald, Pimblett.

Friendly   **Tue 5th August**
Bristol Rovers 2   **Aston Villa 0**
Cumbes, Robson, Aitken, Ross, Nicholl, Phillips, Graydon, Little, Leonard, Hamilton, Carrodus.

Friendly   **Sat 9th August**
Aston Villa 2   **Walsall 1**
Leonard, Little
Cumbes, Gidman, Robson, Ross, Nicholl, Phillips, Graydon, Little, Leonard, Hamilton, McDonald, Sub Aitken.

Friendly   **Tue 4th November**
Aston Villa 11   **SK Brann (Norway) 0**
Deehan 4, Aitken, Graydon, Gray 3, Hamilton, own goal
Burridge, Gidman, Aitken, Ross, Nicholl, Phillips, Graydon, Robson, Gray, Deehan, Hamilton.

Fred Turnbull Testimonial   **Mon 26th April 1976**
Aston Villa 0   **West Bromwich Albion 1**
Att 15,800
Burridge, Gidman, Masefield (McDonald), Phillips, Nicholl, Mortimer, Graydon, Little, Gray (Deehan), Robson, Carrodus.

Tour of Norway

Friendly   **Tue 27th April**
SK Brann 0   **Aston Villa 1**
Gray
Att 7,000
Team from: Burridge, Findlay, Gidman, Robson, McDonald, Phillips, Nicholl, Young, Mortimer, Evans D, Hunt, Graydon, Little, Deehan, Gray.

Friendly   **Wed 28th April**
FC Vard 2   **Aston Villa 5**
Gray 2, Deehan, Little 2
Att 3,647
Team from: Burridge, Findlay, Gidman, Robson, McDonald, Phillips, Nicholl, Young, Mortimer, Evans D, Hunt, Graydon, Little, Deehan, Gray.

End of Season Tour (Central America) May 1976

Squad, Burridge, Findlay, Gidman, Robson, Ross, McDonald, Phillips, Nicholl, Young, Mortimer, Masefield, Evans D, Hunt, Graydon, Little, Deehan, Gray, Carrodus.

Martinique 1   **Aston Villa 0**
No team line-up available.

Guadeloupe 0   **Aston Villa 1**
Hunt
No team line-up available.

[Right] Aston Villa return from their tour of Guadeloupe with a few unusual souvenirs

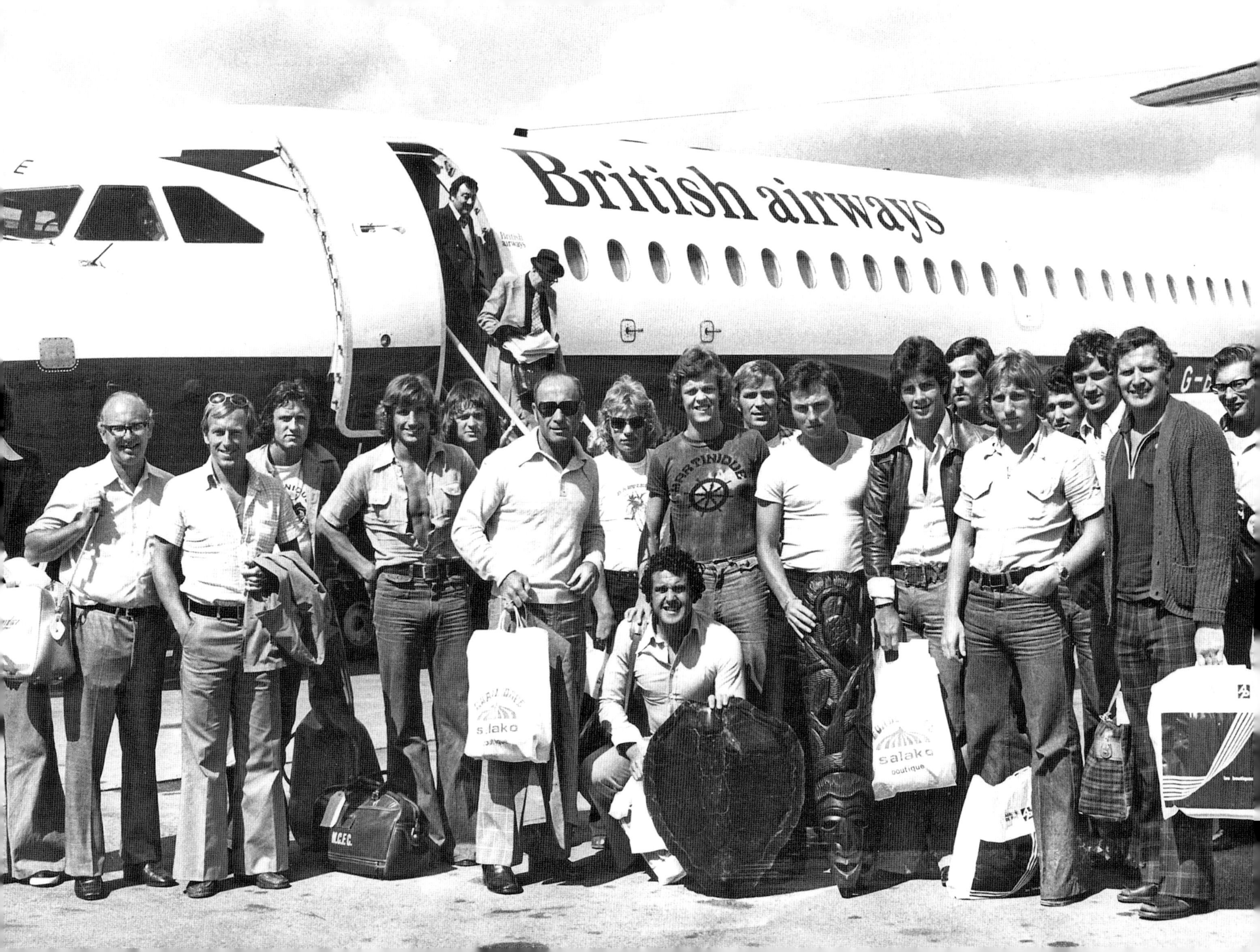
British airways
salako
boutique

1976-77 PRE-SEASON FRIENDLIES AND OTHER NON-COMPETITIVE MATCHES

Pre-Season Tour (France & Portugal)

Friendly   **Fri 30th July**
St Etienne 1   **Aston Villa 2**
Gray, Mortimer

Burridge, Gidman, Masefield (McDonald), Phillips, Nicholl, Mortimer, Graydon, Little, Gray (Deehan), Robson, Carrodus.

Friendly   **Sun 1st August**
Rheims 0   **Aston Villa 0**
Att 18,000

Burridge, Masefield, McDonald, Phillips, Nicholl (Ross), Mortimer, Graydon, Little (Young), Gray, Robson, Carrodus (Deehan).

Friendly   **Wed 4th August**
Oporto 1   **Aston Villa 1**
Little

Burridge, Gidman (McDonald), Masefield, McDonald, Phillips, Nicholl (Ross), Mortimer, Graydon, Little (Young), Gray, Robson, Carrodus (Deehan).

Friendly   **Wed 11th August**
Aston Villa 3   **Royal Antwerp 1**
Gray, Little 2
Att 15,000

Burridge, Gidman, Smith, Phillips, Nicholl, Mortimer, Graydon, Little, Gray, Robson, Carrodus.

[Right] Action from the abandoned match with Rangers

Friendly   **Sat 9th October**
Aston Villa 2   **Glasgow Rangers 0**
Mortimer, Carrodus
Att 18,258
abandoned after 53 minutes

Burridge, Gidman, Smith, Phillips, Young, Mortimer, Graydon, Little, Deehan, Cropley, Carrodus.

Friendly
Aston Villa 3
Deehan, Little 2
Att 26,615

Mon 22nd November
Eintracht Frankfurt 1

Findlay, Gidman, Smith, Phillips, Nicholl, Mortimer, Deehan, Little, Gray, Cropley (Robson), Carrodus.

Charlie Aitken's Second Testimonial
Midland Select XI 1
Evans A
Att 5,129

26th May
Aston Villa 6

Burridge (Findlay), Smith, Robson, Evans D, Young, Mortimer, Graydon, Little B, Evans A, Linton, Cowans (Hughes D).

1977-78 PRE-SEASON FRIENDLIES AND OTHER NON-COMPETITIVE MATCHES

Pre-season International Tour Spain

Friendry   **Mon 8th August**
Athletic Bilbao 2   **Aston Villa 0**

Burridge (Findlay), Gregory, Robson, Phillips, McNaught, Mortimer, Deehan, Little, Cowans, Cropley, Carrodus, Subs Buttress, Evans.

Friendly   **Wed 10th August**
Anderlecht 4   **Aston Villa 3**
Mortimer, Deehan, Gray

Burridge, Gregory, Buttress, Phillips, McNaught, Mortimer, Little, Evans, Findlay, Cowans, Carrodus, Subs Gray, Deehan.

Jake Findlay played upfront until the half-time interval and took over in goal from Burridge for the second half. Both Deehan and Gray came on for the second half.

Friendly at Bodymoor Heath   **Early Aug**
Aston Villa 2   **Saudi Arabia 0**
Gray, Deehan

No team line-up could be found other than the following who definitely played. Buttress, Evans, McNaught, Deehan, Gray

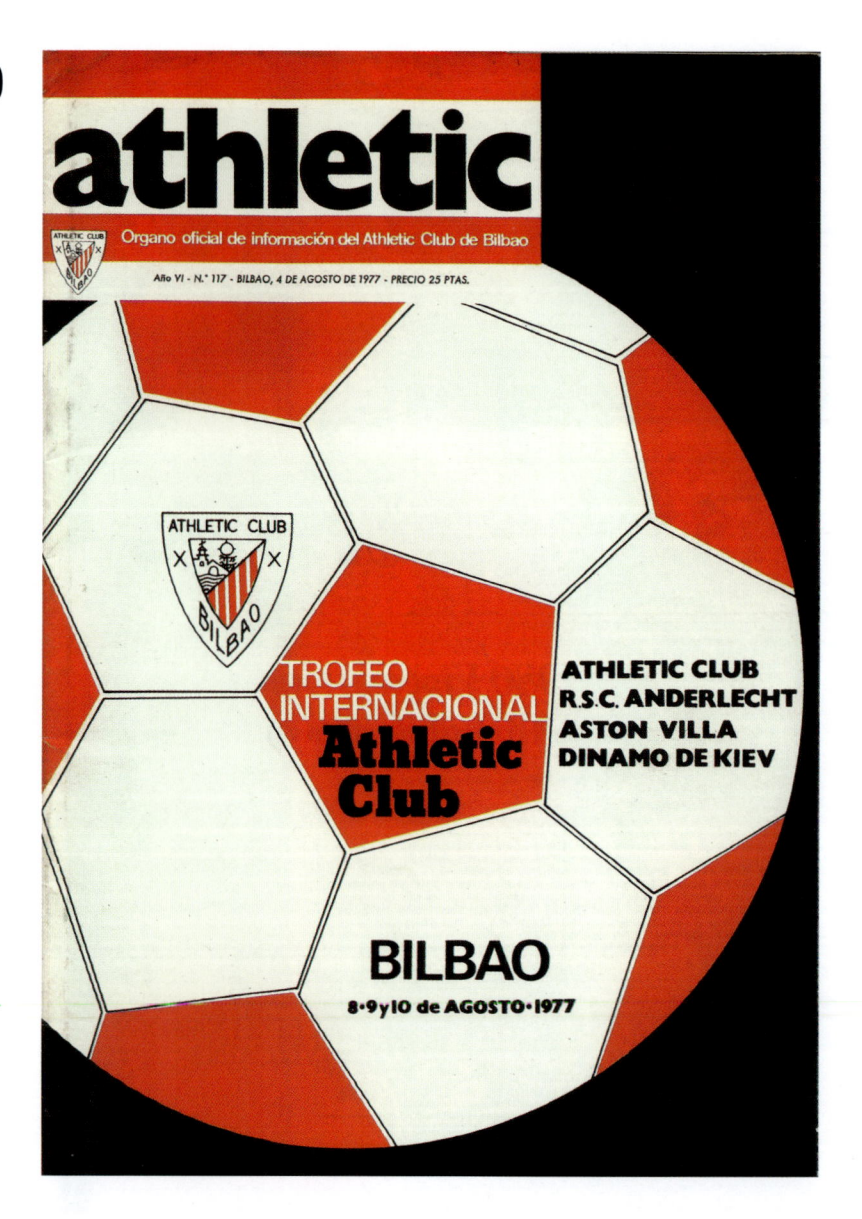

Bob Davies Testimonial — Fri 5th May
Walsall 0 — Aston Villa 3
Att 4,474
Gidman, Evans, Shelton

As listed on programme: Rimmer, Gibson, Smith, Phillips, McNaught, Mortimer, Deehan, Little, Gregory, Cowans, Carrodus, Subs Findlay, Evans, Shelton.
Below are definite players.
Rimmer, Gidman, 3, Evans, Phillips, 6, 7, Little, Deehan, 10, Shelton

Gothenburg

Friendly — Wed 17th May
Sweden World Cup XI 1 — Aston Villa 0
Rimmer, Gidman, Smith, Evans A, McNaught, Mortimer, Deehan, Little, Gregory, Cowans, Carrodus, Subs Shelton, Evans D.

THE BIG ASTON VILLA BOOK OF THE SEVENTIES

1978-79 PRE-SEASON FRIENDLIES AND OTHER NON-COMPETITIVE MATCHES

Pre-Season Tour (Yugoslavia)

Jurica Jerkovic Testimonial   **Tue 1st August**
Hajduk Split 4   **Aston Villa 0**
Att 23,000
Rimmer, Gidman, Smith, Phillips, McNaught, Mortimer, Craig, Little, Gray, Cowans, Carrodus, Subs Evans A, Shelton, Deehan, Gregory, Findlay.

Friendly   **Sat 5th August**
NK Rijeka 2   **Aston Villa 0**
Att 6,000
Rimmer, Gidman, Smith, Phillips, McNaught, Mortimer, Craig (Shelton), Little, Gray (Deehan), Cowans, Carrodus, Subs Evans A, Gregory, Findlay.

Friendly   **Sun 6th August**
NK Olimpija Ljubljana 3   **Aston Villa 5**
Little 2, Deehan, McNaught, Gregory
Att 8,000
Findlay, Gidman, Smith, Evans A, McNaught, Mortimer, Craig, Little, Deehan (Gregory), Shelton (Cowans), Carrodus.

Friendly   **Sat 12th August**
Aston Villa 1   **NEC Nijmegen 1**
Cowans
Att 10,929
Findlay, Gidman, Smith (Gregory), Phillips (Evans), McNaught, Mortimer, Craig (Shelton), Little, Gray, Cowans, Carrodus.

Before Robson's testimonial match at Villa Park

Keith Leonard Testimonial   **Mon 25th September**
Aston Villa 1   **Aston Villa '74-'75 2**
Jenkins   **Graydon (pen), Nicholl**
Att 6,481

Rimmer, Williams, Shelton, Evans A, McNaught, Mortimer, Craig, Shaw (Ormsby), Cowans, Gregory, Jenkins.
Villa '74-'75: Cumbes, Robson (Evans D), Aitken, Ross, Nicholl, McDonald, Graydon, Phillips, Graham, Young, Hunt (Hendry).

John Robson Testimonial   **Mon 30th October**
Aston Villa 6   **International XI 6**
Deehan 4, Gregory, Cropley
Att 14,699

Rimmer, Gidman (Shelton), Williams (Phillips), Evans A, McNaught, Gregory, Craig, Little, Gray, Deehan, Shelton (Cropley).

THE BIG ASTON VILLA BOOK OF THE SEVENTIES

1979-80 PRE-SEASON FRIENDLIES AND OTHER NON-COMPETITIVE MATCHES

Pre-season Tour (Scotland)

Friendly **Thur 2nd August**
Heart of Midlothian 1 **Aston Villa 3**
Deehan, McNaught, Evans (pen)
Att 7,599
Rimmer, Linton, Williams (Gibson), Evans, McNaught, Mortimer, Morley, Little, Deehan (Ormsby), Cowans, Swain, Subs Cropley, Shelton.

Friendly **Sat 4th August**
Dundee United 3 **Aston Villa 0**
Rimmer, Linton, Gibson, Ormsby, McNaught, Mortimer, Morley, Little, Deehan, Cowans, Swain (Shelton).

Friendly **Fri 10th August**
Aston Villa 2 **FC Twente 0**
Shelton, Donovan
Rimmer, Swain, Gibson, Evans, McNaught, Mortimer, Morley, Little, Deehan (Donovan), Cowans, Shelton (Cropley).

Ron Saunders Test **Wed 7th May**
Aston Villa 2 **Birmingham City 3**
Geddis, Gibson
Att 18,204
Rimmer, Swain, Gibson, Evans, Ormsby, Heard (Cropley), Bremner, Shaw, Geddis, Cowans, Linton (Morley).

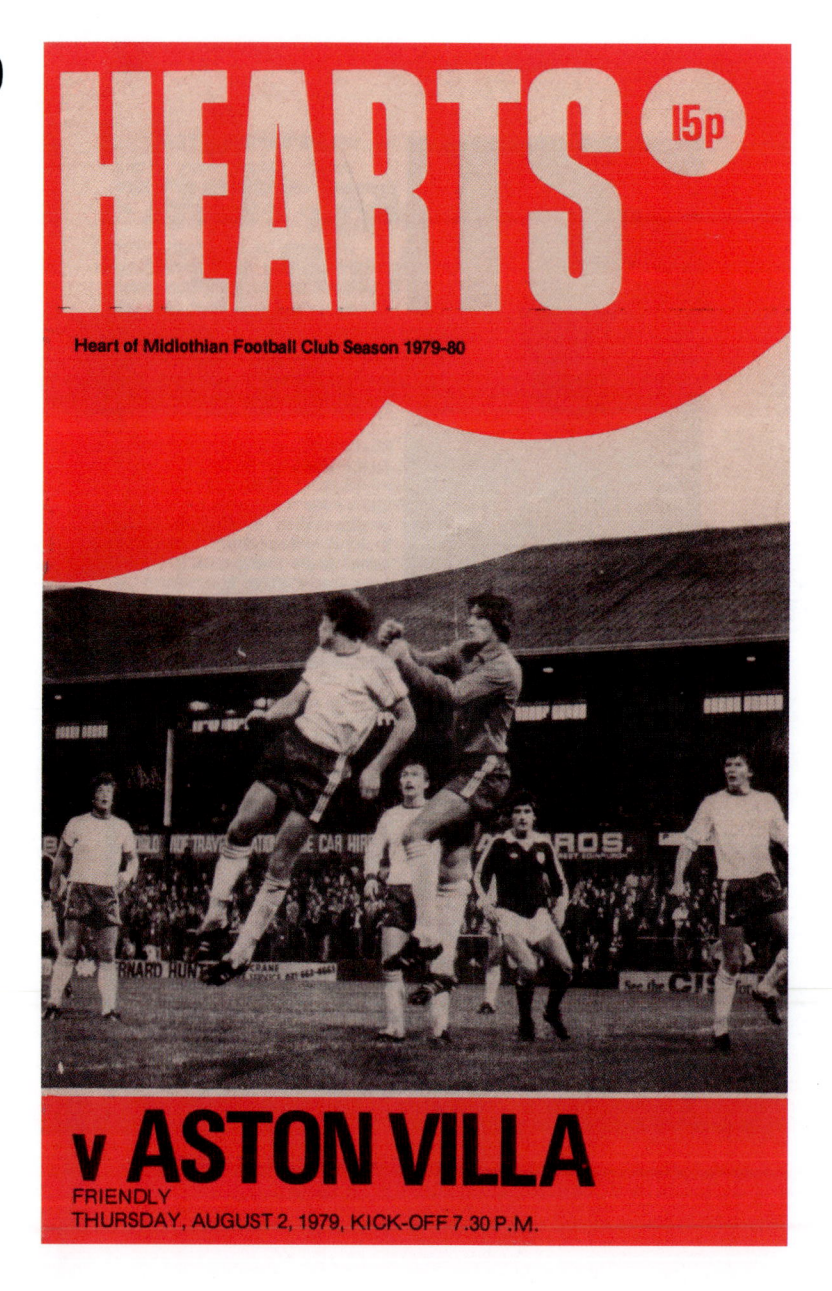

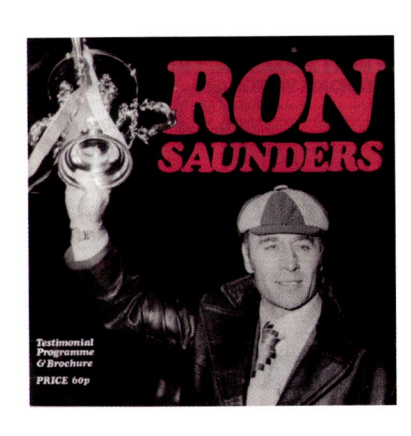

RON SAUNDERS

Testimonial Programme & Brochure
PRICE 60p

TEAM SQUADS

ASTON VILLA	BIRMINGHAM CITY
JIMMY RIMMER	JEFF WEALANDS
KENNY SWAIN	NEIL FREEMAN
COLIN GIBSON	KEVAN BROADHURST
NOEL BLAKE	MARK DENNIS
BRENDAN ORMSBY	ALAN CURBISHLEY
PAT HEARD	JOE GALLAGHER
DES BREMNER	COLIN TODD
DAVID GEDDIS	ALAN AINSCOW
GORDON COWANS	FRANK WORTHINGTON
GARY SHAW	KEITH BERTSCHIN
IVOR LINTON	ARCHIE GEMMILL
BRIAN LITTLE	KEVIN DILLON
TONY MORLEY	STEVE LYNEX
TERRY DONOVAN	TONY EVANS
EAMON DEACY	TERRY LEES

Bruce Rioch watching from the side-lines at Bodymoor Heath

RESERVES

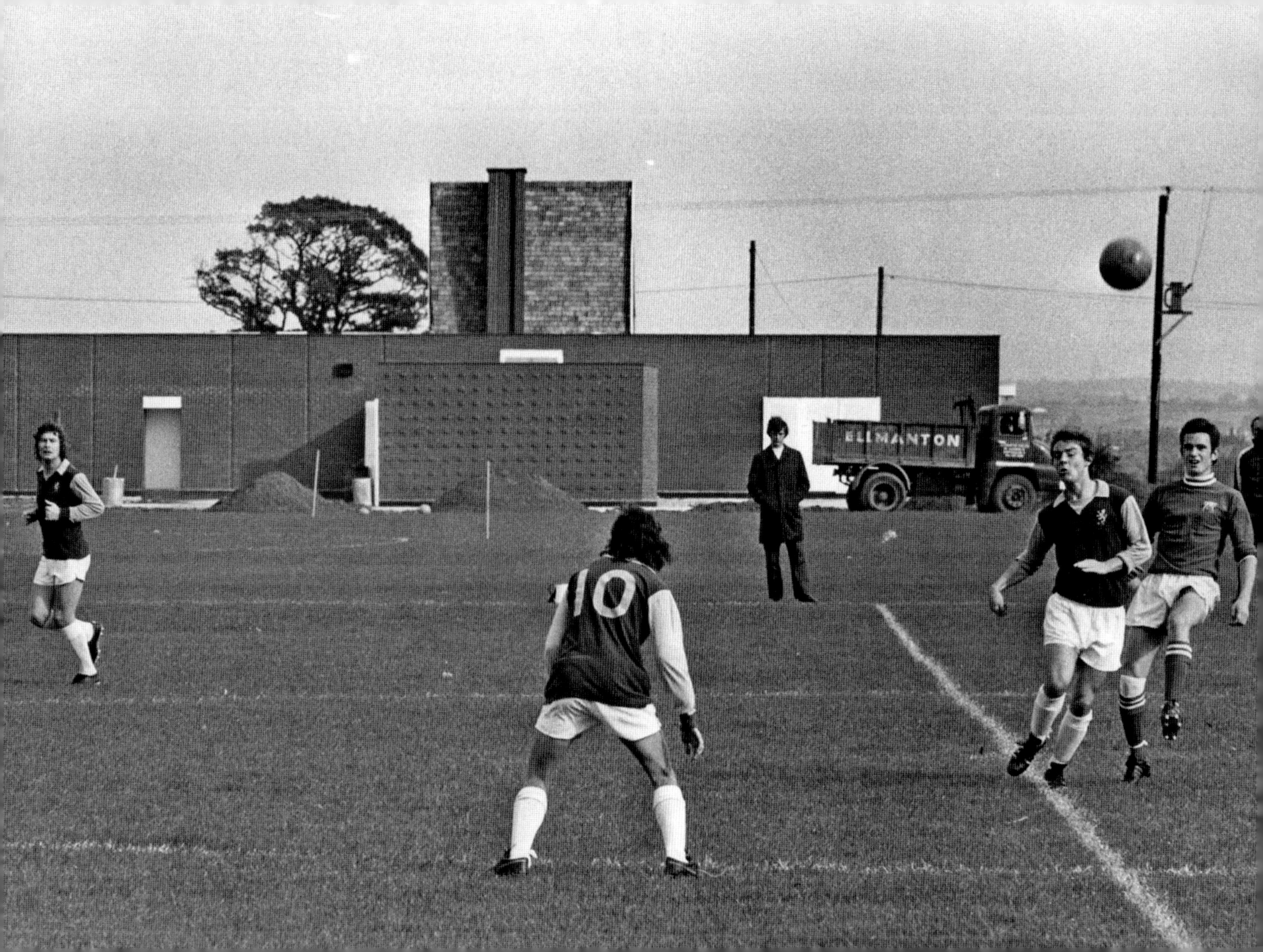
ELLMANTON
10

1970/71

Central League

Sat 15th August
West Bromwich Albion (H) Lost 0-2
Crudgington, Bradley, Hughes, Rioch N, Turnbull, Common, Hoban, Ellery, Melling, Kearney, Simmons, Sub Smith.

Tue 18th August
Coventry City (A) Drew 1-1
Simmons
Crudgington, Bradley, Hughes, Hoban, Rioch N, Turnbull, Melling, Common, Simmons, Brown, Martin, Sub Ellery.

Sat 22nd August
Preston North End (A) Lost 0-3
Crudgington, Bradley, Hughes, Rioch N, Turnbull, Common, Hoban, Rowan, Melling, Simmons, Martin, Sub Ellery.

Wed 26th August
Derby County (H) Drew 1-1
Bradley
Crudgington, Bradley, Hoban, Turnbull, Hughes, Child, Rioch N, Brown, Melling, Simmons, Martin, Sub Common.

Sat 29th August
Burnley (H) Drew 2-2
Rioch N, Simmons
Crudgington, Bradley, Hoban, Turnbull, Hughes, Child, Rioch N, Common, Melling, Simmons, Fellows, Sub Little B.

Wed 2nd September
Wolves (A) Lost 0-2
Crudgington, Bradley, Hoban, Turnbull, Hughes, Child, Rioch N, Common, Melling, Simmons, Fellows, Sub Little B.

Sat 5th September
Nottingham Forest (A) Drew 3-3
Simmons, Child 2
Crudgington, Bradley, Rioch N, Turnbull, Burns, Common, Hoban, Child, Melling, Simmons, Martin, Sub Hughes.

Tue 8th September
Everton (A) Lost 1-2
Hughes
Crudgington, Bradley, Hoban, Rioch N, Burns, Child, Hughes, Rowan, Melling, Simmons, Martin, Sub Common.

Sat 12th September
Everton (H) Lost 1-3
Rowan
Crudgington, Bradley, Hoban, Rioch N, Ellery, Common (Smith), Hughes, Rowan, Melling, Child, Fellows.

Sat 19th September
Bolton Wanderers (A) Lost 0-3
Crudgington, Bradley, Curtis, Rioch N, Hughes, Child, Hoban, Gibson, Melling, Simmons, Rowan, Sub Burns.

Sat 26th September
Stoke City (H) Lost 1-2
Rioch N
Crudgington, Bradley, Hoban, Rioch N, Burns, Hughes, Rowan, Little B, Rudge, Simmons, Melling, Sub Brady.

Sat 3rd October
Manchester United (A) Lost 0-2
Crudgington, Burns, Hoban, Rioch N, McMillan, Lynch, Child, Rowan, Little B, Fellows, Rudge, Sub Ellery.

Sat 10th October
Sheffield Wednesday (H) Won 2-0
Martin, Rowan
Knowles, Bradley, Hoban, Curtis, Lynch, Rowan, Brown, Little B, Rudge, Simmons, Martin (Burns).

Sat 17th October
West Bromwich Albion (A) Lost 0-2
Knowles, Rowan, Hoban, Curtis, Bradley, Lynch, Rioch N, Chatterley, Little B, Simmons, Rudge, Sub Burns.

Sat 24th October
Liverpool (A) Lost 0-3
Knowles, Rowan, Hoban, Chatterley, Lynch, Melling, Burns, Hackett, Rudge, Simmons, Martin, Sub Little B.

Sat 31st October
Manchester City (H) Lost 1-2
Wright
Knowles, Wright, Hoban, Lynch, Rowan, Brown, Gibson, Rudge, Rioch N, Fellows, Martin, Sub Burns.

Sat 7th November
Bury (A) Drew 1-1
Martin
Crudgington, Wright, Hoban, Lynch, Rowan, Chatterley, Gibson, Rudge, Rioch N, Fellows, Martin, Sub Ellery.

Sat 14th November
Newcastle United (H) Drew 1-1
Martin
Crudgington, Bradley, Hoban, Rioch N, Rowan, Common, Gibson, Little B, Rudge, Fellows, Martin, Sub Ellery.

Sat 21st November
Sheffield United (A) Lost 0-2
Crudgington, Rowan, Ellery, Hoban, Burns, Child, Melling, Little B, Rudge, Smith, Brady, Sub Common.

Sat 28th November
Blackpool (H) Lost 1-3
Crudgington, Rowan, Ellery, Rioch N, Burns, Child, Gibson, Rioch B, Rudge, Gregory, Martin, Sub Melling.

Sat 5th December
Blackburn Rovers (A) Lost 0-2
Crudgington, Rowan, Hoban, Rioch N, Burns, Chatterley, Rioch B, Melling, Little B, Fellows, Rudge, Sub Smith.

Sat 12th December
Leeds United (H) Lost 0-1
Crudgington, Rowan, Hoban, Rioch N, Ellery, Melling, Rioch B, Chatterley, Rudge, Fellows, Martin, Sub Smith.

Sat 19th December
Preston North End (H) Lost 0-2
Crudgington, Rowan, Rioch N, Lynch, Ellery, Melling, Brown, Rudge, Gregory, Fellows, Martin, Sub Smith.

Sat 26th December
Huddersfield Town (A) Lost 0-2
Crudgington, Rowan, Rioch N, Chatterley, Ellery, Melling, Brown, Rudge, Smith, Fellows, Martin. Sub required

THE BIG ASTON VILLA BOOK OF THE SEVENTIES

Sat 9th January
Coventry City (H) Won 1-0
Gregory

Knowles, Rowan, Hoban, Curtis, Lynch, Melling, Chatterley, Little B, Gregory, Rioch N, Rudge, Sub Ellery.

Sat 16th January
Derby County (A) Drew 1-1
Brown

Knowles, Wright, Hoban, Curtis, Lynch, Rowan, Chatterley, Brown, Gregory, Rioch N, Rudge, Sub Martin.

Sat 23rd January
Huddersfield Town (H) Drew 1-1
Rioch N

Crudgington, Wright, Hoban, Curtis, Lynch, Rowan, Chatterley, Gibson, Rudge, Rioch N, Martin, Sub Burns.

Sat 30th January
Blackpool (A) Drew 0-0

Crudgington, Wright, Hoban, Curtis, Lynch, Rowan, Chatterley, Brown, Rudge, Rioch N, Martin, Sub Burns.

Sat 6th February
Blackburn Rovers (H) Drew 2-2
Rioch N, Rudge

Crudgington, Wright, Hoban, Curtis, Lynch, Rowan, Brown (Melling), Gibson, Rudge, Rioch N, Martin.

Sat 13th February
Leeds United (A) Won 1-0
Child

Crudgington, Rowan, Hoban, Curtis, Lynch, Little B, Chatterley, Child, Rudge, Rioch N, Martin, Sub Burns.

Sat 20th February
Sheffield United (H) Lost 1-2
Rudge

Crudgington, Wright, Hoban, Curtis, Lynch, Brown, Chatterley, Gibson, Rudge, Rioch N, Martin, Sub Burns.

Sat 6th March
Liverpool (H) Won 1-0
Rioch N

Crudgington, Rowan, Hoban, Curtis, Lynch, Gregory, Brown, Gibson, Rudge, Martin, Rioch N, Sub Burns.

Tue 9th March
Manchester City (A) Lost 0-3

Crudgington, Rowan, Hoban, Curtis, Lynch, Vowden (Little B), Brown, Gibson, Gregory, Rioch N, Rudge.

Sat 13th March
Newcastle United (A) Drew 0-0

Herriot, Wright, Hoban, Curtis, Lynch, Rowan, Brown, Gibson, Rudge, Little B (Burns), Rioch N.

Sat 20th March
Bury (H) Lost 0-1

Knowles, Wright, Hoban, Curtis, Lynch, Child, Brown, Gibson, Rudge, Rioch N, Melling, Sub Burns.

Sat 27th March
Nottingham Forest (H) Drew 1-1
Little B

Herriot, Wright, Hoban, Curtis, Lynch, Child, George, Brown, Rudge, Little B, Rioch N, Sub Rowan.

Sat 3rd April
Burnley (A) Won 2-0
Rioch N, Little B

Herriot, Lynch, Hoban, Curtis, Burns, Child, George, Brown, Rudge, Little B, Rioch N, Sub Brady.

Tue 13th April
Manchester United (H) Drew 1-1
Gregory

Herriot, Wright, Curtis, Rioch N, Gregory, Burns, Brown, Rioch B, Rudge, McMahon, Allner, Sub Child.

Sat 17th April
Sheffield Wednesday (A) lost 1-2
Little B

Knowles, Hughes J, Ellery, Little A (George), Burns, Child, Brown, Rioch B, Rudge, McMahon, Little B.

Tue 27th April
Wolves (H) Lost 0-1

Crudgington, Wright, Ellery, Curtis, Burns, Child, Gibson, George, Rudge, McMahon, Little B, Sub Upton.

Sat 1st May
Stoke City (A) Won 3-0
Martin, Little B, Gibson

Crudgington, Hughes J, Curtis, Chatterley, Burns, Child, Martin, Gibson, Rudge, Lochhead, Little B, Sub George.

Thur 6th May
Bolton Wanderers (H) Drew 2-2
Allner, Rudge

Knowles, Dolby, Curtis, Chatterley, Burns, Wright, Child, Gregory, Rudge, Martin, Allner, Sub Little B.

Central League Table 1970 - 71

Pos	Team	P	W	D	L	F	A	GD	Pts
1	Liverpool	42	30	6	6	82	29	53	66
2	Derby County	42	23	12	7	71	45	26	58
3	Everton	42	22	12	8	69	41	28	56
4	Manchester United	42	18	15	9	67	42	25	51
5	Burnley	42	18	15	9	77	61	16	51
6	Wolverhampton Wanderers	42	16	13	13	68	54	14	45
7	Blackpool	42	17	11	14	60	55	5	45
8	Coventry City	42	14	16	12	69	50	19	44
9	Bolton Wanderers	42	16	12	14	73	71	2	44
10	West Bromwich Albion	42	15	13	14	65	59	6	43
11	Newcastle United	42	12	17	13	45	43	2	41
12	Sheffield United	42	15	11	16	64	64	0	41
13	Sheffield Wednesday	42	12	16	14	45	60	-15	40
14	Huddersfield Town	42	14	11	17	71	72	-1	39
15	Leeds United	42	11	17	14	52	56	-4	39
16	Manchester City	42	16	6	20	61	83	-22	38
17	Nottingham Forest	42	9	16	17	53	65	-12	34
18	Stoke City	42	10	14	18	52	64	-12	34
19	Bury	42	11	9	22	50	75	-25	31
20	Preston North End	42	11	8	23	53	90	-37	30
21	Blackburn Rovers	42	11	6	25	47	84	-37	28
22	**Aston Villa**	42	6	14	22	34	65	-31	26

1971/72

Central League

Sat 14th August
Stoke City (A) Drew 0-0
Crudgington, Wright, Gidman, Curtis, Rioch N, Chatterley, Beard, Rioch B, Rudge, Little B, Martin, Sub Child.

Mon 16th August
Liverpool (H) Drew 0-0
Crudgington, Wright, Gidman, Hoban, Rioch N, Beard, Rioch B, Lynch, Little B, Fellows (Child), Martin.

Sat 21st August
Everton (H) Lost 1-2
Rioch N (pen)
Crudgington, Wright, Gidman, Curtis, Lynch, Chatterley, Hoban, Gibson, Child, Little B, Rioch N, Sub George.

Mon 23rd August
Manchester City (A) Drew 1-1
Gibson
Crudgington, Gidman, Lynch, Curtis, Chatterley, George, Hoban, Gibson, Child, Little B, Rioch N, Sub Fellows.

Sat 28th August
Newcastle United (A) Drew 1-1
Little B
Knowles, Gidman, Lynch, Curtis, Rioch N, Beard, Hoban, Gibson, Child, Martin, Little B, Sub George.

Sat 4th September
Manchester United (H) Lost 0-2
Knowles, Wright, Lynch, Curtis, Rioch N, Hoban, Beard, Gibson, Child, Little B, Martin, Sub George.

Mon 6th September
Wolves (H) Won 2-1
Hamilton 2
Crudgington, Wright, Gidman, Beard, Curtis, Rioch N, Hoban, Brown, Martin, Hamilton, Little B, Sub Lynch.

Sat 11th September
Sheffield Wednesday (A) Drew 2-2
Rudge, Gibson
Crudgington, Wright, Gidman, Rioch N, Curtis, Brown, Hoban, Gibson, Rudge, Martin, Little B, Sub Lynch.

Sat 18th September
Leeds United (H) Drew 1-1
Child
Crudgington, Wright, Gidman, Rioch N, Curtis, Brown, Hoban, Gibson, Fellows (Child), Little B, Martin.

Sat 25th September
Nottingham Forest (A) Drew 3-3
Little B 2, Gregory
Findlay, Lynch, Gidman, Rioch N, Hoban, Child, Gibson, Rudge, Gregory, Little B, Martin, Sub George.

Sat 2nd October
Stoke City (H) Won 3-0
Little B, Child 2
Findlay, Wright, Lynch, Rioch N, Hoban, Child, George, Gibson, Gregory, Little B, Martin, Sub Fellows.

Sat 9th October
Preston North End (A) Won 3-1
Rioch N (pen), Martin 2
Findlay, Wright, Gidman, Tiler, Turnbull, Child, Rioch N, Gibson, Gregory, Fellows, Martin, Sub George.

Sat 16th October
Burnley (H) Lost 1-2
Child
Findlay, Wright, Gidman, Rioch N, Little A, Child, Brown, Gibson, Betts, Gregory, Martin, Sub George.

Sat 23rd October
Blackpool (H) Won 4-0
Martin, Child, Rioch N (pen), Little B
Crudgington, Gidman, Lynch, Rioch N, Hoban, Child, Brown, Gibson, Gregory, Little B, Martin, Sub George.

Sat 30th October
Coventry City (A) Drew 1-1
Brady
Crudgington, Lynch, Aitken, Hoban, Turnbull, Gidman, George, Brown, Brady, Gregory, Child, Sub Melling.

Sat 6th November
Derby County (H) Lost 0-2
Crudgington, Gidman, Aitken, Turnbull, Beard, Child, George, Brown, Rudge, Little B, Martin, Sub Brady.

Sat 13th November
Blackburn Rovers (A) Lost 0-1
Crudgington, Wright, Gidman, Hoban, Little A, McMahon (George), Child, Gregory, Rudge, Little B, Martin.

Sat 20th November
Bolton Wanderers (H) Won 4-0
Little B, Rudge 2, McMahon
Crudgington, Wright, Gidman, Rioch N, Hoban, Lynch, McMahon, Gregory, Rudge, Little B, Martin, Sub Child.

Sat 27th November
Bury (H) Won 4-0
Martin, Rioch N (pen), Rudge 2
Crudgington, Gidman, Lynch, Hoban, Rioch N, McMahon, Gregory, Gibson, Rudge, Little B, Martin, Sub Beard.

Sat 4th December
Sheffield United (A) Won 3-1
Rioch N, Little B, Martin
Hughes, Hoban, Rioch N, Tiler, Lynch, McMahon, Gregory, Beard, Rudge, Little B, Martin, Sub Child.

Sat 11th December
Huddersfield Town (H) Drew 0-0
Hughes, Gidman, Lynch, Rioch N, Tiler, McMahon, Gregory, Gibson, Rudge, Little B, Martin, Sub Child.

Sat 18th December
Everton (A) Lost 2-3
Child, Rioch N
Hughes, Bradley, Lynch, Rioch N, Tiler, Gregory, Beard, Child, Rudge, Little B, Martin, Sub George.

Mon 27th December
West Bromwich Albion (H) Lost 0-1
Hughes, Gidman, Bradley, Rioch N, Beard (George), Child, Lynch, Gibson, Gregory, Little B, Martin.

339

THE BIG ASTON VILLA BOOK OF THE SEVENTIES

Sat 1st January
Manchester United (A) Won 2-1
Rudge 2

Knowles, Gidman, Lynch, Rioch N, Tiler, Gregory, George, Beard, Rudge, Little B (Hoban), Martin.

Sat 8th January
Newcastle United (H) Lost 0-1

Hughes, Gidman, Lynch, Rioch N, Tiler, Gregory, Hoban (Child), George, Rudge, Little B, Martin.

Sat 22nd January
Liverpool (A) Lost 0-2

Hughes, Hoban, Lynch, Rioch N, Tiler, George, McMahon, Brown, Rudge, Little B, Betts, Sub Stark.

Sat 29th January
Manchester City (H) Drew 2-2
Child 2

Hughes, Hoban, Lynch, Rioch N, Stark, George, McMahon, Tiler, Martin, Little B, Child, Sub Melling.

Sat 5th February
Wolves (A) Lost 0-1

Hughes, Lynch, McDonald, Hoban, Stark, George, Rioch N, Tiler, Rudge, Child, Martin, Sub Brady.

Sat 12th February
Blackpool (A) Drew 1-1
Rioch N

Hughes, Gidman, Lynch, Hoban, Stark, George, Rioch N, Tiler, Martin, Child, Little B, Sub Melling.

Sat 19th February
Coventry City (H) Lost 1-2
Child

Hughes, Gidman, Lynch, Bottomley, Hoban, George, Stark, Martin, Brady, Little B, Child, Sub Little A.

Tue 29th February
Derby County (A) Drew 0-0

Hughes, Bradley, Lynch, Rioch N, Tiler, Gregory, Martin, Vowden, Rudge (Gidman), Child, Anderson.

Sat 4th March
Blackburn Rovers (H) Won 5-2
Child 2, Rioch N 2, Tiler

Hughes, Bradley, Lynch, Stark, Rioch N, George, Tiler, Brown, Gregory, Child, Martin, Sub Gidman.

Sat 11th March
Sheffield Wednesday (H) Lost 1-2
Child

Findlay, Bradley, Lynch, Gidman, Stark, George, Gregory, Brown, Hamilton, Child, Martin, Sub Melling.

Sat 25th March
Nottingham Forest (H) Won 2-0
Hamilton 2

Hughes, Williams, Bradley, Hoban, Lynch, Gregory, Martin, Hamilton, Whittaker, Child, Leonard, Sub Francis.

Wed 29th March
West Bromwich Albion (A) Lost 1-2
Leonard

Hughes, Bradley, Lynch, Hoban, Curtis, Gregory, Vowden (George), Tiler, Martin, Leonard, Child.

Sat 8th April
Bolton Wanderers (A) Drew 1-1
Child

Hughes, Bradley, Lynch, Hoban, Beard, Gregory, Martin, Brown, Whittaker, Leonard, Child, Sub George.

Wed 12th April
Preston North End (H) Drew 0-0

Hughes, Bradley, Lynch, Hoban, Dyer, Place, Martin, Gregory, Child, Leonard, Hunt, Sub Whittaker.

Sat 15th April
Bury (A) Drew 0-0

Hughes, Bradley, Lynch, Tiler, Curtis, Place, Hoban, Martin, Hamilton, Leonard, Child, Sub Dyer.

Thur 20th April
Leeds United (A) Drew 0-0

Hughes, Bradley, Lynch, Curtis, Tiler, Gregory, Hoban, Brown, Martin, Leonard, Child, Sub Place.

Sat 22nd April
Sheffield United (H) Won 1-0
Brady

Hughes, Bradley, Lynch, Hoban, Beard, Gregory, Tiler, Place, Leonard, Child, Brady, Sub Smith.

Sat 29th April
Huddersfield Town (A) Drew 1-1
Fellows

Hughes, Bradley, Lynch, Tiler, Beard, Gregory, Hoban, Martin, Fellows (Williams), Leonard, Child.

Thur 4th May
Burnley (A) Won 1-0
Martin

Hughes, Bradley, Lynch, Beard, Tiler, Gregory, Stark, Martin, Smith D, Leonard, Betts, Sub Place.

Central League Table 1971 - 72

Pos	Team	P	W	D	L	F	A	GD	Pts
1	Derby County	42	26	10	6	84	39	45	62
2	Everton	42	25	9	8	82	41	41	59
3	West Bromwich Albion	42	18	18	6	70	43	27	54
4	Liverpool	42	21	10	11	70	42	28	52
5	Newcastle United	42	19	13	10	68	54	14	51
6	Stoke City	42	17	13	12	59	49	10	47
7	Blackpool	42	17	12	13	53	60	-7	46
8	Coventry City	42	16	12	14	71	55	16	44
9	Sheffield United	42	14	15	13	53	48	5	43
10	Manchester City	42	15	12	15	59	56	3	42
11	**Aston Villa**	42	12	17	13	55	43	12	41
12	Burnley	42	16	8	18	61	73	-12	40
13	Leeds United	42	12	15	15	47	43	4	39
14	Manchester United	42	13	12	17	55	50	5	38
15	Nottingham Forest	42	15	8	19	74	73	1	38
16	Huddersfield Town	42	13	12	17	46	63	-17	38
17	Bolton Wanderers	42	12	14	16	39	57	-18	38
18	Sheffield Wednesday	42	9	16	17	44	53	-9	34
19	Wolverhampton Wanderers	42	9	15	18	53	73	-20	33
20	Preston North End	42	11	8	23	45	83	-38	30
21	Bury	42	5	18	19	40	76	-36	28
22	Blackburn Rovers	42	9	9	24	39	93	-54	27

1972/73

Central League

Sat 12th August
Preston North End (H) Won 4-1
Leonard 2, Rudge, Brown
Hughes, Gidman, Stark, Turnbull, Tiler, Gregory, George, Brown, Rudge, Leonard, Little B, Sub Betts.

Tue 15th August
Huddersfield Town (A) Drew 2-2
Gidman, Brown
Hughes, Gidman, Stark, Turnbull, Tiler, Gregory, George, Brown, Rudge, Leonard, Little B, Sub Betts.

Sat 19th August
Burnley (A) Won 1-0
Rioch N
Hughes, Gidman, Stark, Tiler, Beard, Rioch N, George, Brown, Leonard, Hamilton, Little B, Sub Betts.

Mon 21st August
Blackpool (A) Lost 1-2
Leonard
Findlay, Gidman, Turnbull, Tiler, Beard, George (Stark), Rioch N, Brown, Leonard, Evans, Little B.

Sat 26th August
Newcastle United (H) Won 2-0
Leonard 2
Findlay, Bradley, McDonald, Turnbull, Stark, George, Beard, Brown, Leonard, Little B, Betts, Sub Fellows.

Wed 30th August
Wolves (A) Lost 1-2
Little B
Hughes, Bradley (Stark), McDonald, Tiler, Turnbull, George, Beard, Brown, Leonard, Hamilton, Little B.

Sat 2nd September
Stoke City (A) Lost 1-3
Hamilton
Hughes, Bradley, McDonald, Stark, Turnbull, George, Tiler, Brown, Leonard, Hamilton, Child, Sub Hoban.

Sat 9th September
Sheffield Wednesday (H) Drew 0-0
Hughes, Hoban, McDonald, Tiler, Turnbull, Bradley, Beard, Brown, Leonard, Hamilton, Little B, Sub Stark.

Sat 16th September
Bolton Wanderers (A) Won 2-0
Leonard, Little B.
Hughes, Bradley, Hoban, Tiler, Turnbull, Rioch N, Beard, George, Leonard, Hamilton, Little B. Sub Child.

Sat 23rd September
Manchester United (H) Won 2-0
Leonard, Little B.
Hughes, Hoban, Bradley, Tiler, Turnbull, Rioch N, Beard, Brown, Leonard, Little B, Child, Sub George.

Sat 26th September
Everton (A) Lost 0-4
Hughes, Hoban, Bradley, Tiler, Turnbull, George (Child), Rioch N, Brown, Leonard, Hamilton, Little B.

Sat 30th September
Liverpool (A) Lost 1-4
Child
Hughes, Bradley, McDonald, Hoban, Beard, George, Rioch N, Tiler, Leonard, Child, Betts, Sub Stark.

Sat 7th October
Bury (H) Won 2-1
Anderson, Child
Hughes, Hoban, McDonald, Turnbull, Tiler, Beard, Rioch N, Brown, Child, Little B, Anderson, Sub George.

Sat 14th October
Manchester City (A) Drew 2-2
Child, Rioch N (pen)
Hughes, Hoban, Bradley, Tiler, Turnbull, George, Beard, Brown, Child, Rioch N, Little B, Sub Stark.

Sat 21st October
Everton (H) Lost 1-2
Hamilton
Hughes, Bradley, McDonald, Hoban, Stark, George, McMahon, Brown, Child, Leonard, Hamilton, Sub Fellows.

Sat 28th October
West Bromwich Albion (A) Lost 0-1
Hughes, Hoban, McDonald, Stark, Beard, George, McMahon, Brown, Child, Leonard, Hamilton, Sub Bradley.

Sat 4th November
Blackpool (H) Won 2-0
Graydon, George
Hughes, Hoban, Bradley, Stark, Beard, George, Rioch N, McMahon, Graydon, Lochhead, Hamilton, Sub Child.

Sat 11th November
Blackburn Rovers (A) Won 2-0
Leonard 2
Hughes, Hoban, Beard, Stark, Rioch N, George, McMahon, Brown, Child, Leonard, Hamilton, Sub Wright.

Sat 18th November
Leeds United (A) Won 1-0
Brown
Findlay, Hoban, Wright, Rioch N, Stark, George, Beard, Brown, Child, Leonard, Hamilton, Sub Bradley.

Sat 25th November
Sheffield United (home) Drew 1-1
Child
Hughes, Hoban, McDonald, Stark, Beard, George, Child, Place, Fellows, Leonard, Hamilton, Sub Betts.

Tue 28th November
Coventry City (A) Drew 1-1
Stark
Hughes, Hoban, Wright, Rioch N, Stark, Beard, George, Brown, Child, Leonard, Hamilton, Sub Betts.

Sat 16th December
Nottingham Forest (A) Lost 0-3
Hughes, Wright, McDonald, Stark, Rioch N, George, Child, Hamilton, Little B, Leonard, Anderson, Sub Hoban.

Sat 23rd December
Huddersfield Town (H) Won 2-0
Stark, Fellows
Findlay, Wright, McDonald, Stark, Overton, George, Brown, Child, Fellows, Leonard, Hamilton, Sub Betts.

THE BIG ASTON VILLA BOOK OF THE SEVENTIES

Sat 30th December
Burnley (H) Won 1-0
Fellows
Hughes, Wright, McDonald, Stark, Beard, George, Rioch N, Hamilton, Fellows, Little B, Anderson, Sub Overton.

Sat 6th January
Newcastle United (A) Lost 0-2
Hughes, Wright, McDonald, Hoban, Rioch N, George, Vowden, Brown, Child, Fellows, Anderson, Sub Overton.

Sat 13th January
Preston North End (A) Won 2-1
Fellows, McDonald
Hughes, Wright, McDonald, Hoban, Stark, George, McMahon, Beard, Rioch N, Fellows, Hamilton, Sub Child.

Sat 27th January
Sheffield Wednesday (A) Drew 3-3
Lochhead 3
Hughes, Wright, Gidman, Turnbull, Beard, George, Hoban, McMahon, Rioch N, Lochhead, Anderson, Sub Stark.

Sat 3rd February
Blackburn Rovers (H) Won 2-1
McMahon 2
Findlay, Wright, McDonald, Rioch B, Stark, Turnbull, McMahon, Beard, Rioch N, Lochhead, Anderson, Sub George.

Sat 10th February
Bolton Wanderers (H) Won 3-2
George, McDonald, own goal
Findlay, Wright, McDonald, Turnbull, Hoban, George, McMahon, Beard, Rioch N, Betts, Anderson, Sub Stark.

Wed 14th February
Derby County (H) Won 1-0
Lochhead
Findlay, Gidman, Wright, Turnbull, Rioch N, George, McMahon, Beard, Lochhead, Anderson, Hamilton, Sub Hoban.

Sat 24th February
Liverpool (H) Drew 1-1
Hamilton
Findlay, Gidman, McDonald, Turnbull, Hoban, George, Beard, Betts, Rioch N, McMahon, Hamilton, Sub Stark.

Wed 28th February
Wolves (home) Lost 1-3
Betts
Findlay, Gidman, Stark, Hoban, Rioch N, George, Beard, Betts, Baker (Child), McMahon, Hamilton.

Sat 3rd March
Bury (A) Won 2-1
Betts, Hamilton
Findlay, McDonald, Gidman, Stark, Beard, George, Hoban, Betts, Rioch N, McMahon, Hamilton, Sub Child.

Sat 10th March
Manchester City (H) Lost 0-1
Hughes, Dyer, McDonald, Stark, Overton, George, Little A, Beard, Betts, Fellows, Hunt, Sub Place.

Mon 12th March
Manchester United (A) Lost 0-1
Hughes, Hoban, McDonald, Stark, Rioch N, George, Beard, Overton, Betts, Lochhead, Hamilton, Sub Little A.

Sat 24th March
West Bromwich Albion (H) Lost 0-2
Hughes, Wright, Aitken, Stark, Beard, George, Hoban, Overton, Little B, Child, Betts, Sub Little A.

Wed 28th March
Stoke City (H) Lost 0-3
Hughes, Wright, Gidman, Overton, Beard, George, Child, Betts, Fellows (Dyer), Hamilton, Little B.

Sat 31st March
Sheffield United (A) Won 2-1
George, Overton
Hughes, Wright, Gidman, Ross, Stark, George, Hoban, Overton, Campbell, Betts, Child, Sub Dyer.

Sat 7th April
Coventry City (H) Lost 1-2
Own goal
Hughes, Hoban, McDonald, Little A, Beard, George, Graydon, Overton (Smith), Kirk, Betts, Child.

Sat 14th April
Derby County (A) Lost 2-7
Kirk, Child
Hughes, Hoban, McDonald, Little A, Beard, George, Betts, Overton, Kirk (Hunt), Campbell, Child.

Mon 16th April
Nottingham Forest (H) Drew 0-0
Hughes, Gidman (Place), McDonald, Stark, Turnbull, George, Graydon, Hoban, Betts, Beard, Child.

Sat 21st April
Leeds United (H) Won 3-1
Betts 2, Stark
Hughes, Hoban, McDonald, Barnes, Beard, George, Stark, Barley, Parsons, Betts, Child, Sub Rochester.

Central League Table 1972 - 73

Pos	Team	P	W	D	L	F	A	GD	Pts
1	Liverpool	42	21	14	7	82	44	38	56
2	Stoke City	42	23	8	11	86	55	31	54
3	Coventry City	42	23	8	11	77	50	27	54
4	Derby County	42	21	10	11	80	54	26	52
5	West Bromwich Albion	42	20	11	11	72	51	21	51
6	Sheffield Wednesday	42	20	9	13	77	51	26	49
7	Everton	42	20	9	13	55	41	14	49
8	Wolverhampton Wanderers	42	18	10	14	60	55	5	46
9	Newcastle United	42	18	8	16	70	58	12	44
10	**Aston Villa**	**42**	**18**	**8**	**16**	**55**	**61**	**-6**	**44**
11	Sheffield United	42	17	9	16	59	49	10	43
12	Nottingham Forest	42	15	13	14	59	54	5	43
13	Manchester United	42	17	9	16	49	51	-2	43
14	Blackpool	42	17	8	17	54	51	3	42
15	Manchester City	42	13	13	16	58	67	-9	39
16	Burnley	42	15	8	19	57	60	-3	38
17	Bury	42	15	8	19	55	78	-23	38
18	Leeds United	42	15	7	20	50	55	-5	37
19	Huddersfield Town	42	12	9	21	61	88	-27	33
20	Bolton Wanderers	42	7	11	24	44	89	-45	25
21	Preston North End	42	6	11	25	40	92	-52	23
22	Blackburn Rovers	42	7	7	28	34	80	-46	21

THE BIG ASTON VILLA BOOK OF THE SEVENTIES

1973/74

Central League

Sat 25th August
West Bromwich Albion (A) Drew 0-0
Findlay, Gidman (Masefield), McDonald, Turnbull, Stark, McMahon, Little A, Overton, Pelosi, Rioch N, Betts.

Tue 28th August
Sheffield United (A) Drew 2-2
Stark, Masefield
Findlay, Masefield, McDonald, Turnbull, Stark, McMahon, Little A, Betts, Graydon, Rioch N, Hamilton. Sub required

Sat 1st September
Burnley (H) Drew 1-1
McMahon
Findlay, Masefield, McDonald, Stark, Turnbull, Hamilton, Little A, McMahon, Pelosi, Rioch N, Betts, Sub Dyer.

Wed 5th September
Blackburn Rovers (H) Drew 0-0
Findlay, Beard, McDonald, Turnbull, Stark, McMahon, Graydon, Hamilton, Morgan, Rioch N, Betts, Sub Little A.

Sat 8th September
Sheffield Wednesday (A) Lost 0-1
Findlay, Wright, McDonald, Turnbull, Stark, Hamilton, Little A, Beard, Betts, Rioch N, Campbell, Sub Masefield.

Wed 12th September
Leeds United (A) Won 2-0
Morgan, McMahon
Findlay, Beard (Little A), McDonald, Turnbull, Stark, Graydon, McMahon, Betts, Hamilton, Rioch N, Morgan.

Sat 15th September
Huddersfield Town (H) Won 1-0
Hamilton
Findlay, Wright, McDonald, Turnbull, Little A, McMahon, Betts, Overton, Hamilton, Rioch N, Morgan, Sub Masefield.

Sat 29th September
Everton (H) Won 2-0
Betts, Rioch N (pen)
Findlay, Wright, Gidman, Beard, Stark, McMahon, Little A, Betts, Campbell, Rioch N, Hamilton, Sub Hunt.

Tue 2nd October
Nottingham Forest (A) Drew 1-1
Betts
Findlay, Wright, Gidman, Beard, Turnbull, McMahon, Little A, McDonald, Campbell (Betts), Rioch N, Hamilton.

Sat 6th October
Manchester United (A) Won 2-0
Rioch N, Betts
Findlay, Gidman, McDonald, Turnbull, Stark, McMahon, Wright, Beard, Rioch N, Evans, Betts, Sub Hunt.

Sat 13th October
Bolton Wanderers (H) Drew 1-1
Wright
Findlay, Wright, McDonald, Turnbull, Beard, McMahon, Little A, Betts, Campbell, Rioch N, Hamilton, Sub Overton.

Mon 15th October
Wolves (H) Lost 0-2

Peyton, Wright, McDonald, Turnbull, Beard, Betts, Little A, Overton, Rioch N, Hamilton, Leonard, Sub Pimblett.

Sat 20th October
Liverpool (A) Drew 0-0

Findlay, Robson, McDonald, Turnbull, Stark, McMahon, Wright, Beard (Little A), Leonard, Rioch N, Betts.

Sat 27th October
Bury (H) Won 2-0
Campbell, Morgan

Findlay, Robson, McDonald, Turnbull, Stark, Little A, Betts, Beard, Morgan, Campbell, Leonard (Hunt).

Wed 7th November
Blackpool (A) Drew 0-0

Findlay, Robson, McDonald, Turnbull, Stark, Little A, Vowden, Beard, Morgan, Rioch N, Leonard, Sub Betts.

Sat 10th November
Manchester City (H) Won 2-1
Rioch B, McDonald

Findlay, Robson, McDonald, Turnbull, Stark, Rioch B, Little A, Betts, Rioch N, Leonard, Campbell, Sub Overton.

Wed 21st November
West Bromwich Albion (H) Won 1-0
Betts

Findlay, Robson, McDonald, Turnbull, Stark, Rioch B (Betts), Graydon, Little A, Rioch N, Vowden, Campbell.

Sat 24th November
Derby County (H) Won 2-0
McDonald, Little A

Findlay, Robson, McDonald, Rioch N, Stark, Betts, Little A, Beard, Campbell, Leonard, Hunt, Sub Overton.

Sat 8th December
Leeds United (H) Won 2-1
Robson, Beard

Findlay, Robson, McDonald, Turnbull, Stark, Beard, Little A, Overton, Campbell, Betts, Hunt, Sub Leonard.

Sat 15th December
Newcastle United (H) Drew 0-0

Findlay, Robson, McDonald, Rioch B, Stark, Beard, Little A, Overton, Morgan, Evans, Campbell, Sub Hunt.

Sat 22nd December
Stoke City (A) Lost 1-3
Campbell

Findlay, Robson, McDonald, Turnbull, Stark, Vowden, Little A, Betts, Morgan, Evans, Campbell, Sub Hunt.

Sat 29th December
Nottingham Forest (H) Drew 1-1
Betts (pen)

Findlay, Robson, McDonald, Little A, Stark, McMahon, Vowden, Overton, Morgan, Campbell, Betts, Sub Hunt.

Tue 1st January
Burnley (A) Won 2-1
Little A, Campbell

Findlay, Robson, McDonald, Turnbull, Stark, Betts, Little A, Overton (Williams), Rioch N, Campbell, Hunt.

347

THE BIG ASTON VILLA BOOK OF THE SEVENTIES

Sat 12th January
Huddersfield Town (A) Lost 1-5
Campbell
Findlay, Stark, McDonald, Turnbull, Rioch N, McMahon, Little A, Hunt, Campbell, Pelosi, Betts, Sub Overton.

Sat 19th January
Sheffield Wednesday (H) Won 2-0
Hunt, Campbell
Findlay, Stark, McDonald, Turnbull, Rioch N, Betts, Little A, Brown, Campbell, Pelosi, Hunt, Sub Overton.

Sat 2nd February
Everton (A) Drew 1-1
Campbell
Findlay, Robson, McDonald, Turnbull, Stark, Betts, Pimblett, Little A, Overton, Rioch N, Campbell, Sub Masefield.

Wed 13th February
Sheffield United (H) Drew 1-1
Betts
Findlay, Robson, McDonald, Turnbull, Stark, Betts, Little A, Brown, Overton, Campbell, Rioch N, Sub Masefield.

Sat 23rd February
Stoke City (H) Won 2-0
Stark, McDonald
Findlay, Robson, McDonald, Stark, Turnbull, Williams, Little A, Pimblett, Brown, Campbell, Rioch N, Sub Deehan.

Tue 26th February
Bolton Wanderers (A) Won 1-0
Little A
Findlay, Robson, McDonald, Turnbull, Stark, Overton (Pimblett), Little A, Brown, Leonard, Campbell, Rioch N.

Sat 2nd March
Newcastle United (A) Lost 0-1
Findlay, Robson, McDonald, Turnbull, Stark, Betts, Pimblett, Little A, Overton, Campbell, Rioch N, Sub Williams.

Sat 9th March
Bury (A) Lost 0-1
Cumbes, Masefield, Robson, Stark, Little A, Pimblett, Brown, Overton, Campbell (Deehan), Rioch N, Betts.

Wed 13th March
Blackburn Rovers (A) Lost 0-1
Peyton, Masefield, Robson, Stark, Rioch N, Betts, Little A, Pimblett, Brown, Campbell (Overton), Deehan.

Sat 16th March
Liverpool (H) Won 2-0
Betts 2
Findlay, Masefield, Little A, Stark, Rioch N, Robson, Graydon, Hockey, Campbell, Vowden (Overton), Betts.

Tue 19th March
Coventry City (A) Lost 0-2
Findlay, Masefield, McDonald, Stark, Rioch N, Robson, Little A, Beard (Deehan), Overton, Campbell, Betts.

Sat 23rd March
Manchester City (A) Won 1-0
Little A
Findlay, Robson, McDonald, Beard, Little A, Brown, Graydon, Overton (Masefield), Campbell, Hockey, Betts.

Tue 26th March
Preston North End (A) Drew 0-0

Findlay, Robson, McDonald, Stark, Beard (Overton), Vowden, Little A, Hockey, Brown, Campbell, Betts.

Sat 30th March
Blackpool (H) Lost 0-3
Findlay, Robson, McDonald, Beard, Little A, Vowden, Graydon, Hockey, Campbell, Overton, Betts, Sub Pimblett.

Sat 6th April
Derby County (A) Lost 0-4
Findlay, Robson, McDonald, Little A, Beard, Vowden, Graydon, Hockey, Rioch N, Brown, Betts, Sub Overton.

Sat 13th April
Preston North End (H) Won 4-0
Stark, Little A 3
Storrie, Robson, McDonald, Beard, Stark, Hockey, Little A, Overton, Rioch N, Betts, Vowden, Sub Deehan.

Tue 16th April
Wolves (A) Drew 1-1
Vowden
Findlay, Robson, McDonald, Beard, Stark, Vowden, Hockey, Rioch N, Brown, Campbell, Betts. Sub req

Mon 22nd April
Manchester United (H) Drew 1-1
Leonard
Findlay, Robson, Beard, Little A, Stark, Vowden, Hockey, Brown, Leonard, Rioch N, Betts, Sub Campbell.

Sat 27th April
Coventry City (H) Won 1-0
Leonard
Findlay, Masefield, Beard, Stark, Rioch N, Little A, Hockey, Brown, Leonard, Evans, Betts, Sub Overton.

Central League Table 1973 - 74

Pos	Team	P	W	D	L	F	A	GD	Pts
1	Liverpool	42	26	9	7	75	34	41	61
2	Coventry City	42	20	13	9	62	47	15	53
3	Blackpool	42	22	8	12	63	44	19	52
4	Everton	42	20	11	11	68	41	27	51
5	**Aston Villa**	**42**	**17**	**15**	**10**	**43**	**36**	**7**	**49**
6	Manchester City	42	19	10	13	78	52	26	48
7	Wolverhampton Wanderers	42	18	12	12	65	50	15	48
8	West Bromwich Albion	42	18	11	13	62	48	14	47
9	Derby County	42	15	16	11	61	42	19	46
10	Sheffield Wednesday	42	16	13	13	54	45	9	45
11	Sheffield United	42	17	11	14	56	51	5	45
12	Manchester United	42	15	14	13	45	43	2	44
13	Stoke City	42	16	11	15	59	56	3	43
14	Newcastle United	42	13	14	15	55	50	5	40
15	Nottingham Forest	42	12	16	14	49	58	-9	40
16	Bolton Wanderers	42	12	13	17	62	68	-6	37
17	Leeds United	42	11	13	18	43	63	-20	35
18	Blackburn Rovers	42	12	9	21	41	63	-22	33
19	Preston North End	42	9	12	21	49	76	-27	30
20	Burnley	42	12	5	25	38	65	-27	29
21	Huddersfield Town	42	6	12	24	42	81	-39	24
22	Bury	42	8	8	26	39	96	-57	24

1974/75

Central League

Sat 17th August
Preston North End (H) Won 4-1
Campbell 2, Little A, Hunt S
Fletcher, Turnbull, McDonald, Rioch, Stark, Brown, Little A, Overton, Leonard, Campbell, Hunt S, Sub Pimblett.

Mon 19th August
Derby County (H) Drew 1-1
Leonard
Findlay, Masefield, McDonald, Rioch, Stark, Little A, Brown, Overton, Leonard, Campbell, Betts, Sub Pimblett.

Sat 24th August
Sheffield United (A) Won 3-1
Leonard 3
Findlay, Masefield, McDonald, Rioch, Stark, McMahon, Pimblett, Campbell, Leonard, Overton, Betts, Sub Williams.

Tue 27th August
West Bromwich Albion (A) Won 3-2
Little A, Rioch (pen), Hunt S
Fletcher, Masefield, McDonald, Rioch, Stark, Little A, Betts, Evans, Leonard, McMahon, Hunt S, Sub Overton.

Sat 31st August
Newcastle United (H) Won 1-0
Pimblett
Fletcher, Masefield, McDonald, Rioch, Stark, Overton, McMahon, Pimblett, Leonard, Campbell, Hunt S, Sub Deehan.

Tue 3rd September
Wolves (A) Lost 1-3
Evans A
Fletcher, Masefield (Betts), McDonald, Rioch, Stark, Brown, McMahon, Little A, Leonard, Evans A, Hunt S.

Sat 7th September
Huddersfield Town (A) Won 3-2
Betts, Campbell, Rioch
Cumbes, Masefield, McDonald, Rioch, Stark, Brown, Vowden, Campbell, Evans A, Little A, Betts, Sub Overton.

Sat 14th September
Bolton Wanderers (H) Won 3-1
Leonard 3
Findlay, Masefield, McDonald, Rioch, Stark, Brown, Betts, Vowden, Leonard, Evans A, Little A, Sub Overton.

Sat 21st September
Burnley (A) Won 2-1
Leonard, Rioch
Findlay, Masefield, McDonald, Rioch, Stark, Brown, Vowden, Evans A, Leonard, Betts, Little A, Sub Hunt S.

Sat 28th September
Nottingham Forest (H) Lost 2-4
Deehan, own goal
Findlay, Masefield, McDonald, Rioch, Stark, Brown, Vowden, Little B, Deehan, Betts, Little A, Sub Hunt S.

Sat 5th October
Liverpool (H) Drew 1-1
Stark
Findlay, Masefield, McDonald, Rioch, Stark, Evans D (Young), Williams, Pimblett, Deehan, Overton, Hunt S.

Sat 12th October
Sheffield Wednesday (A) Won 3-0
Own goal, Evans A, Little B
Findlay, Rioch, McDonald, Little A, Stark, Brown, Pimblett, Little B, Evans A, Betts, Hunt S, Sub Overton.

Sat 19th October
Leeds United (H) Won 2-1
Hunt S, Campbell
Findlay, Masefield, McDonald, Little A, Stark, Brown, McMahon, Evans A, Betts, Campbell, Hunt S, Sub Pimblett.

Sat 26th October
Blackburn Rovers (A) Won 1-0
Leonard
Findlay, Masefield, McDonald, Young, Stark, Brown, McMahon, Evans A, Leonard, Campbell, Turnbull, Sub Betts.

Wed 30th October
Wolves (H) Won 5-2
Evans A, Vowden, Little B, Hunt S, own goal
Findlay, Masefield, McDonald, Stark, Turnbull, Brown, Vowden, Little B, Hunt S, Evans A, Betts, Sub Overton.

Mon 2nd November
Manchester United (H) Drew 2-2
Leonard, Vowden
Findlay, Masefield, McDonald, Turnbull, Stark, Vowden, Betts, Evans A, Leonard, Little A, Hunt S, Sub Brown.

Wed 13th November
Bury (A) Lost 3-5
Evans A, Leonard, Hunt S
Findlay, Stark, McDonald, Turnbull, Young, Vowden, Pimblett, Evans A, Overton, Leonard, Hunt S, Sub Hughes.

Sat 16th November
Blackpool (H) Lost 0-1
Findlay, Masefield, McDonald, Rioch, Stark, Vowden, Pimblett, Evans A, Campbell, Little A, Hunt S, Sub Leonard.

Sat 23rd November
Everton (A) Drew 1-1
Leonard
Fletcher, Masefield, Buttress, Rioch, Stark, Pimblett, Vowden, Betts, Leonard, Campbell, Hunt S, Sub Deehan.

Sat 7th December
Derby County (A) Lost 0-3
Findlay, Hughes, McDonald, Rioch, Stark, Vowden, Pimblett, Evans A, Leonard, Overton, Hunt S, Sub Deehan.

Sat 21st December
Manchester City (H) Won 2-1
Leonard 2
Findlay (Williams), Hughes, McDonald, Rioch, Stark, Overton, Deehan, Evans A, Leonard, Pimblett, Hunt S.

Sat 28th December
West Bromwich Albion (H) Lost 0-2
Findlay, Masefield, Hughes, Rioch, Stark, Pimblett, Evans A, Campbell, Deehan, Overton, Hunt S, Sub Williams.

Sat 4th January
Coventry City (H) Lost 0-1
Findlay, Masefield, Hughes, Rioch, Young, Williams, Hunt K, Evans A, Overton, Campbell, Hunt S, Sub Wright.

Tue 7th January
Liverpool (A) Lost 2-3
Evans A, Campbell

Findlay, Masefield, Hughes, Rioch, Young, Brown, Hunt K (Williams), Evans A, Overton, Campbell, Hunt S.

Sat 18th January
Coventry City (A) Drew 2-2
Evans A 2
Findlay, Masefield, Hughes, Rioch, Stark, Brown, Williams, Evans A, Overton, Campbell, Hunt S, Sub Deehan.

Sat 8th February
Manchester United (A) Lost 0-3
Findlay, Gidman, Masefield, Rioch, Evans D, Brown, Pimblett, Phillips, Deehan, Overton, Hunt S, Sub Hughes.

Wed 12th February
Leeds United (A) Lost 1-2
Evans A
Findlay, Gidman, Masefield, Rioch, Evans D, Brown, Pimblett, Evans A, Deehan, Phillips, Hunt S, Sub Overton.

Sat 15th February
Everton (H) Won 1-0
Hunt S
Findlay, Gidman, Masefield, Overton, Evans D, Hughes, Pimblett, Phillips, Deehan, Williams, Hunt S, Sub Hunt K.

Sat 22nd February
Blackpool (A) Lost 1-2
Brown
Findlay, Gidman, Hughes, Rioch, Overton, Brown, Pimblett (Evans D), Evans A, Deehan, Hunt K, Hunt S.

Sat 8th March
Huddersfield Town (H) Won 3-1
Deehan 2, Rioch
Findlay, Gidman, Armstrong, Rioch, Overton, Brown, Williams, Evans A, Deehan, Masefield, Hughes, Sub Hunt K.

Sat 15th March
Manchester City (A) Lost 0-1
Findlay, Gidman, Armstrong, Rioch, Overton, Hughes (Masefield), Pimblett, Evans A, Deehan, Williams, Hunt S.

Mon 17th March
Sheffield Wednesday (H) Won 2-0
Evans A, Deehan
Findlay, Gidman, Armstrong, Rioch, Overton, Hughes, Williams, Evans A, Deehan, Phillips, Hunt S, Sub Masefield.

Sat 22nd March
Burnley (H) Won 3-1
Deehan 2, Williams
Findlay, Rioch, Armstrong, Stark, Overton, Pimblett, Williams, Evans A, Deehan, Phillips, Hunt S, Sub Hughes.

Sat 29th March
Nottingham Forest (A) Lost 1-3
Evans A
Findlay, Gidman, Armstrong, Stark, Overton, Rioch, Williams, Evans A, Deehan, Hughes, Hunt S, Sub Evans D.

Tue 8th April
Stoke City (A) Won 1-0
Stark
Findlay, Gidman, Hughes, Stark, Evans D, Brown, Hunt K, Evans A, Deehan, Pimblett, Hunt S, Sub Young.

Mon 14th April
Bury (H) Lost 0-2
Findlay, Gidman, Hughes, Rioch, Stark, Brown, Williams, Hunt K, Deehan, Evans D, Hunt S, Sub Young.

Sat 19th April
Blackburn Rovers (H) Drew 1-1
Stark
Findlay, Gidman, Armstrong, Young, Overton, Brown, Williams, Rioch, Deehan, Stark, Hunt S, Sub Buttress.

Tue 22nd April
Bolton Wanderers (A) Lost 0-1
Findlay, Hughes, Armstrong, Rioch, Overton, Brown, Williams, Peters, Deehan, Stark, Betts, Sub Young.

Thu 24th April
Preston North End (A) Drew 1-1
Betts
Findlay, Masefield, Armstrong, Rioch, Stark, Overton, Williams, Hughes, Deehan, Brown, Betts, Sub Peters.

Mon 28th April
Sheffield United (H) Lost 0-1
Findlay, Masefield, Armstrong, Young, Stark, Overton, Pimblett, Hughes, Deehan, Williams, Betts, Sub Hunt K.

Thu 1st May
Newcastle United (A) Drew 0-0
Findlay, Masefield, Armstrong (Young), Rioch, Stark, Overton, Hunt K, Williams, Deehan, Peters, Evans D.

Tue 6th May
Stoke City (H) Lost 0-2
Fletcher, Masefield, Hughes, Young, Stark, Overton, Hunt K, Williams, Deehan, Brown, Hunt S (Evans D).

Central League Table 1974 - 75

Pos	Team	P	W	D	L	F	A	GD	Pts
1	Liverpool	42	24	11	7	90	51	39	59
2	Derby County	42	23	12	7	90	37	53	58
3	West Bromwich Albion	42	20	15	7	58	36	22	55
4	Manchester City	42	23	9	10	60	39	21	55
5	Everton	42	19	10	13	51	38	13	48
6	Stoke City	42	18	12	12	50	40	10	48
7	Wolverhampton Wanderers	42	22	4	16	63	62	1	48
8	Nottingham Forest	42	18	9	15	81	54	27	45
9	Coventry City	42	16	12	14	70	63	7	44
10	**Aston Villa**	**42**	**17**	**8**	**17**	**62**	**62**	**0**	**42**
11	Leeds United	42	14	14	14	56	60	-4	42
12	Sheffield Wednesday	42	18	6	18	60	69	-9	42
13	Blackpool	42	16	9	17	64	63	1	41
14	Burnley	42	13	13	16	64	68	-4	39
15	Newcastle United	42	14	10	18	43	50	-7	38
16	Bolton Wanderers	42	11	15	16	49	61	-12	37
17	Manchester United	42	11	14	17	55	64	-9	36
18	Preston North End	42	11	12	19	44	66	-22	34
19	Huddersfield Town	42	12	8	22	47	67	-20	32
20	Sheffield United	42	11	7	24	48	75	-27	29
21	Bury	42	10	9	23	53	91	-38	29
22	Blackburn Rovers	42	4	15	23	35	77	-42	23

1975/76

Central League

Sat 16th August
Coventry City (A) Drew 1-1
Morgan
Findlay, Masefield, Armstrong, Overton, Young, Pimblett, Fagan, Peters (Cowans), Morgan, McDonald, Hunt.

Wed 20th August
Manchester City (H) Lost 0-1
Findlay, Masefield (Armstrong), Robson, Overton, Young, Pimblett, Fagan, Peters, Deehan, McDonald, Hunt.

Sat 23rd August
Blackburn Rovers (H) Drew 3-3
Fagan, Deehan, Morgan
Findlay, Hughes, Armstrong, Overton, Young, Pimblett, Fagan, Deehan, Morgan, McDonald, Hunt, Sub Peters.

Tue 26th August
Bury (A) Drew 2-2
Morgan, own goal
Findlay, Hughes, Armstrong, Overton, Young, Pimblett (Williams), Fagan, Deehan, Morgan, McDonald, Hunt.

Sat 30th August
Liverpool (A) Lost 0-4
Findlay, Masefield, Hughes, Overton, Young, Brown, Fagan, Deehan, Morgan, McMahon, Hunt, Sub Pimblett.

Sat 6th September
Bolton Wanderers (H) Won 2-1
Brown, Deehan
Findlay, Masefield, Buttress, Overton, Young, Brown, McMahon, Evans A, Deehan, McDonald, Hunt, Sub Peters.

Sat 13th September
Newcastle United (A) Won 1-0
Peters
Findlay, Masefield, Buttress, Overton, Young, Brown, McMahon (Peters), Evans A, Deehan, Williams, Hunt.

Sat 20th September
Leeds United (H) Lost 1-2
Williams
Cumbes, Masefield, Buttress, Overton, Young, Brown, McMahon, Evans A, Deehan, McDonald, Williams, Sub Armstrong.

Wed 24th September
Wolves (H) Drew 1-1
Deehan
Cumbes, Buttress, McDonald, Overton, Young, Brown, McMahon, Evans A, Deehan, Pimblett, Hunt (Peters).

Sat 27th September
West Bromwich Albion (A) Lost 0-2
Findlay, Buttress, McDonald, Overton, Evans D, Brown, McMahon, Peters, Deehan, Williams, Hunt, Sub Cowans.

Sat 4th October
Sheffield Wednesday (H) Won 2-0
Morgan 2
Cumbes, Buttress, Armstrong, Overton, Young, Brown, Pimblett, Deehan, Morgan, Williams, Hunt, Sub Peters.

Sat 11th October
Preston North End (A) Won 2-1
Pimblett, Hunt
Cumbes, Masefield, Buttress, Overton, Young, McDonald, Williams, Peters, Morgan, Pimblett, Hunt, Sub Fagan.

Tue 14th October
Wolves (A) Won 3-1
Morgan, Hunt, Pimblett
Eyre, Masefield, Buttress, Overton, Young, McDonald, Fagan, Deehan, Morgan, Pimblett (Peters), Hunt.

Sat 18th October
Burnley (H) Won 3-0
Deehan 2, Hunt (pen)
Cumbes, Masefield, Buttress, Overton, Young, McDonald, McMahon, Deehan, Morgan, Evans A, Hunt, Sub Evans D.

Sat 25th October
Everton (A) Lost 0-2
Cumbes, Masefield, Buttress, Overton, Young, McDonald, McMahon, Deehan, Pimblett, Evans A, Peters, Sub Cowans.

Sat 1st November
Sheffield United (H) Won 1-0
Peters
Findlay, Masefield, Buttress, Overton, Young, Pimblett, McMahon, Evans A, Cowans (Price), Peters, Hamilton.

Sat 8th November
Manchester United (A) Lost 0-1
Findlay, Masefield, Buttress, Evans D, Young, McDonald, McMahon, Evans A, Cowans, Peters (Price), Hunt.

Sat 15th November
Nottingham Forest (H) Drew 1-1
McDonald
Findlay, Masefield, Buttress, Overton, Young, McDonald, McMahon, Cowans, Morgan, Peters, Hunt (Evans D).

Sat 22nd November
Burnley (A) Drew 2-2
Hunt, Morgan
Findlay, Masefield, Armstrong, Overton, Young, McDonald, McMahon, Evans A, Morgan, Cowans, Hunt, Sub Buttress.

Wed 3rd December
Huddersfield Town (A) Won 3-0
Evans A 2, Morgan
Findlay, Masefield, Armstrong, Overton, Young, Pimblett, McDonald, McMahon, Morgan, Evans A, Hunt. Sub Cowans.

Sat 6th December
Stoke City (H) Won 2-1
Cowans, Morgan
Findlay, Masefield, Armstrong, Overton, Young, Evans D, McMahon, Evans A, Morgan, Cowans, Hunt, Sub Buttress.

Sat 20th December
Coventry City (H) Drew 1-1
Own goal
Cumbes, Masefield, Buttress, Evans D, Young, Hughes, Fagan, Peters, Cowans, McMahon, Hunt, Sub Overton.

Sat 10th January
Newcastle United (H) Lost 1-3
Hunt
Cumbes, Masefield, Buttress, Evans D, Young, McDonald, Fagan, McMahon, Capaldi, Cowans, Hunt, Sub Hughes.

THE BIG ASTON VILLA BOOK OF THE SEVENTIES

Sat 17th January
Bolton Wanderers (A) Drew 1-1
Capaldi
Findlay, Masefield, Buttress, Overton, Young, McDonald, Fagan, Peters, Capaldi, Cowans, Hunt, Sub Hughes.

Sat 24th January
Liverpool (H) Lost 1-2
Cowans
Findlay, Masefield, Buttress, Overton, Young, Evans D, McDonald, McMahon, Capaldi, Cowans, Hunt, Sub Williams.

Sat 31st January
Manchester City (A) Lost 0-1
Cumbes, Masefield, Buttress, Overton, Young, McDonald, McMahon, Peters, Little, Pimblett, Hunt, Sub Hughes.

Sat 7th February
Bury (H) Won 5-2
Deehan 3, Hunt, Evans
Cumbes, Masefield, Aitken, Evans D, Young, McDonald, Williams, Deehan, Peters, Little, Hunt, Sub Capaldi.

Sat 14th February
Manchester United (H) Drew 1-1
Fagan
Findlay, Masefield, Buttress, Overton, Evans D, Williams, Fagan, Cowans, Peters, Little, Hunt, Sub Young.

Sat 21st February
Nottingham Forest (A) Drew 0-0
Findlay, Masefield, Buttress, Overton, Young, Pimblett, Fagan, Price, Hunt, Peters, Hamilton, Sub Capaldi.

Sat 6th March
Sheffield United (A) Drew 3-3
Hamilton 2, Deehan
Cumbes, Buttress, Short, Overton, Young, Pimblett, Fagan, Hunt, Deehan, Hamilton, Cowans, Sub Capaldi.

Sat 13th March
Preston North End (H) Won 4-1
Masefield, own goal, Buttress, Hunt
Findlay, Buttress, Aitken, Evans D, Young, Williams, Masefield, Cowans, Peters, McDonald, Hunt, Sub Fagan.

Thu 18th March
Everton (H) Won 2-0
McDonald, Hunt
Findlay, Masefield, Buttress, Evans D, Young, McDonald, Fagan (Williams), Cowans, Deehan, Peters, Hunt.

Sat 20th March
Huddersfield Town (H) Won 2-1
Own goal, Peters
Findlay, Hughes, Aitken (Buttress), Phillips, Young, Williams, Cowans, Masefield, Capaldi, Peters, Hunt.

Sat 27th March
Stoke City (A) Won 1-0
Hunt
Findlay, Hughes, Buttress, Phillips, Young, Williams, Masefield, Peters, Capaldi, Evans D, Hunt, Sub Price.

Mon 29th March
Derby County (H) Won 1-0
Deehan
Findlay, Hughes, McDonald, Phillips, Evans D, Williams, Masefield, Cowans, Deehan, Peters, Hunt, Sub Young.

Sat 3rd April
West Bromwich Albion (H) Drew 0-0
Findlay, Hughes, Buttress, Phillips, Evans D, Williams, Masefield, Deehan, Peters, Cowans, Hunt, Sub Wilson.

Wed 7th April
Blackburn Rovers (A) Won 3-0
Deehan 2, Masefield
Findlay, Masefield, Aitken, Hughes, Young, Williams, Peters, Cowans, Deehan, Hamilton, Coleman, Sub Capaldi.

Sat 10th April
Leeds United (A) Lost 0-4
Findlay, Short, Williams, Hughes, Young, Pimblett, Cowans, Deehan, Peters, Wilson, Coleman, Sub Capaldi.

Wed 14th April
Blackpool (A) Won 1-0
Hamilton
Findlay, Hughes, Buttress, Young, Williams, Evans D, Masefield, Cowans, Little, Capaldi, Hamilton, Sub Price.

Sat 17th April
Blackpool (H) Drew 0-0
Parsons, Hughes, Buttress, Ross, Evans, Williams, Pimblett, Little, Linton, Hamilton, Cowans, Sub Price.

Mon 19th April
Derby County (A) Lost 0-3
Parsons, Hughes, Buttress, Young, Evans, Pimblett, Cowans, Peters, Little, Linton, Hamilton, Sub Price.

Sat 24th April
Sheffield Wednesday (A) Lost 0-2
Parsons, Masefield, Short, Evans, Young, Williams, Fagan, Price, Capaldi, Hamilton, Coles, Sub Linton.

Central League Table 1975 - 76

Pos	Team	P	W	D	L	F	A	GD	Pts
1	Liverpool	42	31	5	6	94	32	62	67
2	West Bromwich Albion	42	25	13	4	83	35	48	63
3	Derby County	42	21	13	8	1	40	-39	55
4	Wolverhampton Wanderers	42	21	11	10	82	54	28	53
5	Leeds United	42	21	9	12	76	52	24	51
6	**Aston Villa**	**42**	**17**	**13**	**12**	**57**	**51**	**6**	**47**
7	Coventry City	42	16	13	13	54	46	8	45
8	Everton	42	18	8	16	70	57	13	44
9	Bury	42	14	16	12	64	66	-2	44
10	Manchester United	42	18	7	17	65	55	10	43
11	Stoke City	42	16	10	16	60	55	5	42
12	Sheffield United	42	15	11	16	54	56	-2	41
13	Burnley	42	15	10	17	64	71	-7	40
14	Newcastle United	42	14	1	17	53	58	-5	39
15	Nottingham Forest	42	14	11	17	51	64	-13	39
16	Manchester City	42	11	16	15	47	54	-7	38
17	Sheffield Wednesday	42	9	15	18	42	60	-18	33
18	Blackburn Rovers	42	12	8	22	58	85	-27	32
19	Bolton Wanderers	42	10	9	23	40	72	-32	29
20	Huddersfield Town	42	8	13	21	41	75	-34	29
21	Preston North End	42	10	8	24	36	88	-52	28
22	Blackpool	42	5	12	25	37	83	-46	22

1976/77

Central League

Sat 21st August
Sheffield United (A) Lost 0-1
Findlay, Masefield, Buttress, Ross, Young, McDonald, Fagan, Deehan, Capaldi, Cowans, Price, Sub Williams.

Wed 25th August
Manchester City (H) Won 4-3
Deehan, Capaldi, Fagan, Young
Findlay, Masefield, Buttress, Ross, Young, Price, Fagan, Deehan, Capaldi, Cowans, Hunt, Sub Wilson.

Sat 28th August
Huddersfield Town (H) Won 2-1
Capaldi, Fagan
Findlay, Masefield, Buttress, Ross, Young, Hughes, Fagan, Deehan, Capaldi, Cowans, Price, Sub Wilson.

Sat 4th September
Everton (A) Lost 0-3
Findlay, Masefield, Buttress, Ross, Young, Hughes, Fagan, Deehan, Capaldi, Cowans, Price, Sub Wilson.

Wed 8th September
Bolton Wanderers (H) Drew 0-0
Findlay, Masefield, Buttress, Ross, Young, Price, Hughes, Deehan, Capaldi, Cowans, Hunt, Sub Fagan.

Sat 11th September
Burnley (H) Drew 0-0
Findlay, Masefield, Buttress, Ross, Young, Price, Fagan, O'Dowd, Capaldi, Hughes, Hunt, Sub Williams G.

Sat 18th September
Nottingham Forest (A) Won 2-1
Capaldi, Deehan
Findlay, Masefield, Buttress, Ross, Young, Hughes, Fagan, Deehan, Capaldi, Cowans, Price, Sub Wilson.

Wed 29th September
Bury (H) Won 5-2
Price, Capaldi 2, Deehan, Fagan
Findlay, Masefield, Robson, Ross, Young, Buttress, Hughes (Fagan), Deehan, Capaldi, Price, Hunt.

Sat 2nd October
Coventry City (H) Lost 1-3
Deehan
Findlay, Masefield, Buttress, Ross, Young, Hughes, Fagan, Deehan, Capaldi, Cowans, Hunt, Sub Price.

Wed 13th October
Stoke City (A) Drew 0-0
Findlay, Masefield, Robson, Evans, Young, Williams, Hughes, Deehan, Capaldi, Price, Hunt, Sub Buttress.

Sat 16th October
Preston North End (H) Won 2-1
Hunt, O'Dowd
Findlay, Masefield, Buttress, Evans, Young, Hughes, Cowans, O'Dowd, Capaldi, Williams K, Hunt, Sub Price.

Tue 26th October
Wolves (A) Won 2-1
Fagan, Hunt

Findlay, Masefield, Robson, Young, Williams G, Price, Fagan (Buttress), Cowans, Capaldi, Deehan, Hunt.

Sat 30th October
Sheffield Wednesday (H) Drew 3-3
Deehan 2, Young
Findlay, Masefield, Robson, Young, Williams G, Price, Fagan (Buttress), Cowans, Capaldi, Deehan, Hunt.

Tue 2nd November
Newcastle United (A) Lost 0-1
Spink, Masefield, Buttress, Williams, Young, Price, Hughes, Coles, Capaldi, Cowans, Hunt, Sub Wilson.

Sat 13th November
Blackburn Rovers (H) Won 4-0
Deehan 2, Hughes, Hunt
Findlay, Masefield, Robson, Buttress, Young, Price, Fagan, Deehan, Capaldi, Hughes, Hunt, Sub Williams G.

Sat 20th November
Leeds United (A) Lost 1-2
Williams K
Burridge, Masefield, Buttress, Evans, Young, Williams K, Cowans, O'Dowd, Capaldi, Price (Fagan), Hunt.

Sat 27th November
Blackpool (H) Won 2-1
Coles, Linton
Burridge, Masefield, Hughes, Evans, Young, Williams K (Linton), Price, Coles, Capaldi, Cowans, Hunt.

Sat 18th December
Sheffield Wednesday (A) Won 1-0
Capaldi
Burridge, Masefield, Hughes, Ross, Evans, Williams K, Linton, O'Dowd, Capaldi, Cowans, Hunt, Sub Price.

Sat 8th January
Manchester United (H) Lost 0-2
Findlay, Masefield, Buttress, Evans, Young, Williams K, Williams G, O'Dowd, Capaldi, Hughes, Hunt, Sub Linton.

Sat 15th January
Manchester City (A) Lost 0-3
Spink, Williams K, Masefield, Evans, Young, Williams G, Linton, O'Dowd, Capaldi (Wilson), Price, Hunt.

Sat 22nd January
Sheffield United (H) Won 5-0
Capaldi 2, O'Dowd 2, Hughes
Findlay, Masefield, Buttress, Evans, Young, Williams K, Hughes, O'Dowd, Capaldi, Price, Hunt, Sub Hendry.

Sat 29th January
Derby County (A) Drew 1-1
O'Dowd
Findlay, Masefield, Smith, Evans, Young, Williams K, Price, O'Dowd, Capaldi, Buttress, Hunt, Sub Wilson.

Mon 7th February
Huddersfield Town (A) Won 1-0
Masefield
Findlay, Masefield, Smith, Evans, Young, Buttress, Hughes, O'Dowd, Capaldi, Wilson, Hendry, Sub Price.

Sat 19th February
Burnley (A) Drew 2-2
Buttress, Capaldi
Spink, Masefield, Smith, Evans, Young, Hughes, Graydon,

THE BIG ASTON VILLA BOOK OF THE SEVENTIES

O'Dowd, Capaldi, Cowans, Buttress, Sub Gibson.

Tue 1st March
Preston North End (A) Won 1-0
Price
Findlay, Masefield, Buttress, Evans, Young, Williams G, Graydon, O'Dowd, Capaldi, Price (Wilson), Linton.

Sat 5th March
Bury (A) Lost 1-3
Capaldi
Parsons, Stevenson, Hendry, Williams G, Young, Wilson, Graydon, O'Dowd, Capaldi, Linton, Gibson, Sub Ormsby.

Mon 7th March
West Bromwich Albion (H) Lost 1-2
Wilson
Parsons, Masefield, Hendry, Evans, Young, Williams G, Graydon, Linton, Capaldi, Wilson, Gibson, Sub Price.

Wed 26th March
Liverpool (A) Lost 0-3
Spink, Masefield, Smith, Evans, Williams, Wilson, Graydon, O'Dowd, Capaldi, Hughes, Gibson, Sub Linton.

Wed 30th March
Liverpool (H) Lost 0-1
Findlay, Masefield, Smith, Evans, Buttress, Hughes, Graydon, O'Dowd, Capaldi, Cropley (Wilson), Williams G.

Sat 2nd April
Stoke City (H) Lost 0-1
Findlay, Stevenson, Masefield, Williams G, Young, Evans, Graydon, O'Dowd, Linton, Hughes, Wilson, Sub Capaldi.

Wed 6th April
Nottingham Forest (H) Lost 0-1
Findlay, Masefield, Smith, Evans, Young, Cowans, Graydon, Allett, O'Dowd, Linton, Wilson, Sub Capaldi.

Mon 11th April
West Bromwich Albion (A) Lost 0-2
Findlay, Masefield, Buttress, Evans, Young, Hughes, Smith, O'Dowd, Allett, Linton, Wilson, Sub Williams G.

Thu 14th April
Everton (H) Lost 0-1
Findlay, Masefield, Buttress, Evans, Young, Hughes, Smith, O'Dowd, Allett, Linton, Wilson, Sub Williams G.

Sat 16th April
Newcastle United (H) Won 1-0
Wilson
Spink, Masefield, Buttress, Evans, Ormsby, Wilson, Linton, O'Dowd, Capaldi, Hughes, Gibson, Sub Hendry.

Tue 19th April
Bolton Wanderers (A) Drew 2-2
Hughes 2
Spink, Masefield, Buttress, Evans, Ormsby, Wilson, Linton, O'Dowd, Capaldi, Hughes, Gibson, Sub Hendry.

Sat 23rd April
Blackpool (A) Lost 1-4
Evans
Spink, Stevenson, Buttress, Evans, Ormsby, Williams G, Masefield, O'Dowd, Capaldi, Wilson, Gibson, Sub Hendry.

Wed 27th April
Blackburn Rovers (A) Drew 0-0

Parsons, Stevenson, Buttress, Evans, Ormsby, Williams G, Linton, Hughes, Capaldi, Wilson, Gibson. Sub Hendry

Sat 30th April
Leeds United (H) Lost 1-2
Wilson

Parsons, Stevenson, Buttress, Williams G, Ormsby, Wilson, Linton, Hughes, Capaldi, Hendry, Gibson, Sub Shaw.

Mon 2nd May
Derby County (H) Won 1-0
Hughes

Spink, Stevenson, Buttress, Young, Ormsby, Evans, Linton, Capaldi, Allett, Hughes, Gibson, Sub Hendry.

Thu 5th May
Coventry City (A) Won 1-0
Linton

Findlay, Masefield, Buttress, Young, Ormsby, Evans, Gibson, Capaldi, Linton, Hughes, Hendry. Sub Williams

Sat 7th May
Manchester United (A) Lost 0-4

Findlay, Masefield, Buttress, Young, Ormsby, Williams G, Graydon, Capaldi, Linton, Hendry, Gibson, Sub Wilson.

Wed 11th May
Wolves (H) Lost 1-2
Graydon

Spink, Masefield, Buttress, Young, Ormsby, Evans, Graydon, Capaldi, Linton, Hughes, Gibson, Sub Hendry.

Central League Table 1976 - 77

Pos	Team	P	W	D	L	F	A	GD	Pts
1	Liverpool	42	30	9	3	122	41	81	69
2	Manchester United	42	22	12	8	76	54	22	56
3	Wolverhampton Wanderers	42	22	10	10	70	41	29	54
4	Bury	42	20	11	11	60	45	15	51
5	Nottingham Forest	42	21	8	13	67	53	14	50
6	Manchester City	42	21	7	14	65	56	9	49
7	Leeds United	42	19	10	13	84	54	30	48
8	West Bromwich Albion	42	15	14	13	52	49	3	44
9	Everton	42	15	14	13	51	46	5	44
10	Stoke City	42	13	18	11	49	50	-1	44
11	Derby County	42	15	13	14	48	52	-4	43
12	Coventry City	42	18	5	19	61	65	-4	41
13	Sheffield United	42	16	9	17	46	54	-8	41
14	**Aston Villa**	**42**	**15**	**8**	**19**	**49**	**59**	**-10**	**38**
15	Sheffield Wednesday	42	11	16	15	41	55	-14	38
16	Burnley	42	11	14	17	55	64	-9	36
17	Newcastle United	42	10	15	17	50	55	-5	35
18	Blackburn Rovers	42	13	9	20	51	83	-32	35
19	Blackpool	42	11	11	20	50	66	-16	33
20	Bolton Wanderers	42	9	10	23	44	75	-31	28
21	Huddersfield Town	42	9	9	24	55	85	-30	27
22	Preston North End	42	5	10	27	45	89	-44	20

1977/78

Central League

Sat 20th August
Huddersfield Town (H) Drew 0-0
Burridge, Buttress, Hughes, Capaldi, Ormsby, Williams, Linton, Jenkins, O'Dowd, Shaw, Hendry, Sub Stevenson.

Tue 23rd August
Manchester City (A) Won 1-0
Hendry
Burridge, Buttress, Hughes, Capaldi, Ormsby, Williams, Linton, Jenkins, O'Dowd, Shaw, Hendry, Sub Stevenson.

Sat 27th August
Burnley (A) Drew 0-0
Burridge, Stevenson, Buttress, Capaldi, Ormsby, Williams, Linton, Evans D, Evans A, Shaw, Hendry, Sub Jenkins.

Sat 3rd September
Everton (H) Lost 0-2
Findlay, Stevenson, Buttress, Evans D, Young, Williams, Linton, Cowans, Capaldi, Shaw, Hendry, Sub Jenkins.

Sat 10th September
Sheffield United (A) Won 2-0
Capaldi, O'Dowd
Findlay, Evans D, Buttress, Capaldi, Young, Ormsby, Linton, Cowans, O'Dowd, Shaw, Jenkins, Sub Williams.

Sat 17th September
Nottingham Forest (H) Lost 0-1
Burridge, Evans D, Buttress, Capaldi, Young, Williams, Linton, Hendry, O'Dowd, Shaw, Jenkins, Sub Ormsby.

Sat 24th September
Bolton Wanderers (A) Lost 0-2
Burridge, Evans D, Buttress, Capaldi, Ormsby, Gregory, Linton, O'Dowd, Evans A, Jenkins, Hendry, Sub Ollis.

Sat 1st October
Bury (A) Won 2-1
O'Dowd, Gibson
Findlay, Evans D, Buttress, Capaldi, Young, Williams, Hughes, O'Dowd, Evans A, Jenkins, Hendry, Sub Gibson.

Wed 5th October
Coventry City (H) Lost 0-1
Findlay, Evans D, Robson, Capaldi, Ormsby, Buttress, Linton, O'Dowd, Evans A, Hughes, Hendry, Sub Gibson.

Sat 8th October
Stoke City (H) Lost 2-3
Hughes, O'Dowd
Burridge, Evans D, Robson, Capaldi, Young, Williams, Linton, O'Dowd, Evans A, Hughes, Hendry, Sub Gibson.

Mon 10th October
Preston North End (H) Drew 0-0
Burridge, Evans D, Buttress, Capaldi, Gregory, Williams, Linton, Shaw, Evans A, Hughes, Hendry, Sub Jenkins.

Sat 22nd October
Wolves (A) Lost 1-2
Linton
Burridge, Evans D, Robson, Capaldi, Young, Williams, Linton, O'Dowd, Evans A, Hughes, Buttress, Sub Hendry.

Sat 29th October
West Bromwich Albion (A) Drew 1-1
Evans A

Findlay, Buttress, Robson, Capaldi, Young, Williams, Linton, O'Dowd, Evans A, Hughes, Gibson, Sub Ollis.

Sat 5th November
Blackpool (H) Lost 0-1

Findlay, Evans D, Robson, Buttress, Young, Williams, Linton, Capaldi, Evans A, Hughes, Shaw, Sub Gibson.

Sat 12th November
Leeds United (A) Won 1-0
Evans A

Findlay, Evans D, Hughes, Linton, Young, Williams, Evans A, Shaw, Gibson, Capaldi, Buttress, Sub Hendry.

Sat 26th November
Derby County (A) Drew 1-1
Shaw

Burridge, Evans D, Gibson, Gregory, Young, Linton, Capaldi, Shaw, Evans A, Cowans, Hughes, Sub Williams.

Sat 3rd December
Liverpool (H) Lost 0-1

Burridge, Hughes, Gibson, Williams, Ormsby, Jenkins, Evans A, Deehan (Ollis), Capaldi, Shaw, Hendry.

Sat 10th December
Newcastle United (A) Won 3-2
Capaldi, Evans A, Shaw

Findlay, Hughes, Gibson, Williams, Young, Hendry, Evans A, Shaw, Capaldi, Jenkins, Buttress, Sub Linton.

Tue 13th December
Huddersfield Town (A) Drew 1-1
Capaldi

Findlay, Hughes, Gibson, Williams, Ormsby, Hendry, Evans A, Deehan, Capaldi, Linton, Buttress, Sub Shaw.

Sat 17th December
Manchester United (H) Drew 0-0

Findlay, Hughes, Gibson, Williams, Evans A, Linton, Capaldi, Deehan, Jenkins, Shaw, Hendry, Sub Ollis.

Tue 20th December
Sheffield Wednesday (A) Lost 0-1

Burridge, Evans D, Gibson, Evans A, Young, Linton, Hughes, Capaldi, Shaw, Jenkins, Buttress, Sub Williams.

Sat 7th January
Manchester City (H) Lost 0-1

Spink, Evans D, Gibson, Williams, Young, Linton, Evans A, Hughes, Capaldi, Jenkins, Hendry, Sub Ollis.

Sat 14th January
Burnley (H) Lost 1-2
Shaw

Findlay, Evans D, Gibson, Williams, Young, Hendry, Evans A, Shaw, Capaldi, Ollis (Beech), Jenkins.

Sat 21st January
Everton (A) Drew 0-0

Burridge, Evans D, Gibson, Williams, Young, Linton, Hughes, Shaw (Jenkins), Capaldi, Buttress, Hendry.

THE BIG ASTON VILLA BOOK OF THE SEVENTIES

Sat 18th February
Bolton Wanderers (H) Won 1-0
Young
Findlay, Evans D, Gibson, Williams, Young, Linton, Capaldi, Hughes, Evans A, Buttress, Shelton, Sub Hendry.

Wed 22nd February
Sheffield United (H) Won 10-0
Evans A 6, Shaw 2, Linton, Hendry
Findlay, Evans D, Gibson, Williams, Young, Linton, Shelton, Evans A, Shaw, Gregory, Hendry, Sub Jenkins.

Sat 25th February
Bury (H) Won 1-0
Shelton
Findlay, Evans D, Gibson, Ormsby, Young, Linton, Shelton, Evans A, Shaw, Buttress, Hendry, Sub Hughes.

Sat 4th March
Stoke City (A) Lost 0-4
Findlay, Evans D, Gibson, Ormsby, Young, Hughes, Buttress (Capaldi), Shaw, Linton, Hendry, Jenkins.

Sat 11th March
Preston North End (A) Drew 0-0
Findlay (Jenkins), Evans D, Gibson, Williams, Ormsby, Linton, Hughes, Shaw, Capaldi, Shelton, Hendry.

Mon 13th March
Leeds United (H) Lost 1-3
Hughes
Spink, Evans D, Gibson, Williams, Ormsby, Linton, Evans A, Shaw, Capaldi, Shelton, Hendry, Sub Hughes.

Mon 20th March
Wolves (H) Won 3-0
Evans A, Linton, Hendry
Findlay, Evans D, Gibson, Williams, Evans A, Hendry, Shelton, Hughes, Linton, Shaw, Jenkins, Sub Ormsby.

Wed 22nd March
Blackburn Rovers (H) Won 3-0
Evans A (pen), Linton, Shelton
Findlay, Evans D, Gibson, Williams, Evans A, Hendry, Shelton, Hughes, Linton, Shaw (Ormsby), Jenkins.

Wed 29th March
Sheffield Wednesday (H) Drew 0-0
Findlay, Evans D, Gibson, Williams, Evans A, Hendry, Shelton, Hughes, Linton, Shaw, Jenkins (Capaldi).

Sat 1st April
Blackpool (A) Won 2-0
Linton, Capaldi
Findlay, Evans D, Gibson, Williams, Evans A, Hendry (Capaldi), Shelton, Hughes, Linton, Shaw, Jenkins.

Sat 8th April
Derby County (H) Drew 0-0
Findlay, Evans D, Gibson, Williams, Ormsby, Linton, Graham, Shaw, Hughes, Jenkins, Hendry, Sub Capaldi.

Sat 15th April
Blackburn Rovers (A) Lost 0-1
Findlay, Evans D, Hughes, Williams, Ormsby, Capaldi (Shaw), Jenkins, O'Dowd, Graham, Beech, Ollis.

Mon 17th April
Manchester United (A) Lost 0-1
Findlay, Evans D, Gibson, Williams, Ormsby, Linton, Hughes, Jenkins, Shelton, Graham, Shaw, Sub Ollis.

Wed 19th April
West Bromwich Albion (H) Lost 0-2
Findlay, Evans D, Gibson, Williams, Ormsby, Linton, Hughes, Jenkins, Shelton, Graham, Shaw (Hendry).

Sat 22nd April
Newcastle United (H) Drew 1-1
O'Dowd

Findlay, Gibson, Knight (Ward), Williams, Ormsby, Linton, Hendry, Jenkins, O'Dowd, Capaldi, Shelton.

Tue 25th April
Coventry City (A) Drew 1-1
Ollis

Findlay, Ward, Shelton, Evans D, Ormsby, Linton (Williams), Ollis, Smart, Capaldi, Graham, Beech.

Sat 29th April
Liverpool (A) Drew 0-0
Findlay, Evans D, Shelton, Williams, Ormsby, Linton, Ollis, Capaldi, Graham, Hendry, Beech, Sub Jenkins.

Wed 3rd May
Nottingham Forest (A) Drew 0-0
Findlay, Evans D, Gibson, Williams, Ormsby, Linton, Ward (Ollis), Shelton, O'Dowd, Graham, Hendry.

Central League Table 1977 - 78

Pos	Team	P	W	D	L	F	A	GD	Pts
1	Manchester City	42	27	8	7	92	40	52	62
2	Liverpool	42	24	8	10	85	41	44	56
3	Wolverhampton Wanderers	42	21	12	9	67	44	23	54
4	Everton	42	19	15	8	54	39	15	53
5	Manchester United	42	20	10	12	69	50	19	50
6	West Bromwich Albion	42	18	12	12	56	46	10	48
7	Nottingham Forest	42	17	12	13	66	54	12	46
8	Leeds United	42	16	12	14	69	60	9	44
9	Derby County	42	14	13	15	45	50	-5	41
10	Blackburn Rovers	42	18	5	19	53	70	-17	41
11	Stoke City	42	13	14	15	58	52	6	40
12	Huddersfield Town	42	15	10	17	55	54	1	40
13	Newcastle United	42	14	12	16	51	63	-12	40
14	Coventry City	42	14	11	17	61	70	-9	39
15	Bolton Wanderers	42	14	10	18	57	65	-8	38
16	**Aston Villa**	**42**	**11**	**15**	**16**	**39**	**36**	**3**	**37**
17	Bury	42	10	115	17	57	67	-10	35
18	Blackpool	42	1	13	18	46	60	-14	35
19	Burnley	42	11	12	19	51	67	-16	34
20	Preston North End	42	9	15	18	42	67	-25	33
21	Sheffield Wednesday	42	12	7	23	37	60	-23	31
22	Sheffield United	42	8	11	23	37	93	-56	27

1978/79

Central League

Sat 19th August
Manchester City (A) Lost 1-4
Jenkins
Findlay, Evans D, Gibson, Williams, Ormsby, Craig, Hopkins, Shaw, O'Dowd (Hendry), Jenkins, Young.

Sat 2nd September
Stoke City (A) Drew 0-0
Findlay, Evans D, Gibson, Williams, Ormsby, Craig, Hopkins, Linton, Graham, Jenkins, Young (Hendry).

Sat 9th September
Everton (H) Won 2-0
Shaw 2
Findlay, Evans D, Gibson, Hopkins, Williams, Phillips, Shelton, Shaw, Deehan, Hendry, Young, Sub Graham.

Sat 16th September
Preston North End (A) Won 4-0
Own goal, Shaw 2, Deehan
Findlay, Ward I, Gibson, Crooks, Ormsby, Hendry, Hopkins, Shaw, Deehan, Graham, Young (Jenkins).

Mon 18th September
Blackburn Rovers (H) Won 2-0
Graham 2
Findlay, Ward I, Gibson, Phillips, Williams, Hopkins, Jenkins, Hendry, Young, Deehan, Graham, Sub Crooks.

Sat 23rd September
Huddersfield Town (H) Won 6-2
Shaw 3, Graham 2, Jones
Findlay, Ward I, Gibson, Williams, Ormsby, Jenkins, Hopkins, Shaw, Graham, Jones, Young, Sub Ollis.

Sat 30th September
Nottingham Forest (A) Lost 0-1
Findlay, Evans D, Gibson, Phillips, Ormsby, Hendry, Hopkins, Jones, Graham, Ward I, Young, Sub Heath.

Sat 14th October
Burnley (A) Lost 1-3
Graham
Findlay, Ward I, Gibson, Jones, Heath, Crooks, Hopkins, Graham, Linton, Shelton, Jenkins, Sub Morgan.

Wed 18th October
Coventry City (H) Drew 1-1
Own goal
Findlay, Morgan, Gibson, Heath, Ormsby, Graham, Hendry, Young, Shaw, Jenkins, Shelton.

Sat 21st October
Newcastle United (H) Lost 2-3
Shaw (pen), Deehan
Findlay, Morgan, Gibson, Linton, Ormsby, Graham, Shelton, Shaw, Deehan, Jenkins, Hendry, Sub Heath.

Sat 28th October
Sheffield United (A) Lost 1-3
Deehan
Findlay, Linton, Gibson, Heath, Ormsby, Jenkins, Shelton, Shaw, Deehan, Cropley, Ollis, Sub Hopkins.

Sat 4th November
Wolves (A) Lost 0-2
Findlay, Linton, Smith, Heath, Ormsby, Shelton, Jenkins, Graham, Cowans, Cropley, Ollis, Sub Gibson.

Sat 11th November
Manchester City (H) Won 1-0
Shaw
Findlay, Morgan, Smith, Heath, Ormsby, Craig, Hopkins, Shaw, Graham, Cropley, Gibson, Sub Young.

Sat 18th November
Bury (A) Won 2-0
Graham, Hopkins
Findlay, Morgan, Smith, Heath, Evans D, Craig, Hopkins, Ollis, Graham, Cropley, Young, Sub Jones.

Wed 22nd November
Stoke City (H) Won 4-1
Shaw 2, Gibson, Young
Findlay, Evans D, Gibson, Heath, Ormsby, Craig, Hopkins, Shaw, Graham, Cropley, Young, Sub Ollis.

Sat 25th November
Bolton Wanderers (H) Lost 1-3
Ollis
Findlay, Evans D, Smith, Crooks, Heath, Ollis, Hopkins, Linton, Graham, Cropley, Gibson, Sub Morgan.

Sat 2nd December
Derby County (A) Lost 0-1
Spink, Evans D, Hendry, Heath, Ormsby, Ollis, Hopkins, Jenkins, Graham, Cropley, Young, Sub Linton.

Sat 9th December
Liverpool (H) Drew 1-1
Shelton
Spink, Linton, Gibson, Evans D, Ormsby, Jones, Shelton, Jenkins, Pugh, Gilbert, Young, Sub Morgan.

Sat 16th December
Leeds United (A) Won 3-1
Shaw 2, Jenkins
Spink, Linton, Gibson, Evans D, Ormsby, Ollis, Hopkins, Shaw, Jenkins, Cropley, Cunningham, Sub Jones.

Tue 26th December
West Bromwich Albion (A) Won 2-0
Shaw, Cunningham
Spink, Linton, Gibson, Evans D, Ormsby, Ollis, Hopkins, Shaw, Jenkins, Cropley, Cunningham, Sub Young.

Sat 17th February
Manchester United (A) Drew 1-1
Ward J
Spink, Linton, Gibson, Evans D, Ormsby, Shelton, Ready, Little, Ward J, Cropley, Jenkins, Sub Hopkins.

Sat 24th February
Burnley (H) Won 3-0
Shaw 2, Hopkins
Spink, Linton, Gibson, Evans D, Heath, Jenkins, Hopkins, Little, Shaw, Cropley, Cunningham, Sub Young.

Wed 28th February
Preston North End (H) Won 4-0
Jenkins, Little, Gray 2
Spink, Linton, Gibson, Evans D, Blake, Jenkins, Carrodus, Little, Gray (Young), Cropley, Cunningham.

THE BIG ASTON VILLA BOOK OF THE SEVENTIES

Wed 7th March
Newcastle United (A) Lost 1-3
Shelton
Spink, Linton, Gibson, Heath, Blake, Jenkins, Shelton, Ready, Ward J, Young, Cunningham, Sub Shaw.

Sat 10th March
Sheffield United (H) Won 6-0
Shaw 3, Ormsby, Jenkins, Young
Spink, Morgan, Shelton, Blake, Ormsby, Ollis, Hopkins, Shaw, Jenkins, Young, Cunningham, Sub Jones.

Mon 12th March
Manchester United (H) Won 1-0
Shaw
Spink, Linton, Gibson, Blake, Ormsby, Jenkins, Shelton, Shaw, Deehan, Young, Cunningham, Sub Ollis.

Sat 24th March
Coventry City (A) Lost 0-1
Spink, Linton, Gibson, Blake, Evans D, Young, Hopkins, Shaw, Jenkins, Gilbert, Shelton, Sub Stirland.

Mon 26th March
Huddersfield Town (A) Drew 1-1
Shelton
Spink, Evans D, Gibson, Blake (Linton), Ormsby, Shelton, Young, Shaw, Jenkins, Cropley, Cunningham.

Sat 31st March
Bolton Wanderers (A) Drew 0-0
Spink, Linton, Gibson, Ormsby, McNaught, Jenkins, Shelton, Deehan, Ward J, Cropley, Cunningham, Sub Evans S.

Mon 2nd April
Wolves (H) Lost 2-4
Shelton, Ward J
Spink, Linton, Gibson, Evans D, Blake, Jenkins, Shelton, Deehan, Ward J, Young (Hopkins), Cunningham.

Sat 7th April
Derby County (H) Won 5-2
Ward J 2, Shelton, Cunningham, Linton
Spink, Linton, Gibson, Heath, Ormsby, Jenkins, Shelton, Ward J, O'Dowd, Young, Cunningham, Sub Ollis.

Sat 14th April
West Bromwich Albion (H) Won 3-2
Young 2, Ready
Spink, Linton, Williams, Heath, Blake, Jenkins, Shelton, Craig, O'Dowd, Young, Ready, Sub Hopkins.

Mon 16th April
Blackburn Rovers (A) Lost 0-1
Spink, Jones, Williams, Heath, Ormsby, Hopkins, Deacy, Craig, Ready, Shaw (O'Dowd), Young.

Wed 18th April
Sheffield Wednesday (A) Lost 0-3
Spink, Linton, McGowan, O'Dowd, Williams, Craig, Shelton, Ward J, Ready, Young, Cunningham (Deacy).

Sat 21st April
Leeds United (H) Drew 1-1
Shaw
Spink, McGowan, Williams, Heath, Ormsby, Craig, Hopkins, Shaw, O'Dowd, Young, Ollis, Sub Ready.

Mon 23rd April
Nottingham Forest (H) Drew 0-0
Spink, McGowan, Williams, Heath, Blake, Jenkins, Ollis, Shaw, Ready (O'Dowd), Young, Cunningham.

Wed 25th April
Blackpool (A) Drew 0-0
Spink, Morgan, Heath, Blake, Williams, Deacy, Young (Cunningham), Jenkins, Hopkins, O'Dowd, Shaw,

Sat 28th April
Liverpool (A) Drew 1-1
Shaw
Spink, Linton, Williams, Blake, Ormsby, Deacy, Hopkins, Shaw, Ready, Young, Jenkins, Sub Cunningham.

Mon 30th April
Blackpool (H) Drew 1-1
Little
Kendall, Linton, Williams, Evans D, Ormsby (Cunningham), Jenkins, Deacy, Hopkins, Little, Ward J, Young.

Thu 3rd May
Everton (A) Won 2-1
Deacy, Ready
Spink, Linton, Williams, O'Dowd, Evans D, Craig, Deacy, Ward J, Ready, Young, Cunningham, Sub Jones.

Sat 5th May
Sheffield Wednesday (H) Lost 0-1
Spink, Morgan, Williams, Blake, Evans D, Craig, Deacy, Ward J, Ready, Young, Cunningham, Sub Jones.

Tue 8th May
Bury (H) Lost 2-4
Little, Cunningham
Spink, Morgan, Williams, Blake, Evans D, Craig, Deacy, Little, Ward J, Young, Cunningham, Sub Ready.

Central League Table 1978 - 79

Pos	Team	P	W	D	L	F	A	GD	Pts
1	Liverpool	42	30	7	5	89	34	55	67
2	Nottingham Forest	42	26	6	10	82	38	44	58
3	Stoke City	42	23	11	8	65	45	20	57
4	Manchester City	42	23	9	10	70	45	25	55
5	Wolverhampton Wanderers	42	21	11	10	79	42	37	53
6	West Bromwich Albion	42	18	12	12	80	51	29	48
7	Coventry City	42	19	8	15	87	71	16	46
8	Sheffield Wednesday	42	19	6	17	74	68	6	44
9	Leeds United	42	14	16	12	50	49	1	44
10	**Aston Villa**	42	16	11	15	67	54	13	43
11	Manchester United	42	17	9	16	66	58	8	43
12	Derby County	42	17	9	16	67	64	3	43
13	Everton	42	18	7	17	50	49	1	43
14	Burnley	42	15	9	18	42	56	-14	39
15	Huddersfield Town	42	13	11	18	52	58	-6	37
16	Blackburn Rovers	42	11	13	18	53	69	-16	35
17	Bolton Wanderers	42	11	13	18	61	83	-22	35
18	Sheffield United	42	12	9	21	55	88	-33	33
19	Newcastle United	42	12	8	22	44	72	-28	32
20	Blackpool	42	11	6	25	41	68	-27	28
21	Bury	42	9	4	29	54	104	-50	22
22	Preston North End	42	6	7	29	46	107	-61	19

1979/80

Central League

Wed 22nd August
Newcastle United (A) Won 3-1
Donovan 3
Spink, Gidman, Williams, Blake, Ormsby, Carrodus, Hopkins, Shaw, Donovan, Jones, Young, Sub Ward.

Sat 25th August
Everton (A) Drew 1-1
Shaw
Spink, Gidman, Deacy, Blake, Ormsby, Carrodus, Hopkins, Shaw, Donovan, Jones (Stirland), Young.

Sat 1st September
Sheffield United (H) Won 5-1
Ormsby, Hopkins, Gray, Ward 2
Kendall, Jones, Deacy, Blake, Ormsby, Carrodus, Hopkins, Ward, Gray, Stirland, Young, Sub O'Dowd.

Sat 8th September
Bury (A) Lost 0-2
Spink, Linton, Deacy, Heath, Blake, Carrodus, Hopkins, O'Dowd (Stirland), Donovan, Jones, Young.

Sat 15th September
Manchester United (home) Won 1-0
Donovan
Spink, Jones, Gibson, Williams, Blake, Shelton, Hopkins, Stirland, Donovan, Little, Young, Sub Deacy.

Wed 19th September
Sheffield Wednesday (H) Drew 0-0
Spink, Deacy, Gibson (Jones), Williams, Ormsby, Shelton, Hopkins, Stirland, Donovan, Shaw, Young.

Sat 29th September
Preston North End (H) Drew 0-0
Spink, Linton, Gibson, Blake, Ormsby, Jones, Hopkins, Shaw, Donovan (O'Dowd), Stirland, Young.

Mon 1st October
Derby County (H) Drew 1-1
Shaw (pen)
Spink, Linton, Gibson, Williams, Ormsby, Shelton, Morley, Shaw, Donovan, Jones, Young, Sub O'Dowd.

Sat 6th October
Blackburn Rovers (A) Won 2-1
Morley, Young
Spink, Jones, Deacy, Williams, Blake, Shelton, Morley, Hopkins, O'Dowd, Donovan, Young, Sub Stirland.

Wed 10th October
Newcastle United (H) Won 6-1
Morley 3, Shaw, Donovan, Young
Spink, Jones, Deacy, Williams, Blake, Shelton, Morley, Shaw, Donovan, Hopkins, Young, Sub O'Dowd.

Sat 13th October
West Bromwich Albion (A) Won 1-0
Shelton
Spink, Jones, Deacy, Williams, Blake, Carrodus, Morley, O'Dowd, Donovan, Hopkins, Shelton, Sub Young.

Sat 20th October
Burnley (H) Won 2-0
O'Dowd, Gibson
Spink, Deacy, Gibson, Williams, McNaught, Carrodus, Morley, O'Dowd, Donovan, Hopkins, Jones, Sub Blake.

Wed 24th October
Nottingham Forest (H) Drew 0-0
Spink, Deacy, Gibson, Williams, McNaught, Carrodus, Morley, O'Dowd, Donovan, Heard, Shelton, Sub Hopkins.

Sat 27th October
Wolves (H) Drew 1-1
Morley
Spink, Jones, Deacy, Williams, Blake, Hopkins, Morley, Shelton, O'Dowd, Heard, Young, Sub Stirland.

Sat 3rd November
Bolton Wanderers (A) Drew 1-1
Shelton
Spink, Jones, Deacy, Heard, Blake, Carrodus, Morley, Shelton, O'Dowd, Cropley, Young, Sub Heath.

Mon 5th November
Bolton Wanderers (H) Won 4-2
Morley 2, Donovan 2
Spink, Jones, Deacy, Heard, Ormsby, Carrodus, Morley, Shelton, Donovan, Cropley, Young, Sub O'Dowd.

Sat 10th November
Stoke City (H) Drew 1-1
Donovan
Spink, Jones, Deacy, Williams, Blake, Carrodus, Morley, Hopkins, Donovan, Cropley, Heard, Sub Birch.

Tue 20th November
Huddersfield Town (A) Won 3-1
Donovan 2, Deacy
Spink, Deacy, Gibson, Williams, Blake, Carrodus, Morley, Bullivant, Donovan, Shelton, Young, Sub Hopkins.

Sat 24th November
Liverpool (A) Lost 0-3
Spink, Linton, Gibson, Williams, Blake, Carrodus, Morley, Bullivant, Donovan, Shelton (Hopkins), Cropley.

Sat 1st December
Manchester City (H) Won 2-0
Bullivant, Morley
Spink, Linton, Deacy, Williams, Blake, Bullivant, Morley, Shelton, Donovan, Cropley, Heard, Sub Jones.

Sat 8th December
Leeds United (A) Lost 3-4
Cropley, Shelton 2
Spink, Linton, Deacy, Williams, Blake, Carrodus, Hopkins, Shelton, Donovan, Cropley, Heard, Sub Jones.

Tue 18th December
Coventry City (A) Lost 0-3
Spink, Linton, Jones, Williams, Blake, Heard, Hopkins, Shelton, O'Dowd, Cropley, Young, Sub Stirland.

Sat 29th December
Everton (H) Lost 0-1
Spink, Linton, Deacy, Williams (Young), Evans, Jones, Morley, Shelton, O'Dowd, Cropley, Heard.

THE BIG ASTON VILLA BOOK OF THE SEVENTIES

Sat 5th January
Blackpool (H) Won 2-1
Jenkins, Shelton (pen)
Spink, Deacy, Pejic, Bullivant, Ormsby, Heard, Morley, Shelton, Geddis (Hopkins), Cropley, Jenkins.

Sat 12th January
Sheffield United (A) Won 4-2
Hopkins 2, Blake, Shelton
Kendall, Linton, Pejic, Bullivant, Blake, Mail, Morley, Shelton, Jenkins, Cropley, Hopkins, Sub Jones.

Sat 26th January
Bury (H) Won 1-0
Cropley
Spink, Deacy, Pejic, Bullivant, Ormsby, Blake, Morley, Jenkins (Hopkins), Geddis, Cropley, Young.

Sat 2nd February
Manchester United (A) Lost 1-2
Geddis
Spink, Linton, Pejic, Bullivant, Ormsby, Heard, Shelton, Jenkins, Geddis, Cropley, Young, Sub Deacy.

Wed 20th February
Nottingham Forest (A) Lost 0-1
Spink, Linton, Pejic, Bullivant, Blake, Heard, Hopkins, Shelton, Morley, Deacy. Sub req

Sat 23rd February
West Bromwich Albion (H) Lost 1-2
Young
Spink, Linton, Pejic, Bullivant, Mail, Heard, Shelton, Stirland, Jones, Deacy, Young, Sub Hopkins.

Tue 4th March
Preston North End (A) Drew 1-1
Heard
Spink, Deacy, Pejic, Williams, Blake, Stirland, Shelton, Heard, Jenkins, Linton, Young. Sub Hopkins

Sat 8th March
Wolves (A) Won 2-1
Cropley 2
Spink, Deacy, Pejic, Blake, Mail, Hopkins, Morley, Shelton, Geddis, Cropley, Young. Sub req

Tue 11th March
Burnley (A) Drew 1-1
Geddis
Spink, Deacy, Pejic, Heard, Blake, Shelton, Hopkins, Jones, Geddis, Cropley, Young. Sub req

Fri 14th March
Blackburn Rovers (H) Drew 1-1
Cropley
Spink, Deacy, Pejic, Heard, Blake, Jones (Stirland), Hopkins, Walters, Geddis, Cropley, Young.

Sat 22nd March
Stoke City (A) Drew 1-1
Cropley
Spink, Taylor, Deacy, Mail, Blake, Hopkins, Jones, Geddis, Donovan, Cropley, Young.

Tue 25th March
Derby County (A) Won 1-0
Geddis
Spink, Taylor, Deacy, Mail, Blake, Stirland, Jones, Jenkins, Geddis, Cropley, Young.

372

Sat 29th March
Huddersfield Town (H) Won 3-1
Geddis, Donovan 2

Spink, Taylor, Deacy, Mail, Blake, Bullivant, Geddis, Little, Donovan, Cropley, Young, Sub Jones.

Mon 7th April
Coventry City (H) Lost 0-1

Spink, Taylor, Deacy, Mail, Blake, Bullivant, Ames, Jenkins, Jones, Cropley, Young, Sub Stirland.

Sat 12thApril
Manchester City (A) Lost 1-2
Shaw

Spink, Taylor, Deacy, McNaught, Blake, Bullivant, Shaw, Little, Donovan, Cropley, Young.

Tue 15th April
Sheffield Wednesday (A) Drew 0-0

Spink, Taylor, Deacy, Mail, Blake, Stirland, Hopkins, Bullivant, Ames, Jenkins, Young.

Sat 19th April
Liverpool (H) Lost 1-4
Blake

Spink, Taylor, Jones, Mail, Blake, Stirland, Hopkins, Bullivant, Donovan, Ames, Young, Sub Jenkins.

Sat 26th April
Blackpool (A) Drew 0-0

Spink, Taylor, Jones, Stirland, Walker, Jenkins, Hopkins, Bullivant, Ames, Ready, Young.

Sat 3rd May
Leeds United (H) Drew 1-1
Deacy

Spink, Deacy, Jones, Stirland, Mail, Bullivant, Shelton, Jenkins, Donovan, Cropley, Young, Sub Hopkins.

Central League Table 1979 - 80

Pos	Team	P	W	D	L	F	A	GD	Pts
1	Liverpool	42	21	14	7	92	46	46	56
2	Coventry City	42	23	9	10	96	57	39	55
3	Nottingham Forest	42	22	10	10	69	44	25	54
4	Manchester United	42	20	13	9	70	46	24	53
5	West Bromwich Albion	42	18	15	9	73	49	24	51
6	Everton	42	20	10	12	73	46	27	50
7	Wolverhampton Wanderers	42	21	8	13	70	46	24	50
8	**Aston Villa**	**42**	**16**	**15**	**11**	**59**	**47**	**12**	**47**
9	Burnley	42	18	10	14	46	49	-3	46
10	Manchester City	42	15	15	12	62	56	6	45
11	Derby County	42	14	16	12	59	57	2	44
12	Sheffield Wednesday	42	18	7	17	68	61	7	43
13	Stoke City	42	11	17	14	45	49	-4	39
14	Blackpool	42	13	12	17	60	68	-8	38
15	Huddersfield Town	42	14	10	18	58	66	-8	38
16	Newcastle United	42	14	10	18	41	55	-14	38
17	Blackburn Rovers	42	14	7	21	60	85	-25	35
18	Bury	42	13	8	21	49	86	-37	34
19	Preston North End	42	10	11	21	42	69	-27	31
20	Leeds United	42	9	9	24	47	75	-28	27
21	Bolton Wanderers	42	8	10	24	45	75	-30	26
22	Sheffield United	42	7	10	25	47	99	-52	24

JUNIOR + YOUTH COMPETITIONS

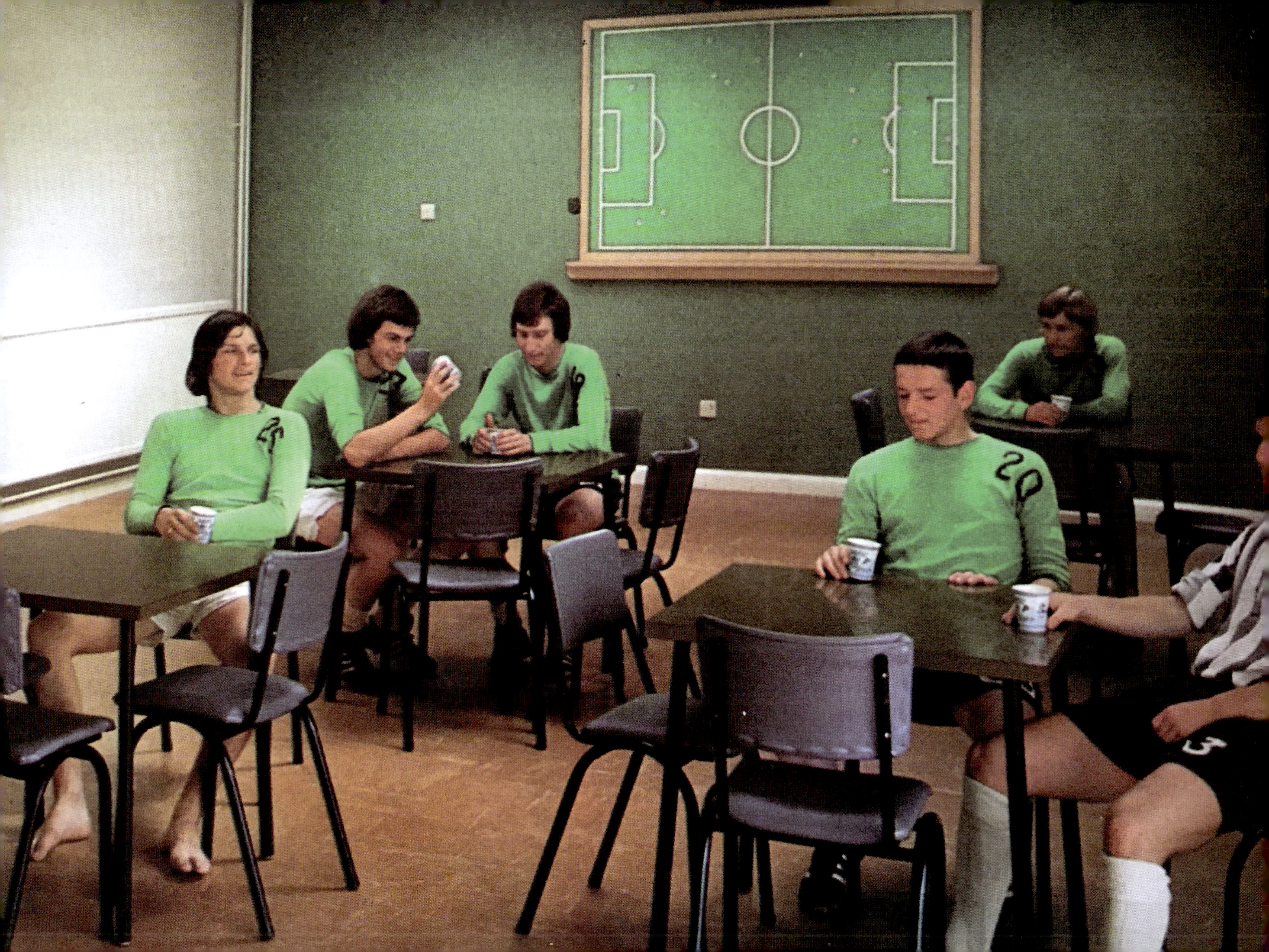
20
3

THE BIG ASTON VILLA BOOK OF THE SEVENTIES

SOUTHERN JUNIOR FLOODLIT CUP

1970/71

Wed 16th September
Oxford United (H) preliminary round Won 4-0
Little B 3, Brady
Knowles, Hughes, Child, Burns, McMillan, Smith, Brown, Melling, Little B, Fellows, Brady, Sub Cook.

Wed 14th October
Crystal Palace (H) 1st round Drew 3-3
Little B, Fellows, Cook
Knowles, Hughes, Child, McMillan, Burns, Brown, Melling, Little B, Fellows, Brady, Cook, Sub Smith.

Wed 4th November
Crystal Palace (A) 1st round replay Won 3-2 after extra time
Brady 2, George
Knowles, Hughes, McMillan, Child, Burns, Brown, Melling, Little B, George, Brady, Cook, Sub Smith.

Mon 23rd November
West Ham United (away) 2nd round Lost 0-2
Knowles, Dorrian, McMillan, Burns, Stark, Child, Melling, Brady, Little B, Smith, Cook, Sub George.

1970/71 Villa's first time in the competition. A young Brian Little, later to be a claret and blue legend, cup winner and manager with 'his club' stole the headlines with a hat-trick in a 4-0 win

---

ASTON VILLA F.C.

President: Mr Pat MATTHEWS
Chairman: Mr Douglas ELLIS   Vice-Chairman: Mr Jim HARTLEY
Directors: Mr Harry KARTZ, Mr Bob MACKAY, Mr Harry PARKES
Secretary: Alan BENNETT   Manager: Vic CROWE   Commercial Manager: Eric WOODWARD
Aston Villa Grounds, Trinity Road, Birmingham 6. Tel.: 021-327 6604

Wednesday, August 16, 1970

Southern Junior Floodlit Cup
Preliminary Round

TODAY'S LINE-UP

ASTON VILLA YOUTHS (Claret and Blue)		OXFORD YOUTHS (Gold and Black)
GORDON KNOWLES	1	DANNY DYMOND
JIMMY HUGHES	2	NEIL HARTIGAN
PAUL CHILD	3	DAVID MILLER
JOE BURNS	4	JIM LIGHT
ALEXIS McMILLAN	5	NICK LOWE
GARY SMITH	6	BOB EVANS
JIMMY BROWN	7	KEN AYRES
BRIAN MELLING	8	DAVID KEMP
BRIAN LITTLE	9	STEPHEN BARNETT
GREG FELLOWS	10	JOHN FLEMING
MICHEAL BRADY	11	DAVID JONES
ALISTAIR COOK	Sub	

Referee: Mr. K. S. Smith (Birmingham)   Linesmen: Mr. C. Smedley (Red Flag)
Mr. B. E. Dickerson (Orange Flag)

Price **3d.**

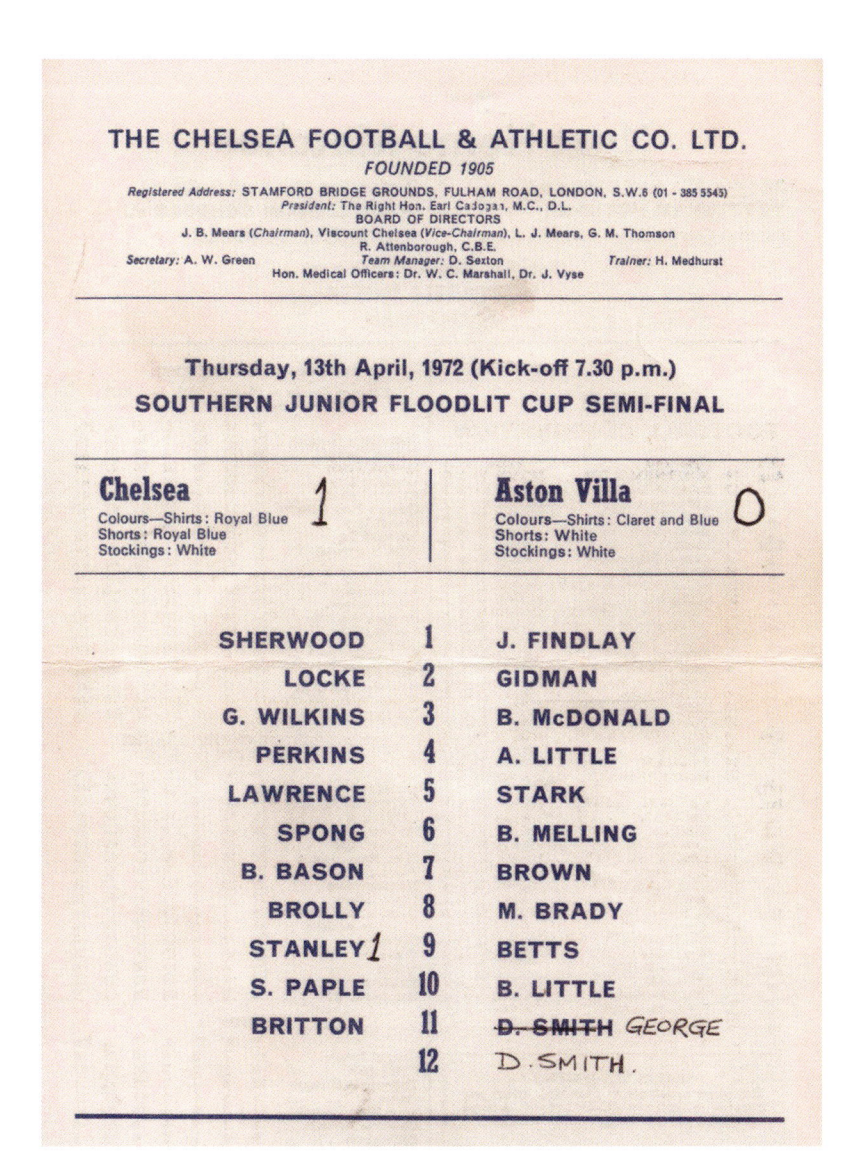

1971/72 Chelsea win 1-0 at Stamford Bridge to gain revenge for their recent FA Youth Cup quarter-final defeat at Villa Park

1971/72

Mon 18th October
Arsenal (H) 2nd round Won 2-1
Little B, Brady (pen)
Findlay, Gidman, Stark, Little A, Dyer, Melling, George, Little B, Betts, Brady, Smith, Sub McDonald.

Thurs 6th April
West Ham United (H) quarter-final Won 2-0
Little B 2
Findlay, Gidman, Dyer, Little A, Stark, Brown, George, Melling, Betts, Little B, Brady, Sub Smith.

Thurs 13th April
Chelsea (A) semi-final Lost 0-1
Findlay, Gidman, McDonald, Little A, Stark, Melling, Brown, Brady, Betts (Smith), Little B, George.

1972/73

Mon 16th October
Oxford United (H) 1st round Won 2-0
Campbell, Place
Peyton, Barrett, McDonald, Little A (Pelosi), Dyer, Overton, Masefield, Smith, Campbell, Place, Hunt.

Wed 22nd November
Cambridge United (H) 2nd round Won 5-0
Dyer, Smith, Hunt 2, own goal
Peyton, Barrett, McDonald, Overton, Dyer, Masefield (Ridley), Pelosi, Smith, Campbell, Place, Hunt.

THE BIG ASTON VILLA BOOK OF THE SEVENTIES

Mon 26th February
West Bromwich Albion (H) 3rd round Won 2-1
Hunt, own goal
Peyton, Masefield, McDonald, Little A, Dyer, Overton, Pelosi, Place, Campbell, Smith, Hunt, Sub Ridley.

Mon 2nd April
Bristol City (home) semi-final Drew 0-0
Peyton, Masefield, McDonald, Little A, Dyer, Overton, Pelosi, Place, Campbell, Smith, (Pimblett), Hunt.

Wed 4th April
Bristol City (A) semi-final replay Drew 1-1 after extra time
Hunt
Peyton, Masefield, McDonald, Little A, Dyer, Overton, Pelosi, Place, Campbell (Pimblett), Smith, Hunt.

Wed 18th April
Bristol City (H) semi-final 2nd replay Won 4-0
Hunt 3, Campbell
Peyton, Masefield, McDonald, Little A, Overton, Pimblett, Pelosi, Place, Campbell, Smith, Hunt, Sub Davidson.

Wed 16th May
Ipswich Town (H) Final 1st leg Lost 0-1
Peyton, Masefield, McDonald, Little A, Dyer, Overton, Pelosi, Pimblett, Campbell, Place, Hunt, Sub Ridley.

Fri 18th May
Ipswich Town (H) Final 2nd leg Won 2-0
Hunt, Campbell
Peyton, Masefield, McDonald, Little A, Barnes, Overton, Pelosi, Pimblett, Campbell, Place, Hunt, Sub Ridley.

Aston Villa lift the Southern Junior Floodlit Cup [pictured right]

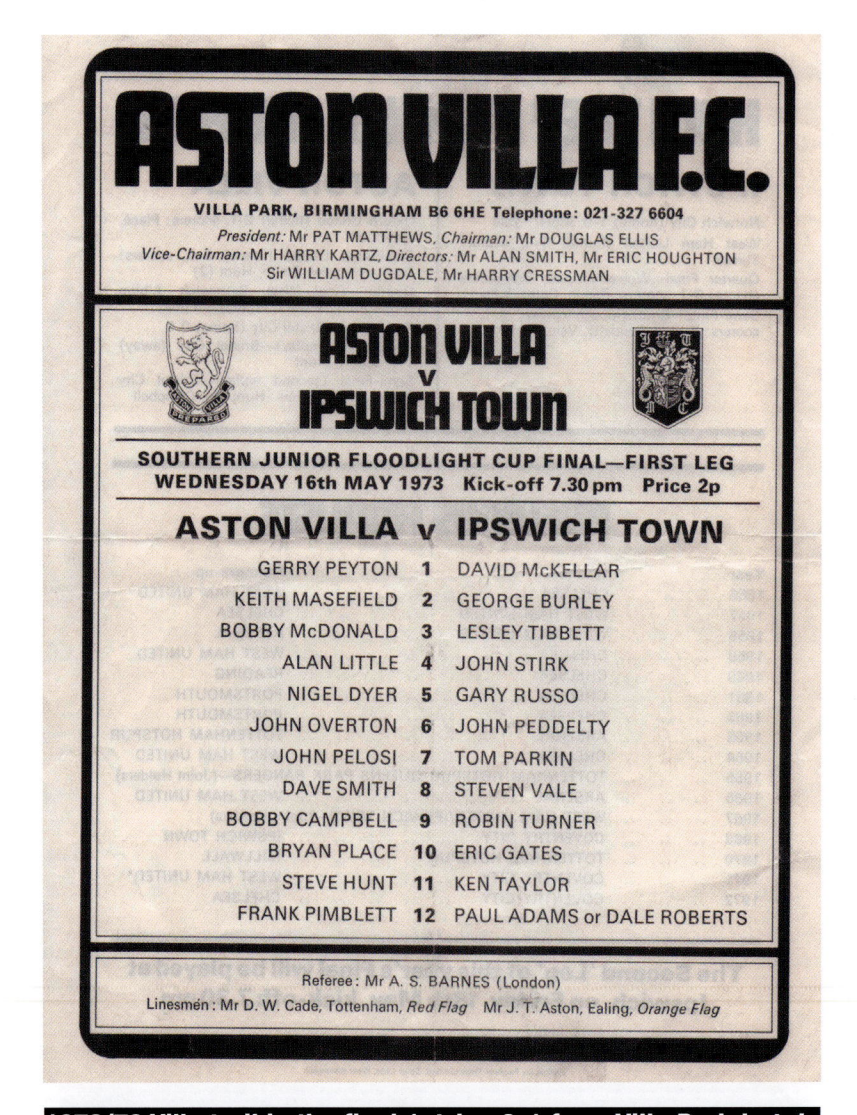

1972/73 Villa trail in the final 1st-leg 0-1 from Villa Park but do the business by winning 2-0 at Portman Road. Ipswich Town's side contains future international players, Burley and Gates, while Steve Hunt would also go on to gain caps for his country

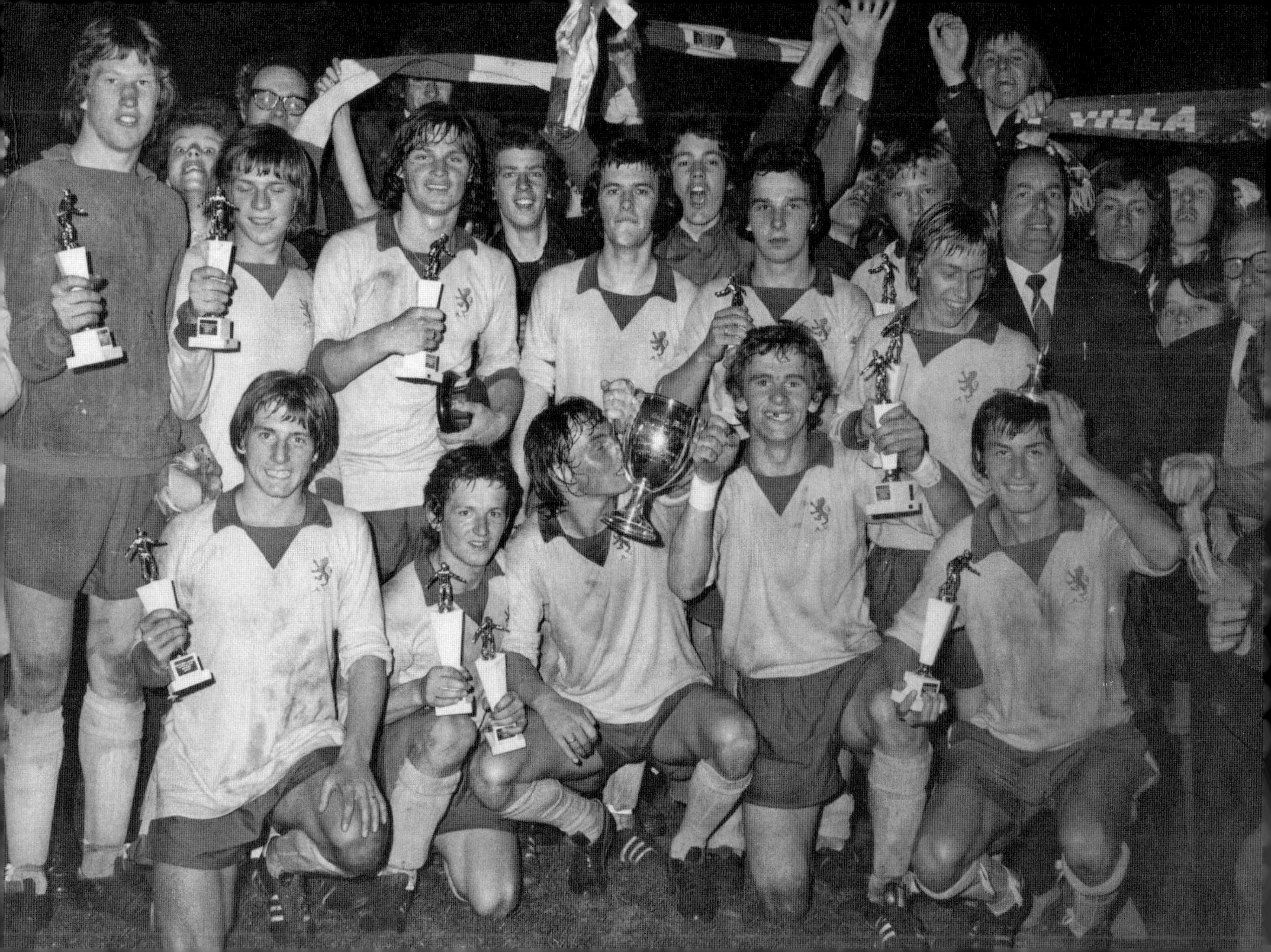
VILLA

THE BIG ASTON VILLA BOOK OF THE SEVENTIES

1973/74

Statement released February 1974.

"Because of a ban on the use of floodlights, this popular and important competition has been suspended until the Government restrictions are relaxed." Villa News & Record 2nd February 1974

Wed 6th March
West Bromwich Albion (H) Lost 2-3
Campbell, Deehan
Lawrence, Masefield, Evans, Pimblett, Overton, Williams, Ridley (Hughes), Davidson, Campbell, Deehan, Sandilands.

1974/75

Mon 16th December
Colchester (A) 1st round Won 1-0
Campbell
Fletcher, Masefield, Hughes, Evans, Young, Pimblett, Purdie, Deehan, Campbell, Williams, Peters, Sub Cowans.

Tue 11th March
Plymouth Argyle (A) 2nd round Won 2-0
Deehan, Hunt K
Fletcher, Masefield, Buttress, Young, Hughes, Williams, Purdie, Peters, Fagan, Wright, Pimblett, Deehan, Hunt K. Team as listed on programme.

Thur 20th March
Bristol City (A) 3rd round Won 2-0
Peters, Hunt K
Team line-up couldn't be sourced.

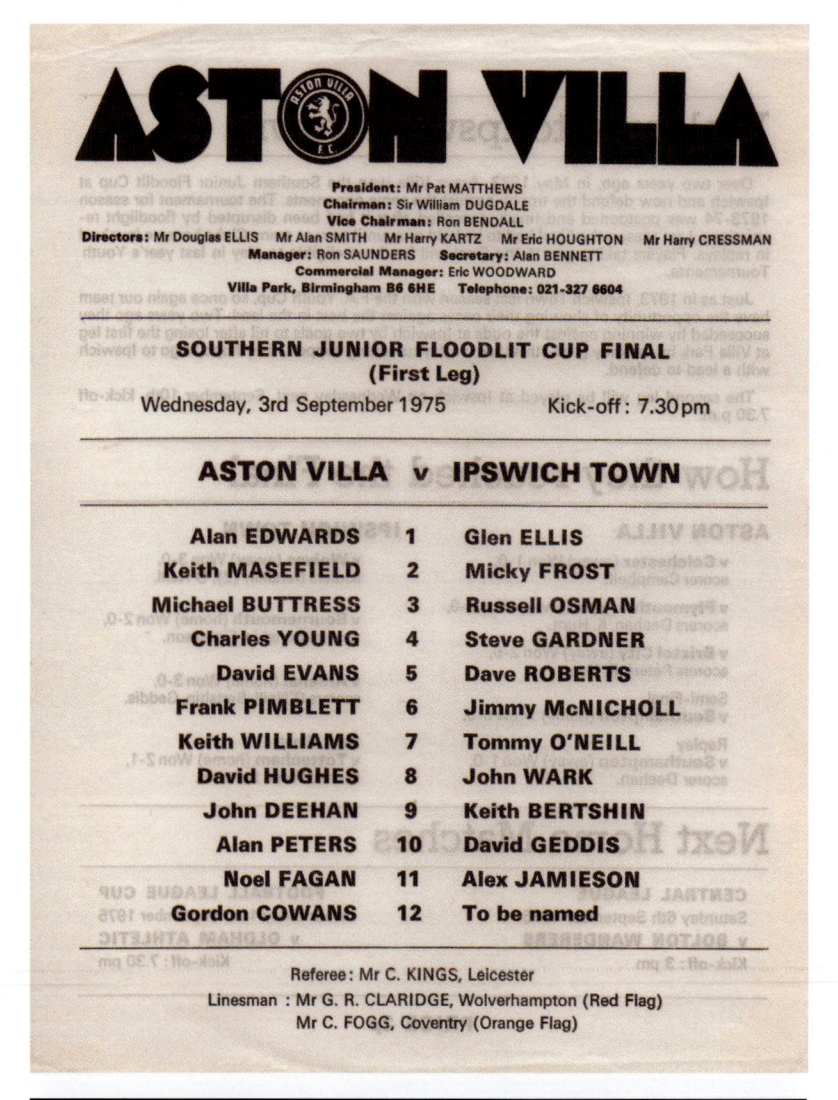

ASTON VILLA

President: Mr Pat MATTHEWS
Chairman: Sir William DUGDALE
Vice Chairman: Ron BENDALL
Directors: Mr Douglas ELLIS Mr Alan SMITH Mr Harry KARTZ Mr Eric HOUGHTON Mr Harry CRESSMAN
Manager: Ron SAUNDERS   Secretary: Alan BENNETT
Commercial Manager: Eric WOODWARD
Villa Park, Birmingham B6 6HE   Telephone: 021-327 6604

SOUTHERN JUNIOR FLOODLIT CUP FINAL
(First Leg)
Wednesday, 3rd September 1975   Kick-off: 7.30 pm

ASTON VILLA   v   IPSWICH TOWN

Alan EDWARDS	1	Glen ELLIS
Keith MASEFIELD	2	Micky FROST
Michael BUTTRESS	3	Russell OSMAN
Charles YOUNG	4	Steve GARDNER
David EVANS	5	Dave ROBERTS
Frank PIMBLETT	6	Jimmy McNICHOLL
Keith WILLIAMS	7	Tommy O'NEILL
David HUGHES	8	John WARK
John DEEHAN	9	Keith BERTSHIN
Alan PETERS	10	David GEDDIS
Noel FAGAN	11	Alex JAMIESON
Gordon COWANS	12	To be named

Referee: Mr C. KINGS, Leicester
Linesman : Mr G. R. CLARIDGE, Wolverhampton (Red Flag)
Mr C. FOGG, Coventry (Orange Flag)

1974/75 With the previous season's SJFC competition suspended due to the electricity shortages, Villa retained the trophy by beating Ipswich Town 5-4 on aggregate. Eight of the listed players for the home-leg would feature in the Villa first-team.

380

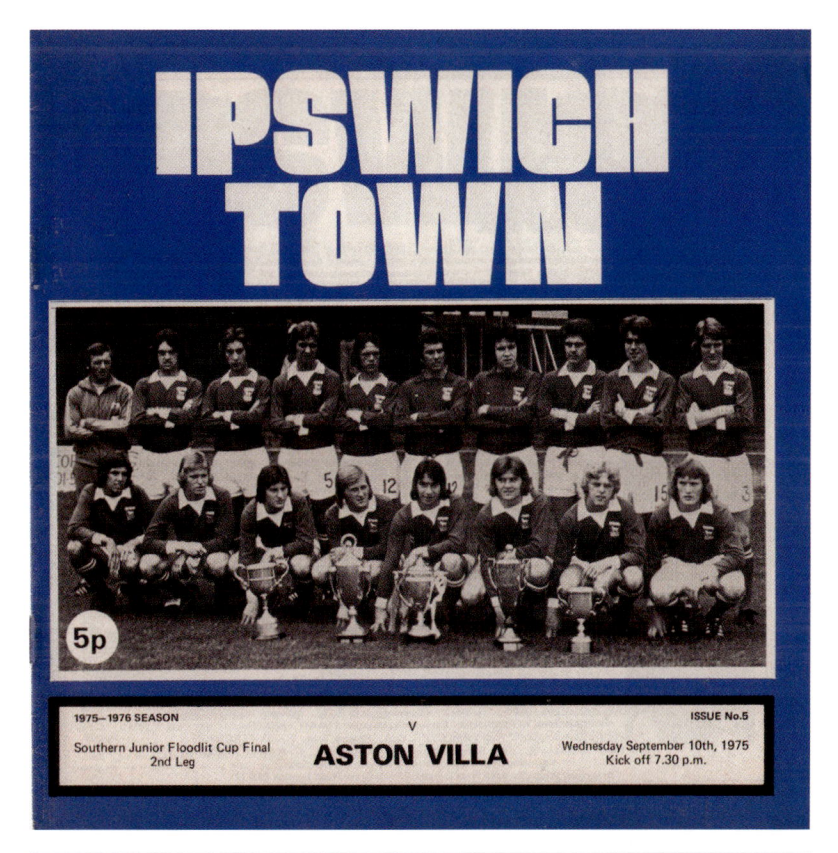

1974/75 Ipswich produced a nice programme for the final 2nd-leg but it wasn't enough to turn the tide as Villa drew 2-2, following their 3-1 win at home.

Mon 21st April
Southampton (H) semi-final Drew 0-0 after extra time
Fletcher, Masefield, Buttress, Williams, Young, Hughes, Pimblett, Purdie, Hunt K, Deehan, Peters, Sub Cowans.

In the programme for the above match it states, 'Aston Villa are the holders of the Southern Junior Floodlit Cup, but the competition was not completed last year because of the power emergency involving the use of floodlights.'

April
Southampton (A) semi-final replay Won 1-0
Deehan
Fletcher, Masefield, Buttress, Williams, Young, Hughes, Pimblett, Purdie, Hunt K, Deehan, Peters, Sub Cowans. Team as listed on programme.

Wed 3rd September
Ipswich Town (H) Final 1st leg Won 3-1
Deehan, Fagan, Pimblett
Edwards, Masefield, Buttress, Young, Evans D, Pimblett, Williams, Hughes, Deehan, Peters, Fagan, Subs Cowans, Price.

In the programme for the above match it states, 'Last season the Final had to be held over until now as many clubs became involved in replays. Players taking part in the Final will be those eligible to play in last year's Youth Tournaments.'

Wed 10th September
Ipswich Town (A) Final 2nd leg Drew 2-2
Williams, Peters
Edwards, Masefield, Buttress, Young, Evans D, Pimblett, Williams, Hughes, Deehan, Peters, Fagan, Subs Cowans, Price.

Aston Villa win 5-3 on aggregate to retain the Southern Junior Floodlit Cup.

THE BIG ASTON VILLA BOOK OF THE SEVENTIES

1975/76

Mon 29th September
Orient (A) preliminary round Won 4-3
Young, Cowans, Deehan, Peters
Parsons, Short, Buttress, Young, Evans D, Cowans, Price, Hughes, Fagan, Deehan, Peters, Sub Walker.

Tue 11th November
Coventry City (A) 1st round Won 2-1
Peters, Short
Parsons, Hughes, Buttress, Young, Evans D, Short, Price, Fagan, Peters, Cowans, Greensmith, Sub Coles.

Mon 26th January
Bristol City (H) 2nd round Won 3-2
Cowans 2, own goal
Wyshnia, Hughes, Buttress, Evans, Young, Wilson, Fagan, Price, Deehan, Cowans, Peters, Subs Coles, O'Dowd.

Mon 16th February
Portsmouth (H) semi-final Won 2-1
Deehan 2
Parsons, Hughes, Buttress, Young, Evans, Price, Fagan, Wilson, Cowans, Deehan, Peters, Subs O'Dowd, Capaldi.

Bottom left clockwise: Keith Masefield, Alan Little, David Smith, Dougie George, Roy Stark and Tony Betts at Villa hostel on the Chester Road ran by Walter and Norma Cowans (parents of Villa legend Gordon)

Mon 5th April
Ipswich Town (home) Final 1st leg Won 2-0
Cowans, Price
Parsons, Hughes, Buttress, Young, Evans, Price, Fagan, Wilson (O'Dowd), Deehan, Cowans, Peters, Sub Capaldi.

Mon 12th April
Ipswich Town (A) Final 2nd leg Drew 1-1
Deehan
Parsons, Hughes, Buttress, Evans, Young, Price, Fagan, Wilson, Deehan, Cowans, Peters, Subs O'Dowd, Capaldi.

Aston Villa win 3-1 over two legs to win the Southern Junior Floodlit Cup for a third time.

1976/77

Mon 11th October
Leicester City (H) 1st round Drew 1-1
Capaldi
Desmond, Mason, Price, Ormsby, Williams G, Wilson (Hendry), Fagan (Linton), Cowans, Coles, O'Dowd, Capaldi.

Mon 18th October
Leicester City (A) 1st round replay Won 3-2
Capaldi 2, Coles
Desmond, Mason, Price, Ormsby, Williams G, Fagan, Wilson (Linton), Coles, O'Dowd (Hendry), Cowans, Capaldi.

Wed 24th November
Queens Park Rangers (H) 2nd round Lost 2-4
O'Dowd, Cowans
Desmond, Mason, Price, Ormsby, Williams G, Wilson, Coles, Cowans, Linton, O'Dowd, Capaldi, Subs Fagan, Hendry.

1977/78

Mon 24th October
Watford (A) 1st round Won 4-0
Williams, Capaldi, Shaw, Gibson
Coton, Morgan, Ormsby, Williams, Gibson, Capaldi, Hendry, Jenkins, Linton, O'Dowd, Shaw, Subs Ollis, Rees.

Mon 14th November
Orient (H) 2nd round Drew 1-1
Shaw
Kendall, Morgan, Gibson, Linton, Ormsby, Williams, Rees, Hendry, Capaldi Shaw, Ollis, Sub Jenkins.

THE BIG ASTON VILLA BOOK OF THE SEVENTIES

Wed 30th November
Orient (away) 2nd round replay Lost 0-2
Kendall, Morgan, Gibson, Williams, Ormsby, Linton, Jenkins, Hendry, Ollis, Shaw, Capaldi Subs Rees, Stevenson.

1978/79

Mon 23rd October
Tottenham Hotspur (H) 1st round Won 2-1
Own goal, Hopkins
Kendall, Morgan, Ward, Heath, Ormsby, Ollis (Beech), Hopkins, Shaw, Ames, Jones, Jenkins.

Tue 7th November
Hereford United (A) 2nd round Drew 0-0
Kendall, Morgan, Ward, Ormsby, Heath, Jones, Hopkins, Ollis, Shaw, Ames, Jenkins, Subs Gilbert, Crooks.

Mon 19th February
Hereford United (H) 2nd round replay Won 3-0
Hopkins, Ollis, Shaw (pen)
Kendall, Morgan, Ormsby, Crooks, Heath, Hopkins, Gilbert, Ollis, Jones, Jenkins, Shaw, Subs Stirland, Pugh.

Tue 20th March
Crystal Palace (A) 3rd round Won 4-0
Shaw 3, Hopkins
Kendall, Morgan, Ward I, Ormsby, Blake, Heath, Ollis, Hopkins, Shaw, Jenkins, Gilbert, Stirland, Subs Wilson, Taylor.

Wed 18th April
Coventry City (H) semi-final Won 2-1
Ollis, Hopkins

Kendall, Morgan, Heath, Blake, Ormsby, Ollis, Hopkins, Shaw, Jenkins, Stirland, Jones, Subs Ward I, Pugh.

Fri 4th May
Leicester City (H) Final 1st leg Won 1-0
Jenkins
Kendall, Morgan, Heath, Ormsby, Blake, Jones, Ollis, Stirland, Hopkins, Shaw, Jenkins, Subs, Birch, Ward I.

Thur 10th May
Leicester City (A) 2nd leg Won 4-1
Ormsby 2, Ollis Jones
Kendall, Morgan, Heath, Blake, Ormsby, Ollis, Hopkins, Shaw, Jenkins, Stirland, Jones, Subs Birch, Ward I. Team as listed on programme.

Villa win the SJFC after beating Leicester City 5-1 on aggregate.

1979/80

Tue 4th September
Watford (A) 1st round Drew 0-0
Kendall, Taylor, Blake, Mail, Heath, Hopkins, Walker, Jones, Birch, Walters, Ames, Subs Hollier, Glover.

Mon 17th September
Watford (H) 1st round replay Won 4-0 after extra time
Blake, Birch, Hutchingson 2
Kendall, Taylor, Heath, Mail, Blake, Birch, Hopkins, Jones, Ames, Pugh Hutchinson, Subs Walker, Walters.

Mon 15th October
Chelsea (H) 2nd round Won 2-1
Ames, Walters
Kendall, Taylor, Jones, Mail, Blake, Birch, Hopkins, Heath, Ames, Hutchinson, Walters, Subs Hollier, Walker.

Wed 7th November
Aldershot (A) 3rd round Won 6-1
Jones, Blake, Birch 2, Hutchingson, Walters
Kendall, Taylor, Jones, Mail, Blake, Birch, Hopkins, Heath, Ames, Hutchinson, Walters, Subs Walker, Hollier.

Mon 10th December
Leicester City (H) 4th round Won 2-1
Jones, Walters
Kendall, Taylor, Jones, Mail, Walker, Hopkins, Rees, Heath, Ames, Birch Walters, Subs Glover, Hill C.

Mon 18th February
Bristol Rovers (A) semi-final Won 2-1
Ames, Walters
Team line-up couldn't be sourced.

Mon 31st March
Queens Park Rangers (H) Final 1st leg Won 3-1
Jones, Walters 2
Kendall, Taylor, Heath, Mail, Blake, Walker, Rees, Hopkins, Walters, Jones, Hutchinson, Subs Ames, Rogers. Team as listed on programme.

Fri 2nd May
Queens Park Rangers (A) Final 2nd leg Lost 2-3
Hopkins, Ames
Kendall, Taylor, Heath, Mail, Blake, Birch, Hopkins, Rees, Jones, Walters, Hutchinson. Team as listed on programme.

FA YOUTH CUP

1970/71

Mon 26th October
Coventry Amateurs (H) 1st round Won 4-0
Brady 2, Smith, Little B
Knowles, Child, McMillan, Dorrian, Burns, Smith, Melling, Little B, Fellows, Brady, Cook, Sub George.

Wed 2nd December
Derby County (H) 2nd round Drew 1-1
Smith
Knowles, Dorrian, McMillan, Child, Burns, Brown, Melling, Little B, Fellows (Smith), Brady, Cook.

Mon 7th December
Derby County (A) 2nd round replay Won 1-0
Child
Knowles, Hughes, McMillan, Child, Dorrian, Stark, Melling, Little B, Fellows Brady, George, Sub Smith.

Mon 21st December
Wolverhampton Wanderers (H) 3rd round Lost 0-2
Knowles, Hughes, McMillan, Dorrian, Stark, Child, Melling, Brady, Fellows, Little B, George, Sub Burns.

1971/72

Mon 1st November
Boldmere St Michaels (H) 1st round Won 8-0
Little B 3, Betts 2, Gidman 2, McDonald
Findlay, Gidman, Dyer, Little A, Stark, McDonald, Melling, Brady, Betts, Little B, George, Sub Smith.

Mon 29th November
Port Vale (H) 2nd round Won 7-0
Fellows 3, Betts 2, Melling, Gidman
Findlay, Gidman, McDonald, Little A, Stark (Smith), Melling, Brady, Betts, Little B, Fellows, George.

Mon 20th December
West Bromwich Albion (H) 3rd round Won 3-2
Gidman, Brown, Fellows
Findlay, Gidman, Dyer, Little A, Stark, Brown, Melling, Little B, Betts, Fellows, Brady, Sub George.

Tue 18th December
Birmingham City (A) 4th round Drew 1-1
Betts
Findlay, Gidman, McDonald, Little A, Stark, Melling, George, Brady, Betts, Little B, Brown, Sub Smith.
Att 21,215

Wed 26th January
Birmingham City (H) 4th round replay Won 2-1
Betts, Little A
Findlay, Gidman, McDonald, Little A, Stark, Melling, George, Brown, Betts, Little B, Smith, Sub Brady.
Att 18,922

Tue 22nd February
Chelsea (A) quarter-final Drew 1-1
Little B
Findlay, Gidman, McDonald, Little A, Stark, Melling, Brown, George, Betts, Little B, Brady, Sub Smith.

ASTON VILLA

President: Mr Pat MATTHEWS
Chairman: Mr Douglas ELLIS **Vice-Chairman:** Mr Jim HARTLEY
Directors: Mr Bob MACKAY Mr Harry PARKES, Mr Dick GREENHALGH
Manager: Vic CROWE **Secretary:** Alan BENNETT **Commercial Manager:** Eric WOODWARD
Villa Park, Birmingham B6 6HE Telephone 021-327 6604

PRICE 1p

F.A. YOUTH CHALLENGE CUP

First Round

Monday, 1st November, 1971.   Kick-off 7.30 pm.

ASTON VILLA		BOLDMERE ST. MICHAEL'S
JAKE FINDLAY	1	STEVE McINDOE
JOHN GIDMAN	2	PAUL BEASON
NIGEL DYER	3	JOHN PAYNE
ALAN LITTLE	4	PAUL CARR
ROY STARK	5	MICHAEL WILLIAMS
BOBBY McDONALD	6	CARL BUFFERY
BRIAN MELLING	7	CHRIS COTTON
MICHAEL BRADY	8	STEVE WATHEN
TONY BETTS	9	PAUL HUGHES
BRIAN LITTLE	10	STEVE HOWES
DOUGIE GEORGE	11	MICHAEL WAROM
DAVID SMITH	12	CHRIS DANGERFIELD

[Above] Mr Sweet serves tea to future first-team stars Bobby McDonald and Jake Findlay at their Stetchford digs

[Right] Villa's FA Youth Cup winners from 1972

THE BIG ASTON VILLA BOOK OF THE SEVENTIES

Mon 28th February
Chelsea (H) quarter-final replay Won 3-0 after extra time
Betts, George 2
Findlay, Gidman, McDonald, Little A, Stark, Melling, Brown, George, Betts, Little B, Smith, Sub Brady.

Thurs 23rd March
Arsenal (A) semi-final 1st leg Drew 0-0
Findlay, Gidman, McDonald, Little A, Stark, Melling, Brown (Brady), George, Betts, Little B, Smith.

Mon 27th March
Arsenal (H) semi-final 2nd leg Won 1-0
McDonald
Findlay, Gidman, McDonald, Little A, Stark, Melling, Brown, George, Betts, Little B, Smith, Sub Brady.
Att 14,540

Mon 17th April
Liverpool (H) Final 1st leg Won 1-0
Gidman (pen)
Findlay, Gidman, McDonald, Little A, Stark, Melling, Brown, George, Betts, Little B, Smith, Sub Brady.
Att 16,463

Tue 25th April
Liverpool (A) Final 2nd leg Won 4-2 after extra time
George, Little B 2, own goal
Findlay, Gidman, McDonald, Little A, Stark, Melling, Brown, George, Betts, Little B, Brady (Smith).
Att 16,612

Villa won 5-2 on aggregate to secure their first ever FA Youth Cup victory.

1972/73

Wed 29th November
Boldmere St Michaels (H) 1st round Won 3-1
Dyer, Campbell, McDonald
Peyton, Barrett, McDonald, Overton, Dyer, Masefield, Pelosi, Smith, Campbell, Place, Hunt, Sub Ridley.

Tue 19th December
Swindon Town (H) 2nd round Drew 2-2
Campbell, McDonald
Peyton, Barrett, McDonald, Overton, Dyer, Masefield, Pelosi, Smith, Campbell, Place, Hunt, Sub Taylor.

Tue 9th January
Swindon Town (A) 2nd round replay Lost 0-4
Storey, Place, McDonald, Little A, Dyer, Overton, Pelosi, Masefield, Campbell, Smith (Pimblett), Hunt.

1973/74

Wed 28th November
West Bromwich Albion (A) 1st round Lost 0-1
Peyton, Masefield, Ridley, Overton, Bates, Pimblett, Pelosi, Williams, Deehan, Campbell, Hunt, Sub Howells.

[Right] Action from Villa's first leg win over Liverpool — Mick Brady and Brian Little lurk as Liverpool's Phil Thompson clears the ball defending the Witton End

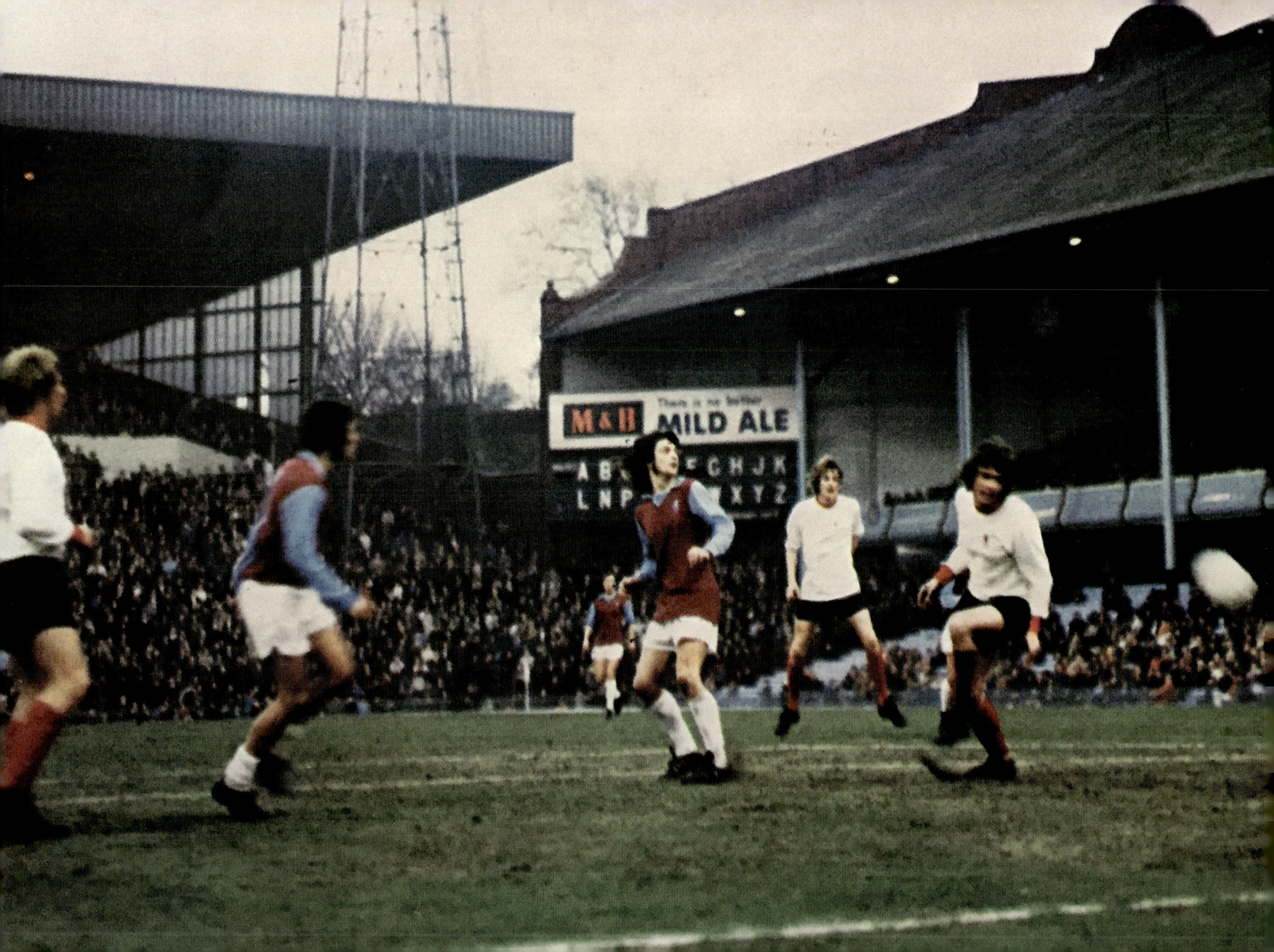
M&B
There is no better
MILD ALE

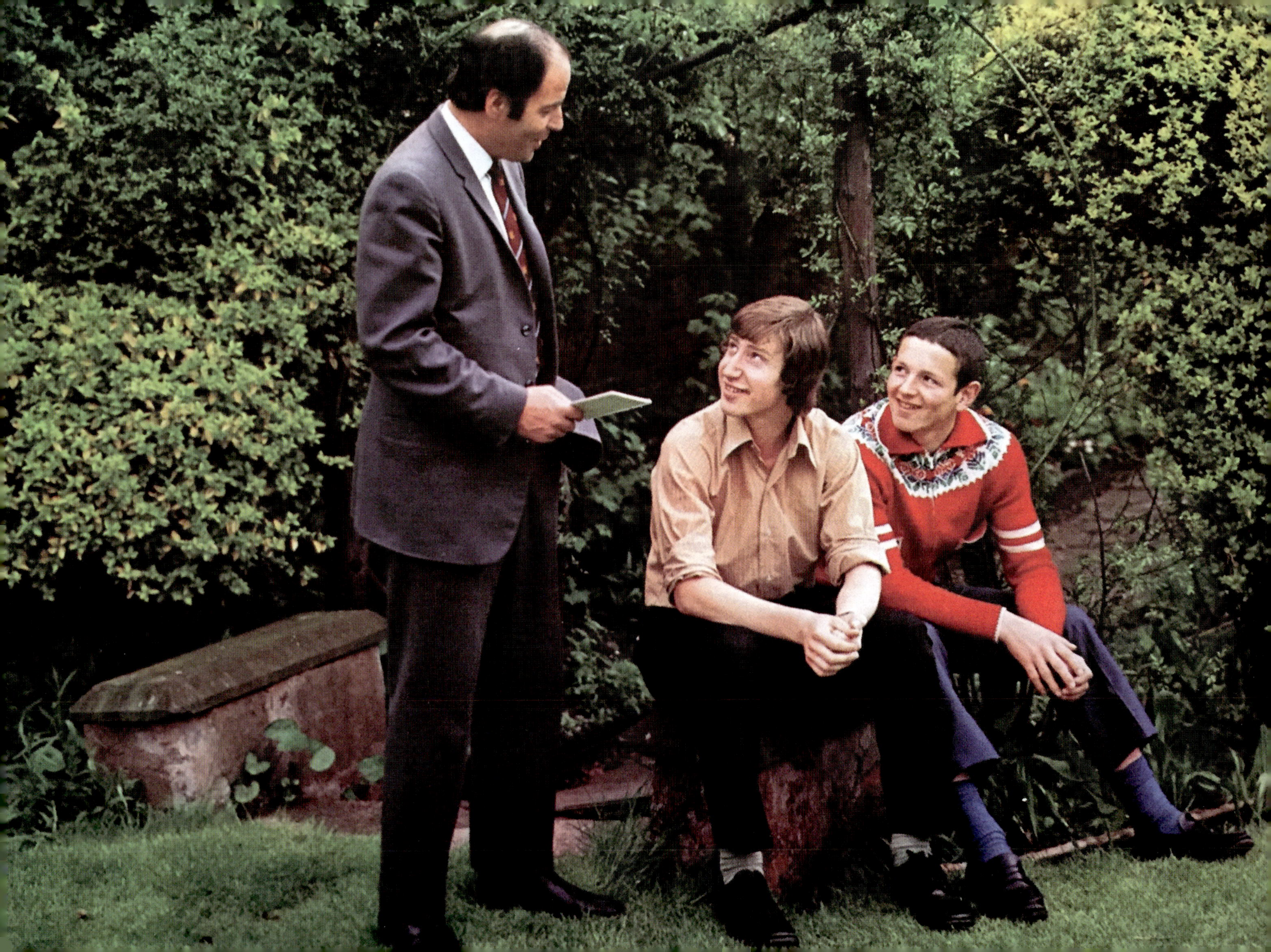

1974/75

Tue 19th November
Coventry City (A) 2nd round Won 2-0
Campbell 2
Fletcher, Masefield, Buttress, Evans D, Young, Pimblett, Purdie, Williams, Deehan, Campbell, Hughes, Sub Cowans.

Mon 23rd December
Bognor Regis Town (H) 3rd round Won 5-0
Deehan, Campbell 2, Williams, Hunt K
Fletcher, Masefield, Hughes, Evans D, Young, Pimblett, Purdie, Williams, Deehan, Campbell, Hunt K, Sub Cowans.

Mon 3rd February
Middlesbrough (A) 4th round Lost 2-3
Campbell, Pimblett
Fletcher, Masefield, Hughes, Evans D, Young, Pimblett, Purdie, Hunt K, Deehan, Campbell, Williams, Sub Peters.

1975/76

Mon 22nd December
Crystal Palace (A) 3rd round Lost 0-1
Parsons, Evans D, Buttress, Short, Young, Price, Fagan, Peters, Coles, Cowans, Hughes, Sub Wilson.

[Left] Villa scout, Neville Briggs, talking to youngsters hopeful of making the grade

1976/77

Wed 8th December
West Bromwich Albion (A) 1st round Drew 1-1
Cowans
Parsons, Stevenson, Wilson, Ormsby, Williams G, Price, Coles, O'Dowd, Capaldi, Cowans, Linton, Sub Gibson.

Wed 5th January
West Bromwich Albion (H) 1st round replay Lost 1-3
O'Dowd
Parsons, Stevenson, Wilson, Ormsby, Williams G, Linton, Gibson (Hendry), Price, Capaldi, Cowans, O'Dowd.

1977/78

Mon 12th December
Nuneaton Borough (H) 2nd round Won 8-0
Ollis, Shaw 4, Capaldi 2, Hendry
Kendall, Morgan, Gibson, Jenkins, Ormsby, Williams, Linton, Hendry, Capaldi, Shaw, Ollis, Sub Rees.

Mon 16th January
Tottenham Hotspur (A) 3rd round Won 2-0
Hendry, Shaw
Kendall, Morgan, Gibson, Jenkins, Ormsby, Williams, Capaldi, Hendry, Linton, Ollis, Shaw, Sub Beech.

Wed 1st February
Southampton (H) 4th round Won 2-1
O'Dowd, Ormsby
Kendall, Morgan, Gibson, Jenkins, Ormsby, Williams, Linton, Shaw, O'Dowd, Hendry, Capaldi, Sub Ollis.

THE BIG ASTON VILLA BOOK OF THE SEVENTIES

Wed 8th March
Grimsby Town (H) 5th round Won 2-0
Shaw, Linton
Kendall, Morgan, Gibson, Jenkins, Ormsby, Williams, Linton, Capaldi, O'Dowd, Shaw, Hendry, Sub Ollis.

Tue 4th April
Burnley (A) semi-final 1st leg Won 3-1
O'Dowd 2, Capaldi
Kendall, Morgan, Gibson, Hendry, Ormsby, Williams, Linton, Shaw, O'Dowd, Capaldi, Jenkins, Sub Ollis.

Mon 10th April
Burnley (H) semi-final 2nd leg Won 1-0
O'Dowd
Kendall, Morgan, Gibson, Hendry, Ormsby, Williams, Linton, Shaw, O'Dowd, Capaldi, Jenkins, Sub Ollis.

Villa go through 4-1 on aggregate.

Thur 27th April
Crystal Palace at Highbury Final Lost 0-1
Kendall, Morgan, Gibson, Linton, Ormsby, Williams, Hendry, Capaldi, O'Dowd, Shaw, Jenkins, Sub Ollis.

Villa lose out in a one-match Final played at Arsenal's Highbury Stadium.

1978/79

Wed 29th November
West Bromwich Albion (A) 2nd round Drew 1-1
Pugh
Kendall, Morgan, Ward, Heath, Ormsby, Ollis, Hopkins, Pugh, Ames, Gilbert, Jenkins, Sub McClean.

Mon 4th December
West Bromwich Albion (H) 2nd round replay Won 1-0
Ames
Kendall, Morgan, Ward, Heath (McClean), Ormsby, Jones, Hopkins, Pugh, Ames, Gilbert, Jenkins.

Mon 8th January
Leicester City (A) 3rd round Drew 1-1
Shaw
Kendall, Morgan (Taylor), Ward, Crooks, Ormsby, Gilbert, Hopkins, Shaw, Pugh, Ames, Jones.

Sat 10th February
Leicester City (H) 3rd round replay Won 1-0
Shaw
Kendall, Morgan, Heath, Crooks, Ormsby, Ollis, Hopkins, Shaw, Pugh (Jones), Gilbert, Jenkins.

Mon 5th March
Luton Town (A) 4th round Lost 1-2
Jones
Kendall, Morgan, Ward I, Crooks, Heath, Ollis, Hopkins, Shaw, Gilbert, Jones, Jenkins, Sub Ames.

1979/80

1st Round - Bye

Mon 3rd December
Derby County (H) 2nd round Won 3-2

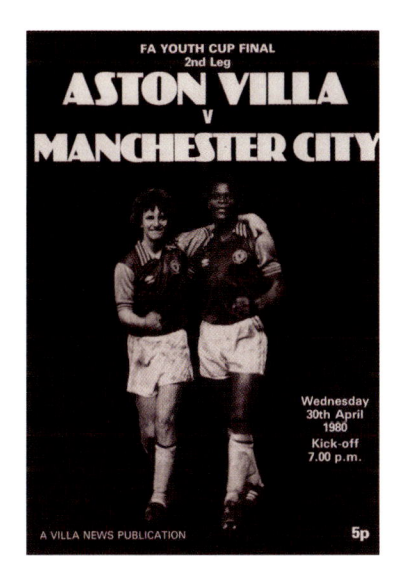

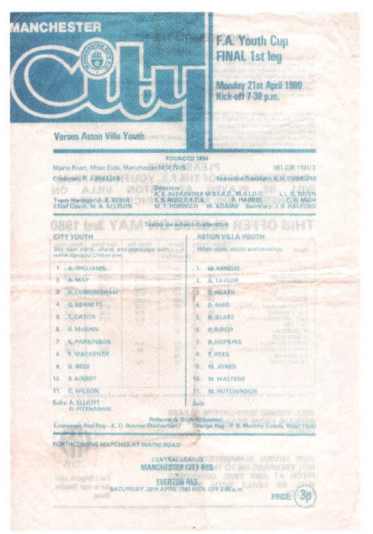

Birch, Heath, Walters
Kendall, Taylor, Jones, Mail, Blake, Birch, Hopkins, Heath, Ames, Walters, Hutchinson, Subs Walker.

Wed 9th January
Hereford United (A) 3rd round Won 5-0
Taylor 2, Birch, Walters, Ames
Kendall, Taylor, Jones, Blake, Mail, Hopkins, Birch, Heath, Hutchinson, Walters (Rees), Ames.

Mon 11th February
Hartlepool United (A) 4th round Won 1-0
Walters
Kendall, Taylor, Blake, Mail, Jones, Hopkins, Birch, Heath, Hutchinson, Ames (Walker), Walters.

Tue 26th February
West Bromwich Albion (A) quarter-final Drew 1-1
Walters
Kendall, Taylor, Jones, Mail, Blake, Birch, Hopkins, Heath, Ames, Hutchinson, Walters, Sub Rees. Team as listed on programme.

Mon 3rd March
West Bromwich Albion (H) quarter-final replay Won 3-2
Own goal, Walters 2
Kendall, Taylor, Blake, Mail, Jones, Hopkins, Rees, Birch, Heath, Hutchinson, Walters, Sub Ames,

Wed 9th April
Millwall (A) semi-final 1st leg Won 2-0
Walters, Hopkins
Kendall, Taylor, Heath, Mail, Blake, Walker, Rees, Hopkins, Walters, Jones, Hutchinson, Sub Ames. Team as listed on programme.

Mon 14th April
Millwall (H) semi-final 2nd leg Drew 0-0
Kendall, Taylor, Heath, Mail, Blake, Birch, Hopkins, Rees, Jones, Walters, Hutchinson, Sub Walker. Team as listed on programme. Villa go through 2-0 on aggregate.

Mon 21st April
Manchester City (A) Final 1st leg Won 3-1
Ames 3
Kendall, Taylor, Heath, Mail, Blake, Birch, Hopkins, Rees, Jones, Walters, Hutchinson. Sub Ames. Team as listed on programme.

Wed 30th April
Manchester City (H) Final 2nd leg Lost 0-1
Kendall, Taylor, Jones, Mail, Blake, Hutchinson, Hopkins, Birch, Heath, Ames, Walters. Sub Rees. Team as listed on programme.

Aston Villa lift the FA Youth Cup for the second time after beating City 3-2 on aggregate.

[Right] Geoff Crudgington arrives at Villa Park – the welcoming committee are Charlie Aitken, Brian Godfrey, Andy Lochhead, with Keith Bradley and Lew Chatterley at the back

FIRST TEAM INFORMATION
APPEARANCES

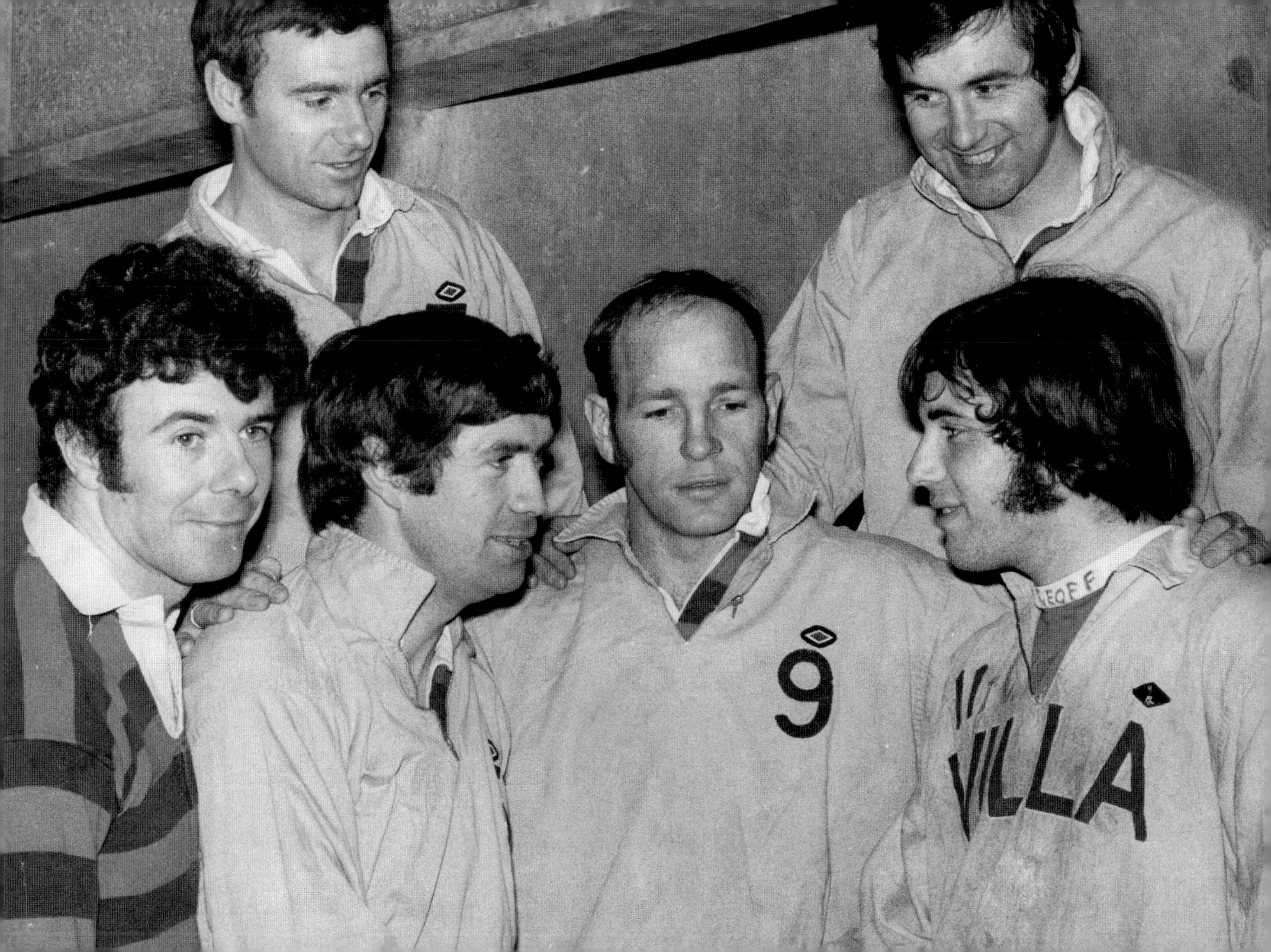
9

THE BIG ASTON VILLA BOOK OF THE SEVENTIES

SEASON 1970-1971

	LEAGUE	GOALS	FA CUP	GOALS	LEAGUE CUP	GOALS	TOTAL	GOALS
CHARLIE AITKEN	44		1	1	10		55	1
BRIAN GODFREY	44	2			9		55	2
IAN 'CHICO' HAMILTON	43+1	9	1		10	3	54+1	12
JOHN DUNN	43		1		10		54	
WILLIE ANDERSON	42	4	1		10	2	53	6
ANDY LOCHHEAD	41	9	1		10	4	52	13
BRIAN TILER	41+1	1	1		9	1	51+1	2
FRED TURNBULL	41	3	1		9		51	3
PAT McMAHON	36+1	8	1		9	4	46+1	12
KEITH BRADLEY	28		1		5		34	
MICHAEL WRIGHT	19				5		24	
BRUCE RIOCH	17+5	5			2		19+5	5
DAVIE GIBSON	13+3	1			4		17+3	1
JIMMY BROWN	9+1		1		4		14+1	
GEOFF VOWDEN	13+1	5					13+1	5
LEW CHATTERLEY	8+1		1		2		11+1	
GEORGE CURTIS	9				2		11	
HARRY GREGORY	10+6	2					10+6	2
GEOFF CRUDGINGTON	3						3	
LIONEL MARTIN	1+1				+1	1	1+2	1
DAVE SIMMONS	1	1					1	1
NEIL RIOCH	+1				+1		+2	

NUMBER OF PLAYERS USED: 22
NUMBER OF GOALSCORERES: 14

[Right] 1970/71: Willie Anderson converts from the penalty spot at home to Fulham in Villa's 1-0 win

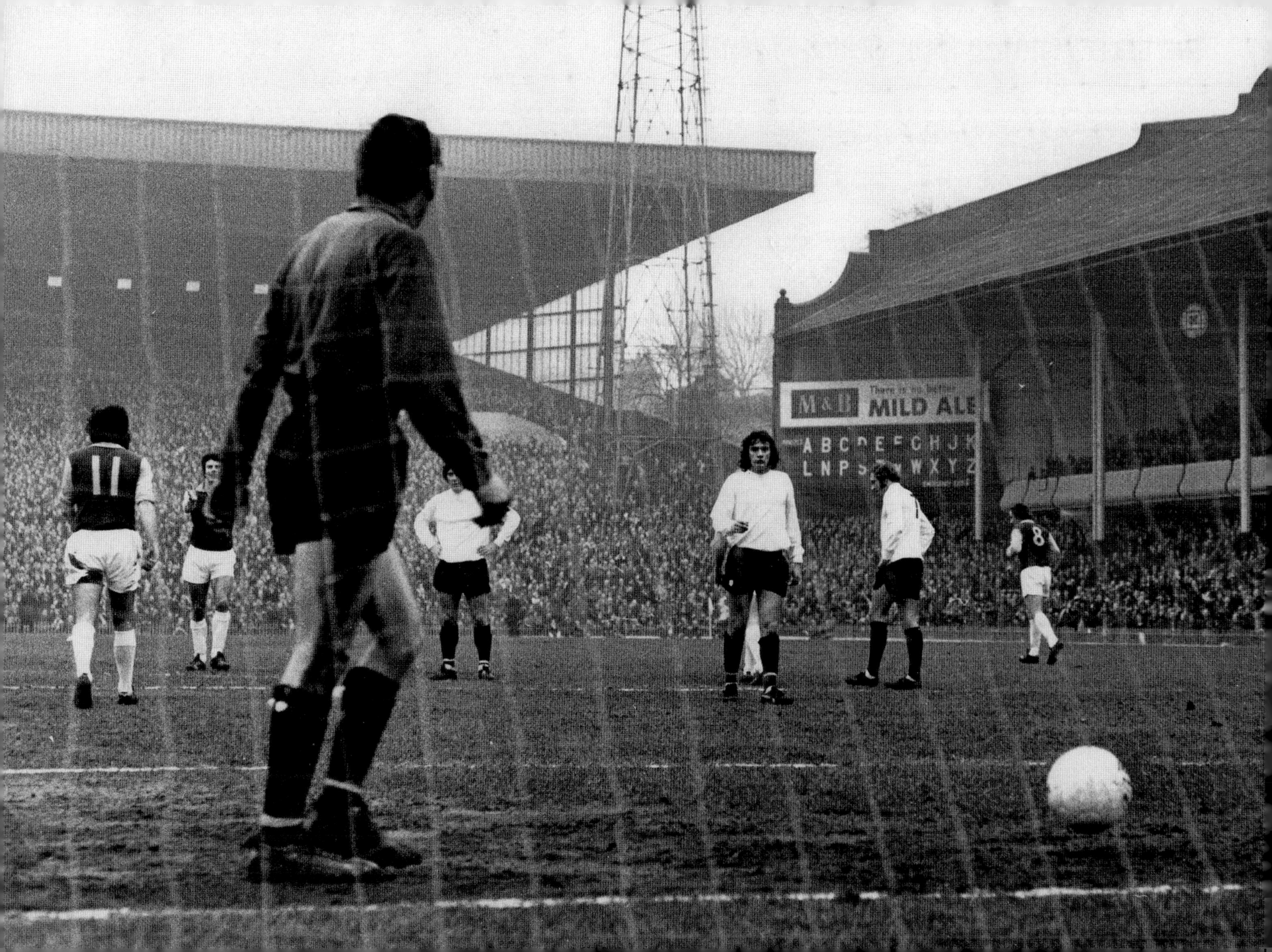
M&B
MILD ALE
A B C D E F G H J K

THE BIG ASTON VILLA BOOK OF THE SEVENTIES

SEASON 1971-1972

	LEAGUE	GOALS	FA CUP	GOALS	LEAGUE CUP	GOALS	TOTAL	GOALS
ANDY LOCHHEAD	45	19	1		7	6	53	25
RAY GRAYDON	45	14	1		6	1	52	15
CHARLIE AITKEN	43	4	1		6		50	4
WILLIE ANDERSON	40	10	1		7	5	48	15
BRUCE RIOCH	40	9			5		45	9
FRED TURNBULL	37		1		5		43	
MICHAEL WRIGHT	31				1		32	
GEOFF VOWDEN	30+3	10	1		7	1	38+3	11
IAN 'CHICO' HAMILTON	25+5	7	1		5	1	31+5	8
JIMMY CUMBES	29						29	
GEORGE CURTIS	24		1		2		27	
KEITH BRADLEY	16		1		7		24	
TOMMY HUGHES	16		1		6		23	
BRIAN TILER	13		+1		6		19+1	
IAN ROSS	17	1					17	1
PAT McMAHON	15+3	5					15+3	5
HARRY GREGORY	8				5		13	
CHRIS NICHOLL	13	1					13	1
JIMMY BROWN	8+1						8+1	
MALCOLM BEARD	4+1				1		5+1	
DAVIE GIBSON	3		1				4	
GEOFF CRUDGINGTON	1				1		2	
NEIL RIOCH	2	2					2	2
BRIAN LITTLE	1+1	1					1+1	1
LIONEL MARTIN	+1				+2		+3	

NUMBER OF PLAYERS USED: 25
NUMBER OF GOALSCORERES: 12

[Right] 1971/72: The Holte End in fine voice as Villa beat promotion rivals Bournemouth in front of 48,110 – a Division Three attendance record

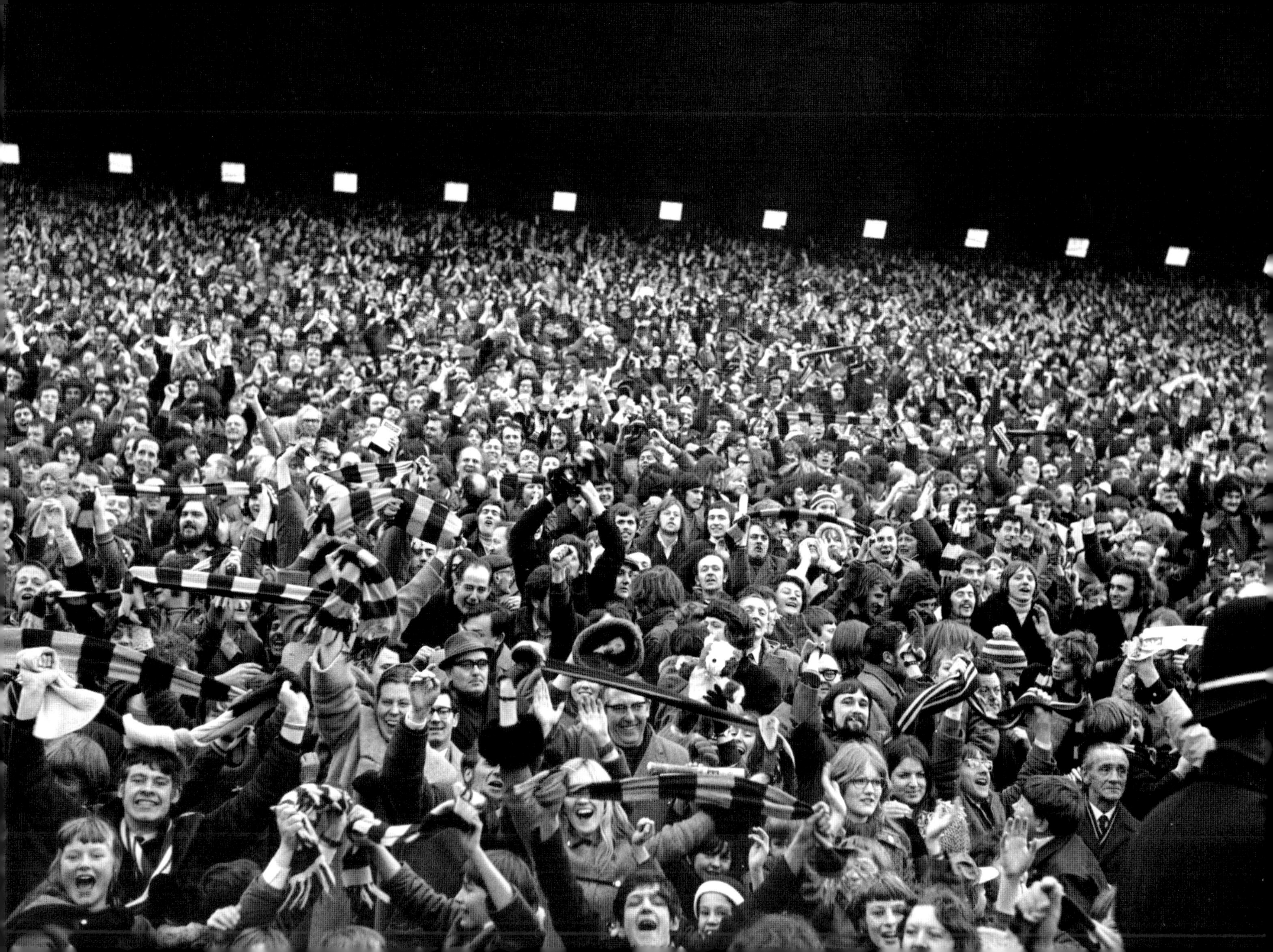

THE BIG ASTON VILLA BOOK OF THE SEVENTIES

SEASON 1972-1973

	LEAGUE	GOALS	FA CUP	GOALS	LEAGUE CUP	GOALS	CHARITY SHIELD	TOTAL	GOALS
JIMMY CUMBES	42		1		4		1	48	
CHRIS NICHOLL	41		1		4		1	47	
IAN ROSS	36		1		4		1	42	
GEOFF VOWDEN	35	5	1	1	4	1	1	41	7
CHARLIE AITKEN	33		1		4		1	39	1
BRUCE RIOCH	32	7	1		4	2	1	38	9
RAY GRAYDON	32	9	1		2+1	1	1	36+1	10
ANDY LOCHHEAD	30+3	6			3		1	34+3	6
ALUN EVANS	29+6	8	1	1	3+1	2	+1	33+8	11
PAT McMAHON	28+1	3			4		1	33+1	3
FRED TURNBULL	21							21	
JOHN ROBSON	19		1					20	
BRIAN LITTLE	17+2	3						17+2	3
JIMMY BROWN	17	1	1					18	1
WILLIE ANDERSON	14	1	+1		2		1	17+1	1
JOHN GIDMAN	13				3			16	
IAN 'CHICO' HAMILTON	9+5	5			2			11+5	5
NEIL RIOCH	6+2	1						6+2	1
BOBBY McDONALD	4							4	
MICHAEL WRIGHT	2				1		1	4	
MALCOLM BEARD	1							1	
BRIAN TILER	1							1	
KEITH LEONARD	+2							+2	

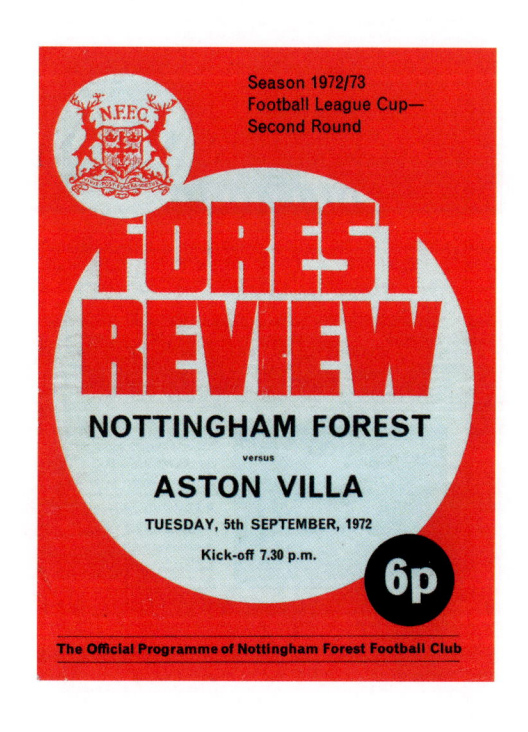

NUMBER OF PLAYERS USED: 23
NUMBER OF GOALSCORERES: 12

[Right] 1972/73: The official team photocall – they're the same team, but from a different angle!

400

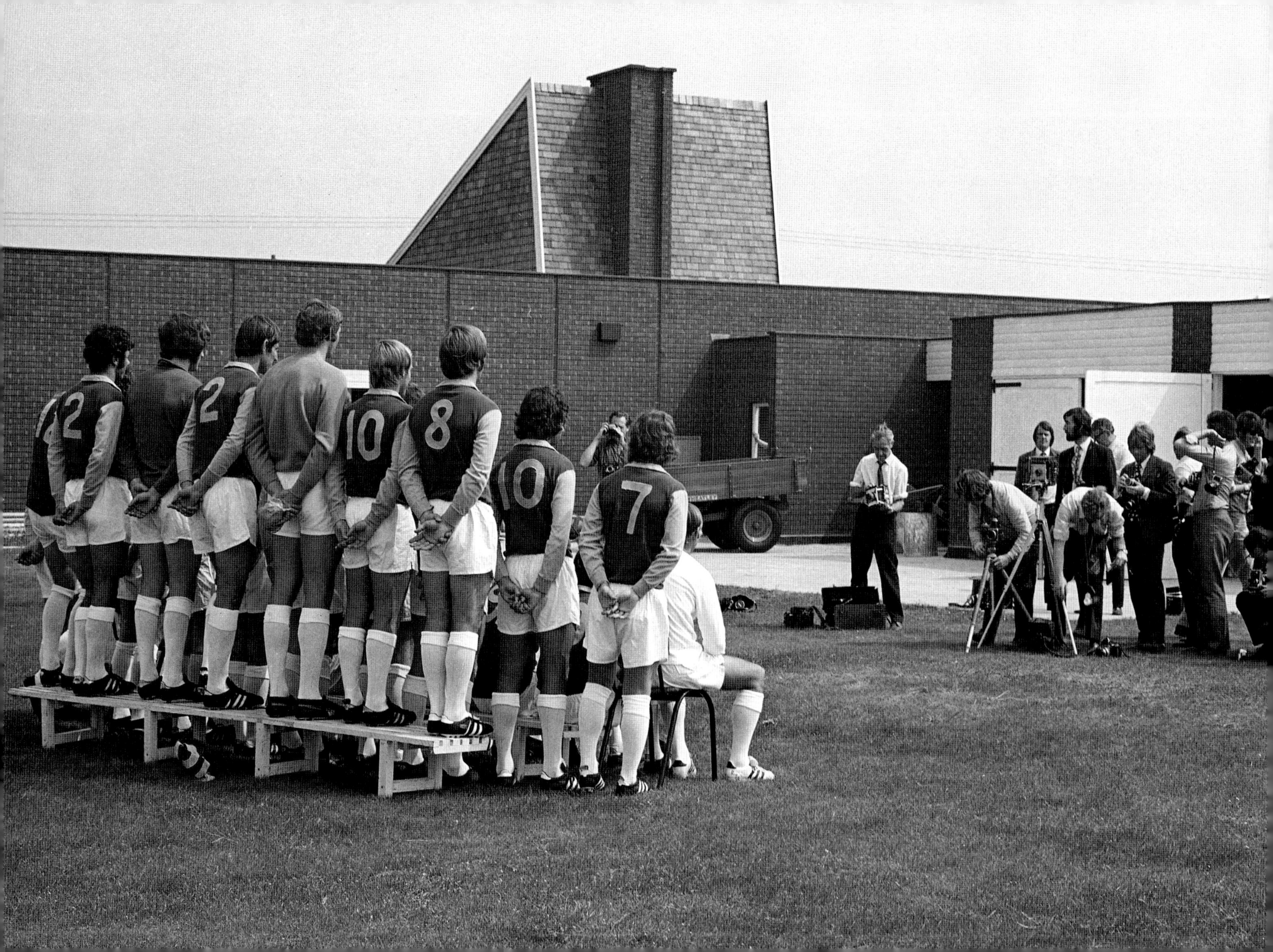

THE BIG ASTON VILLA BOOK OF THE SEVENTIES

SEASON 1973-1974

	LEAGUE	GOALS	FA CUP	GOALS	LEAGUE CUP	GOALS	TOTAL	GOALS
IAN ROSS	42		4		1		47	
JIMMY CUMBES	41		4		1		46	
CHRIS NICHOLL	40		4	1	1		45	1
CHARLIE AITKEN	38	2	4		1		43	2
BRIAN LITTLE	36+1	8	1		1		38+1	8
IAN 'CHICO' HAMILTON	30+1	3	4				34+1	3
JOHN GIDMAN	30		4				34	
ALUN EVANS	24+3	3	4	1			28+3	4
JIMMY BROWN	24		1		1		26	
SAMMY MORGAN	21+4	5	3+1	4	1		25+5	9
TREVOR HOCKEY	24	1					24	1
PAT McMAHON	20	5	3				23	5
BRUCE RIOCH	18	7	4		1		23	7
RAY GRAYDON	19+4	8	2		1		22+4	8
GEOFF VOWDEN	15+1	2	2		1		18+1	2
JOHN ROBSON	12				1		13	
FRED TURNBULL	10						10	
KEITH LEONARD	7	1					7	1
BOBBY McDONALD	4						4	
NEIL RIOCH	3+3						3+3	
ROY STARK	2						2	
BOBBY CAMPBELL	1+2	1					1+2	1
JAKE FINDLAY	1						1	

NUMBER OF PLAYERS USED: 23
NUMBER OF GOALSCORERES: 13

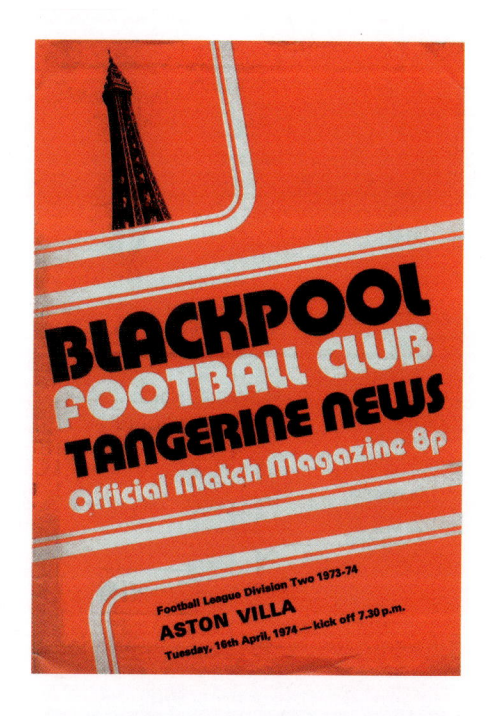

[Right] 1973/74: Charlie Aitken receives silverware from Billy Walker's widow in recognition of surpassing her husband's record appearances in claret and blue – a record still held by Charlie to this day, and one unlikely to ever be beaten

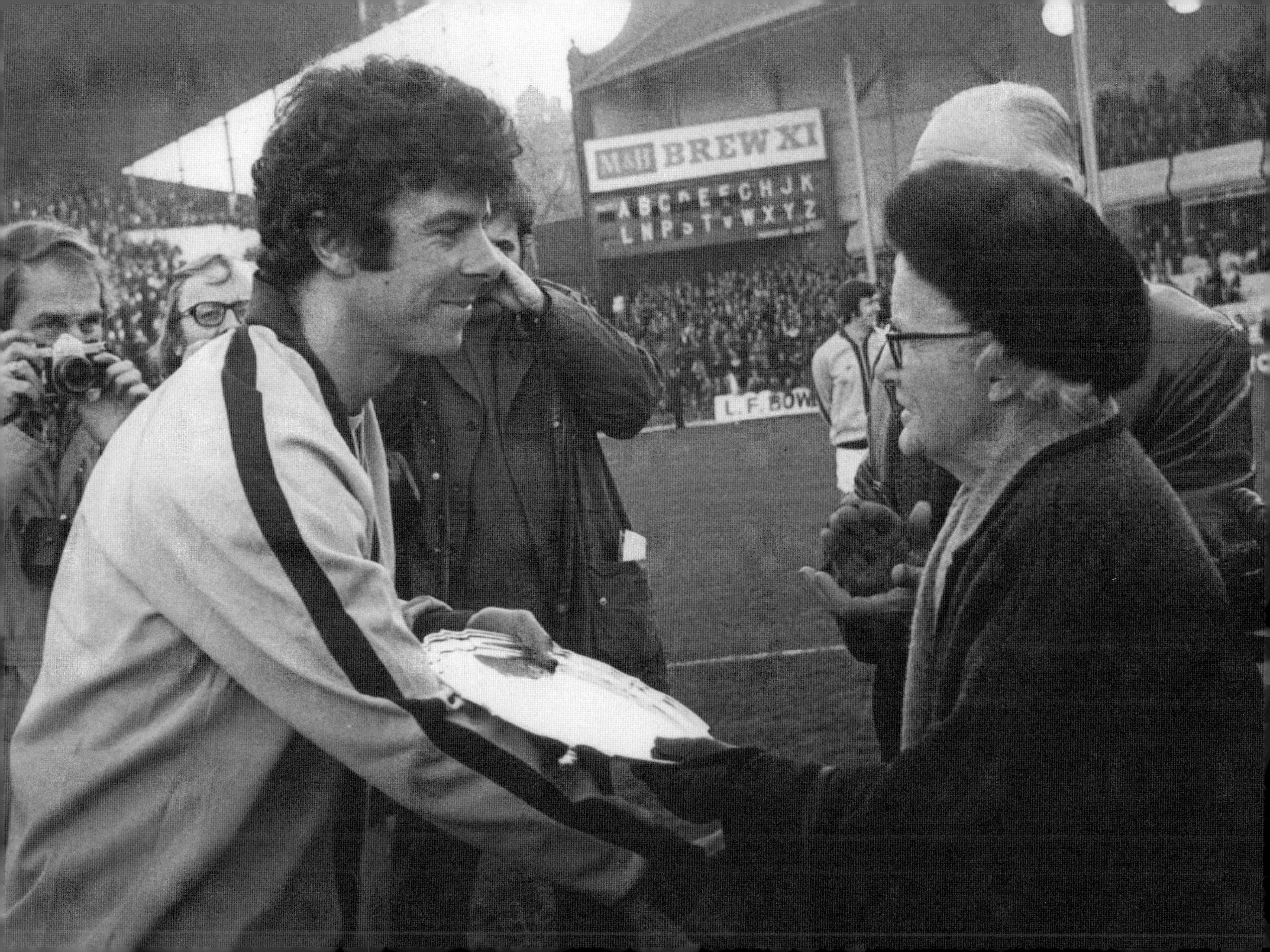
BREW XI

THE BIG ASTON VILLA BOOK OF THE SEVENTIES

SEASON 1974-1975

	LEAGUE	GOALS	FA CUP	GOALS	LEAGUE CUP	GOALS	TOTAL	GOALS
CHARLIE AITKEN	42	1	3		10	1	55	2
IAN ROSS	42	2	3		10		55	2
JOHN ROBSON	41	1	3		10		54	1
CHRIS NICHOLL	41	4	2	2	10	1	53	7
JIMMY CUMBES	38		3		10		51	
IAN 'CHICO' HAMILTON	37	10	3		10	3	50	13
RAY GRAYDON	37	19	3	2	10	6	50	27
FRANK CARRODUS	36	3	2		9	1	47	4
BRIAN LITTLE	33+1	20	2	1	7+1	3	42+2	24
KEITH LEONARD	22	7	3	2	5	3	30	12
LEIGHTON PHILLIPS	23+2	2					23+2	2
BOBBY McDONALD	15+3	1	3	1	3	1	21+3	3
JOHN GIDMAN	13+1	1			3		16+1	1
SAMMY MORGAN	12	4			4	2	16	6
JIMMY BROWN	8+2				3		11+2	
BOBBY CAMPBELL	6+1				2		8+1	
NEIL RIOCH	4		1		1		6	
ALAN LITTLE	2+1				2	1	4+1	1
FRANK PIMBLETT	2		1		1		4	
GRAHAM MOSELEY	3						3	
PAT McMAHON	2						2	
TONY BETTS	1+3				+1		1+4	
ALUN EVANS			1	1	+1		1+1	1
STEVE HUNT	1+1						1+1	
JAKE FINDLAY	1						1	
KEITH MASEFIELD	+1						+1	

NUMBER OF PLAYERS USED: 26
NUMBER OF GOALSCORERES: 15

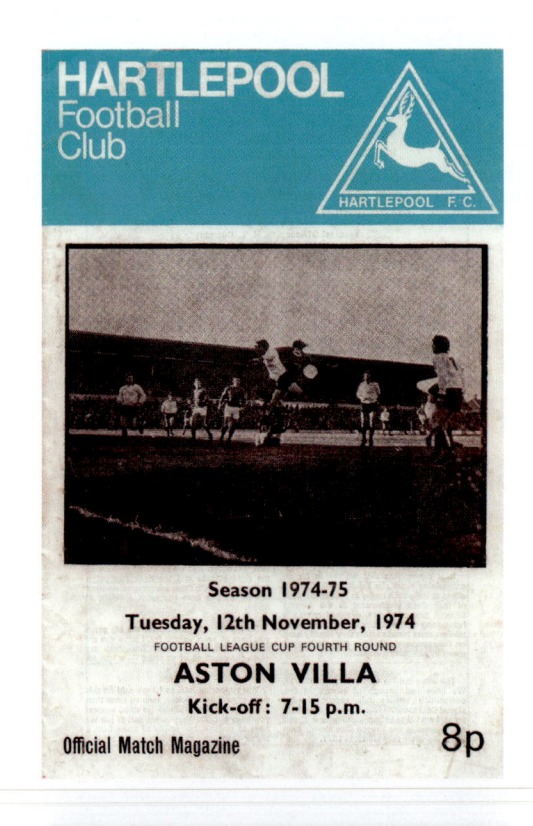

[Right] 1974/75: Jim Cumbes, Ian 'Chico' Hamilton, coach Roy MacLaren, (in front) Chris Nicholl and Frank Carrodus, celebrate lifting the League Cup at the hands of fellow Division Two side Norwich City.

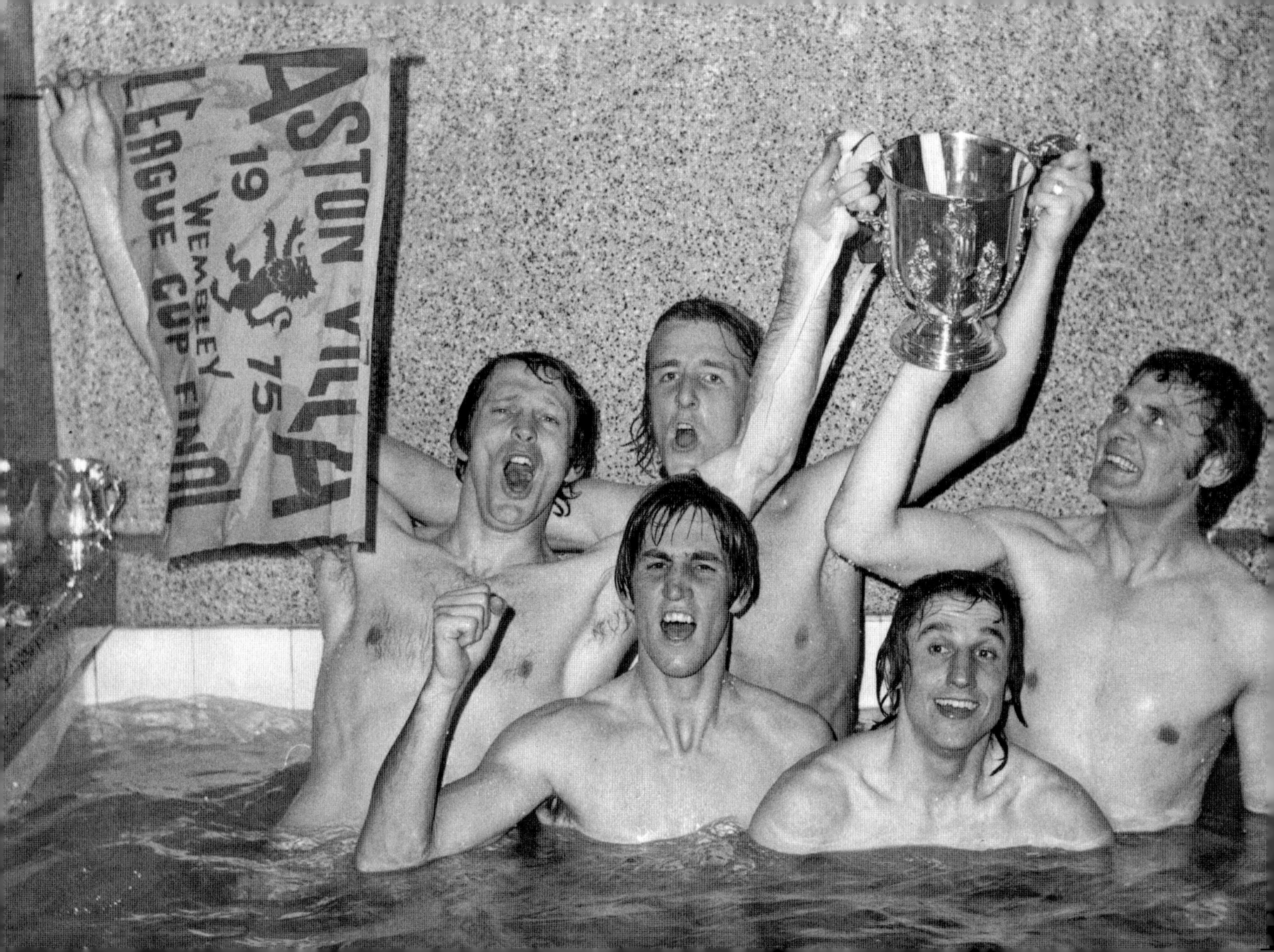
ASTON VILLA
19 75
WEMBLEY
LEAGUE CUP FINAL

THE BIG ASTON VILLA BOOK OF THE SEVENTIES

SEASON 1975-1976

	LEAGUE	GOALS	FA CUP	GOALS	LEAGUE CUP	GOALS	UEFA	GOALS	TOTAL	GOALS
CHRIS NICHOLL	40	4	2		2	1	2		46	5
FRANK CARRODUS	39	1	2		2		2		45	1
JOHN GIDMAN	39		2		1		2		44	
RAY GRAYDON	38	12	2	1	2		2	1	44	14
IAN ROSS	38		2		2		2		44	
LEIGHTON PHILLIPS	33+2	2	2		2		2		39+2	2
JOHN ROBSON	34+2		2		1		1+1		38+3	
IAN 'CHICO' HAMILTON	29+2	4	2		2		2		35+2	4
ANDY GRAY	30	10	2	1	1	1			33	12
JOHN BURRIDGE	30		2						32	
CHARLIE AITKEN	21	1	+1		2		2		25+1	1
BRAIN LITTLE	20	1			2		1		23	1
JOHN DEEHAN	14+1	7	2						16+1	7
DENNIS MORTIMER	14								14	
BOBBY McDONALD	10+3	2					1		11+3	2
JIMMY CUMBES	7				1		1		9	
KEITH LEONARD	7	3			1	1			8	4
JAKE FINDLAY	5				1		1		7	
FRANK PIMBLETT	7								7	
STEVE HUNT	3+1	1					+1		3+2	1
SAMMY MORGAN	2+1						1+1		3+2	
JOHN OVERTON	2+1								2+1	
GORDON COWANS	+1								+1	
KEITH MASEFIELD	+1								+1	

NUMBER OF PLAYERS USED: 24
NUMBER OF GOALSCORERES: 12

[Right] 1975/76: Ray Graydon celebrates as Villa beat rivals Birmingham City 2-1 – Hamilton and Little got the all-important goals

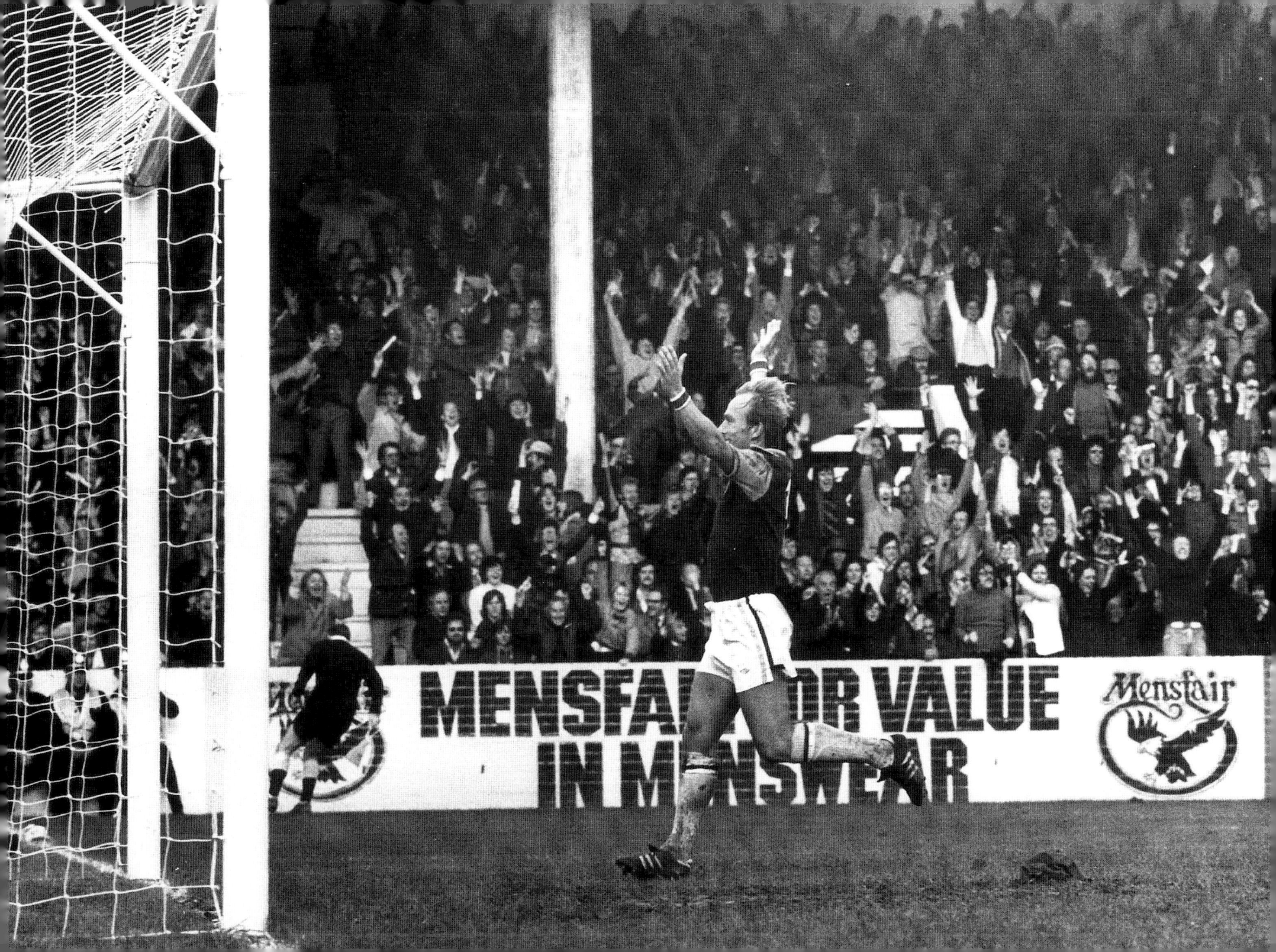
VALUE
Mensfair

THE BIG ASTON VILLA BOOK OF THE SEVENTIES

SEASON 1976-1977

	LEAGUE	GOALS	FA CUP	GOALS	LEAGUE CUP	GOALS	TOTAL	GOALS
BRAIN LITTLE	42	14	4	2	10	10	56	26
DENNIS MORTIMER	41	4	4	1	10		55	5
LEIGHTON PHILLIPS	40		4		10		54	
JOHN BURRIDGE	35		4		9		48	
ANDY GRAY	36	25	3	1	9	3	48	29
CHRIS NICHOLL	35	2	3	1	10	3	48	6
JOHN ROBSON	32+1		4		7		43+1	
FRANK CARRODUS	30		4		9	1	43	1
JOHN GIDMAN	27	4	4		10		41	4
ALEX CROPLEY	32	3	2		6		40	3
JOHN DEEHAN	27	13	4	3	6	2	37	18
GORDON SMITH	32+2				4+1		36+3	
RAY GRAYDON	18	6	1		4	1	23	7
GORDON COWANS	15+3	3	2+1		4+1		21+5	3
CHARLIE YOUNG	9+1		1				10+1	
JAKE FINDLAY	7				1		8	
DAVID HUGHES	3+1	1					3+1	1
STEVE HUNT	+1				1		1+1	
KEITH MASEFIELD	1+1						1+1	
MICHAEL BUTTRESS	+2						+2	
IVOR LINTON	+2						+2	

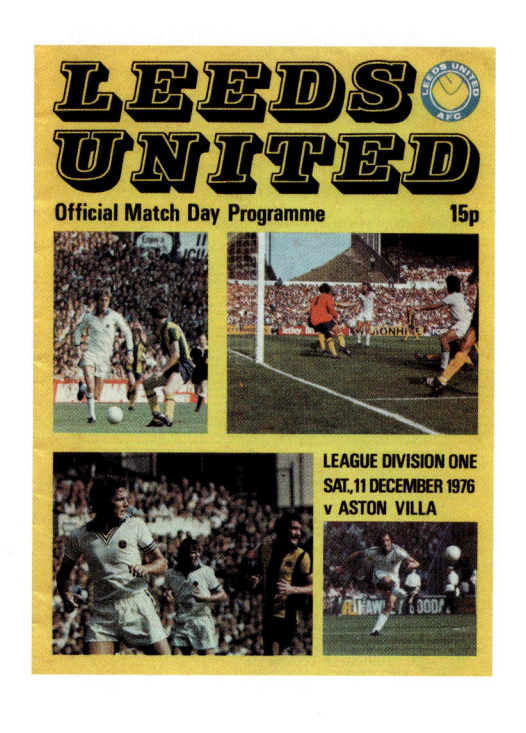

NUMBER OF PLAYERS USED: 21
NUMBER OF GOALSCORERES: 11

[Right] 1976/77: Ex-Villa keeper Kevin Keelan can only watch as Brain Little finds the back of the net in Villa's 1-0 win over the Canaries

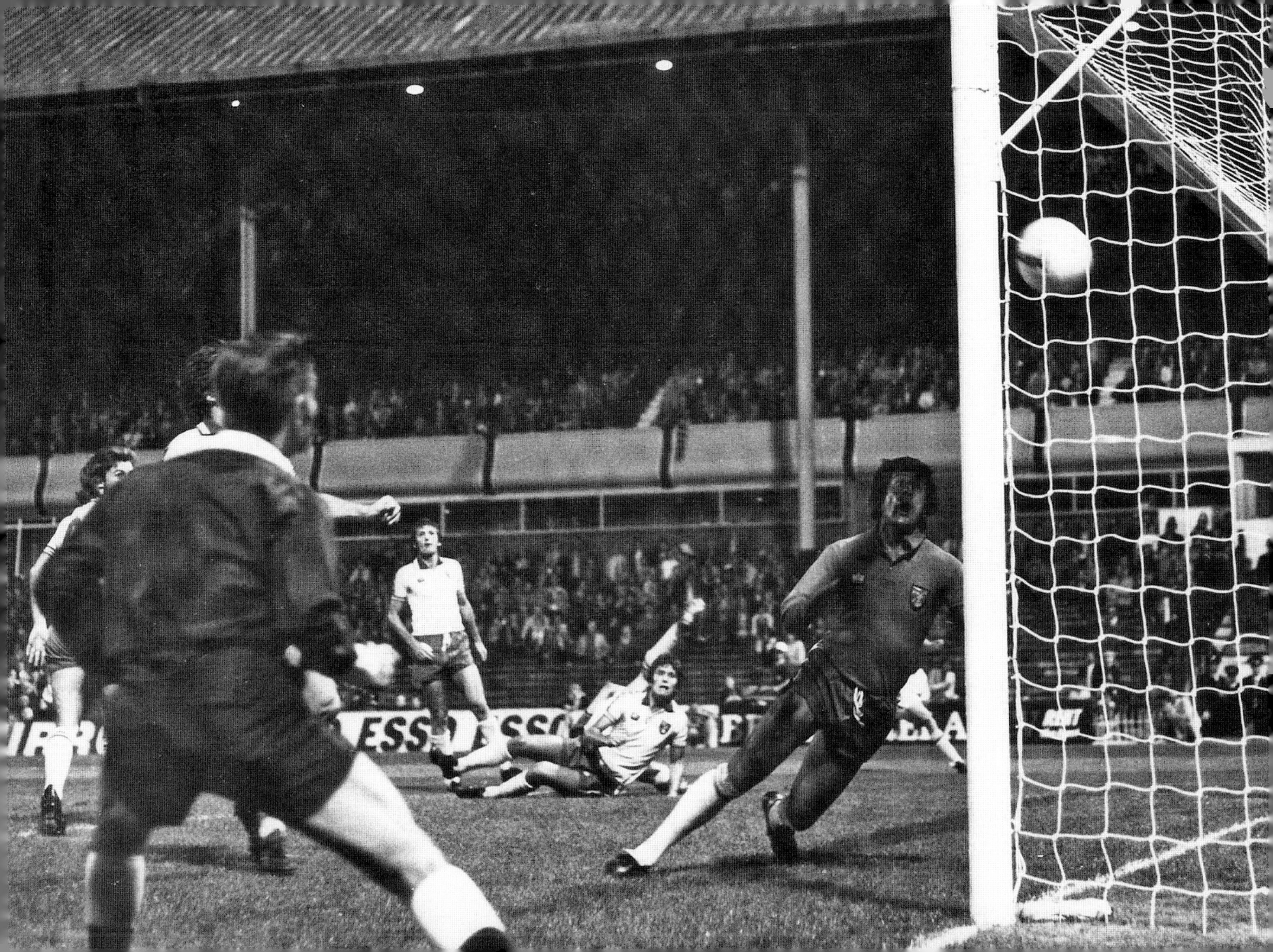
ESSO
ESSO

THE BIG ASTON VILLA BOOK OF THE SEVENTIES

SEASON 1977-1978

	LEAGUE	GOALS	FA CUP	GOALS	LEAGUE CUP	GOALS	UEFA	GOALS	TOTAL	GOALS
DENNIS MORTIMER	42	3	1		3		8	1	54	4
JIMMY RIMMER	41		1		3		8		53	
FRANK CARRODUS	40	3	1		3	1	8		52	4
BRIAN LITTLE	40	7	1		3	1	8	3	52	11
KEN McNAUGHT	40	2	1		3		8	3	52	5
GORDON SMITH	38		1		3		7		49	
LEIGHTON PHILLIPS	35		1		3		8		47	
JOHN DEEHAN	35+1	11	+1		3		7	5	45+2	16
JOHN GIDMAN	34	1	1		2		7		44	1
ANDY GRAY	31+1	13	1	1	3	4	5	2	40+1	20
GORDON COWANS	30+5	7	1		+2		4+1		35+8	7
JOHN GREGORY	21+5	3	1		1		3+1		26+6	3
ALEX CROPLEY	17	2			3		5		25	2
ALLAN EVANS	9	1					+1		9+1	1
TOMMY CRAIG	4								4	
JOHN ROBSON	3						1		4	
MICHAEL BUTTRESS	1								1	
DAVID EVANS							1		1	
IVOR LINTON	+1						+1		+2	
JAKE FINDLAY							+1		+1	

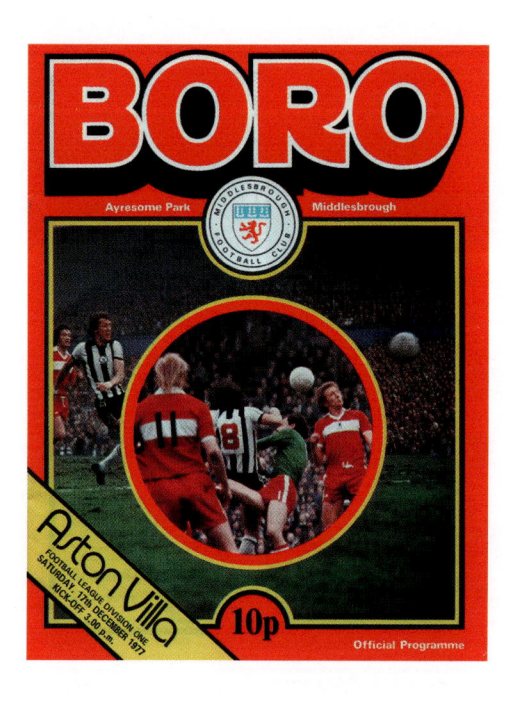

NUMBER OF PLAYERS USED: 20
NUMBER OF GOALSCORERES: 11

[Right] 1977/78: How could Captain Marvel, Dennis Mortimer, be overlooked for a full England cap? Instead, he had to make do with this solitary England B run-out in Prague against Czechoslovakia in November '77

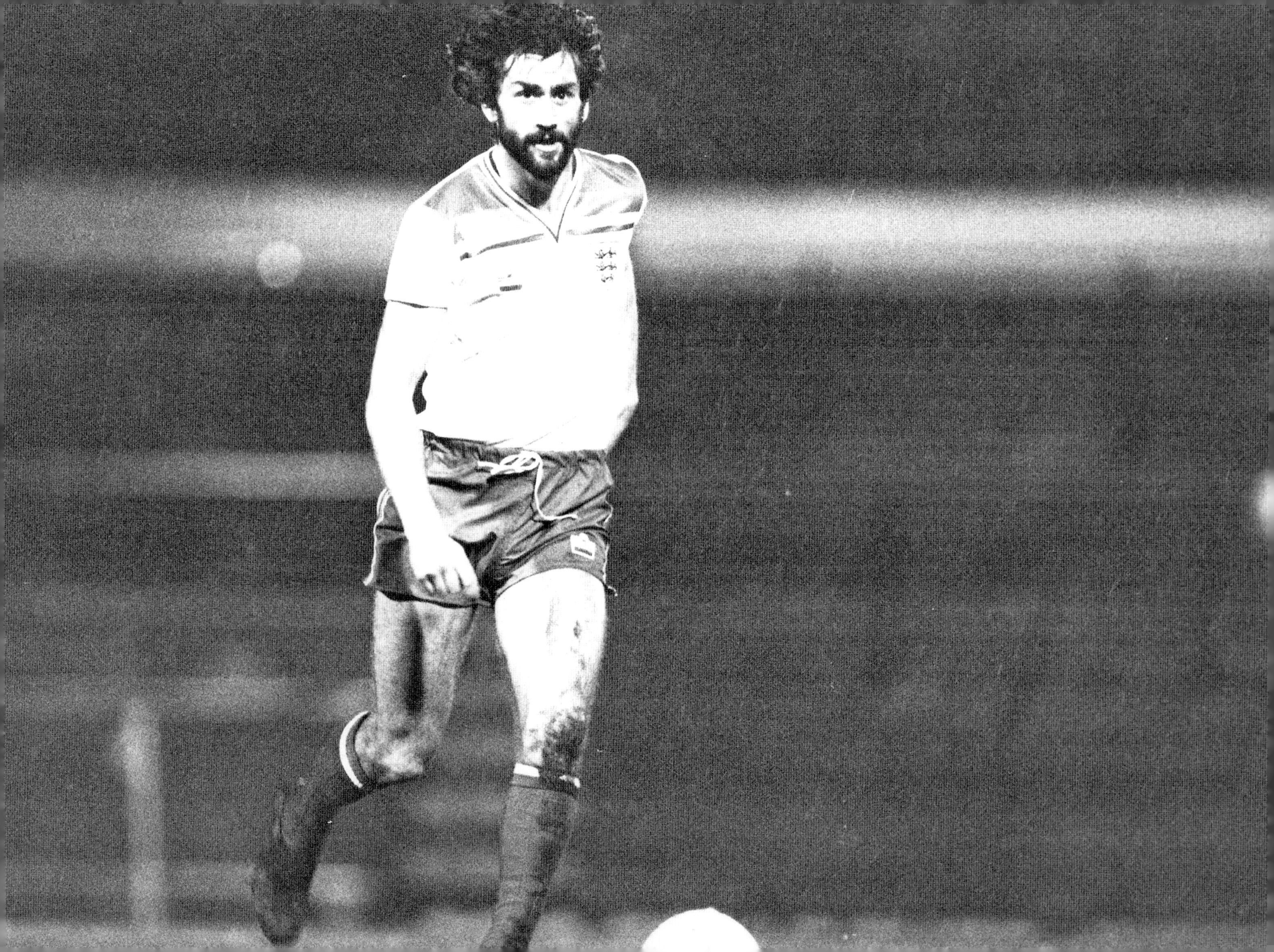

THE BIG ASTON VILLA BOOK OF THE SEVENTIES

SEASON 1978-1979

	LEAGUE	GOALS	FA CUP	GOALS	LEAGUE CUP	GOALS	TOTAL	GOALS
JIMMY RIMMER	42		1		5		48	
DENNIS MORTIMER	38	3	1		5		44	3
JOHN GREGORY	38+1	7	1		4	1	43+1	8
ALLAN EVANS	36+1	6	1		4		41+1	6
JOHN GIDMAN	36	3	1		3		40	3
KEN McNAUGHT	32	1	1		5		38	1
GORDON COWANS	34	4	1		1+1		36+1	4
JOHN DEEHAN	25+1	9	1		3		29+1	9
TOMMY CRAIG	23	2	1		4		28	2
BRIAN LITTLE	24	1			4	1	28	2
GARY WILLIAMS	21+1		1		4		26+1	
KENNY SWAIN	24	4	1				25	4
GARY SHELTON	19	7			2	1	21	8
ANDY GRAY	15	6			4	2	19	8
ALEX CROPLEY	15+2	2					15+2	2
COLIN GIBSON	11+1						11+1	
FRANK CARRODUS	6				4		10	
GORDON SMITH	6+1				1		7+1	
LEIGHTON PHILLIPS	3+2				2+1		5+3	
IVOR LINTON	4+4						4+4	
WILLIE YOUNG	3						3	
BRENDAN ORMSBY	2				+1		2+1	
GARY SHAW	2+1						2+1	
DAVID EVANS	2						2	
JOE WARD	1						1	
LEE JENKINS	+2						+2	

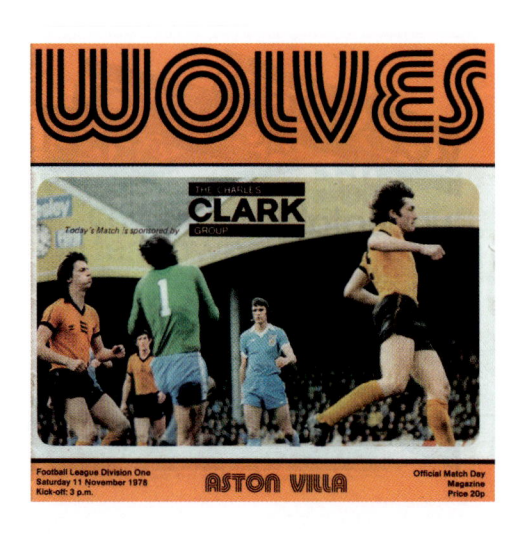

NUMBER OF PLAYERS USED: 26
NUMBER OF GOALSCORERES: 13

[Right] 1978/79: Did somebody forget to tell manager Ron Saunders to smile before the pre-season photocall?

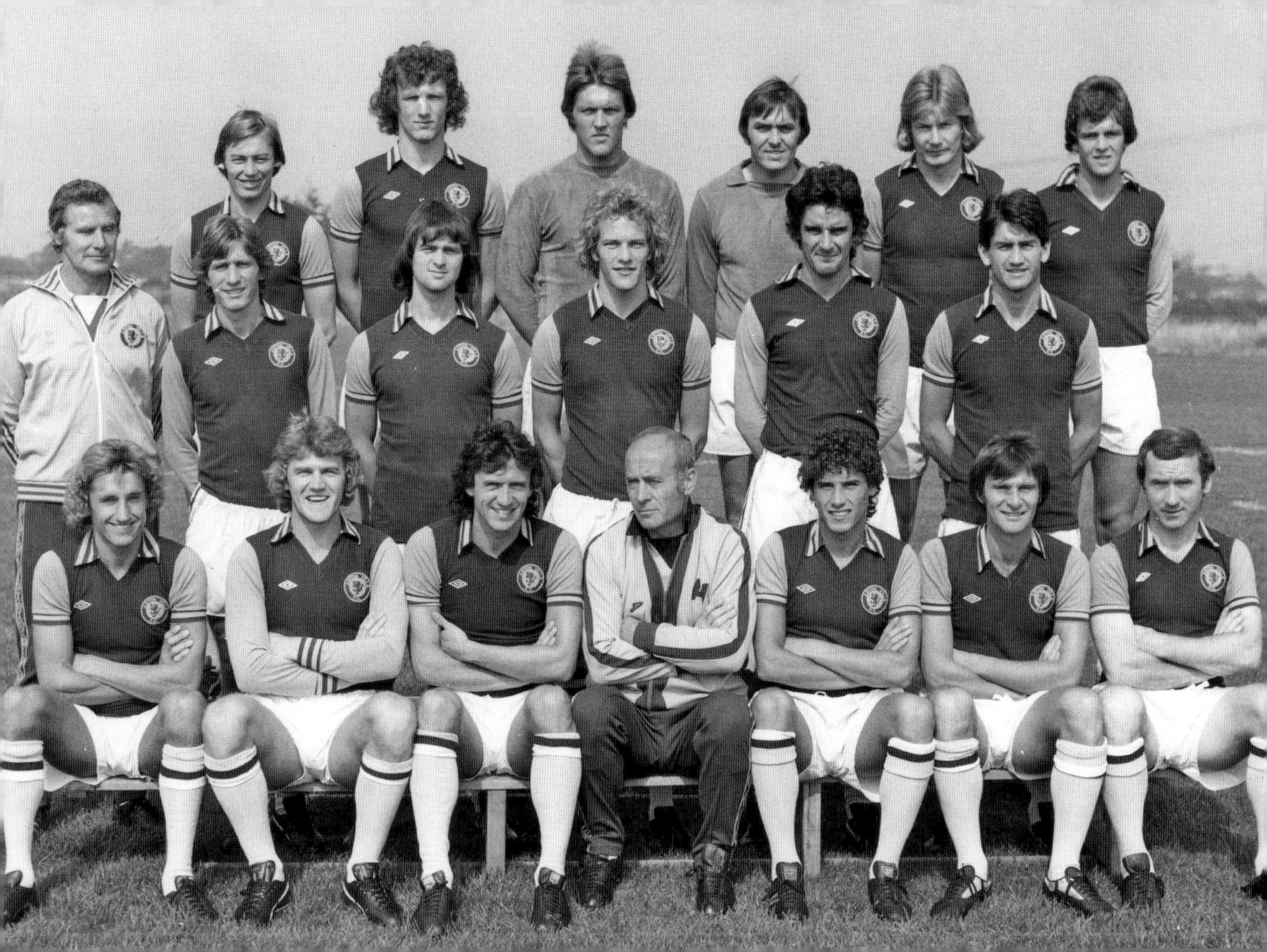

THE BIG ASTON VILLA BOOK OF THE SEVENTIES

SEASON 1979-1980

	LEAGUE	GOALS	FA CUP	GOALS	LEAGUE CUP	GOALS	TOTAL	GOALS
GORDON COWANS	42	6	6	1	4		52	7
JIMMY RIMMER	41		6		4		51	
KENNY SWAIN	41		5		4	1	50	1
DES BREMNER	36	3	6		2		44	3
ALLAN EVANS	35	8	5	2	4		44	10
KEN McNAUGHT	30	1	6		4		40	1
COLIN GIBSON	30+1	2	6		3		39+1	2
BRIAN LITTLE	29	5	6	1	2		37	6
DENNIS MORTIMER	26	6	6		4		36	6
GARY SHAW	28	9	3	1	2	2	33	12
DAVID GEDDIS	19+1	2	2	1	2		23+1	3
BRENDAN ORMSBY	21+2		1+1				22+3	
TONY MORLEY	15+3	3			2		17+3	3
TERRY DONOVAN	9	2	6	3			15	5
IVOR LINTON	12+3		1				13+3	
MIKE PEJIC	10				2		12	
PAT HEARD	9						9	
JOHN DEEHAN	6				2		8	
TERRY BULLIVANT	6		1				7	
JOHN GIDMAN	4				3		7	
GARY SHELTON	4				+1		4+1	
NOEL BLAKE	3						3	
EAMONN DEACY	2+1						2+1	
JOE WARD	1+1						1+1	
GARY WILLIAMS	1+1						1+1	
ALEX CROPLEY	1						1	
NIGEL SPINK	1						1	
ROBERT HOPKINS	+2	1					+2	1
LEE JENKINS	+1						+1	

NUMBER OF PLAYERS USED: 29
NUMBER OF GOALSCORERES: 13

[Right] 1979/80: Kenny Swain and Allan Evans (4) in action against Bolton Wanderers

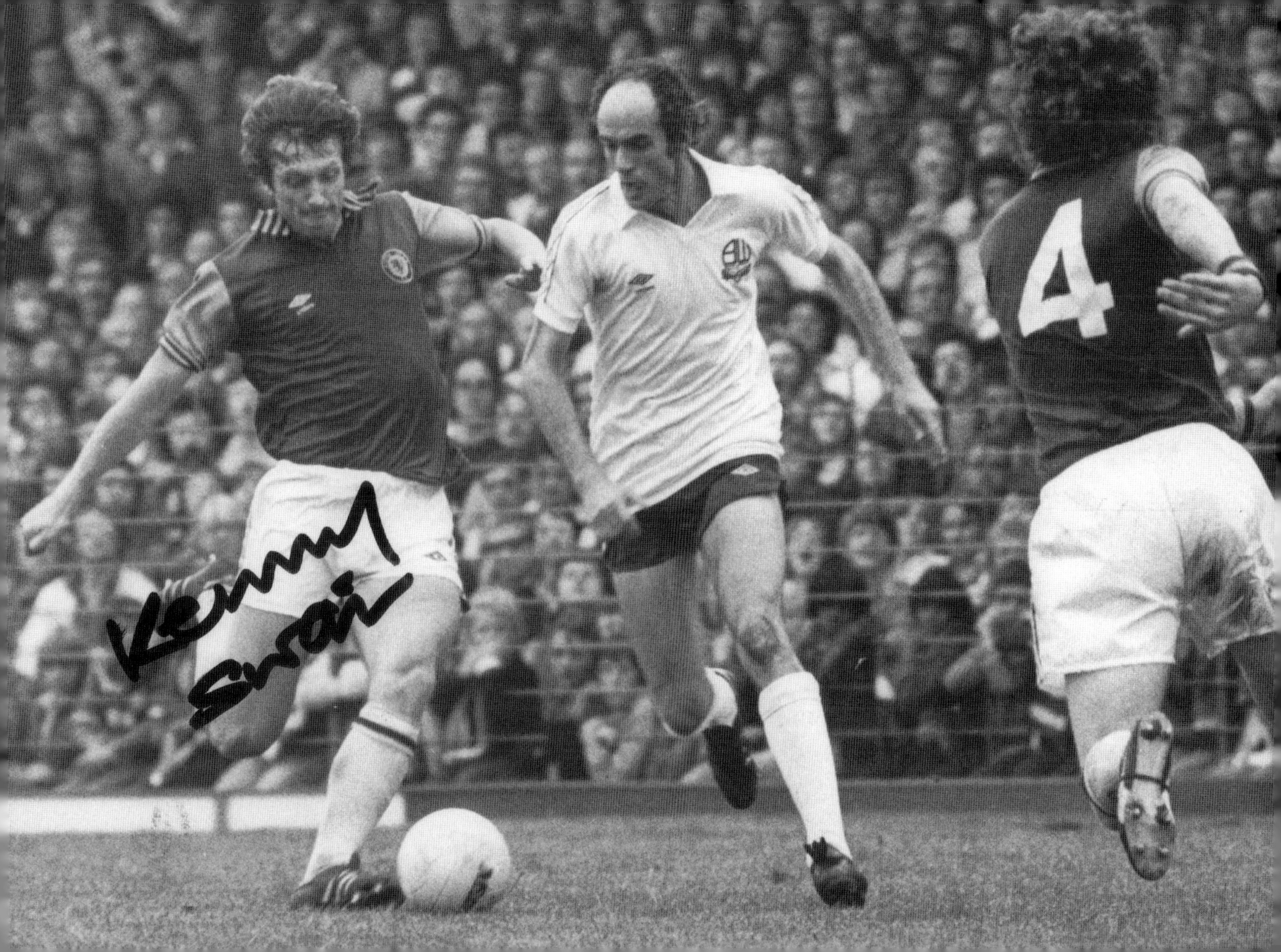
Kenny
Swain

THE BIG ASTON VILLA BOOK OF THE SEVENTIES

DEDICATIONS

Russell Homer
Ray Homer
Talia Homer
Harry Homer
Charlie Homer
Colin J Abbott
Sir Doug Ellis
Mervyn King (Lord King of Lothbury)
John Farrelly
Paul Faulkner
Nicola Keye
Rob Bishop
Garry 'Bruno' Thompson
Gary Shaw
Bob Hinks
Grant Adams
Howard Hodgson
Mat Kendrick
Samuel Kendrick
Steven Stride
John Burridge
Brad & Sammy Abbott
Tilly Abbott
Willie Anderson
David Anderson
Theresa Day
David Lane
Andrew Lane
Gary Dolphin
Nick Harper
Ray Bowers
Sue and Mick Tilt
Winsome and Mike d'Abreu
Andy 'Turnstile' Ullah

Peter Lawrence
Frank Acton (In Memoriam)
Jon Knibb
Pauline Knibb
Thomas Knibb
Graham Cowley
Nathan Cowley
Adam Keith
David Keith
John 'Whiskey' Coniff
Stewart 'Ted' Coniff
Martin Rock
Dennis Rock
Owen William Shutt
Aurora Elisabeth Shutt
Richard Hales
William Hales
Chris Morris
Ernie Morris
Robert R & Mary W Abbott
Harry Moore
Kyle, Sammy & Ryan Colin Abbott
Leon James
Stephen Hill
Michelle Wesley
Charlie Wesley
John Foster
Robert Gough (Daventry)
David Hodges (Southam)
Will Hughes
Terry Hassall
John Rudge
Wayne Bullock
Robin Wilkes

John Ward-Gwilliam
Charles Young
Michael Grayson
Zak Edwards
John Edwards
Graham Boulton
Tim Palmer
Mike Palmer
Nic Palmer
Tom Palmer
Mark Homer
Simon Foxall
Nigel Parsons
Pam Parsons RIP
John Holder
David Lawlor
John Villa Power
Ian Hucker
Peter Ross
Carol Watts
Christopher Greaves
Sally-Anne Harrison
Bob Moore
Riccardo Rossi
Alston Taylor
Robert Price
Lee Bickerton
Derek Day
Martin Moss
Richard & Sue Ford
Stuart Crowe
Knut Kavlie
Paul Matthews
Christopher Turner

Doug O'Brien
Greg Upton
Daniel & Emily Upton
Norman Carless
Keith Carless
Norman Hood
Ron Brunton
John Ward-Gwilliam
Mark Crowe
Chris Nason
Mark Goodwin
Stephen Knott
Steve Bateman
Nige Ainge
Jack Meenan
Peter Stokes
Michael Hoban
Mark Gamble
Colin Brown
Paul Gieron
David Goodwin
Pleaden Family (Denham Villans)
Terry Hassall
Eamon Hamilton
Andy Moyle
Michael Bill
Peter Doolan
John Uttley
David Cross
Alan Edwards
David Nixon
Roger Bunn
Michael Leahy
John Roche
Simon Babb
Rod Guest
Graham Biggs
Larry Byrne

Kevin Piercy
Stephen Rigby
Stephen Rigby Snr
Dave Roberts
Frank Allen
Steve Gough
Mark Judd
Ross Cropley
Dave Wall
Antony Betts
Dougie George
Andy Hooper
Harry Gregory RIP
Benjamin Watts
Sean Collins
Andy Dale
Alec Snook
Yvonne Webb
Maureen Bayliss
Michael Dudziak
Simon Goodyear
Patrick Flynn
Aleksandra Gorbachev
Vincent Mullooly RIP
Sean Mullooly
Philip Gray
Derek Ford
Adrian & Hedda Nevett
Roger Overthrow
Lynda Overthrow
Karl, Sue & Alfie Court
Sean Lynch
Paul Harris
Frank Pattison
Ken Pattison
Stephen Robert Kennedy
Bones from Bristol
Sue Young (Stafford)

Roger Levicki
Paul Lawrence
Steve Fletcher
Brendan Reilly
Mark Shaw
Alex Males
Ross Griffith
Nick Hayes
Steve Lennie
Tony Willis
Ken Baldwin
Nigel Shaw
Bob Spittle
Shaun Cope
Roger Sanderson
Rob Whitney
Peter Robert Hunter
Ian Dobson
Daniel Hutton
Oliver Hutton
James Madden
Peter Hancock
Stephen Walter Stenson
Kevin Gledhill
Robert Garratt
Terence Allen
Paul Williams
John Crawford
Jack Crawford
Mark Holloway
Robert Jones
Duncan, Amy & Ellis
Paul Spooner
Graydon Daley Abbott & Vic
Ruby Abbott
Mick Parker
Leigh Douglas
Jack Douglas

THE BIG ASTON VILLA BOOK OF THE SEVENTIES

Keith Miller
Keith Morris
Julie Wadeson
Graham M Bowden
David John Coley
John Coley
Frank Holt
Dave Hooley
Dave Woodley
Paul Harvey
Mike Davis
Simon Owen
Alun Allsop
Robert Allsop
Darren Jackson
Andrew Dear
Roger (Rogi) Harrison
Phil Bligh
Lewis Bligh
Andy Bigham
Bert Field
Ted Timmins
Tony & Maureen Parton
Frank Hughes
Billy Dumbrell
Chris Berns
Rob McGrath
Wayne Cole
Adam Cole
Mick Dale
Craig, Emma & Sienna Short
Nigel Stevenson
Phil Fellows
Grace Fellows
Ken Knowles
Tony 'The Badgeman' Penn
Dave Roe
Andy Roe

Sheila Maybury
Tommy Cole
David Maybury
Alan Gee
Wayne Homer
Bernard Stokes RIP
Kevin Rollason
John Rollason
Brian C Seadon
Sie Babb
Rob Watkins
Martin Greenslade
Erlend Stavehaug
Vinny Peculiar (Alan Wilkes)
Colin Rose
Elaine Rose
Sean Carroll
Derek Bromwell
Rick Barley
Alan Owen
Lenny Owen
Katie Baragwanath
Andy Thurman
Dale Jarvis
Stephen Green
Jake Yendell
Bob Mooring
Chris Roach
David Wagstaff
Derek Bromwell
Will Hughes
Martin Chrispin
Mick Hoban
Colin Warren
Rob Carless
David Carless
Phil Maddox
Karen Lloyd

Brian Mitchell
Stuart Mitchell

Dedicated to the memory of my younger brother – Paul Stephen Abbott (1968-2008)

THANKS AND ACKNOWLEDGMENTS

Firstly, where the book is concerned, a big thank you to my friend in Italy, Riccardo Rossi, for putting my name forward for this project. It was on his recommendation that Legends Publishing contacted me.

Dave Lane, of the above mentioned Legends Publishing, for giving me the opportunity to write what I genuinely consider to be the most comprehensive and in depth encyclopaedia available today on the 1970s decade of Aston Villa Football Club. Never before has this depth of information been available to hand in one publication.

Good friend, Jon Farrelly, who ably assisted in this project with not only his time, but the use of his vast collection of Villa ephemera; without this the book simply couldn't have got off the ground. Likewise with fellow collector and good friend Mick Tilt for use of personal items.

I also owe a debt of gratitude to the following people, who ably assisted in various ways. In no particular order, Paul Faulkner Aston Villa CEO (former) who was still in place at Villa Park when this book first started taking shape.

Aston Villa Football Club for kindly allowing the use of photographs and to the MirrorPix library staff.

Sir Doug Ellis.

Laura Mansell, former Aston Villa Football Club archivist.

Aston Villa former players; Charlie Aitken, Brian Little, Gordon Cowans, Chris Nicholl, Ray Graydon, Bruce Rioch, Willie Anderson, John Gidman, Jim Cumbes and Neil Rioch.

Aston Villa Former Player's Association.

Ken McNaught and Lions & Legends.

Stuart Crowe (son of Vic Crowe).

Miss T Day for countless hours of support. Amanda Wightman and David Speed, Heart of Midlothian FC.

David Gregory, Communications & Public Relations Officer, Colchester United Football Club and Kevin Drury.

Rick Cowdery Head of Communications Plymouth Argyle, and Russell K Moore.

John Russell, Arthur Bent, Harry Moore, Dave and Pam Bridgewater, Knut Kavlie and Andy Hooper who all helped in various ways.

David Powell, Archive Manager at DC Thomson & Co, Dundee.

The Guernsey Press and Mark Croxford.

Brian Torode and Trevor De La Mare of Guernsey.

THE BIG ASTON VILLA BOOK OF THE SEVENTIES

Paul Grecian, Paul Farley and Alison Styles.

Secondly where the book launch is concerned, a big debt of gratitude to the following:

Total Villa – Grant Adams and Darren Jackson (Trinity Road Box Holder).

Both of these gentlemen kindly offered hospitality tickets and the use of a private executive box at Villa for the ex-Villa players who are coming down to the Villa Park launch.

All the staff at Aston Villa Football Club, particularly Brian Little and Nicola Keye for throwing their backing behind the Villa Park launch, and to Kate Sharp and Alan Williams from the commercial department.

To the former Aston Villa players of the 1975 campaign (all boyhood idols of mine) who are attending the first of several launch events.

And lastly a heartfelt thank you to anyone I have inadvertently overlooked.

Colin J Abbott

The Big Aston Villa Book of the Eighties, and The Big Aston Villa 150 Year Book, are planned to be published by Legends Publishing over the next few years.